Published by Authority

THE
AIR FORCE
LIST

1999

The Stationery Office

ISBN 0 11 772887 X

ISSN 0266 8610

Printed in the United Kingdom for The Stationery Office
J55335 11/98 C26 10170

CONTENTS

NOTES

The Air Force List is published annually. The Royal Air Force Retired List is published separately and biennially. Both Lists are on sale to the public.

This edition of the Air Force List is corrected to include details of officers serving in the Ministry of Defence, Command Headquarters, etc showing the position generally as at 7 July 1998, the date against names being date of postings to the appointments. Later appointments, where known, are also included. The ranks shown are either substantive or acting.

The Gradation Lists show seniority in existing substantive ranks to include changes published in London Gazette supplements up to that dated 7 July 1998. All officers with a common seniority date are shown in alphabetical order. Acting rank is shown only for Air Officers. In addition, most Air Rank Officers are shown under a separate list rather than the Branch Gradation Lists.

Officers who succeed to peerages, baronetcies or courtesy titles, are required to notify the Editor immediately requesting their inclusion in the Air Force List and records of the Ministry of Defence. Such communications should be submitted through the normal channels in order that unit, command and computer records may also be suitably amended. In the case of officers serving at MOD, or on other than a normal RAF administered unit, notification is to be made through the parenting unit.

Entries include honours and awards (as shown on Pages v-vi) and symbols relating to certain courses (as shown on Pages vii-viii). In addition, certain academic and professional qualifications are shown, although not necessarily a complete list of those held on official records. When notifying academic and professional qualifications, attention is drawn to GAI 5094 (The Air Force List—Insertion of Academic and Professional Qualifications) and the need for supporting documentary evidence.

Readers who may notice errors or omissions are invited to notify the Editor quoting the relevant page. Where applicable the procedures detailed in the above paragraphs should be followed. To enable correction of entries for the next edition, all notifications should reach the Editor by 29 June 1999. Such communications should not be sent to the printers or publishers.

The master Distribution List for the free issue of the Air Force List is controlled by the Editor. Central Services Establishment (CSE) at Llangennech is responsible for the issue of the publication strictly in accordance with the Distribution List. Units are asked to ensure the Editor and CSE are informed of any reduction in requirements. Unit requests for additional copies and amendment to the master Distribution List should be addressed to CSE at Llangennech (normally using form MOD 999—Demand for Forms and Publications). Firmly attached to this demand should be a letter with a clear supporting case.

Correspondence for the Editor should be addressed to:

> Editor of The Air Force Lists
> PMA(CS)2a(1)(RAF)
> RAF Personnel Management Agency
> Room 5, Building 248A
> RAF Innsworth
> Gloucester
> GL3 1EZ

LETTERS DENOTING HONOURS AND AWARDS IN ORDER OF PRECEDENCE

VC............. Victoria Cross.

GC .... George Cross.

KG .... Knight of the Garter.

KT............. Knight of the Thistle.

KP............. Knight of the St. Patrick.

GCB .... Knight Grand Cross or Dame Grand Cross of the Order of the Bath.

OM............ Member of the Order of Merit.

GCSI........... Knight Grand Commander of the Star of India.

CI .... Order of the Crown of India.

GCMG .... Knight Grand Cross or Dame Grand Cross of the Order of St. Michael and St. George.

GCIE........... Knight Grand Commander of the Order of the Indian Empire.

GCVO .... Knight Grand Cross or Dame Grand Cross of the Royal Victorian Order.

GBE .... Knight Grand Cross or Dame Grand Cross of the Order of the British Empire.

CH............. Member of the Order of the Companion of Honour.

KCB .... Knight Commander ⎫ of the

DCB .... Dame Commander ⎬ Order of the Bath.

KCSI........... Knight Commander of the Order of Star of India.

KCMG .... Knight Commander ⎫ of the Order of St. Michael

DCMG .... Dame Commander ⎬ and St. George.

KCIE........... Knight Commander of the Order of the Indian Empire.

KCVO .... Knight Commander ⎫ of the Royal Victorian

DCVO .... Dame Commander ⎬ Order.

KBE .... Knight Commander ⎫ of the Order of the British

DBE .... Dame Commander ⎬ Empire.

CB............. Companion of the Order of the Bath.

CSI .... Companion of the Order of the Star of India.

CMG.......... Companion of the Order of St. Michael and St. George.

CIE .... Companion of the Order of the Indian Empire.

CVO .... Commander of the Royal Victorian Order.

CBE .... Commander of the Order of the British Empire.

DSO .... Companion of the Distinguished Service Order.

LVO .... Lieutenant of the Royal Victorian Order.

OBE .... Officer of the Order of the British Empire.

ISO .... Companion of the Imperial Service Order.

MVO.......... Member of the Royal Victorian Order.

MBE.......... Member of the Order of the British Empire.

RRC .... Member of the Royal Red Cross.

DSC .... Distinguished Service Cross.

MC .... Military Cross.

DFC .... Distinguished Flying Cross.

AFC .... Air Force Cross.

ARRC.......... Associate of the Royal Red Cross.

DCM.......... Distinguished Conduct Medal.

CGM.......... Conspicuous Gallantry Medal.

GM .... George Medal.

DSM.......... Distinguished Service Medal.

MM .... Military Medal.

DFM .... Distinguished Flying Medal.

QGM .... Queen's Gallantry Medal.

BEM .... British Empire Medal.

RVM.......... Royal Victorian Medal.

ERD .... Army Emergency Reserve Decoration.

TD............. Territorial Decoration or Efficiency Decoration.

RD............. Royal Naval Reserve Officer's Decoration.

AE............. Air Efficiency Award.

* .... Denotes the award of a bar to a decoration or medal for gallantry. The award of an additional bar is indicated by the addition of a further star for each award.

NOTE—When the recipient of an Order of Knighthood is promoted to a higher rank within the same Order, the lower rank is absorbed in the higher and therefore the designation of the lower rank is omitted after the name.

OTHER HONOURS AND AWARDS

AK...Knight of Australia
QSO ....Queen's Service Order (New Zealand)

LETTER DENOTING APPOINTMENTS TO THE QUEEN

ADC........................... Aide-de Camp
QHS......................... Honorary Surgeon
QHC......................... Honorary Chaplain

QHDS.............. Honorary Dental Surgeon
QHP........................ Honorary Physician
QHNS .... Honorary Nursing Sister

EXPLANATIONS OF ABBREVIATIONS AND SYMBOLS SHOWN IN GRADATION LISTS

a .... Qualified at Specialist Armament Course.

ac .... Qualified in Aircraft Control.

adp .... Qualified Advanced Automatic Date Processing Course.

ae .... Qualified Aero-Systems Engineering Course.

amec .... Qualified Advanced Maintenance Engineering Course. (from Course 8).

asq .... Qualified GD Aero-Systems Course.

awcc .... Graduates of the Air Warfare Commanders' Course, at the Department of Air Warfare. Royal Air Force College Cranwell (including graduates of the Royal Air Force College of Air Warfare Course at the Royal Air Force Flying College).

aws .... Graduates of the Air Warfare Course, at the Department of Air Warfare. Royal Air Force College Cranwell (including graduates of the Royal Air Force College of Air Warfare and graduates of the Air Warfare Course at the Royal Air Force Flying College).

ax .... Qualified at Advanced Armament Course.

cfs* .... General Duties Officers and Master Pilots who have qualified as flying instructors and who hold a Central Flying School A1 instructor category.

cfs .... General Duties Officers and Master Pilots who have qualified as flying instructors and who hold a Central Flying School A2 instructor category.

cfs(c)* .... General Duties Officers and Master Aircrew who have qualified as crewman instructors and who hold a Central Flying School A1 instructor category.

cfs(c) .... General Duties Officers and Master Aircrew who have qualified as crewman instructors and who hold a Central Flying School A2 instructor category.

cfs(n)* .... General Duties Officers who have qualified as navigation instructors and who hold a Central Flying School A1 instructor category.

cfs(n) .... General Duties Officers who have qualified as navigation instructors and who hold a Central Flying School A2 instructor category.

df* .... Officers who have completed a Royal Air Force Diamond Jubilee Fellowship.

df .... Officers who have completed Defence Fellowships.

e .... Qualified at Specialist Engineering Course.

e(t) .... Qualified at Specialist Engineering followed by Torpedo Course.

etps .... Graduate of the Empire Test Pilot's School.

ex .... Qualified at University Course in Engineering in addition to qualifying e.

fc .... Qualified in Fighter Control.

G† .... Qualified at Army Long Gunnery Staff Course (AA).

G(a) .... Qualified at the Army Gunnery Staff Course, Air Defence.

gw .... Qualified at Advanced Guided Weapons Course or Advanced Weapons Course at the Royal Air Force Technical College or the Guided Weapons Course at the Royal Military College of Science or the Graduate Astronautics Course at the United States Air Force Institute of Technology, Dayton, Ohio.

hcsc .... Qualified at Higher Command & Staff course.

i* .... Qualified as 1st class interpreter.

i .... Qualified as 2nd class interpreter.

icc .... Graduate of the Police Staff College (Bramshill) Intermediate Command Course.

idc .... Graduate of the Imperial Defence College, prior to 17 January 1971; or has held an appointment as Commandant or Instructor at the college for a period of one year.

ifp .... International Fellows Programme at the National Defence University in Washington DC.

im .... Supply Officers qualified at an Industrial Management/ Management Science Course at Manchester University.

jsdc .... Graduate of the Joint Service Defence College.

jssc .... Graduate of the—
Joint Services Staff College, prior to 6 August 1971.

met .... Qualified at University Course in Meteorology.

n .... Qualified at Specialists Navigation Course.

nadc .... Graduate of the NATO Defence College.

ndc .... Graduate of the—
National Defence College.

nx .... Qualified at Advanced Specialists Navigation Course.
Graduate of the—

oaws(US) ...... United States Air War College.

ocds(Can) ...... Canadian National Defence College.

ocds(Ind) .... Indian National Defence College.

odc(Aus) .... Australian Joint Service Staff College.

odc(US) .... { United States Armed Forces Staff College.
United States Navy War College.

vii

odc(Fr)	Cours Superieure Interarmes.	qss1	Qualified Staff Studies Module 1.
osc(Fr)	(to include French Ecole Superieure de Geurre).	qtm	Qualified Targeting and Mission Support Course.
odc(Ge)	Command and General Staff	qwi	Qualified Weapons Instructor.
osc(Ge)	College of the Federal German Armed Forces.	qwi(AD)	Qualified Weapons Instructor (Air Defence).
osc(US)	United States Air Command and Staff College.	qwi(SAW)	Qualified Weapons Instructor (Surface-to-Air Weapons).
pfc	Graduate of the RAPC Long Finance and Accountancy Course.	qwi(T)	Qualified Weapons Instructor (Tornado).
ph	Qualified at Specialist Photographic Course.	rcds	Graduate of the Royal College of Defence Studies.
pi	Qualified in Photographic Interpretation duties.	s	Qualified at Specialist Signals Course.
pji	Qualified as a parachutist Instructor.	scc	Graduate of the Police Staff College (Bramshill) Strategic Command Course.
ppetc	Long Petroleum Course.		
psc	Royal Air Force Graduates of the Royal Air Force Staff College and Foreign and Commonwealth Staff Colleges approved by the Director General of RAF Training.	semc	Qualified Senior Engineering Management Course.
		slmc	Senior Logistics Management Course.
psc(a)	Royal Navy and Army graduates of Royal Air Force Staff College.	snc	Qualified Staff Navigation Course. (Series beginning April, 1957).
psc(j)	Graduate of Joint Services Command & Staff College.	sowc	Qualified at Senior Officers War Course. Royal Naval War College.
psc(m)	Royal Air Force graduates of the Army Staff College.	ssc	Senior Supply Course.
psc(n)	Royal Air Force graduates of the Royal Naval Staff College.	sx	Qualified at University Course in Electrical Engineering and Wireless Telegraphy in addition to qualifying s.
psm	Advanced Certificates of the Royal Military School of Music.		
ptsc	Graduate of the Royal Military College of Science.	TIG(a)	Trained in Gunnery (Air Defence).
qab	Qualified Air Battle.	tp	Graduate of Empire Test Pilots' School, United States Air Force Test Pilots' School, United States Navy Air Test Centre or, French Ecole du Personnel Navigant d'Essais et de Reception.
qcc	Qualified at Officers Command Courses.		
qsb	Qualified Support Battlestaff Course.		
qs	Qualified Staff.	ts	Supply Officers who have completed the Cranfield Institute of Technology MSc course in Transport Studies.
qss*	Qualified Staff Studies. (2 year course).		
qss	Qualified Staff Studies. (18 months course).	w	Qualified at the Senior Weapons Course.
qss2	Qualified Staff Studies Module 2.		

SYMBOLS DENOTING AIRCREW CATEGORY AND SPECIALIZATION WITHIN BRANCHES

(P)	Pilot		(A)	Armament	
(N)	Navigator		(E)	Engineer	
(AEO)	Air Electronics Officer	General Duties Branch	(El)	Electrical Engineer	
(Sig)	Signaller		(GS)	Ground Support	
(ENG)	Engineer		(LA)	Electronic Air	Engineer Branch
(ALM)	Air Loadmaster		(LG)	Electronic Ground	
(AG)	Air Gunner		(M)	Mechanical Engineer	
			(MC)	Marine Craft	
(ATC)	Air Traffic Control		(Ph)	Photography	
(FC)	Fighter Control	Operations Support Branch	(S)	Signals	
(INT)	Intelligence		(Sec)	Secretarial	*Administrative Branch
(FLTOPS)	Flight Operations		(Trg)	Training	
(REGT)	Regiments		(Cat)	Catering	
			(P.Ed)	Physical Education	
			(ProvSy)	Provost Security	
			(F)	Medical Officers qualified as Flight Medical Officer.	

* Symbol denotes former specialization for group captains and wing commanders and current specialization for other officers.

ROYAL AIR FORCE

"Per Ardua ad Astra"

THE QUEEN

Air Commodore-in-Chief	Royal Auxiliary Air Force (1.6.53)
Air Commodore-in-Chief	Royal Air Force Regiment (1.6.53)
Commandant-in-Chief	Royal Air Force College, Cranwell (27.5.60)
Honorary Air Commodore	Royal Air Force Marham (11.6.77)

Commonwealth Forces

Air Commodore-in-Chief . . . . Air Reserve (of Canada), Royal Australian Air Force Reserve, Territorial Air Force (of New Zealand)

MEMBERS OF THE ROYAL FAMILY

Her Majesty Queen Elizabeth The Queen Mother

Commandant-in-Chief	Women, Royal Air Force (1.4.94)
Commandant-in-Chief	Royal Air Force Central Flying School (29.6.60)

His Royal Highness The Prince Philip, Duke of Edinburgh, KG KT OM GBE AC QSO

Marshal of the Royal Air Force	(15.1.53)
Air Commodore-in-Chief	Air Training Corps (15.1.53)
Honorary Air Commodore	Royal Air Force Kinloss (11.6.77)

Commonwealth Forces

Marshal of the Royal Australian Air Force
Marshal of the Royal New Zealand Air Force
Air Commodore-in-Chief Royal Canadian Air Cadets

His Royal Highness The Prince of Wales, KG KT GCB AK QSO ADC

Group Captain	(14.11.88)
Honorary Air Commodore	Royal Air Force Valley (1.4.93)

Commonwealth Forces

Air Commodore-in-Chief	Royal New Zealand Air Force
Colonel-in-Chief	Air Reserve Group of Air Command (of Canada)

His Royal Highness The Duke of York, CVO ADC

Honorary Air Commodore	Royal Air Force Lossiemouth (15.9.96)

Her Royal Highness The Princess Royal, KG, GCVO QSO

Honorary Air Commodore	Royal Air Force Lyneham (11.6.77)
Honorary Air Commodore	University of London Air Squadron (2.9.93)

Her Royal Highness The Princess Margaret, Countess of Snowdon, CI GCVO

Honorary Air Commodore	Royal Air Force Coningsby (11.6.77)

Her Royal Highness Princess Alice
Duchess of Gloucester, GCB CI GCVO GBE

Air Chief Marshal . . . . (23.2.90)

Air Chief Commandant . . . . Women, Royal Air Force (1.4.94)

His Royal Highness The Duke of Gloucester GCVO

Honorary Air Marshal. . . . . Royal Air Force (1.9.96)

Honorary Air Commodore . . . . Royal Air Force Odiham (1.4.93)

His Royal Highness The Duke of Kent, KG GCMG GCVO ADC

Honorary Air Chief Marshal. . . . . Royal Air Force (1.7.96)

Honorary Air Commodore . . . . Royal Air Force Leuchars (1.4.93)

Her Royal Highness Princess Alexandra, The Hon. Lady Ogilvy, GCVO

Patron and Air Chief Commandant . . . . Princess Mary's Royal Air Force Nursing Service (1.11.66)

Air Aides-de-Camp to The Queen

Air Chief Marshal Sir Richard Johns, GCB CBE LVO ADC FRAeS
Air Chief Marshal Sir John Allison, KCB CBE ADC

Aides-de-Camp to The Queen

Air Commodore C. R. Fowler, ADC
Air Commodore J. H. Haines, OBE ADC
Air Commodore A. C. Lang, MBE ADC BA CEng FIMechE FRAeS
Group Captain M. R. Bettel, OBE ADC
Group Captain R. H. Lacey, ADC MA BA
Group Captain G. H. Edge, OBE ADC BSc
Group Captain M. Prissick, ADC
Group Captain P. Whalley, ADC
Group Captain J. J. Witts, DSO ADC

Her Majesty's Senior Air Equerry

Air Commodore the Honourable T. C. Elworthy, CVO CBE

Extra Equerries to The Queen

Air Commodore the Honourable Timothy Elworthy, CVO CBE
Air Vice-Marshal Sir John Severne, KCVO OBE AFC DL
Air Commodore Sir Archie Winskill, KCVO CBE DFC* AE MRAeS
Air Commodore Sir Dennis Mitchell, KBE CVO DFC* AFC

Honorary Physicians to The Queen

Air Marshal J. A. Baird, QHP MB ChB FRCP(Edin) FRCS(Edin) FFOM FRAeS DAvMed (F)
Air Vice-Marshal C. J. Sharples, QHP MSc FFOM MRCS(Eng) LRCP DAvMed MRAeS
Air Commodore B. T. Morgans, QHP MB BCh FRCS (Glas.)
Air Commodore W. J. Pike, QHP MSc MB BS MRCGP MRCS MFOM DRCOG DAvMed LRCP

Honorary Surgeons to The Queen

Air Commodore D. J. Rainford, MBE QHS MB BS FRCP FRAeS MRCS
Air Commodore S. A. Cullen, QHS MB ChB FRCPath FRAeS DCP
Air Commodore A. N. Nicholson, OBE QHS PhD MD DSc MB ChB FRCPath FRCP
FRCP(Edin) FFOM FRAeS
Air Commodore T. M. Gibson, QHS PhD MB ChB MFOM DAvMed MRAeS

Honorary Dental Surgeons to The Queen

Air Vice-Marshal I. G. McIntyre, QHDS MSc BDS MGDSRCS(Eng) DDPHRCS FIMgt
Air Commodore R. M. Butler, QHDS MSc BDS MGDSRCS(Ed)

3

FOREIGN SOVEREIGNS
AND
MEMBERS OF FOREIGN ROYAL FAMILIES
who hold Honorary Commissions in the Royal Air Force

Air Chief Marshals

H.M. The King of the Hashemite Kingdom of Jordan, GCVO	19.7.66
HM The Sultan of Brunei Darussalam GCB, GCMG	5.11.92

Air Marshal

H.R.H. Prince Bernhard of the Netherlands, GCB GCVO GBE	15.9.64

4

DEFENCE COUNCIL

The RIGHT HONOURABLE

GEORGE ROBERTSON, MP
Secretary of State for Defence
(Chairman of the Defence Council)

The RIGHT HONOURABLE Dr The LORD GILBERT
Minister of State for Defence Procurement

Mr DOUG HENDERSON, MP
Minister of State for the Armed Forces

Mr JOHN SPELLAR, MP
Parliamentary Under Secretary of State for Defence

General Sir CHARLES GUTHRIE, GCB LVO OBE ADC Gen
Chief of the Defence Staff

Mr KEVIN TEBBIT, CMG
Permanent Under-Secretary of State
(Secretary of the Defence Council)

Admiral Sir JOCK SLATER, GCB LVO ADC
Chief of the Naval Staff

General Sir ROGER WHEELER, GCB CBE ADC Gen
Chief of the General Staff

Air Chief Marshal Sir RICHARD JOHNS, GCB CBE LVO ADC FRAeS RAF
Chief of the Air Staff

Admiral Sir PETER ABBOTT, KCB
Vice Chief of the Defence Staff

Sir ROBERT WALMSLEY, KCB MA FIEE
Chief of Defence Procurement

Professor Sir DAVID DAVIES, CBE FRS F Eng
Chief Scientific Adviser

Mr ROGER JACKLING, CBE
Second Permanent Under Secretary of State

AIR FORCE BOARD OF THE DEFENCE COUNCIL

The RIGHT HONOURABLE

GEORGE ROBERTSON, MP

Secretary of State for Defence

(Chairman of the Defence Council and Chairman of the Air Force Board of the Defence Council)

The RIGHT HONOURABLE Dr The LORD GILBERT
Minister of State for Defence Procurement

Mr DOUG HENDERSON, MP
Minister of State for the Armed Forces

Mr JOHN SPELLAR, MP
Parliamentary Under Secretary of State for Defence

Air Chief Marshal Sir RICHARD JOHNS, GCB CBE LVO ADC FRAeS RAF
Chief of the Air Staff

Mr ROGER JACKLING, CBE
Second Permanent Under Secretary of State

Air Chief Marshal Sir JOHN ALLISON, KCB CBE ADC FRAeS RAF
Air Officer Commanding-in-Chief Strike Command

Air Marshal Sir COLIN TERRY, KBE CB BSc(Eng) CEng FRAeS FRSA FILog FCGI RAF
Air Member for Logistics
Air Officer Commanding-in-Chief Logistics Command. Chief Engineer Royal Air Force

Air Marshal Sir ANTHONY BAGNALL, KCB OBE FRAeS RAF
Air Member for Personnel
Air Officer Commanding-in-Chief Personnel and Training Command

Air Vice-Marshal T. I. JENNER, CB FRAeS RAF
Assistant Chief of the Air Staff

Air Vice-Marshal P. C. NORRISS, CB AFC MA FRAeS RAF
Controller Aircraft
Director General Air Systems 1

The Air Force List 1999

ISBN 0 11 772887 X

ERRATA

Page 377, Right Hand Column. Amend entry 'Henderson, Mr D. . . . 5'
to read: 'Henderson, Mr D. . . . 5, 6, 7'

Page 415, Right Hand Column. Amend entry 'Reid, Dr J. . . . 6-7, 212, 307'
to read: 'Reid, J. . . . 212, 307'

Ministry of Defence
December 1998
LONDON: THE STATIONERY OFFICE

DEFENCE STAFF

SECRETARY OF STATE FOR DEFENCE
The RIGHT HONOURABLE GEORGE ROBERTSON, MP
Private Secretary
Mr T. C. McKane

MINISTER OF STATE FOR DEFENCE PROCUREMENT
The RIGHT HONOURABLE Dr The LORD GILBERT
Private Secretary
Mr R. D. Keen

MINISTER OF STATE FOR THE ARMED FORCES
Mr DOUG HENDERSON, MP
Private Secretary
Mr D. King

PARLIAMENTARY UNDER SECRETARY OF STATE FOR DEFENCE
Mr JOHN SPELLAR, MP
Private Secretary
Dr S. D. Cholerton
Military Assistant
Major C. J. Griggs

CHIEF OF THE DEFENCE STAFF
General Sir CHARLES GUTHRIE, GCB LVO OBE ADC Gen
Principal Staff Officer
Commodore C. R. STYLE, RN
Deputy Principal Staff Officer
Group Captain J. M. M. Ponsonby, RAF
Military Assistant
Lieutenant Colonel M. L. Riddell-Webster
Aide-de-Camp
Captain P. D. Morgan-Davies

PERMANENT UNDER SECRETARY OF STATE
Mr KEVIN TEBBIT, CMG
Private Secretary
Mr M. P. Preston

VICE CHIEF OF THE DEFENCE STAFF
Admiral Sir PETER ABBOTT, KCB
Private Secretary
Dr J. P. Noble
Military Assistant
Wing Commander A. J. Barrett, RAF
Assistant Military Assistant
Lieutenant P. J. Graham

DEFENCE SERVICES SECRETARY
Rear Admiral R B. LEES
Military Assistants
Wing Commander B. J. Walker, RAF
Lieutenant Colonel R. Parkinson

DEFENCE INFORMATION DIVISION

Press Secretary and Chief of Information
Miss O. G. MUIRHEAD, OBE
Private Secretary
Miss K. S. McCarthy

DIRECTOR OF RAF PUBLIC RELATIONS
Air Commodore G. L. McROBBIE, RAF

Personal Assistant
Mrs J. Amour

CHIEFS OF STAFF SECRETARIAT
SECRETARY CHIEFS OF STAFF COMMITTEE
Colonel G. R. Coward, OBE

Assistant Secretaries
Wing Commander I. D. Vacha, RAF
Lieutenant Colonel A. Salmon, MA RM

DEPUTY CHIEF OF THE DEFENCE STAFF (COMMITMENTS)
Air Marshal J. R. DAY, OBE BSc FRAeS RAF

Military Assistants
Commander A. S. Brooks, RN
Major B. Richards

DIRECTOR OF OPERATIONAL CAPABILITY
Commodore C. D. STANFORD, MA MNI

ASSISTANT CHIEF OF DEFENCE STAFF (OPERATIONS)
Rear Admiral S. MOORE

Military Assistant
Major N. Henderson

DIRECTOR JOINT WARFARE
Brigadier M. I. LAURIE, BSc

DIRECTOR NAVAL OPERATIONS
Commodore D. G. SNELSON, FIMgt MNI

DIRECTOR MILITARY OPERATIONS
Brigadier A. D. LEAKEY, MA

DIRECTOR AIR OPERATIONS
Air Commodore P. A. CRAWFORD, AFC BSc RAF

DIRECTOR OF OVERSEAS MILITARY ACTIVITY
Commodore J. M. de HALPERT, RN

DIRECTOR OF FOREIGN & COMMONWEALTH TRAINING
Group Captain M. M. A. Urquhart, RAF

ASSISTANT UNDER SECRETARY OF STATE (HOME & OVERSEAS)
Dr E. BUCKLEY

HEAD OF SECRETARIAT (OVERSEAS)
D. J. BONNER

ASSISTANT CHIEF OF DEFENCE STAFF (LOGISTICS)
Major General G. A. EWER, CBE
Military Assistant
Lieutenant Commander T. G. Davies

DIRECTOR OF DEFENCE SUPPORT POLICY
Brigadier M. KERLEY, CBE QGM

DIRECTOR OF DEFENCE LOGISTICS (PROGRAMMES)
Group Captain C. J. Blencowe, MA BA RAF

DIRECTOR OF DEFENCE LOGISTICS (OPERATIONAL POLICY)
Captain J. L. WILLIAMS, BA

DIRECTOR OF DEFENCE (MOVEMENTS)
Colonel R. I. Harrison

JOINT TRANSPORT AND MOVEMENTS STAFF
Air Commodore N. M. GRIFFITHS, BA FCIPS FIMgt RAF

8

HOME AND SPECIAL FORCES SECRETARIAT
  C. DAVENPORT

JOINT ARMS IMPLEMENTATION GROUP
  Group Captain D. R. E. EVANS, RAF

GULF VETERANS ILLNESS UNIT
  M. J. TONNISON

DIRECTOR OF MEDICAL OPERATIONS AND PLANS
  Brigadier J. R. BROWN

DIRECTOR SECURITY (POLICY)
  Vacant

ASSISTANT UNDER SECRETARY OF STATE (SECURITY & SUPPORT)

Group Captains

  S. H. Anderton, MSc BSc FIMgt
  D. R. Benson, OBE
  N. R. Chandler, MBE LLB
  P. C. Goodman, MBE BSc
  I. S. Hall, BA
  A. J. Kearney, CBE BSc(Econ)
  R. C. Moore, MBE BSc
  A. M. Morris, MSc
  S. L Parkinson
  P. N. O. Plunkett, BSc
  G. W. Pixton, DFC AFC
  A. Sawyer, OBE
  D. J. Stanley
  D. R. Williams, OBE

Wing Commanders

  E. G. N. Acons
  R. J. Allen
  D. A. Angus
  F. F. Amroliwala, OBE MA
  D. F. Archer, MBE MSc MCIPS
  P. A. Atherton
  R. A. Bealer
  P. M. Blee
  D. Bruce
  I. A. Cameron
  D. J. Cleland-Smith
  J. M. Clifford, MSc BSc
  K. L. Cornfield, OBE MA
  I. M. Draper, BA
  M. Djumic, MSc BSc
  J. Faulconer, MA BSc
  N. J. Furniss, MBE
  R. K. Gault, OBE
  D. M. Guest
  P. J. J. Haines, BSc
  A. V. B. Hawken, AFC
  D. J. Hayward
  N. Hutchinson
  W. A. Johnson, BSc
  P. M. Kaye
  D. J. Keenan
  T. Kirkhope, BSc
  M. W. Leaming, BSc
  S. M. J. Macartney, BSc
  G. Moulds, MBE

9

A. K. Mozumder, MB BS MRCGP MRCS(Eng) LRCP DRCOG DTM&H DAvMed
S. Pearson, BA
R. P. Radley
I. M. Robertson
M. G. Saunders
G. T. Scard, BA
S. P. Thompson, BSc
F. Tiernan
C. B. Waitt, BA
D. B. Wallace, MBE
C. M. West, BSc
G. K. Wishart, BSc

Principals and Equivalent Grades

S. Amber-Edwards
A. Barry
N. Blatchley
W. G. Byatt
W. P. Cassell
D. M. Chuter
J. S. L. Garrett
C. A. Gordon
N. Grayston
D. Midgley
G. Morris
R. M. Regan
R. Riordan
K. A. Robertson
S. Schofield
R. Turner
T. Taylor
N. Williams
P. G. Wythe

DEPUTY CHIEF OF THE DEFENCE STAFF (SYSTEMS)

Lieutenant General E. F. G. BURTON, OBE MA

Military Assistants
Commander A. R. Forsyth, RN
Lieutenant C. R. Baller, RN

ASSISTANT CHIEF OF THE DEFENCE STAFF OPERATIONAL REQUIREMENTS (SEA SYSTEMS)
Rear Admiral R. T. R. PHILLIPS, MNI

Military Assistant
Lieutenant Commander S. L. Parton, RN

ASSISTANT CHIEF OF THE DEFENCE STAFF OPERATIONAL REQUIREMENTS (LAND SYSTEMS)
Major General P. J. RUSSEL JONES

ASSISTANT CHIEF OF THE DEFENCE STAFF OPERATIONAL REQUIREMENTS (AIR SYSTEMS)
Air Vice-Marshal S. M. NICHOLL, CBE AFC BA

Military Assistant
Squadron Leader S. P. Russell, RAF

DIRECTOR OF OPERATIONAL REQUIREMENTS (AIR)
Air Commodore A. A. NICHOLSON, CBE LVO MA RAF

DIRECTOR SCIENCE (AIR)
Dr C. PELL

DIRECTOR GENERAL (RESEARCH AND TECHNOLOGY)
Mr M. MARKIN

DIRECTOR RESEARCH (SYSTEMS AND TECHNOLOGY)
Mr A. F. Everett

DIRECTOR RESEARCH (CORPORATE)
 Mr J. Jones

R(LS) HF15 (LIFE SCIENCES)
 Post Gapped

DIRECTOR DEFENCE SYSTEMS
 Commodore G. D. CHALLANDS, BSc MPhil CEng FIEE RN

DIRECTOR DEFENCE FIXED TELECOMMUNICATIONS SERVICE
 Air Commodore A. M. FERGUSON, CEng FIEE RAF

Group Captains

 M. R. Bettel, OBE ADC
 S. D. Black
 I. Evans
 T. G. Hanlon, FRAeS MIMgt
 J. I. Kane, BSc CEng MIEE MIMgt
 M. A. Leakey, BSc
 P. A. Smith, BSc FRIN
 M. D. Stringer

Wing Commanders

 J. P. Anderson
 I. T. Ashcroft
 G. Barber
 N. J. Davis, BSc MRAeS MRIN
 P. J. G. E. McG. Cullum, MIMgt
 R. M. Eastment, OBE MRAeS
 K. J. Harris, BSc CEng MIEE
 G. M. Hewett, MBE
 H. Johnston
 T. R. Kirkin, MRIN
 D. J. Keenan
 P. D. Legg, MA FIMgt MRAeS
 R. A. Lewis
 J. D. Martin, BA
 A. J. Mawby, BSc
 P. C. Osborn
 J. W. Pierce, MRAeS
 J. I. Pigott, MSc BSc CEng MIEE
 J. V. Plumb
 G. T. Scard, BA
 K. K. Thomson, MA
 R. J. Torbet
 C. C. Trundle
 N. P. Willmott
 A. L. Wilson, MSc BSc CEng MBCS

Senior Principals and Equivalent Grades

 G. Butler
 J. C. Copley
 W. J. Couperthwaite
 J. Knight

Principals and Equivalent Grades

 G. Andrews
 Dr G. Bibby
 I. Butcher
 Dr J. Critchley
 M. Geer
 Dr D. George
 P. Gittins
 M. Hepplewhite

11

G. Kirk
S. Lansley
R. Matthews
R. McNee
G. Osborn
Dr A. Witts

POLICY DIRECTOR
R. P. HATFIELD, CBE

Private Secretary
Miss C. Tassell

ASSISTANT CHIEF OF DEFENCE STAFF (POLICY)
Major General C. F. DREWRY, CBE

Military Assistant
Squadron Leader S. D. Pearson

DIRECTOR OF DEFENCE POLICY
J. S. DAY

DIRECTOR OF FORCE DEVELOPMENT
Brigadier D. W. MONTGOMERY

DIRECTOR OF NUCLEAR POLICY
Commodore J. M. PARKINSON, BSc CEng MIEE RN

DEPUTY POLICY DIRECTOR
B. R. HAWTIN, CB

DIRECTOR OF EUROPEAN POLICY
S. SMITH

DIRECTOR NORTH ATLANTIC AND WESTERN EUROPE
Brigadier A. A. MILTON, RM

DIRECTOR FOR CENTRAL AND EASTERN EUROPE
S. POLLARD

DIRECTOR PROLIFERATION AND ARMS CONTROL SECRETARIAT
P. SHULTE

HEAD OF PROTOCOL
Captain M. Bickley, RN Retd

DIRECTOR OF INFORMATION STRATEGY AND NEWS
Ms O. MUIRHEAD, OBE

DIRECTOR OF INTERNAL COMMUNICATION AND MEDIA TRAINING
Mr A. BOARDMAN

DIRECTOR OF PUBLIC RELATIONS (RAF)
Air Commodore G. L. McROBBIE

DIRECTOR OF PUBLIC RELATIONS (NAVY)
Commodore B. LEIGHTON

DIRECTOR OF PUBLIC RELATIONS (ARMY)
Brigadier R. GORDON

Group Captains
S. Chisnall, MPhil BA CertEd
C. P. Igoe

Wing Commanders
M. J. Ellaway
H. F. Gray-Wallis
A. D. Gunby
M. J. M. Jenkins, BSc
P. M. Kaye
M. W. Leaming, BSc
C. J. Leggett
R. P. Radley
J. H. Scholtens, BA
A. J. Stewart, MRAeS MIMgt

Retired Officer
Wing Commander I. C. MacMillan, MA

Senior Principals
T. Downes

Dr P. A. Hollinshead
Dr B. H. Wells

Principals

P. D. Adams
Mrs J. A. Broadhead
J. Chorley
R. Cockram
Dr R. Cornish
R. Davies
R. Holderness
D. Johnson
A. G. Moore
S. Routh
M. Rutter
J. C. Saltmarsh
Mrs A. J. Stevenson
S. J. Willmer
I. Woodman

DEPUTY CHIEF OF THE DEFENCE STAFF (PROGRAMMES AND PERSONNEL)
Air Marshal Sir PETER SQUIRE, KCB DFC AFC FRAeS RAF

Military Assistant
Lieutenant Colonel I. S. James, MBE
Management Planner
Mrs P. Neck

ASSISTANT CHIEF OF THE DEFENCE STAFF
Rear Admiral N. ESSENHIGH

Military Assistant
Squadron Leader M. P. Tomany, BEd RAF

DEFENCE SERVICES SECRETARY
Rear Admiral R. B. LEES

ASSISTANT CHIEF OF DEFENCE STAFF (LOGISTICS)
Major General G. EWER, CBE

Military Assistant
Lieutenant Commander T. Davies, RN

DIRECTOR OF DEFENCE PROGRAMMES
Brigadier R. DANNATT

DIRECTOR OF NAVY PLANS AND PROGRAMMES
Commodore R. McLEAN, RN

DIRECTOR OF ARMY PLANS AND PROGRAMMES
Brigadier A. PALMER, CBE

DIRECTOR OF AIR FORCE PLANS AND PROGRAMMES
Air Commodore S. M. NICHOLL, CBE AFC BA RAF

ASSISTANT UNDER SECRETARY OF STATE (SERVICE PERSONNEL POLICY)
P. M. ALDRED

DIRECTOR SERVICE PERSONNEL POLICY (NAAFI)
Air Commodore A. H. VAUGHAN, OBE BA RAF

DIRECTOR SERVICE PERSONNEL POLICY 1
Commodore D. R. S. LEWIS, CBE FIMgt RN

DIRECTOR SERVICE PERSONNEL POLICY 2
Dr F. PRICE

DIRECTOR SERVICE PERSONNEL POLICY 3
Air Commodore J. C. O. LUKE, CBE BSc RAF

DIRECTOR OF RESERVE FORCES AND CADETS
Brigadier E. R. HOLMES, CBE TD

DIRECTOR OF RESETTLEMENT
Brigadier R. C. WALKER, BSc

DIRECTOR OF DEFENCE SUPPORT POLICY
Brigadier M. KERLEY, CBE QGM

DIRECTOR OF SERVICE LIAISON DEFENCE HOUSING EXECUTIVE
Air Commodore D. C. ANDREWS, MBE FRIN RAF

HEAD OF SERVICE PERSONNEL POLICY (PENSIONS)
Mr R. WILLIAMS

Group Captains

C. J. Blencowe, MA BA
D. A. G. Bremner
N. Brewerton, BA MIMgt
N. R. Chandler, MBE LLB
P. A. Coker, OBE MIMgt
R. J. Hounslow, FRAeS FIMgt

Wing Commanders

S. Abbott, BA
D. F. Archer, MBE MSc MCIPS

L. R. E. Bessant, MHCIMA
C. J. Birks, BSc
G. H. Booth
R. F. Burdett, BA
C. Cordery, BEd
R. I. Elliott, BSc
G. S. Evans, MA MSc CEng MRAeS
A. L. Lewis, BSc
R. A. C. Low
P. M. O'Meeghan
N. B. Randall
J. G. Ross
R. A. Williams, OBE MA BA
G. A. Wright, BSc

SURGEON GENERAL
Air Marshal J. A. BAIRD, QHP MB ChB FRCP(Edin) FRCS(Edin) FFOM FRAeS DAvMed RAF

Military Assistant
Commander G. P. Parker, BEd

DIRECTOR OF MEDICAL PROGRAMMES AND PLANS
Brigadier J. R. BROWN, MA MSc MB BCh FFOM DCH

CHIEF OF STAFF SURGEON GENERAL'S DEPARTMENT
Surgeon Commodore G. H. EVANS, MB BS LRCP FFARCS MRCS

DIRECTOR OF DEFENCE DENTAL SERVICES
Air Vice-Marshal I. G. McINTYRE, QHDS MSc BDS MGDSRCS DDPHRCS FIMgt RAF

DIRECTOR OF DEFENCE NURSING SERVICES
Brigadier J. M. ARIGHO, RRC QHNS

DIRECTOR GENERAL INFORMATION AND COMMUNICATION SERVICES
Mr A. C. SLEIGH, MA

Military Assistant
Lieutenant Colonel A. D. Forster, R SIGNALS

DIRECTOR POLICY, INFORMATION AND COMMUNICATION SERVICES
Commodore J. T. TAMBLYN, ADC RN

DIRECTOR OPERATIONAL REQUIREMENTS INFORMATION AND COMMUNICATION SERVICES
Brigadier D. A. LYNAM, MBE

DIRECTOR ARCHITECTURE AND TECHNOLOGY
Dr R. JUDE

CHIEF EXECUTIVE DEFENCE COMMUNICATIONS SERVICES AGENCY
Major General A. J. RAPER, CBE

DIRECTOR INFRASTRUCTURE INFORMATION AND COMMUNICATION SERVICE
Dr S. H. ALEXANDER

SPECIAL ADVISOR TO DIRECTORATE GENERAL OF INFORMATION AND COMMUNICATION SERVICES
Dr A. J. GRANT

DIRECTOR OPERATIONS INFORMATION AND COMMUNICATIONS SERVICE
Colonel D. J. Lowe

DIRECTOR FINANCE MANAGEMENT AND SUPPORT INFORMATION AND COMMUNICATION SERVICE
Mr M. J. GAMBAZZI

Group Captains
B. G. Bensted, MBE BSc CEng MIEE
R. Camping, BSc
G. A. Paterson, BSc CEng MIEE MRAeS MIMgt
C. A. Suckling, MBE BSc CEng MIEE

Wing Commanders
J. O. Bates, BSc CEng, MIEE MRAeS
S. Brayshaw, BSc CEng MIEE
R. B. Cliffe

J. C. Hay, BA
P. J. Lock
S. D. Ottridge, BSc CEng MIEE MBCS
H. H. Pyper
I. R. Tyrell, BSc
D. Ward, BA BSc

CIVILIAN STAFF

PERMANENT UNDER SECRETARY OF STATE
Mr K. R. TEBBIT, CMG

Private Secretary
M. P. Preston

SECOND PERMANENT UNDER SECRETARY OF STATE
R. T. JACKLING, CB CBE

Private Secretary
Miss K. de Bourcier

DEPUTY UNDER SECRETARY OF STATE (RESOURCES, PROGRAMMES AND FINANCE)
C. V. BALMER

Private Secretary
Miss J. Dawson

DEPUTY UNDER SECRETARY OF STATE (CIVILIAN MANAGEMENT)
J. M. LEGGE, CMG

Private Secretary
Mrs A. Hughes

POLICY DIRECTOR
R. P. HATFIELD, CBE

Private Secretary
R. E. Lingham

ASSISTANT UNDER SECRETARY OF STATE (SERVICE PERSONNEL POLICY)
Miss P. M. ALDRED

Personal Assistant
Mrs L. Hughes

COMMAND SECRETARY LOGISTICS COMMAND
H. GRIFFITHS

Personal Secretary
Mrs Y. May

COMMAND SECRETARY RAF STRIKE COMMAND
C. J. WRIGHT

Personal Secretary
Mrs D. Freeman

COMMAND SECRETARY RAF PERSONNEL AND TRAINING COMMAND
Mrs L. D. KYLE

Personal Secretary
Mrs J. Coker

DEFENCE SCIENTIFIC STAFF

CHIEF SCIENTIFIC ADVISER
Professor Sir DAVID DAVIES, CBE DSc FIEE FEng FRS

PRIVATE SECRETARY
Mr M. A. Sinclair

DEPUTY UNDER SECRETARY OF STATE (SCIENCE & TECHNOLOGY)
Mr G. H. B. JORDAN

PRIVATE SECRETARY
Dr M. C. McCafferty

DIRECTOR GENERAL (RESEARCH AND TECHNOLOGY)
Mr M. MARKIN

DIRECTOR GENERAL (SCRUTINY AND ANALYSIS)
Mr M. EARWICKER

ASSISTANT CHIEF SCIENTIFIC ADVISER (NUCLEAR)
Mr P. ROPER

DIRECTORATE OF SCIENCE (BALLISTIC MISSILE DEFENCE)
Dr M. L. RANCE

DIRECTOR RESEARCH (CORPORATE)
Professor P. SUTTON

DIRECTOR RESEARCH (SYSTEMS AND TECHNOLOGY)
Mr A. EVERETT

DIRECTOR (SCRUTINY & ANALYSIS) AIR (D (S & A) AIR)
Mr I. BARRATT

DIRECTOR (SCRUTINY & ANALYSIS) SEA/CIS (D (S & A) SEA/CIS)
Mr K. SMITH

DIRECTOR (SCRUTINY & ANALYSIS) LAND (D (S & A) LAND)
Dr R. J. POWELL

DIRECTOR (SCRUTINY & ANALYSIS) P & P (D (S & A) P & P)
Mr D. DANIEL

METEOROLOGICAL OFFICE EXECUTIVE AGENCY

CHIEF EXECUTIVE
Mr P. D. EWINS, MSc FEng FRAeS

SENIOR PERSONAL SECRETARY
Mrs A. V. Kent

PROCUREMENT EXECUTIVE

CHIEF OF DEFENCE PROCUREMENT
Sir ROBERT WALMSLEY, KCB MA FIEE

Military Assistant
Captain R. D. FINLAYSON, RN

Private Secretary
Mr S. McCarthy

DEPUTY CHIEF OF DEFENCE PROCUREMENT (OPERATIONS)/MASTER GENERAL OF THE ORDNANCE
Lieutenant General Sir ROBERT HAYMAN-JOYCE, KCB CBE DL

Military Assistant
Lieutenant Colonel P. Jaques, REME

Private Secretary
Dr S. J. Dakin

Director General Aircraft Systems 1/Controller Aircraft
Air Vice-Marshal P. C. NORRISS, CB AFC MA FRAeS RAF

Staff Officer
Squadron Leader C. A. Gill, BSc RAF

Directors
Mr R. LITTLE
Mr S. FRASER
Mr E. GATES
Mr A. N. PEARSE
Air Commodore P. W. GILES, OBE PhD MA RAF
Group Captain J. W. THORPE, AFC RAF

Director General Aircraft Systems 2
Mr I. D. FAUSET

Directors
Mr W. A. DRUMMOND
Dr D. E. COLBOURNE
Mr P. H. PHILLIPS
Ms S. T. LINDSAY

Director General Weapons and Electronic Systems
Mr J. ALLEN

Directors
Air Commodore R. H. FLETCHER, BSc CEng MIMechE MRAeS RAF
Brigadier L. A. WILKES, FIMgt
Mr M. A. PIPER
Mr T. N. STRONG

Director General Command Information Systems
Dr I. WATSON

Staff Officer
Lieutenant Colonel J. A. Terrington, R SIGNALS

Directors
Mr D. TOWERS
Mr T. E. DOROTHY
Mr C. J. U. ROBERTS
Mr A. W. McCLELLAND
Mr S. WADDINGHAM
Brigadier C. BURTON

Director General Surface Ships/Acting Controller of Navy
Rear Admiral P. SPENCER, MA MSc

Secretary
Captain J. Pearce, RN

Directors
Commodore T. S. WITTICH, OBE MSc CEng MIEE RN
Dr J. FANNON
Dr D. R. PATTISON
Commodore N. C. F. GUILD, BA PhD MIEE AFIMA RN
Mr L. HUTCHINSON
Mr A. BEVAN

Director General Submarines/CSSE
Mr G. N. BEAVEN

Naval Assistant
Commander C. J. Longbottom, MEng MSc CEng MIMarE MIMechE RN

Directors
Mr T. R. THOMAS
Commodore C. B. YORK, RN
Mr S. L. SMITH
Mr M. R. OWEN
Mr G. ARMSTRONG
Mr M. FROWDE
Commodore A. J. H. BURBRIDGE, BSc CEng MINucE RN
Mr A. A. WOOLLEY

Director General Land Systems
Major General D. J. M. JENKINS, CBE

Military Assistant
Lieutenant Colonel N. Hutton

Directors
Brigadier P. J. WAGSTAFFE, CBE
Mr M. E. PEDLINGHAM
Mr A. TURNER
Mr G. C. BURRIDGE
Mr D. BALL

Principal Director of Contracts (Air)
Mr J. HARFORD

Principal Director of Contracts (Navy)
Mr S. PORTER

Principal Director of Contracts (Ordnance)
Mr A. V. CAREY

DEFENCE EVALUATION & RESEARCH AGENCY

CHIEF EXECUTIVE DERA
J. A. R. CHISHOLM

Personal Secretary
Miss C. E. Rollings

DIRECTOR OF CORPORATE AFFAIRS DERA
Mrs E. PEACE

DIRECTOR FINANCE DERA
S. PARK

TECHNICAL DIRECTOR DERA
Dr A. L. MEARS

DIRECTOR PERSONNEL DERA
B. HEDLEY

SENIOR MILITARY OFFICER DERA
Air Commodore E. W. TYACK, CBE FRAeS RAF

MANAGING DIRECTOR PROGRAMMES
Dr M. GOODFELLOW

Director Land Systems
Dr D. Anderson
Director Air Systems
M. Steeden
Director Sea Systems
N. J. Helbren
Director Command & Information Systems
A. Middleton

MANAGING DIRECTOR FACILITIES
C. R. STONEHOUSE

Director Test & Evaluation Ranges
Dr C. J. Rigden
Director Aircraft Test & Evaluation
TBA
Director Test & Evaluation Facilities
R. Gould

MANAGING DIRECTOR SCIENCE
Dr G. COLEY

Director Weapon Systems
W. Clifford
Director Chemical & Biological Defence
P. D. Taylor
Director Structural Materials Centre
Dr J. Morton
Director Electronics
Dr N. Apsley
Director Centre For Human Sciences
Mrs M. Walker
Director Chemical & Electronics Systems
Dr J. Widdowson

MANAGING DIRECTOR ANALYSIS
M. EARWICKER

Director Centre for Defence Analysis
Dr A. F. Saunders
MANAGING DIRECTOR DERATEC
J. MABBERLEY

ORDNANCE BOARD

Postal Address—Procurement Executive, Walnut 2c
MOD Abbey Wood, # 67
Bristol BS34 8JH
Telephone No 0117-91-31817

President

Air Vice-Marshal P. J. O'REILLY, BSc CEng FIEE FRAeS RAF 23.2.96

Vice-Presidents

Brigadier L. D. CURRAN, MA CEng FIEE 26.1.96
Dr I. G. WALLACE, PhD BSc 6.10.97

Secretary

Miss C. Bater, MA 4.11.96

Members

Colonel K. J. Farrar 15.9.95
Lieutenant Colonel (Retd) L. W. McNaught 17.11.96
Colonel B. G J. Hutchins, BSc(Eng) MSc CEng FIEE 4.11.96
Colonel P. Davies 19.12.96
Captain J. A. Kongialis, BSc RN 9.5.97
Dr P. H. Collins, PhD BSc 11.6.97
Group Captain S. R. Sims, OBE BSc CEng MRAeS DLUT RAF 12.6.98

OFFICE OF THE
JUDGE ADVOCATE GENERAL OF THE FORCES

(LORD CHANCELLOR'S ESTABLISHMENT)

(Joint Service for the Army and Royal Air Force)

22 Kingsway, London, WC2B 6LE Tel. 0171-218 8079

Judge Advocate General
HIS HONOUR JUDGE J. W. RANT, CB QC

Senior Personal Secretary
Miss E. F. Ruddy

Vice Judge Advocate General
E. G. MOELWYN-HUGHES

Assistant Judge Advocates General (London Office and Overseas)

Judge Advocate D. M. BERKSON (DJAG BRITISH FORCES IN GERMANY)
Judge Advocate M. A. HUNTER
Judge Advocate J. P. CAMP
Judge Advocate Miss S. E. WOOLLAM
Judge Advocate R. C. C. SEYMOUR
Judge Advocate I. H. PEARSON
Judge Advocate R. G. CHAPPLE
Judge Advocate J. F. T. BAYLISS

Grade 6 Legal
T. S. G. Miller

Registrar
D. Murray

DEPARTMENT
OF THE
CHIEF OF THE AIR STAFF

CHIEF OF THE AIR STAFF
Air Chief Marshal Sir RICHARD JOHNS, GCB CBE LVO ADC FRAeS 10.4.97

Private Secretary
I. S. Manson

Personal Staff Officer
Group Captain P. J. Drissell, MA BSc MInstD 1.6.98

Staff Officer
Flight Lieutenant P. C. Brown, BSc. 29.8.96

ASSISTANT CHIEF OF THE AIR STAFF
Air Vice-Marshal T. I. JENNER, CB FRAeS 30.9.95

Personal Staff Officer
Wing Commander N. D. Meyrick 18.11.96

Staff Officer
Squadron Leader S. C. Griffiths, BA 22.9.97

DIRECTOR OF AIR STAFF
Air Commodore C. M. CHAMBERS 3.1.97

HEAD OF AIR HISTORICAL BRANCH (RAF)
J. S. COX, BA MA

HEAD OF SECRETARIAT (AIR STAFF)
M. J. FULLER

INSPECTOR OF RAF FLIGHT SAFETY
Air Commodore E. J. BLACK, FRAeS FIMgt 31.10.97

DIRECTOR EUROFIGHTER PROGRAMME ASSURANCE GROUP
Air Commodore R. S. PEACOCK-EDWARDS, CBE AFC FRAeS FIMgt 31.10.97

Group Captains
P. J. Gooding, AFC 12.6.96
H. R. Corney, OBE BA. 28.4.97
J. Middleton 13.10.97

Wing Commanders
D. A. Angus. 1.9.97
S. B. J. Barber, MA 3.6.97
D. E. Bentley 29.8.95
M. P. Cocksedge 12.5.97
R. Crane 12.12.97
P. J. Daybell, MBE MA BA 2.9.96
S. K. Dobb 9.6.97
N. J. Furniss, MBE. 23.4.93
A. V. B. Hawken, AFC 12.7.97
D. W. Knowles, MBA BA 1.9.97
R. G. Leonard 16.12.96
I. C. Morrison 9.12.96
R. M. Poole 1.9.97
D. G. Robertson 28.4.97
G. D. Soul 26.8.97
T. A. Spandley 14.7.97
J. Whittingham. 9.2.98
P. A. Willis 26.5.98

Principals and Equivalent Grades
J. E. Callcutt
M. Field
J. Lewis

PERMANENT JOINT HEADQUARTERS (UK)

Postal Address—NORTHWOOD, MIDDLESEX, HA6 3TJ
Telephone No 01923 826161

Commander Joint Operations
Lieutenant General Sir CHRISTOPHER WALLACE, KBE 1.10.94

Military Assistant
Wing Commander K. Dennison BSc 27.4.98

Chief of Staff
Air Vice-Marshal R. H. GOODALL, CBE AFC* 1.4.96

Military Assistant
Major T. C. St. J. Warrington 1.4.96

J1/J4 Division
Brigadier P. A. FLANAGAN 1.4.96
Group Captain A. C. Spinks, MILog 1.7.96
Wing Commander D. S. Belmore, MBE MCIPS 16.4.96
Wing Commander R. B. Lindley, MIMgt 1.2.96

J2 Division
Air Commodore P. JEFFERS. 1.4.96

J3 Division
Air Commodore G. L. TORPY, DSO BSc 14.4.98
Group Captain P. W. Day, AFC 1.4.96
Wing Commander J. D. Arkell MA. 13.3.97
Wing Commander N. E. L. Beresford, LVO 22.4.96
Wing Commander A. R. Bown 13.10.97
Wing Commander K. R. Cowieson. 18.5.98

J5 Division
Mr N. J. S. ABBOTT, OBE
Mr M. Truran
Mr G. D. Dean
Mr L. F. Phillips, RD TD
Wing Commander L. J. Irvine, MA DipLaw 8.4.96

J6 Division
Commodore A. C. LYDDON 10.2.97
Wing Commander S. J. Kinder, MBE BSc 11.3.96

J7 Division
Brigadier M. A. RAWORTH 1.4.96
Wing Commander A. P. Kirk. 2.4.96
Wing Commander R. D. Wright, BSc 15.6.98

J8 Division
Commodore P. W. HERRINGTON 1.3.98
Group Captain C. M. Nickols, MA 20.4.98
Mr H. D. Richardson, OBE
Wing Commander M. W. Halsall 6.1.97
Wing Commander P. Lyall, BA 9.3.98
Wing Commander E. J. Scaplehorne, BA MMar 1.4.96

J9 Division
Mr W. M. Jessett

Joint Force Headquarters
Brigadier D. J. RICHARDS 5.5.98
Wing Commander M. W. Brown 1.4.96
Wing Commander D. J. Walker. 1.4.96

DIRECTORATE OF AIRSPACE POLICY

DIRECTOR AIRSPACE POLICY

Air Vice-Marshal R. D. ELDER, CBE FRAeS 1.4.96

Group Captains

D. J. Hodge 8.7.96

T. J. Murray 4.12.95

Wing Commanders

B. E. Bunting 18.11.96

B. Coombs, BA 17.6.96

A. A. Perfect, MIMgt 5.2.96

J. P. Stenson, MBE BSc 5.7.96

M. C. G. Strong 28.6.96

Principal

Mrs E. J. Lewis

27

SOVEREIGN BASE AREAS OF AKROTIRI
AND DHEKELIA ADMINISTRATION

Postal Address—HEADQUARTERS, SOVEREIGN BASE AREAS ADMINISTRATION, EPISKOPI.
BRITISH FORCES POST OFFICE 53

THE ADMINISTRATOR

Major General A. I. RAMSAY, CBE DSO 16.1.98

Military Assistant
Squadron Leader R. J. Cowell, RAF

Aide-de-Camp
Captain M. Luckyn-Malone
Chief Officer of Sovereign Base Areas
P. A. ROTHERAM
Administrative Secretary
J. C. JARVIS

Judiciary
R. J. D. LIVESEY . . . . Senior Judge
F. G. R. WARD, OBE . . . . Resident Judge

Legal
P. W. VISAGIE . . . . Attorney General and Legal Adviser
Akrotiri Area Office
A. Angelides . . . . Area Officer

Dhekelia Area Office
K. A. Demetriades . . . . Area Officer

Sovereign Base Areas Police
E. Vallance, LLB . . . . Chief Constable
Sovereign Base Areas Customs
A. Livingstone. . . . . Fiscal Officer

Administrator's Advisory Board
P. A. ROTHERAM . . . . Chief Officer
Air Commodore P. A. ROBINSON, OBE RAF . . . . . Chief of Staff, British Forces Cyprus
P. W. VISAGIE, ... Attorney General and Legal Advisor
Colonel M. H. H. BROOKE, OBE . . . . Garrison Commander, Dhekelia

DEFENCE AND AIR ATTACHES TO EMBASSIES

ABU DHABI (UAE)—(British Embassy, Abu Dhabi, c/o FCO, Outward Bag Room, King Charles Street, London SW1A 2AH)
Defence, Naval and Military Attaché . . . . . Colonel C. J. B. Copeland 15.9.93
Air Attaché . . . . Wing Commander M. K. Allport MBE RAF. . . 2.5.95

AMMAN—(British Embassy, Amman, c/o FCO, Outward Bag Room, King Charles Street, London SW1A 2AH)
Defence, Naval and Military Attaché . . . . . Colonel R. J. Sandy 12.6.98
Air Attaché . . . . Wing Commander D. M. Sedman, RAF . . . 25.4.96

ANKARA—(British Embassy, Ankara. c/o FCO, Outward Bag Room, King Charles Street, London SW1A 2AH)
Defence and Military Attaché. . . . . Brigadier A. V. TWISS 19.3.96
Naval and Air Attaché . . . . Wing Commander R. G. Blake 15.7.96

ATHENS—(British Embassy, Athens, c/o FCO, Outward Bag Room, King Charles Street, London SW1A 2AH)
Defence and Military Attaché. . . . . Brigadier W. A. McMAHON 17.11.95
Naval and Air Attaché . . . . Captain W. K. Benbow, RN 17.11.95

BANGKOK—(British Embassy, BFPO5)
Defence Attaché. . . . . Colonel J. H. Thoyts 2.12.97

BEIRUT—(British Embassy, Beirut, c/o FCO, Outward Bag Room, King Charles Street, London SW1A 2AH)
Defence Attaché. . . . . Lieutenant Colonel C. J. A. Wilton 30.6.96

BELGRADE—(British Embassy, Belgrade, c/o FCO. Outward Bag Room, King Charles Street, London SW1A 2AH)
Defence Attaché. . . . . Colonel J. H. Crosland, MC 5.8.96

BERNE—(British Embassy, Thunstrasse 50, 3005 Berne, Switzerland)
Defence Attaché. . . . . Lieutenant Colonel E. J. Gould 30.1.98

BOGOTA—(British Embassy, Bogota, c/o FCO, Outward Bag Room King Charles Street, London SW1A 2AH)
Defence, Naval, Military and Air Attaché . . . . Colonel P. C. Maynard, OBE 30.5.97
(also Defence Attaché Lima)

BONN—(British Embassy, Box No 2012, BFPO 105)
Defence and Military Attaché. . . . . Brigadier B. R. ISBELL 30.8.96
Air Attaché . . . . Group Captain S. A. Wrigley 4.5.96

BRASILIA—(British Embassy, Brasilia, c/o FCO, Outward Bag Room, King Charles Street, London SW1A 2AH)
Defence, Military and Air Attaché . . . . . . Colonel D. M. Black 3.6.94

BRATISLAVA—(British Embassy, Grosslingova 35 811 09 Bratislava Slovak Republic)
Defence Attaché. . . . . Wing Commander P. M. Leadbetter, MVO MIMgt RAF
. . . . 14.2.97

BRUSSELS—(British Embassy, BFPO 49)
Defence Attaché. . . . . Colonel T. E. Hall 2.4.98
(also Defence Attaché Luxembourg)

BUCHAREST—(British Embassy, Bucharest, c/o FCO, Outward Bag Room, King Charles Street, London SW1A 2AH)
Defence, Attaché . . . . Lieutenant Colonel R. D. Shaw-Brown . . . 8.11.97

BUDAPEST—(British Embassy, Budapest, c/o FCO, Outward Bag Room, King Charles Street, London SW1A 2AH)
Defence Attaché. . . . . Colonel H. V. C. Stephens 8.12.94

BUENOS AIRES—(British Embassy, Buenos Aires, c/o FCO Outward Bag Room, King Charles Street, London SW1A 2AH).
Defence and Air Attaché . . . . Group Captain D. K. L. McDonnell, OBE . . . 20.12.96
(also Defence Attaché Montevideo)
Naval and Military Attaché . . . . Colonel H. P. D. Massey 7.9.97
(also Defence Attaché Asuncion)

CAIRO—(British Embassy, Cairo, c/o FCO, Outward Bag Room, King Charles Street, London SW1A 2AH)
Defence and Military Attaché. . . . . Colonel A. W. G. Snook, OBE 2.8.96
Naval and Air Attaché . . . . Commander N. P. Smith, RN 23.3.95
(also Defence Attaché Khartoum)

CARACAS—(British Embassy, Caracas, c/o FCO, Outward Bag Room, King Charles Street, London SW1A 2AH)
Defence, Naval, Military and Air Attaché . . . . Colonel P. A. Reynolds, RM 15.12.97
(also Defence Attaché Quito and Panama City)

COPENHAGEN—(British Embassy, 36/38/40 Kastelsvej, DK-2100 Copenhagen, Denmark)
Defence, Naval, Military and Air Attaché . . . .   Commander A. C. Gordon Lennox, RN   . . .   14.2.98

DAMASCUS—(British Embassy, Damascus, c/o FCO Outward Bag Room, King Charles Street, London SW1A 2AH)
Defence Attaché. . . . .   Colonel M. A. Hart, MBE QGM 1.8.97

DOHA—(British Embassy, Doha, Qatar, c/o FCO Outward Bag Room, King Charles Street, London SW1A 2AH)
Defence Attaché. . . . .   Wing Commander W. R. Southcombe, RAF . .   23.7.95

DUBLIN—(British Embassy, Dublin, c/o FCO, Outward Bag Room, King Charles Street, London SW1A 2AH)
Defence Attaché. . . . .   Colonel S. D. Lambe, CBE 5.8.89

GUATEMALA CITY—(British Embassy Guatemala City, Guatemala, c/o FCO Outward Bag Room, King Charles Street, London, SW1A 2AH)
Defence Attaché. . . . .   Colonel D. B Simpson 6.9.96
(also Defence Attaché San Salvador and Tegucigalpa and Managua)

THE HAGUE—(British Embassy, Lange Voorhout 10, 2514 ED, The Hague, Netherlands)
Defence and Naval Attaché . . . .   Captain R. StJ. S. Bishop, RN 13.3.98
Military and Air Attaché . . . .   Lieutenant Colonel C. A. Le Hardy 15.12.95

HELSINKI—(British Embassy, Uudenmaankatu 16,20, 00120 Helsinki 12 Finland)
Defence, Naval, Military and Air Attaché . . .   Lieutenant Colonel G. A. B. Grant 25.4.98
(also Defence Attaché Tallinn)

JAKARTA—(British Embassy, Jakarta, c/o FCO, Outward Bag Room, King Charles Street, London SW1A 2AH)
Defence Attaché. . . . .   Colonel D. S. MacFarlane 8.8.97

KATHMANDU—(British Embassy, Kathmandu, BFPO 4)
Defence Attaché. . . . .   Colonel A. W. Blackett, OBE. 25.10.96

KUWAIT CITY—(British Embassy, PO Box 2, Safat 13001 Kuwait)
Defence Attaché. . . . .   Colonel G. N. R. Sayle, OBE. 22.1.97

LISBON—(British Embassy, Lisbon, BFPO 6)
Defence, Naval and Air Attaché . . . . . .   Commander R. A. Goddard, AFC RN 23.10.96

MADRID—(British Embassy, Madrid, c/o FCO, Outward Bag Room, King Charles Street, London SW1A 2AH)
Defence and Naval Attaché . . . .   Captain P. J. Pacey, RN 4.12.96
Military and Air Attaché . . . .   Colonel R. J. Lawson 19.9.97

MANILA—(British Embassy, Manila, c/o FCO, Outward Bag Room, King Charles Street, London SW1A 2AH)
Defence Attaché. . . . .   Group Captain P. G. Wildman, BA FRAeS RAF .   21.9.95

MEXICO CITY—(British Embassy, Mexico City, c/o FCO, Outward Bag Room, King Charles Street, London SW1A 2AH)
Defence, Naval, Military and Air Attaché . . .   Colonel J. M. C. Watson 1.9.97
(also Defence Attaché Belize and Havana)

MOSCOW—(British Embassy, Moscow, c/o FCO, Outward Bag Room, King Charles Street, London SW1A 2AH)
Defence and Air Attaché . . . .   Air Commodore M. L. FEENAN, CBE MA FIMgt.   28.6.96
(also Defence Attaché Alma Ata, Ashkhabad, Bishkek, Dushanbe and Tashkent)
Assistant Air Attaché . . . .   Squadron Leader A. I. Farmer, MBE BA RAF. .   18.10.96
(also Assistant Defence Attaché Kishinev and Minsk)

MUSCAT—(British Embassy, Muscat, c/o FCO, Outward Bag Room, King Charles Street, London SW1A 2AH)
Defence and Military Attaché. . . . . . .   Brigadier M. I. KEUN 28.6.96
Naval and Air Attaché . . . .   Wing Commander G. R. Warburton RAF . . .   18.7.98

OSLO—(British Embassy, Thomas Heftyesgate 8, 0244 Oslo 2, Norway)
Defence and Naval Attaché . . . .   Lieutenant Colonel P. D. T. Irvine, OBE RM . . .   21.3.96
Military and Air Attaché . . . .   Lietenant Colonel P. H. Gullan, MBE MC . . .   5.8.95

PARIS—(British Embassy, 35 rue du Faubourg St. Honore, 75383 Paris Cedex 08, France)
Defence and Air Attaché . . . .   Air Commodore D. N. ADAMS, BSc MRAeS RAF   18.2.98
Assistant Air Attaché . . . .   Wing Commander S. Gunner, BSc(Eng) RAF .   24.7.95

PEKING—(British Embassy, Peking, c/o FCO, Outward Bag Room, King Charles Street, London SW1A 2AH)
Defence, Military and Air Attaché . . . . .   Brigadier J. G. KERR, OBE QGM 15.6.98

PRAGUE—(British Embassy, Prague, c/o FCO, Outward Bag Room, King Charles Street, London SW1A 2AH)
Defence and Military Attaché. . . . . . .   Colonel A. F. Davidson, MBE 26.6.98

RABAT—(British Embassy, 17 Boulevard de la Tour Hasson, (BP 45), Rabat, Morocco.
Defence Attaché. . . . .   Lieutenant Colonel M. H. Argue, MBE, MC . .   18.6.98
(also Defence Attaché Nouakchott)

RIGA—(British Embassy, Riga, c/o FCO, Outward Bag Room, King Charles Street , London SW1A 2AH)
Defence Attaché. . . . . Lieutenant Colonel N. G. W. Lang 5.1.95
(also Defence Attaché Vilnius)

RIYADH—(British Embassy, Riyadh, c/o FCO, Outward Bag Room, King Charles Street, London SW1A 2AH)
Defence and Military Attaché. . . . . . . Brigadier W. E. STRONG. 20.9.95
(also Defence Attaché Bahrain and Defence and Military Attaché Sana'a)
Air Attaché . . . . Wing Commander C. B. Troke, RAF 26.7.95
(also Air Attaché Sana'a)

ROME—(British Embassy, BFPO 8)
Defence and Military Attaché. . . . . . . Brigadier J. A. ANDERSON 16.10.96
Air Attaché . . . . Group Captain J. N. J. Grisdale MBE RAF . . 16.1.98

SANTIAGO—(British Embassy Santiago, c/o FCO, Outward Bag Room, King Charles Street, London SW1A 2AH)
Defence Attaché. . . . . Captain P. J. Ellis, RN. 2.8.97

SEOUL—(British Embassy, BFPO 3, via BFPO 1)
Defence and Military Attaché. . . . . . . Brigadier C. D. PARR, OBE 12.3.94
Naval and Air Attaché . . . . Group Captain S. J. Coy, OBE RAF 19.10.96

SOFIA—(British Embassy, Sofia, c/o FCO, Outward Bag Room, King Charles Street, London SW1A 2AH)
Defence Attaché. . . . . Colonel R. E. Fielding. 5.12.97
(also Defence Attaché Skopje)

STOCKHOLM—(British Embassy, Box 27819-115-93 Stockholm, Sweden)
Defence and Air Attaché . . . . Wing Commander P. J. G. E. McG. Cullum,
MIMgt RAF 1.8.94

TEL AVIV—(British Embassy, Tel Aviv, c/o FCO, Outward Bag Room, King Charles Street, London SW1A 2AH)
Defence and Military Attaché. . . . . . . Colonel E. H. Houston, OBE. 27.10.97
Naval and Air Attaché . . . . Wing Commander M. B. Whitehouse, BSc RAF. 4.4.97

TOKYO—(British Embassy No. 1 Ichiban-cho. Chiyoda-ku, Tokyo 102, Japan)
Defence and Naval Attaché . . . . Captain N. D. V. Robertson, RN. 12.5.95
Military and Air Attaché . . . . Group Captain P. Edwards, RAF 20.11.95

VIENNA—(British Embassy, Jaucesgasse 12, 1030 Vienna, Austria)
Defence Attaché. . . . . Lieutenant Colonel A. R. Manton 21.3.97
(also Defence Attaché Ljubljana)

WARSAW—(British Embassy, Warsaw, c/o FCO, Outward Bag Room, King Charles Street, London SW1A 2AH)
Defence and Air Attaché . . . . Group Captain M. Mitchell, RAF 9.6.97
Naval and Military Attaché . . . . Lieutenant Colonel P. R. P. Swanson, MBE . . 25.10.97

WASHINGTON—(British Embassy, BFPO 2)
Defence Attaché. . . . . Major General C. G. C. VYVYAN, CBE. . . . 22.4.97
Air Attaché . . . . Air Commodore D. K. NORRISS, RAF. . . . 16.9.95
Assistant Air Attaché . . . . Group Captain R. D. Iveson, AFC 22.3.96

ZAGREB—(British Embassy, Zagreb, c/o FCO, Outward Bag Room, King Charles Street, London SW1A 2AH)
Defence Attaché. . . . . Lieutenant Colonel S. C. H. Cleveland MBE . . 6.12.97

DEFENCE AND AIR ADVISERS TO BRITISH HIGH COMMISSIONS

ACCRA—(British High Commission, Accra, c/o ECO, Outward Bag Room, King Charles Street, London SW1A 2AH)
Defence Adviser. . . . . Lieutenant Colonel E. Glover 30.1.98
(also Freetown and Defence Attaché Lom   and Abidjan)

BRIDGETOWN—(British High Commission, Lower Collymore Rock, (PO Box 676), Bridgetown, Barbados
Defence Adviser. . . . . Captain P. Jackson, RN 18.2.98
(also Defence Advisor St Georges, Kingstown, Castries, Roseau, St Johns, Basseterre, Cayman, Grand Turk, Tortola, The Valley and Plymouth and Defence Attaché Paramaribo)

CANBERRA—(British High Commission, Commonwealth Avenue, Canberra, Australia)
Defence and Naval Adviser . . . . Commodore A. J. LYALL, MBE RN. 12.2.98
Air Adviser . . . . Group Captain A. N. Macgregor, RAF 27.6.96

COLOMBO—(British High Commission, Colombo, c/o FCO, Outward Bag Room, King Charles Street, London SW1A)
Defence Adviser. . . . . Lieutenant Colonel R. N. Kendell, MBE . . . 6.3.98

DHAKA—(British High Commission, Dhaka, c/o FCO, Outward Bag Room, King Charles Street, London SW1 2AH)
Defence Adviser. . . . . Colonel J. M. Phillips 23.6.95

HARARE—(British High Commission. Harare, c/o FCO, Outward Bag Room, King Charles Street, London SW1A 2AH)
Defence Adviser. . . . . Colonel A. J. Reed-Screen, OBE 9.3.95
(also Defence Adviser Gaborone, Lilongwe and Maputo)

ISLAMABAD—(British High Commission, Islamabad, c/o FCO, Outward Bag Room, King Charles Street, London SW1A 2AH Vincent and the Grenadines)
Defence and Military Adviser. . . . . Brigadier B. D. WHEELWRIGHT. 13.6.97
Naval and Air Adviser . . . . Captain M. J. Broadhurst, RN 12.12.97

KAMPALA—(British High Commission, Kampala, c/o FCO, Outward Bag Room, King Charles Street, London SW1A 2AH)
Defence Adviser. . . . . Lieutenant Colonel C. E. Thom, OBE 23.1.98
(also Defence Attaché Burundi and Kigali)

KINGSTON—(British High Commission, Kingston, c/o FCO, Outward Bag Room, King Charles Street, London SW1A 2AH)
Defence Adviser. . . . . Colonel A. L. Moorby 9.4.97
(also Trinidad & Tobago, Georgetown, Paramaribo and Nassau)

KUALA LUMPUR—(Wisma Damansara, Jalan Semantan, 50490 Kuala Lumpur, Malaysia)
Defence Adviser. . . . . Colonel M. B. Cooper. 1.11.96
Assistant Defence Adviser. . . . . Lieutenant Commander R. J. Pharoah, RN . . 10.2.95
(also Defence Attaché Hanoi)

NAIROBI—(British High Commission, BFPO 10)
Defence and Military Adviser. . . . . . . Colonel T. V. Merritt, OBE 12.9.97
(also Defence Advisor Dar-Es-Salaam and Defence Attaché Addis Ababa and Asmara)

NEW DELHI—(British High Commission, New Delhi, c/o FCO, Outward Bag Room, King Charles Street, London SW1A 2AH)
Defence and Military Adviser. . . . . . . Brigadier S. M. A. LEE, OBE. 28.11.97
Air Adviser . . . . Group Captain R. E. Wedge, CBE BSc, RAF . . 26.4.96

NICOSIA—(British High Commission, BFPO 567)
Defence Adviser. . . . . Colonel C. S. Wakelin, OBE 14.5.98

AIR FORCE DEPARTMENT

OTTAWA—(British High Commission, Naval Party 1010, BFPO 487)
Defence and Military Adviser. . . . . Brigadier E. P. O. SPRINGFIELD, CBE 15.1.97
Naval and Air Adviser . . . . Group Captain T. J. Williams, AFC. 14.5.97

PRETORIA—(British High Commission, Pretoria, c/o Outward Bag Room, King Charles Street, London SW1A 2AH)
Defence and Military Adviser. . . . . Brigadier M. L. WILDMAN 8.11.96
(also Defence Adviser Maseru and Mbabane)
Naval and Air Adviser . . . . Commander D. L. Sim, RN 30.11.97
(also Defence Adviser Windhoek)

SINGAPORE—(British High Commission, Naval Party 1022 BFPO Ships)
Defence Adviser. . . . . Group Captain C. B. Le Bas, BSc MIMgt RAF . 20.6.98
(also Defence Attaché Bandar Seri Begawan)

WELLINGTON—(British High Commission, PO Box 1812, (44 Hill Street), Wellington, New Zealand)
Defence Adviser. . . . . Colonel P. R. Barry. 11.2.95
(also Defence Attaché Suva and Nuku'alofa)

HEADQUARTERS IN THE UNITED KINGDOM OF THE AIR FORCES OF COMMONWEALTH COUNTRIES

AUSTRALIA. Australian Defence Staff
Address: Australia House, Strand, London, WC2B 4LA. Telephone: 0171 887 5264

Air Adviser
Group Captain P. B. Layton, RAAF
Staff Officer Engineering (Air Force)
Wing Commander S. C. Sheedy, RAAF

CANADA. Canadian Forces, Canadian Defence Liaison Staff.
Address: 1 Grosvenor Square, London W1X 0AB. Telephone 0171-258 6424

Air Force Adviser
Colonel P. S. Tanton, OMM CD
Assistant Air Force Adviser
Lieutenant Colonel D. E. Cargo, CD

NEW ZEALAND. New Zealand Defence Staff.
Address: New Zealand House, 80 Haymarket, London SW1Y 4TQ. Telephone 0171-930 8400

Head NZDS
Brigadier I. J. DUTHIE, CNZM
Air Adviser
Wing Commander J. B. Jones, RNZAF

INDIA. Staff of the Air Adviser to the High Commissioner for India in the U.K.
Address: India House, Aldwych. London WC2B 4NA Telephone: 0171-836 8484 EXT: 222

Air Adviser
Air Commodore C. S. GILL, VM VSM

BRITISH DEFENCE STAFF WASHINGTON

Postal Address BFPO 2

CENTRAL STAFF

Communications Information Service

Wing Commander B. L. Gray, IEng FIIE(elec) 7.8.95

ROYAL AIR FORCE STAFF

Air Attaché,

Air Commodore D. K. NORRISS 1.9.95

Group Captain

R. D. Iveson, AFC 8.3.96

Wing Commanders

P. J. Hibberd, BA 8.1.96
P. Williams, BSc 1.8.97
D. A. Johncock. 11.9.95
A. B. Crockatt, AFC 1.8.97

DEFENCE STAFF

DE/Air Armaments

Wing Commander G. M. Goddard, MSc BSc CEng MIMechE ACGI 24.1.97

STRIKE COMMAND

Postal Address RAF HIGH WYCOMBE, BUCKINGHAMSHIRE, HP14 4UE
Telephone Nos—01494-461461 (GPTN 95221)

COMMAND HEADQUARTERS

AIR OFFICER COMMANDING-IN-CHIEF
Air Chief Marshal Sir JOHN ALLISON, KCB CBE ADC FRAeS 25.7.97

Personal Staff Officer
Group Captain M. C. Barter, OBE 30.6.96
Deputy Personal Staff Officer
Squadron Leader A. J. Lindsay, BA 13.7.97
Aide-de-Camp
Flight Lieutenant K. S. Muskett, BSc 17.11.97

CHIEF OF STAFF AND DEPUTY COMMANDER-IN-CHIEF
Air Marshal G. A. ROBERTSON, CBE BA FRAeS FRSA 18.3.96

Personal Staff Officer
Squadron Leader M. Rogerson, MBE 27.7.98

SENIOR AIR STAFF OFFICER AND AIR OFFICER COMMANDING 38 GROUP
Air Vice-Marshal P. O. STURLEY, MBE BSc FRAeS 26.1.98

Staff Officer
Squadron Leader G. Tunnicliffe, BA 10.8.98
Air Commodore Operations
Air Commodore N. J. DAY, BSc(Eng) ACGI 7.7.97

AIR OFFICER ENGINEERING AND SUPPLY
Air Vice-Marshal I. BRACKENBURY, OBE BSc CEng FIMechE 1.9.97

Staff Officer
Squadron Leader G. Williams 2.3.98
Air Commodore Communication Information Systems
Air Commodore P. LIDDELL, BSc CEng FIEE FRAeS 17.2.97
Air Commodore Logistics
Air Commodore R. H. O. JOHNSON 17.3.97

AIR OFFICER ADMINISTRATION AND AIR OFFICER COMMANDING DIRECTLY ADMINISTERED UNITS
Air Vice-Marshal A. J. BURTON, OBE BSc FCIS. 27.7.97

Staff Officer
Squadron Leader M. J. Hollingsworth 18.8.97
Aide-de-Camp
Flight Lieutenant P. R. Sanger-Davies 12.1.98
Air Commodore Security and Provost Marshal
Air Commodore J. L. UPRICHARD, CBE 10.3.97

AIR OFFICER PLANS
Air Commodore N. J. SUDBOROUGH, OBE MIPD 6.1.97

COMMAND SECRETARY
Mr C. Wright

Group Captains
N. A. Bairsto, MBE MSc BSc CEng FIMechE FIMgt. 1.4.96
Rev A. P. Bishop, QHC MPhil FRSA LTh 26.8.97
T. Bufton, MSc BSc CEng FIMgt MIEE DIC 31.1.94
G. O. Burton 13.2.95
R. F. R. Carr, MBE 15.12.97

G. C. Daffarn, BSc FIMgt 20.3.98
G. S. Harker 18.10.96
T. C. Hewlett, OBE 14.4.98
J. E. Jeffrey, BA MRAeS 26.8.95
J. A. King, AFC 22.1.96
K. J. Leeson, BSc CEng FIEE 19.7.96
S. P. J. Lilley, MA 5.12.97
J. Mackreath, BSc 10.6.96
R. McConnell, BA 30.1.95
B. G. McLaren, MSc MBA MIMgt 29.1.96
M. J. Perrett, OBE 19.9.94
D. J. Pocock, BA 25.10.96
M. A. Radforth 5.8.96
M. J. Routledge, BSc 21.7.97
N. B. Spiller 20.9.96
R. Springett, FRAeS MILog 31.5.94
I. Travers Smith, DSO 25.3.96

Wing Commanders

C. P. Aber 19.9.94
R. L. A. Atherton 12.1.98
R. Ashenhurst, BSc CEng MRAeS 24.3.97
G. A. Baber, BSc CEng 29.1.96
J. K. L. Babraff 15.2.93
A. T. Bake, BSc 15.7.97
B. J. Beaumont 4.12.95
A. Bentham 17.4.98
G. H. Binfield 3.6.96
T. R. Bonella, MSc BSc 31.3.97
M. J. Bossy 29.8.94
I. K. Buchanan 4.8.97
M. P. Colley 16.2.96
B. A. Cornwell, BSc ARCS 25.3.96
S. J. Court, MBE 6.10.97
J. M. Cruickshank 8.1.96
I. F. Davidson, BA 22.1.96
M. S. Dziuba 7.10.96
K. C. Earnden, BA CEng MRAeS 21.10.96
R. G. Fraser, BSc 2.3.98
M. J. French, MBE BSc CEng MRAeS MIMgt AIL 24.3.98
W. J. Gimblett 5.8.96
B. C. Green 8.7.96
J. A. Hill, BSc 23.5.96
P. S. Hillier, BSc CEng MRAeS 7.10.96
G. J. Howard, MA MCIT MILog MIMgt 16.12.96
E. B. Howlett 2.12.96
D. C. Hyde, MSc BSc 12.9.94
S. S. Keen 7.2.94
R. A. Lewis 18.12.95
S. D. Lungley 3.2.97
J. Maciver 15.1.96
R. J. N. MacKinnon 17.6.96
E. J. MacLean, MBE 7.2.94
B. S. Mahaffey, BA 22.5.95
C. R. Markey 31.7.95
P. Melhuish 6.9.96
M. S. Pearce, BSc CEng MIEE 6.2.95
D. Pollington, AFC 3.9.96
D. L. Prowse, BA 14.7.97
N. B. Randall 22.6.98

S. Randles	11.2.98
P. C. Ridge, BSc	19.5.97
W. A. B. Roberts, OBE	15.1.96
P. H. Rosentall	1.6.96
P. J. Rowney	4.2.95
A. M. O. Scott, BA	4.7.94
R. Shields	27.4.98
I. D. L. Shore, MIMIS MILog	10.9.97
S. L. Singleton	27.4.98
J. P. Squelch, BSc	10.2.97
N. R. Tench, MBE	3.6.95
G. A. J. Tull	13.10.97
C. D. Turner, MSc BSc	8.9.97
A. Ware	27.10.97
M. E. West	15.7.96
S. P. West, MA MSc	1.4.98
J. K. Wheeler, OBE BA	16.9.96
G. A. Williams	1.9.97
C. D. L. Winwood, BSc CEng MIEE	22.3.97

Retired Officers
Group Captain G. W. Gibson, CBE
Wing Commander N. G. Dixon, BA
Wing Commander P. R. Fennell
Wing Commander R. J. C. Green, MRIN MIMgt

Civilians
Miss J. Dupree
Mr J. H. Evans
Mr J Jolly
Mr J. E. Kershaw
Mr E. Martin
Mr M. Ollerenshaw
Mr R. Partridge
Mr K. Proctor
Mr C. Shepherd
Mr G. Sullivan
Mr A. Tindall
Mr P. H. Tipple

HEADQUARTERS LOGISTICS COMMAND

Postal Address RAF BRAMPTON, HUNTINGDON, CAMBS, PE18 8QL
Telephone Number 01480-52151 (GPTN 95331)

AIR OFFICER COMMANDING-IN-CHIEF, AIR MEMBER FOR LOGISTICS AND CHIEF ENGINEER (RAF)
Air Marshal C. G. TERRY, KBE CB BSc(Eng) CEng FRAeS FRSA FILog FCGI 11.7.97

Personal Staff Officer
Wing Commander B. D. Harvey, BSc. 18.5.98

Deputy Personal Staff Officer
Squadron Leader P. G. Hicks, MBE BSc 23.6.97

Aide-de-Camp
Flight Lieutenant J. M. Sanderson, BSc 30.6.97

CHIEF OF STAFF, DEPUTY COMMANDER-IN-CHIEF AND AIR OFFICER COMMANDING DIRECTLY ADMINISTERED UNITS
Air Vice-Marshal M. D. PLEDGER, OBE AFC BSc FRAeS 17.6.97

Personal Staff Officer
Squadron Leader P. D. Hutchinson, BSc 11.8.97

Aide-de-Camp
Flight Lieutenant A. J. Simmonite, BEng 30.6.97

AIR COMMODORE PLANS
Air Commodore A. J. PYE 2.8.96

AIR COMMODORE LOGISTICS POLICY
Air Commodore R. BRUMPTON, BA FRAeS 23.6.97

STAFF OFFICER SERVICE PERSONNEL AND ADMINISTRATION
Group Captain D. M. BAKER, OBE FIMgt 4.4.97

DIRECTORATE OF CATERING (RAF)
Group Captain S. WOOD, MHCIMA 19.5.95

COMMAND SECRETARY
Mr H. GRIFFITHS 1.4.94

DEPUTY COMMAND SECRETARY AND DIRECTOR OF CIVILIAN PERSONNEL (LOGISTICS COMMAND)
Mr S. J. PENFOLD 24.2.97

DIRECTOR OF CONTRACTS (RAF)
Mr J. N. EDDOLLS 6.11.95

ASSISTANT COMMAND SECRETARY (FINANCE AND SECRETARIAT)
Mr D. G. BUTCHER 13.6.94

ACTING CHIEF EXECUTIVE ROYAL AIR FORCE MAINTENANCE GROUP DEFENCE AGENCY
Air Commodore K. J. M. PROCTER, BSc(Eur Ing) CEng FIEE FRAeS FIMgt 9.5.97

Staff Officer
Flight Lieutenant P. J. Baldwin 18.5.98

DIRECTOR MAINTENANCE GROUP DEFENCE AGENCY (FINANCE AND PLANS)
Mr M J HERITAGE-OWEN 5.5.95

DIRECTOR GENERAL OF SUPPORT MANAGEMENT (RAF)
Air Vice-Marshal P. W. HENDERSON, MBE BSc CEng FRAeS 1.10.97

Staff Officer
Squadron Leader C. P. Borrill, BSc. 16.12.96

SECRETARY TO THE SUPPORT MANAGEMENT GROUP (RAF)
Mr B. R. MANN 1.11.97

DIRECTOR OF SUPPORT MANAGEMENT 1 (RAF)
Air Commodore G. SKINNER, MBE MSc BSc CEng FILog FIMechE FIMgt MRAeS 23.6.97

DIRECTOR OF SUPPORT MANAGEMENT 2 (RAF)
Air Commodore P. J. SCOTT, MSc BSc CEng FIMechE 27.10.97

DIRECTOR OF SUPPORT MANAGEMENT 3 (RAF)
    Air Commodore C. F. COOPER, BA MCIPS MIMgt 25.9.95

DIRECTOR OF SUPPORT MANAGEMENT 4 (RAF)
    Mr D. N. BARNETT BTech CEng MIMechE 5.5.98

AIR OFFICER COMMUNICATIONS INFORMATION SYSTEMS AND SUPPORT SERVICES AND AIR OFFICER COMMANDING SUPPORT UNITS
    Air Vice-Marshal B. C. McCANDLESS, CBE MSc BSc CEng FIEE FRAeS 12.1.96

    Personal Staff Officer
        Squadron Leader N. J. Cox, BSc CEng MIMechE 9.12.96

    Aide-de-Camp
        Flight Lieutenant M. R. Wilson 25.9.97

AIR OFFICER COMMUNICATIONS INFORMATION SYSTEMS AND SUPPORT SERVICES (PLANS)
    Wing Commander A. N. Mawston, BSc 16.6.97

CHIEF EXECUTIVE AND DIRECTOR OF LOGISTICS SUPPORT SERVICES (RAF)
    Air Commodore I. SLOSS, CEng FRAeS 1.4.96

AIR COMMODORE COMMUNICATIONS, AND INFORMATION SYSTEMS AND SUPPORT
    Air Commodore C. M. DAVISON, BSc CEng MIEE MIMgt. 1.4.97

DIRECTOR OF COMMUNICATIONS AND INFORMATION SYSTEMS (RAF)
    Air Commodore R. W. CLARK, OBE CEng MIEE 7.1.96

AIR OFFICER LOGISTICS INFORMATION STRATEGY AND INDUSTRIAL INTERFACES STUDY
    Air Vice-Marshal D. C. COUZENS, MA DLUT CEng FIMechE FRAeS 3.3.97

CHIEF EXECUTIVE DEFENCE CODIFICATION AGENCY
    Mr K. A. BRADSHAW, BSc(Eng) CEng MIEE MIExpE RCNC 4.5.96

CHIEF EXECUTIVE AND STATION COMMANDER ROYAL AIR FORCE SIGNALS ENGINEERING DEFENCE AGENCY
    Air Commodore G. JONES, MBE BSc CEng MIEE 14.10.96

Group Captains
    K. E. Archer-Jones, BSc 6.6.96
    B. G. Bate 1.4.94
    R. I. Bateman, BA 28.7.97
    T. P. Brewer, OBE BSc. 13.5.96
    C. C. N. Burwell, MBE. 14.4.97
    D. B. Cannon, MSc BSc MCIT 11.11.96
    J. P. Chitty, OBE MA BSc(Eng) CEng MRAeS ACGI. 13.11.95
    G. Cole, MBA CEng MIMechE 8.10.96
    C. A. Gardiner, BA MCIPS 9.5.95
    D. P. Hedges 15.7.96
    R. I. Hogg 14.4.97
    R. W. Hooper, MBE MSc BSc(Eng) CEng FRAeS 1.4.94
    D. I. Kendrick, MIDPM 26.9.94
    N. J. E. Kurth, OBE 15.11.97
    D. B. Love, BJur MIPD 1.9.97
    P. M. Miles, BSc 16.8.96
    N. S. Morris, MSc BA 20.5.96
    G. Morton, MCIPS 27.5.97
    C. W. Ness, BEng CEng MRAeS 16.12.96
    B. S. Page 16.9.96
    C. W. Pratley, OBE CEng FIEE 10.6.94
    P. D. Rawson, BA IEng MRAes 25.5.98
    M. A. Rogers, OBE. 4.12.95
    S. B. Schofield, MSc BSc CEng MRAeS 10.2.97
    B. L. Sobey, BA CEng MIEE MIMgt 20.4.98
    J. G. Stevenson, MSc BSc CEng FIEE 2.8.96
    Rev I. M. Thomas, MA 4.11.96
    J. A. Upham, MSc BSc CEng FIPD MIEE MBCS DIC CDipAF 15.12.97
    B. Wakely, BSc 30.8.96

D. N. Williams, OBE BSc CEng MRAeS	10.6.96
B. M. Wynn, OBE BSc	18.12.95

Wing Commanders

G. A. Ashcroft	18.11.96
R. R. Ashford	6.1.97
M. A. Ashraf, BSc	4.1.98
I. C. Atkinson, BSc CEng MIMechE DLUT.	19.4.95
S. P. Battley	11.9.95
S. F. Bolam, MHCIMA	27.4.98
M. Brierley, BA	2.10.95
J. Brown, BA	16.9.96
P. M. D. Brown, BSc CEng MRAeS MIMgt	7.4.97
T. C. Burke, MSc BSc	16.12.96
W. D. Butterworth	1.4.94
M. R. S. Chinneck, MSc BSc.	6.1.98
G. S. Clark, IEng MILog MRAeS	1.4.97
M. A. Clark, BSc(Eng) CEng MIEE	3.7.96
T. R. Clark	13.1.97
A. L. Dipper	23.12.96
M. D. Dixon, BSc	27.8.97
A. K. Ebdon, BA CEng MRAeS	1.9.97
D. E. Eighteen, OBE	21.10.96
P. R. Ewen	13.4.98
D. Fairbrother	8.7.96
C. B. Forte	4.4.98
J. A. Foster, MSc BSc CEng MIEE	16.10.95
D. J. Gale, MBE MDA BSc CEng MIEE	10.8.97
S. Gale, BSc.	22.4.96
N. W. Gammon, MA MSc BSc CEng MRAeS MIMgt	20.10.97
A. T. Gell, MBA BA MILog	15.9.97
P. N. Gilbert, BSc CEng MRAeS.	1.4.94
S. A. Griffin, BSc CEng MRAeS.	12.1.98
P. Grimson	7.4.97
J. L. Hancock, MDA BSc CEng MRAeS	6.9.96
A. R. Hannaby, BSc CEng MRAeS	9.12.96
R. M. Harris, BSc CEng MIEE	1.4.94
R. J. Harrison, BA MIMgt DPhysEd CertEd	4.4.97
C. Heithus, MCIPS MILog MIMgt	1.4.94
C. H. Hickman, BSc	16.12.96
P. N. Hubble, MSc BSc	15.12.97
A. S. Humphries, MBA FIMgt MIMIS	17.5.96
P. Johnson	9.9.96
B. A. Jones, BSc	1.1.98
R. J. Kennett, MSc BA FInstPet MCIPS MIDPM	1.4.94
P. C. Knight, MSc	19.2.96
J. G. Leggat	1.7.96
K. MacKenzie, MA MSc CEng MRAeS.	12.1.98
R. MacLeman, BSc	15.10.96
A. W. Madge, BSc	1.7.96
W. E. Mahon, BA	21.10.96
G. C. Martin	6.1.97
I. M. Martin, MPhil LLB MCIT	14.11.96
P. McLachlan, MSc BEng CEng MIEE	21.7.97
M. C. C. Moore	30.9.96
J. V. Morgan, BSc	1.7.96
P. B. Morrell	1.8.96
G. McL. Nisbet, BSc(Eng)	20.7.94
M. W. Norris, MInstPet MRAeS.	21.7.97
C. R. W. O'Connell, MB BCh BAO LLMRCP(Irel) LLMRCS(Irel)	1.4.97

R. Oldaker, BSc.	22.11.96
M. W. Palmer, BSc.	2.12.96
A. J. Parrish, MA MSc BSc CEng MRAeS MIMgt	27.10.97
M. R. Patel, BSc CEng MRAeS	30.6.96
D. A. W. Pearson, MHCIMA	23.3.97
D. Pickavance, MSc BSc(Eng)	10.10.96
A. Proudlove	28.7.97
D. J. Robinson, MA IEng MIEE(Mech).	12.2.96
M. G. Salter, MBE BA MRAeS	10.11.97
P. Short, BSc	16.12.96
R. C. R. Simpson	15.9.97
R. S. Smith, BSc	19.1.98
J. W. C. Spencer, MSc BSc CEng MIMechE	8.4.98
J. E. Stevens, MBE BSc CEng MRAeS MIMgt	20.5.98
M. I. Sturgess	19.12.96
B. L. Swain	19.1.98
R. K. Taplin, MBE BSc(Econ) FILog MCIPS MIMIS MBCS MIL MRAeS MIMgt	12.1.98
P. C. Taylor, OBE BA	18.11.96
K. Thistlethwaite	1.7.98
J. A. Thomas	25.11.96
J. M. Thomas, BA	1.4.97
R. V. Thompson, MSc MILog	12.7.97
I. W. Thomson, BSc(Eng)	6.4.98
D. P. Thow, BSc	14.5.96
R. G. Torrens, OBE BSc CEng MRAeS.	30.6.97
A. J. Towler	9.12.96
D. C. Tudor	6.1.97
R. M. Veale, BA.	24.6.96
R. A. Waldegrave	6.5.97
A. J. Ward, MSc BSc CEng MRAeS MIMgt	11.11.96
J. P. Washington-Smith	11.9.95
A. M. Watson, BSc	25.3.96
R. Watson MBA BA	12.1.98
M. Welburn	14.6.95
S. Welburn, MA MSc BSc CEng MRAeS	15.3.95
J. G. Wheatcroft, MSc BSc(Eng)	23.8.93
M. J. G. Wiles, MILog.	19.1.98
A. G. Willenbruch, MA (Eur Ing) CEng MIMechE MRAeS MIMgt	9.4.96
G. T. Williams	17.3.97
A. Wilson	11.11.96
J. Wiltshire	11.8.97
M. J. Wrigley, MSc BSc	7.10.96
C. A. Wynne, MBE.	24.6.96
J. A. Young, MDA BSc	24.2.97

Retired Officers

Wing Commander H. Binns, OBE MInstPkg MCIPS MILog
Wing Commander A. J. C. MacLachlan, CEng MRAeS
Wing Commander F. Marchington, MIEE DipEE
Wing Commander J. Wells MCIPS

Civilians

L. B. Angove
M. Atkinson
E. Baker
C. J. Ball
D. Baumber
M. J. Bennett
P. Blake
R. P. Bratt
J. Bridgwater

P. E. Broad
C. T. Brown
K. L. Buck
S. Carr
J. Cattier
A. T. Cordory
T. A. Couchman
B. V. Cowell
A. M. Dalton
R. A. Daniels
C. Datchler
C. Ducher
C. J. Dunlop
K. A. Emmings
J. Fall
T. S. P. Flatt
B. Foster
S. H. Freed
P. Gaul
E. A. Gibbins
J. C. Glover
P. A. Kenny
N. Hamilton
M. J. Hannah
W. J. Harcus
D. W. Harding
J. L. Harvey
M. J. Harvey
S. J. Hegley
D. R. Hetherington
P. J. B. Hodgkins
S. Hodgson
B. Holdsworth
J. E. Horner
D. G. Howells
D. Hoyland
J. L. Hunt
J. Hutton
B. R. James
B. L. Johnson
M. P. Loy
C. Mason
J. McDonald
D. B. Macklen
D. M. Monks
B. A. Mowbray
D. J. Mowbray
G. Newton
C. J. Orme
N. Patel
N. K. Payne
A. Perrey
T. W. Pickard
A. Pitts
A. J. Potter
A. Powell
A. Pugh
R. L. Pursey
P. G. Richardson
P. W. Robson

T. Rowntree
J. F. Salmon
S. E. Salmon
C. Seddon
N. Seed
G. Shirra
D. Stewart
D. M. N. Stewart
E. Stewart
S. Swift
C. A. Symms
R. Symms
B. Wadham
A. Walker
M. Webb
M. Weeding
T. E. Weedon
D. Wilkins
P. J. Wilson
M. H. Wittleton
R. N. Venables

ROYAL AIR FORCE PERSONNEL AND TRAINING COMMAND

Postal Address RAF INNSWORTH, GLOUCESTER, GL3 1EZ
Telephone No—01452-712612

AIR MEMBER FOR PERSONNEL AND AIR OFFICER COMMANDING-IN-CHIEF
Air Marshal Sir ANTHONY BAGNELL, KCB OBE FRAeS 7.8.98

Personal Staff Officer
Wing Commander P. Heaton 9.3.98

Staff Officer
Squadron Leader E. J. A. Barclay, BSc 18.8.97

CHIEF OF STAFF/AIR MEMBER FOR PERSONNEL
Air Vice-Marshal R. A. WRIGHT, AFC 2.2.98

Staff Officer
Squadron Leader, C. J. McKiernan, BA MBIFM 24.11.97

PLANS AND POLICY

Air Commodore Policy and Plans
Air Commodore I. S. CORBITT 18.12.95

Chief Scientific Support Officer
Mr D. J. JAMES, BSc

AIR OFFICER ADMINISTRATION AND AIR OFFICER COMMANDING DIRECTLY ADMINISTERED UNITS
Air Commodore O. D. L DELANY, OBE BA FBIFM FIMgt 17.2.97

CHIEF EXECUTIVE TRAINING GROUP DEFENCE AGENCY AND AIR OFFICER COMMANDING TRAINING GROUP
Air Vice-Marshal A. J. STABLES, CBE FRAeS 8.1.97

Staff Officer
Squadron Leader R. D. Gammage, BSc 12.1.98

TRAINING STAFF

Director of Operations
Air Commodore A. P. WALDRON, CBE AFC 15.9.97

Director of Corporate Development
Air Commodore M. J. GILDING, MSc BSc CEng FIEE 21.8.95

Director RAF Sports Board
Air Vice-Marshal R. J. HONEY (Retd), CB CBE FIPD

AIR SECRETARY/CHIEF EXECUTIVE PERSONNEL MANAGEMENT AGENCY
Air Vice-Marshal I. M. STEWART, AFC LLB 28.8.98

Staff Officer
Squadron Leader D. J. Hill 3.4.97

Director of Personnel Management Agency (Officers and Airmen Aircrew) (RAF)
Air Commodore N. E. TAYLOR, BSc FRAeS 1.5.98

Director of Personnel Management Agency (Airmen) and Controller of Reserve Forces (RAF)
Air Commodore C. DAVISON, MBE DPhysEd FIMgt 6.1.97

Director of Personnel Management Agency (Policy)
Air Commodore J. A. COLLIER, CBE BSc. 10.7.98

DIRECTOR-GENERAL MEDICAL SERVICES (RAF)
Air Vice-Marshal C. J. SHARPLES, QHP MSc FFOM MRCS(Eng) LRCP DAvMed MRAeS 3.2.97

Staff Officer
Squadron Leader C. A. Staniforth, DipMgmt 15.9.97

Director Medical Personnel, Policy and Plans
Air Commodore E. J. THORNTON, MB ChB FIMgt MFOM DAvMed 13.10.97

45

Director Primary Health Services
Air Commodore W. J. PIKE, QHP MSc MB BS MRCGP MRCS MFOM DRCOG DAvMed LRCP 27.8.96

Clinical Director (RAF)
Air Commodore D. J. RAINFORD, MBE QHS MB BS FRCP MRCS 1.4.96

Director of Nursing Services (RAF)
Group Captain R. H. Williams, RRC QHNS 6.2.95

DIRECTOR LEGAL SERVICES (RAF)
Air Vice-Marshal J. WEEDEN, LLB 19.6.97

Deputy Director Legal Services (RAF)
Air Commodore R. A. CHARLES, LLB 12.6.97

CHAPLAIN-IN-CHIEF
The Venerable (Air Vice Marshal) P. R. TURNER, QHC MTh BA AKC 21.8.95

Staff Chaplain
Reverend (Wing Commander) P. W. Mills, BD 5.1.98

COMMAND SECRETARY
Mrs L. D. Kyle

Group Captains
T. Mc. Arnot, OBE 1.4.94
J. P. Babington, BA 18.4.98
J. K. E. Barlow 5.6.97
W. Barnett 2.1.96
P. A. Barrett, OBE BSc FRAeS 27.11.95
Rev R. O. Bayliss, QHS SRN RMN 1.4.94
W. H. Boothby, BA. 16.7.97
B. T. Dingle 1.4.96
A. N. Graham-Cumming, MB BS MRCGP MRCS MFOM LRCP DAvMed MRAeS. 1.8.96
I. F. Hendley, FIDPM MILog MBCS 1.4.94
The Rt Rev Mgr E. P. Hill, QHC VG. 15.2.96
P. J. Hilling, MA 14.4.97
P. G. H. Hodcroft, BSc MBCS 24.3.97
D. A. Ingham, OBE BSc 31.10.94
R. D. Iredale. 6.5.97
J. M. Jones, MB BCh DAvMed AFOM. 29.6.96
I. D. Lindsay, MA MSc MB BChir MRCGP DRCOG DAvMed AFOM 29.9.97
G. G. Martin, MBE 3.4.95
I. D. Mitchell, MDA BSc MB BS MRCGP MHSM DRCOG DAvMed AFOM RFN 30.7.96
Rev G. H. Moore 4.5.98
H. M. Randall 11.8.97
M. Ranger, MB BS DAvMed AFOM MRAeS 13.6.95
D. A. Ray 16.1.96
Rev J. Shedden, CBE BD. 1.4.94
W. Smith 26.8.97
J. D. Tonks, BSc 7.4.97
F. L. Turner 23.3.98
P. D. J. Turner, BSc FIMgt FIPD 3.4.97
M. M. A. Urquhart. 13.3.97
R. H. Williams, RRC QHNS 2.4.94

Wing Commanders
R. J. Allaway, BEd 11.5.98
J. D. Allen 18.8.97
S. P. Ayres, BSc 14.7.97
T. T. J. Baker, LLB 16.2.95
D. G. Barton, BSc 8.6.98
S. F. Bolam, MHCIMA. 1.4.98
S. E. Bonell, BA ACIS 18.4.97
K. G. Brackstone, LLB 4.5.98
N. Branagh, OBE BEd. 30.9.96

R. J. M. Broadbridge, MB BS MRCGP DRCOG DAvMed 25.11.96
J. A. Broderick, OBE MCIT MIMgt 15.1.96
K. A. Bull 30.9.96
M. C. Bullock BSc 17.11.97
C. S. Burns 30.9.96
P. A. Burns, BA 6.4.98
C. B. Campbell, BSc ACIS 3.1.96
R. I. Chambers 24.3.98
J. J. Clark 8.6.98
G. A. Clyde, BSc 15.12.97
S. J. Court, MBE 6.10.97
R. G. Cumming. 29.8.95
C. S. Davidson, MA 18.11.96
K. M. Douglas 31.7.95
J. Dyer 3.4.97
S. Edgar, MHCIMA. 6.4.98
D. Ferrar, CertEd 11.9.95
M. G. W. Fisher 3.4.97
K. W. J. Green 30.9.96
J. L. Greenhalgh, MBE 16.9.96
R. A. Harding, MA MDA BA MIPD 9.12.96
I. P. Hamilton 23.9.96
I. Harvey. 26.1.98
A. J. Hayward 24.2.97
C. Hilliker 1.4.94
B. C. Holding, AFC. 23.9.96
M. B. Hutchins 18.12.95
R. R. Innes, OBE MIMgt 4.8.97
M. F. Jordan 3.6.96
J. R. Lees, OBE. 4.12.95
B. P. Ludlow, MMedSci MB BS MRAeS MRCS DAvMed LRCP AFOM 11.12.95
I. J. O. MacEachern, OBE MSc BSc BA CEng CMath FIMA FIPD MBCS MIMgt CDipAF 1.4.96
D. L. McConnell, MSc MB ChB DObstRCOG DAvMed 7.9.95
M. S. Meyer. 7.4.95
Rev P. W. Mills, BD 5.1.98
R. J. Milsom, OBE 1.4.94
F. L. Mogford 1.4.94
G. A. Opie, MDA BSc 7.4.97
G. A. Ordish. 1.7.96
S. J. Orwell 5.5.97
R. G. Parker, BA 6.6.94
D. G. Parry, MBE BA 1.5.97
G. J. Pilgrim-Morris, BSc(Econ) FInstAM 7.4.95
R. A. Reid, OBE ARRC 15.1.98
D. St. Salisbury. 8.6.98
P. J. Schofield, MB ChB MRCGP DA(UK) DAvMed 15.1.98
G. P. Smith 1.4.94
P. H. Steiner, MILog 4.4.98
G. Ware 30.9.96
G. McN. Watson, BSc CEng MIMechE. 1.4.94
N. H. Williams 14.4.97
P. A. Wilson 27.1.97
S. C. Wood, MIMgt 20.5.95
R. N. Woollacott, MBE 1.4.94
C. N. W. Wood, MA 3.11.97

Retired Officers

Air Commodore R. D. Arnott, CBE FIMgt MIPD
Group Captain S. J. Barclay, OBE MIPD
Group Captain D. J. Jones

Group Captain M. A. Molloy
Wing Commander K. W. Baldock, OBE
Wing Commander C. L. Barnfather, BA CEng MIEE MRAeS MIMgt
Wing Commander K. A. Burford
Wing Commander J. I. Gilson
Wing Commander D. J. Magee

Open Grade Structure 6

J. R. Hollands

Open Grade Structure 7

M. E. Court
A. Cowpe
B. P. Fisher
Dr R. Harrison
Ms H. Taylor
P. Wilson

HEADQUARTERS, BRITISH FORCES GIBRALTAR

Postal Address HEADQUARTERS BRITISH FORCES, THE TOWER, GIBRALTAR BFPO 52

COMMANDER

Commodore A. J. S. TAYLOR, BA RN 8.4.97

MA to Commander

Squadron Leader, T. E. Osborne 8.9.97

Station Commander RAF Gibraltar

Wing Commander A. M. Bone, AFC 3.11.97

HEADQUARTERS, BRITISH FORCES CYPRUS

Postal Address HEADQUARTERS, BRITISH FORCES CYPRUS
BRITISH FORCES POST OFFICE 53

COMMANDER

Major General A. I. RAMSAY CBE DSO 16.1.98

Aide-de-Camp
Captain M. P. S. Luckyn-Malone 13.1.98

MA to Commander
Squadron Leader R. J. Cowell 26.3.97

CHIEF OF STAFF
Air Commodore P. A. ROBINSON, OBE 28.3.98

DEPUTY CHIEF OF STAFF
Group Captain B. J, Comina. 8.6.98

Wing Commanders
S. Blackburn, MBE. 10.10.97
J. C. Knights 7.4.97
A. J. B. McGrigor 4.1.96
J. W. Witney, MPhil(Eng) BSc CEng MIEE MIMgt 3.12.96

MISCELLANEOUS ESTABLISHMENTS

D. E. Sibley . . . . Command Secretary
M. Wynne-Jones . . . . Chief Public Relations Officer

HEADQUARTERS INTEGRATED AIR DEFENCE

SYSTEM

(ROYAL AIR FORCE ELEMENT)

Postal Address HEADQUARTERS, INTEGRATED AIR DEFENCE SYSTEM, AIR BASE BUTTERWORTH, c/o GPO PENANG, MALAYSIA

Senior Officer Air Defence
Wing Commander A. P. Childs,. 11.7.94

NATO HEADQUARTERS MILITARY COMMITTEE

(BRITISH ELEMENT—ROYAL AIR FORCE)
Postal Address—BRITISH FORCES POST OFFICE 49
Telephone No.—Brussels 707 72 11

UNITED KINGDOM MILITARY REPRESENTATIVE
Vice Admiral P. K. HADDACKS 28.2.97

Executive Assistant
Wing Commander R. W. Birtwistle. 16.7.98

Aide-de-Camp
Captain M. W. Roddy, RM 20.6.97

DEPUTY UK MILITARY REPRESENTATIVE AND CHIEF OF STAFF
Air Commodore P. W. ROSER, MBE FRAeS 6.7.98

Group Captains
J. L. Buckler. 1.5.95
R. F. Burrough, BA BSc 20.11.95
C. R. Cooper, OBE CertEd MIMgt 1.9.95
D. M. Shannon, OBE 9.5.94

Wing Commanders
A. J. W. Boyd 23.5.98
R. M. Harrison 15.1.96
B. A. Horton. 12.12.94
M. E. Wilson 19.9.94

Admin. Officer
Wing Commander D. M. Casey (Retd)

NATO C3 AGENCY
(Tel (02) 707 81 11)
Group Captain R. J. Whittingham, FRAeS FIMgt 1.2.98
Wing Commander M. Crocombe MIIE(elec) 1.10.97

WEU
(Tel (02) 500 45 29)
Wing Commander G. A. Monaghan 30.10.95

EURO CONTROL
(Tel 7293568)
Wing Commander B. Coombs, BA. 3.6.96

SUPREME HEADQUARTERS ALLIED POWERS EUROPE

Postal Address: BRITISH FORCES POST OFFICE 26
Telegraphic Address: UKNMR SHAPE
Telephone Exchange: SHAPE MILITARY
Telephone No. 00-32-65-447111

DEPUTY SACEUR (UK)
General Sir RUPERT SMITH, KCB DSO OBE QGM 1.10.98

Principal Staff Officer
Group Captain B. W. Newby, AFC 3.11.97

ASSISTANT CHIEF OF STAFF POLICY & REQUIREMENTS DIVISION
Rear Admiral A. B. GOUGH, FIMgt MNI 19.2.97

CHIEF OF SPECIAL WEAPONS BRANCH
Air Commodore A. G. VALLANCE, OBE MPhil 14.12.95

UNITED KINGDOM NATIONAL MILITARY REPRESENTATIVE
Brigadier H. D. C. DUNCAN, MBE 15.7.96

DUKNMR(AIR)
Group Captain D. A. Williams, AFC 6.1.97

Group Captains

R. I. Allan, OBE MSc BSc ACGI 13.11.98
R. J. Fishwick 12.11.96
R. M. Jenner 28.9.98
P. D. Scoffham, AFC 16.5.97

Wing Commanders

C. K. Adams 23.2.98
R. F. Blunden BA MRAeS MBCS MIMgt 3.2.96
M. P. Brzezicki, MPhil MIL 28.7.97
R. J. Cassady 1.4.94
D. A. Donnelly, MRIN 16.9.96
M. V. Godfrey, AFC 14.4.97
A. McP. Gordon, MA 1.3.96
S. G. Griffiths, MBE 15.7.96
W. R. Hartree 16.10.95
G. J. P. Moore 21.10.96
D. M. Rait 13.1.97
M. Rimmer 12.10.98
G. W. Robertson, BSc. 22.6.98
A. W. Semple 28.2.97
S. J. Taylor, MBE MSc CEng MIEE MIMgt 2.9.98
R. E. Todd, BSc(Econ). 28.9.98
I. A. Trewin (Eur Ing) CEng MIEE 24.7.95

NATO School (SHAPE) OBERAMMERGAU
Wing Commander A. J. Gritten, MBE 27.11.95

NATO Programming Centre GLONS
Wing Commander S. A. Gracie, MA BA 5.8.96

ALLIED COMMAND EUROPE RAPID REACTION CORPS (ARRC)

Postal Address: BRITISH FORCES POST OFFICE 40
Telephone Exchange: RHEINDAHLEN MILITARY
Telephone No. 00-49-2161-47100
Direct Dial: 00-49-2161-565-5*** or 00-49-2161-47-****

SENIOR RAF OFFICER
Wing Commander K. J. Parkes, MBE BA BSc 20.11.95

Wing Commander
I. B. Walker, BA. 13.11.96

HEADQUARTERS ALLIED FORCES
NORTHWESTERN EUROPE

Postal Address: RAF High Wycombe, Bucks, HP14 4TZ
Telephone Number: 01494 461461
Direct Dial: 01494 49****

COMMANDER IN CHIEF
Air Chief Marshal Sir JOHN CHESHIRE, KBE CB FRAeS 11.3.97

Aide-de-Camp
Flight Lieutenant F. W. J. Miles. 29.5.95

Group Captains
M. R. H. Connor, OBE MSc 6.6.94
D. Hollin, MIMgt 4.7.94
P. A. Bedford, AFC MRAeS 9.2.98

Wing Commanders
K. J. Burgess 9.2.98
J. S. Douglas, OBE 25.10.97
A. J. Fovargue, BSc 13.4.98
J. N. Kirk. 12.8.98
R. A. Lewis 8.6.98
P. J. McGahan, MISM MIMgt 6.1.97
C. R. Pitt 3.6.96
T. C. Wardill 14.4.98

HEADQUARTERS ALLIED AIR FORCES
NORTHWESTERN EUROPE

Postal Address: RAF High Wycombe, Bucks, HP14 4UE
Telephone Number: 01494 461461
Direct Dial: 01494 49****

COMMANDER ALLIED AIR FORCES NORTHWESTERN EUROPE
Air Chief Marshal Sir JOHN ALLISON, KCB CBE ADC FRAeS 24.7.97
ASSISTANT CHIEF OF STAFF POLICY AND REQUIREMENTS
Air Commodore P. G. JOHNSON, OBE BA FRAeS FIMgt 28.7.97
Wing Commanders
G. J. Goodman, OBE MRIN 22.1.96
C. E. Wade 21.4.97

HEADQUARTERS
ALLIED FORCES CENTRAL EUROPE

KAMP HENDRICK, LIMBURG, NETHERLANDS
(BRITISH ELEMENT: ROYAL AIR FORCE)
BRITISH FORCES POST OFFICE 28
Telephone Exchange: AFCENT
(045 261111)

DEPUTY COMMANDER IN CHIEF
Air Marshal C. C. C. COLVILLE, CB BA FIPD FRAeS 6.8.98

Aide-de-Camp
Flight Lieutenant P. C. Loader, BEd. 8.1.97

Group Captains
W. K. D. Morrow OBE. 17.9.97
R. J. Slater 26.7.92

Wing Commanders
J. B. Bennett 29.7.96
M. W. Brumage, MA CertEd 27.1.96
A. K. Cossar, MSc BSc CEng MIEE 15.2.95
D. N. Crofton 19.1.98
A. McB Davis, OBE 15.2.95
J. H. Easton 21.3.94
Rev R. D. Hesketh, BA 6.3.95
A. J. Little 2.12.96
R. W. Munday 11.11.96
R. N. Randerson, BSc 18.8.96
R. D. Stone, OBE 14.11.94
R. J. Woodroffe, MBE 9.9.96

HEADQUARTERS
ALLIED AIR FORCES CENTRAL EUROPE
AIRCENT

RAMSTEIN AIR BASE GERMANY
(ROYAL AIR FORCE ELEMENT)
Postal Address: British Forces Post Office 109
Telephone Exchange: Ramstein DSN (480 1110-Operator)
Telephone No: 06371–47 (1110-Operator)
IVSN 258 1110
U.K. Support Unit Civil No. 06371–476161

ASSISTANT CHIEF OF STAFF (OPERATIONS)
Air Commodore P. B. WALKER, CBE BA 11.11.96

CHIEF AIR ELEMENT TO LANDCENT
Air Commodore M. J. GOOD, MIDPM MIMgt 29.6.98

EXECUTIVE OFFICER TO COMAIRCENT/SENIOR RAF STAFF OFFICER
Group Captain C. N. Harper, MA FIMgt 7.4.97

Group Captains

A. J. H. Alcock, MBE 8.7.93
M. R. Hallam 11.5.98

Wing Commanders

A. B. Batchelor 6.11.95
R. E. Best, AFC 7.1.98
W. A. D. Carter, BA 29.1.96
P. A. R. Duffin, BA BA MRIN MRAeS 1.6.93
I. Ellison, MIMgt 30.10.95
W. R. Hartree 3.8.98
A. D. Huggett 22.9.97
B. D. Longman, OBE CEng MRAeS MIEE MIMgt 22.1.96
D. W. McCormick, BSc 20.2.97
P. D. G. Milloy, MEng BSc 29.9.97
S. W. StJ. Oliver, BSc 28.10.96
S. G. Rodda 21.2.97
M. Rodgers 26.10.96
D. J. Trembaczowski-Ryder, BSc 19.9.97
L. Turner, BSc 31.3.96
M. C. Valentine 28.7.97

HEADQUARTERS
ALLIED AIR FORCES CENTRAL EUROPE
TACTICAL LEADERSHIP PROGRAMME

AIRCENT/TLP

BASE J. OFFENBERG, FLORENNES, BELGIUM

(ROYAL AIR FORCE ELEMENT)

Postal Address: c/o United Kingdom Support Unit
British Forces Post Office 26
Telephone No: ++32 71681538
IVSN 252 1110

SENIOR RAF OFFICER
Wing Commander
R. M. H. Ellis 22.7.96

Squadron Leaders
J. C. Ball 30.3.98
W. P. Bohill, BSc 15.4.97
J. M. Goatham 29.7.96
I. Hodson 9.12.96
D. A. C. Legg 1.7.96

ALLIED FORCES SOUTHERN EUROPE

Postal Address—HQ ALLIED FORCES SOUTHERN EUROPE, BFPO 8
National Correspondence addressed to—UKNSU, HQ AFSOUTH, BFPO 8
Telephone No.—NAPLES 0039-81-7212046
Fax No.—NAPLES 0039-81-5709053

Group Captain
J. C. Platt, BA 30.10.95

Wing Commanders
S. J. Poyntz 5.1.98
A. G. Reed, IEng FIIE(elec) MIMgt 14.4.97
A. K. Richardson 5.8.96
A. F. Stuart 8.1.96

COMMANDER MARITIME AIR FORCES
MEDITERRANEAN

Postal Address—MARAIRMED, BFPO 8
National Correspondence addressed to—UKNSU, HQ AFSOUTH, BFPO 8
Telegraphic Address—COMARAIRMED
Telephone No.—NAPLES 0039-81-568-3673

Wing Commander
J. L. Morgan 11.9.95

ALLIED AIR FORCES SOUTHERN EUROPE

Postal Address—HQ ALLIED FORCES, BFPO 8
National Correspondence addressed to—UKNSU, HQ AFSOUTH, BFPO 8
Telephone No.—NAPLES 0039-81-7212046
Fax No.—NAPLES 0039-81-5709053

Group Captain
H. Delve 29.9.97

Wing Commanders
M. L. Ashwell, MBE BSc 1.9.97
A. G. Galbraith 13.10.97

HEADQUARTERS
SIXTH ALLIED TACTICAL AIR FORCE
SIRINYER, IZMIR, TURKEY

All correspondence concerning national administration to be addressed to
OC UK Support Unit, NATO/TURKEY, BFPO 599

Postal Address—HQ 6 ATAF PK 527, IZMIR, 35148 TURKEY
Telegraphic Address—UKSUPU TURKEY
Telephone No.—IZMIR 90 232 4875862
IVSN 423-8011 Ext. 2230
Fax No IZMIR 90 232 4875862

Squadron Leader

E. G. J. Candlish, MRIN MIMgt 22.10.91

HEADQUARTERS, SUPREME ALLIED
COMMANDER ATLANTIC

Postal Address—HQ SACLANT, NORFOLK, NAVAL PARTY 1964, BFPO 493
Telegraphic Address—SACLANT, NORFOLK, VIRGINIA, USA
Telephone No.—757-445-3258

Group Captain

C. M. Sweeney 25.4.97

Wing Commanders

A. J. Dear 18.10.96
J. M. Henderson, AMBCS 15.7.96
T. J. Patch, MSc BA CDipAF 31.7.98
P. Roberts, BSc 27.6.97

Squadron Leader

K. L. Thomas, BEng Ceng MIEE 25.8.98

HEADQUARTERS ALLIED COMMANDER-IN-CHIEF EASTERN ATLANTIC AREA AND HEADQUARTERS COMMANDER ALLIED NAVAL FORCES NORTHWESTERN EUROPE

Postal Address—NORTHWOOD, MIDDLESEX, HA6 3EP
Telephone No.—01923-837079

Wing Commanders
M. J. Engwell 2.12.96
N. V. Vaughan-Smith, BSc CEng MIEE MRAeS 4.3.96

Squadron Leaders
P. J. Gow, MSc BSc CEng MIEE 9.1.95
A. P. Myers-Hemingway, BSc 3.2.97

HEADQUARTERS COMMANDER-IN-CHIEF IBERIAN ATLANTIC AREA

(ROYAL AIR FORCE ELEMENT)
Postal Address—HQ CINCIBERLANT, BFPO 6
Telephone No.—003511 440 5135
IVSN 529 5135

Squadron Leader
G. H. B. Laing, MA. 1.10.96

HEADQUARTERS COMMANDER ALLIED MARITIME AIR EASTERN ATLANTIC AREA AND MARITIME AIR FORCES NORTHWEST

Postal Address—RAF BENTLEY PRIORY, STANMORE, MIDDLESEX, HA7 3HH
Telephone No. 0181 838 7000

COMMANDER ALLIED MARITIME AIR EASTERN ATLANTIC AREA AND MARITIME AIR FORCES NORTHWEST

*Air Vice-Marshal B. K. BURRIDGE, CBE BSc 5.6.98

AIR OFFICER MARITIME AIR
*Air Commodore A. E. NEAL, AFC FIMgt. 5.1.96

Group Captains
R. W. Joseph, BSc. 9.12.96
R. W. Henry 12.9.96

Wing Commanders
E. R. Hannaford 16.8.93
L. R. Powell 15.7.94
C. J. Lawrence, MRAeS MRIN 1.6.97

Squadron Leaders
*R. J. Hall, MRIN 28.8.97
C. R. Purser 24.4.97

Retired Officer
Group Captain M. V. P. H. Harrington, CVO BA FIMgt 24.2.92

---

* (Staff serving in national appointments, in HQ No 11/18 Group RAF, with additional NATO duties on the staff of the HQs)

HEADQUARTERS NORTH

BRITISH FORCES POST OFFICE 50
Telephone No: 0047 5157 2689

SENIOR RAF OFFICER

Group Captain M. A. Norris, MBE 1.9.97

Wing Commanders

M. F. F. Common, MBE 1.3.96
M. A. Fulford, MSc MBA BSc CEng MIEE 9.9.96
N. Ross, MB ChB DRCOG DAvMed 11.7.97
W. J. Turner, MA BSc(Eng) MRAeS MRIN MCGI MIMgt 10.3.97
J. R. Whitston 10.11.97

HEADQUARTERS ALLIED FORCES BALTIC APPROACHES

(ROYAL AIR FORCE ELEMENT)

Postal Address—HQ BALTAP, NAVAL PARTY 1004, BFPO 486
Telephone No.—Denmark (0045) 86615111 BALTAP CENTRE (MIL)

Communications and Information Systems Division
Group Captain P. C. Badcock, MBE . . . . *ACOS CIS* *1.7.96*

Operations and Exercises Division
Wing Commander R. W. King . . . . *Staff Officer OCA/AI* *28.8.95*

HEADQUARTERS THIRD AIR FORCE USAF

at RAF Mildenhall, Bury St Edmunds, Suffolk IP28 8NF
Telephone No.—Newmarket (01638) 543000

Senior Royal Air Force Liaison Officer
Wing Commander A. H. C. Dyer-Perry, MInstD MRAeS 28.11.97
Royal Air Force Liaison Officer (Armament)
Squadron Leader R. M. Apps 20.5.96

EUROPEAN AIR GROUP

(ROYAL AIR FORCE ELEMENT)
Postal Address: RAF High Wycombe, Buckinghamshire, HP14 4UE
Telephone No: 01494 497922
Direct Dial: 01494 49****
Fax: 01494 497952

CHIEF OF STAFF
Group Captain A. W. Cope, MBE AFC FRAeS 22.7.96

Wing Commander
P. J. W. Whitaker, BA 26.8.97

Squadron Leaders
J. C. Garstin, BSc 3.2.97
P. G. Miles, MBE 3.6.96

No 1 GROUP

GROUP HEADQUARTERS
Postal Address—RAF HIGH WYCOMBE, BUCKS, HP14 4UE
Telephone No.—01494 461461

AIR OFFICER COMMANDING
Air Vice-Marshal J. H. THOMPSON 30.7.98

Personal Staff Officer
Squadron Leader P. Allan, BA 14.8.98

Aide-de-Camp
Flight Lieutenant J. E. Morton, BA. 10.7.98

SENIOR AIR STAFF OFFICER
Air Commodore P. V. HARRIS, AFC 18.12.95

Group Captains

D. J. Drew 4.8.97
D. H. White 21.7.97
J. W. White, MRAeS MIMgt 6.1.97
*Colonel J. Goodsir, MBE 25.8.97

Wing Commanders

T. L. Boyle 12.8.96
W. G. Evans, OBE 1.6.98
S. W. Exton 15.12.97
R. Foster. 1.1.97
S. D. Greenwood, MDA MInstAM(Dip) ACII 27.8.97
A. Thompson, BSc. 4.8.97

Squadron Leaders

*Major G. R. Akhurst, MBE 24.2.97
R. M. Aspinall, MA 6.7.98
*Major R. P. M. Blake, MIL 31.10.97
J. C. Bottomley, BSc 27.8.97
J. M. Calder, BSc 20.1.98
R. V. Carter, BSc 2.10.92
N. A. Cobb 7.1.98
S. C. Cockbill, BSc. 11.8.97
I. J. Craig, MBE. 29.4.96
D. J. Ekins, BSc 15.1.98
D. A. Foote 26.1.98
M. J. Grout 5.8.96
E. S. J. Hunt 1.9.97
E. S. Huskisson, BSc 10.8.98
A. J. Laidler. 9.2.98
M. T. Lalley 5.5.98
I. J. MacFarlane 9.1.97
P. Martin 31.3.97
G. I. Mitchell 27.1.97
J. D. Paulson 4.5.98
C. M. Peace 26.1.98
R. V. Sanderson, BSc 23.3.98
P. P. Speedy, BSc 2.6.97
M. F. Stangroom 30.5.97
D. J. Stewart, CertEd 7.10.96
G. Stockill 18.11.97
J. G. T. Yarnold. 4.11.93

* Permanent Army Appointment

No 11/18 GROUP

GROUP HEADQUARTERS

Postal Address—RAF BENTLEY PRIORY, STANMORE, MIDDLESEX, HA7 3HH
Telephone No.—0181-838 7000

AIR OFFICER COMMANDING
Air Vice-Marshal B. K. BURRIDGE, CBE BSc 5.6.98
Personal Staff Officer
Squadron Leader M. K. Crayford 1.9.97
Aide-de-Camp
Flight Lieutenant V. P. Gosling, BA. 5.6.98

No 11/18 GROUP

HEADQUARTERS AIR DEFENCE

Postal Address—RAF BENTLEY PRIORY, STANMORE, MIDDLESEX, HA7 3HH
Telephone No.—0181 838 7000

AIR OFFICER AIR DEFENCE
Air Commodore L. A. DOBLE, OBE FRAeS 24.6.96
FRENCH LIAISON OFFICER
Lieutenant Colonel P. Bobbilon
ROYAL NAVAL LIAISON OFFICER (RNLO)
Lieutenant Commander S. Page, BSc 10.9.96
Group Captains
G. G. Cullington, CBE AFC BSc 3.1.96
B. E. Rogers, MBE 17.11.97
Wing Commanders
P. Chambers. 1.4.96
P. R. Hunter, OBE 1.4.96
J. A. Jupp, BA 17.6.96
G. W. MacInnes, BSc 10.1.97
C. C. Nash, BA 1.4.96
J. Pearce. 1.4.97
W. McK. Reid, PhD BSc 9.1.98
P. C. Ridge, BSc 12.5.97
N. I. M. Seward 11.8.97
D. Todd, MBE BSc 18.3.96
Squadron Leaders
J. P. Arden 28.4.97
P. W. Atkinson, BA. 20.5.96
J. A. Child, MMAR. 1.5.96
M. S. P. Coleman 29.4.96
T. J. Divver 1.4.97
M. R. Fixter 22.7.96
J. P. V. Gildersleeves 17.6.96
K. Hann, MBE 27.5.96
D. R. Hartill 1.4.96
T. J. Hill, BA. 1.1.95
S. B. Lewis, BSc 5.5.98
A. G. McFadyen, BA 12.8.96
B. J. McLean 1.4.96
P. Millward 8.7.96

A. J. Morgan	16.3.98
J. C. Prescott	22.8.96
I. R. Price	1.6.98
R. A. Roe	2.9.96
C. J. Stace, BEng CEng MIEE	1.9.97
S. G. Tolley, BSc	1.5.96
P. Taylor, BSc	26.1.98
J. D. Wilmshurst-Smith	14.1.98

USAF Exchange Officer
Major M. E. Matusiewicz

Civilian
R. J. Woodward

GROUP MANAGEMENT ACCOUNTANT
Civilian
Mr. J. Foster

No 11/18 GROUP

HEADQUARTERS MARITIME AIR

Postal Address—RAF NORTHWOOD, MIDDLESEX, HA6 3EP
Telephone No.—01923 826161

AIR OFFICER MARITIME AIR
Air Commodore A. E. NEAL, AFC FIMgt 5.1.96

Staff Officer
Flight Lieutenant C. J. Mace. 18.8.97

Group Captain
R. W. Joseph, BSc. 9.12.96

Wing Commanders

D. J. Ford, BA	7.10.96
C. J. Lawrence MRAeS MRIN	1.6.97
J. H. Plumley, BSc.	3.5.94

Squadron Leaders

A. P. D. Aitken	1.9.97
P. A. B. Basey	11.12.95
P. H. Budd	8.1.96
L. J. Clark, BEd.	25.11.96
R. J. Hall, MRIN	1.9.95
K. L. W. Hughes	27.8.96
D. Kerr-Sheppard	23.2.96
G. Lovegrove	5.1.98
S. P. McNamara	25.11.96
C. R. Purser	24.4.97
S. J. Read	6.1.97
J. C. Walker, BSc	9.3.98
B. R. Withers, AFC.	1.4.96

NO 38 GROUP

GROUP HEADQUARTERS
Postal Address RAF HIGH WYCOMBE, BUCKINGHAMSHIRE HP14 4UE
Telephone No 01494 461461.

AIR OFFICER COMMANDING
Air Vice-Marshal P. O. STURLEY, MBE BSc FRAeS 30.1.98
Personal Staff Officer
Squadron Leader P. Talyor 20.5.98
SENIOR AIR STAFF OFFICER
Air Commodore G. D. SIMPSON, CBE AFC 9.12.96
AO REGT & STO
Air Commodore I. W. P. McNEIL 29.9.95

Group Captains
S. H. Anderton, MSc BSc FIMgt 11.11.96
A. I. B. Beedie 19.9.94
P. P. V. Gaskin, OBE 1.4.96
I. D. Lindsay, MA MSc MB BChir MRCGP DRCOG DAvMed AFOM 1.12.97
J. R. D. Morley, MBE 16.4.96

Wing Commanders
K. S. Balshaw 17.2.97
P. Burt 29.8.98
D. S. Davenall, BSc 15.5.95
A. Davie, MA 22.10.95
J. C. Gardiner, BA DPhysEd 17.2.97
B. D. T. Hay, MILog MRAeS MCIT 12.6.94
C. J. S. Hewat, MBE 16.12.96
M. R. Hooker, MIMgt 1.9.97
F. A. Huddleston 8.5.95
I. E. Shields 23.6.97
M. P. Westwood, OBE 26.5.93
J. G. Williams, MBE 15.5.98

Squadron Leaders
D. E. Ball, BSc 1.10.96
D. M. Beckwith 30.6.97
S. P. Bostock 3.1.96
M. A. B. Brecht, BA 30.3.98
L. B. Brunt 4.8.97
R. Chalklin 19.12.97
S. J. Cloke, BEng 28.3.96
S. H. Crockatt 1.9.97
N. G. Cryer 5.5.97
A. S. Deas, BSc. 2.12.96
D. Dexter, BSc MB ChB DRCOG 1.8.92
P. G. Dixon 3.9.97
A. P. Dobson, BEng 4.8.98
S. P. Fletcher 1.4.96
R. Fogden 22.1.96
G. C. Gair 17.11.97
D. M. Gannon 22.1.96
J. C. Gardiner, MBE 11.5.98
D. F. Goodman 16.11.92
A. J. Hall, MBE 23.7.97
B. T. F. Hall, AE 3.3.97
D. A. Hamilton, BTech 9.6.97

R. L. Harrison, DPhysEd	4.3.96
W. N. King, MDA BA MIPD	4.3.96
D. L. Laws, MSc BA DESEM MCIT MIL MILog	2.7.95
T. Leech, MHCIMA MIMgt	14.10.97
G. I. Lory, BSc	8.4.96
S. B. McBain	8.8.95
A. J. McFarlane	17.11.97
S. S. McFarland	28.4.97
A. McGregor, BA	9.1.95
A. L. McSherry, BSc	28.10.96
C. P. Menage	10.2.97
D. R. Morgan	27.11.92
A. J. Osman.	5.7.96
A. B. Phillips	16.6.97
J. D. Porter, BSc AKC	4.3.96
A. T. Potts	17.2.97
D. M. Pritchard	21.10.96
A. P. Royle, BEng	30.6.97
D. J. Sainsbury, MSc BEd	11.9.95
M. Stewart	11.8.97
P. D. Strachan	8.6.98
A. P. Triccas	16.6.96
J. M. Walsh, BTech	6.8.97
S. J. F. Wright-Cooper, BSc	5.1.98

HEADQUARTERS, MILITARY AIR TRAFFIC OPERATIONS

Postal Address—HILLINGDON HOUSE, UXBRIDGE, MIDDLESEX UB10 0RU
Telephone No.—(01895) 276009
* Postal Address—HQ MATO, CAA House, 45-59 Kingsway, London, WC2B 6TE
Telephone No.—(0171) 8325244
** Postal Address—HQ MATO, Swanwick Centre, Sopwith Way, Bursledon, Southampton, SO31 7AY
Telephone No.—(01489) 6122500

AIR OFFICER COMMANDING

Air Commodore J. R. D. ARSCOTT 18.9.95

Staff Officer

Squadron Leader M. A. Morton, BA 3.2.97

GROUP CAPTAIN OPERATIONS

Group Captain M. J. Fuller 2.10.97

GROUP CAPTAIN PERSONNEL AND RESOURCES

Group Captain R. J. Sturman 4.9.95

GROUP CAPTAIN PROGRAMMES AND PROGRAMME FINANCE

Group Captain N. C. Brewer* 5.1.98

Wing Commanders

A. J. Clare, MIMgt 31.7.95
J. Clark 1.9.97
C. D. Hill, MBE 12.10.98
P. Roberts 16.6.96
K. P. Sherdley, BA 27.1.97
M. R. Wordley* 20.10.97

Squadron Leaders

I. McP. Ainslie 29.1.96
N. J. Alcock, BSc 15.6.98
A. C. Bainbridge 11.5.98
D. Barber, BA 5.10.98
D. A. Bush, BSc 6.10.97
J. D. Cookson*, BEM 19.8.96
D. J. Drake, BA 9.3.98
J. Duncan 29.7.95
F. C. M. Gifford* 15.1.96
D. R. Heaselgrave 3.2.97
J. L. Merriman 9.2.98
D. V. Merryweather* 12.10.98
D. Morrison 6.10.97
A. D. Rapson 7.7.97
M. S. Smailes 6.7.98
C. G. Walker** 28.8.96
C. D. Wood** 8.6.98

Flight Lieutenant

W. A. Clark 20.11.97
R. Flanigan 27.1.97
R. M. James 19.5.97

Royal Navy

Lieutenant Commander D. J. Balchin 17.7.95

THE ROYAL AIR FORCE PERSONNEL MANAGEMENT AGENCY, GLOUCESTER

Postal Address—RAF PERSONNEL MANAGEMENT AGENCY, RAF INNSWORTH, GLOUCESTER, GL3 1EZ
Telephone No.—01452-712612

AIR SECRETARY/CHIEF EXECUTIVE OF THE ROYAL AIR FORCE PERSONNEL MANAGEMENT AGENCY
Air Vice-Marshal I. M. STEWART, AFC LLB 28.8.98

Staff Officer
Squadron Leader D. J. Hill 11.8.97

OC RAF INNSWORTH
Wing Commander A. Spearpoint, MIMgt. 31.10.97

HEADQUARTERS ROYAL AIR FORCE SUPPORT COMMAND HEADQUARTERS PROVOST AND SECURITY SERVICES

(UNITED KINGDOM)

Postal Address—RAF RUDLOE MANOR, HAWTHORN, CORSHAM, WILTSHIRE SN13 0PQ
Telephone No.—01225-810461

HEADQUARTERS

COMMANDING OFFICER
Group Captain C. R. Morgan 15.9.97

Wing Commanders
N. A. S. Cato, BA DipEurHum 2.3.98
G. J. Gardiner, BA 6.6.98

DEFENCE VETTING AGENCY

Hd DVA(RAF)
Mr T. J. Cunniffe, LLB T&G, Grd 7 (PIO)

AIR WARFARE CENTRE
HEADQUARTERS

Postal Address: RAF Waddington, Lincolnshire, LN5 9NB
Telephone No.—01522 720271

COMMANDANT
Air Commodore R. J. HORWOOD, OBE FRAeS RAF 6.7.98
AIR WELFARE CENTRE
Postal Address: RAF Waddington, Lincolnshire LN5 9NB. Telephone No. 01522 720271

Squadron Leaders
W. J. Ramsey 28.10.96
A. W. Walsh. 5.1.98

OPERATIONAL DOCTRINE & TRAINING ELEMENT
Group Captain
R. W. Gault 22.12.95

Wing Commanders
R. J. Dunsford, BSc 13.4.94
P. M. Kelly 15.1.96
P. J. Pharaoh, MSc. 1.7.96
A. P. Stephens 20.5.96
I. D. Teakle 27.4.98
P. N. Voltzenlogel, MCIT 24.6.96

Retired Officer
Wing Commander R. J. C. Green, MRIN MIMgt

Royal Navy
Commander J. A. Lister

Army
Lieutenant Colonel J. M. P. McDonnell

USAF Exchange Officer
Major K. Johnson

OPERATIONAL ANALYSIS ELEMENT
Command Research Officer
Vacant

Principals and Equivalent Grades
Mr A. Cowdale, MSc BSc
Mr R. E. Jarvis, MSc CEng MIMechE
Dr R. C. Wheeler, MA DPhil

AIR WARFARE CENTRE
TACTICS AND ELECTRONIC WARFARE ELEMENT
AND OPERATIONAL EVALUATION UNITS

Postal Address: RAF Waddington, Lincolnshire LN5 9NB
Telephone No.—01522 720271

Group Captain
M. Gleave, OBE 6.1.97

Wing Commanders

D. W. Knowles 4.12.95
C. G. Marrison 5.4.96
A. J. Pulfrey. 13.3.95
W. S. Smyth, BA 12.6.95
N. M. Warrick, FIAP MIMgt 29.9.95
S. D. Forward, BSc 31.8.94

Squadron Leaders

R. Anderson, BSc 18.4.97
R. M. Allchorne. 16.2.98
S. D. Atha, BSc. 6.3.98
R. J. Atkinson 17.7.94
A. Baxter. 30.9.96
P. C. L. Birkbeck, BSc 1.9.96
P. A. Bradbeer 26.4.95
J. H. Brough 4.3.96
S. Buckingham, BA 15.1.98
P. A. Davies 3.4.95
R. W. Davies, BSc 18.3.96
A. M. Eckersley. 8.6.98
P. Evans, BA. 8.6.98
L. T. Hallett, BSc 13.5.96
J. S. Head, BSc. 31.5.95
C. R. Hill 1.5.97
M. C. Huffington, BSc. 1.11.96
A. K. Jeffrey. 19.1.98
C. Jobling 27.1.98
I. Looker, BSc 26.4.95
D. Mason, BSc 5.3.98
E. Middleton 27.5.97
I. A. Myers 1.7.96
T. Newby 16.3.98
G. F. Richardson, BSc 10.4.96
G. G. Riley 4.1.95
I. A. Rose 30.1.95
A. J. Ross, BSc 2.1.96
D. G. Scorer, BSocSc 9.6.97
G. R. Scott 18.4.97
D. M. Shaw 20.5.96
P. R. Smith 26.8.97
M. A. Wakeman 1.2.98
M. R. J. Wescott 27.7.95
R. C. Whitworth 5.8.97

Royal Navy

Commander F. Morris
Lieutenant Commander R. P. Slater

Army
Major D. J. Luckett

CAF Liaison Officer
Major F. C. Castel

AIR WARFARE CENTRE
OPERATIONAL DOCTRINE & TRAINING ELEMENT

Postal Address—RAF Cranwell, Sleaford, Lincs NG34 8HB
Telephone No.—0181 838 7000

Wing Commanders
C. P. A. Hull, BSc 15.4.96
N. S. Yeldham 4.1.94

Squadron Leaders
D. C. Ashton, MSc BSc 8.6.98
P. C. Banks, MBE BSc 1.6.87
B. J. Holley, MSc BSc CEng CPhys MInstP 9.5.94
M. J. Lewis-Morris, MSc BSc 9.9.91
M. J. Lister-Tomlinson 28.5.96
S. A. Mclaren 7.4.97
R. Ross 11.3.98
C. S. Steel 6.4.98

USAF Exchange Officer
Major A. G. Glodowski

RAAF Exchange Officer
Squadron Leader E. Gaschk

ROYAL AIR FORCE SIGNALS ENGINEERING ESTABLISHMENT
Postal address: RAF Henlow, Bedfordshire SG16 6DN
Telephone: 01462 851515

CHIEF EXECUTIVE
Air Commodore G. JONES, MBE BSc CEng MIEE 14.10.96

POLICY AND SERVICES DIVISION
Group Captain H. G. Britten-Austin, MSc BSc CEng FIEE 30.6.97

PROJECTS

Mr A. Palmer, BA CEng FIEE

Wing Commanders

S. Charnock, MSc BSc(Eng) CEng MIMechE MRAeS 1.5.98
N. Little, BSc CEng MIEE. 27.4.98
J. S. Parker, MBE MBA BSc CEng MRAeS 28.10.96
G. E. P. Pattenden, LLB ACIS 13.7.98
E. W. Richards, MSc LLB BSc(Eng) CEng MIEE DIC LTCL ACGI 20.12.96

Heads and Equivalent Grades

Mr J. Broomfield
Mr C. Follenfant
Mr S. Hicks
Mr R. A. J. Hutchinson
Mrs J. S. Jenkins, BSc
Mr J. M. Jones
Mrs A. Quantick

JOINT SERVICES COMMAND AND STAFF COLLEGE, BRACKNELL

Postal Address—JSCSC Bracknell, Berkshire RG12 9DD
Telephone No.—01344-357358

COMMANDANT
Major General T. J. GRANVILLE-CHAPMAN, CBE 1.1.97

Aide-de-Camp
Captain B. Taylor 18.5.98

DEPUTY COMMANDANT
Commodore J. W. R. HARRIS 1.1.97

ASSISTANT COMMANDANT (Navy)
Commodore N. R. OWEN 12.5.98

ASSISTANT COMMANDANT (Army)
Brigadier C. R. WATT, CBE 1.1.97

ASSISTANT COMMANDANT (Air)
Air Commodore M. G. F. WHITE, OBE. 1.4.97

Group Captains

D. H. Anderson, MA 1.1.97
M. N. Lees 1.1.97
S. W. Peach, MPhil BA 21.7.97
J. H. S. Thomas, BA MIL 3.2.97

Wing Commanders

G. J. Bagwell 16.6.97
R. J. Barwell, BSc CEng MRAeS 19.1.98
C. L. Bond 1.1.97
M. A. C. Codgbrook, BSc. 1.1.97
T. Cross, BA. 21.7.97
J. G. Evans, MBE MBA BA 16.2.98
S. G. Footer, MBE 1.12.97
D. J. Foster, MSc BSc 1.1.97
C. H. Green, BSc CEng MRAeS 21.7.97
F. Harbottle 12.5.97
N. C. L. Hudson, MA 1.1.97
G. A. Jermy, OBE 1.12.97
J. R. Jones 5.1.98
M. F. Killen, BSc 1.1.97
J. M. Lyster, MIPD 4.8.97
C. D. Malcolm 1.1.97
B. J. R. Nelson 2.6.97
C. N. Romney, BSc 1.1.97
D. R. Skinner 1.1.97
A. J. Vincent 1.9.97
A. R. D. Welham 1.1.97

Squadron Leaders

T. A. Brady 28.4.97
A. J. Burton, MSc MPhil BEd DIC AMIPD. 1.1.97
A. Campbell. 24.2.97
P. W. Chapman, BSc 1.1.97
R. Collins 1.1.97
M. A. Cowdrey, BA 17.2.97
R. A. Hopkin, BEd 10.2.97
G. Leech, BA CertEd AIPD 21.10.96
J. Lillis 12.1.98
P. J. Morris 6.11.97
N. J. Neal, MSc 1.1.97

A. C. Pearce, MSc BSc PGCE DIC 26.8.97
A. D. Perkins 1.1.97
A. F. Philip, MSc BSc 29.9.97
T. Pickles. 8.3.98
S. J. A. Sharpe 28.4.97
N. D. Wainwright 9.3.98
T. H. P. Wood 23.6.97

Retired Officers

Wing Commander A. G. Corbitt
Wing Commander T. N. King
Wing Commander R. McLauchlin
Wing Commander T. J. Nias, IEng MIIE(mech)
Wing Commander W. M. Parker
Wing Commander R. J. Quarterman
Squadron Leader G. P. Allen
Squadron Leader R. A. Jackson
Squadron Leader K. R. Kendrick, IEng
Squadron Leader D. C. Passby, BA DipEd
Squadron Leader D. A. Petty, MA MA CertEd

OFFICERS COMMAND SCHOOL HENLOW

Postal Address—RAF Officers' Command School, HENLOW, BEDFORDSHIRE SG16 6DN
Telephone No.—01462–851515

Wing Commander

W. Hush, BSc 5.8.96

Squadron Leaders

G. L. Dickson, BA 8.9.97
I. M. McGregor, MA 3.7.95
S. Mitchell-Gears, MILog 28.10.96
S. Murkin 5.1.98
K. W. Park 1.4.97
N. F. Pearson, BSc 24.11.97
D. J. Reed, BA PGCE 31.10.94
C. R. Wood, LLB 4.9.95
J. T. Wright 3.1.97

ROYAL AIR FORCE CRANWELL

(Royal Air Force Personnel and Training Command)
Postal Address—ROYAL AIR FORCE COLLEGE, CRANWELL, SLEAFORD, LINCOLNSHIRE NG34 8HB
Telephone No.—01400-261201

Commandant-in-Chief—HM THE QUEEN

Air Commodore-in-Chief Air Training Corps
Marshal of the Royal Air Force H. R. H. The PRINCE PHILIP, DUKE OF EDINBURGH KG KT OM GBE AC QSO

AIR OFFICER COMMANDING AND COMMANDANT OF RAF COLLEGE
Air Vice-Marshal T. W. RIMMER, OBE MA FRAeS 30.7.98

Personal Staff Officer
Squadron Leader J. J. Faulkes, MHCIMA. 4.9.95

College Secretary
Squadron Leader D. A. Wood, RAFR

DIRECTOR OF RECRUITING AND SELECTION AND INITIAL OFFICER TRAINING
Air Commodore C. R. FOWLER, ADC 15.11.96

Staff Officer
Flight Lieutenant S. P. Braun, MInstAM 14.10.96

COMMANDANT AIR CADETS AND AIR TRAINING CORPS
Air Commodore J. D. KENNEDY, BA 9.4.98

Aide-de-Camp
Flight Lieutenant J. D. Knight, MA. 27.10.97

OFFICER COMMANDING ROYAL AIR FORCE COLLEGE CRANWELL
Group Captain N. E. Threapleton, BSc 7.5.98

DIRECTOR OF ELEMENTARY FLYING TRAINING
Group Captain P. S. Owen 6.1.97

DIRECTOR OF DEPARTMENT OF SPECIALIST GROUND TRAINING
Group Captain D. N. Case, MSc BSc CEng MRAeS. 6.1.97

DIRECTOR OF INITIAL OFFICER TRAINING
Group Captain T. J. Beney, FIMgt 7.5.96

DEPUTY DIRECTORS RECRUITING AND SELECTION
Group Captain I. F. Bruton, BA 14.10.96
Group Captain B. S. Morris, OBE AFC. 13.2.95
Group Captain M. H. Shields, FIMgt 20.10.95

CHIEF OF STAFF AIR CADETS
Group Captain W. M. N. Cross, OBE RAFR

AIR CADETS REGIONAL HEADQUARTERS

Scotland and Northern Ireland (Edinburgh)
Group Captain A. Ferguson, FIMgt RAFR

Wales and West (RAF Cosford)
Group Captain P. S. Kiggell, OBE RAFR

Central and East (RAF Henlow)
Group Captain R. J. Coleman, MMS MIMgt RAFR

London and South East (RAF Northolt)
Group Captain L. Hakin, OBE RAFR

North (RAF Linton-on-Ouse)
Group Captain W. G. Gambold, RAFR

COLLEGES

South West (RAF Locking)

Group Captain R. P. Skelley, RAFR

Wing Commanders

D. C. Fidler	23.10.96
R. N. Halfter, BA	2.3.98
D. R. Herriot	1.10.97
J. Lawlor, BA	4.4.98
R. Marston, AFC	18.3.96
J. P. Mayne, BSc	25.3.96
C. B. Montagu, MSc BSc CEng MIMechE	16.12.96
P. A. Rushmere, MIMgt	28.10.96
C. M. Taylor	2.9.96
P. D. Tindall, BSc	13.4.98

Retired Officers

Wing Commander G. S. Clayton-Jones, MRAeS RAFR
Wing Commander R. B. Crowder, MIMgt RAFR
Wing Commander M. A. Stephens, RAFR
Wing Commander W. W. Wright, BA, BA DipEd RAFR

ROYAL AIR FORCE CENTRAL FLYING SCHOOL
CRANWELL

(Royal Air Force Personnel and Training Command)

Postal Address—HQ CFS, RAF COLLEGE CRANWELL, SLEAFORD, LINCOLNSHIRE NG34 8HB

Telephone No.—01400 261201

Commandant-in-Chief—HM QUEEN ELIZABETH THE QUEEN MOTHER

COMMANDANT

Air Commodore H. G. MACKAY OBE AFC BSc FRAeS. 28.10.96

Aide-de-Camp

Flying Officer V. C. Pearson 4.11.96

Staff Officer HQ CFS

Squadron Leader R. E. Leaviss 23.9.96

DEPUTY COMMANDANT (Station Commander RAF College Cranwell)

Group Captain N. E. Threapleton, BSc 7.5.98

Wing Commanders

J. P. S. Fynes 1.4.96

R. T. Johnston, MA 9.12.96

Squadron Leaders

E. A. Elton, BA 1.9.93

M. J. Hunt 3.3.97

R. L. Maskall 28.10.96

S. C. Meade 12.10.96

J. R. Norton 8.7.96

E. E. Webster 1.6.98

FIXED WING TUTORIAL SQUADRONS

BULLDOG SQUADRON
RAF CRANWELL

Squadron Leader J. F. Gardiner. 7.10.96

TUCANO SQUADRON
RAF LINTON-ON-OUSE

Squadron Leader J. R. Floyd, MA 16.9.96

19(R) SQUADRON
RAF VALLEY

Squadron Leader N. R. Benson, BSc 23.10.95

ROTARY WING TUTORIAL SQUADRON

GAZELLE SQUADRON
RAF SHAWBURY

Squadron Leader I. G. Cahill 15.11.96

RETIRED OFFICER
Editor AP3456

Wing Commander C. R. Deeley, FRIN FIAP MIMgt

ROYAL COLLEGE OF DEFENCE STUDIES

Postal Address—Seaford House, 37 Belgrave Square, London SW1X 8NS
Telephone No. 0171–915–4800

COMMANDANT
Lieutenant General S. C. GRANT, CB MA. 20.12.95

SENIOR DIRECTING STAFF
Major General P. A. CHAMBERS, MBE 20.12.96
Rear Admiral H. W. RICKARD, BSc MIL CBE 20.4.98
Mr R. F. CORNISH, CMG LVO 15.12.97
Air Vice-Marshal K. D. FILBEY CBE FIMgt RAF 5.1.98

JUNIOR DIRECTING STAFF
Wing Commander M. M. Pollitt, BSc 4.11.96
Mr R. d'E. Ward 3.1.95
Wing Commander P. R. Dixon, MBA BSc(Eng) MRAeS 5.5.98
Lieutenant Colonel K. L. de Val, RM 19.7.96
Lieutenant Colonel A. W. Foster 28.4.97

SECRETARY
Brigadier R. TARSNANE, CEng FIMechE FIMgt (Retd) 17.9.93

JOINT WARFARE STAFF

at Maritime Warfare Centre (Southwick)
HMS DRYAD, Nr Fareham, HAMPSHIRE, PO17 6EJ
Telephone No.—01705 284726

Wing Commanders

G. A. Bowerman, OBE 21.4.97
R. A. Forsythe, OBE 2.9.96

AIR OFFICER SCOTLAND AND NORTHERN IRELAND

STATION COMMANDER ROYAL AIR FORCE LEUCHARS
St ANDREWS, FIFE KY16 0JX
Telephone No.—01334 839471

AIR OFFICER
Air Commodore J. H. HAINES, OBE ADC. 18.12.95
Aide-de-Camp and Staff Officer to AOSNI
Flight Lieutenant N. C. J. Brittain, BA 15.12.97

AIR OFFICER WALES

STATION COMMANDER, ROYAL AIR FORCE ST. ATHAN
BARRY, VALE OF GLAMORGAN CF62 4WA

AIR OFFICER
Air Commodore A. C. LANG, MBE ADC BA CEng FIMechE FRAeS 27.10.97
Aide-de-Camp
Vacant

AIR FORCE DEPARTMENT COMMITTEES AND COMMITTEES ON WHICH THE AIR FORCE DEPARTMENT IS REPRESENTED

AIR CADET COUNCIL

President

The Parliamentary Under Secretary of State for the Armed Forces

Vice-President

AOC and Commandant RAF College Cranwell

Members

Commandant of the Air Training Corps (HQ Air Cadets)

Wing Commander P. Guiver RAFVR(T) (Retd) (London and South East Region)

M. J. Marshall Esq, MA DL FRAeS (Central and East Region)

Mr B. J. Acland (South West Region)

Wing Commander D. D. Hemming, MBE BEd RAFVR(T) (Retd) (Wales and West Region)

Wing Commander J. M. Lewington RAFVR(T) (Retd) (North Region)

Mr W. Walker, OBE (Scotland and Northern Ireland Region)

Wing Commander E. Cadden (Northern Ireland)

Reverend D. J. Share

Secretary

Head of AMP (Sec)

In Attendance
The Regional Commandants of each of the six ATC Regions

ADVISORY PANEL ON THE CHAPLAINCY SERVICES

(Arranged in alphabetical order of the Churches represented)

Representing the Church of England
The Rt Rev J. D. G. Kirkham, AKC MA Bishop to the Forces

Representing the Jewish Church
Rev M. Weisman, OBE MA OCF

Representing the Methodist Church
Rev J. B. Sherrington, BD BA CertEd MPhil

Representing the Church of Scotland
Rev Dr I. R. Torrance, TD MA BD DPhil

Representing the Presbyterian Church of Ireland
Rev S. Van Os

Representing the Roman Catholic Church
The Rt Rev F. J. Walmsley, CBE RC Bishop of the Forces

Representing the United Navy, Army and Air Force Board (Baptist and United Reformed Churches)
Rev J. A. Murray—Secretary

Members of the Panel meet under the Chairmanship of the Air Member for Personnel to advise on matters concerning Royal Air Force Chaplaincy. The Chaplain-in-Chief (RAF), and the two Principal Chaplains attend as required.

COMMONWEALTH WAR GRAVES COMMISSION

2 Marlow Road, Maidenhead, Berkshire SL6 7DX
Telephone No.—01628-634221 Telex No.—847526 COMGRA G Fax No.—01628 771208
E-MAIL cwgc@dial.pipex.com

President
  H.R.H. THE DUKE OF KENT, KG GCMG GCVO ADC

Members
  The Secretary of State for Defence in the United Kingdom (Chairman)
  Admiral Sir John Kerr, GCB DL (Vice-Chairman)
  The High Commissioner for the Republic of India
  The High Commissioner for Australia
  The High Commissioner of the Republic of South Africa
  The High Commissioners for Canada and New Zealand
  The Viscount Ridley, KG GCVO TD
  Professor R. J. O'Neill, AO
  Mrs Llinos Golding, MP
  Mr John Wilkinson, MP
  Sir John Gray, KBE CMG
  Mr Paul Orchard-Lisle, CBE TD DL
  Air Chief Marshal Sir Michael Stear, KCB CBE MA
  General Sir John Wilsey, GCB CBE DL

Director-General (Secretary to the Commission)
  D. Kennedy, CMG

Deputy Director-General (Assistant Secretary to the Commission)
  R. J. Dalley

Legal Adviser and Solicitor
  G. C. Reddie

Director of Personnel
  D. R. Parker

Director of Works
  A. Coombe

Director of Finance
  R. D. Wilson, ACMA

Director of Horticulture
  D. C. Parker, Dip Hort (Kew) M (Hort)

Director of Information and Secretariat
  L. J. Hanna

Personal Secretary to Director-General
  Mrs R. M. Truran

UNITED KINGDOM AREA

Area Director
  P. J. Noakes

Area Administration Officer
  A. K. Ghosh

Area Works Officer
  R. J. Bird

Area Horticultural Officer
  C. Griffiths-Hardman

TERRITORIAL, AUXILIARY AND VOLUNTEER RESERVE ASSOCIATIONS

As at 1/1/98
NOTE—In some cases in these lists the rank shown against an officer's name is honorary COUNCIL OF TERRITORIAL, AUXILIARY AND VOLUNTEER RESERVE ASSOCIATIONS
Duke of York's Headquarters, Chelsea, SW3 4SG
Telephone No.—0171-730 6122
MIL: 763 5587
FAX 0171-414-5589
MIL: 763 5589

Patron: Colonel The Rt Hon The Viscount Ridley, KG GCVO TD
President: The Rt Hon Viscount Younger of Leckie, KT KCVO TD DL
Chairman: General Sir Edward Jones, KCB CBE
Vice Chairmen:
    Colonel J. R. G. Putnam, CBE TD DL
    Colonel P. J. C. Robinson, TD DL
    Commodore I. R. Pemberton, RD* DL
    Colonel T. H. Lang, RD* ADC
    Air Vice-Marshal B. H. Newton, CB OBE FIMgt RAF
Secretary: Major General W. A. Evans, CB
Deputy Secretary: Brigadier T. S. Sneyd, OBE

> Note—Each Territorial, Auxiliary and Volunteer Reserve Association is represented on this Council by its President, Vice-Presidents, Chairman, Vice-Chairmen and Secretary.ce of the Chaplain-in-Chief (RAF), The Principal C

EAST ANGLIA ASSOCIATION

President

J. G. P. Crowden, Esq JP

Vice-Presidents

S. C. Whitbread, Esq JP
Lord Braybrooke, JP
S. A. Bowes Lyon, Esq JP
The Right Honourable The Lord Belstead, PC JP
Sir Timothy Colman, KG JP DCL

Chairman

Colonel K. R. FitzGerald, TD DL

Vice-Chairmen

Commander T. C. Haile, RNR** RD (Retd)
Colonel L. J. Rose, OBE DL
Air Vice-Marshal M. J. Pilkington, CB CBE

County Chairmen

Colonel M. J. Simmonds TD (Beds)
Brigadier P. R. G. Williams, DL (Cambs)
Lieutenant Colonel W. I. M. Allan (Essex)
Major P. D. Alexander, CB MBE (Herts)
Lieutenant Colonel R. E. S. Drew (Norfolk)
Major C. J. H. Gurney, DL (Suffolk)

Air Force Members

Ex-Officio

The Officer Commanding, 2620 (County of Norfolk) Squadron Royal Auxiliary Air Force Regiment
The Officer Commanding, 2623 (East Anglia) Training Squadron Royal Auxiliary Air Force Regiment
The Officer Commanding, 7010 (VR) P1 Squadron Royal Auxiliary Air Force
The Officer Commanding, Cambridge University Air Squadron

Selected

The Station Commander RAF Honington
The Regional Commandant, HQ Air Cadets Central and East, ATC
Air Vice-Marshal M. J. Pilkington, CB CBE
Flight Lieutenant N. R. Scammell, RAF (Retd) (Norfolk)

Secretary

Colonel J. S. Houchin, OBE, "Springfield Tyrells" 250, Springfield Road, Chelmsford CM2 6BU Tel No: Civil 01245 354262 FAX: 01245 492398
Tel MIL: Colchester Military FAX MIL: Colchester 4723
Deputy Secretary, Lieutenant Colonel I. G. S. Cartwright, MBE

EAST WESSEX ASSOCIATION

President

Mrs M. Fagan, JP (HM Lord-Lieutenant, Hampshire)

Vice-Presidents

P. L. Wroughton Esq (HM Lord-Lieutenant, Berkshire)
Sir Nigel Mobbs, JP (HM Lord-Lieutenant,
Buckinghamshire)
The Lord Digby, JP (HM Lord-Lieutenant, Dorset)
H. Brunner, Esq (HM Lord-Lieutenant, Oxfordshire)
C. D. J. Bland, Esq (HM Lord-Lieutenant, Isle of Wight)

Chairman

Colonel A. H. Protheroe, CBE TD DL

Vice-Chairmen

C. J. Prideaux, Esq, DL
Colonel W. H. F. Stevens, OBE
Brigadier N. J. B. Mogg, DL
Colonel M. E. Hatt-Cook, CBE RD
Commander D. J. Bellfield, RD
Lieutenant Colonel C. H. Ainsley, TD
Colonel D. G. Thomas

Air Force Members

Ex-Officio

The Officer Commanding, No 7006 RAuxAF Sqn High
Wycombe
The Officer Commanding, Oxford University Air Squadron
The Officer Commanding, Southampton University Air
Squadron
The Officer Commanding, No 2624 (County of Oxford)
RAuxAF Regt Sqn
The Officer Commanding, No 4624 (County of Oxford)
RAuxAF Movements Sqn
The Officer Commanding, Helicopter SP Sqn RAuxAF

Selected

The Officer Commanding, RAF Brize Norton
The Officer Commanding, RAF Benson
The Officer Commanding, RAF High Wycombe
The Officer Commanding, RAF Odiham
The Regional Commandant, South and West Region, ATC

Secretary and Chief Executive

Brigadier R. G. Long, CBE MC DL, Headquarters Offices
30, Carlton Place, Southampton, SO15 2DX
Tel No: (01703) 228661 Fax No: (01703) 334250

EAST MIDLANDS ASSOCIATION

President

Sir John Lowther, KCVO CBE JP (HM Lord-Lieutenant,
Northamptonshire)

Vice-Presidents

Sir Andrew Buchanan Bt. (HM Lord-Lieutenant,
Nottinghamshire)
T. G. M. Brooks Esq, JP (HM Lord-Lieutenant,
Leicestershire)
Mrs B. K. Cracroft-Eley (HM Lord-Lieutenant, Lincolnshire)
J. K. Bather, Esq (HM Lord-Lieutenant, Derbyshire)
Air Chief Marshal Sir Thomas Kennedy, GCB AFC* (HM
Lord-Lieutenant, Rutland)

Chairman

Brigadier M. E. Browne, CBE TD DL

Vice-Chairmen

Colonel G. B. Roper, T. D.
Air Commodore A. J. Griffin, AFC
Colonel A. A. F. Terry, TD DL
Colonel R. Merryweather, TD DL
Colonel J. M. K. Weir, OBE TD DL
Colonel I. R. Keers, OBE DL
Lieutenant Commander P. R. Moore, RD RNR

Air Force Members

Ex-Officio

The Officer Commanding, East Midlands Air Universities
Squadron
The Officer Commanding, 2503 (County of Lincoln) Sqn
RAuxAF Regt
The Officer Commanding, 27 Sqn and 48 Sqn, RAF
Regiment
OCOS Role Support Squadron

Selected

Vacant (Derbyshire)
Air Commodore A. J. Griffin, AFC (Leicestershire)
Wing Commander J. M. Nunn (RAF Regional Liaison
Officer)
Group Captain H. H. Moses, MBE (Lincolnshire)
Group Captain A. D. Turner, JP (Northamptonshire)
Group Captain J. A. F. Ford (Commandant Central and
Eastern Region ATC)

Secretary

Brigadier P. I. B. Stevenson, CBE DL, 6, Clinton Terrace,
Derby Road, Nottingham NG7 1LZ
Tel No: 0115 9476508 FAX: 0115 9473406 Mil: Chilwell
(745) 2670
Deputy Secretary, Colonel R. J. M. Drummond, OBE

GREATER LONDON ASSOCIATION

President

Field Marshal The Lord Bramall, KG GCB OBE MC JP
(HM Lord-Lieutenant of Greater London)

Vice-President

Colonel Sir Greville Spratt, GBE TD JP DL

Chairman

Colonel S. A. Sellon, OBE TD DL

Vice-Chairmen

Commander J. McK. Ludgate RD* DL RNR
Colonel A E Hall, TD DL
Colonel and Alderman C. H. Martin, OBE TD DL
Colonel G. E. Godbold, OBE TD DL
Colonel P. R. H. Thompson, OBE TD DL
Air-Vice Marshal D. R. Hawkins, CB MBE DL

Air Force Members

Ex-Officio

The Officer Commanding, London University Air
Squadron
The Officer Commanding, No 1 MHU, RAuxAF
The Officer Commanding, No 615 Volunteer Gliding
School

Selected

The Officer Commanding, RAF Uxbridge
The Officer Commanding, RAF Northolt
The Regional Commandant, London and SE Region, ATC
Air Vice-Marshal D. R. Hawkins, CB MBE DL

Secretary

Brigadier C. J. Marchant Smith, CBE DL Duke of York's
Headquarters, Chelsea, London SW3 4RY
Tel No: 0171-730 8131 Fax No: 0171 414 5560
Deputy Secretary: Lieutenant Colonel R. J. Redford, DL
Assistant Secretary (Finance), Squadron Leader C. Allison
Assistant Secretary (City & R & P) Major J. B. B. Cockcroft,
DL

HIGHLANDS OF SCOTLAND ASSOCIATION

President

Air Vice-Marshal G. A. Chesworth, CB OBE DFC

Vice-Presidents

Lord Gray of Contin
The Right Honourable Viscount Dunrossil, CMG
The Right Honourable The Earl of Leven and Melville
Mr J. H. Scott
Mr J. A. S. McPherson, CBE JP
The Earl of Airlie, KT GCVO PC
The Lord Provost and HM Lieutenant of the City of
Dundee
Lieutenant Colonel J. Stirling, CBE TD
The Lord Provost and HM Lieutenant of the City of
Aberdeen
Captain C. A. Farquharson, JP
The Viscount of Arbuthnott, CBE DSC FRSE
Captain R. W. K. Stirling of Fairburn, TD JP
Brigadier D. D. G. Hardie, TD JP
Major General D. Houston, CBE
The Earl of Elgin and Kincardine, KT CD
Lieutenant Colonel R. C. Stewart, CBE TD
His Grace The Duke of Argyll
Major G. T. Dunnett, TD
Sir David Montgomery, Bt JP
George Marwick

Chairman

Colonel A. Murdoch, TD

Vice-Chairmen

Group Captain J. P. Dacre
Captain D. J. Ellin, OBE RN
Lieutenant Colonel G. Johnston
Lieutenant Colonel A. R. Cram, TD
Major S. T. Walker, TD
Colonel C. W. Pagan, MBE TD

Air Force Members

Ex-Officio: The Officer Commanding, Aberdeen University
Air Squadron
The Officer Commanding, RAuxAF Regt Sqn Lossiemouth

Selected

The Officers Commanding, RAF Leuchars, RAF Kinloss,
RAF Buchan, RAF Lossiemouth
The Regional Commandant, Scottish and Northern
Ireland, ATC
Air Vice-Marshal G. A. Chesworth, CB OBE DFC
Captain D. J. Ellin, OBE RN

Secretary

Colonel J. R. Hensman, OBE, 365, Perth Road, Dundee
DD2 1LX Tel No: 01382 668283 Fax No: 01382 566442

Deputy Secretary

Major R. B. H. Young, MBE

Assistant Secretary

Squadron Leader E. P. Weatherhead, RAF (Retd)

NORTH WEST OF ENGLAND AND ISLE OF MAN
ASSOCIATION

President

Colonel J. B. Timmins, OBE TD JP (HM Lord-Lieutenant of
Greater Manchester)

Vice-Presidents

Colonel W. A. Bromley-Davenport, JP (HM Lord-
Lieutenant of Cheshire)
His Excellency Sir Timothy Daunt, KCMG (Lieutenant
Governor Isle of Man)
Colonel A. W. Waterworth, JP (HM Lord-Lieutenant of
Merseyside)
Colonel J. A. Cropper (HM Lord-Lieutenant of Cumbria)
Colonel The Right Honourable The Lord Shuttleworth (HM
Lord-Lieutenant of Lancashire)

Chairman

Colonel M. J. E. Taylor, CBE TD

Vice-Chairmen

Commodore R. H. Walker RD** DL RNR
Air Commodore J. Broughton, DL
Colonel A. D. B. Brooks, TD DL

Major D. Gee, TD DL
Major B. Trepess TD DL

Air Force Members

Ex-Officio: The Officer Commanding, Manchester &
Salford University Air Squadron
The Officer Commanding, Liverpool University Air
Squadron

Selected

Air Commodore J. Broughton, DL
Wing Commander D. Forbes RAFVR(T) (Retd)
Group Captain W. G. Gambold, FIMgt RAFR
Group Captain P. S. Kiggell, OBE RAFR
Squadron Leader R. Massey
G. Moore, Esq
Squadron Leader G. J. T. Moore, RAFR

Chief Executive

Brigadier I. R. D. Shapter, DL, Alexandra Court, 28
Alexandra Drive, Liverpool L17 8YE
Tel No: 0151-727 4552 Fax No: 0151 727 8133

Deputy Chief Executive

Lieutenant Colonel R. B. Hawken

LOWLANDS OF SCOTLAND ASSOCIATION

President

Major R. Y. Henderson, TD

Vice-Presidents

The Right Honourable The Lord Provost of the City of
Edinburgh
The Right Honourable The Lord Provost of the City of
Glasgow
The Right Honourable The Earl of Morton
Mr C. H. Parker, OBE
Captain His Grace The Duke of Buccleuch and
Queensberry, KT VRD JP
Lieutenant General Sir Normal Arthur, KCB
Major E. S. Orr Ewing
Major General Sir John Swinton, KCVO OBE
Captain J. D. B. Younger
Captain R. C. Cunningham-Jardine
Mr H. B. Sneddon, CBE JP
Captain G. W. Burnet, LVO
Major Sir Hew Hamilton-Dalrymple, Bt KCVO

Chairman

Brigadier L. Johnman, CBE TD OStJ

Vice-Chairmen

Captain C. J. P. Hall, RD RNR
Brigadier H. A. J. Jordan MBE
Colonel A. J. B. Agnew
Colonel D. A. Scott, OBE TD
Colonel I. W. Williamson
Lieutenant Colonel R. C. Hambleton, TD
Major W. S. Turner, MC

Group Captain D. A. Needham, BA FIMgt

Air Force Members

Ex-Officio

The Officer Commanding, Glasgow and Strathclyde
University Air Squadron
The Officer Commanding, East Lowlands University Air
Squadron
The Officer Commanding, No 2 MHU RAuxAF

Selected

Air Commodore B. N. J. Speed, OBE
The Regional Commandant, Scottish and Northern Ireland
Region, ATC
Group Captain D. A. Needham, BA FIMgt
The Officer Commanding, Royal Air Force Prestwick

Secretary

Colonel R. S. B. Watson, OBE, Lowland House,
60 Avenuepark Street, Glasgow G20 8LW
Tel No: 0141-945 4951 Fax No: 0141 945 4869
Deputy Secretary Major M. R. Knox

NORTHERN IRELAND ASSOCIATION

President

Colonel The Lord O'Neill, TD JP

Vice-Presidents

Colonel J. E. Wilson, OBE JP
The Right Honourable The Earl of Erne, JP
Colonel J. T. Eaton, CBE TD JP
Major W. J. Hall, JP
Sir Michael McCorkell, KCVO OBE TD JP
The Right Honourable The Earl of Caledon JP
His Grace the Duke of Abercorn

Chairman

Colonel G. H. Baird, OBE TD

Vice-Chairmen

Lieutenant Colonel C. T. Hogg, MBE UD JP DL
Colonel W. F. Gillespie, OBE TD JP DL
Major W. B. S. Buchanan, MBE TD
Colonel W. E. Falloon, CBE TD
Captain, R. H. Lowry, DL
Colonel J. M. Steele, CB OBE TD DL
Major S. Irwin, TD
Viscountess Brookeborough
Commander K. Cochrane, RD DL

Air Force Member

Ex-Officio

Wing Commander T. Lyttle RAFVR(T)
Group Captain K. W. Ifould, OBE AFC RAF

Selected

Group Captain B. G. Freeman, OBE
Wing Commander E. Cadden

Squadron Leader A. McClure RAFVR

Secretary

Brigadier I. N. Osborne, OBE, 25, Windsor Park, Belfast
BT9 6FR
Tel No: 01232 6673111 Fax No: 01232 662809

NORTH OF ENGLAND ASSOCIATION

President

Colonel The Lord Gisborough, JP

Vice-Presidents

Colonel Sir Ralph Carr-Ellison, TD
Colonel The Viscount Ridley, KG GCVO TD
Sir Paul Nicholson

Chairman

Colonel C. A. F. Baker-Cresswell, OBE TD DL

Vice-Chairmen

Captain A. I. B. Moffat, RD DL RNR
Colonel R. K. Banerjee, OBE TD DL
Colonel A. A. E. Glenton, MBE TD DL
Colonel W. R. Porteous, OBE TD DL
Air Vice-Marshal A. F. C. Hunter, CBE AFC DL

Air Force Members

Ex-Officio

The Officer Commanding, Northumbria Universities Air
Squadron

Selected

The Officer Commanding, RAF Boulmer
The Regional Commandant, North and East Region, ATC
Air Vice-Marshal A. F. C. Hunter, CBE AFC DL
G. T. Orde, TD JP
Wing Commander N. M. Ridley, MBE

Secretary

Brigadier N. G. R. Hepworth, OBE 53, Old Elvet, Durham
DH1 3JJ
Tel No: 0191-384 7202 Fax No: 0191 384 0918
Deputy Secretary: Lieutenant Colonel D. R. Summers

SOUTH EAST ASSOCIATION

President

Admiral Sir Lindsay Bryson, KCB (HM Lord-Lieutenant for
East Sussex)

Vice-Presidents

The Right Honourable Lord Kingsdown, KG (HM Lord-
Lieutenant for Kent)
Mrs S. J. F. Good, JP
Major General Sir Philip Ward, KCVO CBE (HM Lord-
Lieutenant for West Sussex)

Chairman

Colonel J. R. G. Putnam, TD DL FRICS

Vice-Chairmen

Lieutenant Colonel R. C. B. Dixon, TD DL
Colonel D. E. Stevens, OBE TD DL
Colonel I. W. B. McRobbie, OBE TD DL ADC
Lieutenant Colonel G. H. Wright, TD DL
Captain R. K. Sard, RD RNR
Wing Commander B. Dibb RAFVR(T)
M. C. Griffiths Esq, TD DL

Air Force Members

Selected

The Regional Commandant, London and South-East
Region, ATC

Secretary

Brigadier J. C. Holman, CBE DL, Sandling Place, Sandling
Lane, Maidstone, Kent ME14 2NJ
Tel No: 01622 691888 Fax No: 01622 691944

Deputy Secretary: Lieutenant Colonel C. J. Parslow

WALES ASSOCIATION

President

Sir David Mansel Lewis, KCVO KStJ BA JP (HM Lord-
Lieutenant for Dyfed)

Vice-Presidents

R. E. M. Rees Esq, CBE KStJ JP (HM Lord-Lieutenant for
Gwynedd)
Sir William S. Gladstone, Bt MA JP (HM Lord-Lieutenant
for Clwyd)
Captain N. Lloyd Edwards, GCStJ RD* LLB JP RNR (HM
Lord-Lieutenant for South Glamorgan)
M. A. McLaggan Esq MA KStJ JP (HM Lord-Lieutenant for
Mid Glamorgan)
Commodore R. C. Hastie, CBE RD* RNR (HM Lord-
Lieutenant for West Glamorgan)
M. L. Bourdillon Esq, KStJ JP (HM Lord-Lieutenant for
Powys)
Colonel R. Hanbury-Tenison, KCVO KStJ JP (HM Lord-
Lieutenant for Gwent)

Chairman

Colonel P. L. Gooderson, TD DL

Vice Chairman Naval

Commander J. M. D. Curteis, RD* FCA DL RNR

Vice-Chairmen Military

Colonel D. L. Davies, TD
Lieutenant Colonel D. G. Clarke, TD DL
Colonel P. Eyton-Jones, TD DL

Vice-Chairman Air

Air Commodore A. J. Park, CBE

Air Force Members

Ex-Officio

Group Captain D. S. Griggs, AFC
Air Commodore A. C. Lang, MBE ADC BA
Group Captain P. S. Kiggell, OBE
Squadron Leader A. Cairncross

Selected

Wing Commander D. A. Davies, BA
Squadron Leader D. Warneford, MBE
Group Captain R. F. Grattan, MSc BA

Secretary

Brigadier W. A. Mackereth, DL Centre Block, Maindy
Barracks, Cardiff, CF4 3YE
Tel No: 01222 220251

Deputy Secretary: Lieutenant Colonel D. J. Harding,
WALES TAVR ASSOCIATION, Earl Road, Mold, Clwyd,
CH7 1AD
Tel No: 01352 752782
Assistant Secretary: Major P. J. Mullings, MBE, Centre
Block, Maindy Barracks, Cardiff, CF4 3YE
Tel No: 01222 220251/2 Fax No: 01222 224828

WESTERN WESSEX ASSOCIATION

President

Lady Mary Holborow, JP (HM Lord Lieutenant Cornwall)

Vice-Presidents

J. N. Tidmarsh, Esq MBE JP (HM Lord-Lieutenant City &
County of Bristol)
Major General Sir John Acland, KCB CBE (Acting HM Lord
Lieutenant Devon)
H. W. G. Elwes Esq., JP (HM Lord Lieutenant
Gloucestershire)
Colonel Sir John Wills, Bt KCVO TD JP (HM Lord
Lieutenant Somerset)
Lieutenant-General Sir Maurice Johnston, KCB OBE (HM
Lord Lieutenant Wiltshire)

Chairman

Commander I. R. Pemberton RD**DL RNR

Vice-Chairmen

Colonel M. E. Kelsey, TD (Bristol)
Colonel R. D. Nicholas, OBE (Cornwall)
Colonel P. C. Durbin, OBE TD (Devon)
Lieutenant Colonel D. R. Ayshford Sanford, TD DL
(Gloucestershire)
Brigadier J. Hemsley (Somerset)
Lieutenant Colonel J. R. Arkell, TD (Wiltshire)
Captain G. N. Wood, RD* ADC RNR (Naval)
Colonel R. A. Hooper, MA L/RM (Marine)
Wing Commander J. J. H. Dickson, CVO MBE AE FIMgt
FIPD RAF (Air)

Air Force Members

Ex-Officio

The Officer Commanding, Bristol University Air Squadron
The Officer Commanding, No 3 MHU RAuxAF
The Regional Commandant, South and West Region, ATC
The Officer Commanding, No 2625 (County of Cornwall)
RAuxAF Regt Sqn
The Officer Commanding, 4626 (County of Wiltshire)
Aeromedical Evacuation Squadron RAuxAF
The Officer Commanding, 57 Reserve Squadron RAF
Lyneham

Selected

Station Commander, RAF St Mawgan
Station Commander, RAF Innsworth
Station Commander, RAF Locking
Station Commander, RAF Lyneham

Chief Executive/Secretary

Brigadier B. C. Jackman, OBE MC, 2, Beaufort Road,
Clifton, Bristol, BS8 2JS
Tel No: 0117 973 4045
Fax No: 0117 974 3154

Deputy Chief Executive

Major C. E. Marsh, TD

Deputy Secretary

Colonel C. J. Constable

WEST MIDLAND ASSOCIATION

President

Colonel Sir Thomas Dunne, KCVO KStJ JP

Vice-Presidents

Major J. A. Hawley, TD JP MA
Mr R. R. Taylor, OBE KStJ JP
Mr A. E. H. Heber-Percy
Mr. M. Dunne, JP

Chairman

Colonel P. J. C. Robinson, TD DL

Vice-Chairmen

Commander R. J. Symonds, RD RNR
Lieutenant Colonel W. E. L. Reid, TD
Air Vice-Marshal J. W. Price, CBE FIMgt MRAeS DL
Colonel T. M. Evans, TD DL
Colonel R. L. Cariss, MBE TD
Major S. P. Etheridge, MBE TD JP

Air Force Members

Ex-Officio

The Officer Commanding, University of Birmingham Air
Squadron

Selected

Air Vice-Marshal J. W. Price, CBE FIMgt MRAeS DL

Wing Commander S. D. Little, OBE
Group Captain P. S. Kiggell, OBE
Group Captain A. P. Waldron, AFC

Secretary

Brigadier C. M. J. Barnes, OBE, Tennal Grange, Tennal
Road, Harborne, Birmingham, B32 2HX
Tel No: 0121-427 5221

Deputy Secretary: Lieutenant Colonel J. D. Kane

YORKSHIRE AND HUMBERSIDE ASSOCIATION

President

John Lyles, Esq CBE JP BSc

Vice-Presidents

The Earl of Scarborough
Richard Marriott, TD MA
Sir Marcus Worsley, Bt

Chairman

Colonel E. C. York, TD DL

Vice-Chairmen

Captain J. M. Davies, RD DL RNR
Colonel A. C. Roberts, MBE TD DL JP MPhil PhD FCGI
FIBiol
Colonel R. J. Elliott, TD DL LLB
Wing Commander J. D. Harvey, FIMgt

Air Force Members

Ex-Officio

The Officer Commanding, Yorkshire Universities Air
Squadron
The Officer Commanding, RAuxAF Defence Support
Squadron

Selected

The Officer Commanding, RAF Linton-on-Ouse
The Officer Commanding, RAF Leeming
The Regional Commandant, Air Cadets Regional HQ
(North)
Wing Commander J. D. Harvey, FIMgt
Wing Commander H. R. Kidd, OBE RAFVR(T)
Squadron Leader K. W. T. Noyes, MBE RAF

Secretary

Brigadier W. R. Barker, CBE, 20, St. George's Place, York,
YO24 1DS
Tel No: 01904 623081 and 639008

Deputy Secretary: Lieutenant Colonel M. R. U. McCartney

THE NAVY, ARMY AND AIR FORCE INSTITUTES

Registered Office: London Road, Amesbury, Wiltshire, SP4 7EN Tel 0198 062 7000
(A company limited by guarantee)

PATRON—HM THE QUEEN

COUNCIL

Service Members Appointed by the Admiralty Board of the Defence Council
Admiral Sir John Brigstocke ADC
Rear Admiral P. Dunt

Service Members Appointed by the Army Board of the Defence Council
General Sir Alex Harley, KBE CB
Brigadier A. P. N. Currie

Service Members Appointed by the Air Force Board of the Defence Council
Air Marshal Sir David Cousins, KCB AFC BA
Air Vice-Marshal R. Wright, AFC FRAeS

Other Members Appointed jointly by the Admiralty, Army and Air Force Boards of the Defence Council
Air Marshal Sir Peter Squire, KCB DFC AFC FRAeS (President)
D. J. M. Roberts, MC
Ms. M. Aldred, CBE
Air Chief Marshal Sir David Evans, GCB CBE CIMgt

BOARD OF MANAGEMENT

Directors Nominated Jointly by the Admiralty, Army and Air Force Boards of the Defence Council
D. J. M. Roberts, MC (Chairman)
Air Chief Marshal Sir David Evans, GCB CBE CIMgt (Deputy Chairman)

Directors Nominated by the Board of Management

J. G. A. Irish, CBE
M. B. Bunting
I. W. Lindsey, OBE
G. C. Dart (Chief Executive)
Air Commodore A. H. Vaughan, OBE BA

GRADATION LISTS BY BRANCHES
of Officers Serving on the Active List

Marshal of the Royal Air Force

H.R.H. The Prince Philip, Duke of Edinburgh, KG KT OM GBE AC QSO psc(n)   .   (GD)   15 Jan 53

FORMER CHIEFS OF THE AIR STAFF

Marshals of the Royal Air Force

Grandy, Sir John GCB GCVO KBE DSO idc psc(m) cfs* Born 8/2/13	(GD)	1 Apr 71
Spotswood, Sir Denis GCB CBE DSO DFC idc psc Born 26/9/16	(GD)	31 Mar 74
Beetham, Sir Michael GCB CBE DFC AFC idc psc Born 17/5/23	(GD)	15 Oct 82
Williamson, Sir Keith GCB AFC rcds psc cfs* Born 25/2/28	(GD)	15 Oct 85
Craig of Radley, The Lord GCB OBE MA DSc FRAeS rcds psc cfs Born 17/9/29 .	(GD)	14 Nov 88

Air Chief Marshals

Graydon, Sir Michael GCB CBE FRAeS rcds ndc psc cfs Born 24/10/38 . . .	(GD)	31 May 91

AIR RANK LIST

Air Chief Marshals

H.R.H. Princess Alice, Duchess of Gloucester GCB CI GCVO GBE		23 Feb 90
Johns, Sir Richard GCB CBE LVO ADC FRAeS rcds psc cfs Born 28/7/39 . .	(GD)	30 June 94
Allison, Sir John KCB CBE ADC FRAeS rcds psc qwi Born 24/3/43 . . .	(GD)	8 Mar 96
Cheshire, Sir John KBE CB FRAeS aws psc Born 4/9/42	(GD)	11 Mar 97
Cousins, Sir David KCB AFC BA rcds psc Born 20/1/42	(GD)	1 Aug 97

Air Marshals

Macfadyen, Ian David CB OBE FRAeS rcds psc cfs Born 19/2/42	(GD)	26 Aug 94
Squire, Sir Peter KCB DFC AFC FRAeS psc(n) cfs Born 7/10/45	(GD)	2 Feb 96
Robertson, Graeme Alan CBE BA FRAeS FRSA rcds psc qwi Born 22/2/45 . .	(GD)	18 Mar 96
Bagnall, Sir Anthony KCB OBE FRAeS rcds psc qwi Born 8/6/45 . . .	(GD)	19 June 96
Day, John Romney OBE BSc FRAeS rcds psc cfs Born 15/7/47	(GD)	8 May 97
Terry, Sir Colin KBE CB BSc(Eng) CEng FRAeS FRSA FILog FCGI rcds psc Born 8/8/43	(ENG)	11 July 97

Air Vice-Marshals

Norriss, Peter Coulson CB AFC MA FRAeS hcsc psc psc(m) cfs Born 22/4/44 . . (GD) 1 Jan 92
Coville, Christopher Charles Cotton CB BA FIPD FRAeS rcds psc qwi Born 2/6/45 . (GD) 1 July 92
O'Brien, Robert Peter CB OBE BA FRAeS jsdc psc(m) cfs Born 1/11/41 . . . . (GD) 1 July 92
Feesey, John David Leonard AFC MRAeS hcsc aws oaws(US) psc cfs Born 11/10/42 (GD) 1 Jan 94
Goodall, Roderick Harvey CBE AFC* rcds psc qwi Born 19/1/47 . . . . . (GD) 1 Jan 94
Jenner, Timothy Ivo CB FRAeS rcds psc(m) cfs Born 31/12/45 . . . . . . (GD) 1 July 94
Stables, Anthony James CBE FRAeS rcds psc(m) Born 1/3/45 . . . . (GD) 1 Jan 95
French, Joseph Charles CBE FRAeS rcds psc Born 15/7/49 . . . . (GD) 1 Jan 96
McCandless, Brian Campbell CBE MSc BSc CEng FIEE FRAeS psc Born 14/5/44 (ENG) 1 Jan 96
Elder, Ronald David CBE FRAeS rcds psc Born 27/5/46 . . . . (GD) 1 July 96
Jackson, Michael Richard CB df* aws psc snc Born 28/12/41 . . . . . . (GD) 1 July 96
Spink, Clifford Rodney CBE FIMgt FRAeS rcds ndc qwi(AD) Born 17/5/46 . . . (GD) 1 July 96
Thompson, John Hugh rcds hcsc psc(m) qwi Born 18/9/47 . . . . (GD) 1 July 96
O'Reilly, Patrick John BSc CEng FIEE FRAeS rcds aws psc semc Born 26/4/46 (ENG) 1 July 96
Stewart, Ian Michael AFC LLB psc Born 27/7/45 . . . . (GD) 1 Jan 97
Pledger, Malcolm David OBE AFC BSc FRAeS rcds psc cfs Born 24/7/48 . . . (GD) 1 July 97
Stirrup, Graham Eric AFC FRAeS FIMgt rcds hcsc jsdc cfs qwi Born 4/12/49 . . (GD) 1 July 97
Wright, Robert Alfred AFC FRAeS psc qwi Born 10/6/47 . . . . (GD) 1 July 97
Burridge, Brian Kevin CBE BSc FIMgt hcsc psc(n) cfs Born 26/9/49 . . . . . (GD) 1 Jan 98
Filbey, Keith David CBE FIMgt rcds psc Born 16/12/47 . . . . (GD) 1 Jan 98
Sturley, Philip Oliver MBE BSc FRAeS jsdc Born 9/7/50 . . . . (GD) 1 Jan 98
Brackenbury, Ian, OBE BSc CEng FIEE rcds psc Born 28/8/45 . . . . . (ENG) 1 Jan 98
Henderson, Peter William MBE BSc CEng FRAeS amec psc Born 5/11/45 . . (ENG) 1 Jan 98
Nicholl, Steven Mark CBE AFC BA rcds psc qwi Born 15/11/46 . . . . . . (GD) 1 July 98
Niven, David Miller CBE BSc rcds psc Born 18/9/46 . . . . (GD) 1 July 98

Air Commodores

Bettell, Michael John OBE rcds psc Born 12/3/44	(GD)	1 July 89
Gould, Richard Hugh CBE MA FRAeS df ndc psc asq Born 22/1/45	(GD)	1 Jan 92
McRobbie, Gordon Leslie psc cfs Born 16/6/44	(GD)	1 Jan 92
Tyack, Ernest William CBE FRAeS rcds aws psc(n) asq snc Born 23/4/44 . . .	(GD)	1 Jan 92
Griffiths, Nigel Morane BA FCIPS FIMgt rcds aws psc ssc Born 27/4/44 . .	(SUP)	1 Jan 93
Cooper, Christopher Forrest BA MIMgt MCIPS jsdc ssc Born 5/10/44 . . .	(SUP)	1 July 93
Cruickshanks, Colin John AFC* FRAeS osc(Fr) tp qwi(AD) Born 7/1/45	(GD)	1 July 94
Johnson, Peter George OBE BA FRAeS FIMgt jsdc cfs qwi Born 8/6/44 . . .	(GD)	1 July 94
Nicholson, Antony Angus CBE LVO MA rcds jsdc psc(m) Born 27/6/46 . . .	(GD)	1 July 94
Peacock-Edwards, Richard Skene CBE AFC FRAeS FIMgt psc cfs Born 27/1/45 .	(GD)	1 July 94
Uprichard, James Leslie CBE psc Born 31/12/43	(GD)	1 July 94
Liddell, Peter BSc CEng FIEE FRAeS rcds aws psc amec Born 9/10/48 . . .	(ENG)	1 July 94
Winsland, Christopher George OBE psc Born 21/6/46	(ADMIN)	1 July 94
Chambers, Christopher Maurice ocds(Ind) hcsc aws psc cfs Born 12/2/47 . . .	(GD)	1 Jan 95
Gardiner, Martyn John OBE BSc psc asq Born 13/6/46	(GD)	1 Jan 95
Ferguson, Anthony Malcolm CEng FIEE psc Born 21/3/44	(ENG)	1 Jan 95
Davison, Christopher MBE FIMgt DPhysEd psc Born 26/9/47	(ADMIN)	1 Jan 95
Mackay, Hector Gavin OBE AFC BSc FRAeS rcds psc(n) cfs Born 3/10/47 . . .	(GD)	1 July 95
Couzens, David Cyril MA CEng FIMechE FRAeS DLUT rcds psc ae Born 15/10/49	(ENG)	1 July 95
Fletcher, Richard Holmes BSc CEng MIMechE MRAeS rcds psc ae Born 17/2/47	(ENG)	1 July 95
Skinner, Graham MBE MSc BSc CEng FILog FIMechE FIMgt MRAeS psc Born 16/9/45	(ENG)	1 July 95
Andrews, Derek Charles MBE FRIN jsdc cfs(n) asq snc qs Born 1/4/44 . . .	(GD)	1 Jan 96
Doble, Lloyd Anthony OBE FRAeS rcds psc qwi Born 6/1/47	(GD)	1 Jan 96
Haines, John Harold OBE ADC psc Born 17/10/45	(GD)	1 Jan 96
Jeffers, Peter hcsc aws psc cfs Born 23/1/46	(GD)	1 Jan 96
Norriss, David Kenworthy oaws(US) psc cfs Born 17/6/46	(GD)	1 Jan 96
Rimmer, Thomas William OBE MA FRAeS rcds osc(Fr) cfs Born 16/12/48 . . .	(GD)	1 Jan 96
Scott, Peter John MSc BSc CEng FIMechE rcds psc Born 4/4/49	(ENG)	1 Jan 96
Johnson, Richard Harry Ormond im qss* Born 3/2/44	(SUP)	1 Jan 96
Fowler, Cynthia Ruth ADC jsdc Born 19/11/45	(ADMIN)	1 Jan 96
Corbitt, Ian Stafford hcsc psc Born 30/7/47	(GD)	1 July 96
Crawford, Peter Allan AFC BSc rcds awcc psc Born 11/1/50	(GD)	1 July 96
Feenan, Michael Leonard CBE MA FIMgt psc i* Born 18/9/47	(GD)	1 July 96
Harris, Peter Vernon AFC rcds oaws(US) psc qwi Born 4/3/49	(GD)	1 July 96
Morris, Richard Vaughan AFC rcds qwi qs Born 24/9/49	(GD)	1 July 96
Neal, Andrew Ernest AFC FIMgt rcds nadc psc Born 17/7/48	(GD)	1 July 96
Wilby, David John Gladstone AFC nadc aws psc qwi Born 20/5/47	(GD)	1 July 96
Arscott, John Robert Dare jsdc aws Born 19/4/47	(OPS SPT)	1 July 96
McNeil, Ian William Peter jsdc aws Born 30/9/45	(OPS SPT)	1 July 96
Clark, Roger William OBE CEng MIEE jsdc semc Born 6/4/44	(ENG)	1 July 96
Gilding, Michael John MSc BSc CEng FIEE psc Born 8/8/47	(ENG)	1 July 96
Burton, Andrew John OBE BSc FCIS odc(US) psc Born 11/11/50	(ADMIN)	1 July 96
Adams, David Newton BSc MRAeS rcds hcsc psc asq Born 28/4/46	(GD)	1 Jan 97
Kennedy, John Drummond BA psc cfs Born 23/8/46	(GD)	1 Jan 97
Roser, Phillip Wycliffe MBE FRAeS rcds psc qwi Born 11/7/48	(GD)	1 Jan 97
Torpy, Glenn Lester DSO BSc rcds hcsc psc qwi Born 27/7/53	(GD)	1 Jan 97
Vallance, Andrew George Buchanan OBE MPhil psc Born 7/4/48	(GD)	1 Jan 97
Walker, Peter Brett CBE BA jsdc qwi Born 29/9/49	(GD)	1 Jan 97
White, Malcolm Graham Forrester OBE hcsc psc(n) qs Born 18/11/52 . . .	(GD)	1 Jan 97
Giles, Peter Wilmott OBE PhD MA qs Born 14/12/45	(ENG)	1 Jan 97
Procter, Kenneth John Michael BSc (Eur Ing) CEng FIEE FRAeS FIMgt psc Born 7/3/44	(ENG)	1 Jan 97
Sloss, Ian CEng FRAeS jsdc Born 3/8/46	(ENG)	1 Jan 97
Pye, Alan John rcds psc ssc Born 4/5/47	(SUP)	1 Jan 97
Vaughan, Allan Howard OBE BA rcds psc Born 3/12/49	(ADMIN)	1 Jan 97
Black, Euan James FRAeS FIMgt psc(n) qwi Born 12/7/46	(GD)	1 July 97
Simpson, Geoffrey Dennis CBE AFC rcds psc(n) Born 10/4/48	(GD)	1 July 97
Sudborough, Nigel John OBE MIPD rcds psc Born 23/3/48	(GD)	1 July 97
Brumpton, Rodney BA FRAeS jsdc ae Born 4/1/47	(ENG)	1 July 97

Air Commodores

Davison, Christopher Michael BSc CEng MIEE MIMgt rcds amec psc Born 24/9/48	(ENG)	1 July 97
Jones, Grahame MBE BSc CEng MIEE psc Born 6/7/50	(ENG)	1 July 97
Delany, Oliver David Liam OBE BA FBIFM FIMgt rcds jsdc Born 12/10/49 . .	(ADMIN)	1 July 97
Ford, Anthony Thomas psc Born 18/12/45	(ADMIN)	1 July 97
Connolly, Jerome AFC rcds hcsc jsdc awcc qwi Born 5/2/52	(GD)	1 Jan 98
Day, Nigel James BSc(Eng) ACGI rcds hcsc psc qwi Born 13/2/49	(GD)	1 Jan 98
Dixon, Raymond Lawrence BSc psc qwi Born 7/5/48	(GD)	1 Jan 98
Taylor, Neil Ernest BSc FRAes jsdc Born 6/12/47	(GD)	1 Jan 98
Waldron, Alan Peter CBE AFC jsdc cfs Born 8/9/47	(GD)	1 Jan 98
Lang, Alistair Cochrane MBE ADC BA CEng FIMechE FRAeS rcds semc psc Born 19/10/47	(ENG)	1 Jan 98
Willis, Gerald Edward BSc FRAeS psc semc Born 25/10/49	(ENG)	1 Jan 98
Luke, John Christopher Owen CBE BSc rcds psc Born 7/8/49	(ADMIN)	1 Jan 98
Miller, Graham Anthony jsdc cfs qwi Born 31/10/51	(GD)	1 July 98
Robinson, Paul Anthony OBE psc cfs Born 8/8/49	(GD)	1 July 98
Good, Michael John MIDPM MIMgt jsdc qwi(AD) Born 11/1/49	(OPS SPT)	1 July 98
Thornton, Barry Michael MSc BSc CEng FIMechE FIMgt rcds psc Born 19/11/52	(ENG)	1 July 98
Leaning, Peter Timothy Walter rcds psc Born 6/2/48	(SUP)	1 July 98

GENERAL DUTIES BRANCH

Group Captains

1987

Collier, John Malcolm aws psc Born 5/5/43 . . . . (P)   1 July

1988

H.R.H. The Prince of Wales KG KT GCB AK QSO ADC . . . . (P)   14 Nov

1989

Brindle, Geoffrey psc Born 22/6/44 . . . . (P)   1 Jan
Radforth, Michael Anthony asq ocds(Can) psc Born 3/7/42 . . . . (N)   1 Jan

1990

Day, Peter Warneford AFC jsdc qwi Born 25/1/44 . . . . (P)   1 Jan
Gooding, Peter John AFC psc(m) cfs Born 23/11/43 . . . . (P)   1 Jan
Plunkett, Patrick Noel Oliver BSc psc cfs Born 28/8/45 . . . . (P)   1 Jan
Alcock, Antony John Hamilton MBE psc(n) Born 3/5/44 . . . . (P)   1 July
Edwards, Peter psc cfs Born 22/1/43 . . . . (P)   1 July
Gault, Roger William awcc psc(n) Born 25/9/44 . . . . (P)   1 July
Morris, Brian Sydney OBE AFC psc qwi Born 21/8/45 . . . . (P)   1 July
Wise, Adam Nugent LVO MBE BA jsdc i* Born 1/8/43 . . . . (P)   1 July

1991

Carr, Roger Frederick Richard MBE hcsc psc snc Born 18/5/47 . . . . . (N)   1 Jan
Cullington, George Graham CBE AFC BSc ndc Born 8/5/44 . . . . . (P)   1 Jan
King, Jeremy Andrew AFC aws psc Born 31/12/43 . . . . (P)   1 Jan
Williams, Denys Andrew AFC psc qwi(AD) Born 19/12/44 . . . . . . (P)   1 Jan
Gleave, Malcolm OBE psc Born 5/7/47 . . . . (P)   1 July
Hencken, David Christopher BSocSc aws osc(FR) cfs i* Born 10/3/43 . . . . (P)   1 July
Morris, Christopher John OBE FRIN rcds psc(m) asq snc i* Born 9/7/48 . . . (N)   1 July
Wedge, Roger Edward CBE BSc awcc psc Born 22/6/44 . . . . (P)   1 July

1992

Bedford, Peter Averill AFC MRAeS awcc aws psc cfs Born 28/5/46 . . . . (P)   1 Jan
Macgregor, Alan Norman psc cfs Born 18/7/44 . . . . (P)   1 Jan
Coy, Simon John OBE hcsc aws psc(m) Born 29/11/44 . . . . (P)   1 July
Owen, Philip Stuart psc cfs Born 7/9/47 . . . . (P)   1 July

1993

Horwood, Raymond James OBE FRAeS ocds(Can) psc snc Born 28/9/49 . . . (N)   1 Jan
Kearney, Alan James CBE BSc(Econ) aws psc Born 26/5/45 . . . . . . (P)   1 Jan

Group Captains

1993—contd

Morley, John Robert Douglas MBE hcsc psc Born 28/3/47	(P)	1 Jan
Ray, David Alan hcsc psc(m) qwi Born 23/1/47	(P)	1 Jan
Wildman, Peter Gordon BA FRAeS aws psc cfs Born 10/2/47	(P)	1 Jan
Ball, James Allan AFC asq jsdc Born 14/5/48	(P)	1 July
Beney, Trevor John FIMgt psc qwi Born 20/1/48	(P)	1 July
Burwell, Christopher Charles Nicholas MBE rcds hcsc jsdc cfs Born 12/9/51	(P)	1 July
Doggett, Barry Peter hcsc oaws(US) psc qwi Born 15/5/49	(P)	1 July
Jarron, John Cole aws psc(n) Born 18/1/48	(P)	1 July
Joseph, Robert William BSc psc(n) asq Born 6/10/49	(N)	1 July
Luker, Paul Douglas OBE AFC awcc psc Born 8/7/51	(P)	1 July
Maddox, Nigel David Alan hcsc psc(n) Born 1/4/54	(N)	1 July
Murray, Trevor James jsdc nadc aws Born 4/12/43	(N)	1 July
Rusling, Nicholas Charles BA oaws psc qwi Born 13/12/47	(P)	1 July

1994

Heath, Michael Christopher CBE psc psc(n) qwi snc Born 21/12/50	(N)	1 Jan
Holmes, Michael Stuart jsdc asq Born 11/10/45	(N)	1 Jan
Igoe, Christopher Paul psc cfs Born 15/10/52	(P)	1 Jan
Iredale, Robert David psc(m) snc Born 27/5/47	(N)	1 Jan
Iveson, Robert Douglas AFC psc qwi Born 18/8/47	(P)	1 Jan
Jones, David Martin psc(m) Born 28/6/48	(P)	1 Jan
Lambert, Andrew Peter Noel MPhil awcc psc qwi Born 12/10/48	(N)	1 Jan
McDonnell, David Kenneth Lodge OBE psc asq snc Born 27/1/46	(N)	1 Jan
Milne-Smith, David Henry oaws(US) psc qwi Born 6/2/47	(P)	1 Jan
Mitchell, Michael jsdc Born 3/8/47	(P)	1 Jan
Morris, Angus MacDonald MSc psc cfs Born 12/9/46	(P)	1 Jan
Remlinger, Michael John psc Born 3/1/48	(P)	1 Jan
Smith, Peter Anthony BSc FRIN psc asq snc Born 18/2/47	(N)	1 Jan
Titchen, Barry John MRIN FIMgt aws psc qwi Born 4/8/45	(N)	1 Jan
Trace, Michael Roland OBE MA FRAeS aws psc cfs Born 11/9/47	(P)	1 Jan
Williams, Timothy John AFC psc cfs Born 29/1/48	(P)	1 Jan
Dalton, Stephn Gary George BSc psc qwi Born 25/4/54	(P)	1 July
Grisdale, James Norman John MBE psc(m) cfs Born 4/1/47	(P)	1 July
Hudson, Alan Thomas OBE BSc psc qwi Born 27/4/51	(P)	1 July
Ifould, Keith William OBE AFC FRAeS MIL jsdc osc(GE) cfs qss i Born 14/1/46	(P)	1 July
Metcalfe, Wilson MIMgt psc Born 1/9/48	(P)	1 July
Perrett, Michael John OBE psc cfs(n) snc Born 7/11/44	(N)	1 July
Sweetman, Andrew David OBE BA rcds hcsc psc qwi Born 10/7/53	(P)	1 July
Thirlwall, Colin OBE AFC BA psc cfs* Born 11/7/44	(P)	1 July
Travers Smith, Ian DSO psc qwi Born 14/11/46	(P)	1 July
Vass, David Charles MBE FRAes FIMgt MIPD psc cfs Born 7/3/50	(P)	1 July
Williams, David Richard OBE aws psc Born 12/5/49	(N)	1 July
Witts, Jeremy John DSO ADC psc Born 18/6/50	(P)	1 July

1995

Beedie, Alastair Ian Bartlett psc snc Born 9/8/49	(N)	1 Jan
Buckler, Jonathan Leslie jsdc qwi Born 22/7/46	(P)	1 Jan
Evans, Ivor jsdc qwi Born 22/3/48	(P)	1 Jan
Hanlon, Terence George FRAes MIMgt jsdc qwi Born 10/7/47	(P)	1 Jan
Hewlett, Timothy Chetnole OBE psc qwi Born 9/2/49	(P)	1 Jan

Group Captains

1995—contd

Le Bas, Christopher Brian BSc MIMgt odc(US) Born 28/12/48	(P)	1 Jan
Lees, Mitchell Noel psc(n) Born 3/12/50	(N)	1 Jan
Prissick, Malcolm ADC hcsc psc qwi Born 11/6/49	(P)	1 Jan
Shannon, David Michael OBE aws psc asq cfs(n) snc Born 18/2/45	(N)	1 Jan
White, Andrew David BTech jsdc qwi Born 2/1/52	(P)	1 Jan
Wood, Nigel Richard BSc psc tp Born 21/7/49	(P)	1 Jan
Cliffe, John Alfred OBE FRAeS psc(n) qwi Born 14/6/53	(P)	1 July
Delve, Howard psc Born 22/12/43	(N)	1 July
Hickey, Stanley Albert OBE MRIN MIMgt jsdc nadc snc qs Born 23/5/46	(N)	1 July
Loader, Clive Robert OBE hcsc psc qwi Born 24/9/53	(P)	1 July
Reid, Hamish psc snc adp Born 24/7/43	(N)	1 July
Sweeney, Christopher Michael psc asq snc Born 15/11/48	(N)	1 July
Thomas, Richard Mytton OBE AFC FRAeS psc cfs i Born 3/5/49	(P)	1 July

1996

Barrett, Peter Alan OBE BSc FRAeS psc asq Born 5/7/47	(P)	1 Jan
Burrough, Robert Francis BA BSc jsdc Born 12/8/48	(P)	1 Jan
Campbell, Alasdair BSc jsdc psc(m) asq Born 18/9/49	(P)	1 Jan
Griggs, Derek Stephen AFC BA jsdc qwi Born 1/9/50	(P)	1 Jan
Hall, Ian Stuart BA psc i Born 9/9/48	(P)	1 Jan
Hounslow, Robert John FRAeS FIMgt psc Born 19/11/50	(N)	1 Jan
Lockwood, Alan John AFC psc Born 31/10/51	(P)	1 Jan
McLaren, Brian George MSc MBA MIMgt jsdc Born 3/11/47	(AEO)	1 Jan
Moss, David Malcolm psc(n) Born 24/6/47	(P)	1 Jan
Platt, John Crawford BA psc asq snc Born 2/4/47	(N)	1 Jan
Thorpe, John Winston AFC jsdc tp cfs Born 19/3/45	(P)	1 Jan
Turner, Frank Lester hcsc psc qwi Born 21/10/50	(P)	1 Jan
Wrigley, Stephen Arnold jsdc i Born 19/3/44	(P)	1 Jan
Ades, Andrew Vernon MBE MBA FIMgt odc(US) psc snc Born 29/11/43	(N)	1 July
Brewer, Timothy Paul OBE BSc psc asq qs Born 22/6/53	(N)	1 July
Haward, David Ayton OBE jsdc cfs qs Born 3/12/53	(P)	1 July
Lacey, Richard Howard ADC MA BA psc Born 11/12/53	(P)	1 July
Moran, Christopher Hugh OBE MVO BSc psc qwi Born 28/4/56	(P)	1 July
Peach, Stuart William MPhil BA psc qwi Born 22/2/56	(N)	1 July
Sawyer, Alan OBE osc(GE) qwi i Born 6/11/48	(N)	1 July

1997

Black, Stuart Douglas psc(n) qwi Born 4/1/55	(N)	1 Jan
Blackford, Paul Anthony awcc psc Born 9/7/48	(N)	1 Jan
Butler, Stuart Denham cfs Born 15/1/56	(P)	1 Jan
Clarke, Graham Henry aws psc qwi(AD) Born 11/5/47	(P)	1 Jan
Cope, Arthur William MBE AFC FRAeS psc cfs Born 13/2/47	(P)	1 Jan
Harper, Christopher Nigel MA FIMgt hcsc psc qwi Born 25/3/57	(P)	1 Jan
Hodgson, Peter psc qwi Born 30/7/52	(P)	1 Jan
Hodgson, Raymond Bruce BA psc Born 2/7/49	(P)	1 Jan
McLuskie, Ian Robert OBE MSc psc cfs Born 30/8/48	(P)	1 Jan
McNicoll, Iain Walter BSc psc qwi Born 3/5/53	(P)	1 Jan
Nickols, Christopher Mark MA psc qwi Born 23/7/56	(P)	1 Jan
Ollis, Peter Rennie BSc psc cfs Born 10/2/55	(P)	1 Jan
Roome, David Christopher OBE MRAeS psc cfs Born 30/11/46	(P)	1 Jan

Group Captains

1997—contd

Ruddock, Peter William David psc qwi Born 5/2/54	(P)	1 Jan
Spiller, Nicholas Bertram psc Born 15/8/46	(P)	1 Jan
White, John William MRAeS MIMgt jsdc qwi qs Born 21/2/48	(P)	1 Jan
Brewerton, Nigel BA MIMgt psc cfs Born 7/11/54	(P)	1 July
Bullen, Jeffrey Donald OBE psc Born 12/5/48	(P)	1 July
Coker, Peter Anthony OBE MIMgt jsdc cfs qwi(AD) qs Born 1/4/56	(P)	1 July
Cook, Ronald BTech awcc psc Born 19/2/53	(N)	1 July
Corney, Hugh Richard OBE BA awcc psc Born 1/2/51	(N)	1 July
Dee, Anthony George Oakley psc cfs qs Born 2/1/49	(P)	1 July
Goodman, Philip Charles MBE BSc jsdc qwi qs Born 23/4/54	(N)	1 July
Jeffrey, John Edward BA MRAeS psc asq cfs Born 31/1/44	(P)	1 July
Milne, Ian Alexander MA MA hcsc qwi qwi(T) psc Born 18/9/51	(P)	1 July
Newby, Brian Walter AFC qwi Born 11/9/54	(P)	1 July
Routledge, Martin John BSc psc Born 22/11/52	(N)	1 July
Threapleton, Norman Edward BSc jsdc psc qwi Born 4/11/51	(N)	1 July
Utley, Roger OBE BA jsdc cfs qs i Born 18/9/50	(P)	1 July
Walker, David AFC MA BSc psc qwi qs Born 30/10/56	(P)	1 July

1998

Capewell, Ian BSc psc qwi Born 27/9/52	(P)	1 Jan
Drew, David John aws psc cfs Born 31/7/47	(P)	1 Jan
Edge, Glenn Howard OBE ADC BSc jsdc cfs Born 23/11/51	(P)	1 Jan
Evans, Gordon Roger MRAeS jsdc cfs Born 12/6/56	(P)	1 Jan
Henry, Robert William psc qab Born 20/11/52	(N)	1 Jan
Middleton, John jsdc qwi(AD) qs Born 21/9/48	(N)	1 Jan
Middleton, Richard Hugh psc Born 1/10/51	(N)	1 Jan
Morrow, William Kyle OBE psc Born 6/10/49	(N)	1 Jan
Parkinson, Stephen Leo psc Born 18/7/51	(N)	1 Jan
Scoffham, Peter Douglas AFC psc Born 19/8/48	(P)	1 Jan
Stringer, Martin Derek jsdc awcc cfs(n)* snc qs Born 21/9/52	(N)	1 Jan
Walton, Andrew George jsdc qwi Born 16/12/54	(P)	1 Jan
White, David Harold jsdc qab cfs qs Born 21/2/48	(P)	1 Jan
Wood, Timothy John psc tp cfs Born 16/10/48	(P)	1 Jan
Barter, Michael Carl OBE psc(m) cfs Born 18/8/54	(P)	1 July
Dezonie, Andre Ferdinand Paul psc(m) cfs Born 10/2/56	(P)	1 July
Ponsonby, John Maurice Maynard cfs psc Born 8/8/55	(P)	1 July

Wing Commanders

1983

Engwell, M. J. ndc aws
cfs   (P)   1 Jan
Winkles, A. R. C.
psc   (P)   1 July

1984

Hawken, A. V. B. AFC
psc   (P)   1 Jan

1985

Milsom, R. J. OBE jsdc
awcc psc cfs   (P)   1 Jan
Anderson, J. P. aws psc
qwi   (N)   1 July
Bell, N. G. jsdc qs   (P)   1 July
Felger, C. F. W. psc   (N)   1 July
Horton, B. A. aws
osc(Fr) qs i   (P)   1 July

1986

Dawson, A. F. ndc psc
snc   (N)   1 Jan
Douglas, K. M. awcc
psc   (P)   1 Jan
Grumbley, K. G. jsdc
qwi   (P)   1 Jan
Guest, D. M. aws
psc(m)   (P)   1 Jan
Robertson, I. M.
psc   (P)   1 Jan
Rogers, T. V. aws psc
cfs   (P)   1 Jan
Mahaffey, B. S. BA psc
qab qwi   (P)   1 July
Pollington, D. AFC
psc   (P)   1 July
Whitney, J. R. A. AFC
psc tp   (P)   1 July

1987

Easton, J. H. psc
snc   (N)   1 Jan
Griffiths, S. G. MBE
aws psc cfs   (P)   1 Jan
Henley, I. M. jsdc psc
cfs   (P)   1 Jan

Hudson, N. C. L. MA
jsdc psc(m) cfs   (P)   1 Jan
Mawby, A. J. BSc psc
cfs   (P)   1 Jan
Roberts, W. A. B. OBE
psc qwi   (N)   1 Jan
Smith, G. P. awcc
psc   (P)   1 Jan
Forrester, R. A. OBE BA
jsdc cfs(n) snc   (N)   1 July
Hitchcock, P. G. awcc
psc(n) cfs   (P)   1 July
Johnson, W. A. BSc psc
asq cfs   (P)   1 July
Monaghan, G. A. psc
cfs   (P)   1 July
Thorpe, A. J. psc
cfs   (P)   1 July

1988

Brookes, A. J. MBA BA
FRSA psc   (P)   1 Jan
Cassady, R. J. jsdc nadc
snc   (N)   1 Jan
Dyer-Perry, A. H. C.
MInstD MRAeS
jsdc   (N)   1 Jan
Johnson, B. W. aws asq
snc   (N)   1 Jan
Lloyd, M. G. psc(m)
cfs   (P)   1 Jan
Southcombe, W. R.
qss*   (N)   1 Jan
Whitston, J. R. psc   (P)   1 Jan
Wholey, R. E. jsdc
qwi   (P)   1 Jan
Aber, C. P. psc cfs   (P)   1 July
Beresford, N. E. L. LVO
oaws(US) psc cfs   (P)   1 July
Coop, G. A. MRAeS psc
snc   (N)   1 July
Goodman, G. J. OBE
MRIN psc(n)   (N)   1 July

1989

Common, M. F. F. MBE
osc(GE) cfs i   (P)   1 Jan
Douglas, J. S. OBE psc
cfs   (P)   1 Jan
Miskelly, I. R. jsdc   (N)   1 Jan
Neal, B. R. FIMgt jsdc
psc   (P)   1 Jan
Pulfrey, A. J. psc
qwi   (N)   1 Jan
Stone, R. D. OBE
psc(m) qwi   (N)   1 Jan

Tench, N. R. MBE
qs   (P)   1 Jan
Vacha, I. D. jsdc
odc(US)   (N)   1 Jan
Woollacott, R. N. MBE
psc cfs   (P)   1 Jan
Yeldham, N. S.
psc(m)   (N)   1 Jan
Bannister, D. R.
jsdc   (N)   1 July
Best, R. E. AFC psc
cfs   (P)   1 July
Cocksedge, M. P. rcds
osc(Fr) cfs   (P)   1 July
Eastment, R. M. OBE
MRAeS psc cfs   (P)   1 July
Forsythe, R. A. OBE psc
cfs   (P)   1 July
Godfrey, M. V. AFC psc
qwi   (P)   1 July

1990

Adams, C. K. psc   (N)   1 Jan
Blake, R. G. awcc
cfs(n)* psc snc   (N)   1 Jan
Bonney-James, R. M.
psc cfs   (P)   1 Jan
Bull, K. A. psc(m)   (N)   1 Jan
Channon, J. H. MBE
jsdc   (AEO)   1 Jan
Davis, A. McB. OBE
nadc psc(n) i*   (P)   1 Jan
Donnelly, D. A. MRIN
psc(m) snc   (N)   1 Jan
Eames, C. M. psc
cfs(n)* snc   (N)   1 Jan
Fox, N. G. BA awcc
psc(m) cfs   (P)   1 Jan
Hannaford, E. R. awcc
qss*   (AEO)   1 Jan
Keenan, D. J. psc
qwi   (P)   1 Jan
Martin, J. D. BA psc(n)
asq   (N)   1 Jan
Pitts, J. aws psc cfs (P)   1 Jan
Pixton, G. W. DFC AFC
awcc psc qwi   (P)   1 Jan
Saunders, M. G. jsdc
cfs   (P)   1 Jan
Ware, A. cfs qs   (P)   1 Jan
Williams, D. C. OBE psc
snc   (N)   1 Jan
Blee, P. M. psc(n)
cfs   (P)   1 July
Bowerman, G. A. OBE
psc qab qwi   (P)   1 July
Bruce, D. asq snc
qs   (N)   1 July

Wing Commanders

1990—contd

Cullum, P. J. G. E. McG.
MIMgt psc cfs (P) 1 July
Daffarn, G. C. BSc
FIMgt jsdc asq qab
snc (N) 1 July
Ellaway, M. J. jsdc asq
snc qs (N) 1 July
Flowerdew, B. N.
psc(n) (AEO) 1 July
Foster, R. psc qab
cfs (P) 1 July
Gault, R. K. OBE jsdc
snc (N) 1 July
Haines, P. J. J. BSc rcds
psc asq snc (N) 1 July
Holding, B. C. AFC psc
cfs (P) 1 July
Huckins, N. M. MBE
BSc psc (P) 1 July
Ilsley, C. W. cfs qs (P) 1 July
Mitchell, A. N. MBE psc
cfs (P) 1 July
Mogford, F. L. snc
qs (N) 1 July
Morffew, C. G. psc
psc(n) snc (N) 1 July
Richardson, A. K.
psc[m] (P) 1 July
Roberts, P. BSc psc (P) 1 July
Smith, K. BSc psc
asq (P) 1 July
Stuart, A. F. psc cfs(n)
snc (N) 1 July
Watson, A. M. BSc
odc(Aus) cfs (P) 1 July
Wright, T. C. psc cfs(n)
snc (N) 1 July

1991

Allport, M. K. MBE cfs
qss* (P) 1 Jan
Barber, G. asq snc
qs (N) 1 Jan
Bealer, R. A. jsdc (P) 1 Jan
Burns, C. S. psc (N) 1 Jan
Chambers, R. I. jsdc
cfs(n) snc qs (N) 1 Jan
Crockatt. A. B. AFC psc
qwi (P) 1 Jan
Dickens, C. R. D. psc
cfs(n) snc (N) 1 Jan
Dicks, E. C. R. MRAeS
cfs qss* (P) 1 Jan

Duffin, P. A. R. BA BA
MRIN MRAeS psc
cfs(n) snc (N) 1 Jan
Finn, C. J. awcc jsdc
qwi qs (N) 1 Jan
Goodsell, G. V. psc
snc (N) 1 Jan
Hawes, C. M. H. BA psc
asq snc adp (N) 1 Jan
Hilliker, C. psc cfs (P) 1 Jan
Hurley, D. J. MBE psc
qwi (N) 1 Jan
King, R. W. jsdc qwi
snc (N) 1 Jan
Musgrave, D. awcc psc
snc (N) 1 Jan
Norris, M. A. MBE
odc(Aus) awcc
qs (N) 1 Jan
Pierce, J. W. MRAeS
osc(Fr) tp qwi (P) 1 Jan
Radley, R. P. jsdc tp
cfs* (P) 1 Jan
Ray, P. R. psc (P) 1 Jan
Scard, G. T. BA jsdc asq
snc (N) 1 Jan
Semple, A. W. psc
cfs (P) 1 Jan
Spilsbury, D. A. jsdc
cfs* (P) 1 Jan
Tiernan, F. psc cfs (P) 1 Jan
Westwood, M. P. OBE
psc (P) 1 Jan
Arkell, J. D. MA jsdc
qab qwi qs (P) 1 July
Babraff, J. K. L. cfs
qs (P) 1 July
Bishopp, J. B. psc
cfs (P) 1 July
Childs, A. P. jsdc (P) 1 July
Cumming, R. G. snc
qs (N) 1 July
Elliott, H. T. MA psc(n)
cfs qs (P) 1 July
Gray, P. W. MPhil BSc
LLB MIMgt jsdc
qs (N) 1 July
Harper, T. A. jsdc qwi
qs (P) 1 July
Lawrence, C. J. MRAeS
MRIN awcc psc (N) 1 July
McDonald, T. P. OBE
rcds jsdc cfs qs (P) 1 July
Richey, F. A. BA psc asq
cfs(n) snc (N) 1 July
Sedman, D. M. psc
cfs (P) 1 July
Smyth, W. S. BA awcc
psc qwi (N) 1 July

Stephens, A. P. qab
cfs(n)* snc qs (N) 1 July
Troke, C. B. asq snc
qs (N) 1 July
York, P. psc cfs(n)
snc (N) 1 July

1992

Allen, R. J. jsdc cfs
qs (P) 1 Jan
Angus, D. A. jsdc
qs (P) 1 Jan
Barnes, M. A. J. BSc
psc asq (N) 1 Jan
Blunden, R. F. BA
MRAeS MBCS MIMgt
psc asq snc (N) 1 Jan
Boyd, A. J. W.
psc(m) (N) 1 Jan
Dudgeon, M. G. OBE
psc cfs (P) 1 Jan
Horwood, G. M. psc
asq cfs (P) 1 Jan
Hutchins, M. B. nadc
qss* (P) 1 Jan
Kershaw, J. (N) 1 Jan
Macartney, S. M. J. BSc
awcc psc (P) 1 Jan
Richardson, M. G. OBE
awcc psc (N) 1 Jan
Williams, P. BSc jsdc
snc qs (N) 1 Jan
Collins, B. R. psc
qwi (P) 1 July
Dugmore, I. L. BSc
psc (P) 1 July
Greaves, K. R. C. OBE
BSc qs (P) 1 July
Harte, J. K. OBE qwi
qs (N) 1 July
Leadbetter, P. M. MVO
MIMgt jsdc snc
qs (N) 1 July

1993

Barker, J. asq snc
qs (N) 1 Jan
Boyle, T. L. jsdc qab
qwi qs (P) 1 Jan
Chacksfield, C. C. MBE
qs (P) 1 Jan
Furniss, N. J. MBE psc
ac (P) 1 Jan
Kirk, A. P. psc qab (N) 1 Jan
Marston, R. AFC jsdc
cfs qs (P) 1 Jan

Wing Commanders

1993—contd

Parkes, K. J. MBE BA
BSc psc cfs   (P)   1 Jan
Rycroft, P. W. psc
cfs(n)* snc   (N)   1 Jan
Thompson, A. BSc psc
asq qab snc   (N)   1 Jan
Vincent, A. J. jsdc qwi
qs   (N)   1 Jan
Bryant, S. MA BA
psc   (N)   1 July
Butterworth, W. D. snc
adp qs   (N)   1 July
Cooke, J. A. psc   (ALM) 1 July
Edmonds, C. C. BSc
psc   (N)   1 July
Harbottle, F. jsdc (P)   1 July
Harper, I. F. MBE asq
psc   (N)   1 July
Hartree, W. R. cfs
psc   (P)   1 July
Huddleston, F. A. psc
cfs   (P)   1 July
Hush, W. BSc psc
cfs(n)   (N)   1 July
Jones, J. R. jsdc (N)   1 July
Keating, P. K. MA BSc
MRAeS psc(m)   (P)   1 July
Leaming, M. W. BSc
psc   (P)   1 July
Legg, P. D. MA FIMgt
MRAeS psc(n)
qwi   (P)   1 July
Price, H. W.
DPhysEd   (P)   1 July
Randle, N. C. BSc
MRAeS MRIN psc
asq snc   (N)   1 July
Rodgers, M. snc cfs(n)
qs   (N)   1 July
Rosentall, P. H. psc
cfs   (P)   1 July
Spencer, P. D. psc qwi
qs   (P)   1 July

1994

Almond, T. MBE BA psc
asq qwi   (N)   1 Jan
Bailey, R. M. qs   (N)   1 Jan
Barrett, A. J. jsdc fc
qs   (P)   1 Jan
Bond, C. L. psc cfs(n)*
snc   (N)   1 Jan
Bown, A. R. jsdc qs (N) 1 Jan

Burgess, K. J. psc
qs   (P)   1 Jan
Davidson, I. F. BA snc
qs   (N)   1 Jan
Dixon, G. P. BSc
psc   (P)   1 Jan
Duffill, S. MA MIMgt
psc cfs   (P)   1 Jan
Exton, S. W. psc cfs (P) 1 Jan
Gunner, S. BSc(Eng)
qs   (P)   1 Jan
Halsall, M. W. psc (N)   1 Jan
Harrison, D. I. BSc psc
qwi   (P)   1 Jan
Herriot, D. R. qwi
qwi(T) psc   (N)   1 Jan
Knowles, D. W.
psc   (AEO) 1 Jan
Lamonte, J. MA BSc
CMath FIMA MRAeS
MRIN MIMgt asq
psc   (N)   1 Jan
Leakey, M. A. BSc qwi
psc   (P)   1 Jan
McAlpine, R. I. DFC MA
BSc MRAeS psc qwi
qs   (P)   1 Jan
Pitt, C. R. jsdc psc(n)
qs   (N)   1 Jan
Plumley, J. H. BSc cfs
qs   (P)   1 Jan
Pollitt, M. M. BSc rcds
psc cfs   (P)   1 Jan
Porter, G. R. R. BSc psc
qs   (N)   1 Jan
Pulford, A. D. psc
qs   (P)   1 Jan
Randall, N. B. jsdc qwi
qs   (N)   1 Jan
Rodda, S. G. psc   (N)   1 Jan
Simmonds, B. P. OBE
BSc CPhys MInstP
psc cfs   (P)   1 Jan
Telford, G. M. BSc jsdc
qs   (P)   1 Jan
Williams, M. A. psc cfs
qs   (P)   1 Jan
Ayres, S. P. BSc osc(Fr)
cfs qs i   (P)   1 July
Bates, B. L. BA psc
qwi   (P)   1 July
Bone, A. M. AFC jsdc
asq qs   (N)   1 July
Cobelli, R. D. BSc psc
qwi   (P)   1 July
Cornfield, K. L. OBE MA
psc cfs qs   (P)   1 July
Crowley, J. W. qab
qs   (N)   1 July

Dixon, P. R. MBA
BSc(Eng) MRAeS psc
cfs   (P)   1 July
Evans, W. G. OBE jsdc
tp   (P)   1 July
Ferries, A. I. BSc jsdc
nadc psc asq cfs(n)
snc   (N)   1 July
Fidler, D. C. psc cfs (P) 1 July
Fovarque, A. J. BSc snc
qss   (N)   1 July
Fynes, J. P. S. psc
cfs   (P)   1 July
Hilditch, S. L. BSc jsdc
tp qwi qs   (P)   1 July
Hurst, W. J. psc   (P)   1 July
Kirkhope, T. BSc psc
cfs   (P)   1 July
Lloyd, M. G. psc cfs (P) 1 July
McGeown, M. S. MA
psc qs   (P)   1 July
Powell, L. R. cfs(n) snc
qss   (N)   1 July
Rackham, C. M. cfs
qss   (P)   1 July
Skinner, D. R. psc
snc   (N)   1 July
Stinton, J. MA BA psc
qab qwi   (N)   1 July
Warren, S. F. psc(n)
cfs   (P)   1 July
Whittingham, J. psc cfs
qs   (P)   1 July
Crane, R.   (N)   10 Nov

1995

Armstrong, B. R. psc
qwi   (P)   1 Jan
Bennett, R. J. BSc psc
qwi   (N)   1 Jan
Clifford, J. M. MSc BSc
jsdc asq cfs(n) cfs
qs   (N)   1 Jan
Crawford, G. J. MIMgt
MRAeS psc cfs   (P)   1 Jan
Cunningham, R. B.
MBE MA psc   (N)   1 Jan
Davies, J. S. psc
snc   (N)   1 Jan
Dear, A. J. psc snc (N) 1 Jan
Dennison, K. BSc jsdc
tp qwi qs   (P)   1 Jan
Ellis, R. M. H. qs (N)   1 Jan
Ford, D. J. BA
psc(n)   (AEO) 1 Jan
Fradgley, J. N. AFC BSc
psc qwi(T)   (N)   1 Jan

Wing Commanders

1995—contd

Johnston, H. snc		
qs	(N)	1 Jan
Leggett, C. J. snc		
qss	(N)	1 Jan
Rimmer, J. A. J. BSc		
psc	(P)	1 Jan
Smith, B. BA jsdc asq		
qs	(N)	1 Jan
Squelch, J. P. BSc jsdc		
qab qs	(P)	1 Jan
Tizard, R. W. psc(m)		
cfs	(P)	1 Jan
Vincent, J. C. BSc		
psc(m) qwi	(P)	1 Jan
Wallace, D. B. MBE		
cfs(n) snc qs	(N)	1 Jan
Walne, K. BSc asq		
qs	(N)	1 Jan
Warburton, G. R. snc		
qs	(N)	1 Jan
Whitehouse, M. B. BSc		
qs	(P)	1 Jan
Wilson, D. A. BSc psc		
qs	(P)	1 Jan
Bairsto, C. A. psc qab		
qwi(AD)	(N)	1 July
Birks, C. J. BSc psc	(P)	1 July
Brown, E. S. psc		
snc	(N)	1 July
Dixon, C. W. MBE		
psc	(P)	1 July
Falla, S. O. DSO jsdc cfs		
qs	(P)	1 July
Garwood, R. F. DFC qwi		
qs	(P)	1 July
Malcolm, C. D. psc asq		
cfs(n) snc	(N)	1 July
Marrison, C. G. psc		
qwi(T)	(N)	1 July
McCarthy, W. J. MBE		
qs	(AEO)	1 July
Miller, C. psc	(P)	1 July
Skinner, S. N. BSc psc		
cfs	(P)	1 July
Swan, M. LLB psc		
qwi(T) qs	(P)	1 July
Torbet, R. J. qwi		
psc	(P)	1 July
Wright, R. D. BSc		
psc	(N)	1 July
Young, A. A. MA tp qwi		
qs i	(P)	1 July

1996

Barker, C. M. I. MA psc		
qs	(P)	1 Jan
Bartram, J. A. MSc		
MECI MIMgt psc		
snc	(N)	1 Jan
Bolsover, D. R. jsdc	(P)	1 Jan
Burrett, I. C. psc tp cfs*		
qs	(P)	1 Jan
Cameron, I. A. jsdc	(N)	1 Jan
Cleland-Smith, D. J.		
jsdc qs	(N)	1 Jan
Colley, M. P. psc qab		
qwi	(N)	1 Jan
Coote, J. E. MBE psc		
asq snc	(N)	1 Jan
Davenall, D. S. BSc jsdc		
qs	(N)	1 Jan
Dey, A. J. BSc psc	(N)	1 Jan
Dunsford, R. J. BSc		
qss	(P)	1 Jan
Goodbourn, J. A. BSc		
psc(m) qs	(P)	1 Jan
Green, M. C. BSc cfs		
qs	(P)	1 Jan
Hill, J. A. BSc snc		
qs	(N)	1 Jan
Kelly, P. M. psc qwi	(N)	1 Jan
Lock, R. BSc psc		
cfs*	(P)	1 Jan
Mason, D. R. MBE LLB		
psc	(N)	1 Jan
Maxwell, K. H. MA BSc		
oaws(US) psc(n) asq		
qs	(N)	1 Jan
Powell, R. J. A. psc		
cfs	(P)	1 Jan
Randles, S. psc	(P)	1 Jan
Ryall, F. D. jsdc qab		
qss	(N)	1 Jan
Stapleton, G. M. psc		
qwi	(N)	1 Jan
Thomson, K. K. MA psc		
qwi	(N)	1 Jan
Wylie, M. D. cfs qs	(P)	1 Jan
Bossy, M. J. snc qs	(N)	1 July
Carter, W. A. D. BA psc		
qwi qwi(T)	(N)	1 July
Coulls, C. J. qwi(T)		
qs	(N)	1 July
Cummings, S. jsdc		
qs	(P)	1 July
Elliott, J. G. MBE qss		
i	(P)	1 July
Elliott, R. I. BSc psc		
asq	(N)	1 July
Harwood, M. J. MBE		
MA psc cfs qwi	(P)	1 July
Hillier, S. J. psc cfs	(P)	1 July

Johnston, R. T. MA qwi		
qs	(P)	1 July
Jupp, J. A. BA psc(n)		
qwi(AD)	(P)	1 July
Kirkpatrick, A. S. BSc		
jsdc cfs qs	(P)	1 July
Low, R. A. C. jsdc qwi		
qs	(N)	1 July
Moloney, J. P. MA BA		
psc	(P)	1 July
O'Meeghan, P. M.		
psc	(P)	1 July
Orwell, S. J. psc cfs	(P)	1 July
Pearson, S. BA jsdc		
qs	(N)	1 July
Randerson, R. N. BSc		
psc qwi	(N)	1 July
Readfern, P. A.		
psc(m)	(P)	1 July
Watson, N. J. qwi		
qs	(P)	1 July
Whittingham, D. L. BSc		
psc cfs	(P)	1 July
Williams, J. G. MBE snc		
qs	(N)	1 July

1997

Anderson, T. M. MA		
MRAeS psc	(P)	1 Jan
Bagwell, G. J. psc		
qwi	(P)	1 Jan
Bond, G. R. psc	(N)	1 Jan
Brook, P. J. BA BSc		
MIMgt psc asq		
snc	(N)	1 Jan
Brown, D. A. jsdc		
qs	(P)	1 Jan
Castle, D. A. BSc psc		
qwi	(N)	1 Jan
Culbert, A. S. C. BSc		
jsdc	(P)	1 Jan
Cunningham, P. A. BSc		
cfs psc(m)	(P)	1 Jan
Davis, N. J. BSc MRAeS		
MRIN psc asq	(N)	1 Jan
Golledge, A. BSc		
qs	(P)	1 Jan
Hull, C. P. A. BSc psc		
asq	(N)	1 Jan
Jenkins, R. D. psc tp		
cfs	(P)	1 Jan
Killen, M. F. BSc psc		
qab cfs	(P)	1 Jan
Lawlor, J. BA psc qab		
qwi(T) qwi	(N)	1 Jan
Milburn, T. S. MA BSc		
psc(m)	(P)	1 Jan

Wing Commanders

1997—contd

Morgan, J. L. nadc		
qs	(AEO)	1 Jan
Morris, I. jsdc cfs	(P)	1 Jan
Morrison, I. C. psc		
qwi	(N)	1 Jan
Paton, D. R. BA qs	(N)	1 Jan
Roche, M. J. jsdc cfs		
qs	(P)	1 Jan
Sharp, M. A. psc	(N)	1 Jan
Soul, G. D. qs	(AEO)	1 Jan
Stewart, A. J. MRAeS		
MIMgt cfs psc	(P)	1 Jan
Sudlow, A. J. MBE BSc		
psc qwi	(P)	1 Jan
Turner, L. BSc jsdc		
qs	(N)	1 Jan
Walker, I. B. BA jsdc cfs		
qs	(P)	1 Jan
Wood, D. M. psc		
cfs	(P)	1 Jan
Barmby, A. S. BSc psc		
cfs	(P)	1 July
Barnes, S. G. BSc jsdc		
qwi qs	(P)	1 July
Booth, G. H. psc		
qwi(AD)	(N)	1 July
Cross, T. BA jsdc qs	(N)	1 July
Dobson, W. G. S. BSc		
psc	(P)	1 July
Forward, S. D. BSc jsdc		
qss	(P)	1 July
Garside-Beattie, L. cfs		
jsdc qs	(P)	1 July
Gunby, A. D. psc	(N)	1 July
Jagger, N. R. BSc cfs(n)		
snc psc	(N)	1 July
Kerr, A. W. BA AIL i*		
qs	(N)	1 July
Lungley, S. D. psc	(N)	1 July
Meyrick, N. D. psc	(N)	1 July
Oborn, P. N. psc	(P)	1 July
Simpson, D. A. BSc psc		
tp	(P)	1 July
Stewart, I. R. W. BSc		
jsdc cfs qs	(P)	1 July
Welham, A. R. D.		
psc	(P)	1 July
Whitaker, P. J. W. BA		
osc(Fr) i*	(P)	1 July
Williams, W. D. BA psc		
cfs qs	(P)	1 July
Wright, G. A. BSc		
psc(m) qs	(P)	1 July

1998

Ashcroft, I. T. asq		
cfs(n)* qs	(N)	1 Jan
Atherton, P. A. psc	(P)	1 Jan
Barber, S. B. J. MA		
psc(n)	(N)	1 Jan
Bell, I. K. psc cfs	(P)	1 Jan
Brown, M. W. qwi		
qss	(P)	1 Jan
Buckley, G. C. A. DFC		
psc qwi	(P)	1 Jan
Burley, D. snc qs	(N)	1 Jan
Bye, D. M. I. qs	(P)	1 Jan
Dobb, S. K. psc		
qwi(T)	(P)	1 Jan
Draper, I. M. BA psc		
cfs	(P)	1 Jan
Footer, S. G. MBE jsdc		
qs	(P)	1 Jan
Fox, S. M. AFC MA		
BCom psc cfs		
qwi	(P)	1 Jan
Fryer, A. D. qs	(N)	1 Jan
Goodall, R. jsdc qs	(N)	1 Jan
Harborne, P. N. jsdc	(P)	1 Jan
Hawes, A. P. BSc cfs		
qs	(P)	1 Jan
Hewett, G. M. MBE		
osc(Aus) qwi qs	(N)	1 Jan
Hill, M. R. jsdc	(N)	1 Jan
Horrocks, J. MA psc(n)		
qs	(P)	1 Jan
Howard, S. J. MA		
MRAeS psc qab	(P)	1 Jan
Huggett, A. D. psc		
qwi	(N)	1 Jan
Jenkins, M. J. M. BSc		
jsdc cfs qs	(P)	1 Jan
Kennedy, J. M. BSc		
qs	(N)	1 Jan
Kirkin, T. R. MRIN cfs(n)		
snc qs	(N)	1 Jan
Lloyd, P. O. MBE cfs*		
qs	(P)	1 Jan
MacInnes, G. W. BSc		
jsdc qs	(P)	1 Jan
McCann, K. B. psc(m)		
qab qwi qs	(P)	1 Jan
McWilliams, T. P. psc		
qab snc	(N)	1 Jan
Mercer, M. J. jsdc		
qwi(AD) qs	(P)	1 Jan
Moulds, G. MBE jsdc		
qss	(N)	1 Jan
Newton, S. psc	(P)	1 Jan
Osborn, P. C. psc		
qwi	(N)	1 Jan
Plumb, J. V. qwi qs	(N)	1 Jan

Poole, R. M. psc		
qwi	(N)	1 Jan
Prowse, D. L. BA jsdc		
qab qs	(P)	1 Jan
Robertson, D. G. psc		
qwi(T)	(N)	1 Jan
Scholtens, J. H. BA jsdc		
qs	(N)	1 Jan
Seward, N. I. M. psc		
cfs	(P)	1 Jan
Stevenson, A. D. psc		
qwi	(P)	1 Jan
Sutton, P. R. BA psc		
cfs	(P)	1 Jan
Teakle, I. D. jsdc qwi(T)		
qs	(N)	1 Jan
Thwaites, G. E. psc	(N)	1 Jan
Trembaczowski-Ryder,		
D. J. BSc psc	(N)	1 Jan
Barrass J. A. BSc		
qs	(N)	1 July
Barton, P. R. BSc cfs		
qs	(P)	1 July
Birtwistle, R. W.		
qwi(AD) qs	(N)	1 July
Duell, K. qs	(AEO)	1 July
McAuley, A. W. J.		
qs	(P)	1 July
McLaughlin, A. N. BSc		
qs	(P)	1 July
Morris, P. A. psc	(N)	1 July
Nash, H. W. MBE		
qs	(P)	1 July
North, B. M. MBE MA		
pcs(m)	(P)	1 July
Purkiss, C. C. MBE BSc		
qs	(N)	1 July
Revell, K. A. BA qs	(N)	1 July
Robertson, G. W. BSc		
psc	(N)	1 July
Russell, S. P. jsdc		
qs	(N)	1 July
Shields, I. E. cfs(n)*		
qs	(N)	1 July
Stewart, H. qs	(AEO)	1 July
Stubbs, D. J. qs	(P)	1 July
Suddards, A. J. Q. MA		
BA qab qwi qs	(P)	1 July
Taylor, J. MIMgt		
psc	(P)	1 July
Tull, G. A. J. adp qs	(N)	1 July
Turner, W. J. MA		
BSc(Eng) MRAeS		
MRIN MCGI MIMgt		
asq psc	(N)	1 July
Wade, C. E. asq qs	(N)	1 July
Warner, J. E. AIB cfs		
qs	(P)	1 July
West, P. C. qs	(N)	1 July
Young, S. qs	(P)	1 July

Squadron Leaders

1968

McCluney, J. G. psc
cfs   (P)   1 Jan

1971

Hooper, A. L. cfs qs (P)   1 July

1974

Sayer, M. J. FRIN psc
asq snc   (N)   1 Jan

1975

Elton, E. A. BA cfs
qss*   (P)   1 July

1976

Sollitt, A. G. qs   (P)   1 Jan
Brooks, D. BSc cfs
qss*   (P)   1 July
Day, P. AFC   (P)   1 July
Jarvis, R. H. psc cfs (P)   18 Oct

1977

Hayes, N. P.   (P)   1 July
Laurie, G. H. MVO   (P)   1 July
Webley, D. L. BTech cfs
qss*   (P)   1 July
Wheatley, T. M. K. snc
qs   (N)   1 July

1978

Rouse, E. G. C. cfs
qs   (P)   1 Jan
Martin, D. A. qwi(AD)
qss   (P)   1 July
Adcock, T. R. MRAeS tp
qwi(AD) qss   (P)   29 July
Lovegrove, G. B. snc
qs   (N)   22 Dec

1979

Wright, A. J. BA MIMgt
snc qs   (N)   1 Jan
Butt, L. C. snc qs   (N)   1 July
Culverhouse, P. C. MBE
qss   (P)   1 July
Pegrum, R. G. qs   (N)   1 July
Widdess, J. D. McM.
MBE asq qss   (AEO) 1 July

1980

Bruce, P. R. cfs   (P)   1 Jan
Miles, P. G. MBE qs   (P)   1 Jan
Sitch, T. MBE snc   (N)   1 Jan
Taylor, C. J. MBE cfs
qss   (P)   1 Jan
McCloud, R. C. qs   (P)   18 June
Becker, K. H.   (P)   1 July
Blenkinsop, J. W.   (N)   1 July
Clemett, A. L. BSc snc
qs   (N)   1 July
McKendrick, D. I.
qs   (N)   1 July
Walker, R. S. snc qs   (N)   1 July

1981

Cole, B. F. qss   (N)   1 Jan
Cook, D. F. asq cfs(n)
snc qss   (N)   1 Jan
Hall, R. J. MRIN snc
qs   (N)   1 Jan
Sullivan, L. qs   (N)   1 Jan
Tidball, C. J. qss*   (P)   1 Jan
Waring, D. A. AFC
qs   (P)   1 Jan
Wilcox, P. H. MBE   (P)   1 Jan
Aram, G. D. MBE asq
adp qs   (AEO) 1 July
Wilson, R. M. BA
MRAeS MIMgt
qs   (N)   1 July

1982

Constable, E. C. MIMgt
cfs qs   (P)   1 Jan
Hampton, I. J. snc   (N)   1 Jan
Jones, W. R. D. qs   (P)   1 Jan
Laing, G. H. B. MA
qss   (P)   1 Jan
Lawry, K. J. cfs* qs   (P)   1 Jan
Norbury, E. G. cfs   (P)   1 Jan
Oldham, D. V. cfs
qss   (P)   1 Jan

Pickering, R. J. BSc cfs
qs   (P)   1 Jan
Strang, A. J. M. BA BSc
snc qs   (N)   1 Jan
Bourne, G. F. BA BSc
qs   (AEO) 1 July
Busby, J. M. BSc cfs
qs   (P)   1 July
Hodson, I. qs   (N)   1 July
Hooper, C. A. cfs*
qs   (P)   1 July
King, R. F. MVO cfs   (P)   1 July
Tew, M. R. N. BSc
qs   (P)   1 July
Traylor, A. G. qs   (AEO) 1 July

1983

Baker, J. E. cfs* qs   (P)   1 Jan
Cocking, R. K. BSc snc
qs   (N)   1 Jan
Dixon, P. M. qs   (N)   1 Jan
Kendall, J. F. cfs(n) snc
psc   (P)   1 Jan
Laidler, A. J. snc
qss   (N)   1 Jan
Moody, R. M. cfs
qss   (P)   1 Jan
Sharp, D. J. AFC BSc
cfs qss   (P)   1 Jan
Wright, J. T. qs   (N)   1 Jan
Buckland, M. R. G. BSc
psc cfs   (P)   1 July
Coleman, P. MIMgt cfs
qss   (P)   1 July
Cranswick, C. E. BSc cfs
qs   (P)   1 July
Dobbs, A. C. snc qs   (N)   1 July
Hinton, P. N. qs   (N)   1 July
McNeill-Matthews, J.
H. F. qwi qs   (N)   1 July
Melville-Jackson, A.
qs   (P)   1 July
Mulligan, G. H. MBE
MIMgt qs   (N)   1 July
Phillips, R. A.   (P)   1 July
Seaward, G. L. psc(n)
qwi   (N)   1 July
Shields, R. M. MVO
qss   (N)   1 July
Williams, A. H. BSc
MIMgt qs   (N)   1 July

1984

Collins, R. qs   (ENG) 1 Jan
Daniels, G. A. qs   (N)   1 Jan

Squadron Leaders

1984—contd

Desai, A. K. MIMgt snc		
qs	(N)	1 Jan
Fletcher, A. K. cfs(n) snc		
qs	(N)	1 Jan
Gault, W. MBE qs	(N)	1 Jan
Goodman, D. F. psc(m)		
cfs	(P)	1 Jan
Lee, D. W. cfs qss	(P)	1 Jan
Mason, K. cfs	(P)	1 Jan
O'Connell, C. D. jsdc		
cfs(n) snc	(N)	1 Jan
Ritchie, J. M. B. qss	(P)	1 Jan
Ross, R. asq cfs(n) snc		
qs	(N)	1 Jan
Sharman, P. B. qss	(P)	1 Jan
Snelders, F. M. cfs(n)		
snc qss	(N)	1 Jan
Candlish, E. G. J. MRIN		
MIMgt snc qs	(N)	1 July
Crombie, D. J. C. MBE		
snc qs	(N)	1 July
Fallis, R. J. H. AFC		
cfs	(P)	1 July
James, W. J. M. cfs	(P)	1 July
Poole, N. P. psc cfs(n)*		
snc	(N)	1 July
Rounds, T. W. B. psc		
snc	(N)	1 July
Walters, R. J. BSc asq		
qs	(P)	1 July
Thomas, D. J. cfs		
qss	(P)	30 Aug
Clements, A. N.		
BSc(Eng) ACG		
cfs*	(P)	10 Oct

1985

Boon, T. R. qss	(N)	1 Jan
Da Costa, F. A. cfs*	(P)	1 Jan
Dixon, P. S. AFC cfs		
qs	(P)	1 Jan
Gilbert, J. asq snc	(N)	1 Jan
Hodgson, G. F. BA snc		
adp qs	(N)	1 Jan
Horton, D. qs	(P)	1 Jan
Moule, A. L. BSc adp		
qs	(N)	1 Jan
Norris, D. J. snc qs	(N)	1 Jan
Reay, P. BSc asq snc		
qss	(N)	1 Jan
Carter, R. V. BSc jsdc cfs		
qs	(P)	1 July

Deveson, K. H. BA BSc		
MRAeS asq qs	(P)	1 July
Jacobs, R. cfs(n)*		
snc	(N)	1 July
Lister-Tomlinson, A. D.		
qab qwi qs	(N)	1 July
Murty, J. K. BSc cfs		
qss	(P)	1 July
Paine, M. A. qwi		
qss	(P)	1 July
Peeke, G. BSc MIPD snc		
qs	(N)	1 July
Young, M. BSc(Eng)		
qwi qss	(P)	21 Oct

1986

Alexander, W. J. cfs(n)		
snc qs	(N)	1 Jan
Benn, C. R. qs	(P)	1 Jan
Bennett, D. qwi qs	(N)	1 Jan
Burrows, J. A. cfs(n)		
snc qss	(N)	1 Jan
Gardiner, J. F. cfs		
qs	(P)	1 Jan
Hamilton, D. A. BTech		
qs	(P)	1 Jan
Herbertson, P. S. cfs(n)		
snc qs	(N)	1 Jan
Penny, A. T. snc qs	(N)	1 Jan
Sargent, D. qs	(P)	1 Jan
Sinclair, C. M. BA		
cfs	(P)	1 Jan
Ward, D. BA BSc cfs		
qss*	(P)	1 Jan
Golden, E. snc qss	(N)	21 Apr
Bryan, M. J. BSc(Eng)		
MRAeS MInstD		
MIMgt cfs qs	(P)	1 July
Clark, A. McG. MRAeS		
MIMgt asq psc		
snc	(N)	1 July
Clark, B. M. qss	(N)	1 July
Doig, C. G. qs	(N)	1 July
Hallett, P. Q. MA BSc		
FRGS psc qab	(P)	1 July
Hartley, I. G. qss	(P)	1 July
Heath, C. cfs(n) snc		
qs	(N)	1 July
Henry, B. L. snc qs	(N)	1 July
Jarmain, S. P. cfs		
qss	(P)	1 July
Mander, S. G. qs	(N)	1 July
Procopides, M. D. BSc		
cfs qss	(P)	1 July
Wescott, M. R. J. qab		
qwi qs	(N)	1 July

Hudson, R. A. BA		
CertEd asq cfs(n) snc		
qss	(N)	6 Sept
Calton, S. AFC qs	(P)	24 Dec

1987

Ayres, N. P. BSc asq		
qs	(N)	1 Jan
Bayer, P. qs	(N)	1 Jan
Beard, P. R. cfs(n) snc		
qs	(N)	1 Jan
Budd, P. H. qs	(N)	1 Jan
Burgoyne, H. C.		
AFC	(P)	1 Jan
Calvert, D. P. BSc cfs		
qs	(P)	1 Jan
Cockman, P. R. cfs*		
qss	(P)	1 Jan
Cunningham, J. D.		
MBE	(N)	1 Jan
Davies, P. A. asq		
qs	(AEO)	1 Jan
Ford, R. B.	(N)	1 Jan
Hunt, M. J. cfs*	(P)	1 Jan
Irving, R. BSc cfs*		
qs	(P)	1 Jan
King, R. L. qss	(N)	1 Jan
Lemare, D. A. C. cfs	(P)	1 Jan
May, N. cfs qs	(P)	1 Jan
McNeil, J. J. asq snc		
qs	(N)	1 Jan
Reekie, G. L. cfs	(P)	1 Jan
Rowley, C. M. cfs		
qss	(P)	1 Jan
Slatter, C. BSc(Eng) cfs		
qs	(P)	1 Jan
Smith, P. S. BA asq		
qs	(N)	1 Jan
Smith, R. C. asq snc		
qs	(N)	1 Jan
Viney, G. M. BSc asq		
qs	(N)	1 Jan
Collis, J. J. qss	(P)	2 Apr
Aitken, R. T. cfs(n)		
qs	(N)	15 Jun
Blagrove, C. N. MBE		
BSc psc asq	(N)	1 July
Burges, R. R. cfs(n) snc		
qs	(N)	1 July
Carver, C. C. psc asq		
cfs(n) snc	(N)	1 July
Clephane, W. B. J.		
MIMgt qs	(N)	1 July
Coleman, I. M. cfs(n)		
snc qss	(N)	1 July
Craig, I. J. MBE qs	(N)	1 July
Deane, J. H. asq qs	(N)	1 July
Gledhill, D. J. qs	(N)	1 July

Squadron Leaders

1987—contd

Jones, D. K. qs	(N)	1 July
Landsburgh, A.		
qs	(AEO)	1 July
Lunnon-Wood, A. K.		
qwi (AD)	(P)	1 July
McKenna, M. J. snc qs		
i	(N)	1 July
Reynolds, M. BSc cfs(n)		
qs	(N)	1 July
Robinson, S.	(P)	1 July
Smith, S. P. cfs(n)* snc		
qs	(N)	1 July
Thompson, R. W.		
qss	(AEO)	1 July
Wilder, R. A. BSc		
jsdc	(N)	1 July
Wilkinson, J. BSc cfs		
qwi qss	(P)	1 July

1988

Aspinall, R. M. MA		
qs	(P)	1 Jan
Bolton, M. W. MIMgt		
snc qss	(N)	1 Jan
Clapham, C. M. qs	(N)	1 Jan
Cook, C. J.	(N)	1 Jan
Dobson, M. snc qs	(N)	1 Jan
Frost, D. W. cfs qs	(P)	1 Jan
Lund, R. M. MRAeS asq		
qs	(P)	1 Jan
Macartney, J. K. cfs		
qss	(P)	1 Jan
Medland, W. J. qss	(N)	1 Jan
Milnes, R. A. BSc cfs(n)		
qs	(N)	1 Jan
Newton, H. E. BSc jsdc		
snc	(N)	1 Jan
Parker, A. L. qs	(N)	1 Jan
Rees, M. S. qs	(P)	1 Jan
Rose, V. E. snc qs	(N)	1 Jan
Sparrow, M. V. D. cfs		
qss i*	(P)	1 Jan
Stevenson, J. asq snc		
qs	(N)	1 Jan
Withers, B. R. AFC		
qss	(P)	1 Jan
Yates, R. qss*	(AEO)	1 Jan
Prescot, F. B. qss	(P)	28 May
Alexander, E. C. cfs		
qs	(P)	1 July
Ankerson, R. BTech asq		
qs	(N)	1 July

Boxall, A. C. W. cfs		
qss	(P)	1 July
Cairncross, A. K. cfs		
qs	(P)	1 July
Cowieson, K. R. jsdc		
qs	(N)	1 July
Dart, J. N. qss	(N)	1 July
Davies, R. W. BSc asq		
qs	(N)	1 July
Davy, A. M. J. BA cfs(n)		
snc qs	(N)	1 July
Fallon, R. D. qss	(N)	1 July
Farmer, M. K. cfs i	(P)	1 July
Geddes, H. G. qs	(N)	1 July
Jukes, M. H. BSc cfs		
qss	(P)	1 July
Miall, M. J. D. cfs		
qss	(P)	1 July
Robinson, J. E. BA		
cfs	(P)	1 July
Starling, M. C. cfs		
qss	(P)	1 July
Willey, N. W. cfs qs	(P)	1 July
Williams, S. G. snc		
qss	(N)	1 July
Lakey, M. J. GM		
qss	(P)	16 Aug

1989

Anderson, A. R. L.		
cfs	(P)	1 Jan
Boyle, A. BSc cfs(n) snc		
qs	(N)	1 Jan
Byatt, N. E. qs	(N)	1 Jan
Chapman, J. G. BA BSc		
psc cfs	(P)	1 Jan
Cooper, S. J. qs	(N)	1 Jan
Daughney, R. cfs(n) snc		
qss	(N)	1 Jan
Druitt, R. K. BSc qs	(P)	1 Jan
Francis, A. G.	(N)	1 Jan
Griffin, J. T.	(N)	1 Jan
Heath, R. A. J. qwi		
qs	(P)	1 Jan
Hodgson, I. snc	(N)	1 Jan
King, R. A. cfs qss	(P)	1 Jan
Loveridge, M. J. qs	(N)	1 Jan
MacIntosh, D. R. BA		
qss	(P)	1 Jan
O'Gorman, P. D. snc fc		
qss	(N)	1 Jan
Porter, J. L. snc qs	(N)	1 Jan
Pugh-Davies, M. D. BA		
BTech qs	(N)	1 Jan
Pynegar, P. G. AFC BSc		
qss	(P)	1 Jan
Ramsey, W. J. qab cfs		
qs	(P)	1 Jan

Richardson, G. F. BSc		
asq qs	(N)	1 Jan
Steer, D. H. snc qs	(N)	1 Jan
Sully, A. K. qab cfs(n)*		
snc qs	(N)	1 Jan
Thompson, R. T. N.		
MSc BSc qab qwi		
psc(n)	(N)	1 Jan
Thomson, D. H. BSc		
asq qs	(P)	1 Jan
Todd, R. E. BSc(Econ)		
qs	(N)	1 Jan
Williams, J. K. BA		
psc	(P)	1 Jan
Batson, P. K. cfs*	(P)	1 July
Bradley, D. J. BSc qwi		
qs	(P)	1 July
Bray, A. M. J. tp qs	(P)	1 July
Courtnage, P. J. qwi		
qs	(P)	1 July
Evans, P. A. qss	(P)	1 July
Graves, R. D. cfs qs	(P)	1 July
Haslam, S. J. qs	(N)	1 July
Haworth, P. W. qs	(N)	1 July
Hill, T. J. BA qs i	(N)	1 July
Marsh, D. A.	(N)	1 July
Molloy, G. J. BA cfs		
qs	(P)	1 July
Morgan, D. C. qs	(N)	1 July
Muse, R. C. BSc cfs		
qss	(P)	1 July
Roe, R. A. qs	(N)	1 July
Smith, K. W. snc qs	(N)	1 July
Southwood, D. R. AFC		
BSc tp qwi	(P)	1 July
Trace, B. E. MBE qs	(N)	1 July
Williams, I. R. tp		
qwi(T)	(P)	1 July
Yapp, G. D. qs	(N)	1 July

1990

Anderson, R. BSc		
cfs(n)	(N)	1 Jan
Atherton, I. W. BSc qab		
qss	(N)	1 Jan
Barrett, I. BSc qs	(N)	1 Jan
Boyd, C. J. BSc qwi	(P)	1 Jan
Collier, J. F.	(N)	1 Jan
Cooper, G. qss	(N)	1 Jan
Crichton, C. H. qs	(N)	1 Jan
Davies, C. D. qs	(N)	1 Jan
Flint, P. A.	(P)	1 Jan
Fraser, R. G. BSc qs	(P)	1 Jan
Froude, C. L. BSc		
MIMgt cfs qs	(P)	1 Jan
Gilday, E. J. W. BSc		
qs	(P)	1 Jan

Squadron Leaders

1990—contd

Goodenough, N. J. BSc		
asq qs	(N)	1 Jan
Guest, T. A. qs	(N)	1 Jan
Hall, R. P. W.	(N)	1 Jan
Hartill, D. R. qs	(N)	1 Jan
Knight, C. A. snc qs	(N)	1 Jan
Lillis, J. snc qss	(N)	1 Jan
Mitchell, A. G. BA		
qs	(N)	1 Jan
Moody, J. K. BSc cfs(c)		
qss	(AEO)	1 Jan
Pearce, L. E. F. qs	(N)	1 Jan
Philip, A. F. MSc BSc tp		
qs	(P)	1 Jan
Pierce, H. R. BA qs	(P)	1 Jan
Purser, C. R. qs	(N)	1 Jan
Scarffe, M. G. qwi		
qs	(N)	1 Jan
Scott, G. R. qs	(N)	1 Jan
Smyth, S. G. MBE	(P)	1 Jan
Spandley, T. A. qs	(P)	1 Jan
Ward, R. J. R. MSc BSc		
asq snc qs	(N)	1 Jan
Whitbread, P. C. A.		
cfs	(P)	1 Jan
Wilkin, R. cfs qs	(P)	1 Jan
Leckenby, P. J. MBE		
qs	(N)	15 Jan
Murkin, S. D.	(P)	27 May
Barrett, P. J. qss	(P)	1 July
Bridger, S. P. psc		
qwi(T)	(P)	1 July
Cole, R. A. cfs qss	(P)	1 July
Collins, R. D. qss	(N)	1 July
Fraser, J. C. A. BSc cfs		
qs	(P)	1 July
Gale, G. snc	(N)	1 July
Gillan, J. qs	(AEO)	1 July
Golden, M. J. asq		
qss	(AEO)	1 July
Hargreaves, K. cfs		
qss	(P)	1 July
Harrison, W. P. BSc		
cfs*	(P)	1 July
Hayward, A. J. M. BSc		
MRAeS asq snc		
qs	(N)	1 July
Kirk, G. H. cfs	(P)	1 July
Lander, R. J. snc qs	(N)	1 July
Leaviss, R. E. cfs		
qss	(P)	1 July
MacLennan, K. M.	(P)	1 July
Marshall, J. D. cfs		
qss	(N)	1 July
McBain, S. B. snc	(N)	1 July

McCarthy, R. J. BSc		
cfs(n) qwi(T) snc		
qss	(N)	1 July
McDonnell, N. J. qs	(P)	1 July
Mochan, J. P. qwi(T)		
snc qss	(N)	1 July
Morison, M. C. qss	(P)	1 July
Neal, A. C.	(P)	1 July
Newby, T. asq cfs(n)		
snc qs	(N)	1 July
O'Brien, C. M. P. BA		
qs	(P)	1 July
Richardson, J. G. BSc		
psc cfs	(P)	1 July
Rosie, P. I. cfs qss	(P)	1 July
Vince, S. D. qss	(P)	1 July

1991

Aitken, A. P-D. cfs		
qss	(P)	1 Jan
Barrett, G. J. BSc asq		
qs	(N)	1 Jan
Bentham, A. qss	(N)	1 Jan
Brakewell, C. S. snc	(N)	1 Jan
Brayn Smith, I. A. M.		
cfs qss	(P)	1 Jan
Browne, W. N. DFC	(N)	1 Jan
Bruce, G. J. BSc asq		
qs	(P)	1 Jan
Byron, K. B. qss	(N)	1 Jan
Cairns, J. L. qss	(N)	1 Jan
Cockbill, S. C. BSc		
qss	(N)	1 Jan
Corry, A. qs	(AEO)	1 Jan
Cowling, G. P. BSc asq		
qss	(P)	1 Jan
Dancey, A. N. BA asq		
qs	(N)	1 Jan
Edwards, P. W. MBE		
BSc asq qs	(P)	1 Jan
Ewer, M. H. cfs qss	(P)	1 Jan
Gagen, S. P. qs	(AEO)	1 Jan
Gosling, A. T. BSc asq		
qs	(N)	1 Jan
Green, S. J. jsdc qs	(N)	1 Jan
Gregory, R. D. cfs		
qss	(P)	1 Jan
Gunning, K. E. BSc cfs		
qs	(P)	1 Jan
Guttridge, A. H. MVO		
MBE	(N)	1 Jan
Hedley, A. T. BA cfs		
qss	(P)	1 Jan
Ilett, R. P. cfs qs	(P)	1 Jan
McLeod, J. E. qs	(P)	1 Jan
Menage, C. P. qs	(N)	1 Jan
Morgan, D. T. BSc cfs		
qs	(P)	1 Jan

Read, K. R. L. cfs		
qss*	(P)	1 Jan
Roberts, G. J. qs (ENG)		1 Jan
Smithson, J. D. BSc cfs		
qss	(P)	1 Jan
Snowball, A. J. BSc asq		
snc qs	(N)	1 Jan
Stangroom, M. F.		
qs	(P)	1 Jan
Taylor, C. C.		
qwi(AD)	(P)	1 Jan
Thomas, S. E. MBE		
qss	(AEO)	1 Jan
Whittingham, R. T. BSc		
asq qs	(AEO)	1 Jan
Wilkinson, T. A. MBE		
BSc qs	(N)	1 Jan
Williams, H. M. qs	(P)	1 Jan
Willis, P. A. osc(Fr)		
qwi(AD) qs	(P)	1 Jan
Allan, P. BA cfs*		
qss	(P)	1 July
Bond, R. W. cfs qss	(P)	1 July
Cairns, J. BSc asq		
qs	(N)	1 July
Connor, K. D. qs	(P)	1 July
Crump, D. G. BSc asq		
adp qs	(P)	1 July
Dakin, A. G. BSc qwi		
qs	(P)	1 July
Dawson, N. S.		
BSc(Eng) ACGI		
qs	(P)	1 July
Diamond, D. J. BA		
MRAeS osc(Fr) cfs		
qs	(P)	1 July
Dooley, C. F. BSc asq		
qss	(N)	1 July
Fauchon, T. T. qs	(P)	1 July
Fraser, J.	(AEO)	1 July
Fynes, C. J. S. AFC		
	(ALM)	1 July
Goodison, A. J. BSc		
cfs(n) qs	(N)	1 July
Havelock, K. qs	(P)	1 July
Hudson, D. J. asq	(N)	1 July
Hyslop, R. M. qs	(N)	1 July
Judson, R. W. jsdc		
qs	(P)	1 July
Kessell, J. B. qs	(N)	1 July
Mardon, J. BSc cfs qwi		
qs	(P)	1 July
Marr, J. qss	(N)	1 July
McDermott, C. W. qab		
qs	(N)	1 July
McNamara, S. P. qs		
	(AEO)	1 July
Morgan, D. R.	(ALM)	1 July
Nash, J. A. qs	(N)	1 July
Pick, K. E. qs	(AEO)	1 July

Squadron Leaders

1991—contd

Reeves, C. qs	(ENG)	1 July
Robinson, B. G. M.		
DFC	(P)	1 July
Speight, W. MBE	(ENG)	1 July
Turner, S. C. G.		
BSc(Econ) MIMgt		
jsdc cfs qs	(P)	1 July
Walls, J. A. qss	(AEO)	1 July
Whitworth, R. C. cfs(n)		
qs	(N)	1 July

1992

Avery, D. G. snc		
qss	(N)	1 Jan
Bancroft-Pitman, S.		
C.	(ALM)	1 Jan
Bird, R. C. snc qss	(N)	1 Jan
Brown, D. W. qs	(AEO)	1 Jan
Brunning, I. BSc qs	(N)	1 Jan
Chapman, P. J. snc		
qs	(N)	1 Jan
Chatterton, R. J.		
qs	(AEO)	1 Jan
Deas, A. S. BSc qs	(N)	1 Jan
Greene, R. A. D. cfs		
qs	(P)	1 Jan
Gregory, P. W. MBE BA		
MIL osc(Ge) qs i*	(P)	1 Jan
Hallwood, J. Q. BSc cfs		
qs	(P)	1 Jan
Lawless, A. A. BA		
qs	(P)	1 Jan
Lawrie, I. G. BEng		
qss	(N)	1 Jan
Ledward, D. J. qss	(N)	1 Jan
Loynes, R. A. qss	(AEO)	1 Jan
Mason, R. J. MBE BSc		
cfs(n) snc qs	(N)	1 Jan
McSherry, A. L. BSc asq		
qs	(N)	1 Jan
Nash, A. J. qs	(N)	1 Jan
Newton, R. J. BSc		
cfs(n)	(N)	1 Jan
Oldham, M. G. BSc		
qs	(N)	1 Jan
Pennell, L. J. BSc cfs		
qs	(P)	1 Jan
Perrem T. J. AFC		
qss	(N)	1 Jan
Reeves, K. J. qwi(AD)		
qss	(N)	1 Jan
Reid, S. G. BSc cfs		
qs	(P)	1 Jan

Richards, M. E.		
qss	(AEO)	1 Jan
Roberts, D. G.	(P)	1 Jan
Sanders, J. T. qss	(N)	1 Jan
Smith, N. A. qs	(AEO)	1 Jan
Spreckley, G. C. snc,		
qss*	(N)	1 Jan
Wealleans, E. A.		
qwi	(P)	1 Jan
Wharmby, N. E. BSc		
qwi qs	(P)	1 Jan
Best, D. BSc ALCM tp		
qs	(P)	1 July
Bostock, S. P. qs	(N)	1 July
Chan, D. K. M. qs	(P)	1 July
Christen, J. R. R. MEng		
BSc cfs qs	(P)	1 July
Davey, G. R. qs	(ENG)	1 July
Davis, A. H. cfs		
qss*	(P)	1 July
Hewitt, K. cfs	(P)	1 July
Howe, R. S. snc qss	(N)	1 July
Kinnaird, S. BA qs	(N)	1 July
Millikin, P. M. MBE		
cfs	(P)	1 July
Milne, G. D. qs	(AEO)	1 July
Penrice, C. BSc tp qwi		
qss	(P)	1 July
Powell, R. J. C. qwi		
qs	(N)	1 July
Prior, M. R. tp qss	(P)	1 July
Riley, G. G. qwi(T)		
qs	(P)	1 July
Rose, I. A. qs	(P)	1 July
Setterfield, M. J. snc		
qs	(N)	1 July
Steel, B. B. asq qs	(N)	1 July
Symons, B. R. cfs	(P)	1 July
Wooldridge, J. B. BSc		
qs	(P)	1 July

1993

Baldwin, K. J. qs	(N)	1 Jan
Cairns, T. P. M. cfs	(P)	1 Jan
Carter, J. D. qwi		
qss	(P)	1 Jan
Cunningham, M. asq		
qwi	(AEO)	1 Jan
Errington, M. E.		
qss	(AEO)	1 Jan
Hallett, L. T. BSc		
qwi(AD) qs	(P)	1 Jan
Jefferies, I. S.	(AEO)	1 Jan
Logan, P. S. cfs qss	(P)	1 Jan
Maas, J. D. qs	(P)	1 Jan
MacLeod, D. H. qs	(N)	1 Jan
Marriott, M. B. R.		
cfs	(P)	1 Jan

Morgan, C. N. B. MBE		
asq qs	(N)	1 Jan
Moss, G. P. qss	(AEO)	1 Jan
Pearson, S. D. odc(Ge)		
qs	(N)	1 Jan
Piper, D. cfs qss	(P)	1 Jan
Preston, D. L. qss	(N)	1 Jan
Smith, J. P. snc qss	(N)	1 Jan
Steel, D. J. BSc qs	(P)	1 Jan
Thomas, S. R. cfs qwi		
qss	(P)	1 Jan
Townend, R. J. S. cfs		
qss	(P)	1 Jan
Van Den Berg, G. G. S.		
psc qs	(P)	1 Jan
Wainwright, N. D.		
cfs(n)* qs	(N)	1 Jan
Young, S. J. qab qs	(P)	1 Jan
Ardley, J. C. cfs	(N)	1 July
Ayers, J. H. snc	(N)	1 July
Ball, J. C. qwi qs	(N)	1 July
Blount, C. S. BSc MRIN		
MRAeS asq cfs(n)*		
qs	(N)	1 July
Bremer, G. T. BSc		
qwi(AD) qs	(N)	1 July
Cemm, N. A. BSc		
qs	(P)	1 July
Cliff, M. J. H. qwi		
qs	(P)	1 July
Cockram, S. H. qab qwi		
qs	(P)	1 July
Cottell, P. snc qs	(N)	1 July
Davey, G. J. BSc qs	(P)	1 July
Devlin, H. T. cfs qss	(P)	1 July
Ekins, D. J. BSc qwi		
qs	(P)	1 July
Farley, R. F. qss	(P)	1 July
Fenlon, M. C. BSc(Eng)		
CEng MRAeS asq		
qs	(N)	1 July
Flint, A. P. BA qs	(N)	1 July
Fortune, T. F.	(AEO)	1 July
Guz, N. BSc cfs qs	(P)	1 July
Hobson, R. A. BSc		
qs	(P)	1 July
Hopkins, M. W. G. MBE		
MA cfs qs	(P)	1 July
Hopkinson, M. J. BSc		
cfs qss	(P)	1 July
Howlett, P. W. AFC		
cfs*	(P)	1 July
Jones, K. A. cfs*		
qss	(P)	1 July
Jones, P. J. qwi qs	(N)	1 July
Klein, J. B. qwi qs	(N)	1 July
Lyall, P. cfs qs	(P)	1 July
Masters, S. M.	(P)	1 July
Meade, S. C. qs	(P)	1 July

Squadron Leaders

1993—contd

Pritchard, D. M. cfs
qs (P) 1 July
Randall, A. M. qwi(T)
qs (P) 1 July
Reed, A. D. BSc qss (P) 1 July
Round, P. A. BSc cfs
qs (P) 1 July
Russell, W. H. BSc
qs (N) 1 July
Smith, A. J. qs (N) 1 July
Temple, M. L. L. (P) 1 July
Thomas, C. C. BSc asq
qs (N) 1 July
Tucker, A. qwi(T) qs (N) 1 July
Watson, N. M. (P) 1 July
Wood, I. N. BA qwi
qs (P) 1 July

1994

Baker, M. F. cfs(n)
qs (N) 1 Jan
Basnett, C. qwi(T)
qs (N) 1 Jan
Bell, S. M. BSc(Eng) cfs
qwi qs (P) 1 Jan
Bowman, M. N.
BSc(Eng) tp qwi
qs (P) 1 Jan
Brain, I. B. asq (N) 1 Jan
Collins, A. J. (N) 1 Jan
Connell, N. M. BSc cfs
qs (P) 1 Jan
Coombes, S. R. A. BSc
qs (P) 1 Jan
Cooney, P. J. cfs qs (P) 1 Jan
Cunningham, C. S. cfs
qs (P) 1 Jan
Davies, J. cfs qs (P) 1 Jan
Davis, S. (AEO) 1 Jan
Denning, T. W. E. snc
qss (N) 1 Jan
Dixon, P. G. qs (P) 1 Jan
Docker, P. A. BA MCGI
asq qs (P) 1 Jan
Drewery, C. C. qss (P) 1 Jan
Edwards, A. BSc qs (N) 1 Jan
Emerson, K. J. MPhil
BSc tp qs (P) 1 Jan
Fisher, A. BSc qs (N) 1 Jan
Girling, R. J. cfs qs (P) 1 Jan
Gosling, J. R. qwi
qs (P) 1 Jan
Griffin, G. cfs qss (P) 1 Jan

Hutchings, J. P. qs (N) 1 Jan
Jacobs, P. C. cfs(n)
qs (N) 1 Jan
Kerr-Sheppard, D. A.
cfs qs (P) 1 Jan
Macey, G. qs (AEO) 1 Jan
Mclaren, S. A. qs (N) 1 Jan
Middleton, E.
qwi(T) (N) 1 Jan
Miller, A. D. BSc cfs(c)
qss (N) 1 Jan
Neill, A. BSc cfs qs (P) 1 Jan
Norton, J. R. cfs(n) (N) 1 Jan
Offord, R. J. BCom qwi
qs (P) 1 Jan
Park, K. W. cfs qs (P) 1 Jan
Philpott, C. N. BSc cfs
qs (P) 1 Jan
Rae, D. J. BSc cfs
qs (P) 1 Jan
Reynolds, S. K. P. DFC
cfs qs (P) 1 Jan
Richardson, A. D. (P) 1 Jan
Riddell, G. BSc cfs
qss (P) 1 Jan
Robertson, R. A. D. BSc
qs (P) 1 Jan
Ross, J. W. qs (N) 1 Jan
Shaw, D. M. qwi(AD)
qs (N) 1 Jan
Simmons, I. J. cfs
qs (P) 1 Jan
Smith, F. P. qs (N) 1 Jan
Smith, K. A. BSc qs (N) 1 Jan
Spirit, H. E. BSc
cfs* (P) 1 Jan
Sprague, D. J. qs (N) 1 Jan
Stewart, R. J. snc
qss (N) 1 Jan
Tetlow, M. J. qs (N) 1 Jan
Thorne, G. T. qss (N) 1 Jan
Tomlinson, A. J.
qss (ENG) 1 Jan
Triccas, A. P. qs (N) 1 Jan
Trout, A. J. qss (P) 1 Jan
Turnbull, R. T. cfs (P) 1 Jan
Turner, R. J. cfs(n) snc
qss (N) 1 Jan
Walsh, J. M. BTech
qs (P) 1 Jan
Watson, K. J. BSc
qs (P) 1 Jan
Wilson, S. J. BA cfs(n)
qs (N) 1 Jan
Atkinson, R. J. qwi(AD) (P) 1 July
Birch, P. N. qwi qss (P) 1 July
Birch, R. S. qwi(AD)
qs (P) 1 July

Buchanan, W. D.
cfs (P) 1 July
Carey, R. J. L. BSc qwi
qwi(T) qs (P) 1 July
Clifford, N. LLB cfs
qs (P) 1 July
Cluer, R. J. qss (N) 1 July
Crabb, A. S. G. cfs
qss (P) 1 July
Crawford, J. A. BSc cfs
qss (P) 1 July
Davies, J. H. qs (N) 1 July
Dryburgh, B. A.
qs (AEO) 1 July
Edwards, G. D. qab
cfs(n) qs (N) 1 July
Farmer, A. I. MBE BA
qs (N) 1 July
Fox-Edwards, A.
BSocSc cfs qs (P) 1 July
Garden, S. N. BSc
qs (P) 1 July
Hall, A. N. C. M-M. cfs
qss (P) 1 July
Hillman, G. A. qs (N) 1 July
Hitchcook, J. J.
qwi(AD) (P) 1 July
Hochkins, S. D. qwi
qss (P) 1 July
Jenkins, J. K. qs (P) 1 July
Jochimsen, P. H. C. cfs
qs (P) 1 July
Kingdon, A. A. (ALM) 1 July
Lence, M. S. asq
qss (N) 1 July
Levick, P. asq qss (N) 1 July
Lord, D. P. BSc cfs
qs (P) 1 July
Lunt, C. C. BA qs (P) 1 July
Luxton, P. A. BEng
qs (P) 1 July
Maskall, R. L. cfs qs (P) 1 July
McDonald-Webb, I. D.
cfs qs (P) 1 July
McKay, I. J. BEM (ENG) 1 July
McLean, I. J. qss (P) 1 July
Meadows, N. BSc cfs
qs (P) 1 July
Milne, D. F. BSc cfs
qss (P) 1 July
Neill, F. R. J. qs (P) 1 July
Nielsen, R. E. BA qwi
qs (P) 1 July
Niven, J. G. qs (N) 1 July
Rafferty, M. S. BSc asq
cfs(n) qss (N) 1 July
Reeves, J. W. (AEO) 1 July
Revell, P. R. (ENG) 1 July
Ross, A. J. BSc qss (P) 1 July
Ross, D. McD. tp (P) 1 July

Squadron Leaders

1994—contd

Rousseau, N. A. B.		
(AEO)	1 July	
Ruddock-West, S. C.		
BSc asq qss	(N)	1 July
Scorer, D. G. BSocSc		
cfs(n) qs	(N)	1 July
Sharpe, N. D. qs	(N)	1 July
Spires, B.	(ALM)	1 July
Stockill, G. qwi qs	(P)	1 July
Taylor, P. cfs qs	(P)	1 July
Thompson, C. W. cfs		
qss	(P)	1 July
Toner, A. qs	(N)	1 July
Townsend, S. P. MA cfs		
qs	(P)	1 July
Walker, T. W.	(P)	1 July
Whitehead, M. D.		
BTech qss	(P)	1 July
Whittaker, C. R. cfs		
qss	(P)	1 July
Longstaff, M. C.	(P)	16 Aug

1995

Adams, N. M. cfs		
qs	(P)	1 Jan
Airey, N. D. cfs	(P)	1 Jan
Archer, G. M. BSc tp		
qwi(AD) qss	(P)	1 Jan
Bagnall, R. A.	(AEO)	1 Jan
Ball, M. G. qwi qs	(P)	1 Jan
Basey, P. A. B. qss	(N)	1 Jan
Beet, G. T. W. BSc tp		
qss	(P)	1 Jan
Borland, G. A. qs	(P)	1 Jan
Burn, N. qs	(N)	1 Jan
Byard, J. J. qs	(N)	1 Jan
Collier, P. R. S. BA snc		
qs	(N)	1 Jan
Cookson, N. T. qs	(N)	1 Jan
D'Arcy, Q. N. P. qab		
qs	(N)	1 Jan
Duance, R. C. fc qs	(N)	1 Jan
Eckersley, A. M.		
qss	(P)	1 Jan
Ede, H. snc qss	(N)	1 Jan
Garrett, S. J. BSc		
qs	(N)	1 Jan
Geddes, R. G. BSc	(P)	1 Jan
Groves, A. K. cfs qs	(P)	1 Jan
Harcourt, S. J. R. cfs		
qss	(P)	1 Jan
Hawley, M. D. BSc		
	(N)	1 Jan

Hunt, G. I. qss	(N)	1 Jan
Jeffery, M. A. BSc		
ARCS cfs(n) qs	(N)	1 Jan
Johnston, D. H. BSc		
qab qs	(N)	1 Jan
Last, R. W. BA qwi		
qs	(P)	1 Jan
Lazzari, J. N.	(AEO)	1 Jan
Leviston, A. M. BSc cfs		
qss	(P)	1 Jan
Marshall, L. asq qs	(N)	1 Jan
Middleton, D. J. qs	(P)	1 Jan
Morgan, G. M. BSc asq		
qs	(N)	1 Jan
Morgan, S. H.	(N)	1 Jan
O'Reilly, M. J. BA cfs(n)		
qss	(N)	1 Jan
Sayers, S. R. MA asq		
qs	(N)	1 Jan
Slater, R. C. qs	(N)	1 Jan
Solomon, A. G.		
qs	(AEO)	1 Jan
Sommerville, R. A.		
qs	(P)	1 Jan
Southcott, G. P. asq		
qss	(AEO)	1 Jan
Stainforth, M. A. BSc		
asq snc qss	(N)	1 Jan
Stringer, E. J. BEng qwi		
qs	(P)	1 Jan
Torrance, I. A. cfs		
qs	(P)	1 Jan
Truss, K. P. cfs qs	(P)	1 Jan
Vallance, M. H.		
qs	(ENG)	1 Jan
Wakeman, M. A.		
qwi(AD) qs	(N)	1 Jan
Ward, R. J. BSc cfs		
qs	(P)	1 Jan
Watson, D. C. qwi		
qs	(P)	1 Jan
Wheeler, T. J. cfs		
qs	(P)	1 Jan
White, W. A. qs	(P)	1 Jan
Atha, S. D. BSc cfs		
qs	(P)	1 July
Bland, P. C.	(AEO)	1 July
Bowen, A. P. qwi(AD)		
qs	(N)	1 July
Brecht, M. A. B. BA		
qs	(P)	1 July
Brooks, J. R. qs	(N)	1 July
Brown, J. E. qs	(N)	1 July
Cafferky, P. W. P. qwi		
qs	(P)	1 July
Chambers, P. J. asq	(N)	1 July
Clark, G. BSc qss	(P)	1 July
Coxen, J. BSc cfs		
qs	(P)	1 July
Fitzpatrick, C. qss	(P)	1 July

Fry, D. J. qss	(P)	1 July
Gegg, J. D. J. cfs(n) snc		
ac	(N)	1 July
Graham, M. G. C.		
qs	(P)	1 July
Harrison, G. S. BA		
qss	(N)	1 July
Houlton, J. A. D. cfs		
qss	(P)	1 July
Hughes, W. R. qs (AEO)		1 July
Hulme, L. M.	(N)	1 July
Humphrey, M. H. (AEO)		1 July
Johnston, J. C. M. BSc		
qs	(P)	1 July
Laird, N. W. G. BA		
qs	(P)	1 July
Lea, R. J. BSc cfs	(P)	1 July
Lees, P. D. qs	(P)	1 July
Linstead, A. S. BSc		
qs	(N)	1 July
Mackay, A. J. M. cfs		
qss	(P)	1 July
Martin, P. BA cfs*	(P)	1 July
Munnelly, H. M. qs	(P)	1 July
Pierson, R. M. cfs		
qss	(P)	1 July
Roberts, M. L. qs	(P)	1 July
Seares, M. J. qwi		
qs	(P)	1 July
Shaw, A. J. BEng cfs		
qss	(P)	1 July
Smith, S. L. qs	(P)	1 July
Thomas, K. BSc aqs cfs		
qss	(P)	1 July
Turner, A. M. qs	(P)	1 July
Veitch, C. A. cfs qs	(P)	1 July
Waudby, S. L. cfs		
qs	(P)	1 July
Webb, J. M. L. BSc		
qs	(P)	1 July
Williams, D. I.	(P)	1 July
Wilson, G. K. BSc cfs		
qss	(P)	1 July

1996

Allchorne, R. M. qwi		
qs	(P)	1 Jan
Benson, N. R. BSc cfs		
qwi qss	(P)	1 Jan
Boyland, P. S. AFC BSc		
qs	(P)	1 Jan
Brady, N. H. qs	(P)	1 Jan
Brannan, E. S. qss	(P)	1 Jan
Broome, M. J. BA		
qs	(P)	1 Jan
Brown, G. B. cfs	(P)	1 Jan
Cass, D. N. qs	(P)	1 Jan
Cass, J. M. BA qs	(N)	1 Jan

Squadron Leaders

1996—contd

Chiddention, S. MBE
cfs qss   (P)   1 Jan
Cobb, N. A. qwi
qss   (P)   1 Jan
Comer, P. K. cfs qss (P)   1 Jan
Connolly, B. T. BSc
qss   (N)   1 Jan
Coy, A. BA   (P)   1 Jan
Evans, S. C. cfs qs (P)   1 Jan
Floyd, J. R. MA cfs*
qss   (P)   1 Jan
Fox, P. N.   (P)   1 Jan
Gibson, W. R. BSc
qwi(T) qs   (P)   1 Jan
Green, A. D. BA qs (P)   1 Jan
Grout, M. J. cfs(n) (N)   1 Jan
Gunn, D. J. qs   (N)   1 Jan
Hewson, P. W. BA qs
cfs(n)   (N)   1 Jan
Hill, C. R. qwi qs (P)   1 Jan
Jones, T. W. qss (P)   1 Jan
Knight, M. asq qs (P)   1 Jan
Knowles, D. J. BA cfs
qss   (P)   1 Jan
Marshall, S. BA qwi
qss   (P)   1 Jan
Martin, P. cfs qs (P)   1 Jan
McGuire, K. cfs qss (P)   1 Jan
McMahon, R. M.
qss   (N)   1 Jan
McQuigg, C. J. W. BA
asq   (AEO)   1 Jan
Mitchell, C. T. qss (N)   1 Jan
Monkman, A. BA qwi
qs   (P)   1 Jan
Muskett, A. J. qwi
qs   (P)   1 Jan
Neville, M. C. BSc
qs   (N)   1 Jan
Noel, R. qss   (N)   1 Jan
Norman, I. A. W. qwi
qs   (P)   1 Jan
Physick, M. J. qwi
qss   (P)   1 Jan
Richards, S. I. BSc
qwi(AD) qs   (N)   1 Jan
Richardson, S. A. qwi
qss   (N)   1 Jan
Riches, P. M. snc (N)   1 Jan
Roberts, P. J. asq
qss   (N)   1 Jan
Rose, R. C. cfs   (P)   1 Jan
Smyth, P. J. cfs(n)
qss   (N)   1 Jan

Storey, P. A. BSc
qwi(AD) qs   (N)   1 Jan
Sutcliffe, D. M. cfs (P)   1 Jan
Sutton, M. C. cfs
qss   (P)   1 Jan
Thorogood, A. N. J.
qwi qss   (P)   1 Jan
Trask, L. J. MBE BSc cfs
qs   (P)   1 Jan
Turner, S. C. qwi
qss   (P)   1 Jan
Wesley, C. J. asq cfs(n)
snc qss   (N)   1 Jan
Adlam, R. H. qwi
qss   (P)   1 July
Ager, J. N. qs   (N)   1 July
Appleby, B. K. qss (N)   1 July
Atkins, R. F. BSc asq
qss   (N)   1 July
Bennett, A. A. BSc
qs   (P)   1 July
Benson, N. J. qs (N)   1 July
Bentley, D. A. qwi
qs   (P)   1 July
Blake, S. J. cfs qss (P)   1 July
Bohill, W. P. BSc qwi(T)
qss   (P)   1 July
Bowen, D. K. B. qs (P)   1 July
Broadbent, J. R. BEng
asq qss   (N)   1 July
Byford, A. J. BA qs (P)   1 July
Carr, J. V. BTech
qss   (P)   1 July
Chalmers, I. D. MA cfs
qs   (P)   1 July
Clayton, S. tp qs (P)   1 July
Donovan, C. J. qwi (N)   1 July
Doyle, G. BSc cfs
qs   (P)   1 July
Falvey, M. K. cfs qs (P)   1 July
Gray, A. P. cfs qs (P)   1 July
Head, R. BSc cfs
qss   (P)   1 July
Hogg, J. K. qwi qss (P)   1 July
Hunt, B. D. qwi qss (P)   1 July
Jones, P. A. BTech
qss   (P)   1 July
Jones, R. P. qs   (N)   1 July
Josephy, T. W. cfs (P)   1 July
Legg, D. A. C. qs (P)   1 July
Little, A. H. cfs qss (P)   1 July
Luck, C. J. MBE cfs
qs   (P)   1 July
Newton, R. T. BEng
qs   (P)   1 July
Oddy, R. T. snc   (N)   1 July
Offer, A. C. cfs qwi (P)   1 July
Owers, A. J. BA qwi
qss   (P)   1 July

Pease, A. K. F. BSc cfs
qs   (P)   1 July
Preston, M. MA qwi(T)
qs   (P)   1 July
Scott, C. M. BA qs (P)   1 July
Shankland, D. cfs (P)   1 July
Sinclair, G. A. BSc
qss   (N)   1 July
Smith, S. E. tp qwi
qs   (P)   1 July
Stacey, A. J. AFC (P)   1 July
Stanway, M. F. qss (P)   1 July
Ternouth, M. L. cfs(c)
qss   (N)   1 July
Thrale, T. qs   (N)   1 July
Warren, P. J. BEng cfs
qss   (P)   1 July
Willis, A. S. qss (P)   1 July

1997

Akehurst, R. cfs(n)
qs   (N)   1 Jan
Andrews, M. R. asq
qss   (AEO)   1 Jan
Baker, A. K. AIB qss (P)   1 Jan
Baxter, G. L. qss (N)   1 Jan
Billington, D. P. qwi
qss   (P)   1 Jan
Blockley, M. A.
qs   (AEO)   1 Jan
Boyle, B. qss   (N)   1 Jan
Brailsford, S. qss (N)   1 Jan
Brazier, C. E. J. qwi(T)
qs   (N)   1 Jan
Brooks, J. H. cfs(c)
   (AEO)   1 Jan
Brough, J. H. qss (P)   1 Jan
Cahill, I. G. cfs* qss (P)   1 Jan
Campbell, D. C. cfs
qs   (P)   1 Jan
Constable, D. C. J. snc
qss   (N)   1 Jan
Cooper, D. G. cfs
qss   (P)   1 Jan
Crombie, G. J.
MBE   (P)   1 Jan
Davies, H. B. cfs(n) snc
qss   (N)   1 Jan
De la Cour, G. BSc qwi
qss   (P)   1 Jan
Deas, E. J. cfs(n) (N)   1 Jan
Dixon, J. M. BSc qs (P)   1 Jan
Gillies, S. C. qss (P)   1 Jan
Gray, K. R. BA qss (N)   1 Jan
Harland, M. C. asq
cfs(n)* qss   (N)   1 Jan
Head, J. S. BSc qss (N)   1 Jan
Heames, C. V. J. (P)   1 Jan

Squadron Leaders

1997—contd

Hedley, B. H. qwi		
qss	(P)	1 Jan
Herod, J. R. cfs qss	(P)	1 Jan
Huffington, M. C. BSc		
qs	(N)	1 Jan
Hughes, K. L. W.		
qs	(AEO)	1 Jan
Hunter, C. T. qss	(P)	1 Jan
Kemsley, M. H. M. MBE		
BSc qs	(N)	1 Jan
Kennedy, C. J. cfs	(P)	1 Jan
Laver, M. D. M. BA cfs		
qs	(P)	1 Jan
Lawson, J. BSc qs	(N)	1 Jan
Lloyd, S. J. BA asq		
qss	(N)	1 Jan
Lofts, P. D. cfs qss	(P)	1 Jan
Lord, D. K. qs	(AEO)	1 Jan
McMillen, P. T.		
qss	(AEO)	1 Jan
Notman, S. R. qs	(N)	1 Jan
Prescott, J. C. qwi(AD)		
qs	(N)	1 Jan
Reid, J. P. Q. qs	(ENG)	1 Jan
Sachedina, K. A. BSc		
cfs qs	(P)	1 Jan
Smart, M. A. qs	(N)	1 Jan
Stephens, M. C. BSc		
qwi(AD) qss	(P)	1 Jan
Stewart, D. J. CertEd		
qss	(ALM)	1 Jan
Stewart, N. R.	(P)	1 Jan
Thomson, A. J.	(AEO)	1 Jan
Toft, M. C. qss	(N)	1 Jan
Traynor, E. J. qss	(AEO)	1 Jan
Turnbull, D. T. BSc cfs		
qs	(P)	1 Jan
Walters, A. J. C. BSc		
qs	(P)	1 Jan
Wells, G. R. qss	(N)	1 Jan
Wills, C. J. qwi(AD)		
qss	(N)	1 Jan
Young, R. J. qss	(ENG)	1 Jan
Allton, M. C. BSc		
qss	(P)	1 July
Arden, J. P. qss	(N)	1 July
Barley, M. P. BA qwi(T)		
qss	(N)	1 July
Baxter, I. P. qs	(N)	1 July
Beardmore, M. J.		
cfs	(P)	1 July
Below, T. D. Q. BSc tp		
qss	(P)	1 July
Best, P. K. cfs qss	(P)	1 July
Blair, R. C. qwi qs	(P)	1 July

Brown, M. O. cfs		
qss	(P)	1 July
Brownlow, S. M.		
qss	(P)	1 July
Burr, J. BSc cfs qss	(P)	1 July
Calder, J. M. BSc		
qss	(N)	1 July
Clark, G. qss	(N)	1 July
Cochrane, A. W.		
qwi(AD) qs	(N)	1 July
Cole, M. J. qs	(ALM)	1 July
Crosby, D. M. M.	(P)	1 July
Dalley, G. P. BA qss	(P)	1 July
Dyson, R. K. cfs qs	(P)	1 July
Evans, P. MA BA qwi(T)		
qss	(P)	1 July
Frost, A. S. BSc qss	(N)	1 July
Goatham, J. M. qss	(P)	1 July
Hancock, J. P. qss	(N)	1 July
Hardy-Gillings, B.		
qss	(N)	1 July
Hawkins, R. L.	(N)	1 July
Herbert, G. J. BSc		
qss	(P)	1 July
Hill, A. K. cfs qss	(P)	1 July
Hill, A. P. qwi qs	(P)	1 July
Hindmarsh, S. qss	(N)	1 July
Huckstep, C. R. MA		
FRGS tp qs	(P)	1 July
Hudson, M. J. cfs		
qss	(P)	1 July
Huggett, J. P.	(N)	1 July
Lawrence, R. H. cfs		
qss	(P)	1 July
Lee, N. P. D. BSc qs	(P)	1 July
Lenihan, P. J. D. BSc		
qwi(T) qs	(N)	1 July
Leonczek, M. R. BSc tp		
cfs	(P)	1 July
MacCormack, R. M. J.		
qwi qs	(P)	1 July
MacKenzie, K. J.	(P)	1 July
Norton, C. J. R. BSc qwi		
qs	(P)	1 July
O'Dell, P. M. H. qss	(P)	1 July
Parker, M. R. qss	(N)	1 July
Peters, J. G. BSc		
qss	(P)	1 July
Ramsden, C. P. BSc		
qss	(P)	1 July
Read, S. J. qss	(N)	1 July
Royce, M. J. qwi		
qss	(P)	1 July
Rust, T. J. cfs qss	(P)	1 July
Sampson, M. E. qwi		
qss	(P)	1 July
Simpson, T. D. cfs		
qss	(P)	1 July
Snowden, M. cfs	(P)	1 July

Storer, J. S. cfs(n)*		
qss	(N)	1 July
Swindlehurst, W. (AEO)		1 July
Waterfall, G. M. qwi		
qss1	(P)	1 July
Williams, C. D. BSc tp		
cfs qss	(P)	1 July
Wilson, W. J. qs	(P)	1 July

1998

Adams, R. M. asq		
qss	(N)	1 Jan
Andrew, D. R. qss	(N)	1 Jan
Arathoon, W. J. qss	(P)	1 Jan
Armstrong, D. R. qwi		
qss	(P)	1 Jan
Baalam, A. W. L. BSc		
qss	(P)	1 Jan
Bailey, R. C. cfs qss	(P)	1 Jan
Barker, R.	(N)	1 Jan
Barr, N. J. qss	(N)	1 Jan
Beach, P. J. BSc		
qwi(AD) qs	(N)	1 Jan
Beardmore, S. M.		
qwi(T) qss1	(N)	1 Jan
Bell, P. A. BSc qss	(P)	1 Jan
Bennington, T. BSc cfs		
qss	(P)	1 Jan
Bottomley, J. C. BSc		
qab cfs	(P)	1 Jan
Bowen, J. B. BSc cfs		
qss	(P)	1 Jan
Brown, A. D. qwi(AD)		
qss	(P)	1 Jan
Brown, M. F. cfs		
qss	(P)	1 Jan
Bruce, R. P. BEng		
qss	(P)	1 Jan
Bullement, T. J. BSc		
qss	(P)	1 Jan
Burch, S. C. B. cfs		
qss	(P)	1 Jan
Calderwood, L. D. cfs		
qss	(P)	1 Jan
Cannard, M. W. qss	(N)	1 Jan
Chaskin, S. R. qss	(N)	1 Jan
Clark, R. J. S. G. MBE		
BA cfs	(P)	1 Jan
Cobb, M. R. BSc		
qwi(AD) qss	(P)	1 Jan
Conway, J. B. qss	(N)	1 Jan
Cooper, D. J. E. BEng		
qs	(N)	1 Jan
Craib, J. W. qss	(AEO)	1 Jan
Cryer, N. G. qss	(N)	1 Jan
Cubin, A. MBE		
qss1	(P)	1 Jan
Da'Silva, C. D. qss	(N)	1 Jan

Squadron Leaders

1998—contd

Dalton, R. A. BSc		
qss	(P)	1 Jan
Davis, M. R.	(AEO)	1 Jan
Elliott, E. A. C. MA	(P)	1 Jan
Elliott, H. J. qss	(P)	1 Jan
Fisher, L. qwi qss	(N)	1 Jan
Foote, D. A. cfs qss	(P)	1 Jan
Foote, S. J. BSc cfs		
qss	(P)	1 Jan
Forbes, R. W.	(AEO)	1 Jan
Ford, C. J.	(P)	1 Jan
Fowler, K. E. BSc asq		
qab qss	(N)	1 Jan
Gent, A. J. qwi qss	(P)	1 Jan
Gray, J. J. cfs	(P)	1 Jan
Griffiths, H. M. BSc		
qss	(N)	1 Jan
Grime, J. R. A. qss	(P)	1 Jan
Harrison, P. K. qwi	(P)	1 Jan
Hastings, C. N. BSc		
qs	(N)	1 Jan
Hayler, S. D. BSc cfs*		
qss	(P)	1 Jan
Hinchcliffe, R. A. MBA		
BSc qss	(N)	1 Jan
Jackson, B. G. BSc		
qss	(P)	1 Jan
James, R. S. qss	(N)	1 Jan
James, W. A. W. cfs		
qs	(P)	1 Jan
Jones, C. cfs(n)*	(N)	1 Jan
Jones, C. cfs(n)*		
qss	(N)	1 Jan
Lee, D. J. F. BSc cfs		
qss	(P)	1 Jan
Lines, P. J. qwi qss	(P)	1 Jan
Lovell, A. B. cfs qs	(P)	1 Jan
Lovell, R. H. BA	(P)	1 Jan
Lumb, D. M. V. qwi(T)		
qs	(N)	1 Jan
MacFarlane, I. J.		
qss	(P)	1 Jan
Marson, A. C. snc		
qss	(N)	1 Jan
Mason, D. BSc qwi(AD)		
qss	(P)	1 Jan
Mason, G. qwi qss	(P)	1 Jan
Mavor, R. I. D. qss	(P)	1 Jan
Mitchell, S. A. cfs		
qss	(P)	1 Jan
Naismith, A. cfs		
qss	(P)	1 Jan
Padmore, T. C. qss	(N)	1 Jan
Perkins, C. T. qss (ALM)		1 Jan

Pilling, J. A. BSc qwi		
qss	(P)	1 Jan
Pinner, A. C. BSc qwi		
qss	(P)	1 Jan
Richardson, I. BSc		
qss	(N)	1 Jan
Robertson, D. C. BSc		
qss	(P)	1 Jan
Robson, J. cfs	(P)	1 Jan
Ross, R. A. BSc qss	(P)	1 Jan
Saunders, M. A. qwi(T)		
qss	(P)	1 Jan
Smith, A. G. qss	(N)	1 Jan
Steel, A. qss	(AEO)	1 Jan
Taylor, P. J. BSc qss	(N)	1 Jan
Thomas, D. G. BSc		
qs	(N)	1 Jan
Thomas, G. E. MBE		
FRIN cfs(n)	(N)	1 Jan
Torrance, A. I. MacA.		
qss	(N)	1 Jan
Trapp, D. G. qss	(N)	1 Jan
Uren, J. C. qss	(N)	1 Jan
Vagg, M. J. qss	(P)	1 Jan
Vivian, W. M. cfs		
qss	(P)	1 Jan
Waddington, D. J.		
qwi(T) qss	(P)	1 Jan
Walters-Morgan, R.		
qwi(AD) qs	(N)	1 Jan
Ward, P. M. BSc cfs		
qss	(P)	1 Jan
Webber, W. H. J. BSc		
qss	(P)	1 Jan
Wesley, R. J. qss	(N)	1 Jan
White, D. K. BSc		
qss	(P)	1 Jan
Wilson, J. M. BSc		
qss	(P)	1 Jan
Barnfield, S. K. BSc		
qwi(T) qss	(N)	1 July
Barrett, T. A. qwi		
qss	(P)	1 July
Bartlett, P. J. BEng		
qss	(P)	1 July
Boulden, A.	(P)	1 July
Boyle, S. J. BSc qss	(N)	1 July
Brass, A. J. BEng cfs		
qss	(P)	1 July
Bruce, G. BSc asq		
qss	(N)	1 July
Buckingham, S. C. BA		
qss	(P)	1 July
Carter, D. E. MBE	(P)	1 July
Coope, A. J. BEng cfs		
qss	(P)	1 July
Costello, J. M. BSc	(P)	1 July
Counter, G. C. qss	(N)	1 July
Cowie, A. J. BA qss	(N)	1 July

Craig, A. W. D. BSc		
qss	(P)	1 July
Cross, B. J. qss	(P)	1 July
Cruickshank, W. A. qwi		
qss	(P)	1 July
Dolding, A. E. cfs		
qss	(P)	1 July
Dunn, L. G. BSc qss	(P)	1 July
Evans, J. D. cfs(c)	(N)	1 July
Ferrier, J. A. qss	(N)	1 July
Foster, P. cfs(n) qss	(N)	1 July
Francis, I. R. BSc		
qss	(N)	1 July
Gair, G. C. qss	(P)	1 July
Gallie, D. W. qss	(P)	1 July
Girdwood, K. R. H. BSc		
cfs qss	(P)	1 July
Hargreaves, I. J.		
qwi	(P)	1 July
Harrison, J. J. qs	(P)	1 July
Hay, N. J. qwi(T)	(N)	1 July
Hine, A. C. MA qwi(T)		
qss	(P)	1 July
Hodgson, D. C. qwi		
qss	(P)	1 July
Hoole, P. qss	(AEO)	1 July
Hornby, R. cfs(n)		
qss	(N)	1 July
Jeffrey, A. K. qwi(T)		
qss	(N)	1 July
Kellett, A. J. C. BSc cfs		
qss	(P)	1 July
Kennett, P. D. qwi(T)		
qss	(N)	1 July
Leach, S. C. BSc cfs		
qss	(P)	1 July
Lewis, K. A. BEng qwi		
qss	(P)	1 July
Maunder, C. N. J. BEng		
qwi(T) qss	(P)	1 July
McCarthy, K. R. BSc cfs		
qss	(P)	1 July
McFarlane, A. J. cfs(n)		
qss	(N)	1 July
Moran, E. M. BSc		
qss	(N)	1 July
Neighbour, J. D. E.	(P)	1 July
Peace, C. M. qss	(N)	1 July
Postlethwaite, D. BEd		
cfs(n) qss	(N)	1 July
Pottle, H. W. AFC*	(P)	1 July
Raffles, I.	(P)	1 July
Rycroft, A. S. BSc(Eng)		
qss	(P)	1 July
Savage, S.	(N)	1 July
Shell, S. J. qcc	(P)	1 July
Somerville, A. D. cfs		
qss	(P)	1 July
Sullivan, J. M. qwi		
qss	(P)	1 July

Squadron Leaders

1998—contd

Tank, J. S. R. BSc
qss   (N)   1 July
Wilcock, N. J. BSc
cfs   (P)   1 July
Wistow, M. R. cfs(n)*
qss   (N)   1 July
Woods, T. J. A. cfs
qss   (P)   1 July
Youngman, M. A. cfs(n)
qss   (N)   1 July

Flight Lieutenants

1965

Bradford, D. A. BA
qss*   (N)   30 Oct

1966

Brocklebank, R. A.
cfs(n) qss   (N)   11 Nov

1967

Barradell, D. J. snc
qss*   (N)   12 July

1968

Barnes, F. O. qss   (N)   6 Jan
Marks, P. J. snc qss   (N)   22 Aug
Lane, P. D.   (P)   22 Sept
Leigh, R. G.   (P)   14 Dec

1969

Holmes, R. G. cfs   (P)   6 Mar
Southwould, B. W. BA
snc qss   (N)   29 May
Furr, R. D.   (P)   1 July
Williamson, J.   (N)   28 Aug
Snook, P. snc   (N)   12 Nov
Burnett, D. J.
qss*   (AEO)   22 Nov
Richards, K. D. snc   (N)   22 Nov
Clark, G.   (N)   19 Dec

1970

Brown, S. K. cfs
qss   (P)   15 Apr
Pedley, M. cfs(n)* snc
qss   (N)   5 Aug
Enston, J. N. qss   (P)   2 Oct
Bishop, D. E.   (P)   4 Nov

1971

Dean, T. R. L. BSc
qss   (P)   6 July
Canning, J. A. snc   (N)   2 Aug
Lloyd, J. D. qss   (P)   2 Aug

Payne, A. V. qss   (N)   1 Oct
Waite, G. W. snc   (N)   6 Oct
D'Aubyn, J. A. BSc cfs
qss   (P)   15 Oct
Branthwaite, P. A.   (P)   6 Nov
Knight, R. M. qss   (P)   6 Nov

1972

Chapman, A. D.
snc   (N)   8 Mar
Miller, G. R. cfs(n) snc
qss   (N)   8 Mar
Hawkins, P. J.   (N)   23 Mar
Hammond, S. P. cfs fc
qss   (P)   28 Apr
Jennings, P. T. snc
qss   (N)   28 Apr
Funnell-Bailey, C. C.
cfs   (P)   4 May
Goulding, N. B.   (P)   4 May
Harvey, S. R. cfs   (P)   4 May
Timbers, H. A.   (N)   4 May
Wilkinson, J. N.   (P)   4 May
Pitts, A. cfs qss   (P)   2 June
Hamilton, C. I. qss   (N)   13 July
Gibbons, G. R. qss   (P)   17 Aug
Allen, R. R.   (N)   7 Sept
Glyde, P. L. cfs   (P)   23 Sept
Haggar, N. A. T.   (P)   23 Sept
Sharpe, G. C. BA snc
qss   (N)   23 Sept
Barr, A.   (P)   30 Sept
McCormick, D. G. BSc
MInstP qss   (N)   16 Oct
Davies, R. J. cfs   (P)   28 Oct

1973

Skene, A. J. cfs   (P)   7 Jan
Taylor, P. F. cfs(n)
snc   (N)   7 Jan
Hamlyn, G. M. snc
qss   (N)   15 Mar
Milburn, R. L. BSc   (P)   15 Apr
Grosvenor, L.   (P)   18 May
Edmonds, A. J. snc   (N)   24 May
Goff, D. K. qss   (N)   10 July
Miller, A. S. cfs(c)
qss   (P)   31 July
Dyche, M. W. MA qss
i   (N)   1 Aug
Tredray, N. P. K.   (N)   23 Aug
Bowron, C. F. cfs(n)   (N)   29 Sept
Smyth, P. M. BSc
cfs   (P)   3 Oct
Hughes, A. BSc cfs   (P)   15 Oct
Turbitt, D. BSc cfs   (P)   15 Oct

Flight Lieutenants

1973—contd

Skelton, A. M.	(P)	20 Oct
Hockin, J. W.	(P)	28 Oct
Marshall, D. J. qss	(N)	3 Nov
Cherry, D. F. asq		
snc	(N)	7 Dec
Wheeler, O. J. cfs(n)		
snc	(N)	7 Dec
Rees, G. D. BSc qss	(P)	15 Dec
Wells, T. J. G. BSc cfs		
qss	(P)	15 Dec
Cooper, D. BSc snc		
qss	(N)	30 Dec

1974

Howard, H. J.	(N)	7 Jan
Gulliver, J. cfs(n) snc		
qss	(N)	12 Jan
Slack, A. D.	(N)	12 Jan
Izatt, G. N. AIB cfs	(P)	16 Feb
Priest, J. S. D. snc	(N)	16 Feb
Stilwell, N. J.	(P)	16 Feb
Ward, A. M. qss	(P)	16 Feb
Crick, S. E. cfs(n) snc		
qss	(N)	10 Mar
Todd, P. A.	(N)	20 Mar
Pitchforth, N. A. BSc cfs		
qss	(P)	15 Apr
Horler, D. C. cfs(n)	(N)	16 Apr
Hickin, D. J. T. BSc		
qss	(P)	14 May
Spink, P. L. cfs	(P)	25 May
Verner, A. D. cfs(n) snc		
qss	(N)	29 May
Evans, R. A.	(P)	29 June
Smyth, P. J. snc	(N)	10 July
Whatmore, A. G.	(N)	10 July
Bellingall, J. E.	(P)	25 Oct
Grose, L. A. cfs	(P)	31 Oct
Brandie, W. J. cfs	(P)	30 Nov
Brammer, C. M. BSc		
qss	(N)	2 Dec
Craig, R. E.	(P)	29 Dec

1975

Kennedy, M. H. snc		
qss	(N)	4 Jan
Hobkirk, B. D.	(P)	8 Feb
Hamilton, S. P. cfs	(P)	25 Feb
Barnes, D. A.	(N)	15 Mar

Muir, I. BSc cfs(n) snc		
qss	(N)	13 Apr
Fowler, S. M. cfs(n)		
qss	(N)	28 May

1976

Harris, D. J. cfs	(P)	17 Jan
Emptage, J. A. BSc		
cfs	(P)	19 Jan
Puncher, A. W.	(N)	10 Mar
Smith, A. J. qss i	(P)	15 Mar
Edwards, D.	(P)	16 Mar
Kirkup, A. P. J.	(P)	16 Mar
Bonner, P. B. BSc		
MRAeS asq qss	(N)	15 Apr
Jackson, P. B. BA		
qss	(N)	6 July
Lingard, D. I. snc	(N)	7 July
Bendall, D. H.	(P)	1 Oct
Chatterton, M. J.		
BSc	(P)	15 Oct
Wood, M. A. cfs ac		
snc(n)	(N)	29 Oct

1977

Ayliffe, A. C. MBE BA		
asq cfs(n) snc		
qss	(N)	19 Jan
Blackie, G. C. AFC cfs		
qss	(P)	22 Jan
Russell, B. L. BTech cfs		
qss	(P)	7 Feb
McNichol, P. qss	(N)	19 Feb
Thomas, A. S.	(N)	16 Mar
Hinton, B. K. MA cfs(n)		
snc qss	(N)	15 Apr
Palmer, P. E.	(P)	11 May
Wensley, C. C. cfs(n)		
snc	(N)	9 June
Walters, P. S. qss	(N)	12 June
Hawker, J. BSc qss	(P)	3 July
Wilson, G. C. qss	(P)	13 July
Rooney, J. BSc cfs		
qss	(P)	7 Aug
Easthope, N. C. V.		
cfs	(P)	10 Aug
Needham, E. G. cfs(n)		
qss	(N)	10 Aug
Hendy, J. W. MIPD		
cfs(n) snc qss	(N)	6 Oct
Kidson, M. qss	(N)	6 Oct
Watkins, B. J. BSc cfs		
qss	(P)	15 Oct
Abbot, A. C. cfs	(P)	4 Nov
Ireland, B. J. snc		
qss	(N)	4 Nov

Looseley, M. cfs(n)	(N)	4 Nov
Partridge, S. M. qss	(P)	1 Dec

1978

Elliott, S. W.	(ENG)	8 Jan
Saunders, I. R. cfs		
qss	(P)	27 Jan
Hildred, K. BSc	(P)	7 Feb
Crymble, M. J.	(P)	24 Feb
Huskie, A. J.	(P)	24 Feb
Dewhurst, A. R.		
BSc	(N)	2 Apr
Benke, R. N. BSc cfs		
qss	(P)	11 Apr
Dixon, A. BSc	(N)	15 Apr
Goodman, R. N.		
BSc	(P)	15 Apr
Hext, A. BA qss	(N)	15 Apr
Burley, G. cfs(n)		
snc	(N)	19 Apr
Atkins, S. R. BSc asq		
qss	(P)	6 June
Clarke, D. J. BA asq		
qss	(N)	3 July
Best, J. L. snc	(N)	18 July
Young, G. L.	(P)	17 Aug
Rooke, S. G.	(N)	15 Sept
Warmington, N. B. BSc		
cfs qss	(P)	19 Sept
Robertson, I. W.		
BSc	(P)	15 Oct
Warren, M. D. A.		
qss	(N)	22 Nov
Wrigley, C. M. BSc(Eng)		
ACGI asq qss	(N)	6 Dec
Smith, G. cfs	(P)	7 Dec

1979

Evans, H. F. J. MBE PhD		
BA qss	(P)	5 Jan
Strevens, N. C.	(P)	5 Jan
Hale, M. D. BSc cfs		
qss	(P)	15 Jan
Jones, A. G. qss	(AEO)	27 Jan
Dyer, P. J. BSc	(P)	15 Apr
Sanderson, R. V. BSc		
qss	(N)	17 Apr
Watson, C. S. H. asq		
snc	(N)	16 May
Rechten, I. O. H.		
cfs*	(P)	23 June
Collins, N. D.	(P)	24 July
Gregory, S. StJ.	(N)	24 July
Harrod, V. W. BA asq		
qss	(N)	6 Aug
Astbury, A. J. qss	(N)	21 Sept

Flight Lieutenants

1979—contd

Emery, S. J.	(N)	16 Nov
Taylor, G. L. cfs	(P)	18 Nov
Frostick, A. T. BA		
qss	(N)	30 Nov

1980

James, T. M. qss (AEO)		5 Jan
Brindley, R. A. qss	(N)	8 Feb
Thorpe, A. A. MMar		
qss	(N)	2 Mar
Kelly, P. J. BSc cfs	(P)	14 Apr
Counter, M. J. BSc		
qss	(P)	15 Apr
Jones, P. C. BA cfs	(P)	15 Apr
Kilgour, J. A. BSc cfs		
qss	(P)	15 Apr
Ferrol, W. A. cfs	(P)	4 May
Creighton, W. H.		
cfs(c)	(ALM)	11 May
Plews, J. G. BA asq		
	(AEO)	11 May
Jones, J. M. G. BSc	(P)	12 May
Armstrong, G. R. BSc		
cfs	(P)	25 May
Bull, D. I BSc qss	(P)	2 June
Taylor, D. A. cfs(n)	(N)	21 June
Bradshaw, P. cfs		
qss	(P)	30 July
Hodgson, S. A.	(P)	31 July
Hornby, L. cfs	(P)	23 Aug
Knowles, R. T. qss	(P)	27 Aug
Pollock, N. D. BSc		
qss	(P)	15 Oct
Coombs, D. C. BSc		
qss	(N)	12 Nov
Finnimore, D. T. cfs	(P)	22 Nov
Whinton, A. J. cfs		
qss	(P)	22 Nov
Somers-Cocks, R. V. BA		
cfs(n) qss	(N)	23 Dec

1981

Howell, D. W. BSc asq		
qss	(N)	8 Jan
Bellis, D. E.	(ALM)	11 Jan
Burrows, P. G.	(N)	17 Jan
Robinson, N. S. BA		
	(AEO)	22 Feb
Quick, P. E.	(P)	1 Mar

Powell, M. BEng		
qss	(P)	28 Mar
Poolman, J. C. BSc asq		
qss	(P)	15 Apr
Scott, D. N. BSc cfs	(P)	15 Apr
Chisholm, R. G. BSc		
asq qss	(N)	12 May
Davies, J. qss	(AEO)	17 May
Jillett, M. S.	(P)	20 May
Chelu, R.	(N)	12 July
Chamberlain, S. J.		
cfs(n)	(N)	1 Oct
Fryer, C. G.	(N)	7 Oct
Castle, M. J. D. BSc cfs		
qss	(P)	15 Oct
Hamlin, D. P. A. BA	(P)	15 Oct
Tunnard, J. J. BSc asq		
qss	(N)	15 Oct
White, R. D. R. BSc		
asq	(N)	26 Oct
Astle, P. W. cfs qss	(P)	1 Nov
Russell, S. F.	(P)	13 Nov
Spratt, A. B. BSc		
asq	(N)	17 Nov
Williams, S. C. qss	(N)	13 Dec

1982

Coxon, K. A. cfs		
qss	(P)	5 Feb
McKernan, P. R. qss	(N)	5 Feb
Petherick, S. T. cfs		
qss	(P)	5 Feb
Johnson, P. A. BSc		
qss	(P)	9 Feb
Carr, P. G. BSc cfs		
qss	(P)	15 Apr
Raymond, M. I.		
BSc	(P)	15 Apr
Dobson, P. S. BSc		
qss	(P)	17 Apr
Davidson, I. cfs	(P)	28 Apr
Aston, M. R. asq		
qss	(AEO)	1 May
Hannam, G. A. BSc		
qss	(N)	17 May
Mills, A. M.	(AEO)	17 May
Davis, H. D.	(N)	9 June
Hyde, K.	(AEO)	28 June
Charlton, G. R. cfs		
qss	(P)	3 July
Challis, P. W. cfs(n)		
qss	(N)	9 July
Batin, M. V. BSc		
qss	(N)	18 July
Jupe, D. B. cfs	(P)	20 July
Morrison, A. F. BSc		
cfs	(P)	9 Aug
Morton, I. R.	(ENG)	14 Aug

Maynard, J. C. BA		
qss	(P)	15 Oct
Paul, H. A. BSc asq		
qss	(N)	15 Oct
Brook, K. H. cfs(n)		
qss	(N)	17 Oct
Binsted, P. D. qss	(P)	21 Oct
Lowndes, R. L. BSc asq		
qss	(N)	8 Nov
Innes, J. E. qss	(ENG)	19 Nov
Dean, C. P.	(N)	2 Dec
Ellis, R. A. cfs	(P)	2 Dec

1983

Taylor, G. qss	(N)	14 Jan
Leddra, I. A.	(ENG)	5 Feb
Avent, S. D. qss	(N)	11 Feb
Wyatt, S. J. cfs	(P)	11 Feb
Busk, D. G.	(AEO)	13 Mar
Neilson, B. J. T. cfs(n)		
qss	(N)	25 Mar
Royle, A. P. BEng		
qss	(P)	4 Apr
Baker, P. BA tp	(P)	15 Apr
McCredie, K. I. BSc	(P)	15 Apr
Weightman, G. R. cfs		
qss	(P)	7 May
Brown, C. V. BSc		
cfs	(P)	6 June
Collins, T. J. qss	(P)	12 June
Morris, G. D. qss	(N)	16 June
McNamara, P. A. M. cfs		
qss	(P)	28 June
Crouchman, M. W. AFC		
cfs	(P)	5 July
Holmes, J. A. M.		
cfs(n)	(N)	5 July
Thirkell, P. A.	(N)	2 Aug
Day, M. qss	(AEO)	14 Aug
Irvine, T. G.	(N)	15 Sept
Andrews, M. T. BSc		
cfs	(P)	15 Oct
Bowell, S. J. P. MBA		
BSc qss	(P)	15 Oct
Colquhoun, W. M. BA		
tp cfs	(P)	15 Oct
Fielding, S. BSc tp	(P)	15 Oct
Walker, S. T. MBE BSc		
asq cfs(n) qss	(N)	15 Oct
Whitworth, P. D. BSc		
cfs qss	(P)	15 Oct
Wright, I. M. BSc i		
qss	(N)	15 Oct
Moseley, N. G. cfs(n)		
snc qss	(N)	11 Nov
Wilson, C. qwi(T)	(N)	11 Nov
Payne, R. A. BA qss	(P)	15 Nov

Flight Lieutenants

1983—contd

Sutton, R. C. cfs(n)
qss   (N) 26 Nov
Masters, M. C. H. BA cfs
qss   (P) 26 Dec
Purse, J. M. BSc cfs (P) 26 Dec
Thomson, G. C. BSc
qwi qss   (P) 26 Dec

1984

Burgon, B. E. A.
qss   (N) 20 Jan
Jenkins, C. D. BSc (N) 7 Feb
Etches, R. A. W. (P) 29 Feb
Milnes, P. R. cfs qss (P) 11 Mar
Donnelly, J. AFM*
cfs(c)   (ALM) 19 Mar
Phillips, B. K. qss (N) 20 Mar
Sully, D. S. BEng asq
qss   (N) 4 Apr
Wilson, P. R. BSc
AMRAeS qss   (P) 4 Apr
Allen, D. W. BSc(Eng)
asq qss   (N) 15 Apr
Biddle, D. R. BSc(Eng)
asq cfs(n) qss (N) 15 Apr
Hamilton, P. D. BMet
cfs qss   (P) 15 Apr
Jones, M. C. BSc (P) 15 Apr
Kenrick, W. R. BSc cfs
qss   (P) 15 Apr
Kettles, A. W. BSc cfs
qss   (P) 15 Apr
Turnbull, K. BSc
qss   (P) 15 Apr
Williams, J. M. BA (P) 15 Apr
Vickers, M. E.
qss   (ENG) 26 Apr
Gear, A. C. J. (P) 29 Apr
Simmons, A. J. qss (N) 2 May
Boundy, P. J. BSc cfs
qss   (P) 13 May
Meikleham, F. G.
cfs   (P) 18 June
Macintyre, R. A. BSc
qwi(AD)   (P) 26 June
Marston, I. C. BSc
cfs   (P) 26 June
James, K. G. BSc
qss   (N) 27 June
Walsh, N. R. BSc (P) 27 June
Watts, R. A. BSc cfs
qss   (P) 27 June

Bennett, K. N.
qss   (AEO) 1 July
McCrea, J. D. cfs (P) 11 July
Rowley, A. E. asq
qss   (N) 11 July
Starr, C. J. qss (P) 20 July
Moxon, N. P. cfs
qss   (P) 22 Aug
Anderson, D. C. E. A.
BSc   (N) 15 Oct
Blood, D. M. W. BSc
cfs   (P) 15 Oct
Brennan, S. D. F. BA
qss   (P) 15 Oct
Davies, N. A. BSc
qss   (P) 15 Oct
Fisk, M. P. BSc (P) 15 Oct
Harris, K. BA qss (N) 15 Oct
Henderson, H. BSc
qss   (P) 15 Oct
Leach, W. T. BSc cfs
qss   (P) 15 Oct
Longhurst, D. N.
BSc   (P) 15 Oct
Macdonald, J. B. BTech
tp qwi qss   (P) 15 Oct
Nightingale, A. L.
BSc(Eng) cfs qss (P) 15 Oct
Parry, G. W. H. BSc
qss   (P) 15 Oct
Skinner, A. W. M. BSc
asq qss   (N) 15 Oct
Baverstock, M. J.
BEd   (P) 13 Nov
Bausor, N. T. (P) 17 Nov
Higginbottom, R. P.
cfs(n) qss   (N) 17 Nov
Moore, K. E. BSc asq
qss   (N) 17 Nov
Newton, D. J. (N) 17 Nov
Weir, A. W. qss (N) 17 Nov
Mason, J. P. qss (N) 20 Nov
Thorne, D. E. qss (AEO) 26 Nov
Hughes, R. P. BSc asq
qss   (N) 19 Dec
Bird, J. C. cfs qss (P) 28 Dec

1985

Jackson, R. (P) 1 Jan
Hill, G. J. BSc qss (P) 11 Mar
Carter, R. W. asq cfs(n)
qss   (N) 13 Mar
Cunningham, J. cfs(n)
qss   (N) 6 Apr
Charnley, N. S. BSc qwi
qss   (P) 15 Apr
Gordon, A. G. BA
qss   (P) 15 Apr

Margetts, P. R. BSc cfs
qss   (P) 15 Apr
Munro, C. A. BSc(Eng)
qss   (P) 15 Apr
Simpson, R. A. C. BSc
cfs qss   (P) 15 Apr
Wood, M. A. BTech (P) 15 Apr
Ayton, C. H. (N) 18 Apr
Thompson, S. G. A. (P) 1 May
Mellor, S. G. BSc asq
cfs(n) qss   (N) 11 June
Moule, J. R. qss (P) 13 June
Johnson, D. A. (N) 15 June
Pring, R. M. (AEO) 1 July
Taylor, M. A. qss (P) 19 July
Haskins, S. W. qss (P) 31 July
Read, W. R. qss (P) 31 July
Robinson, C. P. qss (N) 31 July
Thornhill, A. qss (P) 31 July
Firmin, P. A. BSc
qss   (N) 5 Aug
Underwood, S. C.
cfs   (P) 28 Aug
Roberts, C. T. (AEO) 8 Sept
Warren, J. D. tp qss (P) 8 Sept
Humphreys, P. J. (P) 26 Sept
Harding, M. S. asq
cfs(n) qss   (N) 27 Sept
Cannon, G. J. BSc cfs
qss   (P) 15 Oct
Harwell, G. G. M. BSc
asq qss   (P) 15 Oct
Howard-Vyse, C. A. BSc
qss   (N) 15 Oct
Lancaster, D. E.
BSc   (P) 15 Oct
Boyer, K. qss (P) 24 Oct
Ratcliffe, D. cfs qss (P) 24 Oct
Gibby, R. M. BSc cfs(n)
qss   (N) 27 Oct
Francey, M. D. BSc (P) 7 Nov
Cookson, E. W. qss (N) 22 Nov
Dixon, A. J. cfs (P) 22 Nov
Greer, A. S. qss (N) 22 Nov
Hesketh, J. I. (N) 22 Nov
Palastanga, P. R. cfs(n)
qss   (N) 22 Nov
Wells, R. P. D. cfs(n)
qss   (N) 8 Dec
Johnson, A. R. A. BSc
cfs qss   (P) 19 Dec
Nicholson, P. D. BSc
qss   (N) 19 Dec
Ridley, C. R. A. BSc asq
qss   (N) 19 Dec
Robinson, I. G. BA (N) 19 Dec
Smerdon, G. R. B.
BSc   (P) 19 Dec

Flight Lieutenants

1985—contd

Stewart, D. E. BSc
cfs   (P) 19 Dec

1986

Gamble, N.   (N) 3 Jan
Harrison, D. M. qss (N) 3 Jan
Hawkins, P.   (N) 3 Jan
Pillai, S. N. BSc qss (P) 15 Jan
Pickard, A. C. BA
qss   (P) 31 Jan
Stockton, I. D. BSc
qss   (N) 5 Feb
Brennan, B. qss   (N) 13 Feb
Stevens, V. A. cfs(n)
qss   (N) 14 Feb
Williams, W. qss   (N) 14 Feb
Grindley, G. A. BSc
qss   (N) 2 Mar
Wilson, A. D. BSc asq
qss   (N) 2 Mar
Kelly, G. S. BSc cfs
qss   (P) 11 Mar
Smith, N. P. BSc
qss   (P) 11 Mar
Wright, M. J. BSc
qss   (N) 11 Mar
Moss, D. E. qss   (N) 16 Mar
Powell, P. R. qss   (P) 12 Apr
McGrath, J. G. BSc
qss   (P) 14 Apr
Astill, M. C. BSc cfs
qss   (P) 15 Apr
Parker, M. A. BSc (P) 15 Apr
Rees, N. C. R. BSc cfs
qss   (P) 15 Apr
Burman, M. H. BSc
cfs   (P) 30 Apr
Jones, K. A. BSc
qss   (P) 30 Apr
Witts, C. B. BSc   (P) 30 Apr
Dearden, J. A. qss (P) 5 May
Pitts, R. J. M. cfs(n)
qss   (N) 6 May
Rogers, P. C. H. cfs
qss   (P) 6 May
Baston, I. J. qwi(T)
qss   (P) 10 May
Hendry, R. W. qss (P) 15 May
Baber, C. W. BSc cfs(n)
qss   (N) 25 May
Anderson, D. S.
BSc   (P) 11 June

Gilbert, M. StJ. J.
BSc   (P) 11 June
Moore, M. L. BSc qwi
qss   (P) 11 June
Wilson, W. D. M. BSc
cfs   (P) 11 June
Ross-Thomson, A. J. tp
qss   (P) 18 June
Perry, C. BSc cfs
qss   (P) 5 Aug
Randells, T. M. qss (N) 5 Aug
Seely, P. A. A. BA
qss   (N) 5 Aug
Simm, G. E. asq   (N) 5 Aug
Paton, A. D. qss   (N) 29 Aug
Fullerton, R. G. BSc
cfs(n) qss   (N) 18 Sept
Sinker, D. R. G. BSc
qss   (P) 18 Sept
Campbell, I. M.   (P) 19 Sept
March, K. C. W. cfs
qss   (P) 19 Sept
Brown, G. G.   (N) 11 Oct
Emtage, J. A. BSc (P) 15 Oct
Evans, J. C. BSc cfs (P) 15 Oct
Paul, A. G. BSc cfs
qss   (P) 15 Oct
Hudson, A. M.   (P) 19 Oct
Docker, C. E. BSc
asq   (N) 29 Oct
White, W. B. MSc BSc
MCGI asq cfs(n)
qss   (N) 29 Oct
Meston, J. M. qss (N) 30 Oct
Nicol, L. A.   (P) 30 Oct
Purnell, T. L. G.
qss   (AEO) 30 Oct
Ward, P. L. qss   (N) 30 Oct
Spencer, J. qss   (AEO) 22 Nov
Smalldon, R. J.   (P) 8 Dec
Brand, C. W. BSc   (N) 10 Dec
Staunton, G. J. BSc
qss   (N) 10 Dec
Clark, R. D. qss   (N) 11 Dec
Harvey, D. J. qwi   (P) 11 Dec
Ransome, R. L. qss (P) 11 Dec
Twelvetree, T. qwi (P) 11 Dec
Wright, E. G. qss   (N) 11 Dec
Wynn, J. K. qss   (N) 13 Dec

1987

Simpson, A. C.   (N) 5 Jan
Adam, J. BSc cfs
qss   (P) 15 Jan
Arnold, A. D. BSc
qss   (N) 15 Jan
Dobson, G. J. DFC BSc
qss   (P) 15 Jan

Gibson, J. A. BSc   (P) 15 Jan
Kemp, P. G. BSc cfs (P) 15 Jan
Leach, P. W. BSc qwi
qss   (P) 15 Jan
Smorthit, N. M. BSc
cfs   (P) 15 Jan
Williams, G. W. BSc
qss   (P) 15 Jan
Farrington, P. R.
qss   (AEO) 17 Jan
Millar, H. A. W. G.
qss   (AEO) 17 Jan
Jones, M. P. BSc   (P) 22 Jan
Jones, M. S. BSc   (P) 22 Jan
Nash, J. B. BSc cfs
qss   (P) 22 Jan
Davis, R. A.   (N) 24 Jan
Lewis, R. C. J. cfs (P) 24 Jan
Physick, M. D. BSc cfs
qss   (P) 18 Feb
Settery, G. BSc qss (N) 18 Feb
Sheppard, G. J. cfs (P) 25 Feb
Richards, R. P.
qss   (AEO) 28 Feb
Seaton, C. M.   (AEO) 1 Mar
Brown, D. W. T. BSc
qss   (P) 2 Mar
Churchill, I. M. BSc cfs
qss   (P) 2 Mar
Firth, D. S. J. BSc cfs
qss   (P) 2 Mar
Givern, C. F. BSc   (N) 2 Mar
Holden, A. R. BSc asq
qss   (N) 2 Mar
Jones, G. V. BSc
qss   (N) 2 Mar
Sansford, S. M. BCom
qss   (N) 2 Mar
Stoner, R. A. BSc asq
qss   (N) 2 Mar
Whitmore, M. J. BA
qss   (N) 2 Mar
Oliver, M. A.
qwi(AD)   (P) 4 Mar
Pearson, S. M. asq
qss   (N) 4 Mar
Snowdon, R. E.   (P) 4 Mar
Paish, S. C. BA cfs
qss   (P) 29 Mar
Thomas, A. J.   (AEO) 11 Apr
Carter, C. A. BSc
qss   (P) 14 Apr
Quinlan, M. A. BSc
qss   (N) 14 Apr
Taylor, P. F. BA   (P) 14 Apr
Trott, D. T. BSc cfs (P) 14 Apr
Andrew, A. G. qwi (AD)
qss   (P) 15 Apr
Palgrave, C. W. J.
qss   (N) 15 Apr

Flight Lieutenants

1987—contd

Pullen, S. K. asq
qss (N) 15 Apr
Cauchi, M. J. V. qss (P) 21 Apr
Burnell, P. N. BTech
qcc (N) 10 May
Riley, D. J. BSc cfs (P) 25 May
Taylor, A. H. BSc
qss (N) 25 May
Witts, P. D. BSc (N) 25 May
Evans, A. M. asq (N) 26 May
Hayes, S. P. cfs(n)
qss (N) 26 May
Zanker, M. W. qwi (P) 26 May
Lloyd, D. cfs (P) 4 July
Millbank, P. cfs(c)
qss (ALM) 4 July
Halpin, D. R. BEd
qss (N) 5 July
Powell, M. B. BTech
qss (N) 5 July
Holdsworth, P. cfs
qss (P) 8 July
Parker, T. J. cfs (P) 8 July
Hands, R. L. BSc asq
qss (N) 20 July
Marshall, J. BA qss (N) 20 July
Southern, P. BSc
qss (P) 20 July
Cornes, B. R. cfs
qss (P) 25 Aug
Middleton, G. W.
qss (P) 25 Aug
Wilkins, S. J. cfs
qss (P) 1 Sept
Bulteel, C. J. B. BSc (P) 3 Sept
Harris, D. J. BSc asq
cfs(n) (N) 3 Sept
Hilton, C. E. J. BA (N) 3 Sept
Mortimer, A. P. (AEO) 26 Sept
Smith, A. J. (P) 26 Sept
Couper, P. BSc qss (N) 30 Sept
Pittaway, S. F. (N) 1 Oct
Kinder, J. R. qss (P) 8 Oct
Sheath, N. T. qss (N) 8 Oct
Spence, F. qss (N) 8 Oct
Gow, D. G. BSc cfs
qss (P) 14 Oct
Hart, M. C. BSc cfs
qs (P) 14 Oct
Fogarty, R. J.
BCom (P) 18 Oct
Weston, P. J. qss (P) 21 Oct
Tomlinson, M. I.
qss (N) 7 Nov
Straw, E. T. BA qss (P) 11 Nov

Dearie, I. A. S. asq
qss (N) 20 Nov
Saunders, I. W. (P) 20 Nov
Simpson, M. J.
qwi(AD) (P) 20 Nov
Sanders, P. S. BSc asq
qss (N) 26 Nov
Smith, C. J. BSc (P) 26 Nov
Walker, E. S. (AEO) 19 Dec

1988

Evans, J. M. cfs (P) 1 Jan
Hardy, N. J. (P) 1 Jan
Ims, M. K. qwi (P) 1 Jan
Jarvis, T. cfs (P) 1 Jan
Letton, J. S. (P) 1 Jan
Hargrave, B. W. BSc
qss (N) 7 Jan
Spooner, D. M. J. BSc
asq qss (N) 7 Jan
Vallance, S. F. (P) 12 Jan
Ambury, S. B. BSc (N) 15 Jan
Coulton, L. W. J. BA cfs
qss (P) 15 Jan
Esau, R. G. BSc cfs
qss (P) 15 Jan
Galletly, D. R. W. BSc
cfs qss (P) 15 Jan
Gunn, M. J. BSc asq
qss (N) 15 Jan
Haynes, J. M. BA qab
cfs qss (P) 15 Jan
Jacobs, D. M. H. BSc
cfs qss (P) 15 Jan
Martin, D. J. BSc cfs
qss (P) 15 Jan
McCarry, K. J. BSc
qss (P) 15 Jan
Ritch, D. N. S. BSc
cfs (P) 15 Jan
Wallace, P. J. BSc
qwi(T) qss (N) 15 Jan
Williams, G. J. BSc
cfs (P) 15 Jan
Dairon, L. J. T. BSc (P) 3 Feb
Johnston, N. A. BSc
qwi(T) qss (N) 3 Feb
Robinson, M. N.
BA (N) 3 Feb
Smyth, K. BEd qss (N) 3 Feb
Wolfendale, P. cfs (P) 13 Feb
Beaumont, R. G. BSc
asq cfs(n) (N) 18 Feb
Fairs, M. R. R. BSc
qwi(AD) (P) 18 Feb
Heaton, M. R. BSc (N) 18 Feb
Holmes, R. J. BSc asq
qss (P) 18 Feb

Wharmby, P. W. BSc
qwi qss (P) 18 Feb
Williams, S. C. BSc cfs
qss (P) 18 Feb
Wintermeyer, M. J.
BSc (N) 18 Feb
Toyne, R. C. BA qss (P) 5 Mar
Balshaw, M. J. F. BSc
cfs qss (P) 14 Mar
Cunningham, P. M. BSc
cfs qss (P) 14 Mar
D'Lima, D. J. BEd cfs
qss (P) 14 Mar
Wattam, D. M. BSc
cfs (P) 14 Mar
Macdonald, P. J. S. D.
cfs(n) qss (N) 23 Mar
Scoines, D. A. qss (N) 25 Mar
Berry, M. R. BSc
qss (N) 29 Mar
Cameron, I. BSc cfs*
qss (P) 29 Mar
Carr, G. BSc qss (N) 29 Mar
Daulby, K. J. BSc
cfs (P) 29 Mar
Lacey, D. S. BSc (N) 29 Mar
Mallinson, C. P. BSc
qss (P) 29 Mar
May, J. E. BSc(Eng)
qss (P) 29 Mar
McCormick, R. A. BSc
asq qss (N) 29 Mar
Perrins, R. H. BSc
qss (N) 29 Mar
Warren, M. D. BSc cfs
qss (P) 29 Mar
Crook, R. J. M.
BTech (N) 26 Apr
Fraser, E. C. BSc
qss (N) 26 Apr
Shaw, I. M. BSc (N) 26 Apr
Chafer, S. N. BA (P) 4 May
Clarke, S. R. BSc
qss (N) 10 May
Morris, D. P. BSc
qss (N) 10 May
Speight, M. J. BSc
cfs (P) 10 May
Stout, T. A. BSc qss (P) 10 May
Maginnis, R. J. qss (N) 11 May
Temple, J. G. cfs
qss (P) 5 June
Andrew, N. R. BSc (N) 7 June
Aston, S. N. BEng (P) 7 June
Ball, S. W. BSc cfs
qss (P) 7 June
Dodson, G. A. F. cfs
qss (P) 16 June
Goodrum, R. M.
qss (P) 16 June

Flight Lieutenants

1988—contd

Young, N. F. (P) 19 July
Evans, M. D.
  qwi(AD) (N) 21 July
Thomas, R. K. (AEO) 31 July
Roxburgh, D. K.
  BSc (P) 1 Aug
Glover, A. S. BSc cfs(n)
  qss (N) 4 Aug
Brewer, S. J. qss (N) 10 Aug
Hammond, S. M.
  BSc (P) 16 Aug
Lewis, R. D. BSc
  qss (N) 16 Aug
Rea, S. A. BSc qss (P) 16 Aug
Wilson, C. B. BSc asq
  qss (N) 16 Aug
Mellor, D. J. (AEO) 30 Aug
Howieson, W. B. BSc
  cfs(n) qss (N) 15 Sept
Laws, D. J. BEng (P) 15 Sept
Carr, S. R. cfs qss (P) 24 Sept
Evans, L. N. cfs (P) 24 Sept
Hendry, T. qss (N) 24 Sept
Jenkins, G. P. cfs (P) 24 Sept
Huke, C. W. N. BA (P) 30 Sept
Lawson, D. A. BSc
  qss (N) 30 Sept
Plumb, S. P. BA qss (N) 30 Sept
Smith, P. D. BA qss (P) 30 Sept
Burton, D. P. cfs(n)
  qss (N) 23 Oct
Dunkley, P. A. (P) 23 Oct
Stobie, D. N. cfs qwi
  qss (P) 6 Nov
Tait, J. qss (P) 6 Nov
Trainor, P. R. D. cfs
  qss (P) 6 Nov
Williams, N. P. cfs
  qss (P) 6 Nov
Doherty, G. P. BSc (N) 11 Nov
Liston, G. A. (AEO) 4 Dec
Ferguson, I. D. cfs
  qss (P) 15 Dec
Macfarlane, G. J.
  qss (P) 15 Dec
Ouston, C. M.
  qss (AEO) 15 Dec
Pell, G. W. Y. cfs
  qss (P) 15 Dec
Underwood, R. (P) 15 Dec
Goodwill, W. M. G. BSc
  cfs (P) 22 Dec

Robinson, T. BSc
  qss (P) 22 Dec

1989

Stingemore, G. P. (P) 13 Jan
Bennett, M. W. (N) 15 Jan
Cook, M. J. BSc(Eng)
  cfs qss (P) 15 Jan
Cunningham, W. J. BSc
  cfs qss (P) 15 Jan
Dawe, A. G. BA cfs
  qss (P) 15 Jan
Edwards, G. A. BEng
  qss (P) 15 Jan
Evans, B. A. BSc (P) 15 Jan
Gales, A. J. BA (P) 15 Jan
Howard-Smith, P. M.
  BSc qss (N) 15 Jan
Huskisson, E. S. BSc cfs
  qss (P) 15 Jan
Huskisson, N. D. BSc
  cfs* qss (P) 15 Jan
Kelly, B. R. BEng cfs
  qss (P) 15 Jan
Long, I. J. BSc cfs (P) 15 Jan
Mills, C. J. BA cfs (P) 15 Jan
Mitchell, D. J. G.
  BSc (P) 15 Jan
O'Brien, S. T. MA MSc
  qss (N) 15 Jan
Soffe, C. R. BSc cfs (P) 15 Jan
Ward, J. D. R. BSc qwi
  qss (P) 15 Jan
Waterhouse, C.
  BSc (P) 15 Jan
Welsh, M. BSc qwi (P) 15 Jan
Wilkinson, C. J.
  BSc (P) 15 Jan
Wilson, R. D. BSc
  cfs (P) 15 Jan
Aujla, M. S. BEng asq
  qss (N) 19 Jan
Brown, C. T. BEng cfs
  qss (P) 19 Jan
Gorringe, M. J. BA
  qss (N) 19 Jan
Taylor, N. R. cfs qss (P) 19 Jan
Bates, W. N. cfs (P) 29 Jan
Clover, B. J. qss (P) 29 Jan
Cox, D. N. cfs qss (P) 29 Jan
Fenny, D. R. asq
  qss (N) 29 Jan
Harcombe, O. M. (N) 29 Jan
Mackenzie, N. H. (N) 29 Jan
Mcara, D. cfs(n)
  qss (N) 29 Jan
Mitchell, J. I. qwi(T)
  qss (N) 29 Jan

Noujaim, S. C. J. cfs
  qwi (P) 29 Jan
Pontefract, J. C.
  qss (N) 29 Jan
Wooff, K. C. asq
  qss (N) 29 Jan
Duffin, J. R. (P) 1 Feb
Brennan, R. N. BSc
  qss (P) 3 Feb
Cadman, T. L. BSc
  qss (P) 3 Feb
Firth, S. T. BSc qss (N) 3 Feb
Hoaen, A. J. BA cfs (P) 3 Feb
Thomas, M. L. BSc
  qss (P) 3 Feb
Wigham, R. C. BSc
  cfs (P) 3 Feb
Duncan, G. qss (P) 16 Feb
Garratt, W. H. (P) 25 Feb
Carder, C. D. cfs (P) 8 Mar
Durke, P. qwi(T) (N) 8 Mar
Evans, I. A. qss (N) 8 Mar
Geldard, A. P. (P) 8 Mar
Hathaway, N. T. qss (N) 8 Mar
Hewitt, J. P. qss (N) 8 Mar
Knight, A. E. cfs (P) 8 Mar
Newman, P. G. (P) 8 Mar
Patching, E. J. (P) 8 Mar
Pickavance, M. J. (P) 11 Mar
Carson, B. J. qss (N) 12 Mar
Forbes, A. MacP.
  asq (N) 14 Mar
Phipps, A. L. BSc (P) 14 Mar
Smith, A. M. BSc
  qss (P) 14 Mar
Taylor, R. N. BSc (P) 14 Mar
Taylor, T. J. BSc
  qwi(AD) (P) 14 Mar
Tucker, M. P. BSc asq
  qss (N) 14 Mar
Ware, D. J. qss (N) 14 Mar
Cable, M. (P) 5 Apr
Bearblock, P. D. BSc
  qss (P) 11 Apr
Buckingham, C. F.
  qss (AEO) 11 Apr
Sheard, M. J. B. BSc
  cfs (P) 11 Apr
Gregory, R. J. cfs (P) 20 Apr
Hillsmith, K. R. cfs (P) 20 Apr
Knight, P. cfs (P) 20 Apr
Rodgers, M. P. qss (N) 20 Apr
Smith, M. G. (P) 20 Apr
Tait, S. A. asq (N) 20 Apr
Walker, G. P. qss (P) 20 Apr
Wheatley, R. B. qss (P) 23 Apr
Harris, M. R. BSc
  qss (N) 26 Apr
McCombie, I. M. BSc
  qss (P) 26 Apr

Flight Lieutenants

1989—contd

Smith, B. S. cfs (P) 12 May
Hippman, R. S. (AEO) 4 June
Sarjeant, C. J. qss 4 June
Alexander, D. J. BEng
  cfs qss (P) 7 June
Boag, D. A. BSc qss (N) 7 June
Curry, R. L. S. BSc(Eng)
  qss (P) 7 June
Dowdeswell, J. L. BSc
  qss (P) 7 June
Hartford, C. R. BSc
  qss (N) 7 June
Heaney, S. R. BA (P) 7 June
Kevan, R. M. BA cfs(n)
  qss (N) 7 June
Ready, M. S. BA cfs (P) 7 June
Williams, D. R. BSc (N) 7 June
Dunne, J. P. asq
  qss (N) 8 June
Edwards, K. A. J.
  qwi(T) (N) 8 June
Hodgson, C. P. (P) 8 June
Smith, D. W. qss (P) 8 June
Smith, I. S. cfs (P) 8 June
Speakman, N. A. (N) 8 June
Stobart, G. cfs qss1 (P) 8 June
Tett, P. E. cfs (P) 8 June
Pout, C. L. cfs(n)
  qss (N) 10 June
Wright, W. S. (N) 12 July
Henderson, N. McL.
  cfs(c) (ALM) 17 July
Tuckfield, L. S. (P) 19 July
Bradley, G. M. BSc (P) 1 Aug
Edwards, G. D. BSc cfs
  qss (P) 1 Aug
Hall, A. R. BSc asq
  qss (N) 1 Aug
Wardrop, T. BSc
  asq (N) 1 Aug
Bedford, D.J. qss (P) 2 Aug
Davidson, A. G. G.
  cfs (P) 2 Aug
Houghton, D. A. cfs(n)
  qss (N) 2 Aug
Thomas, J. P. (P) 2 Aug
Brotherton, J.
  BEng (N) 14 Aug
Hooper, R. T. qss (P) 27 Aug
Nichols, W. H. BSc (N) 6 Sept
High, P. A. (N) 7 Sept
Beddoes, S. L. BSc
  qss (N) 15 Sept
Bracken, M. J. qss (N) 15 Sept
Craven, I. W. (P) 15 Sept

Dalton, A. G. (P) 15 Sept
Forrester, C. W. J.
  BSc(Eng) qwi(AD)
  qss (N) 15 Sept
Hayward, S. A. (P) 15 Sept
Heathcote, G. BSc asq
  qss (P) 15 Sept
Hopkinson, P. E. BA
  qss (P) 15 Sept
Jepson, C. D. qwi (P) 15 Sept
Jones, R. R. qss (P) 15 Sept
Potter, D. J. A. BA
  qss (N) 15 Sept
Ridley, M. J. tp qss (P) 15 Sept
Robinson, P. BSc qwi(T)
  qss (P) 15 Sept
Tennant-Bell, N. R. (P) 15 Sept
Thyng, I. F. qss (N) 15 Sept
Wall, S. A. cfs qss (P) 15 Sept
Waring, J. M. R.
  qss (N) 15 Sept
Clarke, S. M. BEng
  cfs (P) 27 Sept
Latham, P. E. S. cfs (P) 8 Oct
Marshall, I. F. (N) 8 Oct
Taylor, J. E. qss (P) 12 Oct
Clark, J. W. qss (P) 26 Oct
Couston, T. qwi qss (P) 26 Oct
Cranstoun, C. D. J.
  qss (P) 26 Oct
Devine, N. BA (N) 26 Oct
Jannaty, Y. BSc (N) 26 Oct
Mangan, M. T. BSc (N) 26 Oct
Miller, P. C. R. BSc cfs
  qss (P) 26 Oct
Parkinson, A. F. (P) 26 Oct
Walsh, I. J. BSc (N) 26 Oct
Ward, K. A. BSc cfs (P) 26 Oct
Lyons, T. P. BEng tp
  qwi (P) 8 Nov
Stellmacher, D.
  BEng (P) 8 Nov
Gray, A. S. qss (N) 11 Nov
Bennett, L. J. BSc
  qwi(T) qss (P) 7 Dec
Creber, D. I. (P) 8 Dec
Gray, D. M. cfs qss (P) 8 Dec
Hambleton, A. E. (P) 8 Dec
McAuley, D. qss (P) 8 Dec
Smith, P. A. cfs (P) 8 Dec
Wigglesworth, D. J. cfs
  qwi qss (P) 8 Dec
Buxton, S. G. cfs (P) 18 Dec

1990

Ashford, A. M. BSc (P) 15 Jan
Bearblock, C. D. A. F.
  BSc cfs qss (P) 15 Jan

Beeston, M. D. MA (P) 15 Jan
Bowland, J. D. R.
  BSc (P) 15 Jan
Davy, J. BEng cfs (P) 15 Jan
Edwards, R. C. BA cfs
  qss (P) 15 Jan
Evans, A. D. E. BEng cfs
  qss (P) 15 Jan
Gell, A. P. BSc cfs (P) 15 Jan
Goldstraw, D. A. BSc
  qss (N) 15 Jan
Harris, J. I. M Eng (P) 15 Jan
Helm, D. A. BEng
  qss (P) 15 Jan
Hopson, P. BSc (P) 15 Jan
Howard, S. M. BSc cfs
  qss (P) 15 Jan
Hugall, D. R. BA
  qss (P) 15 Jan
Hughes, P. J. BA
  qss (P) 15 Jan
Hunter J. H. BSc
  cfs (P) 15 Jan
Hurst, G. J. BEng
  cfs (P) 15 Jan
Kemp, B. V. BEng
  qss (P) 15 Jan
Makepeace, A. D. E.
  BSc cfs qss (P) 15 Jan
Martin, A. T. BSc
  qss (P) 15 Jan
Mobbs, P. W. BEng
  cfs (P) 15 Jan
Nicholson, F. J. BSc
  qss (P) 15 Jan
Owen, W. K. BA (P) 15 Jan
Price, R. S. BSc cfs
  qss (P) 15 Jan
Purves, N. L. BSc
  qss (P) 15 Jan
Robertshaw, N. J. BA
  qss (P) 15 Jan
Ross, A. N. BSc (P) 15 Jan
Rovery, S. W. BA
  qss (P) 15 Jan
Russell, I. J. L. BSc
  cfs (P) 15 Jan
Slatford, T. K.
  BTech (P) 15 Jan
Stocker, S. C. BSc (P) 15 Jan
Tait, A. G. BA (N) 15 Jan
Taylor, D. P. BSc
  qss (P) 15 Jan
Telfer, J. C. BSc (P) 15 Jan
Ward, S. J. BSc qss (P) 15 Jan
Wheeler, D. J. BSc
  cfs (P) 15 Jan
Wright, J. BSc (N) 15 Jan
Wyatt, D. P. P. BSc
  cfs (P) 15 Jan

Flight Lieutenants

1990—contd

Barker, R. A. BSc cfs		
qss	(P)	19 Jan
Colligan, G. R. BEng		
qwi qss	(P)	19 Jan
Cook, I. V. BSc qss	(P)	19 Jan
Grant, S. G. BSc qwi		
qss1	(P)	19 Jan
Harbron, S. E.	(P)	19 Jan
Manwaring, M. T.	(N)	19 Jan
Mullen, A.	(P)	19 Jan
Stockings, J. D. BSc		
qwi(T)	(P)	19 Jan
Whitwood, S. L. cfs	(P)	19 Jan
Russell, N. G. asq	(N)	5 Feb
Kelly, A. M. qss	(N)	12 Feb
Birnie, F. BEng qss	(N)	14 Feb
Dornan, I. S. BA cfs	(P)	14 Feb
Edmunds, K. W.	(AEO)	25 Feb
Griffiths, K. I.	(AEO)	25 Feb
Jones, R. L. MBE (ALM)		25 Feb
Annas, D. R. cfs(n)		
qss	(N)	28 Feb
Ead, I. S. qss	(N)	28 Feb
Fowell, J. P. BSc		
qss	(P)	28 Feb
Frost, P. A. BSc cfs	(P)	28 Feb
Gerrard, P. S. BSc cfs		
qss	(P)	28 Feb
Goodman, P. St. J.	(P)	28 Feb
Jones, J. M. BEng		
qss	(P)	28 Feb
McBryde, D. W.		
qwi(AD) qss	(N)	28 Feb
Oliphant, G. G. BSc	(P)	28 Feb
Presland, R. D. BEng		
qwi(T)	(P)	28 Feb
Saunders, P. BSc	(N)	28 Feb
Stirton, I. N. cfs	(P)	28 Feb
Wood, J. R.	(P)	28 Feb
Yorston, R. A. BEng	(N)	28 Feb
Morris, S. C. cfs(n)		
qss	(N)	2 Mar
Addison, J. M.	(N)	9 Mar
Boulton, M. S. BA		
qss	(N)	11 Apr
Coote, S. M. BSc		
qss	(P)	11 Apr
Eccles, C. J. BSc cfs	(P)	11 Apr
Gibson, I. S. BA	(P)	11 Apr
Humphreys, M. S. BSc		
qwi(T) qss	(P)	11 Apr
Livingston, N.	(P)	11 Apr
Mason, C. R. MPhil BSc		
qss	(N)	11 Apr

McCarthy, S. F. BSc		
cfs	(P)	11 Apr
Myhill, J. S. qss	(N)	11 Apr
Sawyer, G. P. BEng cfs		
qss	(P)	11 Apr
Seal, C. T. BPharm		
cfs	(P)	11 Apr
Shinner, A. M. BSc		
cfs	(P)	11 Apr
Tickle, S. R. qwi qss	(P)	11 Apr
Tucker, D. L. BSc		
qss	(N)	11 Apr
Vicary, P. N. L. BSc		
qwi(AD)	(N)	11 Apr
Walton, I. W. R. BEng		
qwi(T)	(P)	11 Apr
Webb-Dicken, R.		
qss	(N)	11 Apr
Williams, C. D.	(P)	15 Apr
Collins, M. D. qss	(N)	2 May
Bayliss, D.	(P)	5 May
Jones, C. D.	(N)	5 May
Millbank, J. MacD.		
qss	(AEO)	5 May
Rundle, N. C. cfs(c)		
qss	(ALM)	5 May
Taylor, N. qss	(AEO)	5 May
Peacey, S. BSc cfs		
qss	(P)	6 May
Smith, D. A. BSc	(N)	6 May
Hughes, D. K. cfs		
qss	(P)	7 May
Price, R. G.	(N)	11 May
Sheldon, M. cfs qss	(P)	14 May
Clarke, J. W. qss	(N)	21 May
Dover, I. P.	(P)	22 May
Fancett, P. A.	(P)	22 May
Garrod, M. D. cfs	(P)	22 May
Gaughan, P. J. cfs		
qss	(P)	22 May
Sell, A. cfs	(P)	22 May
Heald, T. J. H. qss	(P)	23 May
Warburton, P. L.		
qcc	(N)	8 June
Nash, J. E.	(AEO)	16 June
Mudgway, A. P.	(P)	29 June
Bremer, G. J. BSc asq		
qss	(N)	3 July
Grapes, S. A. R. BSc		
qss	(N)	3 July
Paines, J. D. B. MSc BA		
tp	(P)	3 July
Williams, S. T. BA		
qss	(P)	8 July
Sumner, A. P.	(P)	9 July
Bartle, D. J. cfs qss	(N)	10 July
Lake, A. R.	(P)	17 July
Morris, P. G.	(P)	17 July
Parsons, J. J. qss	(N)	17 July
Stafford, M. I. qss	(N)	17 July

Stradling, C. J. qss	(N)	17 July
Gilbert, N. P.	(P)	24 July
Adkinson, S.	(N)	28 July
Charles, R. L.	(AEO)	28 July
Wesley, N. P. cfs	(P)	28 July
Baxter, M. E. BSc		
qss1	(P)	14 Aug
Bostock, P. J. BA		
qss	(N)	14 Aug
Goold, I. G. BA cfs	(P)	14 Aug
Pugh, J. BEng qss	(N)	14 Aug
Winsor, N. W. BEng		
qss	(N)	14 Aug
Austin, R. P.	(P)	28 Aug
Bell, S.	(P)	28 Aug
Crennell, N. J.		
qwi(T)	(P)	28 Aug
Faulkner, S. C.	(P)	28 Aug
Green, S. C. MCGI asq		
qss	(N)	28 Aug
Hiscox, B. J. qss	(N)	28 Aug
Lings, G. B.	(P)	28 Aug
Sanders, R. H. W.		
cfs	(P)	28 Aug
Willson, S.	(P)	28 Aug
Blundell, S. J. BSc		
qss	(N)	27 Sept
Matthews, M. W.		
BSc	(N)	27 Sept
Ross, A. BSc	(P)	2 Oct
Daft, R. E. qss	(P)	11 Oct
Davey, P. M.	(P)	11 Oct
Dazeley, J. M.	(P)	11 Oct
Garner, R. W. C.		
qss	(N)	11 Oct
Harrington, N. qss	(N)	11 Oct
Hough, C. R. qss	(P)	11 Oct
Jackson, J. A. cfs	(P)	11 Oct
Jeffries, M. J. qss	(N)	11 Oct
Salisbury, D. A. qs	(P)	11 Oct
Williams, P. J.	(P)	11 Oct
Gallagher, J. J.	(N)	13 Oct
Foggo, C. H. qss (ENG)		2 Nov
Ainsworth, D. P.		
BSc	(P)	8 Nov
Audet, D. W. BSc	(P)	8 Nov
Flynn, S. A. BA qss	(P)	8 Nov
Richardson, P. T. BSc		
qss	(P)	8 Nov
Williams, N. P. BSc	(P)	8 Nov
Rooney, A. J. BSc	(P)	11 Nov
Francis, P. J. BEng	(P)	14 Nov
Bowles, S. J. MBE		
qss	(N)	17 Nov
Mannion, D. T. cfs	(P)	17 Nov
Bhatia, R. J.	(P)	23 Nov
Davies, G. C. qss	(N)	23 Nov
Fairbrother, P. J.	(P)	23 Nov
Griffiths, S. M. cfs	(P)	23 Nov
Hare, G. W. J. qss	(P)	23 Nov

Flight Lieutenants

1990—contd

Ludlow, S. cfs	(P)	23 Nov
Perrett, S. D. cfs	(P)	23 Nov
Smith, T. G. asq		
qss	(N)	23 Nov
Webster, P. E. qs	(N)	23 Nov
Wood, M. L. qss	(N)	23 Nov
Howells, I. M. qss	(N)	10 Dec
Dunne, P. J. qss	(ALM)	15 Dec
McLaren, T. M.		
qss	(AEO)	15 Dec
Fascione, T. M. BSc		
qss	(N)	19 Dec
Evans, D. A. W. qcc	(N)	24 Dec
Hunt, E. S. J. qss1	(P)	29 Dec

1991

Bishop, N. A. qss	(N)	4 Jan
Cawthorne, P. qwi(T)		
qss	(P)	4 Jan
Chadwick, G. C.	(P)	4 Jan
Cockerill, D. cfs qss	(P)	4 Jan
Jones, K. R.	(N)	4 Jan
Laing, G. W. cfs	(P)	4 Jan
Mason, R. D.	(P)	4 Jan
McGregor, I. cfs		
qcc	(P)	4 Jan
O'Connor, G. M. cfs(n)		
qss	(N)	4 Jan
Powell, P. J. qss	(P)	4 Jan
Richardson, M. P.	(N)	4 Jan
Robson, M. cfs qss	(P)	4 Jan
Rowley, T. G. S.	(P)	4 Jan
Rumens, K. R. cfs		
qss1	(P)	4 Jan
Smith, P. A. qss	(N)	4 Jan
Westwood, P. G.	(P)	4 Jan
Nelson, N. J.	(ENG)	11 Jan
McNulty, M. D. qss	(N)	13 Jan
Ballance, D. J. BSc		
cfs	(P)	15 Jan
Breddy, P. B. BSc	(P)	15 Jan
Carby, H. R. BSc		
qss	(P)	15 Jan
Fitzgerald, J. F. BEng		
cfs	(P)	15 Jan
Frampton, J. K. MBE		
BA qss	(N)	15 Jan
Greig, D. A. BSc	(P)	15 Jan
Grimshaw, R. D. BSc		
BSc qss	(P)	15 Jan
Hales, D. W. BEng cfs		
qss	(P)	15 Jan
Hossle, T. BA qss	(P)	15 Jan

Johnson, S. A. BSc		
qcc	(P)	15 Jan
Johnstone, R. W. S.		
BSc qss	(N)	15 Jan
Jones, P. R. BSc cfs		
qss1	(P)	15 Jan
Lewis, M. T. MB ChB		
DAvMed	(P)	15 Jan
Linter, J. E. MA qwi(T)		
qss	(N)	15 Jan
Mather, D. A. BA		
cfs	(P)	15 Jan
McEvoy, S. BA qss	(P)	15 Jan
Moor, N. BSc asq	(N)	15 Jan
Phimister, M. S. BSc		
qss	(N)	15 Jan
Pike, H. J. BEng		
qwi	(P)	15 Jan
Potter, D. J. BA	(P)	15 Jan
Preston-Whyte, R. A.		
BA qss	(P)	15 Jan
Roxburgh, S. I.		
BEng	(P)	15 Jan
Ryder, A. S. BA qcc	(P)	15 Jan
Scopes, N. R. MA cfs		
qss	(P)	15 Jan
Sharman, P. R. BSc		
qwi	(P)	15 Jan
Sickling, A. M. BSc	(P)	15 Jan
Smith, H. F. BA cfs		
qwi(T)	(P)	15 Jan
Snashall, S. M. BEng		
qss	(P)	15 Jan
Thirtle, C. B. BSc		
qss	(P)	15 Jan
Thornton, M. J.		
BSc	(P)	15 Jan
Walton, R. I. BSc		
cfs	(P)	15 Jan
Watson, I. BSc qss	(P)	15 Jan
Wilson, M. A. BSc		
cfs	(P)	15 Jan
Easton, M. S.	(P)	17 Jan
Cookson, S.	(ALM)	29 Jan
Day, C. J. qss	(N)	7 Feb
Chattaway, M. S.		
BEng	(P)	14 Feb
Erry, D. S. BEng		
qss	(P)	14 Feb
Hynd, A. N. BSc		
qss	(P)	14 Feb
Kirby, S. BSc	(N)	14 Feb
Sumner-Lockwood, G.		
BA	(P)	14 Feb
Cooper, A. E. R.	(N)	15 Feb
Hadley, S. C. qss	(N)	15 Feb
Jobling, C. L. qss	(N)	15 Feb
Kay, S. T. E.	(N)	15 Feb
Parke, R. J.	(N)	15 Feb
Senior, D. A. qss	(N)	15 Feb

Strookman, R. D.	(P)	15 Feb
Warwick, P. J. cfs	(P)	15 Feb
O'Hora, G. A. qss	(AEO)	16 Feb
Stephens, M. F.		
qss	(AEO)	16 Feb
Booth, J. H. J.		
BEng	(N)	20 Feb
Bradshaw, M. C. BSc		
qss1	(P)	20 Feb
Deboys, R. G. BSc		
qss	(N)	20 Feb
Thombs, D. U. BEd	(P)	20 Feb
Smith, J. A.	(P)	1 Mar
Janaway, C. D. qss	(P)	22 Mar
Clarke, P. cfs qwi(T)	(P)	24 Mar
Beal, M. A. BSc	(P)	25 Mar
Dyson, J. BSc qss	(N)	25 Mar
McInroy, S. D. BSc		
qcc	(N)	25 Mar
Payling, C. A. PhD BSc		
CPhys MInstP asq		
qss	(N)	25 Mar
Stewart, G. BA	(P)	25 Mar
Wright, I. BA cfs	(P)	25 Mar
Allsop, D. A.	(P)	26 Mar
Brown, J. C.	(P)	26 Mar
Collier, S. J. qss	(P)	26 Mar
Edwards, J. K. cfs		
qss	(P)	26 Mar
Fenton, S. D.	(P)	26 Mar
Jarvis, A. R. qss	(N)	26 Mar
Wain, S. qss	(N)	26 Mar
Harris, P. J.	(ALM)	30 Mar
Liivet, P. qss	(AEO)	30 Mar
Pritchard, E. J.		
qss	(AEO)	30 Mar
Gourlay, D. C. MacG.		
BEng	(N)	1 Apr
Letch, M. J. BEng		
qss1	(N)	1 Apr
Ballantyne, A. C.	(P)	4 Apr
Hutchins, G. I.	(P)	3 May
Dyer, I. C. BSc	(N)	6 May
Johnston, N. D. S.		
MA	(P)	6 May
Phillips, P. A. BSc	(P)	6 May
Squires, A. J. BSc	(P)	6 May
Tucker, J. D. BSc		
qss	(N)	6 May
Weedon, G. C. BSc cfs		
qss	(P)	6 May
Woods, R. M. BEng	(P)	6 May
Collins, N. D. cfs		
qss	(P)	7 May
Geeson, C. T. cfs	(P)	7 May
Higgs, S. K.	(P)	7 May
Lowry, M. R. J. cfs	(P)	7 May
Dennis, M.	(P)	11 May
Duffy, C. P.	(AEO)	11 May
Lawson, R. J. tp	(P)	11 May

Flight Lieutenants

1991—contd

Devenish, S. A. BEng		
qss	(N)	12 May
Johnson, D. A. N. BEng		
qwi	(P)	12 May
Morton, N. D. BEng	(N)	12 May
Simmonds, M. A. BEng		
qcc	(P)	12 May
Woodley, P. qss	(P)	26 May
Tinworth, M. R. qss	(N)	27 May
Culpin, R. W. qwi(AD)		
qss	(P)	19 June
Horlock, N. J. cfs		
qss	(P)	19 June
Lovely, P. qss	(N)	19 June
McCowan, N. C.	(P)	19 June
Platt, D. qss	(N)	19 June
Scott, D. W.	(N)	19 June
Brown, G. J.	(AEO)	22 June
Abraham, D. L. BSc	(P)	8 July
Piercey, B. A. BA	(N)	8 July
Sweatman, J. BSc		
qss	(P)	8 July
Nixon, A. qss	(N)	11 July
Vaughan, K. M. D.		
qss	(N)	31 July
Cook, G. C. qss	(P)	13 Aug
Robinson, A. W.		
qss	(N)	13 Aug
Wilson, R. A.	(P)	13 Aug
Withington, D. J.		
qwi(AD)	(N)	13 Aug
Morris, D. J. R.		
qss1	(N)	15 Aug
Cant, A. J. BSc	(P)	18 Aug
Kinrade, I. G. BSc	(P)	18 Aug
Parkinson, F. C. J.		
BA	(P)	18 Aug
Ashworth, D. C.		
BSc	(N)	19 Aug
Hargreaves, A. K.	(N)	22 Aug
Barrett, L. F. qss	(N)	1 Sept
Mason, S. J. qcc	(N)	8 Sept
Taylor, P. J. N.	(N)	10 Sept
Catterall, R. P. qcc	(P)	11 Sept
Butler, T. S. qss	(P)	27 Sept
Hazell, D. J. qss	(P)	27 Sept
Howell, R. J. qwi(T)		
qss	(N)	27 Sept
Kennish, B. E.	(N)	27 Sept
Lalley, M. T. cfs qss	(P)	27 Sept
Rainier, M. D. DFC		
qss	(P)	27 Sept
Sharpe, S. R.	(N)	27 Sept
Tennant, J. A. cfs	(P)	27 Sept
Thorpe, P. A. qss	(N)	27 Sept

Weeks, R. M. H. qss	(P)	27 Sept
Holmes, D. qss	(AEO)	28 Sept
Hulmes, T. A.	(ENG)	28 Sept
Vaughnley, A. G.		
qss	(N)	28 Sept
Preece, W. R. qss	(N)	30 Sept
Bird, A. P. BSc	(P)	1 Oct
Faulds, M. D. MA	(P)	1 Oct
Paterson, N. A. BSc	(P)	1 Oct
Cavey, P. A. BA cfs	(P)	2 Oct
Dowling, S. N.		
BSc(Econ) qwi		
qss	(P)	2 Oct
Skinner, J. qss	(N)	12 Oct
Carver, M. H. G.		
qss	(P)	31 Oct
James, B. F.	(P)	3 Nov
Barnett, J. R. qss	(P)	8 Nov
Bastable, A. D. qss	(P)	8 Nov
Clancy, J. M. E. qss	(P)	8 Nov
Fawcett, S. I.	(N)	8 Nov
Hulley, S. F. qss	(N)	8 Nov
Jonas, W. M. qwi	(P)	8 Nov
Mitchell, F. G. qss	(N)	8 Nov
Othen, M. J. qss	(P)	8 Nov
Williams, R. O. cfs	(P)	8 Nov
Cowe, R. I.	(AEO)	9 Nov
Taylor, E. S. BA	(N)	13 Nov
Smith, I. W. qss1	(N)	18 Dec
Atkinson, R. qss	(N)	19 Dec
Carlton, P.	(P)	19 Dec
Everall, E. J. cfs	(P)	19 Dec
Frost, M. cfs	(P)	19 Dec
Matthews, R. qwi		
qss	(P)	19 Dec
McGlone, A. T. qss	(N)	19 Dec
McLean, K.	(N)	19 Dec
Mewes, A. S. cfs	(P)	19 Dec
Parker, J. G. qwi		
qss	(P)	19 Dec
Poppleton, C. A.	(P)	19 Dec
Smith, A. P. qss	(P)	19 Dec
Uren, J. D. qss	(P)	19 Dec
Waghorne, P. S. cfs	(P)	19 Dec
Ward, N. P. D.	(P)	19 Dec
Winwright, G. A.	(N)	19 Dec
Carter, T. P. qss	(AEO)	21 Dec
Gauntlett, D. W.	(N)	21 Dec
Palmer, A. qss	(N)	21 Dec
Maguire, N. M. BEd	(P)	24 Dec
Jenkins, J. H. BSc		
qwi(T) qss1	(N)	25 Dec

1992

Hughes, J. P. BSc	(P)	8 Jan
Ashfield, J. M.		
BEng	(P)	15 Jan

Barrow, C. BA cfs		
qss	(P)	15 Jan
Beck, J. R. BA	(P)	15 Jan
Chown, M. BSc	(P)	15 Jan
Clayphan, R. J. BSc	(P)	15 Jan
Counter, N. E. BA		
qss1	(P)	15 Jan
Cracroft, P. N. BEng		
qwi(AD)	(P)	15 Jan
Dawson, A. E. L.		
BEng	(P)	15 Jan
Dean, S. J. BSc cfs		
qss	(P)	15 Jan
Fairhurst, M. BEng		
qss1	(N)	15 Jan
Farmer, N. J. BEng		
qss	(P)	15 Jan
Felgate, N. J. BEng		
qwi	(P)	15 Jan
Garrett, M. R. BEng	(P)	15 Jan
Gillespie, A. K. BSc		
qwi(AT) qss	(N)	15 Jan
Gladston, J. G. BEng		
qss	(P)	15 Jan
Grant, R. D. BEng		
qcc	(P)	15 Jan
Harland, G. C. BSc	(P)	15 Jan
Hooper, R. S. BSc		
qss	(N)	15 Jan
Hopkins, P. W. BSc	(N)	15 Jan
Hopkinson, A. M.		
BEng	(P)	15 Jan
Kendall, P. A. BSc		
qss	(N)	15 Jan
Kenworthy, D. I. BSc		
qss	(P)	15 Jan
Kerley, A. A. BEng	(P)	15 Jan
Malcolm, J. M. W.		
BA	(P)	15 Jan
Powell, G. S. BEng	(P)	15 Jan
Reeves, S. E. BEng		
qwi(T) qss1	(P)	15 Jan
Shakespeare, P. B.		
BEng qwi(T)	(P)	15 Jan
Slater, A. M. BSc	(P)	15 Jan
Smith, S. H. BA qss	(N)	15 Jan
Taylor, K. D. BEng		
cfs	(P)	15 Jan
Watkins, P. A. BA		
qcc	(P)	15 Jan
Whyatt, O. B. BSc	(P)	15 Jan
Wigston, M. MA qwi(T)		
qs	(P)	15 Jan
Williamson, P. M.		
BSc	(P)	15 Jan
Wood, D. R. W. BA		
qwi(T)	(P)	15 Jan
King, M. J.	(P)	19 Jan
O'Connor, A. C. qss	(P)	23 Jan

Flight Lieutenants

1992—contd

Appleby, D. J. R.		
qss	(N)	28 Jan
Johnson, S. asq cfs(n)		
qss	(N)	28 Jan
Bullick, G. B.	(P)	31 Jan
Charlton, D. H. qss	(N)	31 Jan
Cullen, A. J.	(P)	31 Jan
Kingscott, R. A. qss	(N)	31 Jan
Neyland, J. T. cfs	(P)	31 Jan
Rochelle, S. P. qss	(N)	31 Jan
Sanders, R. G. qss	(N)	31 Jan
Squires, D. J.	(N)	31 Jan
Thomas, P.	(N)	31 Jan
Stinchcombe, C. G.	(P)	4 Feb
Munro, W. P. qss	(N)	13 Feb
Buckley, J. P. qss (AEO)		15 Feb
Wheeler, M. A.	(P)	17 Feb
Bailey, H. R. BSc	(N)	19 Feb
Brooker, J. G. BEng	(P)	19 Feb
McQuade, S. BSc	(P)	19 Feb
Thomas, C. R. BEng		
cfs	(P)	19 Feb
Tyson, P. J. BEng	(P)	19 Feb
Aspden, S. M. BSc	(N)	20 Feb
Avery, D. K. BEng	(P)	20 Feb
Barr, A. BSc qss	(P)	20 Feb
Flynn, R. J. BSc	(P)	20 Feb
Miller, A. B. BSc		
qss	(P)	20 Feb
Pope, C. C. BSc qss	(N)	20 Feb
Quine, I. J. BSc cfs	(P)	20 Feb
Reade, S. E. LLB	(P)	20 Feb
Wood, N. BA	(P)	20 Feb
Newnham, N. cfs		
qwi	(P)	27 Feb
Laing, I. cfs qss	(P)	1 Mar
Robertson, A.		
MacD.	(P)	6 Mar
Allan, M. S. qss1	(N)	8 Mar
House, G. K. qss	(P)	9 Mar
Burgess, T. J.	(P)	11 Mar
Cowell, J. J. qss	(N)	11 Mar
Davidson, G. S. qss	(P)	11 Mar
Delaney, P. G.	(P)	11 Mar
Duguid, I. W. qwi		
qss	(P)	11 Mar
Green, M. J. qwi	(P)	11 Mar
Hayter, D. P.	(P)	11 Mar
Ingle, N. J. W cfs		
qss1	(P)	11 Mar
Littlejohns, G. E.	(P)	11 Mar
Mansfield, J. J. qss	(N)	11 Mar
Mutty, D. J.	(P)	11 Mar
Plain, C. N. cfs qss1	(P)	11 Mar
Roberts, G. P.	(P)	11 Mar

Wilkins, P. qss	(N)	13 Mar
Holmes, G. M.		
qss	(AEO)	29 Mar
Rogan, J. G.	(ALM)	29 Mar
Shepherd, D. J.	(AEO)	29 Mar
Coolbear, R. A.		
BEng	(P)	30 Mar
Cullen, S. M. BEd	(N)	30 Mar
Edwards, O. E. BSc	(P)	30 Mar
Freeman, S. E. G.		
BEng	(P)	30 Mar
Paton, E. J. BSc	(N)	30 Mar
Quick, A. N. BA	(P)	30 Mar
Hamill, S. J. BA		
qss1	(P)	1 Apr
Oliver, S. C. BSc		
qss1	(N)	1 Apr
Palmer, A. D. BSc	(P)	1 Apr
Seymour, A. J. BSc		
qwi(AD)	(P)	1 Apr
Squires, P. J. M. BSc		
qwi	(P)	1 Apr
Stevens, S. D. BSc	(P)	1 Apr
Trueman, R. E. BEng		
tp	(P)	1 Apr
Watts, P. A. F. BSc		
qss	(P)	1 Apr
McDermott, A. W.	(P)	8 Apr
Adcock, M. R.	(P)	23 Apr
Cartwright, L. J.	(N)	23 Apr
Correia, J. C.	(N)	23 Apr
Dingwall, I. R. qss	(P)	23 Apr
Eves, P. M.	(N)	23 Apr
Glover, A. D. qss	(N)	23 Apr
Gregory, S. P.	(P)	23 Apr
Jackson, R. G.	(N)	23 Apr
Luck, R. K. cfs qss	(P)	23 Apr
Mattinson, R. G.	(P)	23 Apr
Morris, P. A. cfs qss	(P)	23 Apr
Newton, N. D.	(P)	23 Apr
Rea, J. C. qss	(N)	23 Apr
Roberts, G. L. qwi		
qss	(P)	23 Apr
Voigt, P. G. O.	(P)	23 Apr
Reed, A. W. qss	(N)	29 Apr
Brooks, K. A.	(ALM)	10 May
Lewis, I. J. qss	(AEO)	10 May
Yates, T. J. qss	(AEO)	10 May
McWilliams, I. R.		
BEng	(P)	11 May
Wirdnam, G. T.		
BTech	(P)	11 May
Baber, M. A. BSc	(P)	12 May
Bedford, R. W. BSc	(P)	12 May
Cosens, I. J. BEng	(P)	12 May
Hill, J. W. A. BEng		
cfs	(P)	12 May
Manson, J. H.		
BEng	(P)	12 May
Barrett, P. N.	(P)	4 June

Lawson, J. D. qss	(P)	4 June
McLaughlin, S. J.		
qss	(N)	4 June
Millington, J. C. asq		
qss	(N)	4 June
Parry, A. J. qss	(N)	4 June
Pearce, M. D. qss	(P)	4 June
Vallely, I. F.	(P)	4 June
Wilson, D. qwi(T)	(N)	4 June
Hatzel, S. A. qss	(N)	20 June
Bond, C. P. qss	(ENG)	21 June
Burrough, G. D.		
qss1	(AEO)	21 June
Ferris, S. J. qss	(AEO)	21 June
Green, N. M. BA qs	(N)	6 July
Knight, R. A. qss	(N)	6 July
Brockett, J. W. A.		
BSc	(P)	7 July
Hannigan, S. D. BA		
qss	(P)	7 July
Howard, A. BEng	(P)	7 July
Matson, R. C.	(P)	7 July
Morgan, P. R. BEng	(P)	7 July
Littley, B. qss	(ALM)	10 July
Chapman, S. R. qwi(T)		
qss	(N)	17 July
Strode, T. M.	(P)	17 July
Barrett, R. W. qss	(N)	29 July
Beckett, P. C. qss	(N)	29 July
Conner, A. G. qss	(P)	29 July
Crowe, J. A. cfs	(P)	29 July
Curtis, D. M. qss	(P)	29 July
Fazal, P. A.	(P)	29 July
Gray, F. T.	(P)	29 July
Innes, A. J. qwi(AD)		
qss	(P)	29 July
Oliver, M. J.	(P)	29 July
Rumsey, N. K. qss	(P)	29 July
Rutherford, T. W.	(P)	29 July
Smith, A. M. qss	(N)	29 July
Jury, N. M. A.	(P)	31 July
Dack, G. T.	(P)	7 Aug
Munns, P. N. BEng	(P)	17 Aug
Shepherd, P. G.		
BEng	(P)	17 Aug
Sykes, P. C. BSc	(N)	17 Aug
Frost, D. K. BSc qss	(P)	18 Aug
Heycock, S. A. BSc	(N)	18 Aug
Housley, R. S. A.		
BSc	(P)	18 Aug
Pugh, A. D. BEng	(P)	18 Aug
Bradshaw, A. qss	(N)	12 Sept
Fowler, M. L.	(P)	12 Sept
Maggs, C. D. qss	(N)	12 Sept
Merritt, P. J. qss	(P)	12 Sept
Hardwick, M. qss (AEO)		26 Sept
Smyth, D. M.	(N)	26 Sept
Ball, G. R. BEng	(N)	30 Sept
Blake, R. D. BEng	(P)	30 Sept
Dale, A. L. BEng	(P)	30 Sept

Flight Lieutenants

1992—contd

Soul, M. D. MEng	(N)	30 Sept
Baddeley, J. J. G.		
BSc	(P)	1 Oct
Burton, A. BSc		
qss1	(N)	1 Oct
Hadlow, C. D. BSc	(P)	1 Oct
Hadlow, D. M. BSc	(P)	1 Oct
Wootton, W. J. BSc	(P)	1 Oct
Jury, J. G.	(P)	4 Oct
Robertson, R. N. BA		
qss	(P)	6 Oct
Boyd, S. qss	(N)	23 Oct
Burley, C. J.	(N)	23 Oct
Cottle, N. qss	(P)	23 Oct
Davies, M. W.	(P)	23 Oct
Hackett, P. L.	(P)	23 Oct
Harris, T. N. qwi(T)		
qss	(N)	23 Oct
Hopcroft, I. D. qss	(P)	23 Oct
McCallum, D. P.	(N)	23 Oct
Monk, T. I.	(N)	23 Oct
Myers, A. M. qwi(T)		
qss1	(P)	23 Oct
Panter, C. S.	(P)	23 Oct
Wilkie, D. W. qss	(N)	23 Oct
Woolley, M. G.	(P)	23 Oct
Curtis, A. C.	(P)	8 Nov
Griffin, S. J. asq	(AEO)	8 Nov
Jones, N. F. qss	(AEO)	8 Nov
Hodgkison, J. BSc	(N)	13 Nov
Strang, J. R. BSc	(N)	13 Nov
McGarrigle, S. B.	(P)	16 Nov
Morrin, A. J. cfs	(P)	19 Nov
Hamilton, D. J. qss	(P)	30 Nov
Ashton, S. P.	(P)	4 Dec
Aspinall, M. E. qwi(T)		
qss1	(N)	4 Dec
Beresford, A.	(N)	4 Dec
Bolton, P. M. qss	(N)	4 Dec
Boyes, M. S. qs	(P)	4 Dec
Davies, S.	(P)	4 Dec
Gray, A. qss1	(P)	4 Dec
Hardy, I.	(P)	4 Dec
Hockenhull, W. J.		
qwi(AD)	(P)	4 Dec
Hutchinson, P. T.	(N)	4 Dec
Lawrence, M. E.		
qss	(N)	4 Dec
Main, K. B. cfs qss	(P)	4 Dec
Parker, A. M. B.	(N)	4 Dec
Prior, S. C.	(P)	4 Dec
Rodden, M. O. asq		
qss	(N)	4 Dec
Stopforth, P. J.	(N)	4 Dec
Mulgrew, K.	(AEO)	20 Dec

Ring, M. J.	(N)	20 Dec
Stamp, R. J. qss	(ENG)	20 Dec
Truesdale, J.	(AEO)	20 Dec
Cooper, N. R. BSc		
qss	(N)	24 Dec
Donaghue, C. E. BSc		
qss	(N)	24 Dec
Williams, M. P. BSc	(P)	24 Dec

1993

Rees, R. G. qcc	(P)	1 Jan
Sumner, R. A. qss	(N)	1 Jan
Strickland, C. E.	(P)	14 Jan
Bayman, P. MBA		
BA	(P)	15 Jan
Bentley, S. A. BSc		
qcc	(P)	15 Jan
Berkley, R. A. BEng		
qss1	(P)	15 Jan
Blythe, A. N. BEng	(P)	15 Jan
Bradshaw, J. P. BSc		
qss	(P)	15 Jan
Church, S. M. MB	(P)	15 Jan
Cooke, C. V. BSc		
qss1	(P)	15 Jan
Cormack, H. R. C. BA		
qcc	(N)	15 Jan
Cornes, T. A. BSc	(P)	15 Jan
Courtis, N. C. BSc	(P)	15 Jan
Day, M. J.	(P)	15 Jan
Edwards, P. J. BA	(P)	15 Jan
Foley, A. P. BEng	(N)	15 Jan
Harrison, R. A. BSc		
cfs	(P)	15 Jan
Homer, R. StJ.		
BEng	(P)	15 Jan
Hoskinson, R. J. BA		
qss1	(P)	15 Jan
James, B. BEng		
qss1	(P)	15 Jan
Kinnersley, S. J.		
BEng	(P)	15 Jan
Lawrence, M. D.	(N)	15 Jan
Maguire, A. J.		
BEng	(P)	15 Jan
McDermott, A. E. R.		
BEng	(P)	15 Jan
McGregor, C. J.		
BSc	(P)	15 Jan
Nash, M. BSc	(P)	15 Jan
Seymour, R. P.	(P)	15 Jan
Stringer, J. J. BA		
qwi	(P)	15 Jan
Taylor, L. S. BEng		
qcc	(P)	15 Jan
Tomlinson, C. J.		
BSc	(N)	15 Jan
Walker, R. W. BA	(P)	15 Jan

Waller, T. M. BSc	(P)	15 Jan
Weller, T. R. BSc	(P)	15 Jan
Williams, A. J. BSc	(N)	15 Jan
Archer, B. M. cfs	(P)	17 Jan
Cheseldene-Culley, R.		
A. qss	(N)	17 Jan
Craghill, C. M. qss	(N)	17 Jan
Day, M. N.	(P)	17 Jan
Day, S. T. qwi(T)	(P)	17 Jan
Donnelly, I. D. qss	(N)	17 Jan
Duckworth, I. N.		
qss	(P)	17 Jan
Farrar, M. P. qss	(P)	17 Jan
Read, M. P.	(P)	17 Jan
Silcock, M. W.	(N)	17 Jan
Stevens, C. P. qwi	(P)	17 Jan
Webber, R. B. cfs		
qss	(P)	17 Jan
Witcombe, T. J. AFC		
cfs	(P)	17 Jan
Nicholas, M. A. qs	(P)	21 Jan
Bull, A. J. MB ChB	(P)	1 Feb
Pomeroy, A. I. cfs	(P)	2 Feb
Rawnsley, S.	(P)	4 Feb
Rich, C. A. cfs(c)		
qss	(ALM)	14 Feb
Sutton, R. J.	(ALM)	14 Feb
Lay, C. J. qss	(P)	17 Feb
Andrew, R. J.	(N)	18 Feb
Burrows, D. H. BSc	(P)	18 Feb
Doyle, M. G. BA	(P)	18 Feb
Meneely, D. W. BA	(N)	18 Feb
Potter, A. J.	(P)	18 Feb
Bacon, A. D. BSc		
qss1	(P)	19 Feb
Bromley, P. R. BSc	(P)	19 Feb
Cooney, S. qcc	(N)	19 Feb
Formoso, S. G.	(P)	19 Feb
Gilpin, W. J. C. BA	(P)	19 Feb
Hui, D. BEng i*	(P)	19 Feb
Humphrey, P. A.		
BSc	(P)	19 Feb
Knight A. M. BEng	(P)	19 Feb
Lilleyman, S. A. BSc		
qss1	(N)	19 Feb
Moreton, J. BEng	(P)	19 Feb
Reed, S. M. BSc	(P)	19 Feb
Vardy, M. J. BA	(P)	19 Feb
Webster, P. J. BEng	(P)	19 Feb
Atkinson, P. G.	(P)	27 Feb
Butler, J. D.	(P)	27 Feb
Cochrane, J. G. qwi(T)		
qss	(N)	27 Feb
Dunsmore, S. M. cfs(n)		
qss	(N)	27 Feb
Houghton, A. M.		
qss	(N)	27 Feb
Jones, K. R.	(N)	27 Feb
Kosogorin, P. cfs		
qss	(P)	27 Feb

Flight Lieutenants

1993—contd

Traill, D. I. G.	(P)	27 Feb
Williams, L. P. qss	(N)	27 Feb
Richards, N.	(P)	5 Mar
Bundock, P.	(ALM)	28 Mar
Heal, M. D.	(ENG)	28 Mar
McKeith, T. N.	(P)	28 Mar
Millward, A. A.	(AEO)	28 Mar
Beard, D. BA	(P)	29 Mar
Edwards, N. J.	(P)	29 Mar
Holland, J. A. BSc		
qcc	(N)	29 Mar
McDermott, K. W. R.		
BSc	(N)	29 Mar
Monahan, J. F. BA	(P)	29 Mar
Brown, P. J. BSc	(N)	30 Mar
Cavaciuti, K. M.		
BSc(Econ) cfs	(P)	30 Mar
Clancy, N. G. BSc	(P)	30 Mar
Dale, B. E. LLB	(P)	30 Mar
Fryar, D. N. BEng	(P)	30 Mar
McIlfatrick, G. R.		
BEng	(P)	30 Mar
Millns, P. A. BSc	(P)	30 Mar
Parker, G. D. A. BSc	(P)	30 Mar
Parkin, K. BSc	(P)	30 Mar
Poole, B. V. J. BEng		
CEng MRAeS		
qss	(N)	30 Mar
Sharman, S. E. BA	(N)	30 Mar
Smith, A. P. T. BA	(P)	30 Mar
Storr, D. J. BSc	(N)	30 Mar
Whittaker, I. D. BCom		
qwi	(P)	30 Mar
Woodward, J. E. BSc		
qss1	(P)	30 Mar
Wright, R. A. BSc	(P)	30 Mar
Bennison, M. A.		
qss	(N)	8 Apr
Crawley, N. R.	(N)	8 Apr
Dix, R. P. qss	(N)	8 Apr
Dodd, P. A. qss	(P)	8 Apr
Dudman, D. A. qss	(P)	8 Apr
Entwisle, M. J.	(P)	8 Apr
Fewtrell, R. A.	(P)	8 Apr
Hunter, G. M.	(N)	8 Apr
Sheppeck, G. J. qss	(P)	8 Apr
Townshend, A. C.	(P)	8 Apr
Cole, P. W.	(N)	30 Apr
Forster, S. D. qss	(P)	5 May
Nash, M. S. qss	(P)	7 May
Barnsley, S. W.	(N)	9 May
Cripps, G. A. qss (ENG)		9 May
Farci, V. I. A. qss (ENG)		9 May
Gimenez, J. C. qcc	(N)	9 May

Mepham, R. P.		
qss	(AEO)	9 May
Stubbs, D. M. BA		
qss	(AEO)	9 May
Ash, J. C. BEng	(N)	11 May
Ashton, S. E. BA	(P)	11 May
Benham, P. W. BSc	(P)	11 May
Bhasin, D. BEng	(P)	11 May
Cook, M. N. MA BA	(P)	11 May
Eva, R. N. BEng	(P)	11 May
Faulkner, J. R. H.		
BSc	(P)	11 May
Flynn, A. G. G.		
BEng	(P)	11 May
Harden, R. J. BSc	(P)	11 May
James, S. F. MSc		
BEng	(P)	11 May
Jones, J. P. BSc	(N)	11 May
Jurd, M. L. BSc		
qss1	(N)	11 May
Kidd, P. BEng	(P)	11 May
Kinsler, K. A. BSc	(P)	11 May
Melvin, A. J. BA	(P)	11 May
Slow, D. J. BSc	(P)	11 May
Sterritt, J. M. BEng	(P)	11 May
Tarry, M. J. BEng	(P)	11 May
Andrews, N. F.	(P)	18 May
Turner, J. qwi(T)	(N)	18 May
Clegg, A.	(N)	19 May
Cooke, R. qss	(N)	19 May
Daly, C. A.	(P)	19 May
Guy, J. P. cfs qss	(P)	19 May
Robinson, I. D.	(P)	19 May
Lushington, S. F.		
cfs	(P)	16 June
Coates, C. R.	(P)	20 June
Muir, R. asq qss (ENG)		20 June
Nelson, A. W.		
qss	(AEO)	20 June
Noble, A. J. qss (AEO)		20 June
Searle, B. A. T.	(AEO)	20 June
Thurtle, I. C.	(P)	20 June
Watson, J. R. qss(ALM)		20 June
Goodwyn, A. N. cfs		
qcc	(P)	1 July
Beck, K. J. BA	(P)	6 July
Davies, N. F. BEng		
qss	(N)	6 July
Gardiner, H. M. BA	(P)	6 July
Segal, A. P. BEng	(P)	6 July
Badino-Green, J. H.		
qwi	(P)	14 July
Bennett, R. S. qss	(P)	14 July
Bingham, J. H. qs	(N)	14 July
Buckland, H. M.	(P)	14 July
Dodds, A. M. qwi	(P)	14 July
Felix, J.	(P)	14 July
Gilling, P. R. T.	(P)	14 July
Thompson, I. M.		
qss	(N)	14 July

Boulter, D. J.	(AEO)	29 July
Dodwell, G. D.	(AEO)	29 July
Howells, J. MBE	(AEO)	29 July
Valentine, A.	(ENG)	29 July
Brookes, K. P.	(N)	30 July
Wildey, S. K. T. qwi		
qss	(P)	5 Aug
Barlow, P. R. qss	(N)	16 Aug
Farmer, N. A.	(P)	16 Aug
Elliot, M. T. BEng	(P)	17 Aug
Shingles, J. S. BSc cfs		
qwi	(P)	17 Aug
Slingsby, S. B.		
BEng	(P)	17 Aug
Warren, D. J. BSc	(N)	17 Aug
Williams, M. BEng	(N)	17 Aug
Armeanu, A. R.	(P)	25 Aug
Grafton, J. E. qss	(N)	25 Aug
Leighton, J. D. qss	(P)	25 Aug
Manning, S. L. qss	(P)	25 Aug
Waugh, P. qss	(P)	25 Aug
Hodson, R. B. H.		
qss1	(P)	13 Sept
Cooke, D. J. qss (AEO)		26 Sept
Drinkwater, G. M.		
qss1	(P)	26 Sept
Martin, R. C. BEng	(P)	29 Sept
Frecknall, I. T. BA	(N)	30 Sept
Evans, A. D.	(N)	5 Oct
Lismore, M. R.		
qss1	(N)	8 Oct
Auckland, G. W. cfs		
qss1	(P)	5 Nov
Barrow, R. P.	(N)	5 Nov
Binns, P. B. qss1	(P)	5 Nov
Boughton, S. J. qss	(N)	5 Nov
Cairns, S. J. N.	(P)	5 Nov
Davis, G. J. qwi(T)		
qss	(N)	5 Nov
Dickson, A. G. qss	(N)	5 Nov
Everett, M. D. qcc	(P)	5 Nov
Organ, R. W.	(P)	5 Nov
Pearce, R. H. qss	(N)	5 Nov
Platt, C.	(N)	5 Nov
Smith, R. I. qwi(T)	(N)	5 Nov
Williams, H. qcc	(P)	5 Nov
Wilson, M. J.	(P)	5 Nov
Berry, K. P.	(P)	7 Nov
Radford, M. BEng	(P)	12 Nov
Sinclair, D. BSc	(P)	12 Nov
Tiddy, J. N. BSc	(P)	12 Nov
Wall, D. A. BSc	(N)	12 Nov
Toriati, D. J. qss	(P)	22 Nov
Mitchell, N. R.	(P)	1 Dec
Honey, R. J.	(N)	14 Dec
Belham, P. W. cfs	(P)	16 Dec
Collins, S. qss	(P)	16 Dec
Durlston-Powell, C.		
A.	(N)	16 Dec
Ellett, N. S. qss	(P)	16 Dec

Flight Lieutenants

1993—contd

Fellowes, D. A. qwi		
qss1	(P)	16 Dec
Green, A. J. cfs qss	(P)	16 Dec
Hulme, S. J. qss	(P)	16 Dec
Leckey, M. J. cfs	(P)	16 Dec
Lightbody, P. A.	(P)	16 Dec
McDonald, M. qss1	(P)	16 Dec
Mitchell, B. G. qcc	(N)	16 Dec
Norris, R. S.	(P)	16 Dec
O'Rourke, J. P.	(P)	16 Dec
Purkis, E. R. qss1	(N)	16 Dec
Seymour-Dale, S.		
A.	(P)	16 Dec
Stamp, D. A.	(P)	16 Dec
Crosby, G. R. qss (AEO)		19 Dec
Sall, I. qss	(ENG)	19 Dec
Brooks, M. W. BSc		
qss1	(P)	23 Dec
Lamping, S. J.		
BEng	(P)	23 Dec
Warren, C. J. BSc	(P)	23 Dec

1994

Tagg, A. M.	(P)	10 Jan
Baxter, A. MSc BEng		
qss1	(P)	15 Jan
Belton, A. C. MA	(P)	15 Jan
Bradshaw, D. G. BSc		
qss1	(P)	15 Jan
Burge, A. S. BSc	(N)	15 Jan
Burke, T. J. P. MA		
BSc	(P)	15 Jan
Cann, A. D. BA	(P)	15 Jan
Chevli, R. J. MA		
BSc	(P)	15 Jan
Chitty, F. M. BSc	(P)	15 Jan
Conner, A. C. BSc	(N)	15 Jan
Denyer, K. A. BEng		
qss1	(N)	15 Jan
Fletcher, P. A. BEng	(P)	15 Jan
Lawrenson, D. J.		
BA	(N)	15 Jan
Linsley, A. BSc	(P)	15 Jan
May, J. M. BSc	(N)	15 Jan
Molyneux, E. T. U.		
BA	(P)	15 Jan
Pattle, R. E. G. BA		
qss1	(P)	15 Jan
Rendall, M. R.		
BEng	(N)	15 Jan
Ritchie, A. J. BSc	(P)	15 Jan
Sanderson, D. P.		
BSc	(N)	15 Jan

Smith, J. A. BEng		
qss1	(N)	15 Jan
Smith, P. A. BSc	(P)	15 Jan
Stringer, N. J.		
BEng	(N)	15 Jan
Zarecky, C. P. J. MA		
BSc(Econ)	(P)	15 Jan
Oldfield, S. C. R.		
qcc	(N)	20 Jan
Tuck, M. A.	(N)	20 Jan
Mace, C. J.	(P)	21 Jan
Chadderton, D. M.		
qss	(N)	28 Jan
Cutmore, M. R. qwi	(P)	28 Jan
Hamilton, A. E. R.	(P)	28 Jan
Hindley, S. J. qss	(P)	28 Jan
Holleworth, L. A.	(N)	28 Jan
Hurley, A. J.	(P)	28 Jan
Marwood, R. qss	(N)	28 Jan
Mayhew, G. M. D.		
qwi	(P)	28 Jan
Moss, D. R. K.	(P)	28 Jan
Powers, D. R. qwi	(P)	28 Jan
Ward, S. M. R. qss	(N)	28 Jan
Williams, C. C.	(P)	28 Jan
Wright, R. J.	(N)	28 Jan
Slatter, F. G.	(P)	31 Jan
Bloomer, G. A. M.		
	(AEO)	13 Feb
Ramsay, D. G.		
qcc	(AEO)	13 Feb
Armstrong, I. R. B.		
BSc	(P)	16 Feb
Gaskell, A. S. BEng	(P)	16 Feb
Maguire, M. J. BSc	(N)	16 Feb
Rendall, L. J. BSc	(P)	16 Feb
Cowie, A. J. BSc	(P)	18 Feb
Freeman, T. J. BSc	(P)	18 Feb
Hindley, N. J. BEng	(P)	18 Feb
Knight, T. J. BA	(P)	18 Feb
McCombie, P. B.		
BSc	(P)	18 Feb
Richards, D. BEng		
qss1	(N)	18 Feb
Webber, D. J. BEng	(P)	18 Feb
Barker, M. H. R. qss	(P)	22 Mar
Claringbould, S. E.	(P)	22 Mar
Davy, A. J.	(P)	22 Mar
Kennedy, G. G. cfs	(P)	22 Mar
Roberts, D. G.	(P)	22 Mar
Rolfe, S. R.	(P)	22 Mar
Rutter, K. J. qss	(P)	22 Mar
Thompson, D. P.		
cfs	(P)	22 Mar
Watts, R. D.	(N)	22 Mar
Bond, M.	(AEO)	26 Mar
Burlingham, P. A.	(P)	26 Mar
Ackland, P. M. BSc	(N)	29 Mar
Baulkwill, M. R.		
BEng	(P)	29 Mar

Copple, J. A. BEng	(P)	29 Mar
Davis, I. S. BA	(P)	29 Mar
Evans, J. E. MSc		
BEng	(P)	29 Mar
Forster, N. J. BSc	(P)	29 Mar
Hall, D. P. BEng	(P)	29 Mar
McNeil, J. D. BSc	(P)	29 Mar
Smiles, J. A. BSc	(P)	29 Mar
Summers, C. M.		
BSc	(P)	29 Mar
Williams, J. V. BSc	(P)	29 Mar
Faulkner, P. M. cfs	(P)	1 Apr
Cochrane, D. S.		
BSc	(P)	11 Apr
Millar, P. F. BSc	(P)	11 Apr
Morris, J. B. BCom	(P)	11 Apr
Rhind, M. G. BEng	(P)	11 Apr
Shepherd, D. J.	(P)	12 Apr
Cooper, C. C.	(P)	19 Apr
Richardson, J. K.		
qss1	(P)	19 Apr
Rose, M. B. qss	(N)	26 Apr
Carrodus, A. J.	(P)	2 May
Foster-Bazin, S. M.	(P)	2 May
Sealey, A. D.	(P)	2 May
Smylie, P. qss	(N)	2 May
Barnes, P. J. M.	(ALM)	7 May
Cox, S. N. qss	(ENG)	7 May
Hutchinson D. E. K.		
qss	(ALM)	7 May
Kneen, C. T. E.	(AEO)	7 May
Farman, D. J. BSc	(P)	10 May
Harris, R. J. BEng	(P)	10 May
Heaney, N. C. BSc	(P)	10 May
Ip, K. H. LLB	(N)	10 May
Ponting, T. M. BSc	(P)	10 May
Reid, A. I. A. BA	(N)	10 May
Robertson, N. G.		
BEng	(P)	10 May
Squires, C. C. M. MA		
BEng	(P)	10 May
Sodeau, M. D.	(P)	16 May
King, E. N. F. BSc	(N)	6 June
Lewry, J. R.	(N)	15 June
Maddison, R. C.		
qcc	(P)	15 June
Perrin, N. A.	(P)	15 June
Blackburn, C. A.	(ENG)	16 June
Stallwood, G.	(AEO)	16 June
Patounas, R. P. G.		
cfs	(P)	22 June
Mackenzie-Brown, P. E.		
BSc	(P)	29 June
Dixey, M. J. BEng	(P)	5 July
Kilkenny, G. M.		
qss1	(AEO)	30 July
McColl, A.	(N)	9 Aug
Wareham, M. J.	(N)	12 Aug
Brown, L. F. BA	(P)	14 Aug

Flight Lieutenants

1994—contd

Cogley, N. M. B.		
BSc	(P)	14 Aug
MacNaughton, K. BA		
qss1	(N)	14 Aug
Perilleux, G B. J.		
BA	(P)	14 Aug
Faskin, E. J.	(P)	16 Aug
Jhoolun, A. S. J.	(P)	16 Aug
Miller, P. D.	(P)	16 Aug
Williams, C. D. cfs		
qss1	(P)	16 Aug
Witcombe, P. R.		
qss1	(P)	16 Aug
Hunter, N. E. BA	(P)	29 Sept
Pilliner, A. N. MA		
BA	(P)	29 Sept
Breese, D. L. qss	(P)	30 Sept
Brown, S. H. C.	(P)	30 Sept
Cepelak, G. P.	(N)	30 Sept
Colman, J. M. qss	(P)	30 Sept
Denton, R. A.	(P)	30 Sept
MacMillan, I. D.	(P)	30 Sept
Taylor, L. A.	(N)	30 Sept
Tully, D. H.	(P)	30 Sept
Murphy, T. J. L.	(P)	1 Nov
Provost, J. D. cfs	(P)	9 Nov
Diggle, I. J. BEng	(P)	10 Nov
Quinn, M. P. BEng	(P)	10 Nov
Barnes, J. A. F. cfs	(P)	11 Nov
Brogden, D. J. qss1	(P)	11 Nov
Hallam, G. M. J.	(P)	11 Nov
Lilley, A.	(P)	11 Nov
MacDonald, F. J.		
qss1	(N)	11 Nov
Nichols, R. J. qss1	(P)	11 Nov
Shields, J. H.	(N)	11 Nov
Vickers, S. qss	(N)	11 Nov
Leeder, J. D. qss	(N)	15 Nov
Manning, D. P.	(P)	27 Nov
Hake, D. qss1	(N)	30 Nov
Gregory, A. J.	(P)	21 Dec
Baines, M. W.	(P)	22 Dec
Darnley, P. R.	(P)	22 Dec
Dewes, R. J. M.	(P)	22 Dec
Earl, J. cfs	(P)	22 Dec
Gubb, P. J. qss	(P)	22 Dec
James, D. J.	(P)	22 Dec
Pappini, N. J. cfs		
qss1	(P)	22 Dec
Smith, G. N. qss	(N)	22 Dec

1995

Davenhill, J. C. M.		
BEng	(P)	5 Jan
Abra, S. M. BEng	(N)	15 Jan
Barnes, D. M. W.		
BA	(P)	15 Jan
Brosch, I. M. MA		
BSc	(P)	15 Jan
Clarke, D. I. T. BSc	(P)	15 Jan
Crawford, J. B.		
BEng	(N)	15 Jan
Datson, R. I. BSc	(P)	15 Jan
Elworthy, R. J. BA	(P)	15 Jan
Froome, P. D. BEng	(P)	15 Jan
Gambold, K. A.		
BSc	(P)	15 Jan
Gatenby, N. J. BSc	(P)	15 Jan
Glaves, G. R. BA	(P)	15 Jan
Grogan, I. BSc	(P)	15 Jan
Hamilton, T. G. W.		
BA	(P)	15 Jan
Helliwell, J. BSc	(P)	15 Jan
Jones, G. A. BEng	(P)	15 Jan
Laugharne, P. A.		
BEng	(P)	15 Jan
Ling, R. J. D. BSc	(P)	15 Jan
Mackereth, J. E.		
BSc	(N)	15 Jan
Marsh, K. BEng cfs	(P)	15 Jan
Meikle, J. C. BSc	(P)	15 Jan
Milward, R. J.		
BEng	(P)	15 Jan
Mulholland, J. P.		
BSc	(N)	15 Jan
Nelson, J. W. BEng	(P)	15 Jan
Sargent, B. BEng	(P)	15 Jan
Sawbridge, T. C.		
BSc	(P)	15 Jan
Smith, S. H. BSc	(P)	15 Jan
Yates, R. J. BEng	(N)	15 Jan
Bartrip, J. R. L.		
qss1	(P)	27 Jan
Chappell, M. W. J.		
qwi(AD)	(P)	27 Jan
Coombs, D. J.	(P)	27 Jan
Hamilton, S. F.	(N)	27 Jan
Milne, J. D. qwi qss	(P)	27 Jan
Molsom, S. J. qss	(P)	27 Jan
O'Kennedy, P. L.		
qss1	(N)	27 Jan
Oakes, S. L.	(P)	27 Jan
Sheffield, J. A.	(P)	27 Jan
Discombe, M. qss1	(P)	29 Jan
Lindsay, J. W.	(N)	30 Jan
Cowie, M. J.	(ALM)	11 Feb
Hamilton, T. A.	(ALM)	11 Feb
Peebles, A. B. qcc	(N)	11 Feb
Roscoe, M. W.	(P)	11 Feb
Watson, D. C.	(ALM)	11 Feb

Lafferty, J. P. BSc	(P)	15 Feb
Cartlidge, R. BSc	(N)	16 Feb
Eyles, T. BEng	(P)	16 Feb
Gibbs, D. A. BSc		
qcc	(N)	16 Feb
Heald, J. E. BEng	(P)	16 Feb
Hughes, S. G. BEng	(P)	16 Feb
Martin, S. A. BEng	(P)	16 Feb
McKenzie, R. L.		
BSc	(P)	16 Feb
Michael, R. J. BEng	(P)	16 Feb
Moyes, D. R. BEng	(P)	16 Feb
Myers, H. J. MA		
BSc	(P)	16 Feb
Parsons, R. BSc	(P)	16 Feb
Williams, S. P.		
BEng	(P)	16 Feb
Roberts, A. G. qss1	(N)	18 Feb
Castle, B. C.	(P)	25 Feb
Attridge, J. J.		
qwi(AD)	(P)	28 Mar
Aveling, G.	(P)	28 Mar
Ball, J. D. qwi(AD)	(N)	28 Mar
Bensly, R. W. qss1	(N)	28 Mar
Bethell, S. F.	(P)	28 Mar
Frick, R. E.	(P)	28 Mar
Gale, I. D. qwi(T)		
qss1	(P)	28 Mar
Grigg, M. J. cfs qss	(P)	28 Mar
Harbottle, E. G. M.	(P)	28 Mar
Johnson, K. V.	(P)	28 Mar
Lewis, M.	(N)	28 Mar
McKeon, A. J. cfs	(P)	28 Mar
Rosser, A. G.	(P)	28 Mar
Richardson, A. G.	(P)	2 Apr
Dawson, A. J. BA	(P)	10 Apr
McCrory, P. M. BA	(N)	10 Apr
Adamson, J. P. M.		
BSc	(P)	11 Apr
Banks, S. M. BEng	(P)	11 Apr
Best, D. A. BSc	(N)	11 Apr
Downey, J. R. BA	(N)	11 Apr
Gault, G. W. K. BA	(P)	11 Apr
Gibb, R. J. BSc	(N)	11 Apr
Holland, M. R.		
BEng	(N)	11 Apr
Kennard P. K. BA	(P)	11 Apr
Kenyon, D. J. BEng	(P)	11 Apr
Lloyd-Evans, G.		
BEng	(N)	11 Apr
Millward, P. T.		
BEng	(P)	11 Apr
Moore, S. I. BSc	(P)	11 Apr
Morley, N. R. BSc	(P)	11 Apr
Murphy, W. R.		
BEng	(P)	11 Apr
Rushmere, L. D. G.		
BSc	(P)	11 Apr
Singleton, P. R. BSc	(P)	11 Apr

Flight Lieutenants

1995—contd

Stradling, A. P. BSc		
qss1	(P)	11 Apr
Crocker, P. T.	(P)	9 May
Jevons, A. P.	(N)	9 May
Morgan, S. C.		
qwi(T)	(P)	9 May
Reuter, J. S.		
qwi(AD)	(N)	9 May
Sharp, J. M.	(P)	9 May
Skene, R. K.	(P)	9 May
Szymanski, A. R.		
qss	(P)	9 May
Wright, D.	(P)	9 May
Renshaw, M.	(ENG)	3 June
Scott, A. J.	(ENG)	3 June
Dixon, R. S. BSc	(N)	6 June
Flewers, J. A. BSc	(P)	6 June
Hendy, I. D. BSc	(N)	6 June
Mack, A. P. BSc	(N)	6 June
Roberts, B. J. BEng	(N)	6 June
Robinson, J. R.		
BEng	(P)	6 June
Startup, D. J. BSc	(P)	6 June
Barratt, C. D.	(N)	21 June
Hawker, J. R. cfs		
qss1	(P)	21 June
House, G. E. W.		
qss1	(P)	21 June
Lock, G. R.	(N)	21 June
Luggar, A. J.	(P)	21 June
Middleton, D. N.	(P)	21 June
Price, M. C. L.	(P)	21 June
Sheardown, C. N.	(P)	21 June
Tickle, A. qcc	(N)	21 June
Calmus, D.	(AEO)	28 July
Crane, R.	(AEO)	28 July
Robertson, R. L.	(ENG)	28 July
Timbrell, C. P.	(AEO)	28 July
Thomas, D.	(P)	3 Aug
Marston, S. K.	(P)	12 Aug
Bowes, J. P. BEng	(P)	13 Aug
Moss, P. S. BEng	(P)	13 Aug
Wisely, A. C. E. BSc	(P)	13 Aug
Bell, S. J. BSc	(N)	14 Aug
Taylor, P. R. BEng	(N)	14 Aug
Upward, J. BEng	(N)	14 Aug
Geary, N. J.	(N)	15 Aug
Moriarty, E. P. qcc	(P)	15 Aug
Parker, R. S.	(P)	15 Aug
Tyzack, J. E.	(P)	15 Aug
Adey, S. K. qwi	(P)	29 Sept
Burrows, E. J. qss1	(P)	29 Sept
Casabayo, S. P.	(N)	29 Sept
Chan, O. T.	(P)	29 Sept
Cox, P. C.	(N)	29 Sept

Cripps, S. T. qss1	(P)	29 Sept
Daniels, S. M. qss1	(P)	29 Sept
Donnelly, J. A. F.	(P)	29 Sept
Evans, W. L.	(P)	29 Sept
Flynn, M. A.	(P)	29 Sept
Green, E. B. H.	(P)	29 Sept
Iavagnilo, R. G. qss	(P)	29 Sept
Lippiatt, S. D. cfs	(P)	29 Sept
Massey, P. C.	(P)	29 Sept
Maund, J. C.	(P)	29 Sept
Mills, D. W.	(P)	29 Sept
Phillips, P. R.	(P)	29 Sept
Puzey, M. E. qcc	(N)	29 Sept
Savage, S. W.	(N)	29 Sept
Reece, J. MEng	(P)	10 Oct
Hobkirk, J. D.	(P)	9 Nov
Alcock, M. L. qss1	(P)	10 Nov
Applegarth, C. G.	(P)	10 Nov
Barmby, M. I.	(N)	10 Nov
Batey, R.	(P)	10 Nov
Berg, S. E. V.	(P)	10 Nov
Bosworth, P. C.	(P)	10 Nov
Brennan, B. J.	(P)	10 Nov
Chadwick, S. J.	(P)	10 Nov
Clayton, G. J.	(N)	10 Nov
Cullen, A. J. E. qwi	(P)	10 Nov
Cunningham, M. L.		
qss1	(P)	10 Nov
Dann, G. J. qcc	(P)	10 Nov
Dobie, A. F.	(P)	10 Nov
Eaton, D. J. qs	(N)	10 Nov
Edwards, S. S.		
qss1	(P)	10 Nov
Franklin, A. R.	(P)	10 Nov
Hepburn, P. R.	(P)	10 Nov
Howett, D. qss	(P)	10 Nov
Humphries, R. W.	(P)	10 Nov
Kay, D. J.	(N)	10 Nov
Owen, D. E.	(P)	10 Nov
Waller, R. D.	(P)	10 Nov
McCann, B.	(P)	9 Dec
Booth, D. L.	(P)	21 Dec
Coleman, G. P.	(N)	21 Dec
Farrell, D. S.	(N)	21 Dec
Goddard, A. R.	(N)	21 Dec
Haines, D. F. qwi		
qss1	(P)	21 Dec
Hatton-Ward, J.		
qwi	(P)	21 Dec
Marshall, P. B.	(P)	21 Dec
McAdam, W. J.	(P)	21 Dec
Payne, J. C. qss1	(N)	21 Dec
Stinson, R. J.	(P)	21 Dec
Knott, I. J.	(P)	22 Dec

1996

Arthurton, D. S.		
BEng	(P)	15 Jan

Charlton, P. BEng	(N)	15 Jan
Evans, J. C. BEng	(N)	15 Jan
Fraser, N. A. BEng	(P)	15 Jan
Hampson, M. BA	(P)	15 Jan
Houston, R. S. BSc	(P)	15 Jan
MacMillan, A. A.	(P)	15 Jan
Marsden, D. F. BA	(P)	15 Jan
Mason, D. P. BA	(P)	15 Jan
McDonald, P. A.		
BEng	(P)	15 Jan
Paterson, S. A. BSc	(P)	15 Jan
Pollard, N. G. BSc	(P)	15 Jan
Poulter, J. L. BEng	(N)	15 Jan
Priestnall, A. R.		
BEng	(P)	15 Jan
Ratcliffe, B. E. BSc	(P)	15 Jan
Reeks, S. I. BSc	(P)	15 Jan
Rigby, J. D.	(P)	15 Jan
Saunders, R. J.		
BEng	(P)	15 Jan
Sington, D. K. BSc	(P)	15 Jan
Slattery, M. L.		
BEng	(P)	15 Jan
Squire, C. M. BA	(P)	15 Jan
Stanley, J. M. BEng	(P)	15 Jan
Stilwell, J. M. BEng	(P)	15 Jan
Thomas, E. M.		
BEng	(P)	15 Jan
Todd, S. G. BEng	(P)	15 Jan
West, C. R. BSc	(P)	15 Jan
Berris, D. C. D.	(P)	2 Feb
Clement, M. J.	(P)	2 Feb
Conway, N. P.	(N)	2 Feb
Hayes, M. A. qwi	(P)	2 Feb
Holder, I. D.	(P)	2 Feb
Holmes, R. qwi	(P)	2 Feb
Jewiss, S. E.	(N)	2 Feb
McKay, J. G.	(N)	2 Feb
Moir, R. D. qss1	(N)	2 Feb
Sparks, C. D.	(P)	2 Feb
Stead, D. K.	(P)	2 Feb
Stevenson, C.	(P)	2 Feb
Toomey, L. D.	(P)	2 Feb
Jones, S. R.	(P)	4 Feb
Livingstone, D. A.		
BEng	(P)	14 Feb
Fisher, S. A. BEng	(P)	15 Feb
Guest, J. A. BEng	(P)	15 Feb
Harding, P. C. B. BA	(P)	15 Feb
Henderson-Begg, R. I.		
BEng	(N)	15 Feb
Higgins, M. J.		
BEng	(P)	15 Feb
Means, S. W. BSc	(P)	15 Feb
Mounsey, P. N. BSc	(P)	15 Feb
Netherwood, A. G.		
BSc(Econ)	(P)	15 Feb
Pollard, S. M. BSc	(P)	15 Feb
Beddall, J. T.	(N)	26 Mar
Hackland, M. A.	(P)	26 Mar

Flight Lieutenants

1996—contd

Hasted, M. R.	(P)	26 Mar
Holland, A. K.	(P)	26 Mar
Howe, J. B.	(N)	26 Mar
Jess, R.	(N)	26 Mar
Leonard, A. R.	(P)	26 Mar
Marshall, R. D.	(P)	26 Mar
Shirley, S. B.	(P)	26 Mar
Woods, M. J. qss1	(N)	26 Mar
Doncaster, M. R. cfs	(P)	1 Apr
Oxford, M. G.	(N)	2 Apr
Keen, S.	(ALM)	7 Apr
Lilly, P. D.	(AEO)	7 Apr
Donald, C. S. BEng	(P)	9 Apr
Hopkins, G. A. BEng	(P)	9 Apr
Morton, N. C. B. BEng	(P)	9 Apr
Pocock, M. F. BEng	(N)	9 Apr
Stewart, M. J. MA	(P)	9 Apr
Twidell, A. J. BEng	(P)	9 Apr
Averty, C. J. BA	(P)	10 Apr
Baker, M. T. BSc	(P)	10 Apr
Brandon, B. BEng	(P)	10 Apr
Bridge, E. K. L. BEng	(N)	10 Apr
Brown, P. J. BA	(P)	10 Apr
Cook, N. P. BSc	(N)	10 Apr
Frewin, K. R. BSc	(P)	10 Apr
Hardie, J. A. BA	(P)	10 Apr
Holt, C. A. BSc	(P)	10 Apr
Johns, D. E. H. BA	(P)	10 Apr
Oetzmann, D. M. BEng	(P)	10 Apr
Stevens, J. A. BSc	(P)	10 Apr
Towell, A. M. BEng	(P)	10 Apr
Trasler, K. F. MLitt BA	(P)	10 Apr
Turner, J. J. BA	(P)	10 Apr
Williams, J. S. BSc	(N)	10 Apr
Spain, D.	(AEO)	7 May
Ashurst, R. C.	(N)	8 May
Bloom, A. H. qcc	(P)	8 May
Brown, K. P.	(P)	8 May
Buchanan, I. M. qss1	(P)	8 May
Creese, L. B.	(P)	8 May
Crumlish, A. P.	(N)	8 May
Griggs, J. P.	(P)	8 May
Owen, T. E. qss1	(N)	8 May
Rawlins, D. G. qcc	(N)	8 May
Saunders, E. M. qss	(N)	8 May
Shaw, J. M.	(P)	8 May
Smiley, S. L.	(P)	8 May
Shenton, A. G.	(ALM)	9 May
Garland, M. M. E. V.	(P)	1 June
Haskins, J. M. A.	(P)	1 June
Jessett, S. P. qss1	(P)	5 June
Crowther, J.	(P)	10 June
Cockram, M. S. BEng	(P)	18 June
Colman, N. J. qss	(N)	20 June
Fitch, S. A.	(P)	20 June
Forbes, D. R.	(P)	20 June
Gleave, C. qss	(P)	20 June
Kirby, D. J. qwi(T)	(N)	20 June
Moran, K. R.	(P)	20 June
Thompson, J. R.	(N)	20 June
Scott, A. J.	(P)	18 July
Burgess, A. J.	(P)	28 July
Chadwick, L. A.	(ALM)	28 July
Courtaux, N. P.	(ENG)	28 July
Gresham, A. P. qss1	(AEO)	28 July
Harris, L. A. qcc	(ALM)	28 July
Lawrence, I. M.	(ALM)	28 July
Paynton, P. J.	(AEO)	28 July
Rennet, A.	(AEO)	28 July
Steele, P. C.	(ENG)	28 July
Simmons, J.	(AEO)	30 July
Dunn, J. F. BEng	(N)	12 Aug
Berry, R. I. BSc	(P)	13 Aug
Ervine, B. J.	(P)	14 Aug
Fraser, C. L.	(P)	14 Aug
Hirst, J. M.	(P)	14 Aug
Bousfield, R. J.	(P)	28 Sept
Connor, R. A. qss1	(N)	28 Sept
Cree, S. J. S.	(P)	28 Sept
Davies, R. A.	(P)	28 Sept
Moore, G. P.	(P)	28 Sept
Ormiston, J. A.	(P)	28 Sept
Palmer, M. S.	(P)	28 Sept
Smith, R. C. W.	(P)	28 Sept
Whitehill, J.	(P)	28 Sept
Gusterson, L. qs	(P)	29 Sept
Holman, M. J.	(ALM)	6 Oct
Stewart, J. A.	(ENG)	6 Oct
Donaldson, N. S. BA	(P)	9 Oct
Hall, J. T. BEng	(N)	9 Oct
Hollywood, M. J. BSc	(P)	9 Oct
Jones, J. L. H. BA	(P)	9 Oct
Lindsay, H. D. BSc	(N)	9 Oct
Mayo, L. M. MA	(N)	9 Oct
Rae, C. MEng	(P)	9 Oct
Eden, J. K. BSc	(N)	10 Oct
Joel, R. W. H. BSocSc	(N)	10 Oct
McGurk, D. G. BEng	(N)	10 Oct
Walden, D. R. BEng	(N)	10 Oct
Pearce, M. A.	(N)	27 Oct
Appleton, J. L. qcc	(N)	9 Nov
Austin, S. J.	(P)	9 Nov
Bazalgette, G. R. qss1	(N)	9 Nov
Dickens, A.	(P)	9 Nov
Driscoll, N. J. S.	(P)	9 Nov
Edwards, H.	(P)	9 Nov
Farrant, R. P.	(N)	9 Nov
Fraser, R. M.	(P)	9 Nov
Godfrey, P. A.	(P)	9 Nov
Jardine, E. S. R.	(P)	9 Nov
Sharpe, P. R.	(P)	9 Nov
Smith, R. R. qcc	(P)	9 Nov
Smyth, H.	(P)	9 Nov
Stewart, N. R.	(P)	9 Nov
Wood, A. M. qss1	(N)	9 Nov
Heamon, P. J.	(N)	11 Dec
Brewis, S. T.	(P)	20 Dec
Doidge, J. G.	(P)	20 Dec
Jamieson, D. S.	(P)	20 Dec
Lapham, P. A. A.	(N)	20 Dec
Mason, D. C.	(P)	20 Dec
Millar, H. M.	(N)	20 Dec
O'Brien, P. A.	(P)	20 Dec
Olsen, M. P. L.	(N)	20 Dec
Parker, D. A.	(P)	20 Dec
Richards, J. B.	(P)	20 Dec
Simpson, S. P. MA	(P)	20 Dec
Turk, A. D.	(N)	20 Dec

1997

Long, R. C. J. R.	(N)	6 Jan
Bagnall, G. BSc	(P)	15 Jan
Bowlzer, D. J. M.	(P)	15 Jan
Cochrane, P. G. BA	(P)	15 Jan
Cole, S. R. MA	(N)	15 Jan
Crutchlow, P. S. BSc	(P)	15 Jan
Dewar, J. E. BEng	(P)	15 Jan
Johnson, A. M. BEng ACGI	(P)	15 Jan
Lund, A. J. K. BSc	(P)	15 Jan
Marshall, A. P. BA	(P)	15 Jan
McNaught, R. S. BEng	(P)	15 Jan
Percival, I.	(P)	15 Jan
Philpot, T. J.	(P)	15 Jan
Priest, J.	(P)	15 Jan
Sanders, D. T. BEng	(P)	15 Jan
Simpson, K. BSc	(P)	15 Jan
Snaith, C. D. BA	(P)	15 Jan
Stewart, D. I.	(P)	15 Jan
Tandy, M. J.	(N)	15 Jan
Tompkins, S. M.	(P)	15 Jan
Trimble, S. BA	(P)	15 Jan
Whitney, M. A.	(P)	15 Jan
Breeze, J. P.	(P)	29 Jan

Flight Lieutenants

1997—contd

Name		Date
Collings, S. J.	(P)	29 Jan
Cox, S. J.	(P)	29 Jan
Dunn, R. B.	(N)	29 Jan
Gardner, S. cfs	(P)	29 Jan
Nolan, B.	(N)	29 Jan
Read, A. J.	(P)	29 Jan
Simmons, D. J.	(P)	29 Jan
Smith, M. B.	(P)	29 Jan
Wells, R. A. C. qcc	(N)	29 Jan
Hopkins, K. R.	(AEO)	9 Feb
Stainton, L. A.	(ALM)	9 Feb
Toms, J. E.	(ALM)	9 Feb
Dark, E. A. BA	(P)	13 Feb
Dunning, J. R. BA	(P)	13 Feb
Hayes, J. L. BSc	(P)	13 Feb
Hunter, L. J. BEng	(P)	13 Feb
Loughran, S. MA	(N)	13 Feb
McArthur, C. P. D. BSc	(P)	13 Feb
Seymour, C. W. E. BA	(P)	13 Feb
Sutherland, M. J. BCom	(P)	13 Feb
Thomson, J. A. C. BSc	(N)	13 Feb
Beldon, J. R. BSc	(N)	14 Feb
Breeze, H. R. MSc BSc	(P)	14 Feb
Burnet, A. E. BA	(N)	14 Feb
Davison, P. BSc	(P)	14 Feb
Dow, A. V. BEng	(P)	14 Feb
Giles, N. S. BEng	(P)	14 Feb
Hedley Lewis, H. C. LLB	(P)	14 Feb
Hillier, S. W. BEng	(P)	14 Feb
Keenlyside, P. G. BSc	(P)	14 Feb
Lansley, J. M. BSc	(N)	14 Feb
Ludman, A. I. BEng	(N)	14 Feb
Ruscoe, T. J. BEng	(P)	14 Feb
Sagar, G. M. BSc	(P)	14 Feb
Wightman, D. J. BEng	(N)	14 Feb
Challen, A. P.	(P)	26 Mar
Dennis, R. J.	(P)	26 Mar
Hargreaves, V. J.	(P)	26 Mar
Knight, S. G. cfs qss	(P)	26 Mar
O'Brien, T. J.	(P)	26 Mar
Ollis, J. P.	(P)	26 Mar
Paine, R. N.	(P)	26 Mar
Pook, S. A.	(P)	26 Mar
Preece, A. D.	(N)	26 Mar
Smith, M. G.	(P)	26 Mar
Tudge, E. V.	(P)	26 Mar
Williams, D. qcc	(P)	26 Mar
Hazell, C. S.	(N)	1 Apr
Crockett, M. L.	(P)	6 Apr
Jopling, B. W.	(ALM)	6 Apr
Jones, T. T. BSc	(P)	8 Apr
Lenahan, C. A. BA	(N)	8 Apr
Maslin, A. C. BSc	(P)	8 Apr
Middleton, C. S. BSc	(N)	8 Apr
Sheldon, J. B. BSc	(P)	8 Apr
Battersby, N. BEng	(P)	9 Apr
Berry, N. S. BSc	(P)	9 Apr
Blackwell, S. E. BEng	(P)	9 Apr
Bunn, T. BSc	(P)	9 Apr
Carvosso, P. F. BSocSc	(P)	9 Apr
Clayton, S. A. LLB	(N)	9 Apr
Cloke, S. J. BEng	(P)	9 Apr
Davis, I. A. BSc	(P)	9 Apr
Everitt, J. M. BEng	(P)	9 Apr
Goodfellow, P. R. BA	(N)	9 Apr
Hanlon, A. D. BA	(P)	9 Apr
Hough, J. T. W. BSc	(P)	9 Apr
Lindsell, S. BSc	(P)	9 Apr
Murphy, P. R. BSc	(P)	9 Apr
Ogilvie, D. C. BSc	(N)	9 Apr
South, M. R. BSc	(P)	9 Apr
Wells, A. E. BSc	(P)	9 Apr
Wyatt, P. J. BSc	(P)	9 Apr
Allison, R. P. G.	(P)	24 Apr
Carr, T. D.	(N)	7 May
Carter, G. S.	(P)	7 May
Checkley-Mills, A. D.	(P)	7 May
Lassale, F. L. C.	(P)	7 May
Main, S. J.	(P)	7 May
May, B. J. S.	(P)	7 May
Whipp, R. I.	(N)	7 May
Witte, J. M.	(P)	7 May
Wood, D. G. D.	(P)	7 May
Wright, A. J. qss1	(N)	26 May
Page, G.	(N)	3 June
Crawford, J.	(P)	8 June
Braid, B. R.	(P)	19 June
Cartner, J. G. S.	(P)	19 June
Drew, N. R.	(P)	19 June
Horrigan, A. J.	(P)	19 June
Mills, R. M.	(P)	19 June
Molineaux, M. K.	(P)	19 June
Robins, A. C. R.	(P)	19 June
Stuchfield, D. J.	(P)	19 June
Pullen, C. L.	(P)	4 July
Davey, M. F.	(P)	11 July
Hockley, D. C.	(AEO)	28 July
Mackay, A. J.	(ENG)	28 July
Bradford, I. J. BEng	(N)	11 Aug
Dunlop, M. T. MA	(P)	11 Aug
Gillan, C. J. BA	(N)	11 Aug
Haxton, D. J. LLB	(N)	11 Aug
Kovach, S. J. BA	(P)	11 Aug
Rolfe, J. H. BA	(P)	11 Aug
Curzon, R. T. BA	(N)	12 Aug
Graham, M. C. BEng	(P)	12 Aug
Page, M. BA	(N)	12 Aug
Spencer-Jones, M. G. BEng	(P)	12 Aug
Wilkes, J. BA	(N)	12 Aug
Dean, M. S.	(P)	13 Aug
Hickey, S. M.	(P)	13 Aug
Rayne, S. E.	(P)	13 Aug
Wootten, P. W.	(N)	13 Aug
Cole, P. A.	(P)	26 Sept
Cooper, P. D.	(P)	26 Sept
Henning, I. C.	(P)	26 Sept
Kane, D. P.	(P)	26 Sept
Kileen, D.	(P)	26 Sept
McCullagh, J.	(P)	26 Sept
Richardson, D. T.	(P)	26 Sept
Rogers, C. P.	(P)	26 Sept
Lennon, M. M.	(P)	5 Oct
Collins, L. BEng	(N)	7 Oct
Dempster, C. S. BEng	(P)	7 Oct
Phoenix, N. BA	(P)	7 Oct
Ross, S. BSc	(P)	7 Oct
Altoft, P. B. BSc	(P)	9 Oct
Cothill, G. M. J. BSc	(P)	9 Oct
Dales, N. M. C. BA	(P)	9 Oct
English, M. J. BA	(P)	9 Oct
Fegan, G. E. BSc	(N)	9 Oct
Green, R. A. BEng	(P)	9 Oct
Hart, W. BEng	(P)	9 Oct
Ingall, D. A. BEng	(P)	9 Oct
John, C. T. B. BSc	(N)	9 Oct
Lindley, M. C. BCom	(P)	9 Oct
Long, S. C. BA	(P)	9 Oct
Mikellides, A. BEng	(P)	9 Oct
Pickup, A. G. MSc	(P)	9 Oct
Pollard, D. M. BSc	(P)	9 Oct
Richings, S. P. BSc	(P)	9 Oct
Street, M. J. BA	(P)	9 Oct
Warmerdam, P. J. R. BSc	(P)	9 Oct
Brown, M. R.	(P)	7 Nov
Catlow, D. W.	(P)	7 Nov
Curnow, P. R.	(N)	7 Nov
Griffiths, P. L.	(P)	7 Nov
Hough, S. H.	(N)	7 Nov
Lloyd-Jones, E.	(P)	7 Nov
Lord, A. S.	(N)	7 Nov
Lowe, N. A.	(P)	7 Nov
Newberry, W. K.	(P)	7 Nov
Nixon, J. P.	(P)	7 Nov
Robinson, P. J.	(P)	7 Nov
Turner, J. H.	(P)	7 Nov

Flight Lieutenants

1997—contd

Bland, I. D.	(N)	3 Dec

1998

Lambert, I. R.	(P)	14 Jan
Butler, W. S. BSc	(P)	15 Jan
Farquhar, B. W.		
BEng	(P)	15 Jan
Francis, P. S. BSc	(P)	15 Jan
Hodges, B. F. L.		
BSc	(P)	15 Jan
Holmes, E. BSc	(P)	15 Jan
Hurley, D. D. BEng	(P)	15 Jan
Kinsella, A. J. LLB	(P)	15 Jan
Layden, C. J. BA	(P)	15 Jan
MacDougall, K. C.		
BEng	(P)	15 Jan
Shand, R. G. P. BA	(P)	15 Jan
Stanton, N. D. BSc	(P)	15 Jan
Vance, R. M.	(P)	15 Jan
Batt, J. G.	(P)	30 Jan
Grieve, S. N.	(N)	30 Jan
Grimsey, S. R.	(P)	30 Jan
Newcombe, S. L.	(N)	30 Jan
Strasdin, S. R.	(N)	30 Jan
Townsend, I. J.	(P)	30 Jan
Allen, D. J.		8 Feb
Batu, A. BSc	(P)	11 Feb
Dalby, N. L. BSc	(P)	11 Feb
Edmondson, J. M.		
BEng	(P)	11 Feb
James, G. S. BSc	(N)	11 Feb
James, T. R. T. BA	(P)	11 Feb
Morrison-Smith, D. J.		
BA	(P)	11 Feb
Taylor, J. J. BEng	(P)	11 Feb
Austin, J. W. LLB	(P)	13 Feb
Bell, D. BSc	(N)	13 Feb
Blackburn, M. J.		
BSc	(N)	13 Feb
Boulton, D. C. BA	(N)	13 Feb
Butler, S. J. BEng	(N)	13 Feb
Cronin, S. A. BSc	(N)	13 Feb
Dyer, K. B. BA	(P)	13 Feb
Lucas, P. A. BSc	(P)	13 Feb
Martin, D. BEng	(P)	13 Feb
Meakins, S. J. BA	(P)	13 Feb
Millikin, A. P.		
BSocSc	(P)	13 Feb
Stephen, D. M.		
BEng	(P)	13 Feb
Turner, L. BEng	(P)	13 Feb
Webb, O. W. BA	(P)	13 Feb
Done, A. J. P. MEng	(N)	15 Mar

Bethell, R. A.	(P)	24 Mar
Gasson, L. F.	(P)	24 Mar
Hailey, A. T.	(P)	24 Mar
Kilby, S. B.	(P)	24 Mar
Maxey, N. D. qcc	(P)	24 Mar
Wells, R.	(P)	24 Mar
Abrahams, M. D.		
qcc	(ALM)	4 Apr
Cannon, S. R.	(P)	4 Apr
Barley, F. J. R.		
BEng	(P)	6 Apr
Ellacott, D. R. BSc	(P)	6 Apr
Lea, M. R. MEng	(P)	6 Apr
Melville, G. C.		
BEng	(P)	6 Apr
Yeoman, D. BEng	(N)	6 Apr
Borthwick, G. J.		
BEng	(P)	8 Apr
Clague, M. J. BSc	(P)	8 Apr
Daykin, C. R. BSc	(P)	8 Apr
Dibden, R. S. BSc	(P)	8 Apr
Farrell, M. J. BA	(N)	8 Apr
Farrow, J. BEng	(N)	8 Apr
Greenhowe, J. M.		
BSc	(N)	8 Apr
Lyle, A. J. BSc	(N)	8 Apr
Murnane, J. M. BA	(N)	8 Apr
Scully, K. J. BSc	(N)	8 Apr
Street, N. A. BA	(P)	8 Apr
Talbot, T. S. BSc	(P)	8 Apr
Thomas, D. E.		
BEng	(P)	8 Apr
Vickers, L. R. BSc	(P)	8 Apr
Waring, M. W. BSc	(P)	8 Apr
Waterson, J. A. BA	(P)	8 Apr
Wylde, P. F. BSc	(P)	8 Apr
Meadows, J. B.	(N)	6 May
Partridge, G. J.	(N)	6 May
Ritchley, K. M.		
MEng	(N)	1 June

Flying Officers

1989

Chapman, A. P. K.		
	(ENG)	29 Nov

1991

Triccas, R. P.	(ENG)	21 Mar

1992

Croydon, T. G.	(AEO)	20 July
Foster, D. A.	(ENG)	11 Sept

1993

Diacon, P. R. BEng	(P)	15 July
Harris, R. P. BA	(P)	15 July
Wright, I.	(AEO)	30 Sept

1994

Murray, I. R.	(AEO)	10 Mar
Meleady, M.	(AEO)	9 Apr
Wilkinson, S. J.	(ALM)	1 May
Ward, K. N. BSc	(P)	13 Aug
Jones, R. G. BAcc	(N)	6 Oct
Bissett, M. H.	(N)	6 Nov
Farrant, P. J.	(P)	17 Dec

1995

Boardman, R. J.		
BEng	(P)	9 Feb
Cartmell, C. M. BA	(P)	9 Feb
Ixer, J. W. BA	(N)	9 Feb
Baxter, N. J. BEng	(N)	11 Feb
Curtis, W. H. BEng	(P)	11 Feb
Dixon, R. M. BEng	(P)	11 Feb
Fairley, C. T. BSc	(P)	11 Feb
Gilbert, S. J. BA	(N)	11 Feb
Henderson, J. R.	(N)	11 Feb
Jewitt, K. D. BEng	(N)	11 Feb
Johnson, E. J.		
BEng	(N)	11 Feb
Jones, P. J. BEng	(N)	11 Feb
Larkam, D. J. D.		
BSc	(N)	11 Feb
Perks, C. BEng	(N)	11 Feb
Richardson, N. G.		
BSc	(P)	11 Feb

Flying Officers

1995—contd

Stretton-Cox, M. L.		
BSc	(P)	11 Feb
Pumford, S. M.	(P)	24 Mar
Barnett, M. P. C.		
MEng	(P)	6 Apr
Enright, C. B. BSc	(P)	6 Apr
Fisher, A. R. BSc	(N)	6 Apr
Adams, A. L. LLB	(P)	7 Apr
Berry, R. G. BEng	(P)	7 Apr
Biggadike, M. E.		
BSc	(N)	7 Apr
Bowell, S. V. BEng	(P)	7 Apr
Cone, G. E. BSc	(N)	7 Apr
Kilvington, S. P.		
BSc	(N)	7 Apr
Lockyer, S. J. BA	(P)	7 Apr
Rafferty, D. J. BEng	(P)	7 Apr
Scourfield, J. D.		
BSc	(P)	7 Apr
Smyth, M. J. BA	(N)	7 Apr
Ashley, D. A.	(P)	8 Apr
Kay, M.	(P)	8 Apr
Lewis, P. B.	(P)	8 Apr
Pymm, M. L.	(P)	8 Apr
Allsop, A. J.	(P)	3 June
Aspinall, M. J.	(P)	3 June
Jarvis, M. R.	(P)	3 June
Killerby, J. A.	(P)	3 June
Littlechild, G. J. M.	(N)	3 June
Margiotta, C. A.	(P)	3 June
Pemberton, G. A.	(P)	3 June
Roberts, A. J.	(N)	3 June
Roberts, A. N.	(P)	3 June
Warren, C. A.	(P)	3 June
Melen, C. A.	(P)	14 July
Berry, S. A. MEng	(P)	15 July
Chettleburgh, R. R.		
MSc	(P)	15 July
Elliott, R. G. BEng	(P)	15 July
Evans, R. O. BA	(P)	15 July
Gossling, S. M.		
BEng	(P)	15 July
Ireland, N. R. BSc	(P)	15 July
Kimberley, S. D.	(P)	15 July
Lynham, C. R. BA	(P)	15 July
Massie, A. MA	(P)	15 July
McKay, D. J. BSc	(P)	15 July
Nicol, C. S. MA	(P)	15 July
Ormshaw, N. J.		
BSc	(P)	15 July
Smith, W. G. BEng	(N)	15 July
Thomson, M. J.		
MA	(P)	15 July
Walls, J. R. E. MA	(P)	15 July
Graham, A. G.	(ENG)	28 July

Grindlay, J. P.	(P)	28 July
Harvey, G.	(N)	28 July
Morley, S.	(P)	28 July
Mullen, C. A.	(P)	28 July
Stratton, A. K.	(N)	28 July
Webb, K. R.	(P)	28 July
Westwood, M. D.	(P)	28 July
Hynes, J. M. BMedSci		
BM BS	(P)	10 Aug
Keenan, W. MEng	(P)	10 Aug
McAllister, J. BSc	(P)	10 Aug
Robertson, E. A.		
BVMS	(P)	10 Aug
Smith, M. A. BSc	(N)	10 Aug
Airey, A. M. R. BSc	(N)	11 Aug
Anderson, D. I.		
BEng	(P)	11 Aug
Ball, C. D. BSc	(P)	11 Aug
Coyle, G. S. J. BSc	(N)	11 Aug
Duff, G. BEng	(P)	11 Aug
Garlick, D. J. B. BSc	(P)	11 Aug
Greenhalgh, S. D.		
BEng	(P)	11 Aug
Hart, G. F. BEng	(P)	11 Aug
Harvey, G. T. BSc	(P)	11 Aug
Laidlar, R. E. BSc	(N)	11 Aug
Mckee, C. J. BSc	(P)	11 Aug
Mcphee, R. K. J.		
BEng	(P)	11 Aug
Militis, G. M. BEng	(P)	11 Aug
Ollerton, C. L. E.		
BSc	(P)	11 Aug
Phillips, T. L. BA	(P)	11 Aug
Tomala, R. J.		
BPharm	(P)	11 Aug
West, D. J. BEng	(P)	11 Aug
Whiteley, N. O. M.		
BSc	(N)	11 Aug
Whiteman, T. J. BA	(P)	11 Aug
Parker, A.	(N)	28 Aug
Ebberson, N. E.	(N)	28 Sept
Bridges, D. R.		
MPhys	(P)	5 Oct
Cripps, R. B. MEng	(P)	5 Oct
Keys, A. T. J. BEng	(P)	5 Oct
Mallon, B. J. BEng	(P)	5 Oct
Marley, N. J.		
MChem	(P)	5 Oct
Reid, C. S. BEng	(N)	5 Oct
Sheldon, J. A. BD	(P)	5 Oct
Belford, J. S. BSc	(P)	6 Oct
Bundock, G. E. BA	(P)	6 Oct
Caple, L. C. BSc	(P)	6 Oct
Davies, G. T. BEng	(N)	6 Oct
Farrell, N. G. A.		
BSc	(P)	6 Oct
Freeborough, J. A.		
BEng	(P)	6 Oct
Galbraith, M. A.		
BSc	(N)	6 Oct

Gover, K. M. A.		
BScEcon	(P)	6 Oct
Grindal, D. J. BEng	(P)	6 Oct
Haley, M. S. BSc	(N)	6 Oct
Morton, C. J. BSc	(P)	6 Oct
Payne, M. B. BSc	(P)	6 Oct
Smith, J. M. BSc	(P)	6 Oct
Staudinger, S. J.		
BEng	(P)	6 Oct
Wilson, D. C. LLB	(P)	6 Oct
Wright, A. J. BSc	(P)	6 Oct
Clarke, P. A.	(P)	7 Oct
Hale, P. N.	(P)	7 Oct
Redfern, C. C.	(P)	7 Oct
Wilson, B.	(P)	7 Oct
Clark, D. J. BCom	(N)	1 Dec
Fleckney, M. A.		
BEng	(P)	1 Dec
Hague, S. C. BA	(P)	1 Dec
Hurcomb, R. J. BA	(N)	1 Dec
James, D. MEng		
BA	(P)	1 Dec
Missen, R. A. C.		
BSc	(P)	1 Dec
Moon, C. J. BEng	(P)	1 Dec
Plummer, A. L. BA	(N)	1 Dec
Pote, C. F. BEng	(P)	1 Dec
Schofield, J. A. A.		
BSc	(P)	1 Dec
Spencer, R. BSc	(P)	1 Dec
Tano, A. BEng	(P)	1 Dec
Vaughan, M. J. BSc	(N)	1 Dec

1996

Wardrope, A. B.	(P)	7 Jan
Watson, J. A.	(P)	2 Feb
Bateman, S. A.	(P)	5 Feb
Berry, J. E. MA BSc	(N)	9 Feb
Blythe, A. T. BEng	(P)	9 Feb
Boyle, S. J. BA	(P)	9 Feb
Chapple, C. O. BA	(P)	9 Feb
Dickerson, K. N.		
BSc	(P)	9 Feb
Fallon, M. BEng	(N)	9 Feb
Fopp, C. M. BSc	(N)	9 Feb
Forward, G. S. BA	(P)	9 Feb
Haith, L. R. P. BSc	(P)	9 Feb
Hutchinson, I. C.		
BA	(N)	9 Feb
Mordecai, P. D. BA	(N)	9 Feb
Murphy, B. D. BA	(N)	9 Feb
Squires, M. J.		
BEng	(P)	9 Feb
Stainthorpe, I. R.		
BSc	(N)	9 Feb
Williams, D. M.		
BEng	(N)	9 Feb
Scuffham, S. J.	(P)	10 Feb

137

Flying Officers

1996—contd

Arlett, D. J. BEng	(P)	6 Apr
Baker, R. D. F. BA	(N)	6 Apr
Beamond, D. A.		
BSc	(N)	6 Apr
Billingham, K. L.		
BSc	(N)	6 Apr
Crawford, M. J. BA	(N)	6 Apr
Cripps, R. E. BEng	(P)	6 Apr
Dunlop, T. E. BEng	(P)	6 Apr
Kay, A. M. BSc	(P)	6 Apr
McLenaghan, L.		
BEng	(N)	6 Apr
Mitchell, J. G. C.		
BSc	(P)	6 Apr
Peterson, I. M. BSc	(P)	6 Apr
Riches, A. S. BSc	(P)	6 Apr
Risely, A. L. BEng	(P)	6 Apr
Rogers, J. S. BEng	(P)	6 Apr
Sloley, R. BSc	(N)	6 Apr
Young, P. L. BSc	(P)	6 Apr
Holmes, J. D.	(P)	10 Apr
Bury, N. P. BSc	(N)	1 June
Fielding, D. M. A.		
BA	(N)	1 June
Salam, A. BA	(P)	1 June
Stead, E. J. BSc	(P)	1 June
Thomas, D. J. BSc	(N)	1 June
Woodward, J.		
BEng	(P)	1 June
Barraclough, H. E.		
BSc	(P)	15 July
Batt, S. P. BEng	(P)	15 July
Clayton, J. A. BSc	(P)	15 July
Crichton, A. BEng	(P)	15 July
Hillard, R. J. BA	(P)	15 July
Hudson, J. D. BA	(P)	15 July
Lewis, I. S. BSc	(P)	15 July
Lindsay, T. J. BSc	(P)	15 July
Littlejohn, P. A. T.		
BA	(P)	15 July
Mannering, R. E.		
BEng	(P)	15 July
Scott, A. J. BSc	(P)	15 July
Williams, P. J. BSc	(P)	15 July
Cassells, I.	(AEO)	25 July
Mottram, D.	(AEO)	25 July
Caine, R. A.	(P)	28 July
Dahroug, M.	(P)	28 July
Hoare, M. D.	(P)	28 July
Lees, R. M.	(P)	28 July
Beck, J. A. BEng	(P)	10 Aug
Butler, V. R. P. BSc	(P)	10 Aug
Campion, S. J.		
BEng	(P)	10 Aug
Clement, T. J. BSc	(P)	10 Aug

Farndon, C. A. BSc	(N)	10 Aug
French, D. C. BEng	(P)	10 Aug
Hollingworth, J. L.		
BSc	(P)	10 Aug
Kent, J. D. BEng	(N)	10 Aug
Logan, C. R. G. BA	(P)	10 Aug
Marr, P. J. B. BEng	(P)	10 Aug
McCann, S. O.		
BEng	(P)	10 Aug
Ouellette, A. D.		
BEng	(P)	10 Aug
Rutland, M. F. BEng	(P)	10 Aug
Spencer, D. C. P.		
BSc	(N)	10 Aug
Whitnall, M. G. BA	(P)	10 Aug
Bressani, M. J. BSc	(N)	5 Oct
Colley, M. BEng	(P)	5 Oct
Deyes, S. BEng	(P)	5 Oct
Dixon, J. P. BEng	(P)	5 Oct
Ellson, A. M. BSc	(P)	5 Oct
Fothergill, S. R.		
BSc	(N)	5 Oct
Frayling, A. K. BSc	(P)	5 Oct
Graham, N. J. BSc	(P)	5 Oct
Guertin, J. A. BSc	(P)	5 Oct
Hill, T. BSc	(P)	5 Oct
Kelly, C. J. R. BSc	(P)	5 Oct
Kenworthy, E. S.		
BSc	(P)	5 Oct
Macniven, D. J.	(N)	5 Oct
Massingham, D. P.		
BSc	(P)	5 Oct
Melville, C. R. BEng	(N)	5 Oct
Norton, P. S. BSc	(P)	5 Oct
Radley, J. P. BA	(P)	5 Oct
Redican, C. J. BSc	(N)	5 Oct
Shaw, M. R. BSc	(P)	5 Oct
Shorey, T. D. G.		
BA(Econ)	(P)	5 Oct
Wadlow, P. J. BEng	(P)	5 Oct
Walker, S. BSc	(P)	5 Oct
Willers, S. J. BA	(N)	5 Oct
Arch, D. J.	(N)	6 Oct
Baptie, D. C.	(N)	6 Oct
Cavendish, T.	(N)	6 Oct
Evans, G. J.	(P)	6 Oct
Firth, P. T.	(N)	6 Oct
Griffiths, G. O.	(P)	6 Oct
Keer, M. B.	(P)	6 Oct
Lovett, G. S.	(P)	6 Oct
Redman, A. P.	(N)	6 Oct
Jones, B. M. BEng	(N)	30 Nov
Leather, R. W. BA	(P)	30 Nov

1997

Potter, R. D. E.	(P)	6 Apr
Stokes, N. J.	(AEO)	29 May
Monslow, K.	(AEO)	24 July

Brough, C.	(P)	28 July
Moore, R. D. G.	(P)	28 July
Wylie, D. R.	(P)	28 July
Elsey, M. J.	(N)	5 Oct
Epps C. P.	(P)	5 Oct
Everett, A. R.	(P)	5 Oct
Keeling, R. L.	(P)	5 Oct
Wills, B. T.	(P)	5 Oct
Naismith, P. J.	(N)	3 Nov
Cade, A. J.	(P)	18 Nov

1998

Coffey, S. M.	(P)	8 Feb
Pepper, A. E.	(N)	8 Feb
Richley, P. J.	(N)	8 Feb
Wood, J. P.	(P)	8 Feb

Pilot Officers

1997

Elwell, M.	(N)	25 July
Hewer, S. M.	(N)	25 July
Lock, M. D.	(P)	25 July
Lockwood, S. I.	(N)	25 July
Prochera, D. J.	(P)	25 July
Pryor, A. M.	(P)	25 July
Boyce, P. A.	(P)	3 Oct
Cole, G. W.	(P)	3 Oct
Cooper, W. D.	(P)	3 Oct
Fincher, S. J.	(N)	3 Oct
Mason, J. R.	(P)	3 Oct
O'grady, P.	(P)	3 Oct
Saunders, W. D. R.	(P)	3 Oct
Baker, A. C. M.		
BEng	(P)	30 Nov
Purkis, R. J. BEng	(P)	30 Nov

1998

Elliott, N. A.	(P)	6 Feb
Robinson, D. A.	(P)	6 Feb
Currie, D. D. BSc	(N)	8 Feb
Griffiths, T. M. BSc	(N)	8 Feb
Sharpe, D. J. C.		
BSc	(N)	8 Feb
Stevenson, T. L.		
BSc	(N)	8 Feb
Swinton, M. L. BSc	(N)	8 Feb
White, C. A. BA	(N)	8 Feb
Warren, T. J.	(N)	3 Apr
Allen, J. W. BA	(N)	5 Apr
Buxton, K. M. L.		
BEng	(P)	5 Apr
Dean, D. R. BEng	(P)	5 Apr
Flewin, M. R. BEng	(P)	5 Apr
Macbrayne, A. A.		
BVMS	(P)	5 Apr
Marston, L. BEng	(P)	5 Apr
Phillips, D. B. BA	(P)	5 Apr
Stratford, G. BSc	(P)	5 Apr
Webster, C. BEng	(N)	5 Apr
Lucas, C. J.	(N)	29 May

Acting Pilot Officers

1997

Bamford, H.	(N)	1 Sept
Clarke, D. J. BSc	(P)	1 Sept
Coe, A. BSc	(P)	1 Sept
Davies, S. G.	(P)	1 Sept
Durban, P. M. BEng	(P)	1 Sept
Fowler, D. J.	(P)	1 Sept
Garbutt, A. M.	(P)	1 Sept
Knight, C. W. BSc	(P)	1 Sept
Parr, A. J. MEng BA	(P)	1 Sept
Rogers, A. J. BSc	(P)	1 Sept
Shepherd, B. BEng	(P)	1 Sept
Waple, C. A. BSc	(P)	1 Sept
Williams, S. M.	(P)	1 Sept
Wharry, M. G.	(P)	4 Sept
Frazer, M. T.	(N)	2 Oct
Jackson, O. J.	(P)	2 Oct
McDonnell, C.	(N)	2 Oct
Osborne, J. W.	(P)	2 Oct
Staite, N. P.	(P)	2 Oct
Tipper, J. A. MEng	(P)	6 Oct
Howe, C. J.	(P)	27 Nov
Meakin, K. S.	(P)	27 Nov
Owczarkowski, N.		
E.	(P)	27 Nov
Reader, G. S.	(P)	27 Nov
Thorne, I. D.	(P)	27 Nov

1998

Edwards, G. T.	(N)	5 Feb
Green, M. W.	(P)	5 Feb
Beevers, P. D. BSc	(P)	24 Mar

OPERATIONS SUPPORT BRANCH

Group Captains

1988

Buckley, Nicholas John rcds psc Born 1/10/47   (FC)   1 July

1989

Keith, George Thomas jsdc i Born 10/4/47   (FC)   1 July

1990

Fishwick, Robert, John psc G(a) Born 18/6/45   (REGT)   1 July

1991

Bremner, David Alastair Gillan psc Born 11/09/45   (REGT)   1 Jan

1993

Shields, Michael Hedley FIMgt psc qwi(AD) Born 4/3/45   (FC)   1 July

1994

Sturman, Roger John awcc psc Born 4/11/46   (ATC)   1 Jan
Hollin, David MIMgt psc Born 6/4/44   (INT)   1 July

1995

Moore, Richard Charles MBE BSc psc Born 5/8/50   (REGT)   1 Jan

1996

Dingle, Barry Thomas psc Born 24/11/48   (ATC)   1 Jan
Fuller, Malcolm John psc Born 22/10/50   (ATC)   1 Jan
Pearson, Nigel John FRAeS FIMgt qs Born 17/2/46   (INT)   1 Jan

1997

Anderton, Stephen Harper MSc BSc FIMgt psc Born 29/8/50   (REGT)   1 Jan
Bettel, Martyn Roswell OBE ADC jsdc qs Born 16/10/49   (FC)   1 Jan
Hodge, Derek James psc Born 2/6/45   (ATC)   1 Jan
Jenner, Richard Mark jsdc qwi qs Born 22/8/53   (FC)   1 Jan
Lloyd, Stephen James BSc FRAeS FIMgt jsdc qs Born 08/05/51 (INT)   1 Jan
Pellatt, Kevin John MIMgt jsdc qs Born 26/1/52   (FC)   1 Jan
Rodgers, Philip John MBE psc Born 25/11/43   (INT)   1 Jan

Group Captains

1997—contd

Williams, Nigel jsdc qss Born 3/2/51   (ATC)   1 Jan

1998

Evans, David Robert Evan jsdc psc Born 19/10/52   (REGT)   1 Jan
McPhee, Ian Alexander psc Born 17/4/53   (REGT)   1 Jan
Rogers, Brian Edward MBE psc Born 6/1/49   (FC)   1 Jan
Drissell, Peter James MA BSc MInstD jsdc qs Born 24/11/55   (REGT)   1 July

Wing Commanders

1983

Huntley, A. S. qs (FC) 1 Jan

1985

Roberts, D. jsdc qwi
qs (FC) 1 Jan

1986

Gritten, A. J. MBE
jsdc (REGT) 1 July

1987

Valentine, M. C.
qs (REGT) 1 Jan
Fonfe, M. D. C. MBE
G(a) qs (REGT) 1 July
Todd, D. MBE BSc jsdc
qs (FC) 1 July
Williams, N. H.
psc (ATC) 1 July

1988

Barnes, L. J. F. MSc
psc (REGT) 1 Jan

1989

Willmott, N. P. qs (FC) 1 Jan
Acons, E. G. N.
qs (REGT) 1 July
Davie, A. MA
psc (REGT) 1 July

1990

Parker, J. E. psc (FC) 1 Jan
Rodford, J. D. BSc G(a)
qs (REGT) 1 Jan
Singleton, P. M. MIPD
qs (FC) 1 Jan
Hooker, M. R. MIMgt
qs (REGT) 1 July
Nash, C. C. BA qs (FC) 1 July
Pile, B. L. BA qs (REGT) 1 July
Pyper, H. H. psc (FC) 1 July

Shepherd, P. jsdc
qs (FLTOPS) 1 July

1991

Brewer, N. C. nadc
psc (ATC) 1 Jan
Gregory, N. A. BA ACII
psc (ATC) 1 Jan
White, R. W. MBE G(a)
qss (REGT) 1 Jan

1992

Ordish, G. A. jsdc
qs (ATC) 1 Jan
Stacey, C. C. D. BSc
qs (INT) 1 Jan
Gray-Wallis, H. F.
qs (ATC) 1 July
Hunter, P. R. OBE
jsdc (FC) 1 July
Shackell, J. M. jsdc
awcc G(a) qs (REGT) 1 July

1993

Hutchinson, N. qs
i* (FC) 1 Jan
Angus, P. J. M. MBE BA
jsdc qs (FC) 1 July
Denholm, I. T. MBE BSc
jsdc qs (INT) 1 July
Knowles, D. W. MBA
BA qs (REGT) 1 July
Pennington, A. J.
MIMgt psc (INT) 1 July
Whiteway, H. A. qs (FC) 1 July

1994

Cornwell, B. A. BSc
ARCS qab qs (FC) 1 Jan
Evans, J. G. MBE MBA
BA jsdc G(a) (REGT) 1 Jan
Hallam, M. R. psc (INT) 1 Jan
Perfect, A. A. MIMgt
qs (ATC) 1 Jan
Stenson, J. P. MBE BSc
qs (ATC) 1 Jan
Crofton, D. N. qs (INT) 1 July
Hamilton, D. B. qs(INT) 1 July
Leckey, J. jsdc qs (FC) 1 July
Middleton, P. G.
qss (FC) 1 July

Parker, M. K.
psc (REGT) 1 July
Roberts, P. psc (ATC) 1 July
Romney, C. N. BSc psc
qab (FC) 1 July
Sherdley, K. P. BA
qs (ATC) 1 July

1995

Gimblett, W. J. qab
qs (INT) 1 Jan
Grant, B. C. E. qs (ATC) 1 Jan
Scott, A. M. O. BA
qss (INT) 1 Jan
Strong, M. C. G.
qs (ATC) 1 Jan
Trevett, A. D. qs (FC) 1 Jan
Wordley, M. R.
psc (ATC) 1 Jan
Hill, C. D. MBE qs(ATC) 1 July
Middleton, I. S. BA
psc (ATC) 1 July
Stacey, G. E. MBE BSc
psc(m) G(a) qs
REGT) 1 July

1996

Clare, A. J. MIMgt
qs (ATC) 1 Jan
Colgate, J. A. BSc
qs (INT) 1 Jan
Dipper, K. R. MA BSc
G(a) psc (REGT) 1 Jan
Finely, N. H. M.
qss (ATC) 1 Jan
Gordon, N. J. MBE
MIPD psc qwi (FC) 1 Jan
Kennedy, P. A. M.
MIMgt ACII qs(REGT) 1 Jan
McGonigle, N.
psc (REGT) 1 Jan
Trundle, C. C. psc(ATC) 1 Jan
Walker, D. J. qs (INT) 1 Jan
Wilkins, R. A. W.
qs (INT) 1 Jan
Abbott, S. BA jsdc G(a)
qs (REGT) 1 July
Greatorex, M. psc (FC) 1 July
Jenkins, I. P. qs (REGT) 1 July
Sheeley, I. M. qss(ATC) 1 July
Smith, F. J. P. BEd
qs (ATC) 1 July
Strickland, K. N.
qss (REGT) 1 July

Wing Commanders

1996—contd

Wood, P. M. qs (FC) 1 July

1997

Ashwell, M. L. MBE BSc
nadc psc (FC) 1 Jan
Batchelor, A. B. qs(INT) 1 Jan
Brignall, T. A. MBE
qs (INT) 1 Jan
Bunting, B. E. qs (ATC) 1 Jan
Clark, J. jsdc qs (ATC) 1 Jan
Dziuba, M. S. qs (ATC) 1 Jan
Hill, E. J. R. qss (FC) 1 Jan
Kaye, P. M. qs (REGT) 1 Jan
Minns, T. qs (ATC) 1 Jan
Rimmer, M. qab qs(FC) 1 Jan
Steele, A. H. BA PGCE
qs (REGT) 1 Jan
Warrick, N. M. FIAP
MIMgt qab qs (FC) 1 Jan
West, C. M. BSc G(a)
qs (REGT) 1 Jan
Williams, R. N. qs(ATC) 1 Jan
Balshaw, K. S.
qs (REGT) 1 July
Buist, S. L. qs (FC) 1 July
Greville, P. J. qss (ATC) 1 July
Hughes, J. T. BA
qs (REGT) 1 July

1998

Chambers, P. qs (FC) 1 Jan
Galbraith, A. G.
qs (REGT) 1 Jan
Peart, C. J. qs (ATC) 1 Jan
Proudlove, A.
qs (REGT) 1 Jan
Stewart, P. D. T. MBE
adp qs (INT) 1 Jan
Tyrrell, I. R. BSc
qs (INT) 1 Jan
Chambers, M. A.
qs (ATC) 1 July
Coombs, B. BA
qs (ATC) 1 July
Crayford, M. K. qs (FC) 1 July
Lynch, R. D. BA
qs (REGT) 1 July
Peters, N. P. qs (FC) 1 July

Squadron Leaders

1978

Taylor, R. J. M. qs(ATC) 1 Jan

1981

Hunter, G. qs (INT) 1 Jan

1982

Comina, P. S. C.
qss (REGT) 1 Jan
Merriman, J. L.
qs (ATC) 1 Jan
Williams, M. qss (FC) 1 July

1983

Cox, R. E. N. qs (REGT) 1 July
Vass, A. (FC) 1 July
Vernal, J. qss (REGT) 1 July

1984

Grove, A. D. W.
qs (ATC) 1 Jan
Baxter, A. qss (REGT) 1 July
Jackson, M. R. qs(ATC) 1 July
Jasinski, N. Z. R.
qs (REGT) 1 July

1985

Stokes, R. K.
qss (REGT) 1 Jan

1986

Harrison, E. C. MBE
qss (ATC) 1 Jan
Moralee, P. J.
qss (REGT) 28 May
Hutchinson, F. N.
qs (REGT) 1 July

1987

Clough, G. (FC) 1 Jan
Dalley, K. P. qss (ATC) 1 Jan

Handy, R. B. MIPD
qss (ATC) 1 Jan
Thompson, C. P. C.
qs (FC) 1 July

1988

Chalklin, R. qs (REGT) 1 Jan
Duncan, J. C. qs (ATC) 1 Jan
George, A. M. MBE qs
i (ATC) 1 Jan
Gifford, F. C. M.
qs (ATC) 1 Jan
Ingham, J. A. qs(REGT) 1 Jan
Radforth, A. M.
qs (ATC) 1 Jan
Sinclair, P. L. MIMgt
qss (ATC) 1 Jan
Smith, A. R. (ATC) 1 Jan
Tester, D. J. MA
qs (INT) 1 Jan
Tully, K. F. qs (ATC) 1 Jan
Wilkey, R. C.
qs (FLTOPS) 1 Jan
Bartlett, A. (FC) 1 July
Hawkins, B. J. R.
qs (ATC) 1 July
Littlehales, M. P. G.
qs (FC) 1 July
Webster, E. E. adp
qs (ATC) 1 July
Williamson, B. T.
qs (ATC) 1 July

1989

Birkbeck, P. C. L. BSc
qs (FC) 1 Jan
Franklin, C. J. (FC) 1 Jan
Green, B. C. qss (FC) 1 Jan
Gresham, J. W. (ATC) 1 Jan
Preston, G. A. qab
qs (FC) 1 Jan
Revell, C. qs (ATC) 1 Jan
Smith, P. R. qab
qs (FC) 1 Jan
Stevens, P. F. qab
qs (FC) 1 Jan
Strachan, P. D.
qs (REGT) 1 Jan
Sutherland-Scott, R.
BSc qs (ATC) 1 Jan
Walker, C. G. qs (ATC) 1 Jan
Williams, V. J. MBE
BSc (INT) 1 Jan
Worrall, J. A. qs (ATC) 1 Jan
Ainslie, I. McP.
qss (ATC) 1 July

Squadron Leaders

1989—contd

Day, P. N. G(a)
qs   (REGT)   1 July
Hammett, G. G.
qss   (INT)   1 July
Howells, L. qs   (ATC)   1 July
Hurry, A. J. qs   (REGT)   1 July
Jago, P. qs i*   (FC)   1 July
McKeown, G. M.
qs   (ATC)   1 July
McManus, S. J. qss(FC)   1 July
Tolley, S. G. BSc qwi
qwi(T) qss   (FC)   1 July

1990

Burchet, C. R. qs   (INT)   1 Jan
Campbell, I. M.
qss   (ATC)   1 Jan
Diffey, G. E. MBE
qs   (REGT)   1 Jan
Foster, C. A. qs   (ATC)   1 Jan
Fryer, R. P. qs   (ATC)   1 Jan
Hagan, J. G. BSc qs(FC)   1 Jan
Heath, M. A. MIPD G(a)
qs   (REGT)   1 Jan
Perkins, A. D. qs   (ATC)   1 Jan
Yarnold, J. G. T.
qss   (REGT)   1 Jan
Adamson, G. D. W.
MBE TD AE MA
     (REGT)   12 June
Barrowcliffe, I. qss(INT)   1 July
Bateman, J. C. qwi(AD)
qs   (FC)   1 July
Bull, R. M. qss   (ATC)   1 July
Child, J. A. MMAR
qss   (FC)   1 July
Clegg, J. A. qs   (FC)   1 July
Hallett, C. qab qss   (FC)   1 July
Jones, P. A. BSc
qs   (ATC)   1 July
Kiely, C. T. qs   (ATC)   1 July
Lainchbury, D. I.
qs   (ATC)   1 July
Merryweather, D. V.
qss   (ATC)   1 July
Mitchell, G. I. qss (ATC)   1 July
Ronaldson, A. qs   (FC)   1 July
Smith, S. K. psc   (FC)   1 July

1991

Caddick, D. J. MBE BA
MIPD MIMgt qs
     (REGT)   1 Jan
Challenor, G. B. BA
qs   (ATC)   1 Jan
Coggon, M. G. qss (FC)   1 Jan
Cole, J. M. qss   (INT)   1 Jan
Cross, H. C.   (REGT)   1 Jan
McFadyen, A. G. BA
qs   (FC)   1 Jan
Riley, J. J.   (REGT)   1 Jan
Abbott, C. J.
qss   (REGT)   1 July
Day, F. B. W. E.
qs   (ATC)   1 July
Hann, K. MBE qwi
qs   (FC)   1 July
Hidden, C. J. qs (REGT)   1 July
Hodgson, J. W.
qss   (ATC)   1 July
Jones, R. W. qs   (FC)   1 July
Kirk, J. N. qs   (REGT)   1 July
La Forte, R. W. MBE BA
qs   (REGT)   1 July
Loader, J. P. MBE
qss   (INT)   1 July
Payne, T. BSc G(a)
qss   (REGT)   1 July
Powe, M. J. BSc qs(FC)   1 July
Reeve, N. P. qss   (FC)   1 July
Ryan, M. J. MIPD
MIMgt qs   (REGT)   1 July
Stoner, N. B. qs   (ATC)   1 July
Thomas, N. A. qs (ATC)   1 July
Ware, I. H. qs   (REGT)   1 July
Wilmshurst-Smith, J. D.
qss   (FC)   1 July

1992

Burt, P. G(a) qs (REGT)   1 Jan
Duffus, A. A. qs   (FC)   1 Jan
Evans, N. qs   (REGT)   1 Jan
Hill, N. BSc qs   (INT)   1 Jan
Holland, D. A. qs   (INT)   1 Jan
Mellor-Jones, R. A.
BSc   (FC)   1 Jan
Mills, A. R. M. BA
qs   (ATC)   1 Jan
Osborne, T. E. jsdc cfs
qs   (FLTOPS)   1 Jan
Oxley, J. P. qss   (FC)   1 Jan
Pearson, G. J. BA
qs   (INT)   1 Jan
Quin, A. K. qs   (ATC)   1 Jan
Tolman, N. J. qs   (ATC)   1 Jan
Downs, G. D. qs   (INT)   1 July

Edwards, P. qss   (INT)   1 July
Gray, R. W. qs   (FC)   1 July
Hemsley, R. J. T. BA
qs   (FC)   1 July
Marsden, J. W. BSc
MRINA qss   (FC)   1 July
Marsh, R. J. L.
BSc   (FLTOPS)   1 Oct

1993

Allan, D. qs   (INT)   1 Jan
Beck, J. MSc BA
qs   (INT)   1 Jan
Buttery, P. A. MRAeS
asq qs   (FC)   1 Jan
Christie, D. J. qs i (FC)   1 Jan
Cox, P. H. qss   (FC)   1 Jan
George, B. D. qss (ATC)   1 Jan
Gorman, C. J.
qs   (REGT)   1 Jan
Griffiths, B. M. MBA
BSc MIMgt G(a)
qs   (REGT)   1 Jan
Hewett, G. BEd qs (FC)   1 Jan
Nott, R. E. qs   (ATC)   1 Jan
Nuttall, S. V. qs   (INT)   1 Jan
Hall, B. T. F. AE (REGT)   2 Mar
Adey, E. J. BA
qs   (REGT)   1 July
Balaam, D. C. MBE
qs   (INT)   1 July
Beckwith, D. M.
qs   (REGT)   1 July
Casey, J. P. qs   (FC)   1 July
Dunn, M.   (ATC)   1 July
Kay, A. qs   (FC)   1 July
King, A. J. qab qs (FC)   1 July
Knapman, C. S. qab
qs   (FC)   1 July
Morrison, D. qss (ATC)   1 July
Rapson, A. D. qs (ATC)   1 July
Roberts, A. J. BSc
qs   (ATC)   1 July
Robinson, A. qs (ATC)   1 July
Rogerson, M. MBE
qs   (ATC)   1 July
White, J. P. BSc
qs   (REGT)   1 July
Williams, D. A. K.
qs   (REGT)   1 July
Woosey, D. C. qab
qs   (INT)   1 July
Wylde, J. D. BA qss(FC)   1 July

Squadron Leaders

1994

Alexander, J. BA G(a)
 qs (REGT) 1 Jan
Bartlett, S. E. BSc
 qss (INT) 1 Jan
Bennett, P. G. qab
 qss (INT) 1 Jan
Bush, D. A. BSc
 qs (ATC) 1 Jan
Chapman, M. A. (ATC) 1 Jan
Chapman, N. A. MSc
 BA qs (INT) 1 Jan
Cookson, J. D. BEM
 qs (ATC) 1 Jan
Embleton, S. N.
 qss (REGT) 1 Jan
Fearon, J. B. BSc asq
 qss (FC) 1 Jan
Garston, R. J. L. MSc
 qs (REGT) 1 Jan
Jobling, C. qs (FC) 1 Jan
McLean, B. J. qs (FC) 1 Jan
Mullings, N. W. BSc
 qs (FC) 1 Jan
Nicolson, J. A.
 qss (ATC) 1 Jan
Ormerod, C. A.
 qs (REGT) 1 Jan
Ward, G. F. qss (FC) 1 Jan
Kreft, S. N. BA (INT) 17 June
Atkinson, P. W. BA
 qs (FC) 1 July
Bainbridge, A. C.
 qs (ATC) 1 July
Dickson, G. L. BA
 qs (ATC) 1 July
Eaton, J. G. MDA BSc
 qs (REGT) 1 July
Fraser, N. A. S. qss(FC) 1 July
Hyett, S. D. qs (ATC) 1 July
Luton, M. qs (REGT) 1 July
Martin, J. C. P.
 qs (REGT) 1 July
McCombe, A. B.
 qss (REGT) 1 July
McLean, A. (INT) 1 July
Millington, W. J. MA
 asq qs (FC) 1 July
Naworynsky, M. P.
 qs (ATC) 1 July
Paige, J. M. qss (ATC) 1 July
Presley, M. A. qs (FC) 1 July
Rayfield, P. H. qs (FC) 1 July
Smailes, M. S.
 qss (ATC) 1 July

Smith, H. G. BA
 qss (ATC) 1 July
Smith, N. C. qss(REGT) 1 July
Steel, C. S. qs (INT) 1 July
Stewart, M. qs (REGT) 1 July
Watson, R. M. qs (ATC) 1 July

1995

Anthistle, P. qs (ATC) 1 Jan
Davies, J. B. qs (INT) 1 Jan
Dowling, F. K. qs (ATC) 1 Jan
Drake, D. J. BA
 qss (ATC) 1 Jan
Driver, M. N. BSc(Eng)
 MRAeS G(a)
 qs (REGT) 1 Jan
Dunn, J. R. qss (ATC) 1 Jan
Hazelgreaves, G. BA
 qss (ATC) 1 Jan
Jones, P. C. qs (INT) 1 Jan
Mackay, I. T. (ATC) 1 Jan
McLintic, P. J. qss (FC) 1 Jan
Prevett, W. S. qs (ATC) 1 Jan
Price, I. R. qab qwi(AD)
 qs (FC) 1 Jan
Roper, M. L. BA qs (FC) 1 Jan
Saunders, R. J. qss(FC) 1 Jan
Sawyer, S. A. qss(ATC) 1 Jan
Wragg, S. G. BSc
 qs (ATC) 1 Jan
Barrow, S. qs (ATC) 1 July
Catmull, T. P. fc qs (FC) 1 July
Holland, P. L. BSc
 qs (REGT) 1 July
Maguire, P. J. BA
 qs (FC) 1 July
Roberts, P. A. BSc
 qs (ATC) 1 July
Stokes, P. M. qs (REGT) 1 July
Todd, C. R. BSc
 qs (ATC) 1 July
Varley, G. A. qs (ATC) 1 July

1996

Barber, D. BA qs (ATC) 1 Jan
Bray, N. qs (REGT) 1 Jan
Brown, R. P. C. qs (INT) 1 Jan
Corbett, A. S. BA
 qs (INT) 1 Jan
Gibb, P. H. qs (FC) 1 Jan
Johnson, S. BEd
 qs (ATC) 1 Jan
Matyear, A. D. qs (FC) 1 Jan
Morton, M. A. BA
 qs (ATC) 1 Jan
Oldfield, C. I. qss (INT) 1 Jan

Raine, D. W. qss (ATC) 1 Jan
Reid, L. M. qs (FC) 1 Jan
Slater, A. BA
 qss (REGT) 1 Jan
Taylor, C. BA qss (ATC) 1 Jan
Taylor, W. S. MSc BSc
 MIMgt (REGT) 1 Jan
Thompson, K. S.
 qs (INT) 1 Jan
Thornber, S. R. BSc
 qss (INT) 1 Jan
Tottman, M. BSc
 qss (FC) 1 Jan
Austen, D. J. qss (ATC) 1 July
Coffey, J. fc qs (FC) 1 July
Germaney, R. C.
 qss (ATC) 1 July
Heyworth, T. C. BSc
 qss (REGT) 1 July
Johnston, D. C. (REGT) 1 July
King, W. N. MDA BA
 MIPD qs (REGT) 1 July
Martin, K. L. qss (ATC) 1 July
McCallum, A. qss (FC) 1 July
McGregor, A. BA
 qss (REGT) 1 July
McLaren, M. R.
 qss (ATC) 1 July
Millward, P. qss (FC) 1 July
Park, A. R. qs (FC) 1 July
Parsons, B. L. (ATC) 1 July
Pound, M. G(a) (REGT) 1 July
Thorner, M. A. BA
 qss (INT) 1 July
Wells, A. J. qss (ATC) 1 July
Woodward, R. G. G.
 qss (REGT) 1 July

1997

Archer, J. P. qss (REGT) 1 Jan
Bainbridge, A. S.
 qss (ATC) 1 Jan
Ball, D. E. BSc G(a)
 qss (REGT) 1 Jan
Barnes, R. W. qs(REGT) 1 Jan
Blake, F. J. qss (INT) 1 Jan
Bradnam, S. W. BSc
 qab qs (REGT) 1 Jan
Burt, M. J. G(a)
 qss (REGT) 1 Jan
Chalmers, J. E. BA
 qs (ATC) 1 Jan
Fitzmaurice, A. F. N. St.
 J. qss (FC) 1 Jan
Fixter, M. R. qss (FC) 1 Jan
Gildersleeves, J. P. V.
 qss (FC) 1 Jan
Gill, A. C. qss (ATC) 1 Jan

Squadron Leaders

1997—contd

Jones, D. K. qs	(FC)	1 Jan
Kell, G. W.	(ATC)	1 Jan
Kendall, E. S. G(a)		
qss	(REGT)	1 Jan
Kitt, A. P. BA qs	(REGT)	1 Jan
Lawrence, R. J.		
qss	(ATC)	1 Jan
Laws, A. P. qs	(INT)	1 Jan
MacPherson, A. M.		
qss	(FC)	1 Jan
Millington, S. BA		
qss	(REGT)	1 Jan
Newman, N. J.		
qs	(REGT)	1 Jan
Oliver, B. A. qss	(ATC)	1 Jan
Osman, A. J. qs	(REGT)	1 Jan
Owens, T. J. L. qs	(ATC)	1 Jan
Smith, I. R. qs	(REGT)	1 Jan
Todd, I. S. G(a)		
qss	(REGT)	1 Jan
Todd, J. D. qss	(REGT)	1 Jan
Turner, J. A.		
G(a)	(REGT)	1 Jan
Webster, R. J. MBE		
qss	(REGT)	1 Jan
Winstanley, D.		
qss	(ATC)	1 Jan
Bailey, R. qss	(INT)	1 July
Beckley, C. P. BSc(Econ)		
qss	(REGT)	1 July
Bell, I. N. qss	(ATC)	1 July
Bird, M. R. MBE	(REGT)	1 July
Brunt, L. B. qs	(REGT)	1 July
Carter, E. M. A. MBA BA		
qs	(ATC)	1 July
Clark, D. J. qwi(AD) fc		
qs	(FC)	1 July
Clifford, R. F. J.		
qss	(REGT)	1 July
Coleman, M. S. P.		
qss	(FC)	1 July
Fitness, J. H. qs	(ATC)	1 July
Gibson, C. R. qwi	(FC)	1 July
Hall, A. J. MBE		
qs	(REGT)	1 July
Lackey, E. W. M. BSc		
qs	(ATC)	1 July
Madden, M. R. BSc		
MILog MIL G(a)		
qss	(REGT)	1 July
McFarland, S. S.		
qss	(REGT)	1 July
McGregor, G. L.		
qss	(ATC)	1 July
Portlock, J. B. qs	(FC)	1 July

Willson, B. qss	(ATC)	1 July

1998

Belfield, F. D. MBE BSc		
qss	(FC)	1 Jan
Callow, A. R. qss	(FC)	1 Jan
Daisley, R. M. BSc	(FC)	1 Jan
DePolo, M. J. qss	(FC)	1 Jan
Devoy, D. A. qab		
qs	(REGT)	1 Jan
Divver, T. J. qss	(FC)	1 Jan
Dobson, A. P. BEng		
qs	(REGT)	1 Jan
Grayson, K. J.		
qss	(REGT)	1 Jan
Heaselgrave, D. R.		
qs	(ATC)	1 Jan
Jones, S. L. qss	(FC)	1 Jan
Loveday, N. J. BSc		
qss	(FC)	1 Jan
Myers-Hemingway, A.		
P. BSc qss	(INT)	1 Jan
Ploutarchou, A. P.		
qss	(ATC)	1 Jan
Rodgers, J. D.		
qss	(REGT)	1 Jan
Rossiter, G. qss	(ATC)	1 Jan
Speedy, P. P. BSc		
qss	(FLTOPS)	1 Jan
Spencer, J. D.		
BSc	(FLTOPS)	1 Jan
Tomaney, D. A.		
qs	(ATC)	1 Jan
Wann, G. B. D.		
qss	(ATC)	1 Jan
Ware, G. S. qss	(FC)	1 Jan
Wilkins, A. J. qss	(FC)	1 Jan
Alcock, N. J. BSc		
qss	(ATC)	1 July
Crompton, N. A. C.		
qss	(FC)	1 July
Cunningham, D. J.		
MBE qss	(FC)	1 July
Gilroy, A. BA		
qss	(REGT)	1 July
Griffiths, S. MISM		
qwi(SAW) qss	(REGT)	1 July
James, N. G. qss	(ATC)	1 July
Lamont, N. BA	(INT)	1 July
MacLeod, E.	(ATC)	1 July
Meridew, E. J.		
qss	(ATC)	1 July
Phillips, D. C. qss	(ATC)	1 July
Read, D. J. BA		
qss	(REGT)	1 July
Scott, P. qss	(REGT)	1 July
Thomson, I. A. BSc		
G(a) qss	(REGT)	1 July

Walker, J. C. BSc		
qss	(FC)	1 July
Wood, C. D. qss	(ATC)	1 July

Flight Lieutenants

1969

Dixon, J. M. qss (INT) 3 Sept

1972

Sims, P. E. qss (ATC) 8 Mar
Pride, I. McC.
MBE (ATC) 4 May
Muse, R. W. qss (FC) 13 July

1973

Russell, J. R. (ATC) 29 July

1974

Don, J. BSc qss (ATC) 10 Oct

1975

Newall, E. R. (ATC) 7 Feb
Wright, A. R. (ATC) 10 May
Thomson, B. R.
qss (REGT) 1 Oct
Monfort, G. R. (FC) 25 Oct

1976

Gardner, R. S. (ATC) 22 Nov

1977

Arnold, I. qss (ATC) 22 May
Jay, P. A. MSc BSc
qss (INT) 24 June
Hill, M. qss (ATC) 4 Aug

1978

Trist, S. N. qss (FLTOP 21 Mar
McClelland, D. M.(ATC) 29 June
Hartley, P. S. qss (ATC) 16 Sept

1979

La Roche, R. (ATC) 10 Nov

1980

Harrison, J. W.
qss (ATC) 28 Apr
Haughie, J. R. qss (FC) 28 Apr
Ripley, G. (FC) 11 May
Montgomerie, H. C. A.
qss (FC) 29 June
Durkin, P. (ATC) 1 July
Clifford, D. P. qss (FC) 5 Oct
Harrison, D. P. (ATC) 13 Dec

1981

Broadway, S. J. H. (FC) 17 Jan
Day, P. qss (ATC) 8 Feb
O'Carroll, J. V. qss (FC) 23 Feb
Lee, R. R. G. qss (FC) 20 Sept
Reading, A. M. (FC) 27 Sept

1982

McIntyre, A. E.
qss (ATC) 17 Jan
Perry, R. (ATC) 28 June
Nickles, R. C. BSc(ATC) 14 Nov
Beer, R. P. BSc qss (FC) 6 Dec
Williams, M. J. (ATC) 24 Dec

1983

Dring, C. A. qss (ATC) 19 Mar
Webster, D. S.
MBE (ATC) 2 July
Jeffs, A. J.
BSc qss (FLTOPS) 4 Aug
Heeley, J. M. qss (INT) 5 Oct

1984

Williams, P. F. qss(ATC) 18 Apr
Lewis, S. B. BSc
qss (INT) 9 May
Carter, C. N. BSc (FC) 22 Sept

1985

Purchase, S. P. MSc
BSc (INT) 25 Feb

Little, R. (ATC) 10 Mar
Phillipson, P. R. qss(FC) 16 May
Tyas, S. P. J. (ATC) 23 May
Taylor, J. F. BSc qss(FC) 18 July
Brightman, P. S.(REGT) 8 Sept
Sturgess, A. P. (ATC) 20 Oct
Gemmill, T. (FC) 19 Nov
Jones, M. P. (ATC) 15 Dec

1986

Shaw, P. A. (ATC) 29 Jan
Millar, H. E. (ATC) 18 Feb
Howes, D. J. G(a)
qss (REGT) 6 Mar
Hobbs, E. W. BSc MCGI
asq qss (FC) 4 Apr
Lloyd, A. T. BSc
qss (INT) 7 May
Faulkner, H. M. BSc fc
qss (FC) 11 June
Townshend, D. P.
qss (FC) 13 June
Goodwyn, C. R. BA
qss (ATC) 27 June
Horne, I. qss (ATC) 24 July
Higgs, S. M. qss(REGT) 28 Aug
Summers, G. S. BA
qss (FLTOPS) 17 Oct
Sharp, A. P. (ATC) 24 Oct
Green, P. J. qss (ATC) 22 Nov
Harvard, I. C. qss (ATC) 22 Nov
Kyffin, R. G. M. BA
qss (REGT) 19 Dec
Burke, D. G. (ATC) 20 Dec

1987

Stansby, A. W. qss (FC) 14 Jan
Williams, S. B.
BSc (ATC) 31 Jan
Wilson, S. C. BA
qss (ATC) 22 Apr
Wood, M. S. BA
asq (FC) 30 Apr
Print, C. P. MSc (ATC) 25 May
Gray, D. L. BA qss (FC) 11 June
Tape, S. F. (FC) 4 July
Cothey, P. qss (FC) 5 Aug
Giles, A. M. (ATC) 5 Aug
Rosie, K. S. qss (FC) 5 Aug
Hornsby, N. A. asq
qss (FC) 18 Sept
Howie, T. D. (REGT) 19 Sept
Iddles, J. A. D. qss (FC) 19 Sept
Jones, G. qss (REGT) 19 Sept
Power, F. (INT) 19 Sept

147

Flight Lieutenants

1987—contd

Guy, M. R. RD
  BSc   (INT)   3 Oct
Bainbridge, D. J. F. BSc
  G(a) qss   (REGT)   15 Oct
Wheeler, A. J.
  BSc   (FLTOPS)   18 Oct
Richardson, P. D. BA
  MISM MIMgt
  qss   (REGT)   29 Oct
Pendleton, G. qss (ATC)   30 Oct
Hilditch, L. E. qss (ATC)   31 Oct
Sutton, A. J. qss (ATC)   6 Nov
Patrick, S. N. BSc (ATC)   26 Nov
Philipson, R. M. fc
  qss   (FC)   5 Dec
Green, A. J. BSc
  qss1   (ATC)   10 Dec

1988

Garrity, R. D. qss (ATC)   24 Jan
Akehurst, P. L. BSc
  qss   (ATC)   4 Mar
Preedy, J. A. qss (ATC)   4 Mar
Hill, A. A. PhD BSc
  qss   (FC)   14 Apr
Mullan, P. M. BSc
  qss   (FC)   14 Apr
Knight, D.   (FC)   15 Apr
Chambers, M. G.
  qss   (ATC)   26 Apr
Moffat, W.   (FC)   9 May
Pollard, C. S. BSc
  qss   (FC)   10 May
Freeman, R. J. B. BA
  G(a) qss   (REGT)   25 May
Mackay, D. M. BA
  qss   (REGT)   25 May
Young, C. A. BSc
  qss   (FC)   25 May
Johnson, A. W. qwi(FC)   26 May
Pickett, G. R. qss (FC)   26 May
Tunaley, M. A. qss (FC)   26 May
Johnson, L. C.
  qss   (ATC)   27 May
Davies, I. D. qss (FC)   29 May
McGuigan, N. D. BSc
  qss   (FLTOPS)   7 June
Brisdion, G. A. MSc
  BSc qss   (INT)   20 July
Busby, C. A. BSc
  qss   (ATC)   20 July
Hall, N. A.   (ATC)   20 July

Saunders, A. E. J. BA
  qss   (REGT)   30 Sept
Clarke, A. C. qss   (FC)   8 Oct
Garvey, K. qss   (INT)   8 Oct
Henley, P. G. qss   (FC)   8 Oct
Ward, M. J.   (ATC)   11 Oct
Webb, B. P.   (FC)   11 Oct
Whitehead, N. qcc (FC)   15 Oct
Smith, R. F. DPhil BA
  PGCE qss   (INT)   8 Nov
Ortyl, R. I. qss   (FC)   20 Nov
Gillott, S. M. BSc
  qss   (FC)   26 Nov
Catterall, C. qss   (FC)   4 Dec

1989

Coleman, A. J. BSc
  qwi(SAW) qss(REGT)   18 Feb
Gibson, G. J.   (FC)   28 Feb
Scott, C. W. qss (ATC)   23 Mar
Upton, M. N. qss1 (FC)   23 Mar
Walkerdine, I. M.
  qss   (FC)   23 Mar
Breeds, P. W.   (INT)   11 Apr
Brown, A. M. qss (INT)   10 May
Jeffs, G. J. BA qss(ATC)   10 May
Mitchell, F. A.   (ATC)   6 June
Kennedy, A. G. MA
  G(a)   (REGT)   7 June
Clark, T. J. qss (REGT)   29 June
Bingham, J. D.   (ATC)   4 July
Sumal, I. S. qss   (FC)   4 July
Barker, R. J. qss (ATC)   17 July
Dowie, C. H. BSc
  qss   (FC)   16 Aug
Parsons, G. A. BA
  qss   (ATC)   16 Aug
Heron, P. M. qss (ATC)   27 Aug
Thayne, A. G.
  qss   (REGT)   27 Aug
Balmforth-Slater, D. L.
  qss   (FC)   24 Sept
Barmby, C. S. BSc
  qss   (INT)   30 Sept
Clayton, K. R. BSc
  qss   (REGT)   30 Sept
Kimber, C. J. BEd
  qss   (FC)   30 Sept
Lawrence, N. J. BSc
  qss   (FC)   30 Sept
Tait, J. D. BSc qss (FC)   30 Sept
Elsegood, M. J.
  qss   (FLTOPS)   8 Oct
Snellock, C. D. BSc
  qss   (INT)   26 Oct
Scott, C. asq qss   (FC)   1 Nov
MacKenzie, K. D.
  qss   (REGT)   6 Nov

Pulfrey, J. M.   (ATC)   15 Nov
Jackson, D. qss   (ATC)   3 Dec
Riley, P. J. BA qss(ATC)   7 Dec
Lewis, P. E. qss   (ATC)   15 Dec

1990

Greenwood, A. BA
  qss   (FC)   15 Jan
Thorpe, C. P. BSc
  qss   (FC)   15 Jan
Davies, A. J. qss   (FC)   29 Jan
Taylor-Powell, C. L.
  qss   (ATC)   29 Jan
Pattinson, M.
  qss   (REGT)   30 Jan
MacDonald, F. G.
  qss   (ATC)   25 Feb
Harrop, M. D. BEng
  qss   (FC)   28 Feb
Henderson, G. S. BEd
  qss   (ATC)   28 Feb
Nicholson, G. B.
  qss   (ATC)   3 Mar
Chinery, M. A. qss (FC)   8 Mar
Green, I. D. qss   (FC)   8 Mar
McCarney, E. S.
  qss   (ATC)   8 Mar
Weaver-Smith, P. A.
  qss   (REGT)   8 Mar
Brooks, D. P.
  qab   (FLTOPS)   11 Apr
Armstrong, J. T.
  qss   (REGT)   20 Apr
Hunt, D. J. fc qss (FC)   20 Apr
Hand, M. T. qss (REGT)   31 May
Sneddon, S. R.
  qss   (INT)   7 June
Barrett, M. S. qss (ATC)   8 June
Dyson, E. F. qss (REGT)   8 June
Hartle, N. J.   (FLTOPS)   8 June
Ross, J. qss   (FC)   19 June
Disdel, C. A. H.   (FC)   8 July
Brabon, M. D.   (REGT)   25 July
Baker, D. A.   (ATC)   28 July
Cochrane, J. qss (INT)   28 July
Leffler, T. qss   (FC)   2 Aug
Marden, A. J. qss(ATC)   2 Aug
Anthony, S. T.   (INT)   17 Aug
Tilley. E. J. qss   (FC)   1 Sept
Bartlett, S. M. qss(ATC)   12 Sept
Benn, C. qss   (FC)   15 Sept
Harding, C. D. E.(REGT)   15 Sept
Hart, M. P. BA qss(INT)   15 Sept
Jones, A. S. qss   (FC)   15 Sept
Jones, H. W.
  qss   (REGT)   15 Sept
Knowles, A. G. G(a)
  qss   (REGT)   15 Sept

Flight Lieutenants

1990—contd

Richardson, F. S.
qss (REGT) 15 Sept
Tuite, P. F. qss (FC) 15 Sept
Turner, G. J. qss (ATC) 15 Sept
Topham, K. D. (FC) 4 Oct
Brook, S. R. qss (ATC) 26 Oct
Coleman, C. W. T.
qss (FC) 26 Oct
Payne, S. M. qss (ATC) 2 Nov
Hughes, D. L. qss (ATC) 4 Nov
Calvert, S. E. qss (ATC) 4 Dec
Bardell-Cox, T. A.
BSc(Econ) MIMgt
qss (INT) 7 Dec
McKillop, J. A. BSc
qss (ATC) 7 Dec
Griffiths, D. J.
qss (REGT) 8 Dec
Tomkins, S. R.
qss (REGT) 20 Dec

1991

Birnie, R. E. R. BSc
qwi(AD) qss (FC) 15 Jan
Carpenter, P. J. BSc
qss (FC) 15 Jan
Hammond, G. B. T. BA
qss (FC) 15 Jan
Jacob, R. G. BA
qss (ATC) 15 Jan
Stirrat, S. S. BA
qss (INT) 15 Jan
Walker, J. C. BSc
qss (ATC) 15 Jan
Hadden, P. (ATC) 19 Jan
Warren, D. R. qss (ATC) 19 Jan
Wilkinson, A. C. BSc
qwi(SAW) qss (REGT) 19 Jan
Clarke, J. qss (ATC) 27 Jan
Bocking, I. (ATC) 29 Jan
Simpson, J. C. D.
(REGT) 30 Jan
Bridges, S. J. qss (FC) 1 Mar
Cartmell, D. R.
qss (ATC) 1 Mar
Trown, N. J.
qab (REGT) 1 Mar
Allen, M. R. L. (REGT) 6 Mar
O'Hanlon, M. J. (FC) 12 Mar
O'Neill, S. G. P. qss (FC) 30 Mar
Boyle, M. P. BSc (ATC) 11 Apr
Day, P. A. BSc qss (INT) 11 Apr

Evans, P. W. BSc
qss (FC) 11 Apr
MacLennan, S. W.
qwi(AD) (FC) 11 Apr
Bennett, A. R. BA
qss1 (REGT) 6 May
Liston, M. J. (FLTOPS) 11 May
Sandon, R. A. (FC) 11 May
Buchanan, J. W. (ATC) 15 May
Palmer, M. R. K. BSc
qss (FC) 15 May
Dallas, A. W.
qss (REGT) 22 May
Kinnell, R. (REGT) 22 May
Spence, S. qss (REGT) 22 May
Mohammed, H. A. (FC) 4 June
Atchison, J. D. BA
qss (FC) 3 July
Hewson, N. qwi(AD)
qss2 (FC) 3 July
Dunstall, M. R.
qss (ATC) 17 July
Kendall, R. A. (ATC) 17 July
Powell, G. J.
qss (REGT) 17 July
Steele, R. C. (ATC) 17 July
Ewen, G. P. MA (ATC) 14 Aug
Miller, D. qss (INT) 19 Aug
Turner, R. G. qss (FC) 28 Aug
Wrenn, M. J. (ATC) 28 Aug
Walker, S. A. (ATC) 4 Sept
Henderson, S. K. (INT) 5 Sept
Miller, D. W. A. qss(FC) 27 Sept
Payne, M. J. G(a)
qss (REGT) 22 Sept
Thorpe, J. A. BA
qss (FC) 27 Sept
Breedon, C. J. qss (FC) 11 Oct
Noone, J. M. (ATC) 11 Oct
Ryles, S. M. qss(REGT) 11 Oct
Brown, G. P. qss(REGT) 6 Nov
Hall, W. P. BS qss(ATC) 8 Nov
Hickson, P. R. BSc
qss (REGT) 8 Nov
Clyburn, N. P. qss(ATC) 9 Nov
Lewis, J. H. (ATC) 14 Nov
Balfour, J. R. S. G(a)
qss (REGT) 23 Nov
Hunter, D. T. qss (ATC) 23 Nov
Reid, A. G. M. qss (FC) 7 Dec
Currie, P. W. (FC) 10 Dec
Curtis, T. B. qss (ATC) 12 Dec
Collier, A. S. qss1 (INT) 19 Dec

1992

Dickson, M. W.
qss (ATC) 4 Jan
Kirkby, I. G. qss (FC) 4 Jan

Lorraine, A. G. qss (FC) 4 Jan
Throsby, M. qss (ATC) 4 Jan
Laker, C. R. BA (REGT) 15 Jan
Willingham, Y.
qss (ATC) 20 Jan
Craven, J. S.
qwi(AD) (FC) 22 Jan
Brown, T. D. A.
qss (ATC) 29 Jan
McAleer, A. S. qss (FC) 8 Feb
Istance, M. qss (ATC) 12 Feb
Walker, C. P. qss (INT) 12 Feb
Glazebrook, A. J. C. BA
qss (REGT) 14 Feb
McEvoy, J. J.
qss (REGT) 14 Feb
Uren, T. E. BSc G(a)
qss (REGT) 14 Feb
Hellard, G. P.
qss (REGT) 15 Feb
Jackson, J. A. (REGT) 15 Feb
Owen, D. J. qss (INT) 15 Feb
Scott, S. J.
qss (FLTOPS) 15 Feb
Seldon, F. P. (ATC) 15 Feb
Coleman, M. G.
qss (ATC) 15 Jan
Bishop, C. A. M. BA
qcc (REGT) 25 Mar
Eason, A. S. BA (ATC) 25 Mar
Maple, P. D. BA qss(FC) 25 Mar
Rickard, J. E. BSc
qss (INT) 25 Mar
Sawyer, R. N. (REGT) 26 Mar
Cooper, R. A. qss (INT) 29 Mar
Jago, M. (FC) 30 Mar
Treacy, S. M. MSc BA
qss (FC) 1 Apr
Martin, A. J. (ATC) 30 Apr
Taylor, D. BSc (FC) 6 May
Coburn, N. L. qcc (ATC) 7 May
Liggat, A. K. S. G(a)
qss (REGT) 7 May
White, J. J. qss (FC) 7 May
Jackson, A. D.
qss (FLTOPS) 10 May
Reid, J. A. (FLTOPS) 10 May
Rutherford, A. qss(INT) 15 May
Pope, M. S. qss (REGT) 21 June
Rogerson, D. M. (ATC) 8 July
Kanhai, R. I. qss (ATC) 13 Aug
Phillips, I. BSc qss(INT) 18 Aug
Eden, J. J. BSc
qss (REGT) 19 Aug
Farmer, R. N. BA
qcc (INT) 19 Aug
Hare, J. A. BA (ATC) 19 Aug
Gunn, J. H. (REGT) 3 Sept
Nugent, S. G. qss(ATC) 26 Sept
Blake, I. R. (FC) 27 Sept

Flight Lieutenants

1992—contd

Higgins, R. F.	(ATC)	27 Sept
Harris, J. C. BSc	(REGT)	2 Oct
Vine, A. P. qss	(ATC)	8 Oct
Elks, S. J. qss1	(ATC)	11 Oct
Skipp, T. A. qss	(ATC)	26 Oct
Bayley, N. J. qss	(INT)	8 Nov
Beasant, A. J.	(REGT)	8 Nov
Blockley, S. A. qwi(AD)		
qss	(FC)	8 Nov
Donoghue M. P. J.		
	(REGT)	8 Nov
Ford, D. L. G(a)		
qss	(REGT)	8 Nov
Mackenzie, A. K.		
qss	(ATC)	8 Nov
Oughton, M. D. qss(FC)		8 Nov
Durban, S. J.	(ATC)	11 Nov
Lowman, M. E. BSc		
qss	(ATC)	14 Nov
Marshall, P. J.		
qss	(ATC)	3 Dec
Leatham, C.	(ATC)	10 Dec
Attewell, D. J.	(ATC)	13 Dec
Webster, A. J. E.		
qss	(ATC)	14 Dec
Hampson, J. R.	(ATC)	15 Dec
Chappell, M. R. qss(FC)		19 Dec
Crompton, D. A.	(FC)	19 Dec
Dinsley, R. M.	(FC)	19 Dec
Hodgson, R. qss	(INT)	19 Dec
Rowntree, C. W.		
qss	(FC)	19 Dec
Ticehurst, J. qss	(FC)	19 Dec
Walton, K. G.	(FC)	19 Dec
Chick, A. J.	(FLTOPS)	20 Dec
Berners, P. R.		
qss	(FLTOPS)	21 Dec
Davis, C. D.	(ATC)	25 Dec

1993

Hope, N. qss	(ATC)	7 Jan
Parrott, M. A.	(INT)	11 Jan
Brown, R. L. BSc		
qss	(FC)	15 Jan
Carter, S. J. BEng		
qss	(REGT)	15 Jan
Clark, A. B. BSc	(ATC)	15 Jan
Gray, F. J. LLB qss(INT)		15 Jan
Hassan, E. J. BEd		
qss	(ATC)	15 Jan
Johnson, M. R. BSc		
qss	(FC)	15 Jan
Martin, D. A. BSc	(FC)	15 Jan

Lindsey, D. E. qss(ATC)		17 Jan
Cockin, M. D.	(FC)	31 Jan
Keefe, D. B. qss (REGT)		31 Jan
Loveridge, S. M.		
qss	(FC)	31 Jan
Benham, T. M.		
qss	(ATC)	1 Feb
Axford-Hawkes, I. A.		
qss	(ATC)	7 Feb
Jones, A. D. BA		
qss	(INT)	20 Feb
Sharp, J. C. BSc		
qss	(FC)	20 Feb
Walker, J. M. L.		
qss1	(FC)	1 Mar
Bullock, S. T.	(ATC)	5 Mar
MacKay, G. E.	(FC)	11 Mar
O'Connor, S. K. qss(FC)		11 Mar
Philip, M. W. BSc (INT)		14 Mar
Robinson, C. qss1 (FC)		14 Mar
Sharples, S. P.		
qss	(REGT)	14 Mar
Burr, S. J. MILog		
	(FLTOPS)	16 Mar
Kellard, C. A.	(ATC)	30 Mar
McKay, D. S.	(ATC)	30 Mar
Reid, G. S. BSc	(ATC)	1 Apr
Stylianides, A. BSc		
qcc	(FC)	1 Apr
Beat, P. A. qss	(ATC)	14 Apr
Wiggans, I. R. qss(ATC)		18 Apr
Clark, W. A.	(ATC)	23 Apr
Forrester, J. M. qss(FC)		23 Apr
Lindsay, G. H.	(ATC)	23 Apr
Swift, V. S. qss	(FC)	23 Apr
Box, R. C. qss	(FC)	25 Apr
Williams, P. L. qss (INT)		9 May
Fraser, G. M. BSc		
qss	(FC)	11 May
Pulling, B. S. qss (ATC)		2 June
Bourton, M. J. W.		
qss	(ATC)	4 June
Dyer, K. P. qss (REGT)		4 June
Bond, C. N.	(REGT)	15 June
Thomas, P. F. S.		
qss	(ATC)	23 June
Claydon, Z. G. BA(ATC)		7 July
Williams, A. G.		
qss	(REGT)	16 July
Barnes, T. J. qss (ATC)		18 July
Northam, M. P.		
qss	(ATC)	18 July
Prytherch, N. S.		
qss	(INT)	23 July
Rutherdale, R. J.	(FC)	27 July
Watson, A. J.	(FC)	27 July
Allison, A. J. qss	(FC)	29 July
Bolton, P. M. qss	(FC)	29 July
James, D. W. qss (INT)		29 July
MacLeod, G. M.	(INT)	29 July

Miller, S. M. qss(REGT)		29 July
Scott, G. T. E.	(FC)	29 July
Seymour, K. L. qwi(AD)		
qss	(FC)	29 July
Van Vogt, M. A.		
qss	(ATC)	29 July
Hanby, D. J. qss	(FC)	30 July
Douglas, I. J.	(ATC)	4 Aug
White, A. A. F. qss(INT)		25 Aug
Lock, R. K.	(ATC)	5 Sept
Morley, W. J.	(ATC)	5 Sept
Streeton, A. D.		
qss	(ATC)	5 Sept
Cumming, J. D. (REGT)		12 Sept
Fountain, D. G(a)		
qss	(REGT)	12 Sept
Mason, M. I.		
qss	(REGT)	12 Sept
Nuttall, R. M. qcc (INT)		12 Sept
Woolfson, C. A. qss(FC)		12 Sept
Clarke, D. J.		
qwi(AD)	(ATC)	15 Sept
Cosway, D. P. qss (FC)		15 Sept
Nixon, P. T.	(FC)	25 Sept
Riley, B. J. BSc		
qss	(INT)	30 Sept
Bellworthy, A. J. (ATC)		17 Oct
Callander, A. D. (REGT)		23 Oct
Collins, S. E. qss (INT)		23 Oct
Flint, C. D. qss	(FC)	23 Oct
Gibson, D.	(FC)	23 Oct
Johnson, D. R.		
qss	(ATC)	23 Oct
Langley, P. H. qss (ATC)		23 Oct
Lester, P. T. G.		
qss	(REGT)	23 Oct
Newton, K. V. qss (FC)		23 Oct
O'Dell, R. M. qss (FC)		23 Oct
Morris, P. K.	(FC)	27 Oct
Kelly, R. W. qss (INT)		7 Nov
Thomas, R. E. L.		
qss1	(ATC)	10 Nov
Burt, T. BA qss (INT)		13 Nov
Nicholas, J. J. R. MIMgt		
qss	(ATC)	21 Nov
Dodds, M. A.	(ATC)	4 Dec
Moore, C. D. qss (INT)		4 Dec
Watkins, D. M. (REGT)		4 Dec
Ball, J. K. TIG(a)(REGT)		19 Dec
Baxter, K. qss	(ATC)	19 Dec
Dix, R. E. qss	(ATC)	19 Dec
Jones, P. L.	(ATC)	19 Dec

1994

Flanigan, R. qss (ATC)		9 Jan
Burchill, G. M. (REGT)		15 Jan
Robson, N. A. H. (ATC)		15 Jan

Flight Lieutenants

1994—contd

Name	Branch	Date
Taylor, L. B. BA qwi(SAW) qss1	(REGT)	15 Jan
Cox, M.	(FC)	17 Jan
Sharland, R. E. qss	(FC)	17 Jan
Walker, K. qss1	(FC)	17 Jan
Wilczek, D. S. E. P. qss	(FC)	17 Jan
Eden, R. E. qss	(ATC)	13 Feb
Gratton, R. E. J.	(ATC)	13 Feb
Pickering, J. D. qss	(ATC)	13 Feb
Rawsthorne, N. A. BSc qss	(REGT)	18 Feb
Whetnall, H. C. BA	(ATC)	18 Feb
Kenning, J. B. BSc	(INT)	19 Feb
Owens, J. A. qss	(ATC)	25 Feb
Duffy, P. J. qss1	(REGT)	27 Feb
Millar, S. A.	(REGT)	27 Feb
Parkinson, J. H.	(REGT)	27 Feb
Rooney, W. J. qss	(REGT)	27 Feb
Traylen, M. J.	(FC)	27 Feb
Williams, D. K. qss	(REGT)	27 Feb
Wood, P. qwi(SAW) qss	(REGT)	27 Feb
Sheppard, K. J. qcc	(ATC)	28 Feb
Kempster, H. M. BSc qcc	(ATC)	29 Mar
Goodchild, M. C. H. BA qss	(ATC)	30 Mar
Lee, A. J. BA PGCE qss	(REGT)	30 Mar
Taylor, M. R. BSc qwi(SAW)	(REGT)	30 Mar
Caesar, I. R.	(REGT)	8 Apr
Cliff, C. H. G. qss	(ATC)	8 Apr
Cox, J. L. qcc	(FC)	8 Apr
Craddock, G. A.	(FC)	8 Apr
Owens, C. J. qss	(ATC)	8 Apr
Rodger, A. L.	(REGT)	23 Apr
Wymer, R. J. qss	(ATC)	27 Apr
D'Lima, L. J. V. BSc qss1	(ATC)	10 May
Lawrence, P.	(REGT)	10 May
Moon, S.	(ATC)	10 May
O'Brien, T. M.	(ATC)	10 May
Scott, P. A. BA PGCE qss	(REGT)	11 May
Stride, K. J. BA	(ATC)	11 May
Watson, E. J. MSc qss	(INT)	11 May
Wilson, M. BSc	(ATC)	11 May
Brooks, D. J. qss	(FC)	19 May
Povey, A. R. qss	(ATC)	19 May
Preston-Whyte, P. A. qss	(ATC)	19 May
Robb, A. McE.	(ATC)	19 May
Stevens, A. J.	(FC)	19 May
Welling, S. C.	(ATC)	19 May
Ballantyne, D. N. qss	(ATC)	22 May
Harvey, D. G.	(ATC)	25 May
Lutton, D. R.	(ATC)	22 June
Breddy, L. A. qss1	(ATC)	30 June
Clark, G. A. P.	(REGT)	3 July
Adamson, A. P. W. BSc AIL	(FLTOPS)	5 July
Hughes, K. A. MA MISM MInstAM(Dip)	(FLTOPS)	5 July
Godfrey, J. E. A.	(INT)	14 July
Hathaway, S. R. BSc qcc	(INT)	15 July
Boxell, D. M.	(ATC)	2 Aug
McIvor, N. J.	(REGT)	2 Aug
Kendall, W. J. qss	(REGT)	14 Aug
Bruce, C. I. D. qss1	(INT)	17 Aug
Dixon, N. R. A.	(FC)	25 Aug
Gibbs, B. T.	(FC)	25 Aug
Gill, C. M. qss	(ATC)	25 Aug
Horn, N. B. qwi(SAW) qss	(REGT)	25 Aug
Sackley, D. P. qwi(AD) qss	(FC)	25 Aug
Sinclair, S. J. qss1	(ATC)	25 Aug
Dickson, J. C. qss	(ATC)	25 Aug
Hamer, P.	(INT)	22 Sept
Dick, G. J. qss	(FC)	24 Sept
Smart, K. qss1	(ATC)	24 Sept
Johnston, M. J.	(FC)	26 Sept
Griffiths, W. R. BA qss	(INT)	30 Sept
Moss-Rogers, N. B. BSc qss	(ATC)	30 Sept
Lillywhite, R. qss	(ATC)	12 Oct
Raper, S. P.	(ATC)	28 Oct
Beck, N. P.	(FC)	5 Nov
Brooks, J. qwi(AD) qss	(FC)	5 Nov
Formby, M. R.	(REGT)	5 Nov
Hughes, P. R. qss	(INT)	5 Nov
Irvine, A. C. A.	(INT)	5 Nov
Ogden, M. R. qss	(FC)	5 Nov
Tatters, S. D.	(ATC)	5 Nov
Wheeler, S. C.	(ATC)	5 Nov
White, A. J.	(INT)	5 Nov
Ratcliffe, J. J.	(REGT)	8 Nov
Buckby, K. S.	(REGT)	9 Nov
Hayter, G. qss1	(ATC)	10 Dec
Mellings, I. M.	(ATC)	10 Dec
Maxted, S. J. qss1	(ATC)	11 Dec
Larry, S. qcc	(FC)	16 Dec
Stamford, J. M.	(INT)	16 Dec
Karle, D.	(FC)	20 Dec
Mills, C.	(FC)	20 Dec
Atkinson, K. M. BSc	(INT)	23 Dec
Myatt, R. J. BSc	(INT)	23 Dec
Hann, C. D. qss	(FC)	24 Dec

1995

Name	Branch	Date
Derbyshire, J. G. BA qwi(SAW) qs	(REGT)	15 Jan
Grady, S. W. MA	(ATC)	15 Jan
Mayers, M. S. BSc	(ATC)	15 Jan
Smeath, M. J.	(REGT)	15 Jan
Driscoll, E. J.	(ATC)	17 Jan
Metcalfe, J. H.	(ATC)	18 Jan
Boundy, R. A. qcc	(FC)	28 Jan
Calame, A. B. G(a)	(REGT)	28 Jan
Connelly, R.	(ATC)	28 Jan
Cryer, N. C. qcc	(ATC)	28 Jan
Lunn, A. R. qcc	(INT)	28 Jan
Otley, D. L.	(ATC)	28 Jan
Kettle, T. M.	(ATC)	11 Feb
Finch, A. D. BSc	(REGT)	18 Feb
Hughes, J. L. BSc	(FC)	18 Feb
Underhill, S. E. BSc qcc	(ATC)	18 Feb
MacLeod, F. D.	(ATC)	4 Mar
James, P. M.	(ATC)	22 Mar
Langley, R. I. qss1	(REGT)	22 Mar
McLucas, R. I.	(REGT)	22 Mar
Prince, N. C. H. qss1	(REGT)	22 Mar
Tait, D. C. qss	(REGT)	22 Mar
White, J. P.	(REGT)	22 Mar
Carr, R. J. BSc	(ATC)	29 Mar
Gardner, S. BA	(FLTOP)	29 Mar
Graham, D. A. BA	(FC)	29 Mar
Hixson, J. S. BSc qcc	(INT)	8 Apr
McCarney, N. C. qcc	(ATC)	12 Apr
Ratcliffe, H. C.	(ATC)	15 Apr
Seaman, M. R. N.	(FC)	28 Apr
Astley-Jones, G. D. qcc	(REGT)	2 May
Biggs, A. J.	(ATC)	2 May

Flight Lieutenants

1995—contd

Cranshaw, F. D. (REGT)	2 May
Hicks, P. M. qss1 (ATC)	2 May
Hubbard, J. W. qcc (FC)	2 May
Kendrick, S. J.	
qss1	(INT)	2 May
Leaman, M. J.	
qcc	(REGT)	2 May
Purse, M. A. qss (INT)	2 May
Ratcliffe, P. A. (FC)	2 May
Wilson, G. D. qcc (ATC)	2 May
Biddlestone, A. (ATC)	9 May
Greene, G. R. (INT)	9 May
Priddy, W. P. (ATC)	9 May
Evans, C. E. BA (ATC)	10 May
Slough, A. P. (ATC)	17 May
Cholerton, M P.	
BEng (REGT)	6 June
Jackson, S. W. BSc	
(REGT)	6 June
Hamilton, G. A.	
qcc (ATC)	15 June
Shea-Simonds, P. J.	
qs (REGT)	17 June
Bissett, W. C. BA	
PGCE (INT)	5 July
McCall, W. L. BSc (FC)	5 July
Borley, W. D.	
qss1 (ATC)	26 July
Gleeson, R. F. (FC)	26 July
Banks, C. P. (ATC)	28 July
Frost, M. L. qss (ATC)	29 July
Davies, R. A. (REGT)	2 Aug
Hickton, K. N. BEng (FC)	14 Aug
McKay, K. R. BSc (ATC)	14 Aug
Haselden, M. qss (INT)	16 Aug
Soanes, P. J. qss (ATC)	16 Aug
Whitworth, J. M.	
qss1 (ATC)	16 Aug
Addison, E. (FC)	4 Sept
Moss, B. W. (REGT)	8 Sept
Daisley, L. S. BSc (FC)	29 Sept
MacFarlane, A. BSc (FC)	29 Sept
Atherton, S. E.	
qcc (ATC)	30 Sept
Doyle, J. M. qss (ATC)	30 Sept
Dunbar, A. J. (ATC)	30 Sept
Franks, S. qcc (ATC)	30 Sept
Hawtin, P. E. (REGT)	30 Sept
Lyon, S. A. (FC)	30 Sept
Middleton, A. J.	
qss1 (FC)	30 Sept
Oliver, S. J. (ATC)	30 Sept
Pickering, A. N. (ATC)	30 Sept
Sinclair, A. D. qcc (ATC)	30 Sept

Wylor-Owen, R. G.	
qss (REGT)	30 Sept
Charlton, S. C. (INT)	12 Oct
Laing, S. F. (ATC)	28 Oct
Gagnon, F. Y. BA (FC)	5 Nov
Lowman, S. (ATC)	7 Nov
Cox, L. (INT)	11 Nov
Fone, S. (INT)	11 Nov
Lee, R. P. G. (ATC)	11 Nov
Merrick, D. (REGT)	11 Nov
Probert, P. R. (INT)	11 Nov
Short, N. P. qss (FC)	11 Nov
Jones, T. E. (ATC)	12 Nov
Hall, R. A. qss (ATC)	8 Dec
Maddocks, D. (ATC)	19 Dec
Davies, M. (FC)	22 Dec
Dimbleby, A. M.	
qcc (FC)	22 Dec
Fraser, P. D. qss (INT)	22 Dec
Mayhew, S. M. (ATC)	22 Dec

1996

Henrick, D. M. (ATC)	12 Jan
Cartwright, C. D.	
BSc (FC)	15 Jan
Fallon, A. M. BEng	
(Regt)	15 Jan
Lamb, P. R. J. BTh (FC)	15 Jan
Mansell, L. D. C.	
BSc (FC)	15 Jan
Quigley, T. L. LLB	
qcc (INT)	15 Jan
Western, S. M. (INT)	19 Jan
Cyster, J. L. (INT)	20 Jan
Holcroft, S. J.	
qwi(SAW) (REGT)	27 Jan
Capel, D. K. S. (REGT)	3 Feb
Endruweit, D. J. (FC)	10 Feb
Hyde, E. A. MSc BSc	
qss1 (INT)	11 Feb
Sexton, S. R. BEng	
(INT)	16 Feb
Jones, A. N. (REGT)	24 Feb
Darling, S. J. qss1	
(ATC)	17 Mar
King, N. S. qss (ATC)	24 Mar
Bradley, A. C. qss1(ATC)	28 Mar
House, D. (ATC)	28 Mar
McDowell, I. G.	
qcc (ATC)	28 Mar
Davies, R. E. BSc (ATC)	10 Apr
Cooke, G. B. BSc (FC)	11 Apr
Stowers, S. M. LLB	
(ATC)	11 Apr
Stewart, A. E. (INT)	15 Apr
Palmer, M. A. (ATC)	7 May
Goodall, V. L. BSc	
qss1 (ATC)	6 June

Martin, K. M. BA	
qss1 (FC)	6 June
Muir, G. (FC)	15 June
Barclay, A. J. (ATC)	21 June
Cargill, R. J. (REGT)	21 June
Marshall, K. L. (ATC)	21 June
Parsonage, E. C.	
qcc (INT)	21 June
Sutton, J. P.	
qss1 (REGT)	21 June
Johnson, R. O. (REGT)	28 June
Stockbridge, E. (FC)	1 July
Harrison, T. G. S.	
(REGT)	27 July
Smith, S. R. F. (ATC)	28 July
Antrobus, A. E. BA	
qss1 (FC)	14 Aug
Drummond, I. M.	
BSc (FC)	14 Aug
McGregor, D. S. A.	
BSc (REGT)	14 Aug
Bendell, S. A. (FLTOPS)	15 Aug
Flett, T. qcc (FLTOP	15 Aug
Finney, P. A. J. (INT)	29 Sept
Ibbetson, N. (ATC)	29 Sept
Rosier, M. P. (FLTOPS)	29 Sept
Watts, D. L. (INT)	29 Sept
Duncan, B. J. (ATC)	6 Oct
Trott, J. S. BEng	
qss1 (FC)	10 Oct
Wigglesworth, C.	
A. (ATC)	7 Nov
Dalton, M. J. qcc (FC)	10 Nov
Gillespie, C. R. (FC)	10 Nov
Keighley, D. L. (FC)	10 Nov
Smith, A. P. (ATC)	10 Nov
Stead, A. A. (FC)	10 Nov
Stowers, M. J. (REGT)	10 Nov
Wilson, A. (REGT)	10 Nov
McCune, D. (INT)	1 Dec
Burgess, G. S. (ATC)	15 Dec
Robinson D. M.	
qcc (ATC)	15 Dec
Vaughan, S. L. (ATC)	15 Dec
Wilson, N. J. (ATC)	15 Dec
Banbrook, J. M. (REGT)	21 Dec
Lofthouse, G. D. J.	
qss1 (ATC)	21 Dec
McIntyre, S. (FC)	21 Dec
Robinson, P. D. (FC)	21 Dec
Roylance, J. A. (REGT)	21 Dec

1997

Thickett, A. B. M.	
qss1 (INT)	6 Jan
Booth, J. A. BSc (FC)	15 Jan
Doney, M. J. BA (FC)	15 Jan

Flight Lieutenants

1997—contd

Hateley, P. B. BA		
qss1	(REGT)	15 Jan
Donaldson, D.	(ATC)	2 Feb
Honeybun-Kelly, C.		
L.	(ATC)	2 Feb
Parfitt, J. E.	(ATC)	2 Feb
Forster, I.	(REGT)	9 Feb
Fairburn, M. R.	(ATC)	11 Feb
Gunter, S. J.	(ATC)	11 Feb
O'Neill, R. K.	(ATC)	11 Feb
Wood, M. J.	(FC)	20 Feb
Davison, A. B.	(FC)	1 Mar
Burton, M. J. J.	(ATC)	17 Mar
Brown, A. qcc	(REGT)	26 Mar
Sills, M. R. qcc	(ATC)	26 Mar
Walker, G. R.	(INT)	26 Mar
Wallace, J. M.	(INT)	26 Mar
Willis, B. D.	(FLTOPS)	26 Mar
Fry, J. A. BSc	(ATC)	10 Apr
May, M. J. BSc		
qss1	(FC)	10 Apr
Cowieson, K. S.	(FC)	30 Apr
Ingamells, S. E.		
qss1	(ATC)	4 May
Philip, G. A. qss1	(FC)	8 May
Street, G. E.	(ATC)	8 May
Drummond, D. R.	(FC)	10 May
Strefford, A. D.		
BEng	(INT)	13 May
Martin, A. P.	(FC)	8 June
Gavars, J. M.	(REGT)	20 June
Jochum, C. W.	(ATC)	20 June
Powell, M. S.	(REGT)	20 June
McCamley, D. S.	(ATC)	26 June
Greenwood, P. M.	(INT)	28 July
Hooper, J. A.	(INT)	28 July
Reeves, A. J.	(INT)	28 July
Harris, J. BA	(ATC)	12 Aug
Edie, C. J. qcc	(ATC)	17 Aug
Eames, K. S.	(ATC)	13 Sept
Harris, G. P. C. qss1	(FC)	28 Sept
Jacklin, M. J.	(REGT)	28 Sept
Jacques, E.	(FC)	28 Sept
Lain, D. P. J. qss1	(INT)	28 Sept
Todd, H. BA	(ATC)	9 Oct
Barber, A. J. BEng	(INT)	10 Oct
Gilvary, D. R. F. BA		
	(FLTOPS)	10 Oct
Keer, M. BA	(ATC)	10 Oct
Nichols, J. M. BA	(INT)	10 Oct
Pegg. R. MSc	(ATC)	10 Oct
Terry, G. BA	(FLTOPS)	10 Oct
Walton, K. J. BSc	(ATC)	10 Oct
Griffiths, J. A.	(Regt)	13 Oct
Crockford, J. D.	(ATC)	9 Nov

Henley, N. R. qcc	(FC)	9 Nov
Holland, P. T. W.		
qss1	(REGT)	9 Nov
Howard, A. R. J.	(INT)	9 Nov
Pieroni, M. L. qcc	(FC)	9 Nov
Radnall, M. M.		
qss1	(REGT)	9 Nov
Harvey, R. M. BA	(INT)	12 Nov
Morton, D. T.	(ATC)	13 Nov
King, C. J.	(ATC)	28 Nov
Gautrey, D. J. M.	(INT)	14 Dec
Gilmore, S. T.	(FC)	20 Dec

1998

Walford, S.	(ATC)	4 Jan
Hoskins, N. E. BSc	(FC)	15 Jan
Cain, P. S.	(REGT)	29 Jan
Janssen, P. C.	(FC)	29 Jan
Paddison, P.	(ATC)	29 Jan
Shea, K. Y.	(ATC)	29 Jan
Smith, M. C.	(FLTOPS)	29 Jan
Greentree, D. W. MA		
BA	(INT)	13 Feb
Brown, M. J. BSc	(FC)	14 Feb
Davison, P. F. BA	(FC)	14 Feb
Garner, N. BSc		
qss1	(INT)	14 Feb
McGlynn, S. BA	(ATC)	14 Feb
Niven, R. J. BSc	(FC)	14 Feb
Webb, S. F. BA	(FC)	14 Feb
Wilson, R. J. BEng		
	(REGT)	14 Feb
Lindsay, C. J.	(ATC)	25 Feb
Aslett, J. R. qss1	(ATC)	7 Mar
Deane, C. C. qss1	(ATC)	7 Mar
Thomas, E. A.	(ATC)	7 Mar
Crosby, A. P.	(FC)	26 Mar
Hugall, J. J.	(INT)	26 Mar
Lumb, R. P.	(REGT)	26 Mar
Shave, R. J.	(INT)	26 Mar
Smith, M. W. qss1	(INT)	26 Mar
Payne, D. V. BSc	(FC)	8 Apr
Hall, I. D. BSc	(INT)	9 Apr
Sibley, V. E. BA	(INT)	9 Apr
Williams, G. D. BSc		
	(INT)	9 Apr
Alborough, R. A.	(ATC)	11 Apr
Crooks, S.	(ATC)	11 Apr
Moss, G. W.	(ATC)	11 Apr
Woods, H. L.	(ATC)	11 Apr
Brown, T. J. qss1	(FC)	7 May
D Albertanson, K.	(ATC)	7 May
Stewart, W. E.	(INT)	15 May
Rait, P. M. BSc	(Regt)	16 May

Flying Officers

1990

France, J. A.	(ATC)	18 June
Booth, S.	(REGT)	7 Dec

1991

Thorpe, G. K.	(FLTOPS)	25 June
Jones, R. C.	(FLTOPS)	4 July
Greenham, P. M.	(ATC)	22 July
Duffield, P. J.	(FC)	5 Nov

1992

McCarthy, P. G. J.		
	(REGT)	24 May
Sparrow, K. A.	(FLTOP)	24 May
Barnes, D. M.	(INT)	7 July
Lane, R. J.	(REGT)	10 July
Flood, A.	(ATC)	23 Dec

1993

McGhee, W. J.	(Regt)	3 Feb
King, A. G.	(ATC)	8 Apr
Stuart, A. J.	(FLTOP)	24 June
Parker, S. R.	(ATC)	17 Aug
Bottrill, M.	(REGT)	21 Aug
Heenan, J.	(ATC)	27 Oct
Dodd, R. M.	(Regt)	3 Nov
Andrews, S. J.		
	(FLTOPS)	7 Nov

1994

Clark, R. J. BA	(N)	8 Apr
Corner, A. G.	(ATC)	24 May
Sproston, J. A.	(INT)	18 June
Downey, C. P. L.	(ATC)	19 June
Hall, A. J.	(ATC)	19 June
Hindley, A. M.	(FLTOPS)	19 June
Hunt, P. J.	(FC)	19 June
Johnson, L.	(FC)	19 June
Mount, G. J. L.	(INT)	19 June
Parker, E. J.	(ATC)	19 June
Lavis, R. J.	(ATC)	30 June
Underwood, S. J.	(ATC)	4 July
Allen, C. M.	(Regt)	8 July
Harrop, G.	(FLTOPS)	18 July
Derrick, A. M.	(FC)	26 July
Mattocks, S. A. B.		
MA	(INT)	11 Aug

Flying Officers

1994—contd

Nelson, A. B. BEng (REGT)	11 Aug
Shaw, I. S. BSc (REGT)	11 Aug
White, C. E. BSc (ATC)	11 Aug
Paul, S. L. S. BA (INT)	12 Aug
Lutman, A. J. (ATC)	13 Aug
Lambton, N. W. J. (INT)	16 Sept
McCourt, R. D. (INT)	26 Sept
Laing, R. P. MA (INT)	7 Oct
Lloyd-Jones, S. A. BA (INT)	7 Oct
Turner, S. G. BSc (FLTOPS)	7 Oct
Hart, J. A. BSC (INT)	9 Oct
Stott, D. B. BEng (ATC)	9 Oct
Hawker, S. M. (ATC)	16 Oct
Mackintosh, W. A.(ATC)	31 Oct
Prytherch, S. J. (ATC)	31 Oct
Sweeney, M. P. C.(ATC)	31 Oct
Tunstall, M. S. R. (ATC)	31 Oct
Armstrong, A. M. R. qss1 (ATC)	7 Nov
Garwood, F. D. qcc (REGT)	7 Nov
Pearson, V. C. qss1(FC)	7 Nov
Williams, D. O. (REGT)	7 Nov
Hesketh, D. G. (ATC)	4 Dec
Ledger, A. J. (ATC)	16 Dec

1995

Morgan, R. L. BSc (REGT)	15 Jan
Wallace, P. N. R. (FC)	30 Jan
Wienburg, E. F. (INT)	30 Jan
Worthington, D. (FC)	30 Jan
Wright, C. qss1 (INT)	30 Jan
Cannon, S. M. (ATC)	1 Feb
Graham, F. (FC)	9 Feb
Davies, B. (REGT)	10 Feb
Brown, E. E. BA (INT)	11 Feb
Robinson, N. C. MA(SocSci) (ATC)	11 Feb
Smith, D. A. BSc (FC)	11 Feb
Bradley, T. J. BA (REGT)	13 Feb
Kirkpatrick, A. M. BA (REGT)	13 Feb
Smith, E. E. BA (ATC)	13 Feb
Owen, A. K. (FC)	20 Mar
Bailey, J. M. (FC)	24 Mar
Jackson, A. M. (FC)	24 Mar
Jermyn, S. M. qcc (FC)	24 Mar
Phelps, D. L. (FC)	24 Mar

Wheeler, B. qss1 (ATC)	24 Mar
Hollin, R. T. D. MA BSc (INT)	6 Apr
Green, M. A. BSc (INT)	8 Apr
Magee, S. BSc (REGT)	8 Apr
Openshaw, S. BSc (REGT)	8 Apr
Stedman, R. D. BSc (ATC)	8 Apr
Taylor, N. J. L. BA (FC)	8 Apr
Boon, S. A. (ATC)	2 May
Peach, B. J. (FC)	5 May
Thomas, C. M. qss1 (REGT)	6 May
Ling, J. J. (ATC)	21 May
Rhead, M. P. (ATC)	20 June
Roberts, K. (ATC)	7 July
Rumsby, J. T. (ATC)	22 July
Davies, J. C. (Regt)	28 July
Gaskin, L. A. (REGT)	28 July
Ackroyd, R. D. BA(ATC)	9 Aug
Allen, D. T. BSc (FC)	9 Aug
Bailey, M. N. MA BSc (INT)	9 Aug
Hall, N. J. BSc (INT)	9 Aug
Hancock, L. BSc (FC)	9 Aug
Crowther, N. R. BSc (ATC)	11 Aug
Dargan, R. J. (ATC)	11 Aug
Elias, R. A. BSc (ATC)	11 Aug
Fruish, S. O. BSc (ATC)	11 Aug
Hill, A. G. BA (ATC)	11 Aug
Hinde, M. R. BSc (FC)	11 Aug
Jones, J. BA (FC)	11 Aug
Norton, E. M. BSc (FC)	11 Aug
Salmon, V. A. (ATC)	11 Aug
Shirley, G. J. (ATC)	11 Aug
Thorpe, A. D. BSc (INT)	11 Aug
Wilkinson, M. G. BA (INT)	11 Aug
Lynch, J. A. (INT)	21 Aug
Nicholls, K. P. (REGT)	28 Aug
McConnell, S. D. (INT)	11 Sept
Fountain, M. J. (ATC)	3 Oct
Ackland, E. C. MSc (INT)	6 Oct
Bentley, S. A. BA (FC)	6 Oct
Brown, P. N. BA (Regt)	6 Oct
Craig, M. D. BSc (FC)	6 Oct
Duhan, J. P. BA (Regt)	6 Oct
Graham, M. R. MEng (FC)	6 Oct
Mason, P. M. BA (FC)	6 Oct
Neeson, C. G. MA (ATC)	6 Oct
Ratnage, P. D. BA (Regt)	6 Oct
Christian, S. M. BSc (FC)	7 Oct

Cressy, K. P. BEng (REGT)	7 Oct
Deakin, M. R. BSc (FC)	7 Oct
Hall, G. E. BA (FLTOPS)	7 Oct
Hamilton, A. M. BA (INT)	7 Oct
Parr, H. M. BA (REGT)	7 Oct
Stellitano, D. W. BA (REGT)	7 Oct
Fleckney, M. J. (FC)	24 Oct
Hetterley, A. D. BA (INT)	1 Dec
Allcroft, J. M. (FC)	3 Dec
Barnes, A. E. (ATC)	3 Dec
Parker, S. (ATC)	3 Dec
Ramsden, C. D. (Regt)	28 Dec

1996

Thorp, J. M. BSc (REGT)	15 Jan
Gregory, K. J. qss1 (ATC)	28 Jan
Grun, A. B. (FLTOPS)	28 Jan
Harvey, G. B. (FC)	28 Jan
Rennie, S. D. (FC)	28 Jan
Bruce, A. S. BA (Regt)	10 Feb
Quayle, G. E. BA (Regt)	10 Feb
Roberts, B. W. BEng (Regt)	10 Feb
Smith, E. M. BA (ATC)	10 Feb
Timms, D. L. BA (FC)	10 Feb
Atkins, V. L. BA (INT)	11 Feb
Beck, N. J. BA (INT)	11 Feb
Bennee, T. S. BSc (FC)	11 Feb
Fitzsimon, J. P. BEng (REGT)	11 Feb
Hodgson, J. BA (ATC)	11 Feb
Liston, J. H. BSc (REGT)	11 Feb
Mayor, M. D. BSc (ATC)	11 Feb
Robbins, N. H. BSc (FLTOPS)	11 Feb
Wadeson, G. K. BSc (ATC)	11 Feb
Westbrook, A. L. BSc (FC)	11 Feb
Huyton, A. D. (ATC)	19 Mar
Black, D. (REGT)	4 Apr
Conn, A. BSc (FLTOPS)	5 Apr
Wiseman, S. T. BEd (Regt)	5 Apr
Would, C. BSc(FLTOPS)	5 Apr
Hale, N. B. BA (FC)	6 Apr
Ives, L. M. BA (REGT)	6 Apr
Iveson, P. R. BTh (REGT)	6 Apr
Jenkins, G. S. BSc (FC)	6 Apr
Jones, C. R. M. BA (FC)	6 Apr

Flying Officers

1996—contd

Khan, S. B. BSc (ATC)	6 Apr
Siddall, A. J. BA (INT)	6 Apr
Sowter, R. M. BEng (FC)	6 Apr
Thorpe, B. C. B.	
BEng (ATC)	6 Apr
Kiff, H. J. (REGT)	28 Apr
Graham, J. M. (REGT)	2 May
Wilson, C. J. BSc (FC)	30 May
Adrain, J. M.	
BSc (REGT)	1 June
Davenport, D. A.	
BSc (FC)	1 June
Marshall, A. S. BA	
(REGT)	1 June
Parker, J. P. F.	
BMus (FC)	1 June
Smith, A. P. BA (REGT)	1 June
Atkin-Palmer, C. M.	
(FLTOPS)	2 July
Wheeler, J. E. (ATC)	13 July
Finley, E. T. BA (ATC)	9 Aug
Rogers, P. D. BSc (FC)	9 Aug
Williams, M. BA (Regt)	9 Aug
Williamson, J. S.	
BSc (INT)	9 Aug
Middleton, I. (FC)	10 Aug
Hoult, J. J. (ATC)	4 Sept
Black, H. M. BA (FC)	6 Oct
Madden, H. M. BSc (FC)	6 Oct
Parker, C. M. BSc (FC)	6 Oct
Pearce, H. E. BSc (ATC)	6 Oct
Waddilove, C. (FLTOP	23 Oct
Appleby, R. I. BA (Regt)	1 Dec
Barker, R. J. BA (FC)	1 Dec
Bennett, A. M. LLB	
(INT)	1 Dec
Booker, C. J. BSc (Regt)	1 Dec
Chambers, S. C. BA (FC)	1 Dec
Finch, D. R. BA (Regt)	1 Dec
Stewart, J. D. BA (Regt)	1 Dec

1997

Duffy, M. R. (ATC)	14 Jan
Buckle, J. V. BA (ATC)	15 Jan
Ritchie, C. C. BEng (FC)	15 Jan
Tindale, A. R. BSc (FC)	15 Jan
Gray, S. A. (FC)	28 Jan
Wells, J. R. BEng (FC)	4 Feb
Brunton, M. J. BA (FC)	10 Feb
Evans, R. L. S. BSc	
(FLTOPS)	10 Feb
Lynn, C. J. BA (ATC)	10 Feb

Stellitano, R. L. BA	
(INT)	10 Feb
Topping, J. L. BA (INT)	10 Feb
Wyatt, P. D. BSc (INT)	10 Feb
McWilliam, S. (FLTOPS)	21 Mar
Dendy, P. (FLTOPS)	3 Apr
Atkins, N. O. BSc (FC)	5 Apr
Clegg, M. K. GRSM (FC)	5 Apr
Crook, D. J. P. BA	
(Regt)	5 Apr
Davies, J. M. E.	
BSc (ATC)	5 Apr
Locke, J. E. BA (INT)	5 Apr
Picken, T. J. BA (INT)	5 Apr
Sewell, A. J. BSc	
(FLTOPS)	5 Apr
Sproule, G. A. BSc (FC)	5 Apr
Binks, P. E. L. (ATC)	6 Apr
O'Sullivan, K. J. (FC)	6 Apr
Page, T. C. (ATC)	21 May
Boreham, D. P. (ATC)	29 May
Bowen, M. A. (Regt)	29 May
Cook, M. J. (Regt)	29 May
Hughes, M. I. (ATC)	29 May
Meacham-Roberts, D.	
A. M. (FC)	29 May
Cripps, E. A. BSc (Regt)	30 May
Holden, E. A. BSc (INT)	30 May
Hook, J. L. BSc (ATC)	30 May
Lawrence, D. J. BA	
(Regt)	30 May
Misiak, C. L. BSc (FC)	30 May
Stewart, K. D. BA (ATC)	30 May
Coomer, D. L. (ATC)	8 July
Irving, K. G. (FLTOP	24 July
Quigley, I. P. J. (ATC)	24 July
Sweeney, P. F. (INT)	24 July
Ansell, K. M. J. (INT)	28 July
Jones, R. M. (Regt)	6 Aug
Mennell, G. R. (FC)	3 Oct
Matthews, J. P. (ATC)	1 Nov

1998

Maclaren, A. F. (INT)	28 Jan
Pilkington, R. C.	
(FLTOPS)	5 Apr
Thomson, A. M. (REGT)	5 Apr

Pilot Officers

1996

Dixon, S. J. (FLTOPS)	13 May
Vine, S. L. (ATC)	8 Aug
Secker, M. C. (REGT)	11 Sept
Anstey, J. S. (FLTOPS)	3 Oct

1997

Brown, S. M. (FLTOPS)	25 Jan
Cleaver, J. C. (ATC)	25 Jan
Harrild, P. E. (FC)	25 Jan
Hanbury, O. J. (FC)	3 Apr
Hetherington, J. (REGT)	3 Apr
Inglis, A. J. C. (ATC)	3 Apr
Tennant, B. (FC)	3 Apr
Archer, M. E. (ATC)	6 Aug
Butcher, J. N. (ATC)	6 Aug
Deane, Y. J. (FC)	6 Aug
Hallaway, E. H.	
(FLTOPS)	6 Aug
McEachran, A. (FC)	6 Aug
Greene, M. P. (FLTOPS)	3 Oct
Barker, J. R. L. (Regt)	29 Nov
Bland, R. G. (FC)	29 Nov
Harris, S. (FC)	29 Nov
Jones, S. D. M. (Regt)	29 Nov
McKnight, K. (ATC)	29 Nov

1998

Barton, S. A. (Regt)	24 Jan
Wilkinson-Cox, P. M.	
A. (FC)	24 Jan
Brown, S. J. B. BA	
(ATC)	8 Feb
Bulmer, M. G. BA (FC)	8 Feb
Bush, R. J. BSc (FC)	8 Feb
Butterfield, A. J.	
BSc (ATC)	8 Feb
Carrick, J. BSc (FC)	8 Feb
Cockram, R. E. BSc	
(FLTOPS)	8 Feb
Drage, M. N. BA (FC)	8 Feb
Fisher, J. LLB (FC)	8 Feb
Hammerton, G. R.	
BSc (FC)	8 Feb
Hole, M. C. BA (ATC)	8 Feb
Latimer, J. A. BEng	
(ATC)	8 Feb
Miller, J. BEng (ATC)	8 Feb
Nelson, D. LLB (Regt)	8 Feb
Parker, J. C. S. BSc (FC)	8 Feb
Paton, I. S. BSc (FC)	8 Feb

Pilot Officers

1998—contd

Shurmer, M. A.		
BSc	(ATC)	8 Feb
Stewart, A. H. BSc (FC)		8 Feb
Warren Rothwell, P. P.		
BSc	(INT)	8 Feb
Whiteley, D. J. BSc (FC)		8 Feb
Currie, G. J. J.	(ATC)	2 Apr
Hull, M. J.	(FC)	2 Apr
Marshall, D. W. L. (INT)		2 Apr
Willis, A. L.	(ATC)	2 Apr
Wood, G. M.	(Regt)	2 Apr
Woodbourne, M. F.		
	(Regt)	2 Apr
Ahmad, O. BA	(ATC)	5 Apr
Daniel, R. C. BA	(ATC)	5 Apr
Hughes, A. P. MSc (FC)		5 Apr
Hughes, M. D.		
BSc	(INT)	5 Apr
Johns, A. B. BA	(ATC)	5 Apr
McCullough, C. L.		
BA	(FC)	5 Apr
Milburn, R. M. LLB (FC)		5 Apr
Rowe, J. R. BA	(INT)	5 Apr
Stevens, R. A. BSc(INT)		5 Apr
White, N. D. BSc (ATC)		5 Apr
Winkworth, R. M.		
BA	(FC)	5 Apr
Clayton, D. L.	(FC)	27 May
Danso, K. G.	(Regt)	27 May
Hall, B.	(ATC)	27 May

Acting Pilot Officers

1997

Hargreaves, K. L.		
BEng	(FC)	1 Sept
Mankowski, M. K. L.		
BSc	(Regt)	1 Sept
Platts, J.	(ATC)	1 Sept

1998

Berry, N. J.	(ATC)	5 Feb
Brown, A. A. F.		
	(FLTOPS)	5 Feb
Hopkins, M. J.	(ATC)	5 Feb
Jones, A. L.	(Regt)	5 Feb
Stanley, J. P.	(FC)	5 Feb
Ward, G.	(Regt)	5 Feb
Hawthorne, V. J. (ATC)		2 Apr
Howard, K. E. L. (ATC)		2 Apr
Jackson, S. B.	(ATC)	2 Apr
McIntyre, A. J.	(ATC)	2 Apr
Reeve, M. W.	(FC)	2 Apr

ENGINEER BRANCH

Group Captains

1988

Mackichan, Alastair Somerled MSc BSc CEng FIMechE FRAeS aws psc Born 6/9/43   (M)   1 July

1990

Newton, John Kenneth MSc BSc CEng MIMechE MRAeS psc Born 22/4/45   (M)   1 Jan
Burton, Geoffrey Owen psc semc Born 23/7/45   (M)   1 July

1991

Ryall, Martin CEng CPhys MInstP psc Born 17/7/44   (M)   1 Jan
Gilbert, John Cliford MBE BSc psc amec Born 22/1/45   (M)   1 July
Gowing, Keith MA CEng MIMechE MRAeS psc amec Born 14/5/45   (M)   1 July
Lampard, Christopher John BSc(Eng) CEng MRAeS ACGI psc amec Born 22/3/46   (M)   1 July
Whittingham, Robert John FRAeS FIMgt qs Born 16/2/44   (EL)   1 July

1992

Ainge, Derek Richard CEng MIEE MIMgt psc amec Born 26/4/44   (EL)   1 Jan
Turner, Jeffrey MSc BSc CEng MRAeS psc Born 18/9/45   (M)   1 Jan
Dickens, Barry Charles BSc CEng MRAeS MIMgt psc Born 8/2/45   (EI)   1 July
Samuel, Edmond George BSc CEng MIMechE psc amec Born 25/11/48   (M)   1 July

1993

Taylor, William John OBE MRAeS psc Born 31/1/51   (M)   1 July

1994

Camping, Robert Alan BSc psc ae Born 21/9/44   (EI)   1 Jan
Schofield, Stephen Bryan MSc BSc CEng MRAeS jsdc qs Born 26/5/48   (M)   1 Jan
Allan, David Douglas psc semc Born 9/7/46   (EI)   1 July
Badcock, Peter Charles MBE jsdc semc qs Born 15/12/46   (EI)   1 July
Case, David Nathaniel MSc BSc CEng MRAeS psc Born 19/8/52   (M)   1 July
Chandler, John Edgar CBE CEng MRAes qs Born 26/10/47   (M)   1 July
Hooper, Robert William MBE MSc BSc(Eng) CEng FRAeS psc Born 20/11/46   (M)   1 July
Paterson, Graham Austin BSc CEng MIEE MRAeS MIMgt jsdc ae Born 29/5/48   (EI)   1 July
Rennison, David Ralph Gray MSc BSc psc semc Born 28/6/51   (EI)   1 July
Sobey, Bruce Leonard BA CEng MIEE MIMgt psc Born 9/12/48   (EI)   1 July

1995

Bate, Brian George semc qs Born 12/2/49   (EI)   1 Jan
Dye, Peter John OBE BSc(Eng) CEng MRAeS ACGI rcds hcsc psc Born 17/8/53   (M)   1 Jan
Hobart, David Anthony MPhil MIMgt jsdc psc semc Born 24/12/51   (M)   1 Jan

Group Captains

1995—contd

Hogg, Robert Ian jsdc amec Born 14/3/46	(M)	1 Jan
Smith, Alan Jeffrey OBE BSc CEng MIMechE psc Born 13/6/53		1 Jan
Kane, James Ian BSc CEng MIEE MIMgt psc Born 30/10/53	(EL)	1 July
Rogers, Michael Andrew OBE qs Born 3/10/47	(EI)	1 July

1996

Bairsto, Nigel Alexander MBE MSc BSc CEng FIMechE FIMgt psc Born 27/8/53	(M)	1 Jan
Chitty, Jonathan Paul OBE MA BSc(Eng) CEng MRAeS ACGI psc Born 4/8/53	(M)	1 Jan
Ness, Charles Wright BEng CEng MRAeS jsdc semc Born 6/11/57	(M)	1 Jan
Rooms, William Simon OBE BSc (Eur Ing) CEng MIEE MRAeS psc semc qs Born 17/7/54	(EI)	1 Jan
Rawson, Paul David BA IEng MRAeS psc semc Born 13/3/53	(M)	1 July
Warnes, Andrew Everett BSc CEng MIEE jsdc semc Born 11/4/53	(EI)	1 July
Wynn, Bruce Martin OBE BSc psc Born 4/7/52	(EI)	1 July

1997

Archer-Jones, Keith Edward BSc semc psc Born 6/6/54	(M)	1 Jan
Bufton, Terence MSc BSc CEng FIMgt MIEE DIC psc Born 26/11/46	(EI)	1 Jan
Capps, Julian John BSc psc ae Born 4/3/49	(M)	1 Jan
Leeson, Kevin James BSc CEng FIEE psc semc Born 11/6/56	(EI)	1 Jan
Stevenson, John Graham MSc BSc CEng FIEE psc ae Born 7/5/49	(EI)	1 Jan
Stewart, James Wilson psc amec Born 8/10/46	(EI)	1 Jan
Verdon, Andrew Martin BTech CEng MRAeS psc semc Born 14/12/52	(M)	1 Jan
Williams, Dilwyn Nigel OBE BSc CEng MRAeS jsdc semc qs Born 1/10/54	(M)	1 Jan
Benstead, Bruce Graham MBE BSc CEng MIEE jsdc ae Born 11/1/53	(EI)	1 July
Cole, Geoffrey MBA CEng MIMechE psc Born 5/3/48	(M)	1 July
Harker, Gregory Scott psc Born 4/5/50	(EI)	1 July
Mackreath, James BSc psc amec Born 28/4/51	(M)	1 July
Pratley, Charles William OBE CEng FIEE amec qs Born 07/11/45	(EI)	1 July
Stevens, Mark Christopher BSc psc semc Born 2/12/54	(M)	1 July

1998

Burrell, Leslie James BEng CEng MRAeS psc Born 19/9/56	(M)	1 Jan
Kurth, Nicholas Julian Eugene OBE psc Born 13/9/55	(M)	1 Jan
Sims, Stephen Ronald OBE BSc CEng MRAeS DLUT psc ae Born 1/3/52	(M)	1 July
Suckling, Christopher Alan MBE BSc CEng MIEE jsdc adp qs i Born 1/3/48	(EI)	1 July

Wing Commanders

1985

Bates, J. O. BSc CEng
MIEE MRAeS jsdc
amec   (EI)   1 Jan
Izzard, J. OBE CEng
FIMechE jsdc amec
qs   (M)   1 Jan

1986

Bell, C. R. L. BSc CEng
MIMechE amec
qs   (M)   1 Jan
Goddard, G. M. MSc
BSc CEng MIMechE
ACGI jsdc qs   (M)   1 Jan
Longman, B. D. OBE
CEng MRAeS MIEE
MIMgt amec qs   (EI)   1 July
Maunder, M. J. semc
qs   (M)   1 July

1987

Hockley, C. J. MBE
CEng MRAeS df
semc psc   (M)   1 Jan
Hyde, D. C. MSc BSc ae
qss   (EI)   1 Jan
Jones, B. A. BSc semc
qs   (M)   1 Jan
Fozard, M. J. CEng
MRAeS ae jsdc
semc   (M)   1 July
Pearce, M. S. BSc CEng
MIEE amec qs   (EI)   1 July
Wilkins, M. J. BSc CEng
MRAeS amec qs   (M)   1 July

1988

Backhouse, D. H. W.
BTech semc qs   (M)   1 Jan
Brayshaw, S. BSc CEng
MIEE qs   (EI)   1 Jan
Cossar, A. K. MSc BSc
CEng MIEE ae semc
qss   (EI)   1 Jan
Munro, M. R. BSc CEng
MRAeS psc   (M)   1 Jan

Patel, M. R. BSc CEng
MRAeS psc
semc   (M)   1 Jan
Trewin, I. A. (Eur Ing)
CEng MIEE ae qs (E)   1 Jan
Vaughan-Smith, N. V.
BSc CEng MIEE
MRAeS jsdc semc
qs   (EI)   1 Jan
Wakely, B. BSc jsdc
amec adp   (EI)   1 Jan
Walsh, L. M. P. BSc psc
ae   (EI)   1 Jan
Yates, D. P. OBE semc
qss   (EI)   1 Jan
Frith, M. C. IEng semc
qs   (EI)   1 July
Hastings, J. B. jsdc
semc qs   (EI)   1 July
Nelson, B. J. R. qs (EI)   1 July
Wood, C. R. S. amec
qs   (EI)   1 July
Woolford, P. R. MBA
(Eur Ing) CEng FRSA
MRAeS MInstD
MIMgt semc qs   (M)   1 July

1989

Gilbert, P. N. BSc CEng
MRAeS semc qs   (M)   1 Jan
Harris, K. J. BSc CEng
MIEE psc ae   (EI)   1 Jan
Stephens, R. J. BSc
CEng MIEE qss* (EI)   1 Jan
Britten-Austin, H. G.
MSc BSc CEng FIEE
psc ae   (EI)   1 July
Johncock, D. A. qs (EI)   1 July
O'Neill, A. G. MSc
CEng MIEE semc
qs   (EI)   1 July
Woods, C. J. MSc
BSc(Eng) CEng
MIMechE MRAeS
qs   (M)   1 July

1990

Akehurst, P. B. LVO OBE
BTech CEng MRAeS
jsdc semc qs   (M)   1 Jan
Atkinson, I. C. BSc
CEng MIMechE DLUT
jsdc ae qs   (M)   1 Jan
Clark, T. R. semc qs (M)   1 Jan
Lewis, A. L. BSc ae psc
i   (EI)   1 Jan

Lewis, R. A. semc
qs   (EI)   1 Jan
Thow, D. P. BSc psc
semc   (M)   1 Jan
Watson, G. McN. BSc
CEng MIMechE semc
psc   (M)   1 Jan
Wilderspin, K. L. BSc
CEng MIEE MRAeS
DLUT psc ae   (EI)   1 Jan
Hillier, P. S. BSc CEng
MRAeS ae qs   (M)   1 July
MacLean, E. J. MBE
jsdc semc qs   (M)   1 July
Milloy, P. D. G. MEng
BSc semc qs   (EI)   1 July
Montagu, C. B. MSc
BSc CEng MIMechE
psc ae smc   (M)   1 July
Oliver, S. W. StJ. BSc
jsdc semc qs   (M)   1 July
Robertson, G. MPhil BA
CEng MIEE semc
qs   (EI)   1 July

1991

Brown, J. BA jsdc semc
qs   (M)   1 Jan
Evans, G. S. MA MSc
CEng MRAeS
psc   (M)   1 Jan
Kiralfy, R. J. C. MSc BSc
CEng FIMgt MIEE psc
ae   (EI)   1 Jan
Nisbet, G. McL.
BSc(Eng) psc
semc   (M)   1 Jan
Pigott, J. I. MSc BSc
CEng MIEE psc[n] ae
semc   (EI)   1 Jan
Willenbruch, A. G. MA
(Eur Ing) CEng
MIMechE MRAeS
MIMgt jsdc ae   (M)   1 Jan
Alton, J. S. ae qss (M)   1 July
Ashenhurst, R. BSc
CEng MRAeS
psc   (M)   1 July
Bonella, T. R. MSc BSc
psc ae semc   (M)   1 July
Church, F. M. MBE BSc
psc semc qs   (M)   1 July
Gammon, N. W. MA
MSc BSc CEng
MRAeS MIMgt psc
semc   (M)   1 July
Harris, R. M. BSc CEng
MIEE semc qs   (EI)   1 July

159

Wing Commanders

1991—contd

Harvey, B. D. BSc psc
  semc qs   (El) 1 July
Johnson, P. semc
  qss   (M) 1 July
McCormick, D. W. BSc
  nadc semc qs (M) 1 July
Ottridge, S. D. BSc
  CEng MIEE MBCS
  jsdc semc   (EL) 1 July
Phillips, R. A. BSc ae
  semc qs   (EL) 1 July
Robinson, D. J. MA
  IEng MIIE(mech) psc
  semc   (EI) 1 July
Salter, M. G. MBE BA
  MRAeS semc qs (M) 1 July
Turner, C. D. MSc BSc
  qs   (EL) 1 July
Wilson, D. G. MBE BSc
  CEng MIMechE
  qs   (M) 1 July

1992

Allan, R. I. OBE MSc
  BSc ACGI psc ae (EL) 1 Jan
Kilshaw, M. J. OBE
  MSc BSc CEng
  MRAeS jsdc qs (M) 1 Jan
Lane, P. L. MSc BSc
  jsdc semc   (M) 1 Jan
Lythaby, R.   (EL) 1 Jan
Thorne, I. D. OBE BSc
  jsdc qs   (M) 1 Jan
Trigg, C. J. MBE MSc
  BSc CEng MRAeS
  MIMgt ae psc (M) 1 Jan
Turvill, P. A. BSc CEng
  MIMechE psc (M) 1 Jan
Chalmers, G. M. BSc
  CEng psc semc (M) 1 July
MacLean, D. F. BSc
  CEng MIMechE
  psc   (M) 1 July
Renshaw, A. qs   (EI) 1 July
Secker, J. C. psc (EI) 1 July
Simpson, R. C. R. adp
  qs   (M) 1 July

1993

Cliffe, R. B. jsdc (EI) 1 Jan

Field, C. F. MSc BSc
  jsdc ae qs   (EI) 1 Jan
Kirby, T. MBE jsdc semc
  qs   1 Jan
Pickavance, D. MSc
  BSc(Eng) psc (M) 1 Jan
Torrens, R. G. OBE BSc
  CEng MRAeS jsdc
  semc qs   1 Jan
Barker, A. C. MBE psc
  ae qs   (M) 1 July
Deytrikh, A. BSc
  psc   (M) 1 July
Duguid, M. amec
  qs   (M) 1 July
Ebdon, A. K. BA CEng
  MRAeS jsdc semc
  qs   (M) 1 July
Hancock, J. L. MDA BSc
  CEng MRAeS psc
  semc   1 July
Heard, P. J. MBE MSc
  BSc CEng MRAeS
  MIMechE psc(n)
  ae   1 July
Lawrence, C. H. BSc
  CEng MRAeS psc
  semc   (M) 1 July
Parker, S. H. MSc
  BSc(Eng) CEng
  MRAeS ACGI jsdc ae
  semc   (M) 1 July
Pilkington, J. L.
  BSc(Eng) ae semc
  qs   (EI) 1 July
Smith, D. R. MSc BSc
  CEng MRAeS jsdc ae
  qs   (M) 1 July
Washington-Smith, J.
  P. semc qs (M) 1 July
Watson, R. MBA BA psc 1 July

1994

Dean, T. P. MSc BSc
  MRAeS jsdc ae (EI) 1 Jan
Dyson, G. W. BSc CEng
  MIMechE semc
  qss   (M) 1 Jan
Foster, J. A. MSc BSc
  CEng MIEE ae semc
  qss   (EI) 1 Jan
Goody, A. J. MA
  BSc(Eng) CEng
  MRAeS ACGI psc
  semc   (M) 1 Jan
Knight, D. A. MBE MA
  BA psc ae (M) 1 Jan
Lock, P. J. qss (EI) 1 Jan

Meagher, J. K. jsdc
  qs   1 Jan
Munday, R. W. semc
  qss   (E) 1 Jan
Parrish, A. J. MA MSc
  BSc CEng MRAeS
  MIMgt psc (EI) 1 Jan
Richardson, K. MSc
  BSc(Eng) qs (M) 1 Jan
Smith, R. P. BSc(Eng)
  CEng MIEE jsdc semc
  qs   (EI) 1 Jan
Barnes, A. J. BSc
  qs   (EI) 1 July
Coulter, E. G. MSc
  CEng MIEE semc
  qs   (EI) 1 July
Driver, P. J. BSc(Eng)
  psc   (M) 1 July
Fisher, F. E. MBE BSc
  CEng MRAeS qs (M) 1 July
Harrison, R. M. amec
  qs   (EI) 1 July
Mackenzie, K. MA MSc
  CEng MRAeS psc
  ae   (M) 1 July
McCluggage, W. A.
  MSc BSc jsdc ae
  qs   (EI) 1 July
Nethaway, M. F. J.
  MInstD slmc qs (EI) 1 July
Wheatcroft, J. G. MSc
  BSc(Eng) qss (EL) 1 July
Williamson, C. M. MA
  BA CEng MRAeS jsdc
  semc qs   (M) 1 July
Wilson, M. E. semc
  qs   (EI) 1 July

1995

Bollom, S. J. BSc CEng
  jsdc qs   1 Jan
Caffell, A. N. MSc BSc
  ae semc qs (EI) 1 Jan
Little, N. G. BSc CEng
  MIEE semc qs (EI) 1 Jan
Welburn, S. MA MSc
  BSc CEng MRAeS
  psc semc (M) 1 Jan
Edwards, C. R. MSc BA
  CEng MIEE ae
  qss   1 July
Gray, B. L. IEng
  FIIE(elec) jsdc semc
  qs   1 July
Hamilton, I. P. qss (M) 1 July

Wing Commanders

1995—contd

Major, A. C. MSc BTech
CEng MRAeS psc(n)
semc   (M)   1 July
McElroy, G. E. BSc
CEng MRAeS
psc   1 July
Pickerill, R. A. OBE MA
BSc CEng MIMechE
MBCS psc   (M)   1 July
Spencer, J. W. C. MSc
BSc CEng MIMechE
qs   (M)   1 July

1996

Brown, P. M. D. BSc
CEng MRAeS MIMgt
semc qs   (M)   1 Jan
Gill, R. L. BSc psc   1 Jan
Griffin, S. A. BSc CEng
MRAeS qs   1 Jan
Keen, S. S. qs   (EL)   1 Jan
Laybourn, R. A. OBE
BEM BA qss   1 Jan
Sneller, J. A. J. MA
CEng MRAeS psc   1 Jan
Stokes, B. J. IEng
FIIE(elec) semc
qs   (EI)   1 Jan
Tanner, D. J. qs   1 Jan
Ward, A. J. MSc BSc
CEng MRAeS MIMgt
jsdc   1 Jan
Ward, D. A. R. BSc
CEng MIEE qs   (EI)   1 Jan
Welburn, M. slmc
qss   1 Jan
Wilson, A. L. MSc BSc
CEng MBCS jsdc
semc   1 Jan
Young, J. A. MDA BSc
psc ptsc   1 Jan
Baber, G. A. BSc CEng
psc semc   (M)   1 July
Binfield, G. H. qss   1 July
Eighteen, D. E. OBE
semc qss   (EI)   1 July
Green, C. H. BSc CEng
MRAeS jsdc psc   1 July
Hickman, C. H. BSc
psc   1 July
Render, M. E. J. MA
MBA MSc BSc CEng
MRAeS psc   (M)   1 July

Stevens, J. E. MBE BSc
CEng MRAeS MIMgt
qss   (M)   1 July
Taylor, S. J. MBE MSc
CEng MIEE MIMgt ae
qs   (EI)   1 July
Thomas, V. E. BSc
psc   1 July
Wilding, A.C BSc jsdc
qs   1 July
Wishart, G. K. BSc ae
qs   1 July
Wynne, C. A. MBE
qss   (M)   1 July

1997

Gale, S. BSc semc
qss   (EI)   1 Jan
Harris, G. H. BSc(Eng)
CEng MIMechE
MIMgt semc qs   (M)   1 Jan
Madge, A. W. BSc
qs   1 Jan
Martin, G. C. psc   1 Jan
Pallister, I. BSc semc
qs   (M)   1 Jan
Pharaoh, P. J. MSc qab
qs   (EL)   1 Jan
Rait, D. M. semc
qss   (EI)   1 Jan
Richards, E. W. MSc
LLB BSc(Eng) CEng
MIEE DIC LTCL ACGI
psc   1 Jan
Ryder, R. S. MSc BSc
gw qs   1 Jan
Sheard, M. S. MSc BSc
CEng MIEE qs   1 Jan
Shearer, R. A. MA BSc
CEng MRAeS MIMgt
MIEE psc semc   1 Jan
Thomson, I. W.
BSc(Eng) qss   (M)   1 Jan
Ward, M. M. MDA BSc
MIMgt semc qs i*   1 Jan
Witney, J. W.
MPhil(Eng) BSc CEng
MIEE MIMgt qs   (EI)   1 Jan
Wrigley, M. J. MSc BSc
qss   (EI)   1 Jan
Abbott, J. D. F. BSc
CEng MIMeche
psc   1 July
Betteridge, R. BSc
ARCS semc qss   (EI)   1 July
Boyle, A. MSc BSc slmc
qs   1 July

Brandt, I. T. G. MSc BSc
CEng MIMechE
qs   1 July
Burke, T. C. MSc BSc
slmc qs   1 July
Carlin, G. M. semc qs   1 July
Clark, M. A. BSc(Eng)
CEng MIEE psc   1 July
Collins-Bent, N. BTech
psc   1 July
Danks, P. I. BSc CEng
MRAeS MIMgt semc
qss   (M)   1 July
Dipper, A. L. psc   1 July
Earnden, K. C. BA CEng
MRAeS semc qs   1 July
Fulford, M. A. MSc
MBA BSc CEng MIEE
semc qss   (EI)   1 July
Hannaby, A. R. BSc
CEng MRAeS qs   1 July
Kinder, S. J. MBE BSc
jsdc semc qss   (EI)   1 July
Lewis, A. P. qss   1 July
Maciver, J. slmc
qss   1 July
Neal, M. F. IEng
FIIE(elec) semc
qs   1 July
Parker, J. S. MBE MBA
BSc CEng MRAeS
semc qss   (EI)   1 July
Penketh, W. J. BSc
qs   (EI)   1 July
Phelps, S. M. BTech
CEng MIMechE semc
qs   (M)   1 July
Rigby, J. C. MSc BSc
CEng MIEE ae qs   1 July
Sturgess, M. I. psc   1 July
Wilson, A. slmc qss   1 July

1998

Barwell, R. J. BSc CEng
MRAeS psc
semc   (M)   1 Jan
Bishop, T. L. J. MSc
BSc CEng MIEE
qs   1 Jan
Burgess, C. A. R. MSc
jsdc semc qss   1 Jan
Cox, A. F. BSc CEng
MIEE MIMgt slmc
qs   1 Jan
Dixon, M. D. BSc slmc
qs   1 Jan

161

Wing Commanders

1998—contd

Gale, D. J. MBE MDA
BSc CEng MIEE slmc
qs   1 Jan
Long, S. BSc qs   1 Jan
McLachlan, P. MSc
BEng CEng MIEE jsdc
qs   1 Jan
Russell, G. M. BSc
qs   1 Jan
Tudor, D. C. qss   1 Jan
Whittaker, D. A. MDA
BSc psc   1 Jan
Wiltshire, J. qs   1 Jan
Ashraf, M. A. BSc
qs   1 July
Bushell, C. R. BSc CEng
MIMechE qs   1 July
Ewen, P. R. jsdc qs   1 July
Ridge, P. C. BSc qs   1 July
Short, P. BSc qs   1 July
Walker, W. F. IEng
MIIE(elec) semc
qs   1 July
Wall, G. P. MBA
BSc(Eng) CEng
MRAes qs   1 July
Winwood, C. D. L. BSc
CEng MIEE qs   1 July

Squadron Leaders

1975

Hoctor, B. P. CEng MIEE
qs   (EI)   1 Jan
Hoare, W. H. C. amec
qs   (EI)   1 July

1977

Hills, P. L. MSc BSc
CEng MIEE ae semc
qs   (EI)   1 July
Kerrison, P. I. BSc CEng
MIMechE MRAeS
qss*   (M)   1 July
Garden, E. R. BSc(Eng)
CEng MIMechE
MRAeS ae qs   (M)   2 Dec

1978

Fleckney, C. F. MSc BSc
DIC qs   (M)   18 Mar
Norris, P. G. semc   (M)   8 Apr
Adam, I. W. BSc ae (EI)   1 July
Smith, R. M. BSc amec
qs   (EI)   1 July
Woodcock, B. N. BTech
ae qs   (M)   1 July

1979

Haynes, A. R. BSc ae
qs   (EI)   1 July
Myall, D. M. qs   (EI)   1 July
Rowley, E. amec qs (M)   1 July

1980

Fullbrook, D. J. MPhil
CEng MIMechE
MRAeS qs   (M)   1 Jan
De Fleury, C. G. qss (M)   1 July
Mcdowell, C. B. semc
qs   (M)   1 July

1981

Chilvers, A. BSc CEng
MRAeS ae qs   (M)   1 July

Downes, D. T. semc
qs   (EI)   1 July

1982

Rowley-Brooke, P. S. J.
BA qs   (M)   1 Jan
Weight, P. E. semc
qs   (EI)   1 Jan
Shepard, M. J. W. semc
qs   (M)   15 July

1983

Buck, C. W. D. MA ae
qss   (EI)   1 Jan
Bakewell, G. BSc(Eng)
CEng MIMechE
MRAeS semc qs (M)   1 July
Peer, R. C. MBE qs (M)   1 July
Seviour, C. D. BSc
qss   (EI)   1 July
Shaw, T. J. H. BSc CEng
MIMechE qs   (M)   1 July
Walker, K. J. BSc CEng
MIMechE qs   (M)   1 July

1984

Greenwood, B. BSc
CEng MRAeS
qss   (M)   1 Jan
Hay, J. C. BA semc
qs   (EI)   1 Jan
Hulland, G. R. qss (M)   1 Jan
Bright, R. M. semc
qss   (EI)   1 July
Chinneck, M. R. S. MSc
BSc semc qss   (EI)   1 July
Deane, S. T. CEng
MIMechE qss   (M)   1 July
Derbyshire, I. MSc BA
CEng MInstP MIEE ae
qs   (EI)   1 July
Farmer, M. J. qss   (EI)   1 July
Hamilton, C. W. BSc ae
qs   (M)   1 July
Marter, A. D. qss   (EI)   1 July
Morrison, G. J. qss (M)   1 July

1985

Abra, J. E. MBE semc
qs   (EI)   1 Jan
Bradshaw, J. C. MSc
BSc semc qs   (EI)   1 Jan

Squadron Leaders

1985—contd

Cartwright-Terry, L. G. G.		
MBE BA semc qs	(M)	1 Jan
Chappell, D. IEng		
MIIE(elec) qss	(EI)	1 Jan
Christensen, C. K. MBE		
MSc CEng DipEE		
MIEE ae semc qs	(EI)	1 Jan
Evans, M. H. IEng		
FSERT qss	(EI)	1 Jan
Figgures, J. M. F. BSc		
CEng MIEE amec		
qss	(EI)	1 Jan
Lewis, I. V.	(EI)	1 Jan
Pickavance, R. MSc BSc		
CEng MIEE ae		
qss	(EI)	1 Jan
Rutter, A. S. BSc CEng		
MRAeS semc		
qss	(M)	1 Jan
Slater, I. M. BSc CDipAF		
semc qs i	(EI)	1 Jan
Webster, D. M. semc		
qss	(EI)	1 Jan
Ayers, R. S. semc		
qss	(E)	1 July
Davies, H. E. J. BSc ae		
qs	(EI)	1 July
Dunkley, P. R. IEng		
MIIE(mech) qs	(M)	1 July
Giles, W. J. BA semc		
qss	(M)	1 July
Keen, P. J. BA semc		
qs	(EI)	1 July
Peterson, G. K. CEng		
MRAeS qs	(M)	1 July
Ruskell, C. M. BSc semc		
qss	(EI)	1 July
Smith, C. J. L. semc		
qss	(M)	1 July
West, S. P. MA MSc ae		
qss	(M)	1 July

1986

Armstrong, M. H. BA		
qss	(EI)	1 Jan
Costello, M. E. MSc		
BSc CEng MIMechE		
MIMgt semc qs	(M)	1 Jan
Davidson, W. A. IEng		
semc qs	(EI)	1 Jan
Dowds, T. BA semc		
qs	(EI)	1 Jan

Horrocks, P. A. BSc		
CEng MIEE qs	(EI)	1 Jan
Kevan, G. J. qs	(E)	1 Jan
Ladds, R. G. BSc CEng		
MBCS adp	(M)	1 Jan
Trood, B. L. MBE		
qss	(EI)	1 Jan
Barker, P. semc qss		1 July
Bookham, R. P. BA		
qs	(M)	1 July
Hood, I. A. semc		
qss	(EI)	1 July
Stanhope, M. F. BSc		
qs	(M)	1 July

1987

Barnard, P. Q. MBE		
IEng semc	(E)	1 Jan
Brunning, G. BSc CEng		
MRAeS ae qss	(M)	1 Jan
Connolly, E. MSc BTech		
CEng MIEE semc		
qss	(EI)	1 Jan
Daniels, S. R. BSc ae		
slmc qs	(M)	1 Jan
Denham, R. L. MSc BSc		
CEng MIEE semc		
qs	(EI)	1 Jan
Elsom, J. BSc CEng		
MRAeS ae semc		
qss	(M)	1 Jan
Gow, P. J. MSc BSc		
CEng MIEE qs		1 Jan
Howell, A. J. MBE		
BSc(Eng) CEng		
MRAeS ACGI qs	(M)	1 Jan
Humphrey, P. G.		
qss	(EI)	1 Jan
Jenkins, M. R. MBE BA		
IEng MIMgt AMRAeS		
semc qss		1 Jan
Jones, G. B. BSc		
qss	(M)	1 Jan
Jones, R. N. IEng		
MIIE(elec) semc		
qs		1 Jan
Martin, J. PhD MSc		
qs		1 Jan
McHale, J. MDA BSc		
CEng MIEE MIMgt		
semc qs		1 Jan
Page, J. M. MBA BSc		
CEng MIMechE		
MIMgt qss	(M)	26 Apr
Adams, R. M. MBE MSc		
BSc CEng MRAeS		
MIMgt qss	(M)	1 July

Brown, S. P. BSc CEng		
MRAeS qs	(M)	1 July
Dean, P. semc qss	(EI)	1 July
Denwood, V. R. MBE		
amec	(EI)	1 July
Gatenby, G. J. BSc		
qss	(M)	1 July
Goff, N. J. BSc CEng		
MRAeS semc		
qss	(M)	1 July
Matthews, T. J. BSc		
qs	(EI)	1 July
Orme, D. J. MSc BSc		
qs	(EI)	1 July
Reed, A. G. IEng		
FIIE(elec) MIMgt		
qs	(EI)	1 July
Shevels, A. A. qss	(EI)	1 July

1988

Berriman, S. C. BTech		
CEng MIMechE qss		1 Jan
Brough, S. G. BEng		
CEng MRAeS semc		
qss	(M)	1 Jan
Bruce, D. A.	(EI)	1 Jan
Chadwick, G. H. CEng		
MRAeS semc qs	(M)	1 Jan
Chamberlain, S. J.		
BEng CEng MIMechE		
slmc qss	(M)	1 Jan
Crocombe, M.		
MIIE(elec) qss		1 Jan
Harris, P. R. BSc(Eng)		
qss	(M)	1 Jan
Lovejoy, F. MBE		
qss	(E)	1 Jan
Marshall, D. MBE slmc		
qss		1 Jan
Melling, P. BSc CEng		
MRAeS ACGI qs		1 Jan
Mowat, I. semc qs		1 Jan
Parfit, G. R. BA semc		
qs		1 Jan
Priestley, S. D. BSc		
qs	(EI)	1 Jan
Robinson, D. F. BSc qss		1 Jan
Tulloch, R. D. A. MBE		
BSc qs	(M)	1 Jan
Weaver, C. B. MSc MBA		
BSc CEng MIMgt		
MRAeS ae qs	(M)	1 Jan
Dixon, M. F. MSc BSc		
qss		1 July
Hands, S. J. MDA BSc		
CEng MRAeS qs		1 July
Jennings, R. W.		
qss	(M)	1 July

Squadron Leaders

1988—contd

Lambie, P. S. BTech
  MIMgt qss   (EI)   1 July
Ruddlesden, D. N. BA
  qs   (M)   1 July
Tillbrook, R. E. qss   1 July
Whitehead, G. E. BSc
  qss   (EI)   1 July

1989

Butterfield, M. qss   1 Jan
Connorton, J. qss   (M)   1 Jan
Crookston, J. MSc
  CEng MIMechE
  qs   (M)   1 Jan
Durling, R. A. R. MSc
  BSc ae semc qs   1 Jan
Ellis, D. C. MSc BSc
  CEng MIMechE
  qss   (M)   1 Jan
Ford, E. A. BSc qs   (M)   1 Jan
Greenbank, A. R. MSc
  CEng MIEE MIMgt
  semc qs   1 Jan
Harding, M. BSc CEng
  MIMechE MIMgt
  qs   (M)   1 Jan
Hardwick, M.   (M)   1 Jan
Hopton, C. H. MSc BSc
  ae qss   (EI)   1 Jan
McMaster, T. H. L. semc
  qs   1 Jan
Morley, E. MBE qss (EI)   1 Jan
Poulton, S. BSc qss (M)   1 Jan
Reid, W. McK. PhD BSc
  qs   1 Jan
Scotchmer, N. J. BSc
  qs   1 Jan
Scully, J. M. qss   1 Jan
Woodhouse, I. P. MBE
  BSc CEng MRAeS
  semc qs   (M)   1 Jan
Fillingham, D. BSc
  CEng MIEE semc
  qs   (EI)   1 July
Green, G. N. qss   (EI)   1 July
Honey, N. J. MSc BSc
  qs   1 July
Hounsell, L. J. qss (LA)   1 July
Ivory, S. P. BSc qss (EI)   1 July
Kidd, A. M. BSc qss (M)   1 July
Phillips, P. L. BSc CEng
  MRAeS qss   1 July
Twine, N. E. semc   1 July

Whiteley, A. M. qss   1 July
Wingrove, G. E. MSc
  BSc slmc qs   1 July

1990

Adams, R. C. qs   1 Jan
Baker, S. E. MSc BSc
  CEng MIEE MIMgt ae
  qss   1 Jan
Bees, A. R. qss   1 Jan
Buckland, A. J. MA (Eur
  Ing) CEng MIEE   (EI)   1 Jan
Bullen, R. K. qss   1 Jan
Cardy, T. semc qs   1 Jan
Charnock, S. MSc
  BSc(Eng) CEng
  MIMechE MRAeS
  jsdc ae qs   1 Jan
Childs, D. R. MSc BSc
  CEng FBIS MRAeS ae
  qs   (M)   1 Jan
Cooke, G. G. MBE qss   1 Jan
Davis, R. MSc BSc
  CEng MIMechE
  qss   1 Jan
Davis-Poynter, S. P.
  MSc BA CEng
  MRAeS ae qs   1 Jan
Drake, D. W. qs   1 Jan
Dreier, S. A. IEng qs   1 Jan
Dubock, I. M. BEng
  qs   (EI)   1 Jan
Eagles, M. E. BSc semc
  qs   (M)   1 Jan
Farrell, B. G. qss   1 Jan
Gibbons, T. E. qss   1 Jan
Goodall, J. P. qs   1 Jan
Gooden, R. qs   1 Jan
Gray, A. BSc CEng
  MRAeS qs   1 Jan
Hicks, P. G. MBE BSc
  qs   1 Jan
Kerry, C. J. BSc semc
  qss   1 Jan
Liley, S. qss   1 Jan
Lloyd-Roach, D. J. BSc
  qs   1 Jan
Martin, M. L. qss   1 Jan
McCarthy, M. B.
  qss   (EI)   1 Jan
Musselwhite, M. N.
  MBE IEng MIIE(elec)
  qs   (EI)   1 Jan
Pearce, K. N. BSc CEng
  MIMechE qs   1 Jan
Peers, J. slmc qss   1 Jan
Petch, C. S. F. MSc
  BSc   1 Jan

Readman, N. E. semc
  qs   1 Jan
Scott, P. J. MSc BSc
  slmc qss   1 Jan
Stephenson, I. MSc BA
  gw   (EI)   1 Jan
Taylor, A. J. BSc CEng
  MRAeS slmc qs   1 Jan
Thompson, A. J. qss   1 Jan
Thompson, M. J.
  qs   1 Jan
Walton, J. IEng qss   1 Jan
Williams, T. B. MSc BSc
  CEng MIEE qs   1 Jan
Wilson, S. J. BSc qs   1 Jan
Wray, C. F. BSc CEng
  MRAeS qs   1 Jan
Young, S. MA qs   1 Jan
Aldridge, M. R. qs   1 July
Cocksey, J. K. BSc
  qs   1 July
Codling, A. semc
  qs   1 July
Dennay, V. R. BEng qss   1 July
Eckersley, R. B. MBE
  MSc BSc qs   1 July
Gingell, C. E. MBE scc
  qs   1 July
Griffiths, D. K. semc
  qs   1 July
Helliwell, D. MSc BSc
  qs   1 July
James, A. R. BSc CEng
  MRAeS qss   1 July
Kelly, W. J. R. BSc CEng
  MIMechE adp
  qss   1 July
McCreanney, T. MBE
  qs   1 July
McTeague, R. B. BSc
  semc qs   1 July
Prout, K. E. qs   1 July
Robinson, J. C. P. BSc
  CEng MRAeS qss   1 July
Webber, S. semc
  qs   1 July

1991

Allen, R. J. BSc qs   1 Jan
Bailey, S. J. qs   1 Jan
Bottomley, S. D. G. BSc
  qss   1 Jan
Bromehead, J. M. BSc
  slmc qs   1 Jan
Brown, A. qss   1 Jan
Chantry, J. S. MDA BSc
  qs   1 Jan

Squadron Leaders

1991—contd

Cottam, S. BSc CEng MIEE qs	1 Jan
Davidson, M. C. F. MDA BSc CEng MRAeS MIMgt qs	1 Jan
Donohoe, H. G. BSc qs	1 Jan
Dunn, J. F. PhD MSc BSc CEng MIEE MIMechE slmc qs	1 Jan
Flowers, P. A. qs	1 Jan
Foran, P. J. qs	1 Jan
Garner, A. S. BSc CEng MRAeS psc	1 Jan
Gould, C. qs	1 Jan
Gransden, A. W. MBE IEng MIIE(elec) qs	1 Jan
Green, A. J. slmc	1 Jan
Harvey, P. J. R. MSc qss	1 Jan
Hepworth, M. E. qss	1 Jan
Hughes, G. J. MSc ae qss	1 Jan
Hutchinson, R. P. W. BSc semc qs	1 Jan
Keep, D. J. MSc BSc qs	1 Jan
Leach, R. L. F. BSc slmc qss	1 Jan
Leitch, D. O. S. semc qs	1 Jan
Mawston, A. N. BSc qs	1 Jan
Millington, N. G. IEng FIIE(elec) qss	1 Jan
Moody, S. C. BSc qs	1 Jan
Moran, M. qss	1 Jan
Pappa, M. R. qss	1 Jan
Parsons, R. M. slmc qs	1 Jan
Ransom, G. MSc BA qss	1 Jan
Richards, S. R. qs	1 Jan
Rigby, R. P. BSc CEng MIEE qs	1 Jan
Roads, C. BSc qss	1 Jan
Shears, A. J. MBE qss	1 Jan
Sibley, M. A. psc slmc	1 Jan
Skinner, M. W.	1 Jan
Smith, M. D. qs	1 Jan
Squires, P. J. MSc BEng CEng MIEE qs	1 Jan

Storey, R. N. MSc BSc CEng MIEE slmc qs	1 Jan
Tasker, D. R. BA slmc qss	1 Jan
Waller, C. J. N. IEng FIEIE AMRAeS qss	1 Jan
Young, D. J. MSc BSc CEng MIMechE ae qs	1 Jan
Arnold, A. J. qs	1 July
Barton, T. R. slmc qs	1 July
Cox, B. W. MBE slmc qs	1 July
Howard, P. qss	1 July
Lindsay, J. R. qss (EI)	1 July
Mansfield, R. A. MSc BSc (Eur Ing) CEng MBCS qs (EI)	1 July
Mays, E. J.	1 July
Mitchell, N. qss	1 July
Pearce, A. J. qss	1 July
Shaw, D. A. BSc CEng MRAeS qs (M)	1 July
Stammers, M. O. qs	1 July
Wood, R. B. qss	1 July
Wren, C. A. MSc BSc(Eng) ae qs	1 July

1992

Allan, J. McM. MSc BA CEng MIEE qss	1 Jan
Bacon, L. D. MSc BSc CEng MRAeS DIC slmc qs	1 Jan
Barrett, A. H. BSc qss	1 Jan
Bunting, M. E. MSc BSc ae qs	1 Jan
Bush, V. R. qs	1 Jan
Butler, D. P. MSc BSc ae qss	1 Jan
Canning, G. M. BSc slmc qs	1 Jan
Cox, N. J. BSc CEng MIMechE psc slmc	1 Jan
Edgar, J. D. BSc CEng MRAeS qs	1 Jan
Elliott, V. P. MSc BSc CEng MIEE slmc qs	1 Jan
French, M. J. MBE BSc CEng MRAeS MIMgt AIL slmc qs i*	1 Jan

Goslin, I. P. BSc CEng MIEE qs	1 Jan
Guthrie, P. F. qs	1 Jan
Hawley, A. B. MSc BSc ae slmc qss	1 Jan
Humphries, L. J. MSc BA CEng MRAeS gw qss	1 Jan
Moore, A. W. BSc slmc qs	1 Jan
Morgan, C. R.	1 Jan
Nicholls, P. qs	1 Jan
Ousby, R. T. BSc ae qs	1 Jan
Payne, T. A. R. MSc BA qss	1 Jan
Pitkin, J. M. BSc CEng MRAeS qs	1 Jan
Powell, K. BSc CEng MIMechE slmc qs	1 Jan
Rickwood, S. R. qss	1 Jan
Roughsedge, E. IEng MIIE(elec) qs	1 Jan
Royle, G. A. MSc BSc ae qss	1 Jan
Shannon, T. S. BSc qs	1 Jan
Shillito, P. MSc BSc CEng MIEE qs	1 Jan
Straw, K. BSc CEng MIEE qs	1 Jan
Thompson, T. A. qss	1 Jan
Thorne, P. A. MSc BSc qs	1 Jan
Underhill, G. P. BSc CEng MIEE slmc qss	1 Jan
Verth, J. W. MSc BA CEng DIC qss	1 Jan
Waring, M. S. BSc qs	1 Jan
White, P. J. FSERT IEng qs	1 Jan
Woodland, C. R. qss	1 Jan
Wrigley, D. A. qss (EL)	1 Jan
Wynne, M. qss	1 Jan
Bland, G. J. BSc CEng MIEE psc	1 July
Bole, L. T. qss	1 July
Boley, P. G. IEng MIIE(elec) MILog	1 July
Burdess, A. R. E. MSc BSc CEng MIEE qs	1 July
Dale, I. P. MSc BA ae qs	1 July
Forrest, P. F. BSc CEng MIEE qs	1 July

Squadron Leaders

1992—contd

Goodall, M. P. qs	1 July
Harsley, S. J. slmc qs	1 July
Lean, P. A. BA MIIE(elec) slmc qs	1 July
Parton, N. BSc CEng MRAeS qs	1 July
Rope, B. A. qss	1 July
Sandeman, C. A.	1 July
Smith, J. J. slmc qs	1 July
Stead, J. R. MSc BSc qab qss	1 July

1993

Aleandri, M. P. BSc qs	1 Jan
Bargewell, T. A. IEng MIIE(elec) qss	1 Jan
Bray, B. A. J. MIIE(elec) qs	1 Jan
Evans, J. R. MDA BSc CEng MRAeS qs	1 Jan
Gill, C. A. BSc qs	1 Jan
Henwood, C. M. MSc BSc CEng MIMechE qs	1 Jan
Hesketh, R. L. MA MSc qss	1 Jan
Lovell, G. J. slmc qs	1 Jan
Martindale, I. qss	1 Jan
Robinson, M. J. BTech CEng MIMechE qs	1 Jan
Simpson, R. MSc BSc CEng MIEE qs	1 Jan
Smith, N. J. MSc BSc qss	1 Jan
Surtees, I. BSc adp qss	1 Jan
Voss, M. G. BSc CEng MIEE slmc qss	1 Jan
Walsh, J. BSc MDA qss	1 Jan
Webb, C. BSc slmc qs	1 Jan
Beange, P. qs	1 July
Billings, P. A. qs	1 July
Collinge, M. J. qss	1 July
Dawson, G. P. M. IEng MIIE(elec) qss	1 July
Etheridge, J. qs	1 July

Evans, M. A. BA MIMgt qs	1 July
Farr, A. J. R. BA qss	1 July
Gilbert, C. N. R. MSc BEng ae qss	1 July
Gilbert, M. P. BSc qs	1 July
Gill, D. N. BA BSc CEng MRAeS qs	1 July
Holder, S. BSc qss	1 July
Lindsay, P. F. MBE qss	1 July
Liston, G. D. MSc BSc slmc qs	1 July
Martin, P. MSc BSc ae qs	1 July
Myers, I. A. qss	1 July
Nidd, D. A. adp qss	1 July
Powell, D. McA. BSc semc qss	1 July
Sirs, R. C. qs	1 July
Thornley, J. F. BEM IEng FIEIE qss	1 July
Turner, R. M. BSc qs	1 July
Venner, R. qss	1 July
Wade, R. A. MA MSc CEng MIMechE qs	1 July
Williams, J. D. BSc qs	1 July

1994

Appleton, D. P. MSc BSc qss	1 Jan
Barclay, I. G. qss	1 Jan
Bosanco-Mitchell, D. W. qss	1 Jan
Clark, D. R. qs	1 Jan
Dalley, S. L.	1 Jan
Dixon, Q. L. MSc BSc CEng MIEE ae qs	1 Jan
Fletcher, G. J. MSc BSc CEng MIEE DMS ae qss	1 Jan
Harris, A. J. MSc BSc qss	1 Jan
Hill, K. W. M. MSc BSc CEng MIMechE qs	1 Jan
Jameson, S. V. qss	1 Jan
Johnston, J. B. BSc qss	1 Jan
Kirkwood, I. Mcl. A. MSc BSc CEng MIEE qs	1 Jan
Land, A. IEng MIIE(elec) qss	1 Jan

Leech, D. W. MSc BEng qss	1 Jan
Maddieson, G. S. qs	1 Jan
Mercer, B. P. BSc qs	1 Jan
Milligan, D. BSc semc qs	1 Jan
Pennycook, J. A. R. semc	1 Jan
Powell, A. L. MSc BSc CEng MIEE qs	1 Jan
Roberts, J. D. slmc qs	1 Jan
Stokes, J. A. BSc CEng MIEE semc qss	1 Jan
Aunger, D. J. MSc BSc qss	1 July
Crane, D. BSc slmc qs	1 July
Croft, P. J. MSc BSc ae slmc qs	1 July
Cross, A. R. D. BA	1 July
Davies, M. J. MSc qss	1 July
Dunn, G. J. BSc IEng FIIE(elec) qss	1 July
Farnell, G. P. BSc qs	1 July
Gray, S. C. MSc BSc qs	1 July
Hanslow, M. G. qss	1 July
Izard, B. S. MSc BSc CEng MIMechE qs	1 July
Jones, R. A. semc qss	1 July
Kennedy, T. qss	1 July
Lansbury, D. BA qss	1 July
Lee, M. E. qs	1 July
McMillen, W. R.	1 July
Moss, S. A. MSc BSc ae qs	1 July
O'Connell, P. M. slmc qs	1 July
Parkinson, S. J. qs	1 July
Raine, P. D. MSc BSc CEng MIEE ae qs	1 July
Scannell, K. H. E. BSc qs	1 July
Singleton, C. M. qs	1 July
Small, M. K. BSc qss	1 July
Spencer, R. M. J. MBA IEng MIIE(elec) qs	1 July
Stewart, W. J. MSc BA IEng MIIE(mech) qss	1 July

Squadron Leaders

1994—contd

Tarbitten, C. M. BSc(Tech) qss	1 July
Terrett, J. D. qss	1 July
Waldwyn, C. R. MSc BSc CEng MIIE(mech) MRAeS ae qs	1 July
Whitaker, J. qss	1 July
Wilson, G. A. BEM qss	1 July
Windsor, P. J. BSc CEng MRAeS qs	1 July

1995

Bingham, G. K. BSc qss	1 Jan
Butler, A. J. qs	1 Jan
Clouth, P. J. MSc BEng CEng MIEE qs	1 Jan
Currie, R. I. MSc BSc ae qss	1 Jan
Daykin, C. P. BEng qs	1 Jan
Friend, R. qs	1 Jan
Fyffe, J. C. N. MSc BSc gw qs	1 Jan
Gibson, J. M. M. qss	1 Jan
Iddenden, P. qss	1 Jan
James, R. D. BA qss	1 Jan
Jones, F. B. qs	1 Jan
Keeton, P. BSc CEng MRAeS slmc qs	1 Jan
Marshall, K. A. BSc CEng MIMechE qs	1 Jan
Mart, K. BEng qss	1 Jan
Matthews, N. qss	1 Jan
McDermid, B. D. MSc BEng CEng MRAeS ae qs	1 Jan
Melhuish, R. T. K. MSc BEng CEng MIMechE qs	1 Jan
Miller, R. L. BSc CEng MIMechE qss	1 Jan
Newby, M. A. MSc BSc ae qs	1 Jan
Reed, S. C. MSc BSc qss	1 Jan
Summers, N. J. MSc BSc ae qss	1 Jan

Tolometti, G. R. BTech qss	1 Jan
Turner, D. J. MSc BEng CEng MIMechE ae qss	1 Jan
Warmington, M. A. BSc qss	1 Jan
Williams, G. qs	1 Jan
Willis, M. E. qs	1 Jan
Baird, M. J. BSc qs	1 July
Barnes, O. R. J. MSc BSc qss	1 July
Brodie, G. E. BSc qs	1 July
Clark, T. J. MSc BSc CEng MIEE ACGI qs	1 July
Dangerfield, M. J. BSc qss	1 July
De Soyza, K. W. BSc qss	1 July
Donald, P. W. qss	1 July
Emmett, P. C. PhD BSc CEng MIEE qss	1 July
Featherstone, C. J. BSc qs	1 July
Glass, M. R. BEng CEng MIMechE qs	1 July
Headey, G. E. qss	1 July
Hollis, M. BSc slmc qs	1 July
Jones, C. G. IEng MIIE(elec) qss	1 July
Judd, D. G. M. MSc MSc BSc qss	1 July
Lyons, D. qss	1 July
Marks, M. H. qs	1 July
McCloskey, P. W. J. qss	1 July
Moody, D.	1 July
Moore, C.	1 July
Muir, A. G. BSc CEng MRAeS qs	1 July
Peet, K. MSc BEng CEng MIEE qss	1 July
Perry, L. K. IEng MIExpE MIIE(mech) AMRAeS slmc qss	1 July
Rawcliffe, A. P.	1 July
Sarjeant, A. P. qs	1 July
Saunders, E. J. IEng MIIE(elec) qss	1 July
Scott, D. P. P. qs	1 July
Smith, C. R. M. qs	1 July
Thomas, K. L. BEng CEng MIEE qss	1 July
Thomson, C. R. BSc CEng MIEE qs	1 July

Turner, N. J. BSc qss	1 July
Williamson, M. B. BSc CEng MIEE qss	1 July
Wilson, D. J. BSc	1 July
Woods, T. A. slmc qs	1 July

1996

Annal, P. D. BSc CEng MIMechE qss	1 Jan
Box, A. P. R. BSc qs	1 Jan
Conant, A. J. BSc qs	1 Jan
Edmondson, S. J. BSc CEng MIEE qss	1 Jan
Evans, B. R. CEng BEng MIMechE qs	1 Jan
Evans, D.	1 Jan
Gibson, M. BEng CEng MIMechE qss	1 Jan
Grinsted, P. J. qs	1 Jan
Guy, T. J. BEng qss	1 Jan
Hargrave, R. J. BSc qs	1 Jan
Hobbs, M. H. qs	1 Jan
Howitt, M. G.	1 Jan
Johnstone, A. K. MSc BSc CEng MIMechE MRAeS qs	1 Jan
Maher, T. M. BEng qs	1 Jan
March, A. P. BSc qss	1 Jan
McMillan, M. MSc BEng CEng MIEE qss	1 Jan
Murray, N. qs	1 Jan
Phillips, N. J. MBA IEng qs	1 Jan
Russell, S. M. qss	1 Jan
Turner, T. N. MPhil BSc AMIMechE qs	1 Jan
Walder, C. L. qss	1 Jan
Wilkinson, S. R. BSc CEng MRAeS qs	1 Jan
Wray, H. L. BSc qss	1 Jan
Ambrose, I. D. qss	1 July
Apps, R. M. qss	1 July
Bartlett, N. G.	1 July
Bennett, C. R. MIIE(elec) qss	1 July
Brown, A. S. E. qss	1 July
Devlin, T. D. BSc IEng MIIE(elec) slmc qs	1 July
Galkowski, R. A. MSc BEng qss	1 July

Squadron Leaders

1996—contd

Harris, S. J. qss	1 July
Ho, M. Y. K. BSc(Eng)	1 July
Holden, P. J. MA MSc	
qss	1 July
Looker, I. BSc qss	1 July
Mann, T. S. BSc CEng	
MIMechE qss	1 July
Marshall, J. qss	1 July
McAlpine, P. W. BSc	
qss	1 July
Moss, M. S. BEM BA	
qss	1 July
Patel, P. qss	1 July
Pooley, T. T. qss	1 July
Robinson, M. BSc IEng	
AMRAeS qss	1 July
Simpson, A. C. slmc	
qss	1 July
Tassell, D. M. qss	1 July
Taylor, K. R. qss	1 July
Thompson, C. M. BSc	
qs	1 July

1997

Biddington, D. V. W.	1 Jan
Bradbeer, P. A. qss	1 Jan
Bradbury, N. J. BSc	
CEng MIMechE	
qss	1 Jan
Cottrell, N. IEng	
MIIE(mech) qs	1 Jan
Donald, M. H.	1 Jan
Eady, C. J. BSc qss	1 Jan
Griffiths, G. D. MSc BSc	
qss	1 Jan
Ham, G. qss	1 Jan
Horrocks, M. BSc	
qss	1 Jan
Horton, M. qss	1 Jan
Jones, P. qss	1 Jan
Mitchison, B. MSc BSc	
qss	1 Jan
Nesbitt, R. C. slmc	
qss	1 Jan
Northcote-Wright, A.	
qss	1 Jan
Orton, D. G. BSc CEng	
MIEE qss	1 Jan
Palmer, W. J. qss	1 Jan
Pearson, N. F. BSc	
qss	1 Jan
Quigley, M. qss	1 Jan
Satchell, V. J. qss	1 Jan

Stewart, S. BSc qs	1 Jan
Stubbs, M. R. BSc(Eng)	
qss	1 Jan
Tait, A. G. BSc(Eng)	
CEng MRAeS	
AMIMechE qs	1 Jan
Wood, A. qss	1 Jan
Wood, N. C. BSc qs	1 Jan
Armitage, S. R. MSc	
BEng CEng MRAeS	
qss	1 July
Benford, C. BSc	
qss	1 July
Booth, G. A. qss	1 July
Bradshaw, N. T. BEng	
qs	1 July
Burgess, C. M. qss	1 July
Carson, A. V. qss	1 July
Cook, D. R. D. BSc	
qss	1 July
Deacon, R. qss	1 July
Delaney, R. H. MSc qss	1 July
Fallow, D. qss	1 July
Gasson, B. R. qs	1 July
Gilbert, M. R. IEng	
AMRAeS qs	1 July
Gill, J. R. BEng qss	1 July
Holmes, C. N. BSc qss	1 July
Horne, B. P. BA IEng	
FIIE(elec) AMRAeS	
qs	1 July
Hughes, R. G. BSc	
qss	1 July
Jarvis, K. E. BEng	
qss	1 July
Johnson, R. M. BSc	1 July
Keeley, R. F. MSc	
qss	1 July
Lewis, D. qss	1 July
McGlary, S. qss	1 July
Mitchell, P. MSc BEng	
qss	1 July
Murphy, T. G. BEng	
slmc qs	1 July
Pearce, P. BSc qss	1 July
Pettitt, S. J. BSc CEng	
MRAeS qs	1 July
Read, A. B. BSc CEng	
MRAeS qss	1 July
Rees, B. G.	1 July
Richardson, S. A. BSc	
CEng MRAeS qs	1 July
Rogers, D. E. IEng	
qss	1 July
Rose, P. S. MSc BEng	
ae qss	1 July
Sainsbury, N. M.	
qss	1 July
Taylor, C. BSc qss	1 July
Thorley, L. R. qss	1 July

Wariner, J. P. BSc	
qss	1 July
Wilkes, J. G. qss	1 July
Wilson, I. A. BEng ae	
qs	1 July
Wilson, P.	1 July
Young, A. G. BEng	
qss	1 July

1998

Andrews, D. L. qss	1 Jan
Axelsen, M. IEng	
AMRAeS qss	1 Jan
Brook, D. J. BSc	
qss	1 Jan
Bullen, A.	1 Jan
Burn, R. qss	1 Jan
Currie, A. J. A. MSc	
BEng qss	1 Jan
Davies, M. R. BSc	
qss	1 Jan
Day, A. P. BSc qss	1 Jan
Dennis, G. J.	1 Jan
Edge, A. D. BSc qss	1 Jan
Evers, M. C. MSc	
qss	1 Jan
Gowing, A. R. IEng	
MIIE(elec) qss	1 Jan
Grainger, R. BSc(Eng)	
qss	1 Jan
Hand, J. A. qss	1 Jan
Hartley, N. J. BSc CEng	
CPhys MIEE MInstP	
qss	1 Jan
Hurst, I. M. BSc qss	1 Jan
Kelsey, D. BSc qss	1 Jan
Knott, S. qss	1 Jan
Legg, A. R. BEng	
qss	1 Jan
Manger, M. J. MSc	
BEng CEng MIEE ae	
qss	1 Jan
Nicholls, A. P. BEng	
qss	1 Jan
Northover, M. J. MBE	
BEng qss	1 Jan
Powell, N. R. BSc	
qss	1 Jan
Rhimes, D. M.	1 Jan
Roberts, H. MSc BSc	
qs	1 Jan
Sansom, A. M. BEng	
CEng MRAeS ae	
qss	1 Jan
Savage, J. D. C. MSc	
BSc qss	1 Jan
Smith, F. E. A.	1 Jan

Squadron Leaders

1998—contd

Tandy, R. MSc BSc ae qss	1 Jan
Tyrell, A. J. BEng qss	1 Jan
Ward, I. BSc qs	1 Jan
Webster, S. M. J. qss	1 Jan
Weston, A. J. BSc qs	1 Jan
Wray, S. W. BEng qss	1 Jan
Arnold, D. B. BSc qss	1 July
Balderstone, A. W. MSc BEng qss	1 July
Bell, A. S. BSc qss	1 July
Berry, I. F. qss	1 July
Bethell, K. H. R. qss	1 July
Birkenhead, G. B. MSc BSc CEng MIEE qss	1 July
Borthwick, S. P. BA BEng qss	1 July
Brown, M. A. IEng MIIE(Elec) MIMgt qss	1 July
Buckland, P. J. qss	1 July
Coleman, M. J. qss	1 July
Diamond, P. A. BEng CEng MIEE qss	1 July
Edwards, M. A. BSc qss	1 July
Ewbank, T. D. qss	1 July
Firby, N. qss	1 July
Freer, G. W. MSc BSc ae qss	1 July
Gilligan, M. MSc BSc gw qss	1 July
Graham, H. BSc qss	1 July
Green, N. B. BA qss	1 July
Greenway, A. M. MSc BEng qss	1 July
Greenwood, R. J. qss	1 July
Gunn, T. J. qss	1 July
Hands, C. J. BEng qss	1 July
Hawley, G. A. qss	1 July
Holmes, A. G. K. qss	1 July
Hughes, G. K. BSc qss	1 July
Jemmett, R. C. MSc BSc CEng ae qss	1 July

Johnson, C. N.	1 July
Kimber, A. J. qss	1 July
MacRury, D. G. qss	1 July
Machray, R. G. MSc BEng ae qss	1 July
McCann, N. F. BEng qss	1 July
Nelson, A. R. BEng CEng qss	1 July
Parlett, R. B. qss	1 July
Pye, C. D. BEng qss	1 July
Rowsell, M. A. BEng CEng MIMechE qss	1 July
Saunders, D. BEng CEng MIMechE qss	1 July
Slee, P. BEng CEng MIEE qss	1 July
Starr, P. G.	1 July
Tremaine, J. BEng qss	1 July
Watts, D. J. BSc CEng MIEE qss	1 July
Wells, M. C. BEng qss	1 July
Williams, P. L. MSc BSc qss	1 July

Flight Lieutenants

1976

Vale, P. N. BSc semc adp qss	(M)	25 Nov

1982

Caines, C. J.	25 Sept
Rubenstein, M. MSc CEng MRAeS qss	10 Dec

1983

Kohli, R. D. S. BSc qss	13 July

1984

Barnes, N. I.	20 Dec

1985

Skinner, M. D. qss	6 Oct
Perry, A. T. BSc qss	20 Oct
Riddell, J. G. BSc CEng MRAeS qss	20 Oct
Jones, K. C. BSc IEng MIIE(elec)	26 Oct
Harrop, J. M. BSc CEng MRAeS qss	31 Oct
Sneddon, M. I. BSc CEng MIEE qss	1 Nov
Third, A. G. CEng qss	7 Dec
Davies, M. J. BSc qss	19 Dec
McGregor, W. R. BSc qss	19 Dec

1986

Goddard, M. R. BSc qss	23 Feb
Shelton-Smith, K. C. BEng qss	13 Aug
Kreckeler, M. K. BSc qss	15 Sept
Dabrowski, M. R. BSc qss	8 Nov
Evans, M. P. qss	20 Nov

Flight Lieutenants

1986—contd

Lucie-Smith, E. R. BSc
CEng MRAeS
qss   15 Dec

1987

Marshall, T. A. BSc
qss   15 Jan
Roberts, T. M. C. BSc
CEng MIEE qss   17 Jan
Kyte, G. M. BSc qss   26 Jan
Wilby, S. K. qss   28 Feb
Carr, J. H. MSc BSc (Eur
Ing) CEng MIMechE
qss   14 Apr
Brown, J. qss   15 June
Hoskin, D. P. qss   29 July
Dodding, S. D. BSc
qss   3 Sept
Vernon, R. K. BEM   8 Sept
Palmer, G. R. A. BSc
qss   15 Oct
St John-Crees, D. BSc
CEng MRAeS
qss   15 Oct
Chapman, M. A.   18 Oct
Wharrier, I. BSc qss   5 Nov
Kelsey, C. M. qss   27 Nov
Quarmby, D. A. BEng
CEng MIEE   30 Dec

1988

Hegharty, D. BSc(Eng)
qss   15 Jan
Jones, A. S. MSc BSc
ae qss   16 Jan
Greenstreet, D. M. BSc
qss   21 Feb
John, R. S. BSc CEng
MIMechE MRAeS
qss   2 Mar
Panton, A. BSc qss   2 Mar
Jones, C. H. BSc
qss   25 Mar
Thorpe, M. P. BSc qss   14 Apr
Dickinson, P. W. BSc
CEng MRAeS
qss   30 Apr
Smale, M. J. qss   8 May
Mason, D. G. J. BSc
qss   10 May

Budkiewicz, K. S. qss   8 June
Rillie, I. qss   19 June
Lomas, M. MBE
qss   30 June
Seymour, W. S. BEng
qss   15 July
Schoner, N. J. BSc qss   22 July
McLellan, A. M. K.   31 July
Middlewood, M. L.
qss   31 July
Dryburgh, G. D.   11 Oct
Sheffield, C. J.   11 Oct
Flather, N. qss   26 Oct
Ramsey, S. A. BEng
AMIEE qss   29 Dec

1989

Ellis, T. J. R. BSc CEng
MRAeS MIExpE qtm qss   15 Jan
Burgess, M. K.   17 Jan
Norton, B. K.   17 Jan
Rees, P. A. BSc qss   3 Feb
Hill, G. W. BEng   18 Feb
Thomas, P. D. BSc
qss   18 Feb
McKevitt, M. BEM
qss   11 Apr
Lawrence, G. BSc
qss   15 Apr
Ellis, G. BEng qss   3 May
Taylor, A. J. BEng
qss   3 May
Higson, D. W. BEng
qss   10 May
Cornford, D. A.   23 May
Ashman, R. J. L.
BA   4 June
Grace, R. qss   4 July
Perrett, B. J. BA BSc
CEng MRAeS   4 July
Cox, M. G. T. BEng   15 July
Mitchell, J. BEng
qss   15 July
Stewart, J. A. BEng
qss   15 July
Seaton, G. R. BSc CEng
MRAeS   1 Aug
Jackson, D.   15 Aug
Kinsey, A. T. qss   27 Aug
Wells, J. W.   2 Sept
Edwards, C. J. (Eur Ing)
BEng CEng MIEE
qss   18 Sept
Reese, N. P. BSc ae   3 Oct
Ford, A. J. qss   7 Oct
Baughan, D. S. IEng
MIEIE qss   8 Oct

Martland, J. R. BSc
qss   17 Oct
Miller, P. L. BEng CEng
MIEE qss   16 Nov
Edwards, G. D. BSc
qss   7 Dec
Way, C. S. BSc qss   7 Dec
Frieland, C. A. qss   19 Dec
Hopkins, D. J. BEng
qss   22 Dec

1990

Swinney, R. W. MSc
MSc BSc   11 Jan
Jamieson, J. IEng
MIIE(elec) qss   14 Jan
Marshall, R. J. qss   14 Jan
Tudor, N. J. BEng CEng
MIEE qss   15 Jan
Wheeler, P. G. BSc
qss   15 Jan
Anderson, M. G. BSc
CEng MISM MRAeS
qss   19 Jan
Armitage, G. V. R. BSc
qss   19 Jan
Lockhart, P. qss   20 Jan
Elsy, K. BEng CEng
MIEE qss   24 Jan
Shippen, J. M. BSc
qss   29 Jan
Phillips, J. S. BEng
qss   11 Feb
Parker, G. H.   13 Feb
Butt, N. J. BSc qcc   15 Mar
Duncan, E. C. D. BSc
CEng MRAeS
qss   15 Mar
Ellis, S. C. qss   15 Mar
Chandler, J. H. BSc
qss   27 Mar
McCandless, D. C.
qss   27 Mar
Clark, F. S. BSc(Eng)
qss   15 Apr
Jeffrey, D. W. R. BSc
qss   26 Apr
Stace, C. J. BEng CEng
MIEE   26 Apr
Stott, I. R. qss   26 Apr
Hockley, S. P. qss   5 May
Waters, P. J. qss   5 May
Shields, R. G. qss   15 May
Shelton-Smith, C. A.
BEng CEng MRAeS
qss   27 May
Berrecloth, P. C. BSc
qss1   5 July

Flight Lieutenants

1990—contd

Ellard, N. A. BA	8 July
Bolton, G. I. qss	15 July
Fryer, D. qss	15 July
Sandom, C. W. MSc	
BEng CEng MIEE	
qss	15 July
Barber, M. I. BEng	25 July
Bowles, K. N. qss	28 July
Evans, G. H. MSc BSc	
CEng MIEE MRAeS	
ae qss	28 July
Booth, D. M. C. qss	31 July
Hill, J. J.	31 July
Pawson, P. T. qss	31 July
Upton, D. J.	31 July
Hubert, I. L. BSc	
qss	1 Aug
McCann, C. T. BSc	
qss	14 Aug
Terrill, N. S. BEng	
qss	25 Aug
Akerman, C. qss	7 Sept
Snowden, R. W.	11 Sept
Houghton, I. BSc	19 Sept
Hopkins, M. J. IEng	
MIIE(elec) qss	22 Sept
Wright, J. M. qss	22 Sept
Atkins, A. R. qss	9 Oct
Winfield, R. J.	19 Oct
Burke, J. G. qss	23 Oct
Leadbitter, S. J.	22 Nov
Losh, S. qss	25 Nov
Owen, M. J. qss	4 Dec
Aitchison, D. F. qss	15 Dec
Frisch, M. A. F.	15 Dec
Kennedy, M. H. IEng	
MIIE(elec) qss	15 Dec

1991

Senior, K. S. BSc CEng	
MIMechE qss	2 Jan
Bannister-Green, G. M.	
BSc qss	15 Jan
Barratt, P. L. MSc BEng	
qss	15 Jan
Long, C. E. BEng	
qss	15 Jan
Milwright, D. T. P. BSc	
qss	15 Jan
Nicholson, E. H. J. MBE	
BSc qss	15 Jan
Savage, S. J. BEng	
CEng MIEE qss	15 Jan

Tapson, I. R. BEng	
qss	15 Jan
Carroll, M. W. BEng	
qss	19 Jan
Pawsey, A. R. BSc adp	
qss	19 Jan
Grimsley, D. T. A. BSc	
qss	14 Feb
Bagley, D. C. qss	16 Feb
Taylor, I. J. BEng CEng	
MRAeS qss	23 Feb
Stanway, N. A. BEng	
CEng MRAeS	
qss	28 Feb
Cockram, J. D. BEng	
qss	4 Mar
Williamson, N. P.	
qss	11 Mar
Jones, L. J. BSc	
qss	15 Mar
Bathgate, P. BEng	
qss	3 Apr
James, T. R. BEng	12 Apr
Wilcock, S. J. qss	12 Apr
Clarkson, D. BSc	
qss	23 Apr
Macdonald, G. B. qss	23 Apr
Wilkinson, S. N. MSc	
BSc CEng MRAeS ae	
qss	30 Apr
Carleton, R. K. MSc	
BEng CEng MIEE qss	6 May
Walker, R. J. BEng	6 May
Ashcroft, K.	4 June
Ladbrook, P. R. qss	4 June
Wilson, C. J. qss	4 June
Marvell, C. B. BEng	
CEng MIEE qss	21 June
Martin, N. R.	26 June
Mills, J. B. qss	1 July
Khan, R. BEng qss	3 July
O'Connell, S. T. BEng	
qss	8 July
Birch, P. H. B. BEng	15 July
Hampson-Jones, C.	
BEng	15 July
Hill, C. V. BEng qss	15 July
Lainchbury, I. M. BEng	15 July
Mackie, W. S. MSc BSc	
BEng CEng	
MIIE(elec) MIEE	15 July
Narsey, A. K. BEng	15 July
Paris, C. A. BEng	
qss	15 July
Souter, W. G. BEng	15 July
Clarke, K.	17 July
Saldanha, R. C.	17 July
Cunningham, S.	
qss	18 July
Pearce, G. C. qss	26 July

Knight, A. J. qss	29 July
Rowes, R. A. qss	14 Aug
Morgan, D. W. MEng	
qss	19 Aug
Gurden, M. BEng	
qss	21 Aug
Oglesby, D. H. BEng	
CEng MIEE qss	25 Aug
Robbins, C. J.	27 Aug
White, T. A. adp	2 Sept
Nimick, P. G. BEng	
qcc	7 Sept
Barrington, M. P. B.	
qss	14 Sept
Vicary, S. R. BEng CEng	
MIMechE qss	15 Sept
Fielding, D. qss	28 Sept
Callaghan, J. BEng	
CEng MIMechE	2 Oct
Fitzpatrick, J. D. BEng	
qss	3 Oct
Rogers, E. W. qss	8 Oct
Beckett, W. B. M.	17 Oct
Treloar, B. C. qss	26 Oct
Hammond, J. BSc	8 Nov
Vella, R. A. qss	9 Nov
MacDonald, A. T.	
qss	19 Nov
Robinson, D. A. qss	14 Dec
MacLennan, A. R. IEng	
MIIE(elec) qss	21 Dec
Peacock, J. C. qss	21 Dec
Pipe, A. J. IEng	
MIIE(elec) MIMgt	
qss	21 Dec
Studley, G. S. qss	21 Dec
Hill, C. M. BEng qss	25 Dec

1992

Parry, D. T. IEng	
MIIE(elec) MIMgt	14 Jan
Campbell, A. J. BEng	
qss	15 Jan
Dryden, I. BEng qss	15 Jan
Ellard, S. D. BSc qss	
i*	15 Jan
McQuillan, S. D. V.	
BEng qss	15 Jan
McQuillin, K. F. BSc	
qss	15 Jan
Parker, R. M. BA	
qss	15 Jan
Skilton, T. J. BSc	15 Jan
Willis, A. S. BSc	
qss	15 Jan
Beresford, I. M. MBE	
qss	17 Jan
Killick, A. J. qss	15 Feb

Flight Lieutenants

1992—contd

Hewitt, A. K. BEng	
qss	20 Feb
Gates, M. qss1	21 Feb
Haywood, S. J. BEng	
qss	21 Feb
Baldwin, B. F. qss	25 Feb
Lacey, T. A. BSc	25 Feb
Bradgate, J. K.	
BEng	27 Feb
Philliban, J. qss	28 Feb
Wallis, A. D. BSc	
qss	15 Mar
Hillary, N. P. qss	29 Mar
Phillips, A. L. MEng	
AMIMechE ACGI	1 Apr
Herbert, G. S. R.	
qss	26 Apr
Lea, N. J. BEng qss	26 Apr
Gordon, B.	5 May
Howard, J. C. E.	
qss	5 May
Sheppard, P. R.	5 May
Stellitano, W.	5 May
Blades, J. M. BEng	
qss	6 May
Williams, M. J. BEng	
qss	6 May
Austen, R. G. qss	10 May
Clarke, N. IEng	
MIIE(elec) qss	10 May
Cooper, I. R.	10 May
Grace, J. C. BEng	
qss	12 May
Williams, H. J. BEng	
qss1	12 May
Warr, S. A. BEng	
qss	20 May
Murphy, C. J. qcc	15 June
Welberry, J. BEM	16 June
Beech, G. qss	21 June
Longdon, S. J.	21 June
Peters, C. E.	21 June
Ward, C. D.	21 June
Wright, K. M.	21 June
Heath, S. T. BSc	
MRAeS qss	24 June
Hood, M. G. H. qcc	2 July
Chalmers, G. qss	6 July
Marshall, P. S. qss	13 July
Bailey, A. P. BEng	15 July
Chapman, C. R. BEng	
qcc	15 July
Foster, S. F. BEng	15 July
Halliday, S. J. BEng	
qss	15 July

Holmes, R. BEng	
qss1	15 July
Legge, G. P. E. BEng	
qcc	15 July
McLaughlin, W.	
BEng	15 July
Still, W. BEng	15 July
Stockton, N. A. BEng	
qss	15 July
Thompson, T. M.	
BEng	15 July
Robertson, C. D.	
qss	25 July
Cudlipp, R. M.	28 July
Pattison, F.	28 July
Allan, C. J. qss	2 Aug
Jones, C. A. qss	2 Aug
Moss, A. S. qss	2 Aug
Ward, S. K. qss	2 Aug
Whitelegg, P. J.	2 Aug
Empson, J. G. BEng	
CEng MIEE qcc	6 Aug
Watkins, G. D.	
BEng	18 Aug
Watson, B. J. BEng	
qss	18 Aug
Jack, S. A. BEng CEng	
MIEE qss	20 Aug
Miller, S. BEng qss	23 Aug
Brown, D. P. BEng CEng	
MIEE qss	3 Sept
Bailey, C. P. IEng	26 Sept
Le Galloudec, S. J.	
qss	26 Sept
Pennington, G. C.	26 Sept
Tanfield, I. F. qss	26 Sept
Hartland, P. A. BEng	
qcc	1 Oct
Barraclough, R. BEng	
qss	2 Oct
Cooper, A. J. qss1	2 Oct
Sanderson, A. M. BSc	
qss	2 Oct
Cummins, N. J. qss	11 Oct
Martin, P. L. qss	20 Oct
Peck, R. BEng qss1	23 Oct
Block, K. J.	2 Nov
Freeman, G. J. qss	2 Nov
Hunter, K.	2 Nov
Hoyton, D. G. BSc	7 Nov
Boardman, L. D.	
qss	8 Nov
Brandon, V. G. qss	8 Nov
Carlton, D. qss	8 Nov
Carter, S. J. qss	8 Nov
Crowle, A. J. W.	8 Nov
Newton, C. H. qss1	8 Nov
Paice, N. J.	8 Nov
Twine, A. N. H. BTech	
qss	8 Nov

Shears, P. M. qss	25 Nov
O'Brien, P. F. J. IEng	
MIIE(elec)	26 Nov
McCleary, D. P. BSc	
qss	7 Dec
Brown, M. H. qss	15 Dec
Phillips, M. E.	15 Dec
Brudenell, J. P. qss	20 Dec
Duncan, B. C.	20 Dec
Bareham, D. M. BEng	
qss	23 Dec
Kilbride, D. M. IEng	
MIMechIE qss	28 Dec

1993

Dique, M. J. A.	7 Jan
Hurst, T. M. BSc	
qcc	11 Jan
Bell, J. R. BEng	15 Jan
Bradshaw, S. J. MEng	
qss	15 Jan
Brown, M. G. BEng	
qss	15 Jan
Chowns, D. A. BEng	
qss	15 Jan
Di Nucci, S. BEng	
qss	15 Jan
Edmondson, E. A.	
BEng qss	15 Jan
Ellen, R. A. BEng	
qss	15 Jan
Hutchison, P. B. BEng	
qss	15 Jan
Johnson, P. E. C. BEng	
qss	15 Jan
Lloyd, N. J. BSc	15 Jan
Martin, D. V. BEng	
qss	15 Jan
McEwing, M. F. BEng	
qss	15 Jan
Moore, S. J. BEng	
qss	15 Jan
Morris, A. J. S. BSc	
qss	15 Jan
Pitchford, D. A.	
BEng	15 Jan
Rooney, C. M.	
BEng	15 Jan
Sansome, E. A. BEng	
qss	15 Jan
Thurrell, W. M. BEng	
qcc	15 Jan
Waring, S. J. BSc	
qss	15 Jan
Watson, N. BEng	
qss	15 Jan
Woodfine, D. S. BEng	
CEng MIEE qss	15 Jan

Flight Lieutenants

1993—contd

Robinson, I. M.	
qss1	25 Jan
McKenna, S. M.	15 Feb
Molle, D. C.	16 Feb
Vernoum, K. G. qss	16 Feb
Brooks, C. P. BEng	18 Feb
Rowland, D. J. BEng	
qss	20 Feb
Timoney, M. J. BSc	
qss	20 Feb
Alcock, A. BEng	
qss	21 Feb
Allison, P. B. BEng	
qs	21 Feb
Krauze, I. A. BEng	
qcc	21 Feb
Thomas, D. M. BEng	
qss	21 Feb
Spencer, P. M. qss	9 Mar
Houghton, A. P.	
qss1	15 Mar
Beken, D. C. qss	27 Mar
Bowden, J. T. IEng	
AMRAeS qss	28 Mar
Jack, J. A. BEng	28 Mar
Gay, M. A. BEng	
qcc	30 Mar
Leyland, T. J. W.	30 Mar
Watt, K. G. BEng	
qss	30 Mar
Morris, P. D. BEng CEng	
MIIE(mech)	1 Apr
Mitchell, J. C. BEng	
qss	2 Apr
Streatfield, G. P.	
BEng	4 Apr
Dove, E. L. BEng	8 Apr
McCarthy, J. A. BEng	
qss	10 Apr
Daulby, P. R. BEng	
qss	11 Apr
Nesbitt, D. J. qss	15 Apr
O'Dell, S. J. BEng	18 Apr
Oram, G. BEng	20 Apr
Mammatt, J. E. BEng	
qss1	7 May
Palk, R. A. BEng	
qss	11 May
Smith, P. J.	11 May
Trimble, I. C.	11 May
Hart, S. J. BEng	12 May
Pye, G. A. BEng qss	12 May
Scantlebury, P. J. BEng	
qss	12 May

Blackmore, N. J. BEng	
qss	25 May
Campbell, P. E.	19 June
Hatcher, A. I. qss1	20 June
Sadler, A. R. qss	20 June
Williams, D. J. qss	21 June
Evans, D. J. BTech	
qss	25 June
Childs, C. BEn qss	29 June
McKeown, I. D.	
BEng	6 July
Elford, S. B. qss	12 July
Burke, S. BEng qcc	15 July
Connor, S. P. BEng	15 July
Dawes, D. P. BEng	
qss1	15 July
Godbolt, S. D.	
BEng	15 July
Griffiths, S. C.	
BEng	15 July
Lefley, R. BEng	15 July
Munslow, W. BEng	15 July
Reed, S. J. BEng	
qss	15 July
Slaven, D. R. BEng	15 July
Woodgate, A. M. BEng	
qss1	15 July
Hill, I. R.	19 July
Knights, S. A. BEng	4 Aug
Pickard, M. J. BEng	
qcc	5 Aug
Hall, D. A. qss	14 Aug
Kirk, J. qcc	1 Sept
Arnold, J. G.	12 Sept
Challonder, A. S.	26 Sept
Blake, C. BEng	27 Sept
Harvey, S. D. BSc	1 Oct
Pemberton, A. J.	
qss	4 Oct
Smeaton, J. P. R. BEng	
qcc	11 Oct
Horsley, D. R. qss	23 Oct
Arnold, N. J. BEng	29 Oct
Connelly, J. A. BEng	
qss1	2 Nov
Sussex, P. S. BEng	
qss	4 Nov
Stanley, M. BEng	
qss1	5 Nov
Crosby, C. P.	9 Nov
Sallis, B. A. MBE	9 Nov
Johnson, I. C. BEng	18 Dec
Anderson, D.	19 Dec
Exley, M. A. qss	19 Dec
Mackay, D. J. qss	19 Dec
Scott, M. D.	19 Dec
Wilkins, M. E. IEng	
MIIE(elec) qcc	19 Dec
Wood, A. W. qss	19 Dec
Dalton, G. S.	21 Dec

Gibbs, P.	21 Dec
Jones, S. A.	21 Dec
O'Callaghan, P. J.	21 Dec
Poulton, J. C.	21 Dec
Gillespie, W. M.	
BEng	22 Dec
Abbs, M. R.	24 Dec
Taylor, C. M.	26 Dec
Mayo, F. qss	27 Dec

1994

Mockford, A. D.	10 Jan
Hellard, S. M. BEng	
qss	11 Jan
Beverley, S. J. BEng	
qss	15 Jan
Bonser, J. V.	15 Jan
Brennan, M. F. qcc	15 Jan
Coleby, T. B. BEng	
qss	15 Jan
Dalton, G. BSc qs	15 Jan
Danton, S. J. BEng	
CEng MIMechE	
ACGI	15 Jan
Elder, R. P. AMIEE	
qss	15 Jan
Ford, R. J.	15 Jan
Hallam, A. J. BEng	
qs	15 Jan
Hutchison, H. G. BEng	
qss	15 Jan
Johnson, J. A. BEng	
qss	15 Jan
Johnson, J. S. qss	15 Jan
Jones, A. J. BEng	
qss	15 Jan
Lawn, J. E. BEng CEng	
MIEE qss	15 Jan
Leeks-Musselwhite, M.	
AMIEE qss	15 Jan
Martin, J. W. R. BEng	
AMIEE	15 Jan
Mitchell, I. J. BEng	
qss	15 Jan
Moore, C. J. qss1	15 Jan
Owen, P. E.	15 Jan
Pennington, C. A. BSc	
qss	15 Jan
Rule, S. Z.	15 Jan
Stevens, J. E. qss	15 Jan
Thompson, J. P	15 Jan
Weston, C. T. BEng	15 Jan
Wilson, M. R. qss	15 Jan
Woods, R. A. BSc	
qss	15 Jan
Parry, R. M. BEng	1 Feb
Press, J. R. qss	12 Feb
Adams, A. D. qss	13 Feb

Flight Lieutenants

1994—contd

Baldwin, P. J. qcc	13 Feb
Burke, R. T. qcc	13 Feb
Moore, S. N.	13 Feb
Thompson, A. G.	
qcc	13 Feb
Bull, M.	15 Feb
Dodds, F. K.	15 Feb
Duncan, J.	15 Feb
Jones, J. G.	15 Feb
McDermott, D.	15 Feb
Newton, M. D.	15 Feb
Rickards, T. J.	15 Feb
Salmon, R. E. BSc	
qss	15 Feb
Shatford, W. F.	15 Feb
Tyler, P. MBE IEng	
MIIE(mech)	15 Feb
Rogers-Jones, A. BEng	
CEng MIEE qss	18 Feb
Villiers, P. BEng	
qss1	25 Feb
Briggs, S. V. BEng	
qcc	2 Mar
Housby, G. BSc qcc	26 Mar
Blackmore-Heal, D. C.	
IEng MIIE(mech)	
qss	29 Mar
Davies, A. T.	29 Mar
Worth, N. P. qss	29 Mar
Rose, P. M. BEng	
qss	30 Mar
Ramsden, G. P. BEng	
qss1	9 Apr
Poole, G. J. BEng CEng	
MRAeS qss	11 Apr
Frew, D. M. BEng	12 Apr
Mitchell, A. BTech	14 Apr
O'Brien, M. C.	21 Apr
Parry, S. A. BEng	
qcc	29 Apr
Beasley, S. G. qss	7 May
Jones, S. J.	7 May
Meeghan, P. qcc	7 May
Croxford, K. C. A.	10 May
Cruikshanks, R. W.	10 May
Hollins, D. G.	10 May
McNamara, P. V. P.	10 May
Moinet, A. N.	10 May
Thomson, I. R. MBE	
qss	10 May
Crowe, J. A. BSc	11 May
Jones, J. P. BEng	
qcc	11 May
Potterill, S. M. BSc	11 May
Docherty, C. qss	14 May

McMurtrie, S. R. J.	
BEng	31 May
King, J. qss	6 June
Cannon, S. A. qss	16 June
Gidda, G. S. qss1	16 June
Applebee, S.	21 June
Bales, S. J.	21 June
Channon, M. P. qss	21 June
Farrow, P. W.	21 June
Gray, G. H.	21 June
Johnson, T. P.	21 June
Piaggesi, G. P.	21 June
Ricketts, J. M.	21 June
Praag, A. N. qcc	27 June
Armstrong, A. D. BEng	
qss	6 July
Edwards, D. B. BSc	10 July
Baker, S. A.	15 July
Bilney, M. BEng	15 July
Clapham, D. L.	15 July
Dunne, A. J.	15 July
Ingleson, M. S.	15 July
Maxwell, I. D. qss1	15 July
Rosbotham, K.	15 July
Ross, F. G.	15 July
Southall, R. C.	15 July
Withers, R. M.	15 July
Carroll, J. H. qcc	30 July
Green, A. R. qss	30 July
Parsons, C. J.	30 July
Bailey, P.	2 Aug
Dunnett, R. D.	2 Aug
Paling, J. J.	2 Aug
Tanner, A. J.	2 Aug
Iles, A. D. G. qss1	5 Aug
Hanley, R. D. BEng	17 Aug
Poyner, I. K. BEng	18 Aug
Partridge, M. A.	
qcc	20 Aug
Smith, L. F. BEng	10 Sept
Eaton, K. P. BTech	11 Sept
Bateman, G. J.	
qss1	24 Sept
Cotter, G.	24 Sept
Martin, G. qss	24 Sept
Moran, R. F.	24 Sept
Owen, R. M.	24 Sept
Goldsworthy, J. H.	26 Sept
Greenfield, J. M.	26 Sept
Hamilton, E. S. qss	26 Sept
Pick, K.	26 Sept
Richards, B.	26 Sept
McKenzie-Orr, A.	
BSc	29 Sept
Khan, F. MEng	9 Oct
Wincott, S. M.	
BEng	11 Oct
Espie, D. W.	27 Oct
Haynes, P. D. BEng	29 Oct

Marshall, R. S.	
BTech	8 Nov
Whittingham, R. C.	
MBE	8 Nov
Williams, W. J. A.	8 Nov
Webb, C. A. M. qss	12 Nov
Wilson-Smith, G.	
K.	12 Nov
Watford, I. R. qss	13 Nov
Hayes, C. G.	21 Nov
Cunliffe, P.	22 Nov
Coulthard, A. J.	
BSc	10 Dec
Shelley, J. M. qss	20 Dec
Thompson, M. H.	20 Dec
Slater, N. qss1	28 Dec

1995

O'Kane, S. J. BEng	10 Jan
Allan, R. M. BSc	15 Jan
Bolt, A. T. BEng qcc	15 Jan
Bonugli, J. G. BEng	15 Jan
Bradley, M. R.	
BEng	15 Jan
Broderick, C. A. BSc	
qss1	15 Jan
Bunning, S. L. BEng	
qcc	15 Jan
Cooksley, A. P. BSc	15 Jan
Dart, P. G. BEng	
qcc	15 Jan
Eames, D. P. BEng	15 Jan
Goodfellow, R. C. BEng	
qs	15 Jan
Heath, P. A. BEng	15 Jan
Hesketh, S. J. BEng	15 Jan
Knighton, R. J. MA	
CEng MIMechE	15 Jan
Lee, P. B. T. BEng	
qss	15 Jan
Marsh, R. E. MEng	
qss	15 Jan
McNeill, A. D. BEng	
qs	15 Jan
Payne, D. E. BEng	
qcc	15 Jan
Payne, N. G. BSc	15 Jan
Ross, J. M. BEng	15 Jan
Simmonite, A. J. BEng	
qss1	15 Jan
Tamlyn, A. M. BEng	
qss	15 Jan
White, A. J. BEng	15 Jan
Williamson, S. C. BEng	
qcc	15 Jan
Wilson, A. G. A.	
BEng	15 Jan

Flight Lieutenants

1995—contd

Woods, S. B. BEng	
qss1	15 Jan
Walker, M. B.	28 Jan
Jones, D. M. qss1	2 Feb
Lander, D. S. BEng	
qss1	7 Feb
Musk, T. S.	11 Feb
Dourish, G. A.	14 Feb
Pullen, J. R. E. qss1	16 Feb
Smeaton, C. A. BEng	
qss	18 Feb
Mepham, K. D.	
BEng	22 Feb
Pullen, M. P. BEng	
qcc	10 Mar
Watkins, S. C. BEng	
qss1	21 Mar
McLoughlin, A. J.	
qcc	23 Mar
Head, S. D. BEng	25 Mar
Lobley, B.	28 Mar
Mannall, D. M.	28 Mar
Pybus, K. W.	28 Mar
Simpson, I.	28 Mar
Lloyd, P. H. BEng	
qcc	29 Mar
McLaughlin, S. BEng	
qss1	29 Mar
Saul, P. M. BEng	
qcc	29 Mar
Skirving, D. J. BEng	
qss1	29 Mar
Smith, I. T. G. BEng	4 Apr
Eccleston, A. M.	
MEng	10 Apr
McNair, G. W. BEng	
qs	11 Apr
Bowland, J. E.	19 Apr
Wootten, M. J. BTech	
qcc	24 Apr
Noon, A. R. BEng	5 May
McCann, A. M.	9 May
Scott, S.	9 May
Hawkins, F. P. BEng	
qcc	10 May
Davies, S. R.	13 May
Tempest-Roe, R. M.	17 May
Cook, C. M.	31 May
Blogg, D. O.	3 June
Breslin, P. G.	20 June
Doughty, R.	20 June
Belfield, D.	21 June
Harris, S. BEng	
qss1	21 June

Kellaway, E. M. BEng	
qs	5 July
Chapman, P. M.	
BEng	15 July
Hussain, Z. BEng	15 July
Lacey, L. J. BEng	15 July
Longden, R. D.	
BEng	15 July
Osborne, J. B.	
BEng	15 July
Smith, R. L. BEM	
BEng	15 July
Stanley, A. K. BEng	15 July
Wray, P. M. BEng	15 July
Robinson, B.	28 July
Turner, J.	28 July
Bradley, R. N.	29 July
Lilly, P. D. BEng qs	8 Aug
Stanley, R. M.	
BEng	12 Aug
Hodge, M.	13 Aug
Keen, K. M. MEng	14 Aug
Lamont, M. M. BA	14 Aug
McKenzie, A. W.	
qcc	31 Aug
Forbes, G. S. qss	26 Sept
Lowry, W. M. IEng	
MIET	26 Sept
Sadler, B.	26 Sept
Walton, J. R.	26 Sept
Evans, M. S. BEng	29 Sept
Powlson, M. D. BEng	
qcc	29 Sept
Orme, D. I.	10 Oct
Blyth, I. qss	7 Nov
Cann, C.	7 Nov
Cole, M. E.	7 Nov
Roberts, W.	7 Nov
Russell, S. J.	7 Nov
Stevens, C. N.	7 Nov
Wild, J. R.	7 Nov
Russell, J. qss1	11 Nov
Wilson, P.	17 Nov
Bradley, I. M. BEng	
qss1	8 Dec
McGhie, D. C. P.	19 Dec

1996

Baker, S. J. BEng	
qss1	15 Jan
Baldaro, J. L. BEng	
qcc	15 Jan
Barton, S. D. MEng	
qss1	15 Jan
Baxter, D. M. BEng	
qs	15 Jan
Chappell, J. L.	
BEng	15 Jan

Donnellan, S. J.	
BEng	15 Jan
Downey, E. A.	
BEng	15 Jan
Fell, A. T. BEng	15 Jan
Gee, S. BEng	15 Jan
Green, A. S. BEng	15 Jan
Head, A. D. BEng	15 Jan
Janssen, S. J. BEng	
qcc	15 Jan
Ley, E. R. J. BEng	15 Jan
Lindsay, D. R. BEng	15 Jan
Lloyd, R. A. BEng	15 Jan
Lunan, I. BEng	
qss1	15 Jan
Matthew, J. H. BSc	15 Jan
Morley, P. M. BEng	15 Jan
Plant, B. M. BEng	15 Jan
Ross, I. A. BEng	15 Jan
Seymour, A. M. BEng	
qcc	15 Jan
Warren, J. BEng	
qss1	15 Jan
Watkin, J. S. BEng	
qss1	15 Jan
Williams, H. M. BEng	
qss1	15 Jan
Wilson, J. W. I.	
BEng	15 Jan
Hopwell, I. J.	10 Feb
Clancy, D. G. R. BA	15 Feb
Hale, N. J. BEng	16 Feb
Huby, G. M. BEng	
qss1	16 Feb
Regan, P. E.	17 Feb
Tucker, C. D. qss1	27 Feb
Brodie, S. qcc	28 Feb
Harrison, A. R.	
BEng	8 Mar
Doherty, B. D. BEng	
AMIEE	13 Mar
Tapping, J. G. C.	26 Mar
Egan, C. J.	2 Apr
German, A. D.	
BEng	11 Apr
Hunter, C. V. BEng	11 Apr
Potts, M. J. BEng	11 Apr
Wright, R. BEng	11 Apr
Streatfield, P. J.	
BEng	30 Apr
Elliott, A. H. qss	7 May
Munroe, G. M.	
BEng	12 May
Pinckney, N. J. BEng	
qss1	6 June
Higham, N. P.	24 June
Roberts, L. P.	4 July
Barr, R. P. BEng	15 July
Calder, A. P. J.	
BEng	15 July

Flight Lieutenants

1996—contd

Davies, H. B. BEng	15 July
Gadney, A. D. BEng	15 July
Kent, S. E. R. BEng	15 July
Kilday, I. BEng	15 July
Kirk, N. H.	15 July
Russell, S. I. BEng	15 July
Tomlinson, G. G.	
BEng	15 July
Tomlinson, J. I.	
BEng	15 July
Young, J. N.	23 July
Harmer, N. J. BEng	
qss1	14 Aug
Shipley, J. M.	13 Sept
Fielder, R.	16 Sept
Mudd, D. J. W. qcc	29 Sept
Wood, B. D. A.	
qss1	29 Sept
Blevins, P. R.	6 Oct
Green, J. R.	6 Oct
Hodge, C. F. BEM	
qss1	6 Oct
Johnson, T. W. R.	
S.	6 Oct
Bye, D. D. BSc qss1	10 Oct
Graham, K. B.	
BEng	10 Oct
Howard, N. A.	
BEng	27 Oct
Mercer, G. F. BEng	2 Nov
Wild, J. E.	13 Dec

1997

Bradbury, S. P.	
BEng	15 Jan
Gilroy, J. R. BEng	
qss1	15 Jan
Green, C. D. BEng	15 Jan
Hampson, M. C. BEng	
qcc	15 Jan
Joly, R. B. BEng	15 Jan
Kelly, P. BEng qss1	15 Jan
O'Donnell S. M.	
BEng	15 Jan
O'Donnell, T. BEng	15 Jan
Prentice, P. R. BEng	15 Jan
Rolf, J. BA qss1	15 Jan
Shipp, A. M.	15 Jan
Smith, R. L. S.	
BEng	15 Jan
Sobers, P. C. BEng	
qcc	15 Jan
Tozer, D. J. BEng	15 Jan

Wilkinson, P. J.	
BEng	15 Jan
Longley, C. I. BEng	6 Feb
Rayner, K. S. BEng	10 Feb
Copeland, A. W. W.	11 Feb
Webb, C. T. BEng	
qcc	14 Feb
Casey, T. J. BEng	15 Feb
Storer, K. A. BEng	15 Feb
Crook, L. D. BEng	1 Mar
Bedding, S. J. qss1	29 Mar
Hunt, M. BEng	10 Apr
Reid, J. C. BEng	10 Apr
Seddon, J. W.	
BEng	10 Apr
Waggitt, R. D. BEng	
qss1	10 Apr
Brydon, M. F.	14 May
Croft, P. BEng	2 June
McLeod, A. C.	
BEng	13 July
Cowie, I. BEng	15 July
Greenland, S. J.	
BEng	15 July
Hall, G. J. BEng	15 July
Hatten, G. A. BEng	15 July
Lawson, D. M.	
BEng	15 July
Mayo, P. R. BEng	15 July
Nadin, M. A. BEng	15 July
Russell, P. J. BEng	15 July
Swanson, J. BEng	15 July
Wright, M. S. BEng	15 July
Bradshaw, N. J.	28 July
Collins, R.	28 July
Pease, C. T.	28 July
Pridmore, B. J.	
BEng	4 Aug
Clapp, S. E. BEng	8 Aug
Hawley, M. R.	16 Aug
Powley, S. K. BEng	16 Aug
Todd, B. S. BEng	23 Aug
Stephens, D. A.	
BEng	9 Oct
Goddard, A. MSc	
BSc	10 Oct
Lewis, D. A. BEng	10 Oct
Gibson, M. A.	
BEng	11 Nov
Hope, M. A. BEng	2 Dec

1998

Ankers, J. R. BEng	15 Jan
Bobbin, A. J. BEng	15 Jan
Browning, J. L. W.	
BEng	15 Jan
Carter, K. BEng	15 Jan

Collins, L. BEng	
qss1	15 Jan
Hamilton, D. M.	
BEng	15 Jan
Handley, D. A. BA	15 Jan
Hocking, P. J. BEng	15 Jan
Neal-Hopes, T. D. BEng	
qss1	15 Jan
Richards, R. P.	
MEng	15 Jan
Frazer, S. R. BSc	30 Jan
Paris, G. D.	8 Feb
Brown, R. N. BEng	13 Feb
Goodchild, S. P.	
BEng	13 Feb
Bellamy, S. J. BEng	14 Feb
Hamilton, C. J. BSc	14 Feb
Limb, N. P. BEng	14 Feb
Will, D. E. BEng	
qss1	14 Feb
Morris, B. D. BEng	6 Mar
Greenwood, P.	4 Apr
Salter, A. R. qss1	4 Apr
Warren, M. C.	
BEng	5 Apr
Barker, M. A. BEng	9 Apr
Carter, D. J. BEng	
qss1	9 Apr
Hughes, F. J. BEng	9 Apr
Kellett, R. J. BEng	9 Apr
Stone, J. D. BEng	9 Apr
Iddon, J. N. BEng	12 May
Robertson, D.	
BEng	12 May

Flying Officers

1989

Rogers, A.	20 Nov

1990

Beagle, T.	12 Oct
Lusty, R. O. D.	21 Nov

1991

Leech, A. H.	10 Feb
Styles, G. T.	10 July
Shrewsbury, T. J.	31 July
Williams, N. P.	3 Nov

1992

Potter, A. K.	23 Jan
Ditton, R. J.	25 Jan
Schoner, A. L.	9 Apr
Hill, S. W.	7 May
Skelton, P. J.	7 June
Calder, F. J.	13 July
Jackson, D. R.	14 Sept
Greenslade, L. A.	7 Oct
Ellis, S.	7 Dec
Gellini, M.	14 Dec

1993

Nicholson, M. S.	13 Feb
Carrier, P. A.	6 June
Higton, C. N.	8 Sept
Collis, P. H.	12 Sept
Strachan, T. R. A.	10 Oct
Peeters, G. A.	19 Oct
Ward, A. L.	7 Nov
Dunn, B. J.	8 Nov

1994

Harrop, D. G.	2 Feb
Collett, T. G. BEng qcc	13 Feb
Wood, A. J.	24 Mar
Searle, P. J.	15 Apr
Bent, C. G.	27 Apr
Holmes, D. P.	15 May
Corn, J. A.	31 May
McGeorge, M. H.	16 June

Woods, D. K.	8 July
Lowe, D. P.	21 July
Keir, R. H. BEng	5 Aug
Burnham, R. E. BEng	12 Aug
Cooke, A. J. BSc	12 Aug
James, P. BEng	12 Aug
Austin, P. R. BEng	7 Oct
Bremner, S. D. BEng	7 Oct
Stocks, M. C. MSc BEng	7 Oct
Thorley, L. D. BEng	9 Oct
Mews, J. E.	10 Oct
Lambert, T. T. A.	12 Oct
Franklin, J. A. R. BEng	20 Oct
White, N. M. BEng	23 Nov
Cox, B. N.	19 Dec
Jones, C.	25 Dec
Keen, S. D.	25 Dec
Barrett, J. E. B.	31 Dec

1995

Green, D. H. BEng	15 Jan
Rodley, C. I. MEng	15 Jan
Sumner, L. D. BEng	15 Jan
Tinsley, I. K.	15 Jan
Whyte, E. BEng	15 Jan
Birchall, S. T.	18 Jan
Goddard, A. P.	9 Feb
Place, M. J.	9 Feb
Watkins, T. C. S. BEng	13 Feb
Hendry, J. BEng	2 Mar
Colledge, G. G.	15 Mar
Elliott, E. J.	26 Mar
Rudge, W.	26 Mar
Bolton, P. J.	6 Apr
Hartley, S. E. BEng	6 Apr
Lamberton, D. M.	6 Apr
Maisey, D. S.	6 Apr
McBain, R. BEng	6 Apr
Morfee, J. P.	6 Apr
Whitehouse, S.	6 Apr
Catt, M. S. BEng	8 Apr
Chappell, D. C. BEng	8 Apr
Clowes, N. A. BEng	8 Apr
Crichton, I. A. B. BEng	8 Apr
Hansford, J. E. BEng	8 Apr
Marter, P. N. BEng	8 Apr
Race, S. C. BEng	8 Apr
Ralph, S. BEng	8 Apr
Robinson, N. M. BEng	8 Apr

Ratcliffe, J. D. K.	2 July
Atkins, I. E.	28 July
Grigglestone, C. M.	28 July
MacNaught, R. L. F.	28 July
Timms, T. G.	28 July
Balls, R. J. BEng	9 Aug
Bradbrook, D. M. BEng	9 Aug
Neasham, S. BEng	9 Aug
Pescott, K. J. BEng	9 Aug
Brett, S. J. BEng	11 Aug
Moody, I. P. BEng	11 Aug
Sidney, R. BEng	11 Aug
Garrad, J.	23 Aug
Brookes, J.	6 Sept
Gilbert, A. MEng	6 Oct
Armstrong, N. BEng	7 Oct
Dickinson, M. J. BEng	7 Oct
Gow, A. BEng	7 Oct
Keenan, S. N. BEng	7 Oct
Kirby, S.	4 Nov
Rowdon, S. C. BEng	1 Dec
Townsend, D. J.	17 Dec

1996

Blenkinship, D.	6 Jan
Follows, M. W. L. MEng	15 Jan
Rose, L. J. MEng BA	15 Jan
Stringer, T. A. MEng	15 Jan
Fashade, O. A. BEng	10 Feb
Fawcett, P. W. MEng	10 Feb
Young, S. E. MEng	10 Feb
Joy, S. D. BEng	11 Feb
Peters, C. J. BEng	11 Feb
Staveley, M. D. BEng	11 Feb
Trollone, S. M.	2 Mar
Flett, D. P.	4 Apr
Harding, N.	4 Apr
Haygarth, M.	4 Apr
Parkes, D. W.	4 Apr
Day, S. P. BEng	5 Apr
Anderson, R. D. BEng	6 Apr
Geeson, J. A. BEng	6 Apr
Gould, H. L. BEng	6 Apr
Harle, J. E. BEng	6 Apr
Newcombe, L. A. BEng	6 Apr
Reid, D. G. BEng	30 May

Flying Officers		Pilot Officers		Acting Pilot Officers	
1996—contd		**1997**		**1995**	
Rose, P. M. BEng	1 June	Macivor, K. S.	30 Nov	Baker, A. J.	2 Aug
Barnaby, I. J.	25 July			Brooker, P. A.	2 Aug
Hawthorn, N. R.	25 July			Checkley, C. C. T.	2 Aug
Macalister, S. J.	25 July	**1998**		Clarkson, J. E.	2 Aug
Middleton, T. J.				Cooke, P. A.	2 Aug
BEng	9 Aug	Blackie, J. R. BEng	8 Feb	Dixon, J.	2 Aug
Bryant, G. J. BEng	1 Sept	Boorman, E. J.		Dyke, S. J.	2 Aug
Martin-Jones, P. D.		BEng	8 Feb	Harding, M.	2 Aug
BEng	6 Oct	Evans, B. BEng	8 Feb	Keeling, A. C.	2 Aug
Mason, M. I. P.		Heard, G. A. BEng	8 Feb	Nash, J. S.	2 Aug
BEng	6 Oct	Irwin, G. BEng	8 Feb	Neasham, M. A.	2 Aug
Weekes, S. A. BSc	1 Dec	Wass, H. L. BSc	8 Feb	Pearce, P.	2 Aug
		Ede, J. A. BSc	5 Apr	Ponting, R. D.	2 Aug
		Hide, A. K. BSc	5 Apr	Taylor, S. M.	2 Aug
1997		Malcolm, N. I.		Walker, G. J.	2 Aug
		BEng	5 Apr	Williams, E. D.	2 Aug
Johnson, H. M.		Mustoe, K. J. BEng	5 Apr		
BEng	15 Jan	Slater, J. H. BSc	5 Apr	**1996**	
Ruben, R. BEng	15 Jan				
Chapman, S.	4 Feb			Barry, R. J.	1 Aug
Bennett, N. P. BEng	10 Feb			Chesworth, I. D.	1 Aug
Osselton, R. G. S.				Dodwell, J. E.	1 Aug
BEng	10 Feb			Hicks, A. B.	1 Aug
Smith, N. D. BEng	10 Feb			Hutcheon, R.	1 Aug
Braybrook, R. E.				Jackson-Soutter, P.	
BSc	5 Apr			B.	1 Aug
Overthrow, J. T. Q.				Jones, D. L.	1 Aug
BEng	5 Apr			Kennedy, D. M.	1 Aug
Sach, J. L. BEng	5 Apr			Lipscomb, P. R.	1 Aug
Hayes, M. I.	29 May			McMahon, J. D.	1 Aug
Cole, T. M.	24 July			Middleton, G. R.	1 Aug
Farrell, D. M.	24 July			Millne, P. E.	1 Aug
Oughton, P.	24 July			Roberts, N. C.	1 Aug
Hake, B. D.	6 Oct			Smallman, R. L.	1 Aug
Williams, R. J.	13 Oct			Edmondson, S. W.	1 Oct
Fortune, J. H.	1 Dec				
				1997	
				Bleakley, T. J.	1 Sept
				Lowe, M. C. MEng	1 Sept
				Penter, D. A. MEng	1 Sept
				Tillyard, M. S.	
				BEng	1 Sept

SUPPLY BRANCH

Group Captains

1992

Connor, Michael Ralph Hamilton OBE MSc psc ssc ts Born 22/3/45	1 July

1993

Blencowe, Christopher John MA BA rcds osc(FR) qs i Born 27/3/50	1 Jan
Springett, Robin FRAeS MILog ssc qs Born 9/4/44	1 July
Wesley, David Maurice OBE FInstPet jsdc ssc qs Born 29/9/46	1 July

1994

Whalley, Peter ADC psc Born 22/5/51	1 Jan

1995

Armstrong, John Christopher MCIPS psc ssc Born 10/11/46	1 Jan
Gaskin, Peter Patrick Victor OBE psc Born 23/10/47	1 July
Morton, Glenn MCIPS psc ssc Born 2/12/47	1 July

1996

Gardiner, Christopher Anthony BA MCIPS psc ssc Born 14/5/45	1 Jan
Morris, Nicholas Steven MSc BA osc(Fr) ssc qs i* Born 22/2/55	1 Jan
Tripp, Robert Jonathan BSc MIMgt psc Born 15/3/49	1 Jan
Ovens, Allan Jefferson OBE BSc psc ssc Born 12/2/52	1 July

1997

Cannon, Donald Bernard MSc BSc MCIT psc ts Born 1/12/53	1 Jan
Howson, Timothy George MSc BA jsdc im ssc qs Born 13/7/52	1 Jan
Kendrick, David Ian MIDPM jsdc ssc Born 4/2/47	1 Jan
Spinks, Andrew Charles MILog jsdc ssc qs Born 16/9/52	1 Jan
Benson, David Richard OBE psc ssc Born 11/11/46	1 July
Bernard, David Charles MBE MIMgt psc qab ssc Born 19/7/47	1 July
Hedges, Desmond Paul psc ssc Born 2/3/48	1 July
Miles, Philip Mark BSc psc Born 18/4/53	1 July

1998

Chandler, Nicholas Robert MBE LLB psc ssc Born 25/10/58	1 Jan
Thompson, Julian Howard MSc BA MBCS jsdc im Born 11/3/54	1 Jan
Bateman, Richard Ian BA psc Born 8/8/54	1 July
Page, Brian Stephen psc Born 6/11/48	1 July

Wing Commanders

1987

Taylor, P. C. OBE BA
odc(US) ssc qs   1 July

1988

Britton, G. S. qss   1 Jan
MacDonald, J. H. MSc
FInstPet ssc qs   1 Jan
Thomas, J. A. ssc
qs   1 Jan
Trench, B. W. ssc
qs   1 Jan
Knight, P. C. MSc im ssc
qs   1 July
Morrell, P. B. ssc qs   1 July

1989

Bratby, M. J. MSc BA
im ssc qs   1 Jan
Bolton, B. N. psc   1 July
Broderick, J. A. OBE
MCIT MIMgt   1 July

1990

Archer, D. F. MBE MSc
MCIPS jsdc ssc
qs   1 Jan
Babington, J. P. BA jsdc
ssc qs   1 Jan
Clark, G. S. IEng MILog
MRAeS ssc qs   1 Jan
Pemberton-Pigott, T. N.
J. MCIT ssc qs   1 Jan
Hay, B. D. T. MILog
MRAeS MCIT qs   1 July
Hollands, S. A. MIMgt
ssc qs   1 July
Humphries, A. S. MBA
FIMgt MIMIS psc
ssc   1 July

1991

Foster, D. J. MSc BSc
psc im qab   1 Jan
Henderson, J. M.
AMBCS ssc adp
qs   1 Jan

Gibb, I. B. MBE
DipTechEd MILog
MInstPet ssc qs   1 July
Rushmere, P. A. MIMgt
psc   1 July

1992

Micallef, D. MCIT
MIMgt ssc qs   1 Jan
Simpson, F. M. BA MIL
MRAeS ALCM
odc(GE) qs i*   1 Jan
Blomley, D. L. MBE ssc
qss   1 July
Grimson, P. psc   1 July
Thompson, D. R.
qss   1 July
Thompson, R. V. MSc
MILog psc im ssc
qs   1 July

1993

Faulconer, E. J. MA BSc
psc   1 Jan
Howlett, E. B. psc   1 Jan
Armitage-Maddox, S.
E. MBE qs   1 July
Bennett, J. B. ssc
qs   1 July
Bushby, R. D. MDA BA
MInstPet ssc qs   1 July
Cromarty, N. W. psc
ssc   1 July
Kellett, B. M. MSc BSc
psc im   1 July
King, P. M. BSc psc   1 July
Leonard, R. G. OBE ssc
psc   1 July
Morgan, J. V. BSc
qs   1 July
Oldaker, R. W. BSc psc
qs   1 July
Williams, R. A. OBE MA
BA psc   1 July

1994

Ashcroft, G. A. ssc
qs   1 Jan
Caunt, S. F. qs   1 Jan
Elliott, R. P. qs   1 Jan
Sheppard, N. A. MCIPS
psc   1 Jan

Heithus, C. MCIPS
MILog MIMgt ssc
qs   1 July
Mahon, W. E. BA
psc(m) ssc   1 July
Norris, M. W. MInstPet
MRAeS qss   1 July

1995

Belmore, D. S. MBE
MCIPS jsdc qs   1 Jan
Blore, D. J. MSc BSc
MRAeS psc ts
ssc   1 July
Davenport, A. J. R.
psc   1 July
Knights, J. C. psc
ssc   1 July
Mason, A. J. MA jsdc
ssc qs   1 July
Patch, T. J. MSc BA
CDipAF psc(m)
ssc   1 July
Steiner, P. H. MILog ssc
qs   1 July
Wiles, M. J. G. MILog
psc ssc   1 July

1996

Atherton, S. P. jsdc ssc
qs   1 Jan
Kennett, R. J. MSc BA
FInstPet MCIPS
MIDPM im qss   1 Jan
Brierley, M. BA jsdc
qs   1 July
Harris, R. C. qs   1 July
Hicks, C. P. qs   1 July
Howard, G. J. MA MCIT
MILog MIMgt psc(m)
ssc qs   1 July
MacLeman, R. BSc ssc
qss   1 July
Markey, C. R. psc   1 July
Martin, I. M. MPhil LLB
MCIT jsdc ssc qs   1 July
O'Dea, K. L. qs   1 July
Primett, M. N. MA
psc   1 July
Rowney, P. J. ssc
qs   1 July
Thistlethwaite, K. jsdc
qs   1 July
Thomas, J. M. BA qss   1 July
Towler, A. J. psc
ssc   1 July

Wing Commanders

Veale, R. M. BA qs	1 July
Waitt, C. B. BA psc ssc	1 July
Waldegrave, R. A. ssc qss	1 July
Warne, A. P. BA qs	1 July

1997

Djumic, M. MSc BSc psc im	1 Jan
Palmer, M. W. BSc psc slmc	1 Jan
Taplin, R. K. MBE BSc(Econ) FILog MCIPS MIMIS MBCS MIL MRAeS MIMgt ssc adp qs i	1 Jan
Vose, W.L. ssc qs	1 Jan
Ashford, R. R. qss	1 July
Henson, S. W. jsdc qs	1 July
Hewat, C. J. S. MBE qss	1 July
Moore, M. C. C. qs	1 July
Thompson, S. P. BSc qs	1 July
Voltzenlogel, P. N. MCIT qab ssc qs	1 July
Williams, G. T. qs	1 July

1998

Allen, J. D. qs	1 Jan
Cannock, P. J. BSc psc	1 Jan
Gell, A. T. MBA BA MILog qs	1 Jan
Thorogood, P. J. MRAeS MILog semc ssc qs	1 Jan
Atherton, R. L. A. ssc qs	1 July
Forshaw, K. H. MSc BSc ts qs	1 July
Hubble, P. N. MSc BSc qs	1 July
Smith, R. S. BSc slmc qs	1 July

Squadron Leaders

1979

Storey, R. R. BSc im ssc qs	1 Jan
Booth, D. P. ssc qs	1 July
Carmen, T. R. E. ssc qss	1 July

1980

Clucas, B. P. MInstPet qss	1 July

1981

Pickles, T. ssc qs	1 Jan
Yarram, M. F. BSc ssc qs	1 July

1983

Collins, M. W. F. MBE	1 Jan
Kingwill, P. M. ssc qs	17 Jan
Green, D. A. ssc qs	1 July

1984

Garstin, J. C. BSc ssc qs	1 Jan
Martin, S. E. MILog ssc qs	1 Jan
Bolton, G. E. qs	1 July
Carr, M. C. qss	1 July

1985

Bevan, D. L. ssc qss	1 Jan
Grant, T. A. MSc BA qs	1 Jan
Palmer, D. J. ssc qs	1 July
Powling, B. F. E. BA im qs	1 July

1986

Finnegan, R. M. J. BSc ssc qs	1 Jan
Fitt, G. R. ssc	1 July
Hadnett, D. T. J. qss	1 July

Hickey, S. D. MIMgt qs	1 July
Thompson, D. A. qs	1 July
Williams, D. R. MSc BSc im qs	1 July

1987

Britton, P. D. qs	1 Jan

1988

Bentley, N. L. qs	1 Jan
Dorman, T. R. BA slmc qss	1 Jan
Drake, I. P. BA ssc qs	1 Jan
Gallaugher, R. A. MBE qss	1 Jan
Page, J. C. BA MCIPS ssc qs	1 Jan
Swift, A. B. ssc qs	1 July

1989

Beverley, I. M. BA qs	1 Jan
Fulker, M. D. qs	1 Jan
Henry, L. H. ssc qs	1 Jan
Laurent, C. L. T. qss	1 Jan
Manville, K. D. qs	1 Jan
Montague, G. T. CertEd ssc qs	1 Jan
Morgan, A. J. qss	1 Jan
Thomas, H. qs	1 Jan

1990

Cloke, S. R. MSc BA MCIT qs	1 Jan
McTeer, M. M. MSc BA MIDPM MBCS qss	1 Jan
Moody, D. B. qss	1 Jan
Parker, R. J. qs	1 Jan
Phillips, I. R. BA MIPD ssc qs	1 Jan
Potts, A. T. qss	1 Jan
Thompson, M. J. MILog ssc qss	1 Jan
Crockatt, S. H. ssc qs	1 July
Edwards, K. A. BSc ssc qs	1 July
Gannon, D. M.	1 July
Rice, P. BA ssc qs	1 July

Squadron Leaders

1991

Bacon, D. R. qss 1 Jan
Bagnall, A. R. BSc ACA
ssc qs 1 Jan
Berry, P. W. qss 1 Jan
Davidson, P. M. slmc
qss 1 Jan
Heaton, S. M. slmc
qss 1 Jan
Kettell, L. P. qss 1 Jan
Kime, A. G. qs 1 Jan
Laws, D. L. MSc BA
DESEM MCIT MIL
MILog ts ssc qs
i* 1 Jan
Old, R. C. slmc qs 1 Jan
Roberts, O. J. slmc
qs 1 Jan
Russell, I. R. qs 1 Jan
Ward, V. H. qss 1 Jan
Ainsworth, S. J. MDA
BSc MILog MCIPS
MIMgt ssc qs 1 July
Barber, J. R. BA ssc
qs 1 July
Heslin, T. ssc qs 1 July
Hughes, J. I. MSc BSc
MCIPS MILog ssc
qs 1 July
Pike, J. MSc qss 1 July
Watton, R. J. MILog
slmc qss 1 July
Weber, E. R. BA MILog
ssc qs 1 July

1992

Arnold, N. MInstPet
qs 1 Jan
Boyce, C. L. MBE MIL
slmc qs 1 Jan
Coward, M. J. qs 1 Jan
Craib, J. A. BSc qss 1 Jan
Dobson, G. A. qss 1 Jan
Ford, M. S. MSc qs 1 Jan
MacKenzie, G. C. 1 Jan
Morris, W. B. slmc
qs 1 Jan
Newstead, T. J. qs 1 Jan
Selby, G. M. C. ssc qs
i 1 Jan
Simmonds, A. slmc
qs 1 Jan
Stewart, C. E. BSc
qs 1 Jan

Borrill, C. P. BSc slmc
qs 1 July
Buckingham, A. E.
MILog ssc qs 1 July
Grogan, P. ssc qs i 1 July
Hall, S. D. B. slmc
qss 1 July
Hannaway, P. MA
qss 1 July
Hornsby, R. C. BH
qss 1 July
Howard, R. M. ssc 1 July
Parr, N. H. E. MCIPS
qss 1 July
Paterson, P. F. B.
qss 1 July
Payne, P. J. BA qs 1 July

1993

Anderson, K. W.
qss 1 Jan
Baxter, A. D. M. qs 1 Jan
Dabin, N. R. S. ssc
qss 1 Jan
Farnsworth, A. D. slmc
qss 1 Jan
Flippant, P. J. BA
qss 1 Jan
Haywood, P. R. BSc ssc
qss 1 Jan
Jones, C. L. MIMgt
slmc qss 1 Jan
Lester-Powell, D. M.
BSc slmc qs 1 Jan
Clark, B. J. BSc slmc
qs 1 July
Cooke, S. C. BA qs 1 July
Gordon, R. G. H. slmc
qs 1 July
Grimson, A. S. BA
qss 1 July
Guthrie, I. BA qss 1 July
Hardman, A. N. slmc
qs 1 July
Smith, N. A. MDA BSc
MILog ssc qs 1 July

1994

Attrill, M. P. ssc qs 1 Jan
Ayers, D. L. OBE qs 1 Jan
Beanland, A. K. BA
qs 1 Jan
Beresford, M. J. qs 1 Jan
Bleeker, J. D. MBA BA
BSc MCIPS qs i* 1 Jan

Coller, A. J. BA MILog
slmc qs 1 Jan
Gardiner, J. C MBE ssc
qss 1 Jan
Green, M. D. qss 1 Jan
Green, R. D. qs 1 Jan
Hardwick, M. C. slmc
qs 1 Jan
Hornett, M. C. G. BSc
slmc qs 1 Jan
Hurren, D. G. MBA BA
qss 1 Jan
Joseph, J. D. qss 1 Jan
Lea, S. M. BSc slmc
qs 1 Jan
Nichol, H. R. BSc slmc
qss 1 Jan
Sexton, G. MBE adp
qs 1 Jan
Treanor, B. G. qs 1 Jan
Arkle, N. BSc qss 1 July
Barbour, S. R. A. BA
qss 1 July
Dell, C. J. BSc qss 1 July
Gough, P. M. BSc slmc
qs 1 July
Harpum, S. P. MSc BSc
MILog ts qs 1 July
Hill, C. M. J. MILog
MCIT qs 1 July
Honeyman, D. J. M.
BSc qs 1 July
Howlett, D. J. qss 1 July
John, D. H. BEng LLB
slmc qs 1 July
Johnson, M. qss 1 July
Organ, J. W. slmc
qs 1 July
Orr, D. J. slmc qss 1 July
Peacock, E. BA slmc
qs 1 July
Stone, T. MSc MILog
qss 1 July
Topley, N. E. A. MILog
qs 1 July

1995

Doherty, L. A. MBE
qs 1 Jan
Gill, E. A. BSc MILog
qs 1 Jan
Green, J. W. M. BA
slmc qs i* 1 Jan
Luter, B. A. qs 1 Jan
Mickleburgh, A. S. BSc
1 Jan
Pearce, N. G. BSc
qss 1 Jan

Squadron Leaders

1995—contd

Watts, D. BA slmc qs	1 Jan
Young, M. P. MILog slmc qs	1 Jan
Brown, A. G. qs	1 July
Fitness, P. M. BSc qss	1 July
Halliday, D. G.	1 July
Hunter, J. M. qs	1 July
Huxtable, R. D. slmc qss	1 July
Keep, R. P. qss	1 July
McErlean, L. BSc qss	1 July
Pey, P. G. qs	1 July
Phillips, A. B.	1 July
Stark, J. P. BSc qs	1 July
Targett, S. R. qss	1 July
Thomson, A. H. W. slmc qss	1 July

1996

Cook, P. G. qs	1 Jan
Craib, B. L. BSc qss	1 Jan
Firth, H. V. qss	1 Jan
Fletcher, S. P. qss	1 Jan
Henderson, T. A. qss	1 Jan
Higgins, P. BA slmc qs	1 Jan
Jones, K. S. qss	1 Jan
O'Keefe, R. J. qs	1 Jan
Rose, S. J. MCIPS MILog Dip	1 Jan
Serrell-Cooke, P. J.	1 Jan
Ainsworth, A. M. MIMgt DipMgmt qs	1 July
Berry, T. I. BSc qss	1 July
Bessell, J. C. qs	1 July
Bickers, S. M. qs	1 July
Cole, D. qs	1 July
Dack, J. R. qss	1 July
Evans, D. J. qss	1 July
Goss, C. H. qs	1 July
Hardcastle, O. E. qss	1 July
Hudson, P. A.	1 July
Macleod, R. M. IEng MILog AMRAeS slmc qss	1 July
Maddox, A. J. M.	1 July
Martin, A. P. BSc qs	1 July

McCann, M. C. MILog qss	1 July
Pearson, J. M. BSc slmc qss	1 July
Rygalski, S. A. qss	1 July
Sargent, B. BA MIL MILog MIMgt qss i* i*	1 July
Smith, R. D. BA qs	1 July
Thomas, G. D. qss	1 July
Thomson, D. B. qs	1 July
Watson, C. W. MInstPet qs	1 July
Woodward, M. F. qss	1 July
Wright-Cooper, S. J. F. BSc qs	1 July

1997

Clempson, P. qss	1 Jan
Colpus, M. R. MDA BSc qss	1 Jan
Elworthy, B. J. DMS qss	1 Jan
Haseltine, S. J. qss	1 Jan
Lee, R. G. BSc MILog qss	1 Jan
McMillan, N. J. MSc MILog qs	1 Jan
Munday, S. P. qss	1 Jan
Mutton, P. A.	1 Jan
Porter, J. D. BSc AKC qss	1 Jan
Rolfe, A. W. BSc MDA MILog qss	1 Jan
Stevens, N. W. H. BA qs	1 Jan
Widger, W. J. qss	1 Jan
Cowie, G. BSc qss	1 July
Dolan, M. C.	1 July
Ellis, J. qs	1 July
Fogden, R. qs	1 July
Hughes, M. A. qs	1 July
Jones, S. D. BSc qss	1 July
Lory, G. I. BSc qs	1 July
Mitchell-Gears, S. qss	1 July
Osman, M. R. qs	1 July
Picton, D. M. BSc MCIPS qs	1 July
Poppe, A. N. BSc MILog qss	1 July
Read, S. G. qs	1 July
Stobart, R. H. MILog qss	1 July
Tranter, P. BA qss i* i*	1 July

Vincent, M. S. E. BA qss	1 July

1998

Barclay, E. J. A. BSc qss	1 Jan
Curtis, A. R. qs	1 Jan
Dunn, M. K. qss	1 Jan
Flint, R. qss	1 Jan
Hale, R. J. BSc qss	1 Jan
Hill, R. MILog qss	1 Jan
Otley-Doe, C. E. qs	1 Jan
Perryman, J. G. qss	1 Jan
Roberts, R. W. qss	1 Jan
Sharpe, S. J. A. qss	1 Jan
Tempest-Roe, C. B. qss	1 Jan
Alder, I. T. qss	1 July
Crighton, M. BSc qss	1 July
Dainton, S. D. qss	1 July
Duncan, A. W. BA	1 July
Farrer, G. B. J. BSc qss	1 July
Grieves, D. J. qss	1 July
Howard, R. E. BA qss	1 July
Masters, C. W.	1 July
Ogden, S. qss	1 July
Paulson, J. D. qss	1 July
Smith, C. R. BA qss	1 July
Sutton, R. A. qss	1 July
Thompson, G. J. BA ssc qss	1 July
Tripp, I. M. qss	1 July
Walsh, P. BA qss	1 July

Flight Lieutenants

1973

Mumme, I. G. T. qss 18 Mar

1978

Burch, P. F. R. 6 Oct

1983

Richardson, C. H.
  MILog DipMgmt
  qss 19 Mar

1984

Beard, D. M. 13 Dec

1985

Hardingham, P. qss 15 June
Williams, I. S. BSc qss 27 June
Cope, P. 11 July

1986

Pratt, T. F. qss 26 Mar
Wilson, A. J. O. MILog
  AMIPD 30 Aug

1987

Innes, A. G. BSc
  qss 31 Jan
Taylor, A. C. qss 23 May
Adams, I. M. qss 4 July

1988

Bullers, P. M. BA
  qss 2 Mar
Carroll, P. J. qss 4 Mar
Evans, R. D. qss 22 July

1989

Stanford, P. G. qss 26 Mar
Wood, G. P. 23 Apr

Dathan, C. H. BA
  qss 10 May
Dean, M. J. 26 Sept
Arnold, S. 16 Dec

1990

Caldara, S. BEng 15 Jan
Barley, M. J. qss 20 Jan
Aldhous, R. R. qss 21 Jan
Barth, R. O. qss 29 Jan
Stewart, J. G. qss 31 Jan
Morgan, S. J. BSc
  qss 28 Feb
Jones, P. G. MCIT
  qss 8 Mar
Parry, D. W. 8 Mar
Clare, P. E. BA qss 14 Mar
Scire, J. P. qss 20 Apr
Musselwhite, J. BSc
  MILog qss 26 Apr
Huddleston, C. J.
  qss 22 July
Lendon, G. D. C.
  qss 15 Sept
Allen, J. M. 22 Sept
MacPherson, C. J.
  qss 2 Nov
Bell, N. E. BA qss 8 Nov
Tomkinson, P. qss 26 Nov
Hunter-Tod, J. F.
  qss 6 Dec
Carlton, M. R. BA
  qss 7 Dec
Sharples, V. C. BA
  qss 7 Dec

1991

Fisher, S. MA qss 15 Jan
Killey, A. H. BSc DMS
  qss 15 Jan
Larkin, P. J. BA 1 Jan
Duffy, G. J. M. qss 21 Jan
Whitwham, M. D.
  qss 23 Jan
Grice, G. B. 6 Feb
Cooper, D. A. qss 2 Mar
Wareham, F. 12 Mar
Marshall, M. L. qss 11 Apr
Garnham, A. J. BSc
  qss 6 May
Power, R. W. BSc 14 May
Gould, J. C. MBE
  qss 3 July
Mulholland, L. G.
  ACMA 8 July

Christison, D. S. W.
  qss 28 Aug
Harrington, J. M. H.
  qss 28 Aug
Coughlan, J. R. MILog
  qss 28 Sept
Redgwick, C. D. MSc
  BA 12 Nov

1992

Almond, M. BSc MILog
  qss 14 Feb
Cumberland, M. J. qss 15 Feb
Hulls, A. P. 15 Feb
Dover, M. R. AE 28 Mar
Wright, S. Mck. qss 23 Apr
Burn, R. qss 10 May
Dale, D. C. qss 10 May
Beach, T. E. BEd
  qss 12 May
Marshall, A. R. qss 28 May
Grimwood, M. P. 16 June
Streeter, M. J. qss1 21 June
Tyre, G. J. B. BA 7 July
Jiggins, J. M. BSc
  qss 8 July
Gannon, A. S. BSc
  qcc 24 July
Williams, S. K. 28 July
Hutchinson, P. D. BSc
  qss 2 Aug
Davidson, R. B. qss 3 Aug
Smith, D. P. BSc 18 Aug
Maple, G. C. BA
  qss 19 Aug
Rowlands, J. W. BSc
  qss 19 Aug
Scrancher, P. J. 26 Sept
Burman, C. W. qss 27 Sept
Flint, T. D. qss 27 Sept
Norman, G. J. BSc
  qss 2 Oct
Little, R. A. 2 Nov
Wood, M. J.
  MInstPet 2 Nov
Atkinson, N. F. MBE
  qss 19 Dec
Dungate, J. MILog
  qss 19 Dec

1993

Gossow, S. D. 4 Jan
Vine, A. J. qss 31 Jan
Harrop, D. J. BEd
  MInstPet qss 19 Feb
Jacobs, D. E. qss 28 Feb

Flight Lieutenants

1993—contd

Sendell, C. W. J.	
qss	28 Feb
Bowtell, C. MILog	
qss	11 Mar
George, E. R. qcc	11 Mar
Potts, D. J. qss	11 Mar
Talbot, D. J. qss	11 Mar
Morgan-Frise, F. T.	
qss	28 Mar
Turner, C. R. qss	28 Mar
Bathgate, A. qss	31 Mar
Etches, T. J. qss	4 Apr
Twose, S. J. qss	23 Apr
Barclay, I. D. qss	26 Apr
Chatterton, S. A.	8 May
Corby, K. S. qss	9 May
Biggs, P. R.	11 May
Mahon, M. C. qss	11 May
Newland, D. J.	11 May
Williams, M. R.	11 May
Ward, J. L. BA qss	12 May
Forshaw, N. de C.	4 June
Hawker, A. M. qss	4 June
Ireland, D.	4 June
Shields, P. L. qss	8 June
Cameron, J. D. BA	7 July
Jones, G. R. qss	29 July
Johnson, K. qss	15 Aug
Lee, S. W. MILog	12 Sept
Wilcox, R. J.	26 Sept
Bowsher, S. J.	21 Oct
Large, M. L. qss	23 Oct
Udy, J. G.	23 Oct
Winks, K. qss	7 Nov

1994

Lloyd, A. R. qss1	27 Feb
Smith, G. N.	27 Feb
Rose, J. R.	13 Mar
Wilkins, D. E. qss	18 Mar
Tissington, B. R.	29 Mar
Curry, R. J. BA qss	30 Mar
Sykes, I. J. qss	30 Mar
Alexander, G. C.	8 Apr
Bridgman, P. J. MILog	
qss	8 Apr
Comfort, J. L. qss	8 Apr
Dorsett, P.	1 May
Warwick, P. J.	7 May
Louca, J. C. LLB	14 May
Jones, K. A.	19 May
Licence, J. R. qss	19 May
Talbot, R. C. qss	19 May

Wellings, N. D.	19 May
Farmer, R. M. L.	16 June
State, A. J. qss	25 June
Wober, D. U. BA	
qss	6 July
Merrison, K. L.	
MInstPet qss	14 July
Burrows, T. MILog	22 July
Brewer, G. P.	2 Aug
Laurie, J. K.	2 Aug
Bowen, S. M.	17 Aug
Heaton, D. C. BSc	
qss1	17 Aug
Cole, E. J. qss1	25 Aug
Smith, B. J. BSc	30 Sept
Duguid, R. K.	30 Oct
Davies, M. L.	5 Nov
Lansdown, M. L. E.	
A.	8 Nov
Jarvis, D. J. qss1	10 Nov
Wilson, K. J. qss	20 Dec

1995

Veitch, C. C.	
DipTechEd	7 Jan
Wilson, L. M.	8 Jan
Jackson, I. A. MSc BSc	
MILog qss	15 Jan
Moss, T. S. BSc	15 Jan
Savage, E. J. BEng	15 Jan
Wardle, S. J. H. BA	15 Jan
Green, N.	11 Feb
Coote, A. H. BA	16 Feb
Snitch, M. L. BEd	16 Feb
Waterworth, G. K.	
BSc	18 Feb
Young, C. BA	18 Feb
Best, E. L. qss	22 Mar
Prime, R. J.	22 Mar
Brown, S. M. BSc	
qss	29 Mar
Muskett, K. S. BSc	29 Mar
Roberts, R. J. BA	
qss1	29 Mar
Rowland, E. M. BA	
qcc	29 Mar
Allen, R. D.	2 May
Brambles, J. P. qss	2 May
Giles, M. R. qss	2 May
Collins, F. C. M.	
BSc	10 May
Feasey, P. BEng	10 May
Fidler, G. N.	17 May
Arnold, P. J. BSc	6 June
Chilas, A. BSc	6 June
Keith, A. K. BSc	
qss1	6 June
Potts, D. S. qcc	14 June

Alexander, D. R. BSc	
qss1	5 July
Tomlinson, C. M. A.	24 July
Page, A. C.	16 Aug
Lambe, P. A.	21 Aug
Stutters, G. A.	
MILog	26 Sept
Logan, M. J. BSc	
qss1	29 Sept
Oakes, J. S.	30 Sept
Smith, M. G.	1 Oct
Booly, M. I. E.	7 Nov
James, P. A. H.	11 Nov
Matthews, L. A.	
DipHE	11 Nov
Valentine, W. A.	
qcc	11 Nov
Ward, D. N.	11 Nov
Davidson, N.	13 Nov
Jones, N. A.	22 Dec

1996

Pratley, R. D. MA	
qss1	15 Jan
Bewsher, J. E. S. MSc	
qss	27 Jan
Duffy, S. J. qss1	27 Jan
MacKenzie, E. G.	27 Jan
Ford, S. L. BA	15 Feb
Brown, R. G. BEng	
qss1	16 Feb
Florey, I. BSc qss1	16 Feb
Mahony, P. A.	18 Feb
Jinadu, A. O. qss	7 Mar
Reed, G. W.	26 Mar
Alford, S. L.	28 Mar
Simpson, M. qcc	28 Mar
Thurston, P. L. BA	
qs	11 Apr
Randerson, A.	23 May
Dant, A. C.	9 June
Heath, P. J. qcc	21 June
Binns, J. S.	23 June
Drummond-Hay, R. N.	24 June
Henry, D. G.	28 July
Webb, W. M. qss1	15 Aug
Reynolds, I. D. qss1	19 Aug
Robinson, J.	24 Sept
Topley, D. C.	29 Sept
Watkins, S. N.	29 Sept
Campbell-Wood, J. S.	
qss1	6 Oct
Hart, R. J.	6 Oct
Fairgrieve, J. A.	10 Nov

Flight Lieutenants

1997

Rowlands, M. A.	
qss1	6 Jan
Roofe, J. BEng	
qss1	15 Jan
Stepney, M. J. BA	15 Jan
Williams, C. R. BSc	15 Jan
Baxter, K. D.	22 Jan
Nash, R. A. J.	9 Feb
Draper, P. J. BSc	
qss1	14 Feb
Collingswood, P. D.	19 Mar
Frain, I. K. qss	26 Mar
Miller, J. qcc	26 Mar
Leckie T. M. BTech	8 May
Curnow, J. D.	28 July
Garnon-Cox, D. G.	28 July
Thorne, C. J. qss	28 July
Brown, C. G. J. BSc	13 Aug
Lowe, S. J. BSc	13 Aug
Durke, J. MILog	14 Aug
Stuart, P. G.	14 Aug
McGowan, J.	5 Sept
Richins, E. K. L.	
qss1	26 Sept
Beeby, S. C. qss1	28 Sept
Casey, G. A.	5 Oct
Haggett, P. J.	5 Oct
Crewe, J. C. BA	9 Oct
Rands, S. M.	9 Nov

1998

O'Neill, A. J.	4 Jan
Wilson, J. P. MA	15 Jan
Wiseman, F.	15 Jan
Munden, B.	29 Jan
Corriette, R. H.	8 Feb
Hampton, D. J.	8 Feb
Ingram, G. J.	8 Feb
Taylor, D. C.	13 Feb
Crabtree, J. A. E.	
BA	14 Feb
Holmes, S. L. BSc	
qss1	14 Feb
Moorecroft, C. A.	
BSc	14 Feb
Ling, S. J.	4 Apr
Vaughan, S. M. P.	4 Apr
Fletcher, H. S. BA	9 Apr
Hodge, M. BA	9 Apr
Rooke, J. P. qss1	7 May
Sawyer, G. T.	7 May
Johnson, S. L. MILog	29 May
Pook, E. A.	29 May

Flying Officers

1992

Atack, J. E.	26 Nov

1993

Jones, A. D.	27 Jan

1994

Hamilton, D. qss1	19 June
Keith, C. S.	19 June
Langfield, G.	19 June
Connor, P.	6 Aug
Roberts, R. J. qss	6 Aug
Rogers, S. H.	6 Aug
McGrath, T. E. BSc	11 Aug
Penn, S. N. BA	12 Aug
Andrews, N. J.	26 Sept
McComisky, E.	26 Sept
Morrison-Smith, S.	
BSc	7 Oct
Atkinson, V. L. BA	9 Oct
Bullard, G. L. BA	9 Oct
Hubbick, D. J. BA	9 Oct
Stoneley, I. S. BA	9 Oct
Baker, G.	21 Oct
Harding, S. R.	9 Dec
Bell, Q. L.	11 Dec
Knight, S. R.	13 Dec

1995

Hall, T. G.	
BSc(Econ)	15 Jan
Baker, A. M. BA	11 Feb
Chappell, S. J. BSc	11 Feb
Sharp, D. J. W. MA	11 Feb
Kinloch, S. MSc BSc	
PGCE	13 Feb
McGeary, G. P. BA	13 Feb
Presly, A. D. BSc	13 Feb
Reece, L. P. BEng	13 Feb
Rutherford, C. E. MSc	
BSc	13 Feb
Abbott, P. K.	20 Mar
Cane, P. J.	24 Mar
Stewart. A. G.	24 Mar
Kingston, S. L. BA	6 Apr
Wheeler, P. J. qss	6 Apr
Barnes, G. A. BSc	8 Apr
Benjamin, T. M. BA	8 Apr
Turnbull, J. K. BA	8 Apr

Clulo, M. J.	6 May
Craig, P. S. A.	6 May
Evans, D. B. L. BSc	11 Aug
Lewis, C. O. M. BA	11 Aug
Toye, S. E. BA	11 Aug
Kane, I. F.	14 Aug
Eastham, J. F. A.	19 Aug
Cameron, R. C. BSc	7 Oct
O'brien, P. J. BA	7 Oct
Burns, D. E. BSc	11 Oct
Bell, J. H. D. BSc	24 Nov
Brennan, C. BA	1 Dec

1996

Miller, J. J.	28 Jan
Bayley, N. J. BSc	10 Feb
Griffiths, R. G. BA	10 Feb
Brabner, D. J. BEng	11 Feb
Coughlin, K. BEng	11 Feb
McGeachy, F.	
BSc(Econ)	11 Feb
Symons, J. A. BSc	11 Feb
Watkinson, S. J.	
BSc	11 Feb
Brown, D. D. MA	5 Apr
Clarke, P. J. BSc	6 Apr
Gregory, S. J. E.	
BSc	6 Apr
Grist, A. W. J. BSc	6 Apr
Smith, P. D. BA	6 Apr
Doncaster, J. C.	7 Apr
Foulstone, S. BEng	30 May
Harris, R. A. F. BA	1 June
Taylor, L. E. K. BA	1 June
Gray, A. R. BA	9 Aug
Fell, J.	10 Aug
Burcher, G. S.	28 Dec

1997

Males, A. C. BSc	15 Jan
Batey, T. J. BA	10 Feb
Moss, S. J. R. BSc	5 Apr
Tribble, J. L. BA	5 Apr
Grant, A. N.	6 Apr
Huntley, N. J. A.	6 Apr
McLuskie, T. A.	9 Aug
Binns, L. K.	6 Oct

1998

Whelan, G.	28 Jan

Pilot Officers		Acting Pilot Officers	
1996		**1997**	
Kingsman, M. P.	8 Aug	Moore, S. M. BSc	3 Dec
1997		**1998**	
Motley, J. A. K.	25 Jan	Braddick, B. G.	5 Feb
Brooke, J. C. A.	6 Aug		
Matthews, R.	3 Oct		
Maton, A. K.	29 Nov		
1998			
Kean, G. L.	24 Jan		
Sadler, G. M. BA	8 Feb		
Godwin, S. BEd	5 Apr		
Lamb, A. L. BA	5 Apr		
Priestley, J. B. BSc	5 Apr		
Reed, M. BSc	5 Apr		

ADMINISTRATIVE BRANCH

Group Captains

1991

Slater, Robert John qss Born 13/2/45 (Sec) 1 July

1992

Baker, Dennis Michael OBE FIMgt psc Born 4/1/48 (Sec) 1 Jan
McConnell, Richard BA psc Born 12/11/48 (ProvSy) 1 Jan
Collier, James Andrew CBE BSc psc Born 6/7/51 (Sec) 1 July
McLoughlin, John Allan MBE MA psc Born 28/8/50 (Sec) 1 July

1993

Cooper, Clive Richard OBE CertEd MIMgt nadc psc Born 5/3/45 (Sec) 1 July

1994

Thomas, Paul Royston MBE BSc psc Born 16/3/55 (Sec) 1 July

1995

Chisnall, Steven MPhil BA CertEd psc Born 12/6/54 (Trg) 1 July
Harris, Andrew BSc psc Born 12/8/50 (Trg) 1 July
Ingham, David Andrew OBE BSc qs Born 22/3/50 (Sec) 1 July
Martin, Gary Graham MBE psc Born 28/4/54 (Sec) 1 July
Stanley, David John qss Born 28/2/49 (ProvSy) 1 July
Walker, David Allan OBE MVO BSc FBIFM MIPD qs Born 14/7/56 (Sec) 1 July

1996

Hilling, Peter James MA qs Born 1/11/53 (Sec) 1 Jan
Jerstice, Brian James BA psc Born 29/2/52 (Sec) 1 Jan
Lewis, Peter John LLB psc Born 21/1/56 (Sec) 1 Jan
Morgan, Clive Richard jsdc scc Born 7/2/51 (ProvSy) 1 Jan
Pocock, David John BA jsdc df Born 1/6/53 (Sec) 1 Jan
Arnot, Thomas McKenzie OBE qs Born 7/1/47 (Sec) 1 July
Sherit, Kathleen Louise MA MSc CEng FIPD MInstMC jsdc ae qs Born 1/10/53 (Trg) 1 July
Wood, Stephen MHCIMA psc Born 29/6/52 (Cat) 1 July

1997

Anderson, David Hugh MA psc Born 24/6/55 (Sec) 1 Jan
Barnett, Wendy qs Born 24/2/45 (Sec) 1 Jan
Hendley, Ian Francis FIDPM MILog MBCS adp qs Born 22/4/44 (Sec) 1 Jan
Love, David Bernard BJur MIPD qs Born 9/9/47 (ProvSy) 1 Jan
Tonks, John David BSc psc adp Born 2/2/49 (Sec) 1 Jan

Group Captains

1997—contd

Turner, Philip David James BSc FIMgt FIPD jsdc Born 7/5/53	(Sec)	1 Jan
Bruton, Ian Frank BA jsdc qs Born 8/11/50	(Sec)	1 July
Cooper, Ian Robert jsdc qs Born 10/6/49	(Sec)	1 July
Evans, Christopher David OBE qs Born 4/4/48	(Sec)	1 July
Kinzett, Roger Harvey BA psc Born 23/9/49	(Sec)	1 July
Pettifer, Maurice Ian OBE BSc psc Born 4/11/48	(Sec)	1 July
Randall, Helen Mary jsdc psc Born 10/4/52	(Sec)	1 July
Thomas, John Henry Stanley BA MIL jsdc qs i* Born 13/2/54	(Sec)	1 July

1998

Lilley, Stephen Patrick John MA psc Born 3/10/57	(Sec)	1 Jan
Watson, Peter Lindsay FIMgt DPhysEd psc pji Born 11/2/46	(PEd)	1 Jan
Comina, Beverley Jane jsdc qs Born 19/6/52	(Sec)	1 July

Wing Commanders

1985

Hocknell, J. S. MBE
MSc BSc qs   (Trg)   1 Jan

1987

Bullock, M. C. BSc
qss   (Sec)   1 July
Edgar, S. MHCIMA
qss   (Cat)   1 July
Upham, J. A. MSc BSc
CEng FIPD MIEE
MBCS DIC CDipAF
psc   (Trg)   1 July

1988

Jordan, M. F. qs   (Sec)   1 Jan
Poulter, J. M. BSc
qs   (Trg)   1 Jan
Shore, I. D. L. MIMIS
MILog adp qs   (Sec)   1 July

1989

Lindley, R. B. MIMgt
psc   (Sec)   1 Jan
Morgan, J. R. MHCIMA
qs   (Cat)   1 Jan
Pearson, D. A. W.
MHCIMA psc   (Cat)   1 Jan
Dyer, J. qs   (Sec)   1 July
Medford, A. W. BSc
qs   (Sec)   1 July
Parkhurst, C. R. qs(Sec)   1 July
Pilgrim-Morris, G. J.
BSc(Econ) FInstAM
qs   (Sec)   1 July
Skinner, J. D. PhD
BTech
AdvDipEd(Open)
qs   (Trg)   1 July
Urquhart, M. M. A.
qs   (Sec)   1 July
Woodroffe, R. J. MBE
jsdc qs   (Sec)   1 July

1990

August, G. I. BA osc(Fr)
qs   (Sec)   1 Jan

Bentley, D. E. qs   (Sec)   1 Jan
Codgbrook, M. A. C.
BSc qab psc   (Cat)   1 Jan
Hodcroft, P. G. H. BSc
MBCS psc   (Sec)   1 Jan
Maxwell, A. R. psc(Sec)   1 Jan
Bell, J. D. OBE qs (Sec)   1 July
Dawson, C. L. qs (Sec)   1 July
Ellison, I. MIMgt
qs   (Sec)   1 July
Fisher, M. G. W.
qs   (Sec)   1 July
Greenhalgh, J. L.
MBE   (ProvSy)   1 July
Halfter, P. N. BA
qs   (Sec)   1 July
Leatt, M. T. BSc
psc   (Trg)   1 July
Little, A. J. psc   (Sec)   1 July
Salisbury, D. StJ.
psc   (Sec)   1 July
Sharma, D. C. qs (Sec)   1 July

1991

Burdett, R. F. BA
qs   (Sec)   1 Jan
Foster, E. C. qs   (Sec)   1 Jan
Gracie, S. A. MA BA psc
qs i*   (Trg)   1 Jan
Jones, M. H. OBE
qs   (Sec)   1 Jan
MacEachern, I. J. O.
OBE MSc BSc BA
CEng CMath FIMA
FIPD MBCS MIMgt
CDipAF jsdc qs (Trg)   1 Jan
Barton, D. G. BSc jsdc
qs   (Sec)   1 July
Daybell, P. J. MBE MA
BA qs   (Sec)   1 July
Harden, K. J. qss (Sec)   1 July
Lees, J. R. OBE qs(Sec)   1 July
Milnes, J. P. BEd
qs   (Sec)   1 July
Rice, W. qs   (Sec)   1 July
Ross, J. G. qs   (Sec)   1 July
Swain, B. L. qs   (Sec)   1 July

1992

Blackburn, S. MBE jsdc
qs   (Sec)   1 Jan
Bolam, S. F. MHCIMA
qss   (Cat)   1 Jan
Gardiner, J. C. BA
DPhysEd pji qs (PEd)   1 Jan

Harrison, R. J. BA
MIMgt DPhysEd
CertEd psc   (PEd)   1 Jan
Heaton, P. psc   (Sec)   1 Jan
Wardill, T. C.
qs icc   (ProvSy)   1 Jan
Ware, G. qs   (Sec)   1 Jan
Clyde, G. A. BSc
qss   (Sec)   1 July
Hayward, D. J. jsdc
qs   (Sec)   1 July
Hill, C. J. qss   (Sec)   1 July
Jones, A. MBE qs (Sec)   1 July
Kennedy, B. J. O.
qs   (Sec)   1 July

1993

Allen, C. psc qs   (Sec)   1 Jan
Branagh, N. OBE BEd
pji qss   (PEd)   1 Jan
Cordery, C. BEd
psc   (Trg)   1 Jan
Pearce, J. qs   (Sec)   1 Jan
Spearpoint, A.
MIMgt   (Sec)   1 Jan
Hibberd, P. J. BA
psc   (Sec)   1 July
Meyer, M. S. qss (Sec)   1 July
Waring, M. R. MA BSc
FIPD psc   (Trg)   1 July

1994

Amroliwala, F. F. OBE
MA psc   (Sec)   1 Jan
Bale, N. T. BSc qs (Sec)   1 Jan
Davidson, C. S. MA jsdc
qs   (Sec)   1 Jan
Doel, M. T. OBE BEd
psc   (Sec)   1 Jan
Fox, L. MA BA
psc   (Sec)   1 Jan
Harvey, I. qs   (Sec)   1 Jan
McGahan, P. J. MISM
MIMgt psc   (Sec)   1 Jan
Poyntz, S. J. qss (Sec)   1 Jan
Smith, W. jsdc
qs   (ProvSy)   1 Jan
Wood, S. C. MIMgt
qs   (Sec)   1 Jan
Bessant, L. R. E.
MHCIMA psc   (Cat)   1 July
Brackstone, K. G. LLB
qs   (Sec)   1 July
Britton, C. A. MIPD
qs   (Sec)   1 July

Wing Commanders

1994—contd

Brumage, M. W. MA
  CertEd qs   (Trg)   1 July
Bryans, J. C. W. MSc
  BA BSc CEng
  MIEE   (Trg)   1 July
Brzezicki, M. P. MPhil
  MIL qs i*   (ProvSy) 1 July
Codd, M. L. F. qss (Sec) 1 July
Gardner, D. K. BSc
  qs   (Sec)   1 July
Gillingham, N. K. OBE
  BEd qs   (PEd)   1 July
Gordon, A. McP. MA
  qs   (Sec)   1 July
Green, K. W. J.
  qss   (Sec)   1 July
Moore, G. J. P. jsdc
  qs   (ProvSy) 1 July
Murray, C. A. qs (Sec) 1 July
Nash, P. BSc qs (Sec) 1 July
Roberts, C. I. BSc(Econ)
  MIMgt qs   (Sec)   1 July
Wheeler, J. K. OBE BA
  psc   (Sec)   1 July
Wilkinson, N. W. R. BA
  BSc PGCE FIPD FIMgt
  qs   (Trg)   1 July

1995

Harding, R. A. MA MDA
  BA MIPD psc (Sec)   1 Jan
Pollock, A. J. jsdc
  qs   (Sec)   1 Jan
Scaplehorn, E. J. BA
  MMar qs   (ProvSy) 1 Jan
Smith, S. E. MBE MBA
  BEd MIPD MIMgt
  psc   (Sec)   1 Jan
Smyth, A. T. psc (Sec) 1 Jan
Winstanley, T. MA BA
  psc   (Trg)   1 Jan
Bohm, E. B. ACIS pfc
  qs   (Sec)   1 July
Burkinshaw, D. A. MEd
  qs   (Trg)   1 July
Cameron, A. D. C. icc
  qs   (ProvSy) 1 July
Parker, R. G. BA
  qss   (Sec)   1 July
Tofts, S. W. MA BA
  PGCE jsdc qs (Trg)   1 July

Ward, A. W. MBE BSc
  qs   (Sec)   1 July

1996

Castle, R. A. J. MDA BA
  jsdc qs   (Sec)   1 Jan
Clark, R. E. V. BA BSc
  qs   (Sec)   1 Jan
Cruickshank, J. M.
  odc(Aus) qs (Sec)   1 Jan
Hughesdon, P. J.
  psc   (Sec)   1 Jan
Innes, R. R. OBE MIMgt
  qs   (Sec)   1 Jan
Mayne, J. P. BSc
  qss   (Trg)   1 Jan
McNish, A. F. BA
  psc   (Trg)   1 Jan
Murray, The
  Honourable D. P.
  MBE psc   (Sec)   1 Jan
Rooney, P. BA DPhysEd
  qs   (PEd)   1 Jan
Shields, R. psc (Sec)   1 Jan
Wyn-Jones, E. W. BSc
  jsdc qs   (Trg)   1 Jan
Battley, S. P. adp
  qs   (Sec)   1 July
Beaumont, B. J.
  qs   (Sec)   1 July
Campbell, C. B. BSc
  ACIS pfc qss (Sec)   1 July
Cato, N. A. S. BA
  DipEurHum
  qss   (ProvSy) 1 July
Ferrar, D. CertEd
  qs   (Sec)   1 July
Gardiner, G. J. BA scc
  qs   (ProvSy) 1 July
Jermy, G. A. OBE
  qs   (Sec)   1 July
Kemley, M. J. BA
  qss   (Sec)   1 July
Paterson, R. BSc jsdc
  qs   (Trg)   1 July
Singleton, J. R. M.
  qs   (Sec)   1 July
Singleton, S. L. qs(Sec) 1 July
Taylor, M. W. BSc
  qss   (Sec)   1 July
Walker, B. J. qss (Sec) 1 July
Williams, G. A.
  psc   (Sec)   1 July

1997

Andrews, J. R. MA jsdc
  qs   (Sec)   1 Jan
Barnes, N. J. BSc jsdc
  qs   (Trg)   1 Jan
Beet, N. P. BA qs (Sec) 1 Jan
Clark, D. P. C. V. BA
  psc   (Sec)   1 Jan
Hollin, M. A. MBE
  MInstD psc (Sec)   1 Jan
Knight, S. C. qs (Sec) 1 Jan
Lackey-Grant, R. J. BSc
  qs   (ProvSy) 1 Jan
Leggat, J. G.
  qs   (ProvSy) 1 Jan
McAll, D. MDA qs (Sec) 1 Jan
Melhuish, P. qs (Sec)   1 Jan
Parry, D. G. MBE BA
  adp qs   (Sec)   1 Jan
Taylor, C. M. qs (Sec) 1 Jan
West, M. E. qss (Sec)   1 Jan
Williams, M. A. jsdc pfc
  qs   (Sec)   1 Jan
Bake, A. T. BSc qs(Sec) 1 July
Berridge, A. J. qs (Sec) 1 July
Cooper, B. qs (Sec)   1 July
Dingle, A. G. MHCIMA
  qs   (Cat)   1 July
Fairbrother, D.
  qss   (ProvSy) 1 July
Harris, P. G. qs (Cat)   1 July
Hereford, P. J.   (Sec)   1 July
Howard, S. P. MHCIMA
  MIMgt qs   (Cat)   1 July
Leggett, A. E. MDA BA
  MInstAM qs (Sec)   1 July
MacKinnon, R. J. N.
  qs   (ProvSy) 1 July
Milburn, M. J. BEd
  qs   (PEd)   1 July
Sagar, P. J. MBE jsdc
  qs   (Sec)   1 July
Smith, V. MSc MBA
  BEd MIPD MIMgt
  AMBCS psc   (Trg)   1 July
Smout, P. F. AFC
  DPhysEd pji qs (PEd) 1 July
Wilson, P. A. qs (Sec) 1 July

1998

Bonell, S. E. BA ACIS
  pfc qss   (Sec)   1 Jan
Buchanan, I. K. qs
  icc   (ProvSy) 1 Jan
Coombes, D. C. MIMgt
  psc   (Sec)   1 Jan
Harrison, J. qs (Sec)   1 Jan

Wing Commanders

1998—contd

Ogg, D. I. BSc qs (Sec)		1 Jan
Opie, G. A. MDA BSc		
qs (Sec)		1 Jan
Payn, A. L. qs (Sec)		1 Jan
Smith, C. L. MBE		
qs (Sec)		1 Jan
Smithson, P. C. MSc		
BEd psc (PEd)		1 Jan
Archer, T. D. BEd		
qs (Trg)		1 July
Branston, N. G. MBE		
BA MIL MInstAM qs		
i* (Sec)		1 July
Bray, P. L. BEd qs (Sec)		1 July
Court, S. J. MBE		
qss (ProvSy)		1 July
Egerton, A. J. qs (Sec)		1 July
Forte, C. B. qs (Cat)		1 July
Greenwood, S. D. MDA		
MInstAM(AD) ACII		
qs (Sec)		1 July
Lyster, J. M. MIPD		
qs (Sec)		1 July
McCafferty, D. A.		
qs (Sec)		1 July
McMillan, R. MA MSc		
qs (Trg)		1 July
Milroy, W. H. MA BTh		
MIPD qss (Sec)		1 July
Oxland, C. J. ACIS		
qs (Sec)		1 July

Squadron Leaders

1975

Hall, S. R. MA BA MIPD		
MRIN qs i (Trg)		23 Jan
Cooper, D. R. MSc BSc		
gw qss (Trg)		5 Mar

1978

Barnes, D. N. qs (Sec)		1 July

1980

Davies, P. A. G.		
BSc (Sec)		1 July
Leech, T. MHCIMA		
MIMgt qs (Cat)		28 Aug
Styles, J. C. (ProvSy)		18 Nov

1982

Kershaw, M. E.		
DPhysEd MIMgt pji		
qs (Sec)		1 Jan

1983

Symes, G. D. BA		
qss (Sec)		1 Jan
Pritt, M. G. adp qs(Sec)		1 July

1984

Haywood, J. W. MSc		
BEng CEng ae		
qs (Trg)		1 Jan
Fidgett, J. G.		
MIISec (ProvSy)		1 July
McBurney, A. E.		
qs (Sec)		1 July
Tench, I. R. PhD BA		
qs (Trg)		1 July

1985

Nicolle, R. J. Le C.		
DPhysEd (PEd)		1 Jan
O'Donnell, R. E. BSc		
AIB qss (Sec)		1 Jan

Williams, P. R. B.		
qs (Sec)		1 Jan
Brady, T. A. qs (Sec)		1 July
Finney, S. F. MBE		
qs (Sec)		1 July
Gilbert, R. L. BSc MBCS		
qss (Sec)		1 July
Gunn, D. C. E.		
qs (ProvSy)		1 July
Jenkins, N. BSc		
qss (Sec)		1 July
Lyttle, R. E. MIMgt		
qs (Sec)		1 July
McPhee, A. MIMgt		
qs (Sec)		1 July

1986

Donnelly, P. P. MA		
qs (Sec)		1 Jan
Fletcher-Smith, R. D.		
BSc qss (Trg)		1 Jan
Godfrey, P. M. BSc		
qs (Trg)		1 Jan
Harrison, R. L. DPhysEd		
pji qs (PEd)		1 Jan
Makin, B. G. qss (Sec)		1 Jan
Sturgeon, B. qs (Sec)		1 Jan
Galley, B. W. qss (Sec)		1 July
Jeffery, J. M. qss (Sec)		1 July
Melvin, I. BSc adp		
qs (Sec)		1 July
Newcombe, A. M. MBE		
qs (Sec)		1 July
Vizoso, A. F. BSc		
qss (Sec)		1 July
Walton, P. MSc BSc		
ae (Trg)		1 July
Lacey, S. M. (ProvSy)		19 Dec

1987

Browning, C. J. BA		
(Sec)		1 Jan
Chown, B. A. qs (Sec)		1 Jan
Clark, A. qss (Sec)		1 Jan
Devlin, D. BSc CEng		
MBCS ARSM		
qss (Sec)		1 Jan
MacKenzie, M. R. BSc		
qss (Sec)		1 Jan
Wright, E. (Cat)		1 Jan
Asher, D. R. LLB		
qs (Sec)		1 July
Hughes, P. B. qss (Sec)		1 July
Johnston, C. W. H.		
(Sec)		1 July

Squadron Leaders

1987—contd

Macnab, A. J. MA
 BCom FCMA
 MInstAM MIMgt
 AMS qs (Sec) 1 July
O'Sullivan, M. P. BA
 qs (Trg) 1 July
Parmee, R. J. MIMgt
 qs (Sec) 1 July
Scott, W. J. BSc
 qs (Trg) 1 July
Wood, C. R. LLB
 qs (Sec) 1 July

1988

Burton, A. J. MSc
 MPhil BEd DIC
 AMIPD qs (Trg) 1 Jan
Fraser, B. BA DPhysEd
 pji qs (PEd) 1 Jan
Learner, P. F. G. MIMgt
 qss (Sec) 1 Jan
Mann, C. F. MSc BSc
 CPhys CEng qs (Trg) 1 Jan
Morris, P. J. qs (Trg) 1 Jan
Murray, M. J. qs (Cat) 1 Jan
Pattenden, G. E. P. LLB
 ACIS qs (Sec) 1 Jan
Roberts, S. E. BSc
 qs (Sec) 1 Jan
Smith, S. qss (Cat) 1 Jan
Turner, D. J. qss (Cat) 1 Jan
Wynn, D. I. qs (Sec) 1 Jan
Mundy, D. (Sec) 23 Feb
Kenrick, M. C. BSc
 qs (Sec) 1 July
McDonald, I. J. MA
 qs (Sec) 1 July
Sharpe, J. H. MBE
 MISM MInstAM(Dip)
 MIMgt qs (Sec) 1 July
Webster, M. K.
 qss (Sec) 1 July

1989

Anderson, L. E. qs(Sec) 1 Jan
Ashton, D. C. MSc BSc
 qs (Trg) 1 Jan
Bartlett, G. D. BSc
 qs (Trg) 1 Jan
Brooke, R. BSc qs (Sec) 1 Jan

Cullen, A. M. (Trg) 1 Jan
Erwich, K. M. adp
 qss (Sec) 1 Jan
Godfrey, M. F. BSc
 (Sec) 1 Jan
Haslam, A. S. MSc BSc
 CEng MRAeS qs(Trg) 1 Jan
Howell, E. A. BEd
 qs (Sec) 1 Jan
Muir, J. N. qs (Sec) 1 Jan
Potter, D. N. R. BEd
 (Sec) 1 Jan
Prunier, A. P. BSc
 qs (Trg) 1 Jan
South, A. A. MBE
 DPhysEd qs (PEd) 1 Jan
Staincliffe, C. D. qs
 (ProvSy) 1 Jan
Tindall, P. D. BSc
 qss (Trg) 1 Jan
Wilson, J. R. qss (Sec) 1 Jan
Geoghegan, M.
 qs (Sec) 1 July
Lee, G. MSc BSc
 qs (Sec) 1 July
Mellor, D. B. MA DMS
 CertEd pji qss (PEd) 1 July
Pope, C. A. MA PGCE
 FRGS MIPD
 DipEdTech qs (Trg) 1 July
Rawe, C. J. (Sec) 1 July
Read, J. A. pji qs (PEd) 1 July

1990

Banks, P. C. MBE
 BSc (Trg) 1 Jan
Bristow, P. D. BSc
 qss (Sec) 1 Jan
Carey, I. qss (ProvSy) 1 Jan
Chubb, M. A. MA BSc
 MIMgt qs (Sec) 1 Jan
Clark, L. J. BEd qs (Trg) 1 Jan
Clayton, C. A. M.
 qs (Sec) 1 Jan
Cowdrey, M. A. BA
 qss (Sec) 1 Jan
Daughtrey, P. S.
 qs (Trg) 1 Jan
Green, M. D. BSc MMS
 ACIS pfc qss (Sec) 1 Jan
Haywood, V. M. MIPD
 CertEd
 AdvDipEd(Open)
 DPhysEd qs (Sec) 1 Jan
Henderson, H. R.
 qs (Sec) 1 Jan
Johnston, I. A. B.
 qs (Sec) 1 Jan

Russell, R. M. BA
 qs (Sec) 1 Jan
Sainsbury, D. J. MSc
 BEd pji qs (PEd) 1 Jan
Sheldon, K. J. adp
 qs (Sec) 1 Jan
Williams, M. qs (Sec) 1 Jan
Andrews, A. W. PhD
 MSc BSc CPhys
 CChem MRSC
 MInstP MIPD qs (Trg) 1 July
Gillespie, J. R. (Sec) 1 July
Powell, J. B. qss (Sec) 1 July
Taylor, P. A. BSc MBCS
 adp qss (Sec) 1 July

1991

Brooks, D. R. BSc
 qs (Trg) 1 Jan
Davies, J. C. qs
 (ProvSy) 1 Jan
Dezonie, L. J. qss (Sec) 1 Jan
Hobday, P. MSc BA
 qs (Trg) 1 Jan
Johnston, S. J. MBE
 MA qss (Sec) 1 Jan
Mackie, E. D. qss (Sec) 1 Jan
Nicholson, M. J.
 qss (Sec) 1 Jan
O'Donnell, T. K. BSc
 qs (Cat) 1 Jan
Ritchie, N. D. BA
 MIPD (Sec) 1 Jan
Roberts, R. W. qs (Sec) 1 Jan
Schollar, J. S. B.
 qs (Sec) 1 Jan
Walker, A. qs (ProvSy) 1 Jan
Waterfield, B. J.
 qs (Sec) 1 Jan
Wilmers, D. H.
 qss (Sec) 1 Jan
Banks, P. A. BSc
 qs (Sec) 1 July
Brown, I. P. qss (Sec) 1 July
Christie, S. J.
 qs (ProvSy) 1 July
Clews, P. J. MEd BSc
 qss (Trg) 1 July
Copping, G. C. A.
 qss (Sec) 1 July
Everall, N. D.
 qss (ProvSy) 1 July
Finlow, B. H. BSc
 qss (Cat) 1 July
Galloway, A. H.
 qs (Sec) 1 July

Squadron Leaders

1991—contd

Guthrie, J. M. BSc
MISM MInstAM
qss   (Sec)   1 July
Login, B. ACIS qs (Sec)   1 July
Osborne, R. A. qs (Sec)   1 July
Pepper, M. S. MSc adp
qs   (Sec)   1 July
Pollitt, I. S. MBE MDA
qs   (Sec)   1 July
Renshaw, S. MSc BSc
qss   (Trg)   1 July
Simpson, C. BA pji
qs   (PEd)   1 July
Spight, P. J. U.   (Sec)   1 July
Swatkins, I. R. BA
qs   (Sec)   1 July
Townsend, P. A.
qs   (PEd)   1 July

1992

Bown, T. V. qs   (PEd)   1 Jan
Brown, A. M. MSc
qss   (Trg)   1 Jan
Clarke, D. C.
qss   (ProvSy) 1 Jan
Dale, J. icc qss(ProvSy) 1 Jan
Evans, M. G. BEd
qss   (Trg)   1 Jan
Faulkes, J. J. MHCIMA
qs   (Cat)   1 Jan
Grant, K. F. MA MEd
qs   (Trg)   1 Jan
Hermon, C. C. qs (Sec)   1 Jan
Jones, D. M. BSc
qss   (Trg)   1 Jan
Kelly, P. G. qss   (Sec)   1 Jan
Lewis-Morris, M. J.
MSc BSc gw   (Trg)   1 Jan
Lloyd, P. J. qs   (Sec)   1 Jan
Martin, D. L. BSc
qss   (Sec)   1 Jan
McGregor, I. M. MA
qs   (Sec)   1 Jan
McIntosh, J. A. K.
qs   (Sec)   1 Jan
Mullinger, J. R.   (Sec)   1 Jan
Neal, N. J. MSc qs(Trg)   1 Jan
Screech, P. V. BA qs
(ProvSy) 1 Jan
Waygood, S. A. BSc
qs   (Sec)   1 Jan
Whitmell, J. W. qs
(ProvSy) 1 Jan

Wookey, C. K. MHCIMA
qs   (Cat)   1 Jan
Bacon, D. T. qs   (Sec)   1 July
Bellars, B. P. qab
qs   (Sec)   1 July
Cambrook, I. D. BA
qss   (Sec)   1 July
Cook, C. M. qs   (Sec)   1 July
England, J. D. L. MBE
LLB qs   (Sec)   1 July
Evans, B. N. qss (Sec)   1 July
Firth, M. H. BA qs (Sec)   1 July
Harker, J. qss   (Sec)   1 July
Lee, M. K. MBE   (PEd)   1 July
Moran, J.   (Sec)   1 July
Morgan, D.   (Sec)   1 July
Rabagliati, R. O. ACIS
qs   (Sec)   1 July
Shay, S. P. qss   (Sec)   1 July
Slade, J. P. MA BA
qs   (Sec)   1 July
Tyrer, S. qs   (Sec)   1 July
Wolton, A. J. qs (Sec)   1 July
Wright, S. R. A.
qs   (Sec)   1 July

1993

Allen, R. MBE BA
qss   (Sec)   1 Jan
Burton, A. J. MEd BA
qs   (Trg)   1 Jan
Calder, J. ACMA
qs   (Sec)   1 Jan
Clark, J. J. qs   (Sec)   1 Jan
Donald, R. qs   (Trg)   1 Jan
Gilbert, A. I. qs (Sec)   1 Jan
Haywood, M. W. MBE
BA qs   (Sec)   1 Jan
Horscroft, G. D. MSc
BSc qs   (ProvSy) 1 Jan
Lindsay, S. M. BSc
qss   (Trg)   1 Jan
Marley, T. J. BSc
qss   (Sec)   1 Jan
Page, M. L. GradDipMS
qss   (Sec)   1 Jan
Parr, R. M. P. BA
qs   (Sec)   1 Jan
Pearce, A. C. MSc BSc
PGCE DIC qss (Trg)   1 Jan
Peters, S. G. MIPD
qss   (Sec)   1 Jan
Reith, R. G. qs   (Sec)   1 Jan
Rogerson, C. S. BA
qs   (Sec)   1 Jan
Rover-Parkes, S. N.
qs   (Sec)   1 Jan
Sears, R. H. qss (Sec)   1 Jan

Short, M. A. qss (Sec)   1 Jan
Thomas, A. M. MA
qs   (Trg)   1 Jan
Ulhaq, Z. BA qs   (Sec)   1 Jan
Warwick, N. C. qs (Sec)   1 Jan
Bryne, A. M. BA
qs   (Trg)   1 July
Harrison, J. MHCIMA
qss   (Cat)   1 July
Johnston, A.
qss   (ProvSy) 1 July
Leech, G. BA CertEd
AMITD qs   (Trg)   1 July
Meacham, R. L.
qs   (Sec)   1 July
Mountain, P. W. MSc
BSc CEng MRAeS
CertEd qs   (Trg)   1 July
Roberts, C. S. MSc BSc
qs   (Trg)   1 July
Shackleton, M. J. BSc
qss   (Trg)   1 July
Williams, G. D. V.
qss   (Cat)   1 July

1994

Bale, M. A. BA adp
qss   (Sec)   1 Jan
Betteridge, P. A.
DipMgmt qs (ProvSy) 1 Jan
Bull, K. M.   (Sec)   1 Jan
Burton, A. D. CertEd
qss   (Trg)   1 Jan
Caddick, R. P. qs (Sec)   1 Jan
Campbell, A. qss (Sec)   1 Jan
Campbell, P. A. BSc
qs   (Sec)   1 Jan
Cowell, R. J. qs (Sec)   1 Jan
Dean, S. P. BA qs (Sec)   1 Jan
Gatenby, M. H. BSc qss
i   (Sec)   1 Jan
Griffin, M. J. MA BSc
PGCE MIPD qs (Trg)   1 Jan
Hart, P. T.   (Sec)   1 Jan
Heath, R. A. BA   (Sec)   1 Jan
Hedley-Smith, P. C. W.
PhD MBA BSc qs
(Sec)   1 Jan
Henderson, G. G.
qss   (Sec)   1 Jan
Hutchison, B. BA
qs   (ProvSy) 1 Jan
Jones, T. A. qss (Sec)   1 Jan
Lewis, D. J. MSc BA
PGCE qs   (PEd)   1 Jan
Lewis, M. P. D. MSc BSc
qss   (Trg)   1 Jan

Squadron Leaders

1994—contd

Macaulay, L. K. BA
    (Sec) 1 Jan
Marden, V. J. A. BA
qss   (Sec) 1 Jan
McLintock, I. BSc
qs   (Sec) 1 Jan
Ralston, W. qs (Trg) 1 Jan
Sanderson, J. S. BA
qs   (Trg) 1 Jan
Sparks, J. C. BA CertEd
qs   (Trg) 1 Jan
Sumner, E. C. DMS
  MInstAM MIMgt
DMS qss (Sec) 1 Jan
Tagg, P. MIMgt qs (Sec) 1 Jan
Williams, D. V. BA
  PGCE MIPD qs (Sec) 1 Jan
Williamson, I. D. (Sec) 1 Jan
Bate, P. N. qss (PEd) 1 July
Blanchard-Smith, R. M.
qss   (Sec) 1 July
Bryant, P. N. R.
qss   (Sec) 1 July
Chaplin, C. P. FISM
  MBIFM MIMgt
qss   (Sec) 1 July
Collinson, D. P. qs (Sec) 1 July
D'Ardenne, P. J.
    (ProvSy) 1 July
Dean, S. BSc qs (Trg) 1 July
Evans, P. BA qs i i (Trg) 1 July
Exeter, D. W. BA
qss   (Trg) 1 July
Forde, D. J. C. BA
qs   (Cat) 1 July
Gammage, R. D. BSc
qs   (PEd) 1 July
Gibson, D. A. MA MIL
  MIMgt qs i* (Sec) 1 July
Harvey, J. C. BA qs
i   (Trg) 1 July
Hockley, S. J. E. BSc
  MIBiol qs (Sec) 1 July
Holley, B. J. MSc BSc
  CEng CPhys MInstP
ae qs (Trg) 1 July
Hopkin, R. A. BEd
qs   (Trg) 1 July
Horton, P. qss (Sec) 1 July
Jerrard, P. E. BSc
qss   (Sec) 1 July
Kerr, R. A. qs (Sec) 1 July
Lamb, J. A. qss (Cat) 1 July
Lydiate, D. MSc FIPD
qs   (Trg) 1 July

Lyons, D. E. BA
qss   (Sec) 1 July
MacTaggart, R. A. McL.
qss   (Sec) 1 July
Marks, P. C. G(a)
    (ProvSy) 1 July
McCafferty, P. qs (Sec) 1 July
McCullough, D. McC.
qss   (Trg) 1 July
McDevitt, P. M. qs (Sec) 1 July
McKillen, J. D. B.
qss   (Sec) 1 July
Mitchell, R. A. snc (Sec) 1 July
Mitra, A. R. qs (Sec) 1 July
Moos, F. J. BSc MBCS
  adp qss (Sec) 1 July
Morris, D. S. qss (Sec) 1 July
Neild, J. R. qss (Sec) 1 July
Perks, R. J. ACIS
qss   (Sec) 1 July
Rudd, M. J. (Sec) 1 July
Sinfield, A. T. (Sec) 1 July
Stretton, C. J. H. BSc
qs   (ProvSy) 1 July
Surr, R. A. qss i* (Trg) 1 July
Wallis, H. M. BA MIPD
qss   (Sec) 1 July
Walsh, A. W. qss (Sec) 1 July
Wilkinson, M. BA PGCE
  MIL qss i* (Trg) 1 July
Young, M. qs (Sec) 1 July
Youngs, R. A. DMS
qs   (Sec) 1 July

1995

Atkinson, R. D.
qss   (Sec) 1 Jan
Chalmers, N. F. BSc
qss   (ProvSy) 1 Jan
Davies, J. A. BA
qs   (Trg) 1 Jan
Dunleavy, B. T. MBE
qss   (Sec) 1 Jan
Harris, K. A. qs (Sec) 1 Jan
Haughton, S. E. MBE
  BA qs (Sec) 1 Jan
Hill, A. R. FBIFM
qss   (Sec) 1 Jan
Hill, D. J. qs (Sec) 1 Jan
Hoper, B. P. qss (Sec) 1 Jan
Hunter, D. A. BA qs
    (ProvSy) 1 Jan
Little, C. BEd qss (Sec) 1 Jan
Parkinson, W. N. MA
  BSc CEng MIMechE
  MIPD qs (Trg) 1 Jan
Pittson, K. T. (Sec) 1 Jan

Reed, D. J. BA PGCE
qss   (Trg) 1 Jan
Spencer, K. A. BH
qs   (Sec) 1 Jan
Tomany, M. P. BEd
qs   (Sec) 1 Jan
West, I. J. qs (ProvSy) 1 Jan
Whitfield, K. H. adp
qs   (Sec) 1 Jan
Bain, D. D. BSc qs (Trg) 1 July
Battersby, R. S. H. BA
qs   (Sec) 1 July
Bishop, R. S. qss
    (ProvSy) 1 July
Cobley, L. W. G. BSc
qs   (Trg) 1 July
Field, T. W. J. qs (Sec) 1 July
Fish, M. BA qss (Trg) 1 July
Flynn, K. G. M. BSc
  ACMA qs (Sec) 1 July
Johnston, G. A.
qs   (Sec) 1 July
Leadbeater, N. C. LLB
qs   (Sec) 1 July
Lindsay, A. J. BA
qss   (Sec) 1 July
Mackenzie, D. P.
qs   (Sec) 1 July
Mahoney, N. G. A. BSc
qss   (Sec) 1 July
McGuigan, M. P. BA
qss   (Sec) 1 July
McLean, J. F. BA
qs   (Sec) 1 July
Organ, M. J. BEd
qss   (Sec) 1 July
Patching, C. BSc
qss   (Sec) 1 July
Radcliffe, A. J. qs (Sec) 1 July
Riseley-Prichard, J. M.
  BSc qs (ProvSy) 1 July
Seymour, P. S. AIB
qss   (Sec) 1 July
Smith, C. M. qs (Sec) 1 July
Thompson, R. M.
  MSERT qs (Sec) 1 July
Tippett, C. M. qss (Sec) 1 July
Tofi, P. M. qs (Sec) 1 July
Tolfts, I. R. qss (Sec) 1 July
Warby, D. A. J. MBE
  BEd pji (PEd) 1 July

1996

Boston, J. qss (Sec) 1 Jan
Bowles, D. J. qss (Sec) 1 Jan
Carver, L. BA qss (Trg) 1 Jan
Collett, T. G. BA
qss   (Cat) 1 Jan

Squadron Leaders

1996—contd

Coombes, R. E. qss		
	(ProvSy)	1 Jan
Crowder, S. J. qs	(Sec)	1 Jan
Flatt, H. BSc qs	(Sec)	1 Jan
Garwood, M. qss	(Sec)	1 Jan
Good, J. BSc qs	(Cat)	1 Jan
Gough, A. A. MSc BEd		
qs	(Trg)	1 Jan
Griffiths, S. C. BA		
qs	(Trg)	1 Jan
Heffron, M. D. qs	(Sec)	1 Jan
Highmore, R. A. qs		
	(ProvSy)	1 Jan
Mahoney, P. J. BA		
qss	(Sec)	1 Jan
McKiernan, C. J. BA		
MBIFM qs	(Sec)	1 Jan
Montellier, C. A.		
qss	(Sec)	1 Jan
Nicholson, A. S.		
qs	(Sec)	1 Jan
Read, R. C. qss	(Sec)	1 Jan
Roberts, N. J. FISM		
MInstAM MIMgt		
qs	(Sec)	1 Jan
Selway, K. qs	(Sec)	1 Jan
Smith, D. M. BA		
qss	(PEd)	1 Jan
Spence, S. J. qs	(Sec)	1 Jan
Stanfield, J. W. MA BA		
qss	(Sec)	1 Jan
Stewart, A. G.	(Sec)	1 Jan
Walker, A. BA qs	(Sec)	1 Jan
Weight, M. J.	(Sec)	1 Jan
Yorke, D. J. FBIFM		
qss	(Sec)	1 Jan
Arnold, L. E. BA MIPD		
qss	(Sec)	1 July
Atkins, S. qss (ProvSy)		1 July
Barlow, P. E. qs	(Sec)	1 July
Bowen, S. J. FIL		
qs i	(Sec)	1 July
Bray, C. M. qs	(Sec)	1 July
Brinkworth, D. A.		
qss	(Cat)	1 July
Butler, S. J. MBE	(Trg)	1 July
Chant, T. J. qs	(Sec)	1 July
Clarke, P. K. BEd		
qs	(PEd)	1 July
Dickinson, C.	(Sec)	1 July
Edgcumbe, G. D. T.		
qss	(ProvSy)	1 July
Erskine, J. W.		
icc qss	(ProvSy)	1 July

Evans, M. W. BSc		
MIMgt qs	(Trg)	1 July
Fuller, M. A. qss	(Sec)	1 July
Fuller, S. BSc qss	(Sec)	1 July
Holden, T. I. qs	(Sec)	1 July
Hunter, A. J. BA		
qss	(Sec)	1 July
Kellachan, P. A.		
BSc	(Trg)	1 July
Lawlor, A. E. M.	(Cat)	1 July
Lock, D. M.	(Sec)	1 July
MacLean, D. A.		
qss	(Sec)	1 July
Reynolds, R. G. BA		
qs	(Sec)	1 July
Roberts, O. D. BEd		
qs	(PEd)	1 July
Robins, P. D. BA		
pji qss	(Sec)	1 July
Townend, I. A.		
qss	(Sec)	1 July
Webster, J. T. qss	(Sec)	1 July
Willox, K. W. qs	(Cat)	1 July
Wilson, G. BSc		
qss	(Sec)	1 July

1997

Bird, T. G. BEd pji		
qss	(PEd)	1 Jan
Bolton, G. BA AdDipEd		
qss	(Trg)	1 Jan
Bulman, C. G. MBE		
qss	(Sec)	1 Jan
Chapman, P. W. BSc		
qss	(Sec)	1 Jan
Cornish, C. S. qss (PEd)		1 Jan
Evans, M. A. BA		
qss	(Sec)	1 Jan
Jackman, S. M. icc		
qs	(ProvSy)	1 Jan
Jewsbury, M. R. MSc		
BSc MIPD qss	(Trg)	1 Jan
Keetley, A. E. qss	(Sec)	1 Jan
Lawson, E. BSc icc		
qs	(ProvSy)	1 Jan
Leighton, G.	(Trg)	1 Jan
Lunan, M. qs (ProvSy)		1 Jan
Martin, M. J. qss	(Sec)	1 Jan
Pearson, A. qs	(PEd)	1 Jan
Salway, J. E. BA		
qss	(Trg)	1 Jan
Taylor, H. D. BA		
qss	(Trg)	1 Jan
Tracey, M. A. BA ACIS		
qss	(Sec)	1 Jan
Tunnicliffe, G. BA		
qss	(Sec)	1 Jan

Walcot, B. V. H. BA		
qs	(Sec)	1 Jan
Wilkinson, K. BA		
qss	(Sec)	1 Jan
Willerton, A. qss	(Sec)	1 Jan
Cairns, S. L. qss	(Sec)	1 July
Chadwick, S. P. qs (Sec)		1 July
Cunliffe, R. P. BEd		
qss	(PEd)	1 July
Curry, D. BA qss	(Sec)	1 July
Elliott, D. J. McC		
BA	(Sec)	1 July
Groves, J. A.	(Sec)	1 July
Logan, K. A. FISM MIPD		
qss	(Sec)	1 July
Louth, J. P. W. BSc		
qss	(Sec)	1 July
McCracken, T. S.	(Sec)	1 July
Mulready, C. P. qs (Sec)		1 July
Palmer, I. L. qs	(Sec)	1 July
Paul, R. J. BA qs	(Sec)	1 July
Prescott, K. qs	(Sec)	1 July
Seabright, A. J. BA		
qs	(ProvSy)	1 July
Southern, S.	(ProvSy)	1 July
Sugden, G. H. B. MSc		
FIISec qs	(ProvSy)	1 July
Taylor, M. F. H.	(PEd)	1 July
Vincent, H. J. C.		
qss	(Sec)	1 July
Wheeler, M.		
qss	(ProvSy)	1 July

1998

Aderyn, A. A. MA		
qss	(Sec)	1 Jan
Anderson, P. W.		
qss	(Sec)	1 Jan
Ashworth, D. R.		
qss	(Sec)	1 Jan
Ball, L. P. qss	(Sec)	1 Jan
Beaton, J. E. BA	(Sec)	1 Jan
Bradstock, J. BA		
qss	(Cat)	1 Jan
Bruce, G. J. qs	(Sec)	1 Jan
Bruff, K. J. qss	(Sec)	1 Jan
Campbell, C. J. A.		
qss	(ProvSy)	1 Jan
Daniels, J. C. BSc		
qss	(Cat)	1 Jan
De Soyza, N. A.		
qss	(Sec)	1 Jan
Fane De Salis, H. J. A.		
BA qss	(Sec)	1 Jan
Fenton, T. J.	(Sec)	1 Jan
Fiddy, P. C.		
qss	(ProvSy)	1 Jan

Squadron Leaders

1998—contd

Gracey, D. G. T. BSocSc		
qss	(ProvSy)	1 Jan
Hobkirk, C. A. qss	(Sec)	1 Jan
Hollingsworth, M. J.		
qss	(Sec)	1 Jan
Isaac, S. A. qss	(Trg)	1 Jan
Jackson, P. A. qss	(Sec)	1 Jan
Jennings, R.	(Sec)	1 Jan
Morgan, A. N. BEd qab		
qss	(Trg)	1 Jan
Palomeque, A. G. BA MHCIMA DipAT		
qss	(Cat)	1 Jan
Peoples, S. F. BSc		
qs	(Trg)	1 Jan
Riches, A. W. MA		
qss	(Trg)	1 Jan
Todd, C. W. BA		
qs	(Sec)	1 Jan
Tudor, R. I. C. BA		
qss	(Trg)	1 Jan
Turner, M. J. qss	(Sec)	1 Jan
Williams, I. A. BEd		
qss	(ProvSy)	1 Jan
Ainsworth, M. S. A.		
	(Sec)	1 July
Allan, S. BA qss	(Sec)	1 July
Bell, N. J. D.	(Sec)	1 July
Black, P. BA		
qss	(ProvSy)	1 July
Carten, J. B. qss	(Sec)	1 July
Dryburgh, D. S. MSc		
BSc qss	(Trg)	1 July
Ellis, R. A. BA CertEd		
qss	(Sec)	1 July
Gorman, N. R. BEd pji		
qss	(PEd)	1 July
Johnstone, S. C. BEd		
qss	(PEd)	1 July
Jones, A. qss	(Sec)	1 July
Khepar, B. S. qss	(Sec)	1 July
Loxton, W. T. BEd pji		
qss	(PEd)	1 July
Marshall, P. J. qss	(Sec)	1 July
McCord, A. A. BA adp		
qss	(Sec)	1 July
McGill, A. qss	(Sec)	1 July
Mennie, B. G. qss	(Cat)	1 July
Mitchell, J. K. H.		
qss	(Sec)	1 July
Page, M. R.	(ProvSy)	1 July
Potts, D. A. BA		
qss	(Sec)	1 July
Stewart, D. E. M.	(Sec)	1 July
Trollen, A. F. qss	(Sec)	1 July

Wain, W. J. qss	(Sec)	1 July
Wilson, A. R. BA		
qss	(Sec)	1 July
Wood, T. H. P. qss	(Sec)	1 July
Young, C. MHCIMA		
qss	(Cat)	1 July

Flight Lieutenants

1971

McIntyre, W. J. J. H.	(Sec)	17 Mar

1974

Seaward, P. V. A. MRIN MIMgt qss	(Sec)	28 Dec

1976

Dickson, W. H. E. DPhysEd pji	(PEd)	29 Aug

1978

Clarke, P. M. MSc		
qss	(Trg)	6 Oct

1980

Evans, C. J. BSc		
qss	(Trg)	18 Sept

1981

Hinchliffe, N. B.	(Trg)	20 Jan
Cardwell, M. A. BSc		
qss	(Trg)	14 Oct

1982

Hutchinson, L. J. BEd		
qss	(Trg)	2 Mar
Walling, G. BA		
qss	(Trg)	14 June
Lodge, A. M.	(Trg)	20 Sept

1983

Cassels, J. D.		
qss	(ProvSy)	16 Mar
Singleton-Hobbs, G. A.		
qss	(ProvSy)	28 Apr
Stock, I. M. BSc		
qss	(Trg)	11 June

Flight Lieutenants

1983—contd

Holden, R. P. BSc
qss   (Trg)   5 July

1984

Alfandary, C. M. BA
qss   (Trg)   16 Feb
Langstaff-Ellis, J. W.
BEd qss   (Sec)   17 Feb
Skuodas, L. J. BEd BSc
qss   (PEd)   14 Apr
Wilkinson, K. MA BSc
CertEd qss   (Trg)   3 July
Revell, M. FRSA FIPD
MIMgt qss   (Sec)   17 July
Morgan, G. R.   (Trg)   3 Aug
Heathershaw, C. M. pji
qss   (PEd)   17 Aug
Overton, D. G. BA
CPhys MInstP
qss   (Trg)   7 Dec

1985

Jarvis, R. A.   (Trg)   1 Feb
Barrett, J. BSc qss (Trg)   19 Feb
Freak, D. C. BSc adp
qss   (Trg)   18 Apr
Denner, P. O. H. BA
qss   (Trg)   30 Apr
Kerr, R. J. gw   (Trg)   3 July
Lamb, R. A. qss   (PEd)   6 Sept
Merrick, R. E. MIPD
AIB   (Sec)   17 Oct
Cooper, J. D. BSc
qss   (Trg)   26 Oct

1986

Pim, R. S. BSc qss (Trg)   29 Mar
Elmes, R. I.   (Cat)   30 Mar
Ashton, C. C. BA
qss   (Trg)   30 Apr
Allcock, G. BA pji
qss   (PEd)   7 May
Bullock, C. G. qss (Sec)   19 July
Grieve, D. J. W. BA qss
i   (Trg)   18 Sept

Blackburn, G. J. BA qss
i*   (Trg)   20 Oct

1987

Griffiths, M. A. BEd
pji   (PEd)   4 Jan
Goatham, J. MSc BSc
PGCE qss   (Trg)   15 Jan
Marsh, H. BEd
qss   (PEd)   3 Feb
Curwen, D. J. BSc
qss   (Trg)   1 Mar
Turner, J. A. BEd
qss   (PEd)   11 Mar
Cannon, M. J. BSc
PGCE CBiol MIBiol
MIPD   (Trg)   29 Mar
Jackson, M. L. BSc
qss   (Trg)   26 Apr
Doonan, D. K. BSc
qss   (Sec)   30 Apr
Hudson, M. BA   (Trg)   30 Apr
Sutherland, D. J. L.
BSc   (Sec)   30 Apr
Kindell, F. J. BA qss
i*   (Trg)   25 May
Hemingway, C. J.
qss   (Sec)   31 May
Amis, S. A.
qss   (ProvSy) 4 July
Newton, E. J. C. BA
qss   (Trg)   16 Sept
James, I. MHCIMA
MRSH qss   (Cat)   27 Sept
Amos, S. A. qss   (Trg)   3 Nov
Cottew, T. A. J. ACMA
adp qss   (Sec)   25 Nov
Walker, R. S. qss (Sec)   11 Dec

1988

Gorton, A. P. BA qss
i   (Trg)   7 Jan
Battey, F. J. BA
qss   (Trg)   15 Jan
Smith, D. B. MSc BSc
PGCE CEng MIEE
qss   (Trg)   1 Feb
Earle, P. J. BSc   (Trg)   16 Feb
Haggarty, E. BSc
qss   (Trg)   11 Apr
Kirman, C. K.   (Sec)   26 Apr
Stanyon, P. qss   (Trg)   19 June
Hunt, B. J. MSc
qss   (Sec)   23 June
Sunderland, S. J. E.
BSc qss   (Trg)   20 July

Bauer, J. C. MA BA
qss   (Trg)   1 Aug
Burbridge, J. M. BEd
qss   (PEd)   1 Aug
Clarke, R. M. P. G. BEd
qss   (PEd)   18 Aug
Jones, W. A. qss   (PEd)   30 Aug
Healey, J. R. qss (Cat)   11 Sept
Shuttleworth, M. R.
qss   (PEd)   14 Sept
O'Shea, P. F. A. BA
qss   (Sec)   14 Oct
Dalton, S. M.
qss   (ProvSy) 25 Oct
Colgan, A. J. BEd
qss1   (PEd)   10 Nov

1989

Day, M. BSc qss   (Trg)   7 Jan
Huddlestone, J. A. BEd
qss   (Trg)   15 Jan
Ousby, S. E. BSc
qss   (Trg)   15 Jan
Morris, P. M. BA adp
qss   (Trg)   1 Feb
Painter, R. E. PhD BSc
qss   (Trg)   14 Feb
Brake, C. R. BSc
qss   (ProvSy) 18 Feb
Richards, N. M. BSc
qss   (Trg)   18 Feb
Buchanan, N. J. BEd
qss   (PEd)   7 Mar
Cowsill, J. R. qss (PEd)   14 Mar
Heathfield, A. J. BEd
qss   (Trg)   14 Mar
Wadsworth, S. E. BA
qss   (Trg)   26 Mar
Rich, S. J. MA BSc
qss   (ProvSy) 30 Mar
Bailey, J. P. BSc
CertEd   (Trg)   1 Apr
Petersen, C. J. BA
qss   (PEd)   26 Apr
Burge, G. P. qss   (Cat)   29 Apr
Plume, J. M. (ProvSy)   14 May
Bon, D. A. BEd pji
qss   (PEd)   30 May
Hicks, D. A. BEd
qss   (PEd)   3 June
Jardim, M. P. MBE
BA   (Trg)   3 July
George, R. M. A. pji
qss   (PEd)   1 Aug
Keane, C. BSc adp
qss   (Trg)   1 Aug
Brown, G. BEd   (PEd)   18 Aug
Manktelow, A. J.   (Sec)   8 Oct

Flight Lieutenants

1989—contd

Pulford, J. F.	(PEd)	8 Oct
Quick, D. M.	(Sec)	19 Nov
Bateman, S. A. BH		
PGCE qss	(PEd)	7 Dec
Kendell, M. R. J. B.		
	(Sec)	19 Dec
Saunders, P. C. H.		
qss	(PEd)	19 Dec
Bunce, A. R. BA qss		
	(ProvSy)	22 Dec

1990

Cusack, E. P. BSc		
PGCE	(Trg)	5 Jan
Nicholls, B. A. BEd		
qss	(PEd)	19 Jan
Parkinson, G. E. BSc		
qss	(Trg)	3 Feb
Snape, C. J. S.	(Sec)	3 Feb
Jarvis, S. N. P. BEd pji		
qss	(PEd)	14 Feb
Burns, P. BSc	(Trg)	20 Feb
Payne, D. W. BSc	(Trg)	20 Feb
Bowman, M. A.	(Sec)	27 Mar
Paveley, D. J. BA		
qss	(PEd)	11 Apr
Jones, R. A. BA		
adp	(Sec)	18 Apr
Spiller, A. W. J.	(Sec)	19 Apr
Glendinning, P. J.		
BSc	(Trg)	26 Apr
Hill, J. S. BA qss	(Trg)	26 Apr
Alker, M. A. BA		
qss	(Trg)	7 June
Thomas, D. G. MSc BSc		
qss	(Trg)	7 June
Garnett, I. M. BSc		
qss	(Sec)	26 June
Bryce, S. BA pji	(PEd)	8 July
Hewitt, S. L.		
qss	(ProvSy)	1 Aug
Rowlinson, D. I.		
BEd	(Sec)	1 Aug
Atcheson, C.		
qss	(ProvSy)	14 Aug
Mountain, A. R.		
qss	(Sec)	15 Sept
Roberts, A. R. MInstAM		
CertEd	(Sec)	22 Sept
Gwillim, J. M. D.		
	(ProvSy)	24 Sept
Incledon-Webber, P. D.		
qss	(Cat)	17 Oct

Bland, M. qss (ProvSy)		26 Oct
Milburn, E. J. BA		
qss	(Sec)	26 Oct
Hayllor, P. A. BSc	(Trg)	30 Oct
Stewart, G. K.		
qss	(ProvSy)	2 Nov
Ward, J. M. MSc BSc		
PGCE qss	(Trg)	1 Dec
Mathieson, P. BSc		
qss	(Sec)	7 Dec
Hannaford, G. E.		
qss	(Sec)	8 Dec
Palmer, W. V. qss (Sec)		15 Dec
Potts, A. J. qss	(Cat)	22 Dec
Newbould, H. C.		
qss	(Sec)	25 Dec

1991

Hughes, A. M. qss (Cat)		5 Jan
Bissell, R. J. BA qss		
	(ProvSy)	8 Jan
Gudgeon, A. C. MSc		
BSc CEng MIEE		
qss	(Trg)	15 Jan
Marshall, I. G. BSc (Trg)		19 Jan
Taylor, S. qss	(Sec)	19 Jan
Scott, S. C. W. qss (Cat)		27 Jan
White, K. M. BEd		3 Feb
Luton, S. BSc qss (Trg)		28 Feb
Adams, M. P. BSc (Sec)		1 Mar
Coton, C. C.	(Sec)	1 Mar
Gillies, J. R. C. BSc		
qss	(Trg)	25 Mar
Gillies, R. L. MA		
qss1	(Trg)	25 Mar
Parry, J. A. BSc		
qss	(Trg)	25 Mar
Baber, J. D. BEd (PEd)		6 May
Hunt, A. C. BEd pji		
qss	(PEd)	6 May
Petty, M. J.	(Cat)	11 May
Williams, S. G. BA		
CertEd	(PEd)	12 May
Chauhan, A. R. BA		
qss	(Sec)	24 May
Chadwick-Higgins, S.		
G. qss	(Sec)	21 June
Brown, H. J. qss (Sec)		22 June
Harris, A. W. D.	(Sec)	22 June
MacInnes, A. J. E. BA		
qss	(Sec)	3 July
Dyson, P. J. qss	(Cat)	19 July
Jamieson, B. W.		
qss	(Sec)	3 Aug
Overend, D. T.		
qss	(Sec)	3 Aug
Brooks, G. S. BA FRGS		
qss	(Sec)	14 Aug

Guthrie, M. E. G. BEng		
adp	(Trg)	19 Aug
Brebner, R. A. qss (Sec)		14 Sept
Dunn, J. J. BEd		
qss	(PEd)	27 Sept
MacAlpine, A. T. MA		
qss	(Sec)	27 Sept
Peel, D. B. qss	(PEd)	28 Sept
Couzens, M. C. A.		
qss	(ProvSy)	1 Oct
Williams, K. D.		
qss	(ProvSy)	4 Oct
Fox, D. A. BA		
qss	(ProvSy)	8 Nov
Heathcote, A. J.		
qss	(ProvSy)	11 Nov
Godsland, M. BEd		
pji	(PEd)	14 Nov
Logsdon, C. L.		
MHCIMA qss	(Cat)	7 Dec
Beanlands, S. M.		
MInstAM(Dip) MISM		
MIMgt AInstBA		
qss	(Sec)	21 Dec
Pilkington, G. S.		
qss	(Cat)	21 Dec

1992

Suggett, D. M. H.		
qss	(Sec)	1 Feb
Draper, L. M. LLB		
qss	(Sec)	14 Feb
Fairbrass, P. qss	(Sec)	16 Feb
Dalby, R. P. BSc		
PGCE	(Trg)	19 Feb
Seaton, A. D. I. BSc		
PGCE qss	(PEd)	20 Feb
Western, G. R. adp		
qss	(Sec)	25 Feb
Astley-Jones, J. G. MSc		
BSc	(Trg)	25 Mar
Moorcroft, P.	(PEd)	29 Mar
Wiener, J. S. adp (Sec)		29 Mar
Crennell, J. qss	(Sec)	23 Apr
Loader, P. C. BEd (Trg)		5 May
Newcombe, E. P.		
qss	(Trg)	10 May
Peart, J. W. qss	(Trg)	10 May
Sayer, J. P. qss	(Trg)	10 May
Brown, R. B. qss	(Sec)	11 May
Paton, M. A. qss	(Sec)	11 May
Willis, S. R. MSc BSc		
qcc	(Sec)	12 May
Barnes, S. A. K.		
qss	(Sec)	4 June
Armstrong, B. L.	(Sec)	7 June
Doherty, J. N. qss (Sec)		21 June

Flight Lieutenants

1992—contd

MacDonald, A. R.
qss (Sec) 22 June
Holland, E. J. BSc (Trg) 5 July
Horne, S. R. BSc
qss (ProvSy) 6 July
Jones, M. G. BSc
adp (Trg) 6 July
Buchan, E. M. BEd
qss (PEd) 7 July
Kearney, J. S. BSc
qss (Trg) 7 July
Cowley, R. L. R. BA
qss (Sec) 8 July
Sanderson, J. M. BSc
qcc (Sec) 8 July
Tribe, D. M. qss (Sec) 19 July
Trevey, S. G. (Sec) 28 July
Brennan, P. S. BA PGCE
MIPD MIMgt
qss (Trg) 2 Aug
Tanner, D. B. qss1 (Cat) 14 Aug
Blane, A. E. MSc (Trg) 17 Aug
Pollock, D. M. (Trg) 12 Sept
Ball, H. J. (Cat) 26 Sept
Charnock, P. M.
qss (PEd) 26 Sept
Evans, D. C. (Trg) 26 Sept
Wright, N. D.
qss (ProvSy) 27 Sept
Young, R. BSc qss (Trg) 1 Oct
Forbes, L. MSc BSocSci
MIPD qss (Trg) 2 Oct
Hamilton, I. G. BSc
qss1 (Trg) 2 Oct
Mandley, C. J. BA
RGN (Sec) 2 Oct
Parker, K. L. MSc (Trg) 10 Oct
Dickinson, K. (PEd) 2 Nov
Harwood, R. W. (Sec) 2 Nov
Ramsey, B. P. qss (Sec) 8 Nov
Vaughton, P. A.
qss (PEd) 8 Nov
Jones, W. A. BEd
(ProvSy) 11 Nov
Heffer, R. J. MA (Trg) 13 Nov
Whitty, M. A. BA (Sec) 14 Nov
Fyfe, P. D. qss (ProvSy) 25 Nov
Murphy, C. M. MBE
pji (PEd) 15 Dec
Lynch, B. G. BA CertEd
qss (Trg) 20 Dec

1993

Bell, P. N. BA (Sec) 15 Jan
Morris, G. BSc
PGCE (Sec) 15 Jan
Cockerill, G. S. MIL
qss1 (Sec) 21 Jan
Balmer, M. T. qss (Sec) 24 Jan
Thomson, C. G. A.(Sec) 7 Feb
Broadley, S. M. qss
(ProvSy) 10 Feb
Sloan, N. P. (Sec) 10 Feb
Boyes, H. R. BEM
qss (Sec) 14 Feb
Ditch, O. qss (Cat) 16 Feb
Dixon, S. A. qss (Sec) 18 Feb
Hyde, R. M. BMus (Trg) 19 Feb
Leckenby, D. BA
qss (Sec) 19 Feb
Mason, T. R. BA
qss (Trg) 20 Feb
Simmonds, A. BA (Sec) 20 Feb
Barry, S. qss (ProvSy) 11 Mar
Johnston, G. A.
qss (ProvSy) 11 Mar
Meal, R. G.
qss (ProvSy) 11 Mar
Stalker, A. D. J.
qss (Sec) 11 Mar
Ripley, B. E.
qss (ProvSy) 21 Mar
Howard, K. L. qss (Cat) 27 Mar
Ellis, M. J. BEd pji(PEd) 30 Mar
Maskell, P. BEng PGCE
qss (Trg) 30 Mar
McCormack-White,
C. (Cat) 30 Mar
Burgess, P. D. C.
BEng (Trg) 1 Apr
Carder, T. C. BSc (Sec) 1 Apr
Dharamaj, S. J.
BSc (Trg) 1 Apr
Forster, D. BA qss (Sec) 1 Apr
Harrison, A. G. BSc
qss (Sec) 1 Apr
McCleery, S. BSc
qss (ProvSy) 1 Apr
Norey, M. BA (Trg) 1 Apr
Parker, J. R. qss (Sec) 23 Apr
Gibson, E. A. (Sec) 8 May
Halliday, R. J. qss (Sec) 9 May
Stacey, A. M. qss (Sec) 9 May
Miller, R. M. BA
qss (Sec) 10 May
Clifton, H. R. MA
qss (Sec) 11 May
Faulkner, N. (ProvSy) 11 May
Simmonds, J. R. BA
pji (PEd) 11 May

Booth, R. J. BEd pji
qss (PEd) 12 May
Wright, S. qss (ProvSy) 12 May
Mabey, A. V. qss (Sec) 18 May
Harper, S. A. qss (Sec) 25 May
Carter, S. G. qss (Sec) 4 June
Fancourt, I. J.
qcc (ProvSy) 4 June
Gavin, M. K. qss (Sec) 7 June
Lewis, D. L.
MInstAM(Dip) (Sec) 17 June
McSherry, P. BSc
qss (Sec) 19 June
Harrison, D. E. qss(Cat) 25 June
Taylor, M. V. MSc
BSc (Trg) 5 July
Turner, K. A. BA (Trg) 6 July
McKeen, P. W. qss(Sec) 29 July
Oswald, N. G. pji (PEd) 29 July
Richards, A. C. (Sec) 29 July
Sykes, P. qss (PEd) 8 Aug
Morris, D. S. (Cat) 14 Aug
Bill, N. J. BA
GradIPD (Sec) 17 Aug
Fenemore, A. M.
BEng (ProvSy) 17 Aug
Holcroft, K. M. LLB
qss (Sec) 18 Aug
Moss, D. S. MSc BA
qss (Trg) 18 Aug
Taylor, I. B. BSc
qss (Sec) 18 Aug
King, I. D. qss (Sec) 21 Aug
Rossiter, G. A. qss(Sec) 21 Aug
Yarwood, J. T. (ProvSy) 26 Aug
Jackson, S. J. qss (Cat) 25 Sept
Battye, A. E. BSc (Trg) 26 Sept
Morris, I. J. (Sec) 28 Sept
O'Donnell, N. (Sec) 28 Sept
Wotton, R. E. qss (PEd) 28 Sept
Alvey, M. J. qss (Sec) 29 Sept
Fuller, A. D. qss (Sec) 23 Oct
Appleton, M. R. qss
(ProvSy) 6 Nov
Kelly, J. A. C. qss (Cat) 6 Nov
Eamonson, J. M.
(ProvSy) 7 Nov
Watt, A. W. (Sec) 9 Nov
Bamford, R. (Sec) 19 Nov
Ackroyd, C. A.
qss (Sec) 2 Dec
Harrison, I. M.
qss (Sec) 2 Dec
Barratt, W. T. (Sec) 12 Dec
Gibson, G. V. qss1 (Trg) 19 Dec
Wallace, P. J. qss (Sec) 19 Dec
Morrow, A. M. H. BA
qcc (Sec) 23 Dec

Flight Lieutenants

1994

Carpenter, R. L.
  MHCIMA qss (Cat) 8 Jan
Sheppard, R. BA (Trg) 8 Jan
Binns, M. A. H. BA
  qcc (Sec) 15 Jan
Penelhum, J. P.
  (ProvSy) 15 Jan
Savage, J. E. BSc (Sec) 15 Jan
Sexton, M. S. BA
  (ProvSy) 15 Jan
Stringer, L. M. BSc
  PGCE qss1 (Trg) 15 Jan
Timbers, C. J. (Sec) 15 Jan
Miles, F. W. J. qss (Sec) 17 Jan
Brooks, N. N. BA (Trg) 13 Feb
Hill, D. J. qcc (Sec) 13 Feb
Doughty, A. M. qss
  (ProvSy) 14 Feb
Hebden, M. A. BA
  PGCE qss (Trg) 18 Feb
McFetrich, M. S. BSc
  MIPD MHCIMA
  qss1 (Trg) 18 Feb
Shieber, K. J. qcc
  (ProvSy) 18 Feb
Lawrence, C. S. BA
  (ProvSy) 19 Feb
Perkins, J. M. BA
  qcc (Sec) 19 Feb
Turner, B. A. (ProvSy) 23 Feb
Thomson, W. J.
  BEd 25 Feb
Rignall, A. J. (Sec) 7 Mar
Best, M. C. LLB (Sec) 10 Mar
Churchman, N. J.
  qss (Sec) 16 Mar
East, R. G. qss1 (Sec) 16 Mar
Gaynor, J. (Sec) 26 Mar
Greaves, J. M. BA
  qss1 (Trg) 29 Mar
Tobin, K. R. BSc (Sec) 30 Mar
Gibson, S. J. qss1 (Cat) 2 Apr
Bailey, K. R. BA
  (ProvSy) 13 Apr
Lavender, M. D.
  qss (Sec) 8 May
Ward, M. A. BA (Cat) 10 May
Wright, I. N. BSc (Sec) 10 May
Bogg, A. BSc (Trg) 11 May
Perry, K. W. BSc
  qss (Sec) 11 May
Cook, J. A. qss (Cat) 12 May
Rowntree, R. A.
  qcc (Sec) 15 May
Snell, R. A. (Sec) 18 May

Nicholas, A. K. qs
  (ProvSy) 19 May
Bushell, K. J. qss (Sec) 15 June
Dean, P. N.
  AInstAM(Dip) (Sec) 21 June
Egglestone, M.
  (ProvSy) 21 June
Evans, T. J. qcc (Cat) 2 July
Hayes, M. J. BA
  qss1 (Sec) 5 July
Lushington, R. D. L. BA
  qss1 (Sec) 5 July
Prichard, K. A. BSc
  qss (ProvSy) 5 July
Wardle, C. R. BSc
  qss1 (Cat) 5 July
Allen, P. A. BSc (Trg) 6 July
Clucas, A. W. BSc
  qss (Sec) 6 July
McMillan, D. R. (Sec) 14 July
Owens, P. J. (Sec) 20 July
Moore, C. qss (Sec) 30 July
Searles, S. M. (Sec) 30 July
Young, S. R. (Sec) 30 July
Bayliss, D. G. (Sec) 2 Aug
Limbert, J. J. (PEd) 2 Aug
McCormack-White, P.
  A. (Cat) 2 Aug
Smith, P. A. (Sec) 2 Aug
Quinn, A. M. qss
  (ProvSy) 21 Aug
Cheeseman, N. D.
  qss1 (ProvSy) 24 Sept
Wardlaw, K. (PEd) 26 Sept
Hadley, S. MA (Sec) 29 Sept
Williams, D. BSc
  PGCE (Trg) 29 Sept
Eichenberger, M. T. BA
  qss (Sec) 30 Sept
Fowler, J. D. BSc (Sec) 30 Sept
Marsh, D. W. R. BSc
  pji (PEd) 30 Sept
Gerry, S. T. qss (Sec) 23 Oct
Ashmore, G. J. BEng
  qss1 (Sec) 12 Nov
Connolley, R. J. BA
  GradIPD qss1 (Sec) 12 Nov
Dixon, M. C. (ProvSy) 30 Nov
Wood, S. M.
  qss (ProvSy) 8 Dec
Scott, S. H. (Trg) 17 Dec
Braun, S. P. MInstAM
  qcc (Sec) 20 Dec

1995

Bishop, J. N. (Cat) 7 Jan
Walters, J. (Sec) 7 Jan

Sutherland, W. D.
  qss (Sec) 8 Jan
Brown, P. C. BSc
  qss (Trg) 15 Jan
Cleary, D. J.
  BSocSc (Sec) 15 Jan
Ratcliff, P. M. de G. BSc
  qss (Sec) 15 Jan
Ardron, A. qss1 (Sec) 11 Feb
Scott, A. E. M.
  qss1 (Sec) 11 Feb
Larter, M. H. (Sec) 13 Feb
Peebles, L. D. BEd (Trg) 16 Feb
Burton, A. D. BSc
  qss (Sec) 18 Feb
Chipperfield, G. A.
  BA (Trg) 18 Feb
Rothery, W. BA (Sec) 18 Feb
Cooper, J. R. qss (Sec) 8 Mar
Sharp, R. A. (Sec) 8 Mar
Taylor, D. A. (Sec) 8 Mar
Dunn, R. (Sec) 17 Mar
Barnes, C. R. (ProvSy) 19 Mar
Cross, L. qcc (Sec) 20 Mar
Lyons, N. J. (Sec) 22 Mar
Simon, R. J. (Sec) 22 Mar
Jones, K. G. BA (Sec) 29 Mar
Purdom, C. J. BA
  qs (Sec) 29 Mar
Sawyer, H. E. BSc (Sec) 29 Mar
Turner, J. P. BA (Sec) 29 Mar
Wyeth, G. L. BSc
  qss1 (Sec) 29 Mar
Collins, M. A. qcc (Cat) 1 Apr
Gilroy, K. M. (Sec) 7 Apr
Tullock, E. P. qss (Sec) 2 May
Smith, M. T. (Cat) 9 May
Dole, W. E. BA
  qcc (Sec) 10 May
Lovelace, S. K. BA
  (ProvSy) 6 June
Wannell, H. M. (Sec) 9 June
Hathaway, J. S.
  qss (Sec) 21 June
Beech, J. A. qss1 (Sec) 2 July
Jenkins, A. G. L.
  (ProvSy) 9 July
Gulliver, A. D. (Sec) 19 July
MacDonald, P. D.
  qcc (Sec) 19 July
Dawling, R. I. RVM
  (Cat) 28 July
Gadbury, T. M.
  qss1 (Sec) 28 July
Jones, A. G. (Trg) 28 July
Marshall, A. P. (Cat) 28 July
Mitchell, P. W. (ProvSy) 29 July
Groombridge, R. D.
  BA (Trg) 8 Aug
Clayton, N. J. BSc (Sec) 14 Aug

Flight Lieutenants

1995—contd

Lumsdon, M. BEng		
qcc	(Sec)	14 Aug
Millington, C. H.		
BSc	(Sec)	14 Aug
Bell, A.	(ProvSy)	18 Aug
Martin, J. W.	(Sec)	20 Aug
Hogarth, D. R.		
BEng	(Trg)	10 Sept
Gange, D. K. pji	(PEd)	26 Sept
Jones, H. L. qss	(Sec)	27 Sept
Salmon, D. R.	(Sec)	27 Sept
Morton, J. E. BA		
qss1	(Sec)	29 Sept
Rice, P. H. BA	(Sec)	29 Sept
Hindmarsh, H. C.	(Sec)	30 Sept
McWilliam, I. A. B.		
	(Sec)	30 Sept
Bettridge, A. V. R.	(Sec)	2 Oct
Parlor, S M.	(PEd)	4 Oct
Armitage, G. J.	(Trg)	7 Oct
Knight, J. D. MA		
qss1	(Sec)	10 Oct
Duffy, J. S.	(ProvSy)	11 Nov
Myers, M.	(Sec)	11 Nov
Rose, S. M.	(Sec)	11 Nov
Wheeler, I. R.	(ProvSy)	11 Nov
Smith, M. I. qss	(Sec)	12 Nov
Wright, J. M. BSc	(Sec)	15 Nov
McEvoy, D. A. T.		
qcc	(Sec)	19 Nov
Bowie, I. J. qss	(Sec)	20 Dec
Brown, A. D. qss1	(Sec)	20 Dec
Cook, R. W. qss	(Sec)	20 Dec
Logan, S. W. qcc		
	(ProvSy)	22 Dec

1996

Treweek, A. J. MSc		
	(PEd)	2 Jan
Davies, J. A. qss1	(Sec)	6 Jan
Schollar, A. D. B.		
qss1	(ProvSy)	6 Jan
Headland, G. C.		
qss1	(Sec)	12 Jan
Parkhouse, T. E.		
BSc	(ProvSy)	15 Jan
Rimmer, L. F. BA		
qss1	(Sec)	15 Jan
Gillespie, A. J.	(ProvSy)	19 Jan
Bowditch, M.	(Sec)	27 Jan
Gunther, J. C. BSc	(Trg)	11 Feb
Wood, V. BSc	(Trg)	11 Feb
Parry, A. BSc	(Cat)	15 Feb

Mitchell, A. K. BSc		
	(Trg)	16 Feb
Moore, T. BA	(Sec)	16 Feb
Turner, D. J. M. qcc		
	(Sec)	17 Feb
Parker, C. qss1	(Sec)	9 Mar
Burston, K. A. D.		
qss	(Sec)	26 Mar
O'Neill, P. E. MIPD	(Sec)	29 Mar
Pruden, J. R. BA	(Trg)	10 Apr
Welborn, J. M. BA	(Sec)	10 Apr
Brittain, N. C. J. BA		
	(Sec)	11 Apr
Corbett, G. BA	(Sec)	11 Apr
Stewart, D. E. BA ALCM		
qcc	(Sec)	12 Apr
Dorsett, S. J. qss1	(Sec)	9 May
Rowlands, D. C.		
qcc	(Sec)	9 May
Schmalenbach, M. R.		
BEng	(Trg)	13 May
Parkins, E. A.		
qcc	(ProvSy)	26 May
McLafferty, G. BSc		
	(Sec)	6 June
Harrison, R. J. T.		
	(ProvSy)	21 June
Egan, P. J. BA	(Sec)	13 July
McNamara, A. J.	(Sec)	13 July
Roulston, S. P.	(ProvSy)	28 July
Disley, J. BA	(ProvSy)	14 Aug
Haskell, S. L. BA		
	(ProvSy)	14 Aug
Hincks, J. E. BA	(Sec)	14 Aug
McEwan-Lyon, S. R.		
BA	(Sec)	14 Aug
Ewer, R. P. qss1	(Sec)	15 Aug
Thacker, S. L. McD.		
	(Sec)	15 Aug
Coombes, C. A.	(Sec)	29 Sept
Adey, D. D. qs	(Sec)	6 Oct
Akred, R. L.	(Sec)	6 Oct
Beer, P. qss1	(Sec)	6 Oct
Brickwood, R. P.	(Trg)	6 Oct
Cross, N. G.	(Trg)	6 Oct
Smith, M. G. qss1	(Sec)	6 Oct
Arkless, N.	(ProvSy)	10 Oct
Brown, J. T. BA	(Sec)	10 Oct
Corbould, R. J. BA BA		
qss1	(Trg)	10 Oct
Ellwood, C. J. BSc		
qss1	(Trg)	10 Oct
Gosling, V. P. BA		
qss1	(Sec)	10 Oct
Griffiths, N. R. BA	(Ed)	10 Oct
Rea, S. K. BA		
qss1	(Sec)	10 Oct
Sanger-Davies. P. R. BA		
qss1	(Sec)	10 Oct
Selby, H. K. BSc	(Sec)	10 Oct

Whyte, S. J. BA		
qss1	(Sec)	10 Oct
Michael, T. J. BSc	(Sec)	29 Oct
Gillespie, A. L.	(Sec)	10 Nov
Blakeley, P.	(Sec)	21 Nov
Moorhouse, R. W.		
qss	(Sec)	21 Nov
Barrett, M. E. MA		30 Nov
South, D. E. BA	(Trg)	7 Dec
Petticrew, G. A		
qcc	(Sec)	21 Dec

1997

Alabaster, M. J. BSc		
qcc	(ProvSy)	15 Jan
Burns, A. S. BSc		
qss1	(Sec)	15 Jan
Hamilton-Wilks, J. L.		
BSc	(Sec)	15 Jan
Havercroft, R. I.		
BSc	(Sec)	15 Jan
Read, P. J. BSc	(Sec)	15 Jan
Sharp, C.	(PEd)	15 Jan
Ellison, A. M. qcc	(Sec)	23 Jan
Rolfe, M. J.	(Sec)	23 Jan
Dempsey, K. C.		
qs	(Sec)	2 Feb
Morin, R. A. DMS		
qss	(Sec)	2 Feb
Sumner, G. BA		10 Feb
De-La-Hunty, T. S.	(PEd)	11 Feb
Baskeyfield, A.		
BSc	(Sec)	13 Feb
Moore, I. D.	(Sec)	21 Feb
Brown, S. A. MECI		
qss1	(Sec)	26 Mar
Bryden, L. P. qss1	(Sec)	26 Mar
Treharne, S. M.		
	(ProvSy)	26 Mar
Smith, C. A.	(Sec)	29 Mar
King, D. R. qcc	(Sec)	31 Mar
Duffy, J. F.	(ProvSy)	6 Apr
King, J. R. MBE		
qss1	(Sec)	6 Apr
Nichols, R. M.	(Cat)	6 Apr
Riddell, J. W.	(Sec)	6 Apr
Howells, K. L. BSc		
qss1	(Sec)	9 Apr
Mardon, P. D. BA	(Sec)	9 Apr
Nicholson, S.	(Sec)	8 May
Clarke, I. P.	(ProvSy)	12 May
Edwards, E. S. BA		
	(PEd)	1 June
Jackson, T. I.	(Sec)	3 June
Cartmell, G. H.		
qss1	(Sec)	20 June
Gillett, K. D. L.		
qss1	(Sec)	20 June

Flight Lieutenants

1997—contd

Hartley, N. A. qcc (Sec) 20 June
Anstee, S. D. (Sec) 28 July
O'Donnell, P. K.
  qcc (Trg) 28 July
Scott, J. B. (Trg) 28 July
Whyborn, C. M.
  (ProvSy) 28 July
McClelland-Jones, M.
  A. BA (Sec) 1 Aug
Fall, J. J. H. BEng 8 Aug
Neaves, M. G. BSc
  (Cat) 12 Aug
Knight, J. BSc (ProvSy) 13 Aug
Stephenson, A. BA 11 Sept
Bill, A. M. (Sec) 28 Sept
Hornby, G. P. qcc (Sec) 28 Sept
Norris, R. H. (ProvSy) 28 Sept
McClurg, P. A. (Sec) 5 Oct
Doyle, E. M. BEM (Sec) 7 Oct
Weir, C. A. BA (PEd) 9 Oct
Goodwin-Baker, J.
  BEng (Sec) 10 Oct
Louca, N. A. BA (Sec) 10 Oct
Morgan, A. L. BA (Sec) 10 Oct
Sharp, S. D. BSc (Sec) 10 Oct
Lyttle, R. B. M. (Sec) 12 Oct
Cooper, M. qcc (Sec) 17 Oct
Jennings, R. S. (Sec) 17 Oct
Bennett, K. M. (Sec) 9 Nov
Baird, W. Y. qcc (Sec) 20 Nov
Sandilands, A. P. (Sec) 20 Nov
Holder, D. M. BA
  pji (PEd) 11 Dec
Cowan, T. W. (Sec) 20 Dec
Jolliffe, G. J. R. (Sec) 30 Dec

1998

Butler, I. (Sec) 29 Jan
Harland, D. P. MIPD
  qss1 (Sec) 29 Jan
Kidd, P. D. (Sec) 29 Jan
Pitter, A. M. (Sec) 29 Jan
Trotter, L. R. A. (Sec) 12 Feb
Gibson, A. L. BSc (Trg) 13 Feb
Neasom, R. J. BSc
  (Trg) 13 Feb
Scott, S. L. BA (Sec) 13 Feb
Stembridge, H. M.
  BSc (Sec) 13 Feb
Yates, J. A. BA (Sec) 13 Feb
Allcock, S. A. BA
  (ProvSy) 14 Feb

Britten, J. E. BSc
  qss1 (Sec) 14 Feb
Chalkley, T. G. BSc
  (Sec) 14 Feb
Roberts, S. J. (Sec) 14 Feb
Stoker, S. E. BA (Trg) 14 Feb
Hansell, C. L. (Sec) 1 Mar
Barnes, T. M. (Sec) 5 Mar
Gilbert-Simpson,
  A. (Sec) 5 Mar
Read-Jones, A. M. (Sec) 5 Mar
Sturtridge, K. N.
  qss1 (Sec) 11 Mar
Brayshaw, J. P.
  LicIPD (Sec) 18 Mar
Ball, R. F. (Sec) 26 Mar
Clark, A. C. qss1 (Sec) 26 Mar
Harper-Davis, D. P.
  qcc (Sec) 29 Mar
Pearson, K. W. BSc
  (Trg) 7 Apr
Casebury, J. S. BA
  (Trg) 8 Apr
Floyd, A. D. C. BEd
  pji (PEd) 8 Apr
Manvell, S. P.
  BSocSc (ProvSy) 9 Apr
McClean, J. BA (Sec) 9 Apr
Posthumus, L. C.
  BSc (Trg) 9 Apr
Priestnall, S. J. BSc
  (Sec) 9 Apr
Hobbs, M. K. qcc (Sec) 7 May
Lloyd, E. R. qss1 (Sec) 7 May
Lovett, Z. K. (Sec) 7 May
Parke, F. S. (ProvSy) 7 May
Woolley, J. E. MInstAM
  MISM (Sec) 7 May
Reed, W. A. (Sec) 27 May

Flying Officers

1989

Warner, S. R. BSc (Trg) 17 May

1990

Hall, A. F. (Trg) 28 Feb
Smith, M. (ProvSy) 19 Dec

1991

Brearley, J. F. (PEd) 6 Apr
Green, A. C. MBE
  BSc (Trg) 10 May

1992

Roberts, B. A. (Trg) 13 Jan
Solomon, G. E. (Sec) 14 July
Johnstone, I. A. (Trg) 2 Nov

1993

Lovatt, I. M. (PEd) 27 Feb
Harrison, P. A. (Sec) 26 May
Harrison, C. A. (Trg) 22 Sept
Meenan, K. (ProvSy) 29 Sept

1994

Full, S. M. (Sec) 12 Jan
Malone, M. (Sec) 30 Apr
Buttery, M. J.
  qss1 (Sec) 19 June
Blake, A. G. (Sec) 29 June
Dear, R. A. (Sec) 17 July
Chalk, J. A. BA (PEd) 9 Aug
Collier, E. L. BA (Sec) 11 Aug
Parker, M. L. MA (Sec) 11 Aug
Webster, J. D. BSc (Ed) 11 Aug
Beck, G. BSc (Trg) 12 Aug
Finn, N. J. BA (ProvSy) 12 Aug
Graham, S. A. BA (Sec) 12 Aug
Armstrong, S. J.
  (ProvSy) 13 Aug
Hannam, R. (Sec) 16 Aug
Webber, P. N.
  qs (ProvSy) 16 Aug
Wooler, D. V. (Sec) 11 Sept
South, A. C. (Sec) 26 Sept
Tomlin, N. D. (Sec) 26 Sept

Flying Officers

1994—contd

Eley, S.	(Trg)	6 Oct
Palmer, K.	(Sec)	6 Oct
Worsfold, D. L.	(Cat)	6 Oct
Brown, J. E. BA	(Sec)	9 Oct
Craggs, J. V. BSc	(Sec)	9 Oct
Paterson, C. P. BA		
	(ProvSy)	9 Oct
Aston, A. D.	(Sec)	1 Nov
Bown, M.	(Sec)	7 Nov
Boyle, M. qss1	(Sec)	7 Nov
Davis, M. Y. qcc	(Sec)	7 Nov
Jones, N. A.	(ProvSy)	7 Nov
Orr, S. A.	(Sec)	7 Nov
Pickering, A. K.		
qcc	(Sec)	7 Nov
Ploutarchou, L. M.	(Sec)	7 Nov
Rogers, E.	(Sec)	7 Nov

1995

Renton, P. D.	(PEd)	11 Jan
Bettington, G. J.		
BA	(Sec)	15 Jan
Lynam, N. C. BSc		
	(ProvSy)	15 Jan
Davies, A. J.	(Sec)	30 Jan
Hodder, M. A.		
qss1	(Sec)	30 Jan
O'Neill, K. M.	(ProvSy)	30 Jan
Perry, A. J.	(Sec)	30 Jan
Allen, A. C.	(Sec)	9 Feb
Irwin, R. W.	(ProvSy)	9 Feb
Whiting, P. D. BEd(PEd)		10 Feb
Gunn-Wilson, C.		
BA	(Cat)	11 Feb
Lannie, F. P. BA		11 Feb
Pearce, J. L. BA	(PEd)	11 Feb
Razzaq, S. BA	(Sec)	11 Feb
Walker, G. M. BEd(PEd)		11 Feb
Barnett, J.	(Cat)	12 Feb
Foster-Jones, R. A.		
BA	(ProvSy)	13 Feb
Fox, C. A. BA	(Sec)	13 Feb
Newland, R. J. BA(Sec)		13 Feb
Wilkinson, D. J. BA		
	(ProvSy)	13 Feb
Dennis, J. L.	(Sec)	28 Feb
Charlesworth, K. H.		
BSc	(Trg)	6 Apr
Kitson, B. BA	(ProvSy)	6 Apr
Carroll, N. D. BA		
	(ProvSy)	8 Apr
Mayes, T. M. BSc		
	(ProvSy)	8 Apr

Morgan, P. J. BA	(Sec)	8 Apr
Baker, C.	(Sec)	28 July
Allen, M. C. BSc	(Sec)	9 Aug
McMillan, S. N. MA		
	(Sec)	9 Aug
Truswell, D. BA	(Trg)	9 Aug
Drake, A. Y. BA		
	(ProvSy)	11 Aug
Elliott, D. R. BA	(Sec)	11 Aug
Humphrey, G. D.		
BSc	(Sec)	11 Aug
Martin-Mann, A. C.		
BSc	(Ed)	11 Aug
McDougall, P. F.	(Sec)	11 Aug
O'Donnell, S. J.		
BSc	(Sec)	11 Aug
Trasler, J. qss1	(Sec)	11 Aug
Willis, S. C. BA	(Sec)	11 Aug
Hodder, B. qss1	(Cat)	14 Aug
Daly, B. J.	(ProvSy)	20 Aug
Hoskison, P.	(Sec)	20 Aug
Jones, J. C. BA	(Trg)	1 Sept
Campbell, S. E.		
BEng	(Trg)	7 Oct
Potter, M. S. A. BSc		
	(ProvSy)	7 Oct
Draper, T. C.	(Sec)	8 Oct
Edwards, D. K.		
qcc	(Sec)	8 Oct
Furness, S. L.	(Cat)	9 Oct
Edwards, P. W.	(Sec)	14 Oct
Kendall, J. M.	(Sec)	24 Oct
Goodwin, J. P.		
BEng	(Trg)	1 Dec
Jones, M. I. BA	(Sec)	1 Dec
Warwick, K. MA	(Sec)	1 Dec

1996

Payne, R. B. BEng (Trg)		9 Jan
Westcott, S. J. BA(PEd)		15 Jan
Backus, T. W. qcc	(Sec)	28 Jan
Boyle, M. M. qss1	(Sec)	28 Jan
Curzon, R. S.		
qss1	(ProvSy)	28 Jan
Evans, C. A. S.	(Sec)	28 Jan
Jeffery, C. R.	(ProvSy)	28 Jan
Lumb, E.	(Sec)	28 Jan
Sharman, N. J.	(ProvS	31 Jan
Lynch, H. A. M. BA		
	(Sec)	10 Feb
Reeves, J. E. BA	(Sec)	11 Feb
Allan, N.	(ProvSy)	4 Apr
Brown, A. J. BA	(Cat)	5 Apr
Clifford, M. BEd	(Trg)	5 Apr
Huntley, D. M.		
MSci	(ProvSy)	5 Apr
Matthews, K. L.		
BSc		5 Apr

Nesbitt, J. A. BA	(Trg)	5 Apr
Radford, J. MA BA(Trg)		5 Apr
Jelfs, R. J. BA	(Sec)	6 Apr
Slater, E. A. M. BSc		
	(Sec)	6 Apr
Dobbing, T. J.	(Sec)	7 Apr
Davies, G. B. H.		
BEd	(PEd)	30 May
Gillespie, S. G. BA(Sec)		30 May
Nicholl, E. J. BEd	(Trg)	30 May
Williams, O. A. BA(Trg)		30 May
Bolton, L. M. LLB	(Sec)	1 June
Dickens, P. BSc	(Trg)	1 June
Lowe, P. S. BSc	(Cat)	1 June
Watkins, T. K. BA	(Sec)	1 June
Walls, J. A. BA	(Sec)	8 July
Mansell, A. C.	(Sec)	25 July
Collinge, M. J. BA(Sec)		9 Aug
Harris, K. R. BSc	(Sec)	9 Aug
Henry, L. C. BSc	(Sec)	9 Aug
Rowlands, S. LLB	(Sec)	9 Aug
Gue, R. W. M.	(Sec)	10 Aug
Knox, A. J.	(Cat)	13 Aug
Parry-Sim, J. A.	(Sec)	27 Sept
Howie, D. A. MBE(PEd)		3 Oct
Gleave, B. J. BA	(Sec)	5 Oct
Bowles, S. J. BSc	(Trg)	6 Oct
Bunce, N. J. E. BSc		
	(Sec)	6 Oct
Garratt, A. J. BA	(Sec)	6 Oct
Selway, M. A. BSc(Sec)		6 Oct
Abdy, D. L. BA	(Sec)	1 Dec
Floyd, S. BA	(Sec)	1 Dec
King, N. A. BSc	(Sec)	1 Dec
Macdonald, F. M.		
BA	(Sec)	1 Dec
Woodrow, S. C. BA		
	(Sec)	1 Dec

1997

Portlock, A. J. BSc		
	(Sec)	15 Jan
Brewer, L. J. BA	(Sec)	10 Feb
Cordock, M. A. L.		
BA	(Cat)	10 Feb
Hampson, M. D.		
BA	(Sec)	10 Feb
Jarvis, A. S. J. BSc		
	(ProvSy)	10 Feb
McIntosh, K. M. BA		
	(Sec)	10 Feb
Thomas, G. R. F.		
LLB	(Sec)	10 Feb
Todd, P. M. BSc	(Sec)	10 Feb
Lovejoy, A. F.	(Sec)	11 Feb
Marks, D. J.	(Sec)	13 Mar
Edensor, L.	(Cat)	5 Apr
Parr, J. N. BSc	(PEd)	5 Apr

Flying Officers

1997—contd

Pilgrim-Morris, L. S.		
BA	(Sec)	5 Apr
Sinclair, R. A. BA	(Sec)	5 Apr
Bailey, E. L.	(Sec)	6 Apr
Rickard, M. W.	(Sec)	6 Apr
Condren, M. A.	(PEd)	29 May
Brown, A. J. BA	(Sec)	30 May
Cross, T. A. BA	(Sec)	30 May
Davis, A. G.		
BA	(ProvSy)	30 May
Gabb, N. BSc	(Sec)	30 May
Glover, T. M. BSc	(Sec)	30 May
Mullen, M. J. BA	(Sec)	30 May
Reardon, A. J. BSc		
	(Sec)	30 May
Weavill, R. G.	(PEd)	24 July
Mahon, K.	(Sec)	9 Aug
Hone, J. A.	(Sec)	11 Aug
Moody, G. A.	(Sec)	6 Oct
Wood, N. M.	(Sec)	6 Oct

1998

Hamilton, J. J.	(ProvSy)	28 Jan
Milnes, J. A. J.	(Sec)	28 Jan
Putland, K. A.	(ProvSy)	5 Feb
Green, N.	(Sec)	5 Apr
Scales, D. J.	(Sec)	26 Apr

Pilot Officers

1996

Evans, A. J.	(Sec)	29 June
Cairns, S. L.	(Sec)	4 Oct
Higgins, J. M.	(ProvSy)	4 Oct
Bird, S. A.	(Sec)	7 Nov

1997

Morris, A. L.	(Sec)	25 Jan
Roe, J. E.	(Sec)	18 Mar
Ward, A. J.	(Sec)	18 Mar
Mann, D. D.	(Sec)	3 Apr
Beel, D. E.	(Sec)	29 July
Brandwood, S. J.		
	(ProvSy)	26 Sept

1998

Bailes, C. A. BA	(Sec)	8 Feb
Dengate, N. S. BSc		
	(Sec)	8 Feb
Eason, R. M. BA	(Trg)	8 Feb
Jones, P. A. BA MA		
	(ProvSy)	8 Feb
Lomas, V. A. BA	(PEd)	8 Feb
McDonnell, C. L.		
BEd	(PEd)	8 Feb
Milledge, E. C. BA	(Sec)	8 Feb
Outteridge, G. J.		
BA	(ProvSy)	8 Feb
Park, C. S. BSc	(Sec)	8 Feb
Peddle, L. V. LLB	(Sec)	8 Feb
Thorburn, J. I. R.		
BA	(Trg)	8 Feb
Tipping, C. J. BSc	(Trg)	8 Feb
Lawrence, S. J. L.	(Sec)	26 Mar
Bremner, K. D. LLB		
	(Trg)	5 Apr
Hiller, L. J. BA	(Sec)	5 Apr
Hinton, R. J. BSc		
	(ProvSy)	5 Apr
Humphries, S. J.	(Sec)	5 Apr
Macinnes, F. C. L.		
BSc	(Trg)	5 Apr
Morefield, C. E.		
BSc	(Trg)	5 Apr
Scott, S. BA	(Sec)	5 Apr
Whitehead, N. H.		
BA	(Sec)	5 Apr
Wright, M. J. BA	(Sec)	5 Apr
Bryan, K. P.	(Sec)	2 May

Acting Pilot Officers

1998

Butler, J. R.	(Sec)	5 Feb
Logan, J. C.	(Sec)	5 Feb

MEDICAL BRANCH

Air Marshal

1997

Baird, John Alexander QHP MB ChB FRCP(Edin) FRCS(Edin) FFOM FRAeS DAvMed
Born 25/7/37   (F)   24 Feb

Air Vice-Marshal

1997

Sharples, Christopher John QHP MSc FFOM MRCS(Eng) LRCP DAvMed MRAeS rcds
Born 9/4/42   (F)   1 July

Air Commodores

1990

Nicholson, Anthony Norman OBE QHS PhD MD DSc MB ChB FRCPath FRCP FRCP(Edin) FFOM
FRAeS Born 26/7/34   18 July

1992

Cullen, Stephen Anthony QHS MB ChB FRCPath FRAeS DCP Born 18/7/39   6 Apr

1996

Pike, Warwick John QHP MSc MB BS MRCGP MRCS MFOM DRCOG DAvMed LRCP qss
Born 31/12/44   (F)   1 July
Morgans, Brian Thomas QHP MB BCh FRCS(Glas) Born 31/5/43   21 Aug
Rainford, David John MBE QHS MB BS FRCP FRAeS MRCS Born 27/7/46   21 Aug

1997

Gibson, Terence Michael QHS PhD MB ChB MFOM DAvMed MRAeS psc Born 6/3/47   (F)   1 July

1998

Thornton, Eric John MB ChB FIMgt MFOM DAvMed psc Born 24/8/48   (F)   1 Jan

Group Captains

1986

Reader, David Cedric PhD BSc MB BS MRCS LRCP Born 7/6/35   3 Mar

Group Captains

1989

Chakraverty, Amaresh Chandra MB BS MChOrth FRCSEd Born 5/9/36   31 May

1991

Merry, Robert Thomas George MB BS FRCP MRCPsych DRCOG Born 25/10/37   20 Sept

1993

Long, Peter James MB ChB DPhysMed Born 14/11/44   27 July

1994

Coles, Peter Keith Lindsay MB ChB MRCGP DRCOG DAvMed AFOM Born 31/1/48   (F)   1 July

1995

Jones, John MSc MB BCh MRCPath DRCOG Born 15/4/48   (F) 11 Aug
Batchelor, Anthony John BSc MB BS FRCP DRCOG DAvMed Born 27/6/47   30 Nov

1996

Abbott, Christopher James Alan MBE MB BS MRCGP MHSM MRCS LRCP DObstRCOG DAvMed
   AFOM jsdc Born 11/7/48   (F)   1 Jan
Dougherty, Simon Robert Charles MSc MB BS FFOM DRCOG DAvMed MRAeS jsdc qs
   Born 26/2/49   (F)   1 Jan
Coker, William John OBE MB ChB BA BSc FRCP Born 28/8/46   12 Mar
Jones, John Meirion MB BCh DAvMed AFOM Born 14/10/46   (F) 1 July
Laundy, Trevor John BSc MB BS FRCP DAvMed qss Born 11/4/48   7 Oct

1997

Lindsay, Ian David MA MSc MB BChir MRCGP DRCOG DAvMed AFOM psc Born 1/3/48 (F) 1 Jan
Mitchell, Ian Duncan MDA BSc MB BS MRCGP MHSM DRCOG DAvMed AFOM RFN psc
   Born 22/1/48   (F)   1 Jan
Ranger, Michael MB BS DAvMed AFOM MRAeS qss Born 23/8/49   (F)   1 Jan

1998

Graham-Cumming, Andrew Nesbitt MB BS MRCGP MRCS MFOM LRCP DAvMed MRAeS psc
   Born 17/12/48   (F)   1 Jan

Wing Commanders

1988

Dharmeratnam, R. MB
  BS FRCR DCH   20 June
McConnell, D. L. MSc
  MB ChB DObstRCOG
  DAvMed qss   (F) 30 June
Reid, G. E. MB ChB
  FRCPsych DAvMed
  MRAeS qs   1 Aug

1989

Jones, D. W. MRCP(UK)
  MRCS(Eng)
  LRCP   14 Aug
Morris, C. B. MB BS
  DRCOG   (F) 18 Aug

1991

McManus, F. B. MB BS
  MRCPsych qss   10 Mar
O'Connell, C. R. W. MB
  BCh BAO
  LLMRCP(Irel)
  LLMRCS(Irel)   3 July
Watkins, M. J. G. BA
  MB BChir FRCS(Edin) 30 Aug
Keatings, B. T.
  MMedSci MB ChB
  DAvMed AFOM
  qs   (F) 31 Dec

1992

Cromarty, I. J. MSc MB
  ChB MRCGP DRCOG
  DAvMed psc   (F) 1 Aug
Evans, C. P. A. MB BCh
  DAvMed psc   (F) 1 Aug
Ludlow, B. P. MMedSci
  MB BS MRAeS
  MRCS DAvMed LRCP
  AFOM psc   (F) 1 Aug

1993

Ferriday, D. W. MB BCh
  MRCGP DRCOG
  qs   13 Feb

Elphinstone, L. H. MB
  ChB MRCGP qs   15 Feb
Lenoir, R. J. MA MB
  BChir FFARCS
  DRCOG   10 May
Smyth, D. G. BA MB
  BCh BAO   16 July
Mcloughlin, K. H. MB
  ChB BAO
  FFARCS(Ire)   1 Aug
Skipper, J. J. MB BCh
  FRCS(Ed) qss   1 Sept
Blake, D. C. S. BSc MB
  ChB FFARCS   1 Nov

1994

Jenkins, D. I. T. BSc MB
  BS MRCP DRCOG
  DAvMed qs   (F) 24 May
Marshall, D. N. F. MB
  ChB MRCGP DRCOG
  DAvMed qs   (F) 18 July
Reynolds, M. F. MB ChB
  MRCGP DRCOG
  qss   (F) 2 Aug
McGuire, N. M.
  BMedSci BM BS   3 Aug
Groves, F. J. MBE MB
  BCh MRCGP DRCOG
  DAvMed MRAeS
  qs   (F) 10 Aug
Macauley, S. J. BSc MB
  BS   2 Sept
Kilbey, J. H. BSc MB
  BS   28 Sept

1995

Phillips, R. C. MB ChB
  MRCGP DRCOG (F) 8 Jan
Cugley, J. OBE MB
  BS   8 Feb
Peterson, M. K.   17 Feb
Jagdish, S. MB BS   11 May
Mozumder, A. K. MB
  BS MRCGP
  MRCS(Eng) LRCP
  DRCOG DTM&H
  DAvMed qs   (F) 29 July
Anderson, A. M. MB
  ChB MRCGP (F) 1 Aug
Gradwell, D. P. PhD BSc
  MB ChB DAvMed
  MRAeS   1 Aug

1996

Scerri, G. V. G. J.
  FRCS(Eng) LRCP   1 Feb
Skinner, T. A. MB
  BS   19 Feb
Green, A. D. MB BS
  MRCPath
  DTM&H   27 Feb
Hackney, R. G. MB ChB 1 May
Lucas, M. A. MB ChB 20 May
Broadbridge, R. J. M.
  MB BS MRCGP
  DRCOG DAvMed
  qss   (F) 1 Aug
Lewis, D. M. MB ChB
  MRCGP DAvMed (F) 1 Aug
Vardy, S. J. FRCSEd MB
  ChB   1 Aug
Neal, L. A. MB BCh
  MRCGP DRCOG   18 Oct
Aitken, J. BSc MB ChB
  DAvMed   (F) 13 Nov
Schofield, P. J. MB ChB
  MRCGP DA(UK)
  DAvMed qss   (F) 17 Nov

1997

Connolly D. M. MB BS
  MRCGP MRAeS
  DAvMed qs   (F) 2 Mar
Khan, M. A. MB BS
  MRCP   19 May
Bell, I. F. MB ChB
  qss   (F) 30 June
Whitbread, T. MB BS 4 July
Barney, J. S. MR
  ChB   (F) 1 Aug
Mason, P. F. MB ChB
  FRCS(Edin)
  DAvMed   1 Aug
Ross, N. MB ChB
  DRCOG DAvMed (F) 1 Aug
Ryles, M. T. MB ChB
  MRCGP DRCOG   1 Aug
Spittal, M. J. MB ChB   1 Aug
Wilcock, A. C. MB ChB
  MRCGP DRCOG
  DAvMed qss   (F) 1 Aug
Lupa, H. T. BSc MB ChB
  DAvMed MRAeS   2 Aug
Wingham, A. MB BS
  DRCOG   3 Aug
Seddon, P. J. BSc MB
  BS   15 Aug
Carr, N. J. MB BS
  MRCPath   22 Sept

Wing Commanders

1997—contd

Cousins, M. A. MB ChB MRCGP	8 Oct
Webster, T. M. MB BS MRCGP DRCOG (F)	16 Oct
Allison, G. E. MB BS (F)	17 Nov
Bone, C. E. MB ChB	25 Nov

1998

Gaffney, J. E. BSc MB ChB MRCGP DCH DRCOG DAvMed qss (F)	11 Jan
Bhullar, T. P. S. MBBS FRCPRCS(Glas) FRCS(Edin)	12 Jan

Squadron Leaders

1990

Bruce, D. L. MBE MSc MB BS MRCGP DAvMed DiplMC DOccMed MRAeS AKC qss (F)	1 Aug
Matthews, R. S. J. BSc MB BS MRCGP qs (F)	19 Aug
Sheldon, K. J. MB ChB DOccMed	9 Sept
Gomes, P. J. BM MRCP	16 Sept

1991

Roberts, A. J. BSc MB BS MRCGP DAvMed qss (F)	1 Feb
Wallace, V. J. MB ChB MRCGP DRCOG qs (F)	2 Mar
Kirkpatrick, R. B. J. MB BS DAvMed (F)	26 Apr
Reid, A. N. C. MB ChB MRCGP DRCOG	27 June
Shapland, W. D. MB BS MRCPsyc DA DRCOG	27 June
Greenish, T. S. MB BS DAvMed qss (F)	1 Aug
Farmer, D. J. BSc MB ChB	6 Aug
Kilbey, S. C. MB ChB MRCGP DRCOG DAvMed DOccMed qss (F)	12 Aug
Amos, A. M. MB BCh MRCGP DRCOG DAvMed MRAeS qss	5 Sept
Gilbert, T. J. MB BS	10 Sept
Allen, G. M. BM MRCGP MRCP DCH	9 Dec

1992

Cartwright, J. MB BS DAvMed (F)	13 Jan
Dexter, D. BSc MB ChB DRCOG qs (F)	1 Aug
Hurley, A. V. A. BA BA BM DoccMed	1 Aug

Sargeant, I. D. MB BS qss		1 Aug
Boden, J. G. MB ChB qss	(F)	3 Aug
Ross, D. E. MB ChB	(F)	4 Aug

1993

Archer, G. A. MB BS	1 Aug
Houghton, J. A. MB BS	1 Aug
Warren, A. Y. MSc MB BS MRCPath	1 Aug
Winfield, D. A. BSc MSc MB ChB MRCGP DCH DRCOG DCH DPhil ARCS qss	2 Aug
Hall, I. S. MB BS	27 Aug
Burling, P. M. MB ChB	30 Nov

1994

Scott, R. A. H. MB BS		26 Feb
Hutchinson, M. R. MB BS qss	(F)	1 Aug
Paish, N. R. MB BS		1 Aug
Hill, N. J. MB ChB		9 Aug
Carter, N. D. R. MB ChB		21 Aug
Connor, M. P. MB ChB		25 Aug
Hansford, N. G. MB ChB	(F)	27 Aug
Green, N. D. C. BSc MB BS		1 Sept

1995

Bartlett, D. W. MB ChB		25 Feb
Wright, P. MSc MB BCh BAO DAvMed qcc		25 Feb
Pathak, G. MB BS FRCS		22 Mar
Trudgill, M. J. A. MB ChB MRCGP DAvMed DiplMC MRAeS	(F)	1 Aug
Walton, C. S. BSc MB BS MRCGP DRCOG	(F)	1 Aug
Low, N. J. MB ChB		7 Aug

Squadron Leaders

1995—contd

Bastock, J. M. MB
ChB 26 Aug
Holdcroft, A. J. MB ChB
MRCGP DRCOG 26 Aug
Lewis, M. E. MB
BCh 18 Nov

1996

Maidment, G. MA BM
BCh DAvMed MRAeS
qss 24 Feb
Rowland, P. O. MD
FRCS 15 Mar
Barr, E. J. MB ChB 1 Aug
Dyer, M. F. MB ChB 1 Aug
Fox, E. V. MB BS 1 Aug
Hodgson, J. MB ChB 1 Aug
Kennish, N. P. MB BCh
MRCGP 1 Aug
McLoughlin, D. C. MB
BCh BAO MRCGP
DRCOG 1 Aug
Procter, D. B. MB BCh 1 Aug
Ruth, M. J. MB ChB 1 Aug
Timperley, A. C. BSc
MB ChB 1 Aug
Wright, L. J. BSc MB
BS (F) 25 Aug
Lasrado, I. F. N. MB
BS 24 Sept
Caldera, S. R. M. BSc
MB BS FRCS 25 Nov

1997

Burton, T. BSc MB BS
MRCGP DCH
DiplMC 1 Aug
Cotton, S. J. MB
ChB 1 Aug
Forde, S. C. O. MB ChB
FRCA DA(UK) 1 Aug
Fox, G. C. MB BS
MRCPsych 1 Aug
Gregory, K. L. MB
ChB 1 Aug
Hill, K. P. MB BS 1 Aug
Khan, R. MB BS 1 Aug
Stitson, D. J. MB
BS 1 Aug

Thomson, N. J. MB
ChB 1 Aug
Brunskill, J. M. E. MB
BS 5 Aug
Monnery, P. M. MB
BS 27 Aug
McGrath, R. D. MB
BCh 3 Sept

1998

Pickering, P. M. MA BSc
MB BChir MRCGP
DRCOG 1 Feb

Flight Lieutenants

1993

Stammers, J. B.
MB 28 June
Baker, J. E. MB BS 1 Aug
Berry, R. D. BSc BM
BS 1 Aug
Ferris, D. S. MB BS 1 Aug
Flucker, C. J. R. BSc 1 Aug
Geary, K. G. 1 Aug
Hastle, J. A. BM BS 1 Aug
Hocking, G. MB
ChB 1 Aug
Hughes, P. R. MB
ChB 1 Aug
Sareen, S. D. MB
BCh 1 Aug
Williams, M. MB
ChB 1 Aug
Withnall, R. D. J. MB
BS 1 Aug
Durrani, A. MB BS
FRCS 14 Aug
Daborn, D. K. R. BSc
MB BS 3 Sept

1994

Craig, J. P. MB ChB 1 Feb
Sheehan, J. P. A. MB
BCh 6 Mar
Lewis-Russell, J. M. MB
ChB 1 Aug
Smith, S. A. MB
BCh 1 Aug
Trimble, K. T. MB
ChB 1 Aug
Smith, M. B. MB
BS 3 Aug

1995

Evriviades, D. MB
ChB 1 Aug
Sparks, S. E. MB
ChB 1 Aug
Avory, G. M. BM 2 Aug
Birch, K. MB 2 Aug
Brown, D. J. G. MB
ChB 2 Aug
Dynan, Y. M. BSc MB
ChB 2 Aug
Naylor, J. R. MB
ChB 2 Aug

Flight Lieutenants

1995—contd

Temple, M. J. MB	
ChB	2 Aug
Davies, M. T. BSc MB	
ChB	7 Aug
Jackson, C. E. MB	
ChB	10 Aug

1996

Timperley, J. MB	
ChB	7 Feb
Singleton, J. F. MB	
ChB	22 Feb
Griffiths, J. S. MB	
BCh	1 Aug
McLaren, R. M. BM	
BCh	1 Aug
Butt, A. BSc MB BS	7 Aug
Cartwright, A. J. MB	
ChB	7 Aug
Chapple, S. A. MB	
ChB	7 Aug
Dalrymple, P. M. MB	
ChB	7 Aug
Grimmer, P. M. MB	
ChB	7 Aug
Whittle, C. L. MB	
BS	7 Aug
Woodcock, M. G. L.	
BM	8 Aug

1997

Huntbach, J. A. BSc BA	
BChir	13 Feb
Shepard, C. L. BM	1 Aug
Kendrew, J. M. MB	
BS	6 Aug
Knights, A. L. MB	
BS	6 Aug
Tagg, C. E. MB BS	6 Aug
Haseldine, D. C. MB	
ChB	7 Aug

1998

Becker, G. W. MB	
BChir	4 Feb

Flying Officers

1997

Hughes, S. N. MB	
BS	15 July
Mollan, I. A. MB	
ChB	6 Oct

Pilot Officers

1995

Houghton, L. J. MB	
ChB	26 Sept
Nicol, E. D. MB BS	26 Sept
Ostler, A. M. MB	
BS	26 Sept

1996

Bradley, J. C.	25 Nov
Drew, J. L.	25 Nov

1997

Hendriksen, D. A.	6 Oct
O'Reilly, D. J.	6 Oct
Tipping, R. D.	6 Oct

1998

Brown, A. M. R.	26 Jan
Mollan, S. P.	26 Jan
Smith, E. J. D.	26 Jan
Davy, A. P.	16 Mar
Shepherd, B. D.	
BSc	16 Mar

DENTAL BRANCH

Air Vice-Marshal

1997

McIntyre, Ian Graeme QHDS MSc BDS MGDSRCS(Eng) DDPHRCS FIMgt psc Born 9/7/43   1 July

Air Commodores

1994

Negus, Timothy Wilfred OBE BDS FDSRCS(Ed) LDSRCS Born 10/1/43   1 Jan

1997

Butler, Richard Michael QHDS MSc BDS MGDSRCS(Ed) qss Born 20/5/44   1 July

Group Captains

1987

Shepherd, Robert George BDS FDSRCPS LDSRCS MIMgt qss Born 16/1/41   29 July

1992

Reid, John BDS MGDSRCPS(Glas) psc Born 11/9/46   1 Jan

1994

Allen, Derrick Raymond MSc BDS MGDSRCS(Ed) Born 23/12/42   1 Jan

1996

Amy, David James MSc BDS MGDSRCS(Ed) qss Born 17/6/50   1 July
Armstrong, David Brian BDS DGDP(UK) LDSRCS Born 21/9/46   1 July

1997

Richardson, Peter Sandiford MSc BDS MGDSRCS(Eng) MGDSRCS(Ed) LDSRCS(Eng)
    DDPHRCS(Eng) Born 29/9/48   1 Jan
Ollivere, P. T. R. MSc BDS Born 16/4/47   6 Aug

1998

Rees, David John MSc BDS MGDSRCS(Eng) qs Born 5/5/53   1 July

Wing Commanders

1977

Hughes, J. C. BDS qss	23 June
Hobkinson, J. T.	
LDSRCS	13 July

1981

Swain, J. G. G. BDS qss	18 Dec

1984

Knowles, R. C. BDS	
LDSRCS	15 Dec

1989

Cornthwaite, P. W. BDS	
MGDSRCS(Ed]	
qs	6 Nov

1990

Gallagher, P. M. BDS	
BA MGDSRCS(Ed)	
qs	28 Feb

1992

Mellor, T. K. MB BCh	
BDS FDSRCPS	
FRCS(Ed)	13 Feb
Nottingham, J. A. BDS	
MGDSRCS(Ed)	
qs	2 Apr
Mayhew, M. T. MSc	
BDS DDPHRCS jsdc	
qs	5 Dec

1994

Monaghan, A. M. BDS	
FDSRCS(Eng)	
qss	12 Jan

1995

McCarthy, D. BDS	
LDSRCS qss	21 Apr

Brown, R. T. M. BDS	
MGDSRCS(Ed)	
qs	18 June
Gibson, D. G. BDS	29 Oct

1996

Knight, H. I. MSc BDS	
MGDSRCS(Eng)	
DDPHRCS	
LDSRCS	30 Jan
Senior, N. J. BDS	
MGDSRCS(Eng)	31 July
Harper, K. A. MSc BDS	
FDSRCS(Eng)	
MGDSRCS(Eng)	
MRD qss	1 Aug
Bows, R. W. BDS	
MGDSRCS(Ed)	
qss	22 Aug

1997

O'Donnell, J. J. BDS	
LDSRCS	3 Mar
Gibbons, A. J. MA BDS	
MB BChir FDSRCSEd	
FRCS (Edin) LDSRCS	
qss	16 Mar
Bambridge, D. E.	
BDS	5 Aug

1998

Birkett, A. C. BDS	2 Jan
Nelson, T. A. B. BChD	
FDSRCS(Eng)	3 Feb
Allan, K. T. BDS	4 Mar
Fleming, J. C. MSc BDS	
MGDSRCS(Eng)	
LDSRCS	4 Apr

Squadron Leaders

1990

Saunders, M. B. MSc	
BDS MGDSRCS(Eng)	11 July
Mitchell, M. BDS	19 July
Chadwick, A. R.	
BDS	10 Sept
Duffy, S. BDS	29 Oct

1991

Cox, J. J. LDSRCS	1 Apr
Brooks, E. A. S.	
BDS	6 July
Hamshaw, G. BSc BDS	16 July
Boyle, L. M. BDS	8 Sept
McDavitt, J. N. MSc	
BDS	
MGDSRCPS(Glas)	18 Dec

1992

Cook, C. BDS qss	4 Jan
Gowing, S. T. J. BDS	
qss	4 Jan
Rhodes, C. E. BDS	
MGDSRCPS(Glas)	4 Jan
Cook, E. BChD	23 Feb
Jones, T. W. MSc	
BDS	6 Mar
Frick, T. BDS	2 Aug
King, J. M. BDS	11 Aug
Austin, J. F. BDS	
MGDSRCPS(Glas)	
qss	13 Sept

1993

Andrews, N. A. G.	
BDS	20 Feb
Reith, M. J. BDS	10 Aug
Porteous, J. W.	
BDS	1 Dec

1994

Richardson, M. H.	
BDS	29 Jan
Feasey, J. M. M.	
BDS	1 Dec

Squadron Leaders

1995

Peak, J. D. BDS	
FDSRCSEng	1 Jan
Lloyd, M. V. BDS	20 Jan
Cooper, D. J. BDS	4 Feb

1996

Byford, M. BDS	13 Jan
Macbeth, N. D.	
BDS	25 Jan
Pratt, A. C. BDS	5 Feb
Laird, L. M. BDS	23 Aug
Hurst, S. E. BDS	25 Aug
Neppalli, R. P. K. BDS	
DGDPRCS	25 Aug
Doyle, S. B. BDS	1 Sept
Ilsley, J. D. BDS	1 Nov

1997

Wynne, J. E. BDS	17 Jan
Towlerton, A. J.	
BDS	23 May
Savage, A. BDS	
DGDP(UK)	17 Sept
Foster, M. R. BDS	
DGDP(UK)	14 Dec

Flight Lieutenants

1994

McLelland, R. G.	
BDS	12 Jan
Renfrew, A. H. BSc	
BDS	6 Mar
Scott, L. A. BDS	9 July

1995

Jones, I. R. BDS	23 June

1996

Clare, M. D. BDS	8 Aug
Clayton, D. R.	
BChD	8 Aug
King, M. L.	8 Aug

1997

Butler, S. R. BChD	7 Aug
Robb, S. M. BMSc	
BDS	7 Aug

1998

Burn, R. L. BDS	5 Feb
Ritchie, K. L. BDS	5 Feb
Smith, R. M. BDS	5 Feb

PRINCESS MARY'S ROYAL AIR FORCE NURSING SERVICE

AIR CHIEF COMMANDANT H.R.H. PRINCESS ALEXANDRA, The Hon. Lady Ogilvy, GCVO

All Officers of Princess Mary's Royal Air Force Nursing Service hold the qualification of Registered General Nurse or Registered Mental Nurse

Air Commodore

1994

Williams, Robert Henry RRC QHNS Born 13/10/44 +Ld.   1 July

Group Captain

1998

Forward, Bernard John BA ARRC RNT CertEd qs Born 27/1/48 + Ld.   1 July

Wing Commanders		Squadron Leaders			
				1993	
				McCulloch, J. qs	18 Feb
				Williams, W. B. RM	18 Feb
1992		**1981**		Eastburn, E. A.	30 May
Scofield, A. J. ARRC		Goodfellow, N. S. RM			
qss	1 Jan	qs	22 June	**1994**	
Welford, A. M. RRC RM					
qss	1 July			Gross, J. L. qs	10 Apr
		1987		Weir, H. ARRC RM	16 June
				Harper, P. J.	3 Nov
1994		Smith, J. A. RM qss	22 July		
Reid, R. A. OBE ARRC				**1995**	
RM	1 July	**1990**			
				Hurst, L. MA BSc	
1997		Massey, L. A. qs	24 June	CertFE	3 Feb
				Cromie, S. E.	6 Apr
Chew, L. RRC qs	1 Jan	**1991**		Baker, C. A. RM	4 Oct
				Beaumont, S. P. qs	12 Dec
		Laurence, R.	23 May		
1998		Wroe, B. CertEd qs	18 Sept		
		Henderson, C. A. ARRC		**1996**	
White, M. E. ARRC qs	1 July	RM qss	26 Dec		
				Devenport-Ward, A.	
				BSc RM DipN	14 Jan
		1992		Day, J. A. RM	27 Jan
				Callcott, S. T. RM	
		Warburton, A. M.	26 Feb	qss	2 Apr
		Shaw, M. J. MSc BSc		Barnes, M.	8 Apr
		CertEd(RNT)	3 Dec	Stewart, H. M.	15 Apr
				Gullidge, K. A.	9 June
				Ferguson, P. G.	25 June

Squadron Leaders

1996—contd

Roscoe, F. G. qss	5 July

1997

Petter-Bowyer, D. A. RM	21 Mar
Taylor, M. J. BSc	24 July
Oakley, S. J.	17 Nov

1998

Dickin, L.	10 Jan
Ward, P. J. ARRC qss	21 May

Flight Lieutenants

1990

Hutton, D. J.	10 July

1991

Burgess, D. A.	9 Jan
Merritt, J. C. RM	13 Jan
Cushen, P. B.	9 Feb
Mackie, K. C.	21 May
Evans, A. W.	26 June
Smith, P. A. RM	8 Aug
Hopper, T. M.	31 Dec

1992

Edwards, D. R.	14 Jan
Tue, N. S. DipN	18 Jan
Lockton, L. A.	31 Jan
Gibson, L. K.	5 Feb
Priestley, M. J.	5 Feb
Jones, D. C.	6 Mar
Meath, P.	29 May
Spragg, P. M.	15 Oct
Preece, A. D. RCSN	27 Nov

1993

Smart, C. A.	6 Feb
Denkowycs, I. L. RM	25 Apr
Timothy, N. F. M. BA	28 June
Jenner, B. C.	6 Sept
Ewart, A. P. G.	16 Sept
Payne, D. A.	17 Sept
Gardner, J.	8 Oct

1994

Ball, S. J. RM	6 Jan
Covill, L. M.	13 Jan
MacPherson, A. P.	3 Feb
Hymas, P. B. RM	8 Feb
Cuthbert, S. J.	20 Feb
Griffiths, T. A.	22 Feb
Wallace, J. H. RM	8 May
Raper, A.	21 May
Van Zwanenberg, G. qcc	9 June
Duffy, K. M.	26 June
Hecht, D. A. RSCN	28 July

Davenport, J. RM	3 Aug
Aird, B. G. BSc DipN	2 Sept
Edmondson, M. J.	18 Oct
Bedwell, L. C.	8 Nov
Whiting, D.	14 Nov
Harrison, R. J.	15 Nov

1995

Lamb, D. W.	2 May
Rapson, K.	21 June
Reilly, B. A.	7 Aug
English, M. E.	3 Sept
Rimmer, V. A. RM	27 Sept

1996

Hold, C. K.	15 Jan
Hutchison, F. M.	22 Apr
Brennan, K. D. BSc	7 May
Dyson, N. C.	27 July
Lester, A. J.	15 Oct

1997

Hill, M. K.	28 Apr
Pascoe, S. W.	27 May
Kiddey, V. K. RSCN RM	20 Aug
Phythian, S. M.	20 Aug
Swain, I. S.	1 Sept
Stratford-Fanning, P. J.	10 Oct

Flying Officers

1994

Bathgate, Y.	15 June
Ducker, S. J. BSc	11 Nov

1995

Pavitt, A. J.	24 June

1996

Lynn, S. B.	5 Mar

MEDICAL TECHNICIAN BRANCH
(MEDICAL SECTION)

Wing Commanders		Squadron Leaders		Flight Lieutenants	
1995		**1991**		**1993**	
Mayes, R. W. OBE PhD BSc CChem FRSC qss	1 Jan	Farmer, T. P.	11 Jan	Hill, D. M. W. MSc BSc FISM RMN qss	4 June
1998		**1994**		**1994**	
Stacey, J. qss	1 July	Murray, I. R.	20 Dec	Bain, R. MSc	4 June
				1995	
				Lawson, S. P. BSc qss	11 May
				1996	
				Jones, R. J. BA MCSP CertEd	1 June
				Dray, M. D.	2 Aug
				Earp, M. T.	2 Aug
				Beach, C. J.	27 Sept
				1997	
				Nixon, J. R. M.	22 Apr
				Mitchell, W. A. MIPD	26 July
				Biggs, C. J.	27 Dec

MEDICAL TECHNICIAN BRANCH

(DENTAL SECTION)

Flying Officers

1994

Culpan, D. S.	17 Aug
Maynard, M. R.	24 Sept
Tilling, E. J.	26 Nov

1996

Ulke, D.	10 Feb
Stezaker, M.	6 Oct

MEDICAL SECRETARIAL BRANCH

Wing Commanders		Squadron Leaders		Flight Lieutenants	
1990		**1986**		**1990**	
Bush, P. J. qs	1 Jan	Booker, T. T. qs	1 July	Court, P. G. BSc	31 Jan
				Baird, W. P.	22 Sept
				Ellis-Martin, P. qss	2 Nov
1992		**1992**		Acres, S. P.	21 Nov
Woods, T. L. qss	1 Jan	Allaway, R. J. BEd qss	1 Jan		
		Burgess, P. MSc		**1991**	
		DipMgmt qs	1 Jan		
1993		Williams, K. MIMgt		Fleetwood, W. M. qss	1 Feb
		qs	1 Jan		
Jarvis, J. A. MBE					
MHSM RMN qss	1 July			**1992**	
		1994			
				Robinson, J. SRN RMN	
1997		Cowan, A. DipMgmt		qss	21 Jan
		MRIPHH MIMgt		Choppen, P. I. BSc	
Lane, K. MBA DipMgmt		qs	1 Jan	CBiol MIBiol	8 Nov
qs	1 Jan	Quincey, N. J. qs	1 July		
Rippon, D. qss	1 July			**1993**	
		1995			
				McCay, D. D.	9 Nov
		Dalby, A. P. MSc MHSM		Smith, H. A. qss	4 Dec
		MIMgt DipHSM			
		qs	1 July	**1994**	
		Hoyle, D. L. qs	1 July		
				White, J. E.	2 June
		1997		Quinn, A. C.	
				DipMgmt	24 Sept
		Cranfield, A. qss	1 Jan		
		Batley, R. J. qss	1 July	**1996**	
				Covill, J. A.	21 Mar
		1998			
		MacDonald, G. W. B.		**1998**	
		MSc FICD qs	1 Jan		
		Staniforth, C. A.		Carlin, N. J.	19 Feb
		DipMgmt qs	1 Jan		

Flying Officer

1994

Miranda, D. A.   6 Oct

CIVIL CONSULTANTS

Mr P. Banks BDS MB BS FDSRCS MRCS LRCP (Oral and Maxillo-Facial Surgery)

Professor R. W. Beard MD MB BChir FRCOG (Obstetrics and Gynaecology)

Professor R. J. Berry RD Ost.J DPhil MD FRCP FRCR (HON FACR) FFOM (Radiobiology)

Professor R. S. Bluglass CBE MD FRCPsych FRCP DPM (Psychiatry)

Dr A. J. Boakes MSc MB BS FFARCS (Genito-Urinary Medicine)

Mr J. B. Booth FRCS (Otology)

Mr P. D. Burge FRCS (Orthopaedic (Hand) Surgery)

Dr A. K. Clarke BSc MB BS FRCP (Rheumatology and Rehabilitation)

Professor R. C. D. S. Coombes MD PhD FRCP (Medical Oncology)

Mr M. J. Coptcoat ChM FRCS(Urol)(Urology)

Mr C. B. Croft FRCS FRCS(Ed)(Laryngology)

Dr A. R. Cummin DM MRCP (Respitory Physiology)

Mr D. J. Dandy MD MChir FRCS (Knee Surgery)

Professor D. M. Denison PhD FRCP (Applied Physiology)

Mr M. A. Edgar MA MChir MB FRCS (Orthopaedic Surgery)

Professor P. H. Fentem MSc BSc MB ChB FRCP (Aviation Medicine)

Dr P. R. Goddard MD BSc MB BS FRCR DMRD (Computed Tomography and Magnetic Resonance Imaging)

Dr F. Stc. Golden OBE Phd MB BCh DAvMed (Survival Medicine)

Mr P Goldstraw FRCS(Eng) FRCS(Ed) (Thoracic Surgery)

Professor E. C. Gordon-Smith MA MSc MB FRCP FRCPath (Civil Consultant in Haematology)

Dr I. W. F. Hanham FCRP FRCR MA MB BChir MRCP FFR DMRT (Radiotherapy)

Professor J. M. Harrington CBE BSc MSc MD FRCP FFOM RCP (Epidemiology)

Professor J. Hayden FRCP FRCGP DCH DRCOG (General Practice)

Dr I. R. Hill OBE MA MD PhD MRCPath MRAeS LDS (Forensic Medicine)

Dr J. M. Holt MD FRCP (Medicine)

Dr G. R. V. Hughes MD FRCP (Rheumatology)

Professor H. S. Jacobs BA MD MB BChir FRCP FRCOG (Metabolic and Endocrine Disorders)

Mr D. H. A. Jones FRCS FRCSEd(Orth)(Paediatric Orthopaedic Surgery)

Dr J Keenan MA MB BChir FRCPath (Clinical Chemistry)

Mr B. G. H. Lamberty MA FRCS FRCSEd(Plastic Surgery)

Professor W. R. Lees FRCR FRACR(Hon) (Radiology)

Dr D. G. Lowe MD FRCS FRCPath FIBiol (Histology)

Dr E. B. MacDonald MB ChB FRCP(Glas) FRCP FFOM DIH (Occupational Medicine)

Professor D. G. McDevitt DSc MD FRCP FRSC FFPM (Experimental Medicine)

Dr C. M. Mckee MD MSc FRCP(UK) FFPHM (Public Health Medicine)

Professor D. McLeod FRCS FRCOphth (Ophthalmology (Retinal Surgery)

Dr A. T. Mitchell MB BS MRCP (Paediatrics)

Dr D. Murray FRCP (Dermatology)

Professor A. J. Newman Taylor OBE FRCP FFOM (Chest Diseases)

Professor Sir Keith Peters FRS (Renal Disorders)

Professor I. Phillips MA MD FRCP FRCPath (Microbiology)

Mr M. Powell FRCS (Neurosurgery)

Dr A. F. Rickards MB BS FRCP (Cardiology)

Dr D. Rule FDS DOrth MCCD RCS (Post Graduate Education)

Mr M. D. Sanders MB BS FRCP FRCS (Ophthalmology)

Dr J. W. Scadding BSc MB BS MD FRCP (Neurology)

Professor C. D. Stephens MDS FDSRCS(Edin) FDS DOrthRCS(Eng) (Orthodontics)

Dr J. M. Thomas MS MRCP FRCS (Oncology)

Mr J. P. S. Thomson DM MS FRCS (Surgery)

Mr J. K. H. Webb MB BS FRCS (Spinal Trauma)

Mr P. Worlock DM FRCS (Orthopaedic Trauma)

Dr G. B. Wyatt MB BS FRCP FFCM DTM&H DCH (Tropical Medicine)

HONORARY
CIVIL CONSULTANTS

Air Commodore A. J. C. Balfour CBE MA MB BChir FRCPath LMSSA DCP DTM&H MRAeS RAF (Retd) (Aviation Pathology)

A. J. Barwood OBE MRCS LRCP DPH DIH FRAeS Group Captain (Retd) (Accident Investigation)

B. J. Bickford MB BS FRCS (Thoracic Surgery)

Professor W. Burns DSc ChB FRCP DRCOG (Acoustic Science)

Professor S. Brandon MD MB BS DPM FRCPsych MRCP DCH (Psychiatry)

Dr S. J. Carne CBE MB BS MRCS LRCP FRCGP DCH (General Practice)

Air Vice Marshal J. Ernsting CB OBE PhD MB BS BSc FRAeS MFOM MRCS FRCP RAF(Retd) (Aviation Medicine)

Dr M. R. Geake FRCP (Chest Diseases)

Dr J. Harper MBE MB ChB FRCP(Edin) FRCPsych DPM (Psychiatry)

Dr J. C. Hasler OBE MD MA BS FRCGP DA DCM (General Practice)

Mr P. L. James FDS FRCS LRCP (Oral and Maxillo-Facial Surgery)

Dr R. C. Kocen TD FRCP (Neurology)

T. F. Macrae OBE DSc PhD (Nutrition)

Mr M. A. Makey MS FRCS (Thoracic Surgery)

Professor J. R. E. Mills DDS FDS DOrthRCS (Orthodontics)

Air Vice Marshal P. J. O'Connor CB OBE MD BCh FRCP(Edin) FRCPsych DPM, RAF (Retd) (Neuropsychiatry)

Professor J. P. Payne MB ChB FFARCS DA (Anaesthetics)

Dr D. A. D. Slattery MBE FRCP FFOM DIH (Occupational Medicine)

Dr Walter Somerville MD FRCP (Cardiology)

Dr A. G. Stansfeld MA(Cantab) MB BChi FRCPath (Histopathology)

Professor Sir Eric Stroud BSc MB BCh FRCP DCH (Paediatrics)

Air Commodore P. D. Sutton MB BS FRCR DMRD RAF (Retd) (Radiology)

Mr K. Till MA MB BCh FRCS (Paediatric Neurosurgeon)

Mr J. E. A. Wickham MS MD BSc FRCS FRCP FRCR (Urology)

Professor Sir Brian Windeyer MB BS FRCS FRCS(Edin) DMRE FFR (Radiotherapy)

CHAPLAINS BRANCH

The Air Member for Personnel administers the Chaplains Branch on behalf of the Minister of Defence for the Armed Forces

The Chaplains belonging to the Church of England are under the control of the Chaplain-in-Chief

Chaplains belonging to Churches other than the Church of England are under the control of the respective Principal Chaplains

Chaplains are known and addressed by their eccleciastical titles and not by the rank titles equivalent to their relative status in the RAF (QR 73)

Chaplain-in-Chief with the relative rank of Air Vice-Marshal

1995

The Venerable Peter Robin Turner QHC MTh BA AKC Born 8/3/42   .   .   .   .   26 Aug

Principal Chaplain: with the relative rank of Group Captain

1994

Church of Scotland—
Rev John Shedden CBE BD Born 23/6/43 .   .   .   .   1 Aug

1997

Roman Catholic—
The Rt Rev Mgr Edward Peter Hill QHC VG Born 8/8/43 .   .   .   .   3 Feb

1998

Methodist—
Rev R. O. Bayliss QHC SRN RMN Born 21/7/44 .   .   .   .   27 Mar

Chaplains with the relative rank of Wing Commander

1983

Church of England—
Rev N. A. Bryan BA. . . . . 11 Aug

1985

Church of England—
Rev R. Noble BA . . . . . 26 Sept

1988

Church of England—
Rev D. S. Mackenzie . . . . 21 Apr

Church of England—
Rev P. J. Abell . . . . . . 1 Sept

1989

Church of England—
Rev R. W. Bailey qs. . . . . 21 Apr

Church of England—
Rev R. D. Hesketh BA . . . 29 June

Church of England—
Rev A. P. Bishop QHC LTh . . . 5 Oct

1991

Church of England—
Rev I. M. Thomas MA qs . . . 2 Jan

Church of England—
Rev I. J. Weston MBE . . . . 18 Sept

Church of England—
Rev P. Sladen MA . . . . . 11 Dec

1992

Church of England—
Rev A. P. R. Fletcher BTh DipPasTh 14 May

1994

Church of England—
Rev T. R. Lee AKC qss . . . . 20 Jan

1996

Church of England—
Rev C. W. Long BA BTh . . . 6 June

Church of England—
Rev S. J. Ware BA . . . . . 6 June

Church of England—
Rev R. A. P. Ward qss . . . . 19 July

Roman Catholic—
Rev T. J. Devany . . . . . 14 Nov

1997

Methodist—
Rev G. H. Moore . . . . . 22 May

Church of England—
Rev. A. L. Willis BA. . . . . 14 Aug

Church of England—
Rev M. P. Roemmele MA . . . 13 Nov

1998

Church of England—
Rev C. Parnell-Hopkinson . . . 19 Feb

Church of England—
Rev I. F. Greenhalgh qss . . . 13 May

Church of Scotland—
Rev P. W. Mills BD qss . . . . 13 May

Church of Scotland—
Rev D. Shaw LTh . . . . . 13 May

Chaplains with the relative rank of Squadron Leader

1986

Roman Catholic—
Rev J. A. Daly . . . . . . 21 Jan

Baptist—
Rev J. R. Russell . . . . . 17 Mar

§ Temporarily holding the relative rank of Group Captain

Chaplains with the relative rank of Squadron Leader

1987

Church of England—
Rev E. Core BTh . . . . . 19 Jan

Church of England—
Rev C. W. K. Berry-Davies . . . 3 Mar

Church of England—
Rev J. W. G. Hughes MBE . . . 25 May

Church of England—
Rev M. F. Loveless . . . . . 28 Sept

1988

Church of England—
Rev D. J. Mckavanagh MA BD AKC 26 Jan

Church of England—
Rev L. E. D. Clark MBE . . . . 15 Feb

Church of England—
Rev N. P. Heron BA BTh . . . 10 May

Church of England—
Rev W. L. F. Mounsey . . . . 19 June

Church of England—
Rev L. E. Spicer. . . . . . 1 Aug

Church of England—
Rev D. T. Osborn BD AKC . . . 1 Nov

1989

Church of England—
Rev D. Wynne-Jones . . . . 31 Jan

Church of England—
Rev K. Maddy GRSM MA . . . 6 Mar

Church of Scotland—
G. T. Craig BD . . . . . . 3 Apr

Church of England—
Rev J. E. Coyne BA. . . . . 21 Aug

1990

Church of England—
Rev M. J. Elliott MTh PGDipTh . 15 Jan

Church of England—
Rev A. C. Gatrill BTh . . . . 15 Jan

Church of England—
Rev A. J. D. Gilbert BA qs . . . 15 Jan

Church of England—
Rev A. J. Davies MTh BA PGCE qss 21 May

Church of England—
Rev I. McFadzean MA BD . . . 21 May

Church of England—
Rev I. S. Ward BD qss . . . . 21 May

United Reform Church—
Rev J. G. Petrie. . . . . . 25 June

Methodist—
Rev R. J. Taylor. . . . . . 25 June

Roman Catholic—
Rev A. J. Wilson . . . . . . 27 Aug

1991

Church of England—
Rev N. B. P. Barry BA . . . . 25 Feb

Church of England—
Rev J. P. Chaffey BA qss . . . 20 May

Presbyterian—
Rev D. A. Edgar. . . . . . 20 May

Roman Catholic—
Rev P. A. Owens . . . . . 20 May

Church of England—
Rev A. D. Hewett BA . . . . 1 July

Church of England—
Rev A. B. McMullon BSc . . . 1 July

Church of Scotland—
Rev A. J. Jolly qcc . . . . . 9 Aug

Church of England—
Rev R. J. Pentland . . . . . 26 Aug

1992

Church of England—
Rev J. K. Wilson . . . . . 13 Jan

Church of England—
Rev C. E. Hewitt MA BA . . . 24 Feb

Church of England—
Rev G. Williams . . . . . 6 Mar

Methodist—
Rev R. B. Hardman . . . . . 25 Aug

Church of England—
Rev A. J. Turner . . . . . 25 Aug

1993

Roman Catholic—
Rev J. M. White BSc . . . . 12 Jan

Chaplains with the relative rank of Squadron Leader

1993—contd

Church of England—
Rev A. D. Bissell . . . . . 23 Aug

Roman Catholic—
Rev D. C. Hewitt . . . . . 23 Aug

Roman Catholic—
Rev C. Webb . . . . . . 15 Nov

Church of England—
Rev J. W. K. Taylor MSSc BD BTh. 7 Dec

1994

Church of England—
Rev I. R. Colson BSc . . . . 21 Feb

Church of England—
Rev S. P. Iredale BA . . . . 21 Feb

Church of England—
Rev J. C. Hetherington . . . . 5 Sept

1996

Church of England—
Rev J. F. Hudghton BA . . . . 10 Aug

1997

Church of England—
Rev A. T. Coates . . . . . 8 Aug

Church of England—
Rev I. A. Jones BA . . . . . 8 Aug

Chaplains with the relative rank of Flight Lieutenant

1993

Roman Catholic—
Rev J. E. Caulfield BD . . . 7 Aug

Roman Catholic—
Rev M. W. Hodges MTh . . . 7 Aug

Methodist—
Rev M. A. Olanrewaju MA . . . 7 Aug

Church of England—
Rev P. A. Rennie BSc LTh . . . 7 Aug

1994

Church of England—
Rev J. M. Beach BA BSc . . . 3 July

1998

Methodist—
Rev K. M. Hart . . . . . . 5 Feb

Church of England—
Rev T. Wright BSc . . . . . 5 Feb

LEGAL BRANCH

Air Vice-Marshal

1997

Weeden, John LLB Born 21/6/49   (Solicitor)   1 July

Air Commodore

1998

Charles, Richard Anthony LLB Born 24/2/54   (Solicitor)   1 Jan

Group Captains

1998

Barlow, Jonathan Kim Edward Born 21/4/54   (Solicitor)   1 Jan
Boothby, William Henry BA Born 18/9/51   (Solicitor)   1 Jan

Wing Commanders	Squadron Leaders	Flight Lieutenants
1992	**1991**	**1996**
McGrigor, A. J. B. (Solicitor) 14 Mar	Howard, A. C. LLB (Barrister) 25 Oct	Dunn, R. J. LLB qs (Solicitor) 8 Feb
		Dureau, S. LLB qcc (Solicitor) 8 Feb
1993	**1993**	Foster, M. S. LLB qab qcc (Solicitor) 8 Feb
Burns, P. A. BA (Solicitor) 9 June	Connell, P. J. BA (Barrister) 2 July	Leonard, I. LLB (Solicitor) 8 Feb
		Donington, S. J. LLB (Solicitor) 8 Aug
1994	**1994**	Moore, N. J. LLB (Barrister) 8 Aug
Baker, T. T. J. LLB (Solicitor) 21 July	Kell, S. J. LLB (Barrister) 25 Aug	Spinney, P. C. LLB (Solicitor) 8 Aug
		Wood, T. J. LLB (Solicitor) 8 Aug
1995	**1997**	
Wood, C. N. W. MA (Barrister) 4 Jan	Rowlinson, S. P. LLB (Solicitor) 18 Aug	**1997**
Harding, G. J. LLB (Solicitor) 21 Jan		Mardell, A. LLB (Solicitor) 6 Feb
Ash, D. LLB (Solicitor) 3 Feb		
Irvine, L. J. MA Dip-Law (Barrister) 5 Nov		

Flight Lieutenants

1998

Baird, N. J. LLB (Solicitor)	5 Feb
Cowley, A. M. LLB (Barrister)	5 Feb
McKendrick, A. G. LLB (Solicitor)	5 Feb

DIRECTORS OF MUSIC

Wing Commander	Squadron Leader	Flight Lieutenants
1998	**1997**	**1991**
Wiffin, R. K. BA FTCL LRAM ARCM 1 July	Stirling, S. L. MA BMus FTCL LRAM ARCM 15 Aug	Compton, D. W. ARCM 17 Aug
		1992
		Stubbs, D. J. G. BA PGCE ARCM LGSM 29 Mar
		1994
		Bain, G. J. BA MIL LRAM ARCM 10 Oct

WARRANT OFFICERS

1979

Beasley, E. J. MBE BEM	13 Jun

1981

Harrison, C. J.	22 June

1982

Rose, R. E. BEM	4 May
Withers, R. M.	19 July
Griggs, D. F. C. MBE	23 Aug

1983

Hodson, J. C.	31 Jan
Park, T. B. B.	23 June
Willis, R. J. AFM	19 Sept
Hetherington, D.	3 Oct
France, H. J. AFM	10 Dec

1984

Bacon, D. J.	28 Feb
Kilroy, G. R.	22 Mar
Goodman, K. R. J. MBE	9 Apr
Andrews, J. B. BEM	30 Apr
Thorrowgood, I. G.	9 July
Ellis, G. L.	23 July
Carter, B. J.	1 Oct
Cocker, D. J.	1 Oct

1985

Tipper, P. T. V.	21 Jan
Ash, G. D. MBE	28 Jan
Valentine, J. C.	20 Feb
Cornett, A.	1 Mar
Leese, S. MBE	6 Mar
Stock, C. J.	8 July
Williams, A. T. MBE	19 Aug
Higginson, E. J. MBE	27 Aug
Clouston, M.	9 Sept
Neale, D.	16 Sept
Seddon, J.	8 Oct
Angood, D. A. BEM	14 Oct
Berry, I. W.	4 Nov

Davies, D. E.	11 Nov
Cooper, R. G.	13 Nov
Weeks, R. A. F.	25 Nov

1986

Ballantyne, T. B. MBE	3 Feb
Jones, K. L.	25 Feb
Hooper, R. C.	1 Apr
Martin, P. H. MBE	2 Apr
Tainsh, K. J. MBE	7 Apr
Lewis, K. A. C.	19 May
Winfield, A. P.	19 May
Gipson, P. S.	30 May
Hughes, R.	2 June
Sweeney, E. W. T.	2 June
Peel, D. G. MBE	9 June
Benford, A.	16 June
Hodgson, D.	16 June
Leslie, A. W.	30 June
Hunter, J. J. MBE BEM	14 July
Wills, C. R.	28 July
Bradford, I. D. R. H.	1 Aug
Austen, N. E. P.	4 Aug
Morris, W.	11 Aug
Figgins, T. J.	26 Aug
Chandler, R. A. BEM	3 Nov
Burgess, H. H. M.	10 Nov
Turner, T. J.	10 Nov
Brailey, D. O. MBE	13 Nov
Wells, P. A.	24 Nov
Coppenhall, L. V.	15 Dec
Vince, L. R.	15 Dec

1987

Holdsworth, S.	12 Jan
McGrath, S. C.	27 Jan
Wishart, R. T.	16 Mar
McCombie, S.	15 Apr
Reddell, D. J.	24 Apr
Patrick, A. K. MBE	27 Apr
Melville, A. D. BEM	2 May
Rudling, B. J.	11 May
Voisey, D.	18 May
Harris, T. C.	19 May
Cutler, C. J.	1 June
Sweeney, P. MBE	1 June
Plaxton, G.	15 June
Whitbourn, P. J. MBE	15 June
Kavanagh, J. J.	17 June

Turner, B. M.	22 June
Heat, M. A. R.	6 July
Parkin, K. E.	6 July
Facey, D. W.	20 July
Gough, A. J. MBE BEM	20 July
Kendall, V. C.	20 July
Sparrow, B.	27 July
Blair, J. R.	3 Aug
Jarrel, P. A. MBE	3 Aug
Lacey, D. M.	3 Aug
Roffey, J. M. MBE	3 Aug
Coppell, D. J. A. BEM	10 Aug
Ogilvie, L. W.	13 Aug
Goodlad, D.	17 Aug
Standley, J. F.	17 Aug
Kellas, J.	24 Aug
Marshall, T. C.	2 Sept
Parker, B. BEM	7 Oct
Scullion, C. J.	3 Nov
Hamilton-Wilks, B. P.	6 Nov
Kearney, W. J. C. MBE BEM	30 Nov
Blair, T. F. BEM	1 Dec
Wheeler, B. BEM	9 Dec

1988

Ralph, P. J.	2 Feb
Black, G.	15 Feb
Oswald, I. W.	15 Feb
George, I. H.	29 Feb
Gray, R. C.	1 Mar
Munro, D. R. MBE	7 Mar
Siggs, G. S. BEM	14 Mar
Day, E. C. MBE	11 Apr
Beaty, R. B.	18 Apr
Williams, D. H.	20 Apr
Hardie, A. G.	2 May
Kirkbride, J. S.	2 May
Anderson, E. T. L.	9 May
Bailey, P. W.	9 May
Taylor, K. L.	9 May
Hughes, B. W.	23 May
Wallace, S. E.	23 May
Wass, M.	23 May
Libby, R. L.	31 May
Harding, D. A.	1 June
Palmer, R. P. A. BEM	13 June
Males, D.	27 June
Bradley, A. C. BEM	4 July
Hodgetts, R. D.	4 July
Penrose, B. L.	4 July
Powell, M.	4 July
Baker, H. J.	11 July

1988—contd		White, W. MBE	26 June	Roberts, R. G.	8 Jan
		Gore, M. F.	3 July	Woods, K. W.	9 Jan
Johnston, T. A. MBE		Allcock, M. W.	10 July	Allgood, D. T.	22 Jan
BEM	11 July	Dixon, M. G.	10 July	Chalmers, M. A.	29 Jan
Ryan, K. R.	12 July	Morgan, W. BEM	10 July	Radford, A. J.	5 Feb
Fray, R. A.	18 July	Hutchinson, W.	17 July	Smith, J. A.	5 Feb
Hicks, C. J. G. BEM	18 July	Lee, P. J.	17 July	Smith, J. D.	16 Feb
Bailey B. J. BEM	19 July	Leigh, R. A.	17 July	Cain, B. BEM	26 Feb
Lay, P. C.	19 July	Skelton, M.	17 July	Angus, E. B. BEM	5 Mar
MacDonald, A.	1 Aug	Steadman, K.	27 July	Goodwin, A. R. P. BEM	5 Mar
Munro, V. H.	1 Aug	Knowles, A.	30 July	Turley, E. P.	5 Mar
Smith, N. P.	7 Aug	Evans, M. J.	31 July	Walley, I. J.	19 Mar
Ford, J.	8 Aug	Smith, D.	31 July	Fields, B. G.	26 Mar
Dawson, P. J.	14 Aug	Welsh, B. H.	31 July	Herd, I.	29 Mar
Nott, J. L.	22 Aug	Brennan, N. P.	7 Aug	Dix, G.	1 Apr
Shaw, R. G. MBE BEM	30 Aug	Tappin, D. BEM	7 Aug	Blyth, R.	2 Apr
Norman, W.	5 Sept	Kidd, R. D.	10 Aug	Cloke, C. J.	2 Apr
Ayres, P. C. R. MBE	8 Sept	Menzies, H. D. P.	10 Aug	Short, R. M.	2 Apr
Johnson, P. E.	12 Sept	Last, A. K.	14 Aug	Smith, M. R.	2 Apr
Pashley, D. A.	28 Sept	Burgess, R. D.	21 Aug	Truelove, A. S.	2 Apr
Saker, G.	30 Sept	Curzon, P.	21 Aug	Dickinson, M. D.	4 Apr
Francis, R. A.	21 Oct	Macrae, A. R.	22 Aug	Wattam, P.	11 Apr
Anderson, P. J.		Sinclair, J. G.	30 Aug	Stephens, D. L.	
MBE	24 Oct	Fletcher, E. T.	4 Sept	BEM	16 Apr
Connell, O. BEM	24 Oct	Snitch, P. A. BEM	8 Sept	Tonkin, R. J.	21 Apr
Turner, L. G.	24 Oct	Hyde, J. F.	11 Sept	May, J. H. MBE	
Raw, M. G.	28 Oct	Hyde, R.	18 Sept	BEM	24 Apr
Reddick, G.	7 Nov	Herbert, J. M.	25 Sept	Bilner, C. J. BEM	29 Apr
Pittard, G.	14 Nov	Hannah, K.	28 Sept	Smith, E. MBE	2 May
Bradbury, M. J.	30 Nov	Collins, J. P. BEM	1 Oct	Griggs, J.	9 May
Dunthorn, D. R.	5 Dec	Fosh, G. E. BEM	2 Oct	Hedinburgh, R.	21 May
McHugh, R. MBE	9 Dec	Hare, L. G.	3 Oct	Garfoot, B. R.	25 May
		Mullen, J. L.	6 Oct	Crisp, J. A.	28 May
		Philp, G. H. G. C. BEM	9 Oct	Green, D. E. MBE	
1989		Simons, T. C.	9 Oct	BEM	4 June
		Leiper, E. A.	16 Oct	Anderson, C. C.	8 June
O'Reilly, M. V. MBE	16 Jan	Davies, T. R. W.	18 Oct	Norris, I. M.	11 June
Thompson, W. W.	8 Feb	Greer, D. W.	23 Oct	Gorman, J. W.	18 June
Hughes, S. BEM	14 Feb	Butcher, D. J.	30 Oct	Bowskill, A. S. P.	25 June
Aitken, J. O.	20 Feb	Farr, N.	30 Oct	Smith, C. MBE	
Wright, J. R. B. BEM	20 Feb	Costello, G. BEM	3 Nov	BEM	29 June
Campbell, K. A.	13 Mar	Page, D. C.	6 Nov	Lee, D. M. J. MBE	
Flinn, W.	13 Mar	Roberts, P.	6 Nov	BEM	2 July
Morris, W. R. J.	13 Mar	Stewart, A. B. MBE	27 Nov	Watling, N. D.	2 July
McGilligan, M.	28 Mar	Clark, A. J.	29 Nov	Gibson, W. M.	13 July
Livesey, G. BEM	31 Mar	Collins, W.	2 Dec	Salisbury, E. MBE	
Kelly, P. J. MBE	3 Apr	Houlden, D.	4 Dec	BEM	16 July
Hanson, J.	17 Apr	Lunnon, D. W. J. MBE		Squire, D. E.	16 July
Sansome, J. S.	17 Apr	BEM	4 Dec	Nicholson, R.	18 July
Prior, A. S.	19 Apr	Hopkins, M. J. K.	5 Dec	Lynch, G. T.	23 July
Gormley, A.	27 Apr	Barnsley, C. J.	11 Dec	Allen, D. E.	30 July
Gardner, D. H.	4 May	Wilce, R. T.	20 Dec	Lee, P. V.	30 July
Marcer, P.	8 May	Campbell, R. G.	25 Dec	Steel, J. D.	30 July
Carnan, B. N.	22 May			Woodley, B. W.	30 July
McNalty, T. A. BEM	22 May			Norton, G.	5 Aug
Lamb, C.	27 May	**1990**		Carter, R.	6 Aug
Howard, J.	30 May			Millward, G.	6 Aug
Braithwaite, T.	12 June	Aitken, R. C.	3 Jan	Grimshaw, G. A.	13 Aug
Gant, R. W.	19 June	Hampson, A. J.	8 Jan	Jordan, M. R.	20 Aug
Haveron, A. B. BEM	19 June	Martin, J.	8 Jan	Cheshire, A. J.	28 Aug

1990—contd		Sparks, B. J.	17 June	Hocking, D. S.	6 July
		Marr, I. R. W.	24 June	Curson, R. G.	20 July
Julian, P. J. MBE		Bloomfield, P. R.	1 July	Gass, I.	20 July
Born	28 Aug	Carr, A. L. BEM	11 July	Winspear, R. I.	27 July
Rose, M. R.	28 Aug	Eversden, P. W. A.	15 July	Tyler, C. R.	2 Aug
Smith, M. I.	28 Aug	Akers, P. A.	22 July	Bigham, J. C.	10 Aug
Vater, J. BEM	28 Aug	Walker, J. M.	22 July	Evans, G.	10 Aug
Wesley, D. A.	28 Aug	Jones, B. J.	29 July	Jones, D.	10 Aug
Whitelaw, H.	28 Aug	Whyte, P. MBE	29 July	McGill, B.	10 Aug
Belshaw, P. J.	10 Sept	Lamb, J.D. BEM	7 Aug	Palmer, N. R.	10 Aug
Dodd, D. J.	28 Sept	Giles, G. G.	12 Aug	Tibble, C. G.	14 Sept
Blackett, P.	1 Oct	Smailes, M. J.	19 Aug	Jones, M. B.	25 Sept
Daniels, R. A.	1 Oct	Walkett, D.	26 Aug	Mc Cune, T. BEM	5 Oct
Tyler, P. A.	1 Oct	Claypole, A.	27 Aug	Waterhouse, A. H.	5 Oct
Ashwood, A. J.	4 Oct	Gillett, P.	2 Sept	Jones, D. R.	12 Oct
Day, A. J. MBE BEM		Taylor, M.	2 Sept	Love, A. J.	12 Oct
Born	8 Oct	Fry, R. P.	4 Sept	Andrew, K. MBE	
Telford, B.	8 Oct	Jones, R.	9 Sept	BEM	23 Nov
Cowling, N. W. F.	10 Oct	Hutchinson, R. C.		Streek, M. A.	30 Nov
Foulds, R. J.	17 Oct	MBE	30 Sept	Crossman, A. A.	
Smooker, E. P.	22 Oct	Price, I.	30 Sept	MBE	18 Dec
King, M. R.	5 Nov	Owen, T. W. BEM	7 Oct	Goswell, B.	21 Dec
Fuller, S.	19 Nov	Wilson, R. B.	14 Oct		
Chaplin, A. J. MBE	3 Dec	Graham, W. J. BEM	21 Oct		
Hinkley, R. W.	3 Dec	Crump, S. A.	4 Nov	**1993**	
John, G. L.	4 Dec	Williams, W. E. R.	4 Nov		
McKenzie, K.	10 Dec	Shakespeare, N. R.		Andrews, T. B.	4 Jan
		BEM	18 Nov	Green, T. J.	4 Jan
		Pearce, J. M.	25 Nov	Threlfall, M.	11 Jan
1991		Hargreaves, R.	16 Dec	Smith, K. A. MBE	31 Jan
		Shand, G. S.	17 Dec	Morris, K. J.	25 Feb
Gray, B. T.	7 Jan			O'Brien, D. J.	1 Mar
Renwick, D. T.	7 Jan			Singfield, J. T.	15 Mar
Walters, M.	7 Jan	**1992**		Percy, D. W. BEM	5 Apr
Peacock, A. M.	11 Jan			Sainty, P.	5 Apr
Hughes, R.	21 Jan	Bainbridge, J. W.	1 Jan	Sanderson, J. A.	5 Apr
Dunphy, A. J. MBE	4 Feb	Goddard, M. J.		Walker, D.	5 Apr
Tombs, F. E.	4 Feb	BEM	6 Jan	Callaghan, A. J.	19 Apr
Dowding, H. J.	5 Feb	Lewis, K. G.	6 Jan	Andrews, N.	26 Apr
Bolderson, G.	25 Feb	Williams, N. E.		Williams, J. H.	4 May
Churchyard, A. C.	1 Mar	BEM	13 Jan	Mason, J. P.	1 June
Shiells, A. D.	4 Mar	Palmer, A. P. K.		Mitchell, R.	1 June
Honey, S. J.	14 Mar	BEM	1 Feb	Olphert, J. M. B.	1 June
Pointon, D.	25 Mar	McMurdo, J. M.	27 Feb	Short, E. J. BEM	1 June
Nightingale, J. A. BEM	2 Apr	Stockdale, P. H. MBE	9 Mar	Fleming, R. J.	7 June
Jones, T. I.	3 Apr	Ferris, E. J.	6 Apr	Hurd, A. A. BEM	14 June
Billingsley, J. L.	8 Apr	Haward, B. T.	6 Apr	Hope, D. R.	21 June
Eden, G. C.	8 Apr	Ingledew, V. E. MBE		Lowe, R. F. BEM	22 June
Tappenden, B. P.	8 Apr	BEM	27 Apr	Ayres, M. F. W.	28 June
Lane, A.	15 Apr	Luckhurst, A. R.	27 Apr	Hannis, J.	28 June
Rees, D. A. BEM	15 Apr	Mallison, J. G.	11 May	Williams, R. J.	29 June
Stevens, J. H.	7 May	Gill, K.	18 May	Lambert, S. W.	5 July
Boissel, T. K.	13 May	O'Neill, P. J. BEM	18 May	Tully, R. C.	5 July
Ward, B. J.	13 May	Pitt, W. R.	18 May	Bunnett, P. S.	12 July
Davidson, M. A.	21 May	Sparks, C. J.	18 May	Dark, W. J.	12 July
Brown, A. F.	28 May	Hall, R. R. J.	1 June	Macrae, J. C. MBE	12 July
Cale, B.	28 May	Molyneaux, R. C.	8 June	Brooks, C. BEM	19 July
Dring, M. C.	28 May	Low, W. R.	15 June	Duff, J.	19 July
Robinson, P.	3 June	Turnbull, S. W.	29 June	Follett, S. K.	19 July
Robertson, D.	17 June	Farrell, T. D. BEM	6 July	Hall, K. E.	19 July

1993—contd

Milne, A. P. R.	26 July
Thompson, D. J.	26 July
Young, R.	26 July
Sowerby, P. J.	29 July
Osbourne, A. M.	30 July
Wylie, J. S.	2 Aug
Scott, R.	9 Aug
Kennedy, I.	16 Aug
Murray, D. G.	23 Aug
Sewell, C. P.	23 Aug
Summersgill, J. R. BA	23 Aug
Collins, J. A.	31 Aug
Edgeworth, J. R.	1 Sept
Holmes, S. W.	13 Sept
Cruze, D. J.	15 Sept
Scott, P. K.	20 Sept
Williamson, J. A.	27 Sept
Gaynor, J. F.	4 Oct
Hoban, C.	4 Oct
Kirton, W. S.	4 Oct
Shipley, R.	25 Oct
Harrison, M.	29 Oct
Farrell, I.	1 Nov
Winters, I. S.	1 Nov
Shepherdson, D.	8 Nov
Clements, M. M.	9 Nov
Pengilly, D. F.	15 Nov
Owen, P.	13 Dec
Wilson, K. MBE	13 Dec

1994

Bray, J. H.	14 Jan
Crane, S. M.	17 Jan
Wilcox, J. A.	17 Jan
Hancock, M. J.	23 Jan
Hutchinson, D.	1 Feb
Gard, B. J.	7 Feb
Wood, J. R.	7 Feb
McVey, F.	8 Feb
Harper, J. C.	21 Feb
Williams, K.	21 Feb
Crowe, D. J.	28 Feb
Kynaston, T. G.	28 Feb
Peirce, D.	28 Feb
Regan, D.	7 Mar
Bromley, A. F.	18 Mar
Thom, I.	21 Mar
Downe, D. F.	22 Mar
Lloyd, R. C.	28 Mar
Lynch, C.	28 Mar
Wellstead, V. J.	28 Mar
Forster, L. E.	5 Apr
Gardiner, R. C.	5 Apr
Heaton, R. J.	5 Apr
Thomas, A. G. MBE	11 Apr

Powell, P. J.	25 Apr
Ramsdale, L. J.	25 Apr
Ayling, J. R.	3 May
Meakin, D. R. MBE	9 May
Pickering, H. K.	13 May
Cardy, B. M. MBE	16 May
Dutton, G. W. MBE BEM	16 May
Lines, R.	16 May
Nelson, J.	16 May
Frame, O. G. MBE	23 May
Long, S. M. BEM	31 May
McKee, J. J. BEM	31 May
Chapman, M. L.	1 June
Hall, M. Mc L.	6 June
Champion, D. R.	13 June
Fell, G.	13 June
Stewart, J. B.	13 June
Mackie, J. P.	16 June
Attard, J.	4 July
Bate, R. A.	4 July
Coughlan, M. J.	4 July
Exton, N. P.	4 July
Finbow, B. C.	4 July
Robson, T.	4 July
Hull, P. BEM	10 July
Magee, B. MBE	18 July
Whitfield, C.	18 July
Fryer, K. P.	25 July
Jones, P.	25 July
Rawle, A. P. MBE BEM	25 July
Cairns, E. J.	1 Aug
Morgan, D. W. MBE BEM	1 Aug
Hopkins, B.	15 Aug
Williams, G. M.	15 Aug
Hunt, G. R.	30 Aug
McAllister, G.	31 Aug
Clarkson, J. D.	5 Sept
Mikolajewski, J. MBE	5 Sept
Hunter, I. N.	12 Sept
Brimacombe, K. P.	3 Oct
Moore, L.	3 Oct
Gray, J.	13 Oct
Clarke, T.	17 Oct
Johnson, C. G.	31 Oct
Kane, F. H. Mc.	31 Oct
Keng, F. T.	31 Oct
Ruhle, C. J. K.	31 Oct
Smith, J. B.	31 Oct
Ashman, W. L.	1 Nov
Walliman, C. G. M.	1 Nov
Pullen, C. R.	7 Nov
Davidson, J. H.	21 Nov
Hamilton, G. V.	28 Nov
Kilner, I. F.	4 Dec
Feeney, P. J.	5 Dec

Wark, S.	12 Dec

1995

Byford, M. C.	3 Jan
Moss, P. G.	3 Jan
Trangmar, J. M.	3 Jan
Jones, C. W.	4 Jan
Ledsham, T. A.	9 Jan
Bennett, D. G.	16 Jan
Wilson, J.	21 Jan
Fewings, P. A.	20 Feb
Asty, W.	27 Feb
Meldrum, D. H. A. BEM	27 Feb
Edwards, J. C. MBE	1 Mar
Hull, D.	6 Mar
Maggs, J. N.	20 Mar
Beal, N. P.	21 Mar
Fox, T.	27 Mar
Moulton, L. P.	5 May
Woodbridge, F. D.	9 May
Neal, P. L.	30 May
Baker, A. J.	5 June
Kerr, A. McA. MBE	5 June
Crawford, W. F. C.	12 June
Jennings, M. D.	12 June
McQuiston, C. A.	12 June
Anderson, B. M.	19 June
Thain, D. J.	19 June
Marjoram, R. A.	26 June
Green, N. MBE	3 July
Hardinges, D. A.	3 July
Lord, B. D.	4 July
Bennett, G. J.	17 July
Acton, A.	28 July
Harrison, R. A.	1 Aug
Kirkham, B. M.	1 Aug
Davis, A. P.	2 Aug
Purvis, M. QGM	29 Aug
O'Reilly, D. F.	1 Sept
Gascoigne, P. G.	4 Sept
Taylor, R.	4 Sept
Sherry, J. F. MBE	1 Oct
Cahill, D. P.	2 Oct
Williams, L. F.	2 Oct
McMath, J. G. F. BEM	23 Oct
Pollard, J. S.	6 Nov
Barton, T. F.	12 Nov
Nightingale, P. W.	13 Nov
Robertson, M.	20 Nov
Pettitt, D. J.	27 Nov
Boyd, W. J.	4 Dec
Hebert, C. J.	4 Dec
Horsburgh, J.	4 Dec
Mason, M. K.	4 Dec

1996		Houghton, T. A.	5 Aug	Smith, G.	2 Dec
		Nicol, B.	5 Aug	Tarran, J. V.	2 Dec
Layton, D. J. H.	2 Jan	Ogilvie, W.	5 Aug	Thorne, W. G.	2 Dec
Taylor, M.	2 Jan	Steen , G.	5 Aug	Bradfield, S. P.	9 Dec
Hassall, B.	3 Jan	Webb, T. W.	5 Aug	Clark, P. A.	9 Dec
Jackson, J.	3 Jan	Burton, P. R.	12 Aug	Blackman, C. A. R.	9 Dec
Bennett, A. E.	8 Jan	Fitzgerald, G. G.	12 Aug	Pepper, G. A.	9 Dec
Burns, W. J.	8 Jan	Blanchard, W. J.	19 Aug	Chopping, D. V.	16 Dec
Knowling, C. C.	8 Jan	Currie, W. R.	19 Aug	Peace, M. J.	16 Dec
Morrisroe, T. G.	8 Jan	Hynam, R. A.	19 Aug	Lang, D. J.	23 Dec
Sealy, K. A.	8 Jan	Jordan, M. B.	19 Aug	Mepham, K. D.	30 Dec
Battersby, P. G.	22 Jan	Spicer, A. D.	19 Aug	Stoddart, D. R.	30 Dec
Martin, A. J.	25 Jan	Williams, G.	26 Aug		
Clarkson, D.	5 Feb	Armitage, R.	27 Aug		
Hardy, D. P.	5 Feb	Smaldon, C. R. E.	1 Sept	**1997**	
Norman, G. L. BEM	12 Feb	Dennis, R. H.	2 Sept		
Looen, D. J. F.	26 Feb	Ditty, J. M.	2 Sept	Wightwick, D. R.	3 Jan
Edward, J. G.	4 Mar	Payne, J. K. H.	2 Sept	Blackburn, A. J.	6 Jan
Guest, A. H.	4 Mar	Saul, A. W.	2 Sept	Gwilliam. M. J.	6 Jan
Russell, B.	4 Mar	Smith, S. P.	2 Sept	Kelly, B. S. E.	6 Jan
Yelland, D. J.	4 Mar	Collicut, G. J.	9 Sept	Loker, T. J. A.	6 Jan
Trew, A. N. F.	11 Mar	Hockley, T. G.	9 Sept	Mahoney, B. R.	6 Jan
Hand, T. R. BEM	12 Mar	Logue, M. J.	9 Sept	Nash, T. M.	6 Jan
Tipler, G. C.	13 Mar	Copsey, L. J.	16 Sept	Rollings, G. M.	6 Jan
Burgess, R. W.	18 Mar	Dykes, P. A.	16 Sept	Cradock, W.	13 Jan
Ralph, R. R.	18 Mar	Hodgett, P.	16 Sept	Nuttall, G.	20 Jan
Simmonds, A. M.	18 Mar	Nash, W. V.	16 Sept	Browne, M. S. BEM	27 Jan
Slowey, J. L.	18 Mar	Sheppard, A. B.	16 Sept	Spencer, B. R.	27 Jan
Salmon, A. C.	31 Mar	Staton, E.	16 Sept	Strange, J. M.	27 Jan
Smith, F. W. J. BEM	31 Mar	Shipley, S.	18 Sept	Werndly, S.	29 Jan
Harris, J. R.	1 Apr	Dadds, J.	23 Sept	Bennett, R. J. MEB	3 Feb
Ramsay, W.	12 Apr	Granger, T. W.	23 Sept	Davies, T. B.	3 Feb
Bowden, J.	3 Apr	Muncey, R. D.	23 Sept	Farmer, W. G.	3 Feb
Gilbert, P. C. BEM	7 Apr	Taylor, D. J.	23 Sept	Gilroy, F. A.	3 Feb
Donald, P. H.	15 Apr	Toyne, D.	23 Sept	Morning, J. L. BEM	3 Feb
Bray, T. A. G.	7 May	Blackledge, W. E.	30 Sept	McDonald, P. R.	3 Feb
Lowry, W. S.	13 May	Dunn, R. G.	30 Sept	North, H. S.	3 Feb
Anderton, N. H.	20 May	Hogg, R. J.	30 Sept	Pritchard, R. D.	3 Feb
Harding, M. H. R.	20 May	Credland, A. C.	7 Oct	Richardson, W. L.	3 Feb
Murray, A. BEM	20 May	Goldsmith, C. R.	7 Oct	Cartwright, L. F.	10 Feb
Hiscoke, D. L.	23 May	Jackson, P.	7 Oct	Liptrot, J.	10 Feb
Wells, M. J.	1 June	Restall, D. I.	7 Oct	Loughlin, R. B.	10 Feb
Marklew, M. J.	17 June	Taylor, D. G.	14 Oct	Hulbert, A. R.	24 Feb
Fallows, J.	24 June	Cilia la Corte, F.	21 Oct	Claxton, R. M.	3 Mar
Hodgson, S. J.	30 June	Edwards, L. W.	21 Oct	Clayton, P.	3 Mar
Brydon, J. W.	4 July	Sluggett, R. P.	21 Oct	Gardner, A. H.	3 Mar
Howell, R. A.	8 July	Walton, D. M.	28 Oct	Hunter, A. M.	3 Mar
Sutton, T.	14 July	Vincent, D. J.	4 Nov	James, C. M.	3 Mar
Hartis, N. MBE	15 July	Day, D. W.	11 Nov	Rouget, D. J.	3 Mar
Morris, I. S. MBE	15 July	Fraser, I. B.	11 Nov	Tulloch, T. C.	8 Mar
Ogden, B.	15 July	Hobbs, R. J.	11 Nov	Horner, K. MBE	10 Mar
Rodger, D. I.	21 July	Hughes, R. J.	11 Nov	Knight, J. G.	17 Mar
Duke, M. W.	22 July	Shorthose, P. C.	11 Nov	Meadows, G. P.	20 Mar
Ricketts, M. R. BEM	22 July	Stuart, R. M.	11 Nov	Amos, K. W.	24 Mar
Tansley, A. D.	22 July	Corton, D. W.	18 Nov	Rudling, R. S.	24 Mar
Watkins, M. W.	22 July	Payne, D. C.	18 Nov	Vaughan, E. A.	26 Mar
Barnes, P.	29 July	Shrimpton, P. J.	18 Nov	Wolford, M. J.	31 Mar
Conlin, B. J.	29 July	Taylor, J. W.	18 Nov	McKay, M. J.	1 Apr
Pryce, P. G.	29 July	Stebbing, C. R.	25 Nov	Hannah, R. G.	2 Apr
Campbell, H. A.	5 Aug	Donovan, G.	2 Dec	Jaques, R. A.	2 Apr

1997—contd

		Watkins, J. D.	22 Dec
Nicol, A. W.	2 Apr		
Sperring, A. P.	2 Apr	**1998**	
Snowden, G. N.	7 Apr		
Winter, R. A.	7 Apr	Swanson, R. L.	2 Jan
Yeaman, E.	7 Apr	Chapman, A. E. W.	5 Jan
Allan, G. F.	14 Apr	Ingram, M. J.	5 Jan
Brown, C.	14 Apr	McCaffrey, J. P. M.	5 Jan
Davies, B.	28 Apr	Oswin, J.	5 Jan
Main, A.	28 Apr	Siddle, D.	19 Jan
Norris, S. M.	28 Apr	Bishop, C.	21 Jan
Payne, A. G.	5 May	McTavish, J. C.	26 Jan
Hughes, J. J	6 May	Phillips, M. J.	2 Feb
Ince, P. H.	6 May	Kilby, S. A.	3 Feb
Stout, E. J.	6 May	Murphy, S. J.	11 Feb
Lynskey, M. F. BEM	12 May	Ellis, D. G.	16 Feb
Harper, T. W. RVM	2 June	Holmes, A. M.	3 Mar
Hutton, I. D.	9 June	Brown, S.	9 Mar
Birt, M. J.	7 July	Foster, F. T.	9 Mar
James, G. R.	7 July	Harris, D. A.	9 Mar
Chivers, P. K.	14 July	Thomas, G. J.	9 Mar
Harrhy, D. P.	21 July	Fletcher, R. A.	16 Mar
Bowyer, A. D.	28 July	Hembry, G. H.	16 Mar
Hunt, J. L.	28 July	Bailie, A.	30 Mar
Myton, R.	28 July	Norrish, G. C.	30 Mar
Jones, P. BEM	31 July	Symonds, C. L.	30 Mar
Frizzell, G. H.	4 Aug	Grieves, A.	1 Apr
Horseman, D. C.	4 Aug	Walton, K. D.	13 Apr
Burhouse, M. N.	6 Aug	Kilner, A.	14 Apr
James, D.	11 Aug	Smith, M. A.	15 Apr
Bryden, J. D.	2 Sept	Piddington, M. J.	17 Apr
Ricketts, D. A.	8 Sept	Assanand, K. K. K.	20 Apr
Rutherford, J.	8 Sept	Carr, G.E.	27 Apr
Butt, M. A.	11 Sept	Jackson, V.	27 Apr
Muir, J. M.	16 Sept	McQuigg, C. W.	27 Apr
Jones, S. M. W.	29 Sept	Durrant, I.	1 May
Shanks, W. N. MBE	29 Sept	Marsden T. G.	8 June
Smyth, J.	29 Sept	Wilmott, M.	8 June
Ash, I. R.	6 Oct	Barnes, D. J.	15 June
Lucas, B.	13 Oct	Moffat, J. A. BEM	15 June
Bradshaw, J.	20 Oct	Southcott, D.	15 June
Harmer, G. R.	27 Oct	Smith, K. M.	29 June
Harfield, G. D.	3 Nov	Bindloss, A. C.	6 July
Martin, I. D. M.	3 Nov	O'Donoghue, J.	6 July
McMahon, S. M.	3 Nov		
Dunlap, A. C.	17 Nov		
Austin, P. J.	24 Nov		
Moss, N.	24 Nov		
Roberts, A.	1 Dec		
Smith, W. K.	1 Dec		
Edwards, J. C.	5 Dec		
Brompton, J. A.	8 Dec		
Lovell, D. J.	8 Dec		
Wilson, D. C. BEM	8 Dec		
MacDonald, N. Mc. K.	15 Dec		
Waite, C. A.	15 Dec		
Oram, J. B.	16 Dec		
Rumbell, D. E.	22 Dec		

MASTER SIGNALLERS

1979

Stevenson, J. M.	28 Feb

1980

Luke, P.	10 Jan

1982

Rigby, M. BEM	9 Aug

1983

Carpenter, M. E.	7 Aug
Watts, P. H.	18 Aug

1985

Wade, A. P.	3 Apr

1988

Cleminson, A.	1 July
Rock, D.	1 Nov

1994

Gibney, J. C.	1 July

1996

Oliver, D.	1 July

1997

Cook, M. D. A.	1 Jan

1998

Halliwell, M. R.	1 July
Waterfield, W. E.	1 July

MASTER ENGINEERS

1976

Barnes, C. J. MBE	1 July

1977

Morley, C. A.	1 Jan

1978

Othen, J. E. A.	13 Oct

1979

Hardy, H. R.	1 July

1980

Evans, L.	6 June
Murrell, J. R. MBE	1 July

1981

Smith, D. J.	1 Jan

1982

Jones, N. C.	1 Jan
Hall, R.	1 July

1983

Reddcliff, J. H.	5 Jan

1984

Quick, K. J.	22 Aug
Furneval, H.	20 Sept
Vince, G. R.	27 Sept
Skate, J. A.	16 Oct
Smith, C. A.	2 Nov

1985

Newton, N. J. MBE	1 Jan

1986

Pace, K.	17 Jan
Crosland, J. D.	23 Feb
Hampson, G. R.	4 May

1987

Wishart, W. S. C.	24 Jan
Dodd, D. M.	1 July
Herman, G. M.	1 July

1988

Nobbs, P. D.	1 Jan
Riley, N. J.	1 June
Baker, C. J.	29 June
Sheldon, S. J.	29 July

1989

Mitchell, K.	1 Jan
Saunders, P. R. C.	14 May
Sutton, A.	14 June
Carter, R. A.	1 July
Saxby, T. J. cfs(c)	1 July

1990

Gregson, P.	1 July
Iddon, R. P.	1 July
Keable, M. J.	1 July
Nurse, K.	1 July

1991

Blackburn, C.	1 July
Rockley, A. P. B.	1 July
Scott, A. J.	1 July
Simpson, D. W.	1 July
Winner, P. C.	1 July
Sheather, M. C.	5 Sept

1992

Docherty, A. J.	1 Jan
Garrett, J. T.	1 July

1992—contd

Paull, N. MBE   1 July

1993

Lee, T.	1 Jan
Hamill, M.	1 July

1994

Mohun, A. R.	1 Jan
Morris, J.	1 Jan
Whapples, G.	18 Apr
Pogue, T.	1 July

1995

Hall, C. I.	1 Jan
Cheese, I. L. MBE	1 July
Murray, A.	1 July

1996

Warrilow, J. T. W.	1 Jan
Chicken, P. A.	1 July

1997

Moxon, M. D.	1 Jan

1998

Allan, J. W.	1 July
Deepan, N. K.	1 July

MASTER AIR ELECTRONICS OPERATORS

1975

Hamilton, R.	1 July

1976

Knight, G. J.	1 July

1978

Smeed, J.	1 July
Slade, M. J.	10 July

1979

Bree, P. M.	1 Jan
Harber, J. E.	22 Oct

1980

Pewton, A. V.	16 Jan
Clack, M. E.	18 Jan
Torrance, D. A.	1 July
Little, E. B. BA BSc	30 July

1981

Kitchingham, I. D.	1 Jan
Whittaker, E. MBE	19 Mar
Abbott, P. L.	1 July
Hunt, B. I. S.	1 July
Miller, R. A.	1 July

1982

Jerry, D. I.	1 Jan

1983

Thompson, M. S.	1 Jan
Morrice, J. C.	21 Jan
Moys, W. R.	1 July
Cornes, M. R.	5 July

Turner, M. E.	14 Dec

1984

Rath, N. T.	1 Jan
Flint, R. G.	7 Apr
Dobson, M. B.	28 Apr
Antley, F. J.	4 May
Webb, R.	1 July
Scott, D.	6 July
Fielding, M. W.	1 Sept

1985

Birnie, C. E. MBE BEM	1 Jan
Knight, K. M.	1 Jan
Tamblyn, C. W.	26 Mar
Bramley, R. W.	10 May
Davies, K. A.	1 July
McGregor, I. J.	29 July

1986

Cox, E. P. cfs(c)	1 Jan
Edwards, G. MBE	1 Jan
Halley, W. L.	1 Jan
Moore, S. P.	1 Jan
Davies, A. E.	24 Feb
Dewfall, A.	28 Mar
Abbott, J. E.	25 Apr
Lofts, D. A.	12 May
Amos, R.	30 May
Brown, C. M.	1 July
Muir, D.	1 July
Bush, J. A.	11 Dec

1987

Clay, S.	1 Jan
Ward, S. J.	1 Jan
Holdway, P. MBE	18 Mar
Burns, B.	1 July
Thompson, K. T.	27 July
Headland, M. J.	10 Aug
Nichols, B. G.	7 Oct
Brown, R. E.	23 Nov

1988

Hallett, D.	1 Jan
Silvester, E. A.	29 Mar
Woolfson, A. J. MBE	22 Apr
Reid, W.	8 Sept

1988—contd

Masson, A.	3 Nov
Ramsay, D. McC.	10 Nov

1989

Wade, W. H.	1 Jan
Wetherell, M. J.	1 Jan
Lawrence, R. A.	1 July
Smedley, P.	1 July
McCabe, A. J. M.	4 July
Fennell, R. S.	14 Sept

1990

Pratt, E. J.	16 May
Edwards, A. J.	1 July
Wilkinson, R. A.	1 July

1991

Dewar, A. J. M.	1 Jan
Loosemore, A. R.	1 Jan
Nicholson, D. C.	1 Jan
Lloyd, B. J.	1 July

1992

Crouch, M. J. B.	1 Jan
Parrish, W.	1 Jan
Ashby, B. J.	1 July
Bird, J.	1 July
Keracher, R. I.	1 July

1993

Dixon, D.	1 Jan
Hitchin, D. K.	1 Jan
Schiavone, A. P.	1 July

1994

Benton, N. J.	1 Jan
Curtis, A. J.	1 Jan
Paterson, J.	1 Jan
Bruce, D. W.	1 July
Clarke, A. J.	1 July
Forbes, W. B.	1 July

1995

Dewar, I.	1 Jan
Vongyer, G. G.	1 Jan
Woodland, A. L.	1 Jan
Berry, R. W.	1 July
Geary, S. G.	1 July
Haynes, R. B.	1 July

1996

Jeffrey, D. S.	1 Jan
Penlington, D. W. E.	1 Jan
Cullimore, S. R.	1 July
Oates, S. T.	1 July

1997

Bayne, J. T.	1 Jan
Cross, M.	1 Jan
Stansfield, D.	1 Jan

1998

Hawksworth, I. R.	1 Jan
Silvey, C. E. P.	1 Jan
Walker, J. A.	1 Jan
Jones, N. P.	1 July
Warren, P. L.	1 July

MASTER AIR LOAD-MASTERS

1976

Dally, M. J.	1 Jan
Bain, A.	1 July
Caddick, R.	1 July

1977

Bond, T. A. MBE	1 Jan
Bearham, G.	14 Mar
Pringle, N. cfs(c)	1 July
Unwin, C.	1 July

1978

McArthur, J. L.	1 July
Murphy, P.	1 Dec

1979

Hynes, G. A. MBE	3 Feb
Purvis, G. L.	10 Mar
Graham, F. H. cfs(c)	21 Apr
Gattrell, R. A. AFM	1 July
Whiting, D. T.	1 July
Payne, W.	12 Oct

1980

Felton, M. J.	1 Jan
Mursell, K. T.	22 Feb
Wright, S.	26 Feb
Broome, I. M.	31 Mar
Robertson, I. P. MBE cfs(c)	28 May
Evans, R. E.	1 July
Amor, R. J. AFM cfs(c)	27 Aug

1981

Collings, K.	1 Jan
Graham, R. S.	1 Jan
Maggs, C. M.	1 Jan
Milburn, P.	1 Jan
Scott, A. R. cfs(c)	1 July
Lynn, R. H. cfs(c)	10 Sept
Glenton, C. I.	16 Sept

1981—contd

Michael, E.	22 Oct
Connolly, B.	18 Nov

1982

Tyas, P. D.	1 Jan
Mead, M. J.	6 Jan
McKee, M. T.	15 Apr
Whitehead, C. M.	9 May
Hegarty, A. P. J.	1 July
Willis, C. W.	1 July
Samwell, T. J.	9 Nov
Armstrong, J. MBE MIPD cfs(c)	13 Dec

1983

Venn, B. F.	1 Jan
Shepherd, R. A.	16 Jan
Allen, D.	23 Jan
Bush, L. M.	1 July
Mills, R. A.	1 July
Clements, D.	1 Oct
Todd, R. H.	1 Oct

1984

Edwards, K. D. V. cfs(c)*	1 Jan
Brakes, E. N.	26 Jan
Rowe, S. A.	25 May
Payne, A. D.	1 July
Lowe, S.	6 July

1985

Goodall, A. D. cfs(c)	1 Jan
Cross, K. J.	8 Mar
McLeod, A.	6 May

1986

Jones, H. O.	1 Jan
Porter, D. R.	6 Jan
Colley, P. C.	7 Mar
Cuthell, T. M.	28 Apr
Ball, A. L.	22 May
Davies, G.	22 June
Maddison, M. J.	11 Sept

Jones, A. W.	31 Dec

1987

Bateson, G.	1 Jan
Birkin, B. M.	1 Jan
Lester, D. R.	1 Jan
McCullough, K. D.	1 Jan
Magee, T. M.	1 Jan
Wain, A. G.	1 Jan
Webster, N. J. R.	1 Jan
Lewis, M. H.	4 May
Andrews, G. P. cfs(c)	2 June
Davidson, R. BSc MISM MIMgt LCGI LicIPD	1 July
Dowell, P. D.	1 July
Morrison, H. C.	1 July
Taylor, K. J.	28 Aug
Morris, C. M.	3 Sept
Laken, W. E.	30 Sept
Stanhope, I. W.	1 Nov
Gudgin, G. D.	26 Nov

1988

Bragg, R. J. AFM cfs(c)	1 Jan
Colven, P. McL.	1 Jan
Gosney, P.	1 Jan
Tucker, K. C. cfs(c)	1 Jan
Buxton, R.	7 Jan
Guttridge, I.	1 Mar
Mellor, J. R. D.	1 July
Seward, G. N.	1 July
Thomas, H. MBE cfs(c)	1 July
Thraves, P. T.	11 Nov
Milward, R. G.	30 Nov

1989

Corner, G. R.	1 Jan
Mackenzie, G. T.	9 Feb
Crawford, M. L. cfs(c)	7 Mar
Nightingale, P. R.	12 Apr
Lynch, S. C.	7 June
Jones, C. J.	1 July
Thompson, A. R. cfs(c)	1 July
Connell, P. R. C.	18 July
Roberts, G. W.	23 July

1990

Blake, P. K.	1 July

Clabby, M. J.	1 July
Turnbull, P. A. cfs(c)	1 July

1991

Read, M. C. J.	1 Jan
Watts, S. H.	1 Jan
Kinnimont, F. I.	1 July

1992

Coombes, D. N.	1 Jan
Robinson, R. F.	1 July

1993

McLaughlin, K. J.	29 Jan
Ritson, A.	1 July
Rodham, C. L.	1 July
Whittle, H. G. MBE	1 July

1994

Evans, D. J.	1 Jan
Hamilton, I. D.	1 Jan
Muir, J. D.	1 Jan
Aitken, D. S.	1 July
Mitchell, R. J.	1 July

1995

Bottomley, M.	1 Jan
Gale, R. D.	1 Jan
Grogan, A. P.	1 Jan
Walmsley, D. A.	1 Jan
Dodsworth, V. G. S.	1 July
Franks, N.	1 July
Mahef, G. M.	1 July

1996

Maxwell, D. F. A.	1 Jan
Tait, M. W.	1 Jan
McDonagh, S. cfs(c)	1 July
Morgan, G. N.	1 July
Sampson, F. J.	1 July

1997

Bridge, M. V.	1 Jan

1997—contd

Pearson, B. G.	1 Jan
Prall, T. G. E.	1 Jan
Archard, P. W. MBE	1 July

1998

Bence, A. J.	1 Jan
Dearing, G. J.	1 Jan
Galloway, J. R.	1 Jan
McKay, W A.	1 Jan
Davies, G.	1 July
Docherty, T. G.	1 July
Hunter, B. H.	1 July

ROYAL AIR FORCE RESERVE
GENERAL DUTIES BRANCH

Squadron Leaders

1993

Bridges, A. G. CBE	(P)	1 Oct
Hughes, C. W. G.	(P)	1 Oct
Mayer, W. L. M. AFC	(P)	1 Oct

1994

Purchase, W.	(P)	20 Nov

1995

Turgoose, R. BSc	(P)	4 Sept
Neil, M. J. MBE	(P)	18 Sept

1997

Jewiss. J. O.	(P)	1 Apr
Steen, B. A. MBE	(P)	6 Oct

Flight Lieutenants

1982

Hopwood, C. G. BSc cfs	(P)	22 June

1983

Bletcher, J. R. BA	(P)	13 May
Fessey, M. J. BSc qwi(AD)	(P)	26 Dec

1984

Mew, P. BEng cfs	(P)	13 May

1985

Davidson, M. F. MA	(P)	11 June
Allan, S. D.	(P)	10 Dec

1986

Bodie, C. S. BSc	(P)	15 Jan
Curry, P. D. BA	(P)	11 Mar
Fortune, M. BSc	(N)	11 Mar
Seymour, M. A. BSc tp	(P)	11 Mar
Hill, M. J. R. BSc	(N)	11 June
Linney, M. V. cfs	(P)	19 Sept
Keefe, R. J. BSc	(P)	29 Oct

1987

Hart, R. W. BSc cfs	(P)	22 Jan
Airey, S. M. BSc	(P)	2 Mar
Croshaw, J. BSc cfs	(P)	2 Mar
Dutton, N. C. BEng	(P)	2 Mar
Watson, R. A. H. BSc cfs	(P)	29 Mar
Cousins, P. T. BSc cfs	(P)	14 Apr
de Savigny-Bower, R. A. BSc	(P)	14 Apr
Smith, L. P. L. BSc	(P)	14 Apr
Flinn, P. D. BSc	(N)	25 May
Wells, N. M. cfs	(P)	16 June
Boyd, F. D. S. BSc	(P)	16 Aug
Reynolds, G. R. BSc	(N)	11 Nov
Arundell, P. A. MSc cfs	(P)	3 Sept

1988

Hill, A. G. BA cfs	(P)	15 Jan
Keays, D. K. BA cfs i	(P)	18 Feb
Rowlinson, P. J. BSc tp	(P)	18 Feb
Cooper, A. H. C. BSc	(P)	29 Mar
Haigh, W. D. P. BSc cfs	(P)	29 Mar
Siddall, P. J. BSc	(P)	29 Mar
Sheridan, R. J. BEng	(P)	26 Apr
Hawkins, M. D. BSc	(P)	10 May
Kelly, S. M. BA	(P)	10 May
Thorington, A. J. BSc	(P)	10 May
McSkimming, F. W. J.	(N)	16 June
Boyle, D. St J. BSc	(P)	16 Aug

1989

Gill, C. S. BSc	(P)	15 Jan
Smiles, P. W. BTech	(P)	19 Jan
Capon, G. A.	(P)	29 Jan
Watson, A. T. N. BSc	(P)	3 Feb
Loftus, P. BEng	(P)	28 Feb
Shenton, P. J. BSc	(P)	14 Mar
Bartlem, K. A. BSc	(P)	11 Apr
Langman, A. R. MEng	(P)	11 Apr
Adair, P. G. BSc	(P)	7 June
Bonwitt, A. J. BEng	(P)	3 July
Sowery, C. D.	(P)	2 Aug
Hazzard, C. I.	(P)	8 Dec

1990

Arnold, M. S. BSc	(P)	28 Feb
Weatherly, S. A. BA	(P)	25 Mar
Batey, N. R. qwi	(P)	17 July
Cleaver, S. H. BSc	(N)	27 Sept
Rose, D. A. BSc	(P)	14 Nov
Beresford, G.	(P)	23 Nov
Cheesbrough, P. D. cfs	(P)	23 Nov

1991

Madgwick, I. A.	(P)	15 Feb
Gallon, J. C. BEng	(N)	6 May
Walker, A. R. BSc	(P)	6 May
Fox, C. J.	(P)	13 Aug
Spencer, J. J.	(P)	13 Aug
Williams, D. M. P.	(P)	13 Aug

1992

Fryett, R. P. cfs	(P)	31 Jan
Spratt, C. J. BEng	(P)	19 Feb
Archer, J. W.	(P)	27 Feb
Lees, D. M. BSc	(P)	1 Apr
Steele, F. P. BSc	(P)	1 Apr
Wood, C. M.	(P)	23 Apr
Phelps, M. A.	(P)	4 June
Baker, M. J.	(N)	29 July
Liebers, J.	(P)	29 July
Caley, J. J.	(P)	23 Oct
Mackle, T.	(P)	23 Oct

1992—contd

Hamer, P. M.	(P)	4 Dec

1993

Pullen, M. J.	(P)	17 Jan
Leigh, C. J.	(P)	27 Feb
Pearcy-Caldwell, J. L. D.	(P)	27 Feb
Watson, B. L.	(P)	19 May
McLean, E. F.	(N)	14 July
Harris, M. R. cfs	(P)	25 Aug
Hurt, T. S. BSc	(P)	30 Sept
Duffy, C. E. cfs	(P)	5 Nov
Marshall, J. E.	(P)	5 Nov

1994

Bonser, A. C. L.	(P)	22 Mar
Lear, M. J. cfs	(P)	2 May

1995

Bielby, M. C.	(P)	28 Mar
Hillyer, K. S.	(P)	28 Mar

1997

Johnson, M. C.	(P)	24 Mar
Skipp, J. S.	(P)	24 Mar
Morley, P. R.	(P)	1 Apr
Bowen, A. J.	(P)	7 Apr
Edenbrow, R. A. O. BSc	(P)	7 Apr
Janiurek, J. D.	(P)	7 Apr
Mannings, E. J.	(P)	7 Apr
McDougall, D. J. DipEd	(P)	7 Apr
Woods, R. D.	(P)	7 Apr
Johnson, H. R. BSc	(P)	14 Apr
Pearce, A. G.	(P)	16 Apr
Marshall, A. S.	(P)	21 Apr
Patrick, K. N.	(P)	21 Apr
Stanton, S.	(P)	21 Apr
Kennedy, G. S.	(P)	28 Apr
Wiseman, R. A. BSc	(P)	6 May
Patterson, L. J. BSc	(P)	7 May
Danby, C. I.	(P)	12 May
Ford, M. A.	(P)	19 May
Selman, A. C.	(P)	27 May
Clark, D. H.	(P)	28 May
Stewart, J. R.	(P)	10 June
Gent, A. M. BSc	(P)	16 June
Sumner, A. W.	(P)	2 July

Barbour, T. M. BA	(P)	4 Aug
Fletcher, R. M. BSc	(P)	26 Aug
Sproul, E. C.	(P)	26 Aug
Campbell, D. A.	(P)	2 Sept
Chew, C. P. BA BArch	(P)	8 Sept
Eeles, T. BA	(P)	15 Sept
Clements, R. E.	(P)	22 Sept
Shuster, R. C. AFC	(P)	27 Sept
Garton, A. C.	(P)	7 Oct
Wood, M. H. MBE	(P)	11 Oct
Hall, M. R. BA	(P)	18 Oct
Newman, R. A.	(P)	21 Oct
Newton, R. J. BSc	(P)	26 Oct
Taylor, G. T.	(P)	7 Nov
Logan, S. T. BSc	(P)	3 Dec
Brown, J. R.	(P)	9 Dec
Mathieson, D.	(N)	20 Dec

1998

Clark, M. A.	(P)	5 Jan
Williams, M. A.	(P)	5 Jan

OPERATIONS SUPPORT BRANCH

Group Captains

1992

Keers, J. F. Born	(FLTOPS)	13 July

1998

Jones, D. J.	(FLTOPS)	20 Jan

Wing Commanders

1986

McQueen, W. R. MBE AE	(FLTOPS)	23 Jan

1987

Read, N. R.	(FLTOPS)	26 Aug

1989

Nunn, J. M.	(FLTOPS)	14 Aug

1993

Grange, M. J.	(FLTOPS)	1 Jan
Buchanan, P. J.	(FLTOPS)	28 May

1995

Green, R. J. C.	(FLTOPS)	6 Mar
Houghton, A. W.		11 Sept
Gibb, R. W.	(FLTOPS)	4 Dec

1996

Moses, H. H.	(FLTOPS)	29 Jan

Wing Commanders

1996—contd

Campbell, A. D. K.
(FLTOPS) 10 June

1997

Vary, C. E. (FLTOPS) 3 Feb

Squadron Leaders

1985

Philpott, J. H. AE
(FLTOPS) 15 Aug

1988

Crane, D. L. (INT) 11 July

1990

Cook, J. B. MILog (INT) 2 Apr

1991

Dixon, R. S. (FLTOPS) 9 Dec

1992

Blackburn, G. J. OBE
(INT) 1 June

1994

Austin, T. S. (FLTOPS) 17 Jan
Hudson, C. P. M.
(FLTOPS) 16 May
Noyes, S. G. (FLTOPS) 30 Aug
Williams, R. G. C.
(FLTOPS) 10 Oct

1995

Wilson, H. (FLTOPS) 17 Nov

1996

Nicolle, B. P. (FLTOPS) 31 Jan
Squires, J. V. (FLTOPS) 15 Apr
Whelan, J. B. D.
(FLTOPS) 15 Apr
Deepan, K. V. (FLTOPS) 3 June
Campbell, C. H.
(FLTOPS) 23 Sept
Goodman, P. J.
(FLTOPS) 3 Oct

1997

Ashton, J. M. (FLTOPS) 6 Jan
Glasspool, I. D.
(FLTOPS) 8 July
Coles, R. G. (FLTOPS) 9 July
Bray, D. B. (FLTOPS) 3 Dec
Hartley, J. (FLTOPS) 17 Dec

Flight Lieutenants

1983

Hopkinson, D. L. AE
(FLTOPS) 1 Dec

1986

Hind, P. J. (FLTOPS) 4 Aug

1988

Leach, K. L. BA (ATC) 18 Feb
Hamilton, B. A. BEd
(ATC) 10 May
Browne, N. T. (FC) 26 May
Hay, W. P. (FLTOPS) 26 Sept

1989

Tudor, K.E. BSc (ATC) 7 Jan
Tweed, P. L. AE
(FLTOPS) 16 June
Tayler, J. S. (FLTOPS) 3 July
Hargreaves, C. M.
BSc (ATC) 1 Aug

Price, A. E. BSc (FC) 30 Sept
Roper, L. (FC) 17 Dec

1990

Easton, S. T. BSc (ATC) 14 Mar
Nicholls, B. G.
(FLTOPS) 2 Apr
Cartwright, B. A.
(FLTOPS) 18 Apr
Welsh, D. BSc (ATC) 7 June
Burslem, J. C. (ATC) 8 June
Horn, K. (FLTOPS) 14 Aug
Cheetham, J. D.
(FLTOPS) 24 Sept
Corby, S. C. (FC) 1 Dec
Chislett-McDonald,
E. M. R. BSc (ATC) 7 Dec
Newsome, C. P. BA
(ATC) 7 Dec

1991

Barnes, P. N. AE
(FLTOPS) 1 Feb
Sharp, F. (ATC) 1 Mar
Jack, A. E. (ATC) 11 Apr
Wallis, C. M. (ATC) 11 Apr
Ross, D. A. (REGT) 16 July
Chisholm, H. J. BA
(INT) 14 Aug
Hammond-Doutre, G. I.
(FLTOPS) 14 Oct
Ager, L. J. (ATC) 6 Dec

1992

Ings, J. T. LLB (REGT) 25 Mar
Harrington, R. BA
(REGT) 6 May
Martindale, J. D. BSc
(ATC) 6 May
Wright, M. A. BA (FC) 12 May
Adkin, M. E. (FLTOPS) 25 Sept
Chapman, N. (FLTOPS) 25 Sept
Hurst, I. P. (FLTOPS) 25 Sept
Robins, C. G. AE
(FLTOPS) 6 Oct
Goodman, C. J. (ATC) 11 Oct
Williams, D. P. (ATC) 8 Nov
Mallinson, C. L. (FC) 19 Dec

1993

Armstrong, A. E. AE
(FLTOPS) 4 Feb

243

Flight Lieutenants

1993—contd

Dane, M. B. MBE AFC		
(FLTOPS)		15 Feb
Cameron, I.	(FLTOPS)	4 Mar
MacDonald, E. D.		
(FLTOPS)		4 Mar
Merrell, J. C.	(FLTOPS)	4 Mar
Carpenter, F. J.	(FC)	23 Apr
Kerley, M.L.A. BA	(ATC)	12 May
Pace, R. J. BSc	(ATC)	12 May
Phillips, G. A. AE		
(FLTOPS)		13 July
Hussey, P. J.	(FLTOPS)	3 Aug
Norman, R. E. J.		
(FLTOPS)		3 Aug
West, D. J.	(FLTOPS)	3 Aug
Bishop, S. M.	(FC)	12 Sept
Burgess, C. BSc	(FC)	1 Oct
Griffiths, M. C. BSc		
(INT)		13 Nov
Wood, L. G.	(ATC)	21 Nov

1994

Linton, M. G.	(FLTOPS)	1 Jan
Donnelly, M. G.	(ATC)	17 Jan
Gabriel, S. L.	(REGT)	20 Jan
Hickmore, G. G. A.		
(FLTOPS)		24 Jan
Scott, I. C.	(FLTOPS)	27 Jan
Lloyd, T. E. L.	(FLTOPS)	3 Feb
Maeer, K. W.	(FLTOPS)	3 Feb
Steel, M. K.	(FLTOPS)	3 Feb
Watson, J. R. AE		
(FLTOPS)		9 Feb
Warren, J. J.	(FLTOPS)	14 Feb
Jones, D. J. R.	(FLTOPS)	9 Mar
Pearson, G. M.	(ATC)	19 Mar
Hanley, K. D. BA	(ATC)	30 Mar
Sherry, R.	(ATC)	2 Apr
Wynne, M. C.	(ATC)	8 Apr
Stewart, K. J. BSc	(FC)	10 May
Dunbar, L.	(FC)	2 July
Bennett, A. BA	(INT)	17 Aug
Clark, A. C. BSc	(FC)	17 Aug
Beeby, H. M.	(ATC)	5 Nov
Turner, P. W.	(ATC)	5 Nov

1995

Davies, R. W.	(FLTOPS)	3 Apr
Cook, R. M. S. MBE		
(FLTOPS)		31 July

Dawson, K. J. BA		10 May
Illing, C. L. BSc	(FC)	10 May
Bartram, I. M. G.		
(FLTOPS)		16 June
Paul, A. G.	(FLTOPS)	16 June
Buckman, J.	(FLTOPS)	28 June
Gallon, J. D.	(FLTOPS)	1 Sept
Gresty, P. J.	(FLTOPS)	8 Sept
Matthews, I. D.		
(FLTOPS)		8 Sept
Nott, J. M. BSc	(ATC)	10 Nov
Lowman, C.	(ATC)	22 Dec

1996

Cowell, R. W.	(ATC)	5 Feb
Kiggel, L. J.	(ATC)	5 Feb
Howell, D. K.	(FLTOPS)	7 Feb
Burdekin, P. A.		
(FLTOPS)		19 Feb
McFarland, C. A.	(ATC)	28 Mar
Mason, I. M.	(FLTOPS)	11 Apr
Brown, T. C.	(FLTOPS)	13 May
Delahunt-Rimmer, H. F.		
RGN	(ATC)	19 May
Collins, G. E.	(ATC)	16 Sept
Quick, M. C.	(ATC)	14 Oct
Jones, J. N.	(FLTOPS)	28 Oct
Kent, S. L.	(FLTOPS)	1 Nov
Ward, J. F.	(FLTOPS)	1 Nov

1997

Lucking, R. R.	(FLTOPS)	20 Jan
Locke, G. H.	(FLTOPS)	27 Jan
Baker, H. M.	(FLTOPS)	1 Apr
Byrne, M. S.	(FLTOPS)	14 Apr
Davis, J. A.	(INT)	8 May
Johnston, G. J. BEd		
(FLTOPS)		10 July
Young, A C. M. N.		
(FLTOPS)		18 Aug
Laybourne, K. R.	(REGT)	28 Oct
Kent, K. J. BSc	(ATC)	3 Nov
Hallowes, S. D.	(ATC)	8 Nov

1998

McKeown, J. D. P.		
(FLTOPS)		19 Jan
Sumner, D. G.	(ATC)	23 Feb
White, D. A. C.	(ATC)	1 Mar
Tournay, R. N. A. J.		
(REGT)		1 Apr
Culmer, B. E.	(ATC)	4 Apr
Baker, B. A. F.	(ATC)	8 Apr

George, G. H. E.	(ATC)	8 Apr

Flying Officers

1990

Ross, J. M.	(FC)	16 Feb
Harrison, S. R.	(ATC)	9 July

1991

Mattinson, E. A.	(ATC)	28 Jan
McGregor, K. J.	(FC)	28 Jan
Kutub, M. V. A.	(FC)	11 Nov

1992

Haigh, J. L. BA	(ATC)	11 Apr
Dale, J.	(ATC)	9 May
Laing, B.	(FLTOPS)	25 Sept
D'Albertanson, S. R.		
	(ATC)	18 Oct
Davis, A. S.	(ATC)	10 Nov

1993

Thompson, S. M.		
(FLTOPS)		4 Mar
Osborne, A. P.	(ATC)	26 Mar
Saunders, R.	(ATC)	4 May
Trapp, J.	(ATC)	20 June
Reeve, P. D.	(FLTOPS)	3 Aug
Davis, A. L.	(INT)	9 Nov

1994

Gunn, C.	(REGT)	14 Feb
Gerrard, C. P.	(ATC)	26 Sept

1995

Main, V. J.	(ATC)	30 Jan

1996

Edmeston, M. C.	(ATC)	28 Jan

ENGINEER BRANCH

Squadron Leaders

1990

Tweedley, J. McM.	1 June

1992

Swan, A. J.	13 July

1994

Carrington, D. J.	10 Oct

1997

McKenzie, I. BA CEng MIEE MRAes	6 Jan
Thorpe, G. S. E.	17 Mar

Flight Lieutenants

1987

Rawal, A. BSc	31 Jan
Wood, G. R. BSc	22 Dec

1988

May, S. L.	14 Sept

1989

Payne, S. BSc	26 Apr
Kirby, B. C. BA	2 May
Morris, C. V. BSc	7 June

1990

Summers, B. H. BSc	3 Feb

Waddington, S. P. BSc	7 June
Mann, S. S. BSc	1 Aug
Wilkinson, L. R. BSc	27 Sept
Sproat, J. R.	14 Nov

1991

Russell, M. S. BSc	14 Feb
Hill, M. N.	20 Apr
Turner, P. D. C.	3 Aug

1992

Lazenby, P. BSc	17 Feb
Loizou, I. D. BEng	25 Mar
Betterton, J. M. BSc	12 May
Vernon, M. J. BEng	18 Aug
Whitfield, M. M. MEng	18 Aug
Wilson, T. J. BEng	18 Aug
Powell, A. D.	30 Sept
Perks, K. S. BEng	19 Oct
Lewis-Morgan, A. C. BSc	14 Nov

1993

Whitbread, K. M BEng	20 Feb
Darling, T. BEM	29 Mar
Stewart, K. L. BEng	30 Mar
Williams, S. BEng	30 Mar
Stidolph, R. L. BEng	11 May
Donlon, C. J. BEng	12 May
Filby, J. E. MEng BA	6 July
Davies, A. R. BEng	18 Aug
Barrett, C. L. BSc	30 Sept

1994

Allinson, M. MEng	19 Feb
Hall, D. E. BEng	19 Feb
Relf, M. N. BEng	10 May
Ascott, S. BEng	11 May
Patel, I. M. BEng	11 May
Watkins, D. L. BEng	11 May
Hogan, N. BSc	10 July
Collie, P. D. BSc	12 Nov

1995

de Rouffignac, C. BEng	15 Jan

Broatch. D. M. BSc PGCE	29 Sept
Jayne, B. M. BEng	29 Sept

1998

Watson, C. R.	10 Mar

Flying Officer

1990

MacLeod, S. I.	1 Nov

SUPPLY BRANCH

Wing Commander

1997

Wells, J. MCIPS   2 Sept

Squadron Leader

1998

Ayers, C. R.   5 Jan

Flight Lieutenants

1990

Strang, D. L. BSc	7 June
Hale, S. L. BSc	1 Aug

1991

Cook, N. M.	25 Mar
Tucker, M. BSc	11 Apr
Britten, M. C.	23 Apr
Finding, J. A.	16 Nov
Lindley, J. E.	22 Dec

1992

Alcock, M. J. BSc   6 May

1993

Tindley, S. E.	31 Jan
Bennett, K. BSc	7 July
Gladwin, K. J. BSc	19 Aug
Potter, C. BSc	1 Oct
Ashurst, S. J. BSc	24 Dec
Robertson, C. S. A. BSc	24 Dec

1994

Lenihan, J. H.	20 Feb
Fisk, C. L. BSc	29 Mar
McGrath, L. J.	15 May
Healey, M. R.	19 May
Rich, A. W. G.	19 May
Laurent, N. A.	25 Aug
Cooper, J. P.	13 Sept

1995

Gibbons, R. J.	22 Mar
Robbins, T. S.	22 Mar
Tobin, F. K.	15 June
Wilby, N. S.	22 Dec

1996

Stamp, S.	9 May
Lane, S. R.	30 June

Flying Officers

1990

Parsons, R. D. BSc   19 Jan

1991

Carpenter, D. H.   16 Aug

1992

Howarth, R. M.   28 Mar

1993

Brown, S.	2 Feb
Paish, J. R.	8 May
Freear, D. J.	28 Sept
Hawkins, T. R. A.	9 Nov

1994

Stephens, T. A.   29 Jan

ADMINISTRATIVE BRANCH

Squadron Leaders

1991

Boyne, R.   (Sec)   29 July

1994

Edmunds, D. J.	(Sec)	17 Jan
Monte, G. H.	(Sec)	1 Feb

1996

Morgan, M. L.	(Sec)	2 Jan
Bacon, T. J. OBE	(Sec)	3 June

1997

Campion, P.	(Sec)	7 Apr
Wilson, W. J.	(Sec)	1 Oct
Pritchard, M. MIMgt		
	(Sec)	4 Oct

Flight Lieutenants

1988

Higgins, D. J.   (Sec)   3 Sept

1990

Bessant, S. E. BEd (Trg)		17 Feb
Anderson, G. I. BA		
	(Sec)	28 Feb
Wilson, D. A. W. BSc		
	(Trg)	28 Feb
Davies, R. J. MInstAM		
AMIPD	(Sec)	11 June
Heyes, W. J. BEd	(Trg)	7 July
Rich, V. M. BSc	(Trg)	7 Dec
Smith, S. J. BA(ProvSy)		7 Dec

Flight Lieutenants

1991

Dyer, S. P. BEd pji(PEd)		14 Feb
Dempsey, S. L. BA(Trg)		14 Feb
Glass, M. P. BA	(Cat)	14 Feb
Hood, H. J. BSc	(Trg)	28 Feb
Rodger, S. R. BA	(Trg)	3 July
Lane, S. BSc PGCE(Trg)		5 July
Jones, G. M. BEng(Trg)		7 July
Buckley, J. N. V. BSc		
	(Trg)	19 Aug
Oakley, P. C. BSc	(Trg)	19 Aug
Brown, S. L. BSc		
CertEd	(Trg)	1 Oct
Whitbread, A. J. BA		
	(Sec)	8 Nov
Eaves, A. L.	(Sec)	7 Dec
Langley, S. J. BA	(Trg)	19 Dec

1992

Petty, T. J. R. BSc		
PGCE	(Trg)	6 Jan
Lee, C. BA	(Sec)	20 Feb
Manhire, L. J. BSc(Trg)		20 Feb
Evans, J. J. BSc	(Trg)	25 Mar
Harrison, J. M. MSc		
BEng ae	(Trg)	25 Mar
Jones, S. H. BSc	(Trg)	1 Apr
Hansford, F. H. BA(Sec)		6 May
Frame, L. V. BSc	(Sec)	7 July
Serrell-Cooke, T. BSc		
	(Sec)	8 July
Larsson, E. A. BA	(Sec)	18 Aug
Berry, S. J. MA	(Sec)	1 Oct
Barker, S. J. BSc	(Sec)	2 Oct
Payn, J. A. R.	(Sec)	15 Oct
State, N. J.	(Sec)	24 Oct
Tandy, S.	(Cat)	1 Nov
Wells, C. E. BA	(Sec)	13 Nov
Wallace, G. A. BSc		
	(Sec)	1 Dec

1993

Gunn, Z. M.	(Sec)	4 Jan
Sullivan, M. L. BSc		
	(Sec)	18 Feb
King, A. J. BEd	(Sec)	19 Feb
Lake, R. J. N. BA	(Trg)	20 Feb
Walsh, J.	(Sec)	27 Feb
Bosworth, A. J. BSc		
	(Sec)	1 Apr
Wignall, P.	(Sec)	23 Apr

Crompton, J. M. BA		
	(Cat)	11 May
Campbell, G. J. BSc		
	(Trg)	12 May
Fragel, K.	(Sec)	10 June
Hyde, S. M. BSc	(Trg)	7 July
Tyler, J. H. BSc	(Trg)	7 July
Green, G. E. BSc	(Trg)	17 Aug
Anderson, A. J. T.	(Sec)	30 Aug
Dempsey, D. A. BA		
	(Sec)	1 Oct
Punshon, R. BA	(Cat)	1 Oct
Hall, T. W. BA	(Sec)	24 Dec

1994

Johnson, A. M. BA(Trg)		6 Jan
Eagger, G. R.	(Sec)	17 Jan
Davidson, H. R. BSc		
	(Cat)	29 Mar
Gilley, R. M. BSc	(Trg)	30 Mar
Burden, L. A.	(Sec)	8 Apr
Lopez, D. A.	(Sec)	8 Apr
Moore, A. J.	(Sec)	19 May
Morris, N. J.	(Cat)	25 June
Sully, P. D.	(Sec)	14 July
Wellard, C. J.	(Sec)	14 July
Hollett, S. J. L. BA(Sec)		17 Aug
McLeod, J. P. LLB (Sec)		30 Sept
Russell J. BA	(Sec)	30 Sept
Thompson, Y. BA (Sec)		30 Sept

1995

Jackson, R. A.	(Sec)	1 Apr
Coyne, S. A.	(Cat)	17 May
Ashby, T. A. GradIPD		
	(Sec)	15 June
Cheesbrough, D.	(Sec)	25 Oct
Corrie, N. C. BA	(Sec)	10 Nov
Sutherland, A. J. BSc		
	(Sec)	10 Nov

1996

Mackmurdie, R. L.(Sec)		9 May
Davis, W. MBE	(Sec)	1 July
Cradden, B. P.	(Sec)	16 Oct

1997

Blackburn, N. J. S.(Sec)		27 Jan
Stanton, R. H. MVO		
MRAeS MRIN	(Sec)	27 Aug

Ginnever, J. D.	(Sec)	28 Sept

Flying Officers

1990

Baldwin, N. R.	(Cat)	21 Dec

1991

Gerrard, E. L.	(Sec)	28 Jan
Grundy, S. K.	(Sec)	18 Apr
Stowell, B. E. M.	(Sec)	15 Oct
Bain, C. A.	(Sec)	20 Dec
Roberts, J. E.	(Sec)	20 Dec

1992

Skuodas, P. A.	(Sec)	19 Feb
Gwillim, F. J.	(Sec)	28 Mar
Struthers, W. J. R. (Cat)		23 June

1993

Cunningham, L. N.(Cat)		5 Jan
Kennedy, S. M.	(Sec)	23 Jan
Phillips, K. M.	(Sec)	23 Jan
Prole, N. M.	(Sec)	23 Jan
McTaggart, H. A.	(Sec)	26 Mar
Scurrah, P. J.	(ProvSy)	24 May
Steadman, D. R.	(Sec)	14 Aug
Hardy, D. N.	(ProvSy)	17 Aug
McNea, P.	(Sec)	28 Sept
Lisney, P. J.	(Sec)	20 Nov

1994

Rawnsley, L. M. BSc		
	(Sec)	14 Feb
Bruce, T. J.	(Sec)	7 Nov
Lilleyman, A. M. (Sec)		7 Nov

MEDICAL BRANCH

Squadron Leaders

1985

Walters, J. N. MB BCh
MRCGP DA
DRCOG   14 Jan

1988

Cook, C. C. H. BSc MB
BS MRCPsych   18 Nov

1990

Laliwala, M. A. H. MB
BS DTM&H   14 May
Maclachlan, D. A. C.
BM BCh   1 Aug

1992

Arathoon, D A. MB
BS   12 Jan

1993

Hammond, K. C. MB BS
FRCP MRCP(UK)   18 Nov
Houlder, A. R. MB ChB
FRCS(Edin)
FRCS(Eng)   6 Dec

1994

Barrow, A. S. MB ChB
DRCOG   4 Jan

1995

Graham, D. J. M. MB
ChB   1 Aug
Jones, J. W. M. BSc MB
ChB   1 Aug
Speight, H. M. BM BS
                          1 Aug

Findlay, G. P. MB ChB
                          15 Aug
Middleton, S. B. MB
ChB   26 Aug
Jackson, T. M. MB BS
                          6 Sept

1996

Morris, J. A. C. MB
BS   1 Feb
Licence, K. A. M. MB
BS   1 Aug
Watermeyer, S. R. BSc
MB BCh   1 Aug

Flight Lieutenants

1990

Dean, A. D. P. BSc MB
BChir   1 Aug
Withington, B. S. MB
BCh   1 Aug

1991

Foley, S. J. MB BS   4 Feb
Anees, W. M. MB BS   1 Aug
Brazier, J. C. MB BS   1 Aug
Gorton, M. G. MB
ChB   1 Aug
Price, S. V. MB BS   1 Aug

1992

Howell, J. R. MB BS   1 Aug
Watt, D. A. L. MB ChB
                          1 Aug

1994

Ambler, L. C. MB BS   1 Aug

DENTAL BRANCH

Squadron Leaders

1994

Howe, M. BDS   1 Jan

1996

Dearing, J. BDS
FDSRCPS   3 Aug

Flight Lieutenants

1991

Minall, P. A. BDS   25 Aug

1993

Belcher, K. A. BDS   9 Dec

PRINCESS MARY'S ROYAL AIR FORCE NURSING SERVICE

All Officers of Princess Mary's Royal Air Force Nursing Service hold the qualification of Registered General Nurse and/or Registered Mental Nurse

Flight Lieutenants

1982

Olliver-Cook, S. E.	29 Jan
Howie, J. M. C.	15 Mar

1983

Eatwell, S. A.	9 Jan

1984

Ellis, S. A. RM	6 Aug
Whitfield, S.	18 Aug
Cooke, M. A. RM	7 Dec

1985

Parker, M. J. RSCN	30 Apr
Bull, A. M. C. RM	22 Dec

1986

Wingham, A. E.	10 June

1987

Ralph, E. A. RM	3 Apr
Pullen, J. D. RM RHV	12 Apr

1988

Simpson, D. A. RM	21 July

1989

Butterworth, C. T. RSCN	12 July
Bray, L. M. RM	17 July

1990

Churchill, C. M. RSCN	16 Mar
Pardoe, A. L. RM	1 June
Norman, J. E.	19 Aug

1991

Trayler, J. E.	17 Feb
Slaughter, I. R.	10 Mar
Tarplett, L. J.	2 Aug
Edwards, J. T.	24 Aug
Hensey, J. V.	2 Oct
Percival, R.	20 Nov

1992

Lewis, J. L.	5 Jan
Toomer, S. F. RM	13 Feb
Allen, W. C. RM	15 Feb
Skinner, S. E.	2 June
Cox, A. J.	25 July
Grainger-Birkholz, J. A. RM	25 July
Stribley, J. E.	13 Oct
King, M. L.	6 Dec
Fitzmaurice, P. A.	18 Dec
Orr, K. D. M.	21 Dec

1993

Gormley, S. RM	1 May
Smith, K. A.	7 June
Pierpoint, V. J. RSCN	7 July
Lee, P.	29 Sept
Drynan, P. G. RM	3 Oct
Noble, A. D. RM	18 Nov

1994

Woodfine, D. M. RM	9 Jan
Tilley, L. H. A.	19 Nov

1995

Taylor, S. E. BNurs	7 July
Hughes, D. A. RM	15 Aug
Lord, J. S. RM	17 Nov

MEDICAL SECRETARIAL BRANCH

CLASS "CC"

Wing Commander

1998

Fares, D. B. MInstAM
MHSM MIMgt   1 May

Group Captains

1993

Skelley, R. P. Born   7 June
Gambold, W. G.   25 Oct
Ferguson, A. FIMgt   6 Dec

1994

Kiggell, P. S. OBE   6 Apr

1997

Cross, W. M. N. OBE   26 May
Hakin, L. OBE Born   10 July

1998

Ford, J. A. F. FIMgt   25 May

Wing Commanders

1988

Herd, H. D. OBE   24 Nov

1991

Woods, G.   22 Apr

1992

Seymour, C. C. B.   14 Sept
Sewell, J. BA FRGS   9 Nov

1993

Evans, J. P.   3 June
Canning, P. F. A.   31 Aug

1995

Kermeen, R. W.   2 Oct

1996

Stephens, M. A.   1 Apr
Thorley, M. A.
MRAeS   1 Apr
Wright, W. W. BA BA
DipEd   1 Apr
MacLachlan, A. J. C.
CEng MRAeS   20 Sept

1997

Jones, M. J. OBE
MIMgt   3 Mar
Carter, P. R.   1 Sept
Clayton-Jones, G. S.
MRAeS   1 Dec

Squadron Leaders

1985

Moorhouse, M. G.
BSc   2 Sept
Miller, R. W. A.   4 Oct

1986

Goldstein, M. MBE
BA   17 Mar
Cunnane, A.   4 Aug
Murray, P. G. E. FIMgt
MRAeS   3 Nov
Le Moine, J. MBE   19 Dec

1987

Stock, B. MIMgt   18 May
Dunstan, P. N.   1 Sept
McEwan, A. R.   4 Sept

1988

Butler, B. J. McG.   26 Aug
James, F. D.   31 Oct
Gibson, A. J.   2 Dec

Squadron Leaders

1989

Ross, A.	5 June
Morris, H. R.	25 Oct
Gibson, D. W.	27 Nov

1990

Reep, M. F.	12 Mar
Tutin, F.	4 June
McMichael, A. F.	7 Sept
Wood, D. A.	15 Nov
Foley, T.	10 Dec

1992

McFarlane, S. C.	12 May
Dinmore, G. W.	1 Sept
Davies, W. G.	30 Oct
Douglass, M. P.	23 Nov

1993

Johnson, D. L. MIPD MIMgt	4 Mar
Grant, T.	1 June
McCluskey, R. AFC DPhysEd pji qs	6 Sept
Butler, V. P. L.	1 Oct
Booth, R. E.	21 Oct

1994

Roberts, R. E.	14 Feb
Johns, L. T.	25 Mar
Taylor, R.	5 Apr

1995

Abbott, R. J.	6 Mar
Crowder, R. B. MIMgt	6 Mar
Maddocks, B. J.	18 Apr
Dole, T. F.	8 May
Foster, J. E.	19 June
Hastings, A.	4 July
Fairhead, I. F. BSc(Eng)	17 July
Grand-Scrutton, J.	4 Sept
Griffiths, A.	16 Oct

1996

Bruce, A. J.	8 Jan
Bird, P. R.	15 Feb
Lang, B.	8 Mar
Bayliss, J. A. MBE	29 Apr
Nadin, J. L.	1 July
Durack, C. B.	8 July
Ramsay, I. A.	12 July
Wright, R. C.	19 Aug
Lunt, J. D. BA	24 Sept
Locke, M. A. MIMgt	16 Oct
Cobb, J. W. MBE	11 Nov
Carr, E. MILog MIPD	18 Nov
Broom, B. A.	27 Nov
English, J. P.	1 Dec
Yarrow, S. W. S. MIMgt	9 Dec

1997

Shorter, B.	27 Jan
Chalkley, K. B. MBE	3 Mar
Spence, B. G. BA IEng MIIE(elec)	21 Apr
Low, I. N.	9 June
Hathaway, J. H. T.	11 Sept
Collins, R. M. MIMgt	6 Oct
Joose, C. A.	3 Dec
Massey, R. G. MIMgt	11 Dec

1998

Duguid, M. D. MIMgt	5 Jan
Margiotta, G. L.	2 Feb
Campbell, R. S.	7 Feb
Moore, G. J. T.	17 Mar
Livingston, R. J.	27 Apr

Flight Lieutenants

1975

Tapson, B.	3 Jan
Eyre, T.	24 Nov

1978

Throssell, M. G.	5 Apr

1981

Coombes, C.	7 Sept

1982

McCulloch, T.	4 Jan
Ward, T. J.	6 Aug

1985

Burge, W. J.	7 Jan

1986

Plummer, J. A.	25 Apr

1987

Westwell, D. K.	6 July
Hood, L. S.	13 Aug

1989

Taylor, J. E.	15 May
Cliff, M. E.	1 Sept
Taylor, N. H.	4 Sept
Reed, K. B.	28 Dec

1990

Pleasant, D. M.	12 Mar
Shepherd, J. M. P.	13 Aug
Jessiman, W.	15 Oct
Lawrence, I.	5 Nov

1991

Vernon, J.	7 Jan
Leech, B. J.	20 May
Rigby, C. M. R.	16 Sept
Exley, B. J. A.	4 Oct
Parrini, A. L.	4 Nov
Brooks, P. E. BA	11 Nov
Jackson, G. H.	18 Nov

Flight Lieutenants

1991—contd

Dutton, M. J. R.	25 Nov

1992

Preston, N. G.	6 Apr
Parratt, R. MBE	14 Sept
Pennington, G. J.	17 Nov

1993

Hermolle, M. A.	19 Aug
Barkway, R. J.	23 Aug
Davies, D. E.	14 Sept

1994

Anderson, J. D.	5 Apr
Dalling, R.	26 Nov

1995

Welch, F. I.	3 Jan
Rowe, D. H. W.	3 Apr
Bell, J. J.	10 Apr
Foster, A. F.	1 May
Samme, R. J.	1 June
Hack, K. S.	4 July
James, J. R. BA	3 Aug
Wood, M. J.	31 Aug
Miller, R. E. BA PGCE FRGS	25 Sept
Watkins, M.	13 Nov
Coker, J. D.	4 Dec

1996

Webber, G. R.	9 Jan
McCran, J. B.	19 Feb
Morris, D. G.	22 July
Shephard, R. G.	2 Sept
Pelcot, A. F.	7 Oct
Fahey, J. B.	28 Oct
Halford, P.	11 Nov
Meadows, C. J.	11 Nov

1997

Morris, P. L.	20 Feb

Hamon, S.	18 Apr
Inman, P. G.	6 June
Bartle, C. J.	30 Sept
Ross, D. FInstAM	1 Oct
Lawrenson, A. J. BA	25 Nov
Flaherty, S. D.	8 Dec

1998

Marshall, R. A.	23 Feb

Flying Officers

1987

Young, G. A.	19 Oct

1989

Mason, A. D.	12 Sept

ROYAL AUXILIARY AIR FORCE

Air Commodore-in-Chief .... H.M. THE QUEEN

**Honorary Inspector-General of the Royal Auxiliary Air Force
The Right Honourable Lord Monro of Langholm, AE JP DL**

Inspector — Group Captain R. T. W. Mighall, OBE ADC MSc BA RAUXAF

Honorary Air Commodores

Sir Adrian Swire, AE MA DL No 1 (County of Hertford) Maritime Headquarters Unit

The Right Honourable Lord Selkirk of Douglas QC, MA LLB No 2 (City of Edinburgh) Maritime Headquarters Unit

His Honour Judge Neville No 3 (County of Devon) Maritime Headquarters Unit

Air Vice-Marshal T. P. White CB CEng FIEE No 2503 (County of Lincoln) Squadron RAuxAF Regiment

Marshal of the Royal Air Force Sir Michael Beetham, GCB CBE DFC AFC DL FRAeS Strike Attack Support Squadron RAuxAF

The Right Honourable Lord Monro of Langholm, AE JP DL No 2622 (Highlands) Squadron RAuxAF Regiment

His Grace the Duke of Grafton, KG DL No 2623 (East Anglia) Squadron RAuxAF Regiment

Sir John Graham, Bt GCMG, Air Transport and Air-to-Air Refuelling Support Squadron RAuxAF

Mr. J. M. Williams, No 2625 (County of Cornwall) Squadron RAuxAF Regiment

Sir Mark Norman, Bt DL No 4624 (County of Oxford) Movements Squadron RAuxAF

Air Vice-Marshal R. A. Riseley-Prichard, MA BM BCh FFCM FIMgt No 4626 (County of Wiltshire) Aeromedical Evacuation Squadron RAuxAF

Dame Stella Rimington, DCB No 7006 (VR) Intelligence Squadron RAuxAF

Air Vice-Marshal B. H. Newton, CB OBE Helicopter Support Squadron RAuxAF

GENERAL DUTIES BRANCH

Flight Lieutenants

1991

Graham, K. P. BSc   (P)   4 Nov

1994

Burgess, J. G.	(P)	1 Sept
Garrod, S. J.	(P)	1 Sept
Prince, I. A.	(N)	24 Oct
Chandler, H. T.	(P)	21 Nov

1996

Hawkins, P. W. BSc	(P)	30 Aug
Jordan, R. J. B. BSc	(P)	30 Aug

Roberts, H. D. BSc(Eng)	(P)	30 Aug
Ford, J. A. BSc	(P)	1 Oct
Cook, C. E. BSc	(P)	12 Nov
Wildeman, M. BA	(P)	26 Nov

1997

Lawrenson, A. J. BA	(P)	25 Feb
White, M. J. H. BSc		5 Mar
Fitzgerald, P. E. BSc	(P)	7 Apr
Baatz, A. P.	(N)	30 May
Shiells, I. M.	(N)	30 May
Harper, H. R.	(N)	17 June
Finch, G. P.	(P)	1 July
Walton, M. M. W.	(P)	1 July
Kingsford, P. G. BSc	(P)	5 July
Crawford, J. A. BSc cfs qss	(P)	15 Sept
Pinnington, A.	(ENG)	19 Sept

Black, I. C.	(P)	29 Sept
McLea, C. D.	(P)	3 Oct
Sully, D. S. BEng asq qss	(N)	5 Oct
Knapp, P. D.	(N)	6 Oct
Dixon, D. P.	(N)	7 Oct
Vaughan, T. A. G.	(P)	11 Nov
Bell, J. V. CBE	(N)	12 Nov
Lewis, D. H.	(N)	8 Dec
Coulson, D. L.	(N)	17 Dec

1998

Morison, I. C.	(P)	5 Jan
Marshall, R. A.	(P)	23 Feb
Brown, G. P.	(N)	27 Feb
Mackay, L. W.	(N)	16 Apr
Jones, P. D.	(P)	8 May
Nichol, G. R.	(P)	14 May

OPERATIONS SUPPORT BRANCH

Wing Commanders

1992

Kemp, R. G. MIMgt
    (FLTOPS) 13 July

1996

Partridge, E. F. AE
    BEd   (FLT OPS) 21 Apr

1997

Colver, R. J. OBE
    (FLT OPS)   4 Dec

Squadron Leaders

1987

Blanche, J. B. AE MSc
    BSc DIC   (INT)   1 Feb

1988

Dawson, S. AE MRIN
    (FLT OPS) 16 Sept

1989

Melling, T. J. AE (INT) 1 July

1990

Carr, F. R.   (REGT) 1 Mar
Londesborough, A.
    (FLT OPS) 1 Sept

1991

Wells, J. C. A. AE MA
    BA RGN RMN RNT
    (INT)   1 Feb

1992

Dulson, P. P. AE
    (FLT OPS) 1 May
Lussey, D.   (REGT) 26 Oct

1993

Marshall, I.   (INT) 16 June
Hodgson, P. AE MA
    (INT)   1 July
O'Shaughnessy, K. M.
    P. AE   (FLT OPS) 1 Oct

1994

Beamish, O. T.
    (FLT OPS) 1 Aug
Matheson, D. AE
    (REGT) 1 Aug
Park, A. S. (FLT OPS) 1 Oct

1995

Roberts, S. G. AE BA
    (INT)   3 Mar
Graham, M. B.
    (FLT OPS) 30 June
Ward, J. R. AE (REGT) 1 Nov

1996

Muir, R. W. (FLTOPS) 1 Jan
Cullpitt, J. V. (INT) 1 Feb
Pattenden, S. M. (INT) 1 Oct
Beaton, A. J. (FLT OPS) 22 Nov
Ashton, D. (INT) 27 Nov
Bevan, J. H. (INT) 27 Nov

1997

White, D. J. (FLTOPS) 29 Jan
Ridge, M. C. FIMgt
    MILog   (INT) 1 Apr
Main, A. P. T. OBE MIPD
    MRAeS MIMgt
    (FLTOPS) 15 May
Moncaster, C. J. BSc
    (FLTOPS) 9 July
Bunkell, G. W. AE
    FCII   (REGT) 1 Sept
Plumridge, D. L. AIB
    (INT)   1 Oct

1998

Wallbank, D. J. (INT) 1 Feb

Flight Lieutenants

1980

Graham-Green, V. M. T.
AE   (INT)   1 May

1983

Harrison, A. J. AE MRIN
MIMgt   (INT)   15 Aug

1985

Wright, W. F. AE BSc
BArch RIBA(FLT OPS)   1 Sept

1986

Gray, N. M. BSc   (INT)   3 Jan
Horn, J. A. BSc   (INT)   12 Jan

1987

Mackay, F. TD   (INT)   1 Jan
Colhoun, D. N. T.
              (FLT OPS) 18 May
Reid, J. C. BA   (INT)   18 May
Laird, B. C.   (FLT OPS) 26 June
Ailes, M. K. G. BSc
                  (INT)   7 Nov
Tingle, D. AE
DipElEng   (INT)   7 Nov

1988

van Geene, R. G.
              (FLT OPS) 29 Mar
Tooze, R. J. W. AE
IEng   (FLT OPS)   3 May
Shields, D.   (INT)   16 Dec

1989

Tomlinson, P. F. BEd
                  (INT)   5 Feb
Fraser, C. BEd   (INT)   1 July
Matthews, J. T. BA
              (REGT)   16 Dec

1990

Gray, J.   (FLT OPS) 13 Jan
Davies, C. W.   (INT)   15 Mar
Crudgington, S. AE
              (FLT OPS)   2 July
Platt, K. J. G. BSc(Eng)
CEng MIEE   (INT)   24 Sept
Bratton, E. G. R. AE
              (REGT)   1 Oct
Purdy, R. B. MA MITI
qss i   (FLT OPS)   6 Nov

1991

Shaw, R. J. AE RIBA
                  (INT)   1 Jan
McGettrick, J. J.(REGT)   2 July
Ashbee, D. J. AE (INT)   1 Aug
Everitt, A. J. (FLT OPS) 22 Aug

1992

Lynn, T. DMS FIMgt
MRIN   (FLT OPS)   1 July
Byrne, J. D. AE MA
                  (INT)   1 Aug
Creed, N. R. E.   (INT)   1 Aug
Drew, J. L. BSc MIPD
GradIPD   (INT)   1 Aug
Meiklejohn, I. R. BA
BA   (INT)   1 Nov
Buxton, R. S.(FLT OPS)   10 Nov

1993

Chappell, J. I. BSc(INT)   1 Jan
Magan, J. BA   (INT)   29 June
Martin, L. A. AE (INT)   11 July
Hellyer, R. J. (FLT OPS) 27 July

1994

Langston-Jones, P. G.
              (REGT)   7 Feb
Oliver, A. J.   (INT)   1 Apr
Whiteley, H. E. LLB
                  (INT)   4 Apr
Quaintmere, P. J. (INT)   11 Apr
Weekes, N. C. F. MA
psc(m)   (INT)   5 May
Lewis, A. D. BA LLB
JP   (INT)   21 June
Gardner, M. J. MBA
BSc   (REGT) 22 June

Eves, D. G. E. D. (INT)   2 Aug
Beynon, G. G(FLT OPS)   18 Oct
Currie, J. H.   (INT)   31 Oct
Lovegrove, G. B.
              (FLT OPS)   1 Nov

1995

Bruster, A. G.(FLT OPS)   25 Jan
Collins, K.   (FLT OPS) 27 Jan
Lyall, G. AE BA   (INT)   1 May
Morrison, D.   (INT)   1 May
Murray, B. A. BA (INT)   1 May
Verril, M.   (FLT OPS) 29 Nov

1996

Alldritt, D. P. G. (REGT) 16 Jan
Woodhead, S. J. M.
BSc   (FLT OPS) 21 Jan
Alderson, B.   (INT)   30 Jan
Davies, J. C.   (INT)   1 Feb
Daniel, N. S.   (ATC)   29 Feb
Livingstone, S. BSc
MIMgt   (FLT OPS) 15 Mar
Retallic, J.   (INT)   28 Mar
Andrews, S. C.   (INT)   15 Apr
Launder, W. A. AE
              (REGT)   1 May
Bradshaw, P. N. MSc
                  (INT)   26 May
Shaw, G.   (INT)   1 June
Zervoudakis, A. BA
                  (INT)   1 June
Slingsby, E. T. BEng
              (FLTOPS) 26 June
Greenhalgh, S. B.
              (FLT OPS) 25 Sept
Niven, M. L. (FLT OPS)   26 Sept
Ryan, G. A. E. AE
              (FLT OPS)   1 Oct
Nichol, D. A. BA
              (FLT OPS)   9 Oct
Rice, K. R.   (REGT)   9 Oct
Owens, N. R. BSc
              (REGT)   15 Oct
Park, S. J. BA
              (FLT OPS) 27 Nov
Payne, A. J. MA BA
                  (INT)   27 Nov

1997

Anning J. E.   (INT)   1 Jan
Baker, J. E.   (REGT)   2 Jan
Turnbull, J. G.
              (FLT OPS) 21 Jan

Flight Lieutenants

1997—contd

Lowe, P. R. AE MEd
    (REGT)   7 Feb
Londesborough, L. A.
  AE   (FLT OPS) 19 Feb
Reeves, A. C.   (INT) 11 Mar
Redgrave, M. S. (INT) 14 Mar
Stothard, C. A. (REGT) 16 Apr
Greenfield, C. W.
  BEng   (INT) 20 Apr
Abram, E. A.   (INT) 28 Apr
Bayne, P. BSc (FLTOPS) 4 May
Whichelo-Page, E. A.
         (INT) 3 June
Partridge, S. J.   (INT) 16 June
Berryman, C. W.(REGT) 25 June
Rigby, J. C. H. BA
       (REGT) 27 June
Winter, C. B.   (REGT) 22 July
Stenson, R. BA   (FC) 19 Nov
Broome, T. J. (FLTOPS) 24 Nov

1998

Nicoll, R. F.   (INT)   1 Jan
Gilbert P. N.   (INT) 12 Jan
Arnold, A. J. (FLTOPS) 13 Jan
Newman, R. D.
     (FLTOPS) 29 Jan
Austin, P. D.   (INT)   1 May
Wilson, A. D. BA BSc
     (FLT OPS)   1 May

Flying Officers

1991

Bell, A. D. BSc(Eng)
      (REGT) 18 Oct

1992

Crisp, R. J. (FLT OPS)   1 Feb
Nokes, S. M.   (INT)   2 Apr
Talton, S. J. S. (INT) 16 July
Smith, S.   (FLT OPS) 6 Aug
Pike, S. BA   (INT) 25 Nov

1993

Morcom, B. W. (REGT) 27 June
Dye, A. P.   (REGT) 30 July
Metcalfe, J. W. (REGT) 19 Aug
Avery, J. W. L. S. (INT) 20 Sept
Parker, J. E. BA PGCE
  (INT)   2 Oct
Kewish, C. R. M. (INT) 26 Oct
MacFadyen, S. (INT) 19 Nov

1994

Somerville, J. (INT) 17 Feb
Tabbron, J. W.
     (FLT OPS) 21 June
Moir, A. G. C. BSc (INT) 6 Aug
Owen, C. M.   (INT)   8 Oct
Smith, T. F. MA BA
        (INT) 18 Nov

1995

Waite. I. P.   (INT)   5 Jan
Hayes, D.   (INT) 15 Jan
Austin, T. N.   (INT) 19 Jan
Comfort, S. B. RM(INT) 2 July
Fox, S. BA   (INT) 14 July

1996

Moore, M. A. S. (INT) 16 Feb
Johnson, J. C. (INT)   1 Mar
Roche, J. A.   (INT) 25 Mar
Weaver, P. M. G. (INT) 18 Apr
Morley, D. M. BEd
       (REGT) 24 May
Leyshon, T. J. R. (INT) 25 May
Cavie, G. R.   (INT)   1 July
Skidmore, T. R. (INT) 18 July
McDonald-Webb, R. N.
       (INT) 16 Aug
Bolton, C. L. (FLT OPS) 29 Oct
Pearson, N. R.
     (FLT OPS) 19 Dec

1997

Gale, P. S.   (INT) 24 Feb
Fines, G. J.   (REGT)   1 Mar
Bagley, J. V.   (INT)   1 June
Farrant, W. F. (INT) 31 July
Chegwidden, P. (REGT) 21 Sept

Jones, J. A.   (INT) 10 Dec

1998

Thompson, S. P. BA
      (INT) 13 Apr

Pilot Officers

1995

Bowden, L. M. (REGT) 1 May

1996

Ince, N. D.   (INT) 16 Mar
Drye, T. J.   (REGT) 11 Sept
Horwood, J.   (INT) 15 Oct
Cowling, J. T.(FLT OPS) 16 Dec

1997

Cooper, J. P. (REGT) 24 Apr
Bowles, C. M. (REGT) 7 Nov
Padgett. L.   (INT) 21 Nov
Walters, T. J. MA BA
      (INT) 21 Nov

Acting Pilot Officers

1996

Patel, R. C.	(INT)	30 Mar
Crayford, K. A. J.	(INT)	14 Apr
Barnes, R. A.	(INT)	20 Apr
Moore, G. L.	(INT)	18 May
Warren, R. J. R. K. BA		
BSc	(INT)	16 July
Featherstone, R. A. J.		
	(INT)	4 Sept
Brooksbank, A. J.		
	(FLT OPS)	16 Dec
Nicholds, D.	(FLT OPS)	16 Dec

1997

Gooch, N. I.	(FLTOPS)	16 May
Paton, R. A.	(REGT)	13 Oct
Coulson, S. G.	(INT)	12 Nov

1998

Claesens, A. P.	(INT)	16 Feb
Hanson, S. C.	(INT)	5 Mar

ENGINEER BRANCH

Squadron Leader

1996

Ahearn, A. S. AE	1 Feb

Flight Lieutenants

1996

Place, C. S. BTech	7 Aug
McMahon, D. BSc	23 Sept
McAnally, A. D. BSc	
CEng MIMechE	30 Sept

Flying Officer

1996

Greig, A. D. C.	1 Oct

SUPPLY (MOVEMENTS) BRANCH

Group Captain

1994

Mighall, R. T. W. OBE	
ADC MSc BA	28 July

Wing Commander

1994

Dixon, R. OBE MCIPS	
MInstPet MIMgt aws	
psc im	16 May

Squadron Leaders

1995

Freeman, F. A. AE qs	20 Apr
Symonds, M. L. AE	20 Oct

1996

Gingell, A. S. BSc	27 Nov

1997

Willis, A. P.	26 Mar

1998

Mallon, M. G.	15 Feb

Flight Lieutenants

1996

Anderson, C. G. BEd	22 Feb
Willmot, P. S.	23 Sept
Dunn, M. J. AE	1 Oct

1997

Saddington, J. P.	1 Jan
Williams, R. B. BSc MIPD MIMgt	1 Apr

Flying Officers

1994

Hammond, B. K.	3 Feb

1996

Morgan, B. E.	31 Jan

1997

Morgan, D. L.	14 May

Pilot Officers

1997

Stephens, J. C.	21 Nov
Wheeler, J. A.	21 Nov

ADMINISTRATIVE BRANCH

Wing Commanders

1987

Dickson, A. OBE AE	(Sec)	25 Nov

1997

Ducker, G. H. AE	(Sec)	14 Feb
Hyde, C. B.	(Sec)	2 June

Squadron Leaders

1989

Gower, C. AE	(Sec)	24 May
Skues, R. K. AE	(Sec)	24 Nov

1993

Merrick, V. E.	(Sec)	28 July

1994

Gwyn, R. T.	(Sec)	5 July

1995

Mitcham, D. T.	(Sec)	9 Aug

1996

Beighton, S. AE PhD BSc	(Sec)	21 Oct

1997

Lamonte, E. S. M.	(Sec)	1 Apr

Forde, W. L. T. MIMgt (Sec)		11 June

1998

Cunningham, G. C.	(Sec)	1 May

Flight Lieutenants

1982

Allen, D. L. AE MA MSc BA CEng MIM MIProdE i	(Sec)	28 Oct

1987

Storey, C. B. BSc	(Sec)	23 Nov

1989

Difford, H. AE MA BA (Sec)	5 Apr

1991

Morgan, I. D. AE MB ChB MRCGP	(Sec)	4 Sept
Moult, C. J.	(Sec)	8 Nov

1992

Norman, D.	(Sec)	17 Jan
Johnston, P. T.	(Sec)	22 Nov

1993

Darby, S. J. BSc	(Sec)	1 Aug
Craig, T. J. CertEd	(Sec)	1 Sept
Cairns, M. J.	(Sec)	1 Nov

1994

Seaword, R. W.	(Sec)	25 Feb
Lynch, J. R.	(Sec)	12 Apr
Taffinder, S. J. S.	(Sec)	17 July

Flight Lieutenants

1994—contd

Dargan, S.   (Sec)   25 Nov

1995

Masson, D. G. MA
     (Sec)   17 Jan
Power, C. S.   (Sec)   25 Sept
Corbett, A. J.   (Sec)   6 Nov

1996

Willis, R. J. BA   (Sec)   29 Apr
Burgess, S. F. BSc (Sec)   1 May
Pell, K. L. BA   (Sec)   22 July
Parr, J. L. AIB   (Sec)   23 Sept

1997

Chitty, D. A. MA   (Sec)   12 Apr
McNulty, K. BA   (Sec)   1 Aug
Shrubsole, S. C.   (Sec)   1 Aug

1998

Hearn, P. J. MBE
   MIMgt   (Sec)   1 Jan

Flying Officers

1991

de Banzie, S. E. BA
   MIL   (Sec)   21 June

1994

Dorey, P. M.   (Sec)   25 Feb

1995

Bryant, I. M.   (Sec)   1 Dec

1997

Bishop, L.   (Sec)   7 Mar
Leach, J. W. P.   (Sec)   23 Apr
Sawers, L.   (Sec)   1 May
Mitchell, G.   (Sec)   21 Sept

1998

Pemberton, A. L.   (Sec)   26 Mar

Pilot Officers

1996

Loosemore, C. S. A.
     (Sec)   26 Mar

1997

Radcliffe, N. J. R.   (Sec)   1 Apr

Acting Pilot Officers

1997

Buckley, D.   (Sec)   6 Feb
Dalboozi, F. BA   (Sec)   6 Feb
Grattan, M. P. BA   (Sec)   28 Apr
Thomas, C. D. I. BA
     (Sec)   7 Aug

1998

Walsh, M. C. F.   (Sec)   7 May

MEDICAL BRANCH

Wing Commanders

1997

Curnow, J. BMedSci
   BM BS   1 Sept
Almond, M. K.
   BMedSci BM BS
   MRCP   28 Nov

Squadron Leaders

1980

Vital, M. F. MRCS LRCP
   DRCOG   13 June

1986

Pote, J. BSc MB BS
   MRCGP   22 June
Whitmey, R. J. BSc MB
   ChB   17 Aug
Lee, C. P. MSc BSc MB
   ChB DRCOG DPH
   DTM&H   10 Nov

1991

Martin, T. E. BSc MB BS
   MRCGP MRCS LRCP
   DRCOG MRAeS   11 June
Elcock, S. M. MB BCh
   MRCGP DRCOG
   DA   29 Oct

1992

Thomas, H. F. MSc BSc
   MB ChB   19 July

Squadron Leaders

1995

Hannaford, P. F. MB
  ChB MRCGP DRCOG
  DCH DAvMed   26 Jan
Guly, U. M. V.   17 Feb
Smith, P. C. T. MB BCh
  MRCGP DRCOG   19 July
Charlwood, G. P. MB
  BCh BAO MRCGP
  DCH   12 Sept
Mowbray, A. BSc MB
  ChB FRCA   21 Oct

1996

Pugsley, W. B. BA MB
  BS FRCS   19 Mar
Bannister, J. MB ChB
  FRCA   26 Mar
Barlow, P. BSc MB ChB
  FRCS   26 Mar
Day, T. K. MChir MB
  MRCP   10 Jun

1997

Stewart, A. V. G. MB
  ChB FRCA DA   2 July
McCormack, P. J. MB
  ChB MRCGP DRCOG
  DOrthRSCEng   3 July

1998

Douglas, A. F.   13 Feb

Flight Lieutenants

1993

Smart, K. T. BA MB
  ChB   1 Aug

1995

Shirley, P. J. MB ChB
  FRCA DA DipIMC   2 Nov

1997

Ratnasabpathy, U.   9 Sept
Akhatar, S.   21 Oct

PRINCESS MARY'S ROYAL AIR FORCE NURSING SERVICE

Squadron Leaders

1990

Sparkes, P. J. AE   27 Oct

1994

Orzel, M. N. F. RSCN   1 Aug

1996

Kyte, D. I.   1 Aug

Flight Lieutenants

1987

Stephens, E. M. RM   15 May

1990

Warncken, B. C. RMN
                   19 Feb

1993

Baranski, P. B. RM   1 Sep

1994

Haggo, S. J.   18 Aug

1995

Charters, S. E.   18 Feb
Thornhill, P. A.   30 Nov

Flight Lieutenants

1996

Moodie, A. M.	7 Feb
Horton, H. J.	18 June
Bond, E. F.	12 Sept

1997

Horburgh, M. W.	13 May
Woodbridge, V. T.	20 Aug

Flying Officers

1994

Iheagwaram, E.	2 May

1995

Farrell, L. N.	14 Dec

1997

Arroyo, H. G.	4 Aug

MEDICAL SECRETARIAL BRANCH

Wing Commander

1995

Donaldson, A. S. AE BA psc(m) s G(a)	1 Oct

Squadron Leaders

1988

Walker, S. AE RNT	3 May

1996

Hird, J. C. M.	1 Oct

Flight Lieutenants

1995

Walden-Hughes, P. P.	1 Dec

1996

Pottie, C. R.	9 Dec

1997

Edwards, N. H.	24 Apr

1998

Hawthornthwaite, J. M.	1 Mar
Heaton, B. G.	1 Mar

Flying Officer

1997

Mathieson, C. A. C. AE	2 May

1998

Irwin, M. J.	2 Feb

Acting Pilot Officer

1997

Borgman, P. S.	1 Jan

(UNIVERSITY AIR SQUADRONS)

GENERAL DUTIES BRANCH

Acting Pilot Officers

1996

Flewin, M. R.	(P)	1 Sept
Rickards, J. A.	(P)	1 Sept
Aspin, K. P.	(P)	12 Nov
Barrett, M. P.	(P)	12 Nov

1997

Spencer, D. C. P.	(N)	28 Jan
Thomson, A. R. H.	(P)	28 Jan
Butler, V. R. P.	(P)	1 Mar
Baron, A. P.	(P)	1 Aug
Lee, P. J.	(P)	1 Oct

1998

Pengelly, O. J.	(P)	1 Jan

ROYAL AIR FORCE VOLUNTEER RESERVE

(Training Branch)

Flying Officers		1967		1970	
1959		Badham, J. W.	14 Jan	Darrant, J. G.	1 Apr
		Gillett, F. R.	26 Jan	Fawkes, R. E. MIMgt	
Clarke, J. K.	11 Nov	Edwards, G.	25 Feb	MInstAM	27 June
		Trotman, C. S.	3 Mar	Emmerson, B.	16 July
1960		Wallace, P. R.	10 Apr	Sims, A. W. BSc	16 Aug
		Green, R. W.	4 May	North, StJ. D. B.	5 Sept
Crowdy, B. A. BA	25 Sept	Fraser, R. L. OBE	18 May	Allcoat, M. L.	9 Sept
		Scott, J. A.	18 Aug	Shepperd, K. H.	10 Sept
		Selwyn-Yates, I. M. P.	15 Sept	Briton, T.	12 Sept
1961		Croucher, D. M.	28 Sept	Pomeroy, D. E. BSc	28 Oct
Smith, G. MIMgt	6 Aug			Howard, A. A. MBE	20 Nov
		1968			
1963		Beavis, J. R. BA	7 Jan	**1971**	
		Grierson, S. W. MA	8 Jan	King, J. P. BA	10 Jan
Blunn, K.	30 June	Briar, L. A. MBE	14 Jan	Brackenborough, K.	1 Mar
Beeley, G. R. LLB	9 Aug	Smith, B. C.	8 Feb	Starling, R. H.	23 Apr
Higgins, B. T. MBE	16 Dec	Ireland, E. G.	7 Mar	Jones, I. D. L. MBE BSc	25 June
		Jeffcoate, R. C.	21 May	Richards, D. J.	25 June
		Sollars, A. J. MA	12 July	Ramsden, G.	10 July
1964		Wood, B.	2 Aug	Speed, D. R.	10 July
Willis, M. R.	5 May	Dawson, C. J.	22 Aug	Williams, B. C. MA	10 July
Austin, A. W. MBE	22 June	Giles, P. OBE	22 Aug	Sutton, M. J. F. C.	1 Aug
Scott, P. G. BSc	9 July	Bartram, I.	19 Nov	Broad, I. H.	10 Oct
Boyce, P. E. BA	25 July	McMaster, R. S.	13 Dec	Robinson, G. F.	20 Oct
Fleetwood, A. V.	6 Oct	Lobb, T. A.	17 Dec	Gallup, S. BSc	23 Oct
Lowe, E. H. OBE	10 Oct			Price, B. V.	5 Dec
Lowes, R.	10 Oct	**1969**		Prescott, R. M. BSc	18 Dec
		Gillen, D. A. BA	12 Jan		
		Alleyn, W. G.	27 Jan	**1972**	
1965		Howard, J.	27 Feb	Beaven, J. P.	27 Jan
		Coombes, M. C. R. MBE	23 Mar	Bacon, C. J. BA MCIPS	29 Jan
Lemm, D. H. W.	29 Apr	Moor, R. G. BSc	29 Mar	Watson, M. W.	24 Feb
Farron, J.	17 July	Arnold, R. W. MBE	6 Apr	Brown, R. W.	4 Mar
Hearn-Grinham, M. C.		Stedman, K. B.	4 May	Tiller, N.	11 Mar
V.	14 Sept	Allen, T. J. BA	26 June	Fox, R.	24 Apr
Copas, R. N. K. BA	21 Sept	McCarroll, P. J.	30 June	Sturman, H.	30 Apr
Gilbert, M. J. BA	6 Nov	Hunt, V. J.	20 July	Wiggins, A.	30 Apr
		Murray, A. V. M. MA	14 Sept	Axhorn, P. C.	9 May
		Young, K. A.	14 Sept	Bonney, E. V.	25 June
1966		Pennock, N.	10 Oct	Jackson, K.	25 June
		Jones, F. M. P. BSc		Harrison, D. L.	30 June
Cotton, M. J.	28 Jan	ACGI	1 Nov	Endean, B. W.	1 July
House, B. N. M.	11 June	Strickland, C. S. P.	29 Nov	Fuller, J.	1 July
Carter, R. O.	11 Nov	Todd, I. F. OBE	29 Nov	Shepherd, P. W. BSc	
				CEng MIMechE	3 July
				Singleton, J. E.	
				DPhysEd	3 Aug
				Coulam, M. G. BSc	11 Sept

Flying Officers

1972—contd

Mott, B. G.	4 Oct
Murphy, B.	14 Oct
Kerr, I. S.	15 Oct
Mallett, C. W.	14 Nov
Curry, J.	1 Dec
Hayler, P. BA	7 Dec
Bowles, I. R.	16 Dec
Yarrow, P. N. S.	16 Dec

1973

Mobey, R.	3 Feb
Harris, J. C.	15 Feb
Brand, A. D.	22 Mar
Porter, G. C. BSc	1 Apr
Vass, R. I.	6 Apr
Arnold, I. D.	21 Apr
Pepper, J.	5 May
Gilmour, C. R.	7 May
Bowen, D. I.	27 May
Broadwith, B. E. BSc	2 June
Bullock, J.	8 June
Bomphrey, J. S. BSc	21 June
Johns, T. J. OBE	7 July
Hotston, P. R.	14 July
Laver, M. R.	6 Aug
Arnott, R. H. C.	30 Sept
Abbott, P. L.	24 Oct
Lyall, G. BA	22 Nov
Short, T. W.	25 Nov
Wallis, P. S. BA	10 Dec
Doust, R. J. C.	13 Dec

1974

Lloyd, D. M.	4 Jan
Scott, R. J. I.	4 Jan
Beaumont, R. A.	14 Jan
Young, M.	14 Jan
Talbot, K.	27 Jan
Connolly, T. E.	14 Feb
Campbell, G.	15 Feb
Williams, F. S.	1 Mar
Gray, T. D.	20 Mar
Walsh, R. H.	28 Mar
Quartly, A. F. BSc	29 Mar
Colebrook, M. C.	1 May
Olver, J. N.	12 May
Smith, K. R. J.	18 May
Flood, C. J. MA	26 May
Whitestone, A. E. N. BA	7 July
Benson, P.	4 Aug

Walton, J. N.	4 Aug
Protheroe, L.	10 Aug
Greer, A. T. BSc	18 Aug
Hearle, E. M.	20 Aug
Gridley, M. J.	4 Sept
Pertwee, M. N.	9 Sept
Scott, C. R.	18 Sept
Talbot, R. K. DPhysEd	29 Sept
Broom, B. N.	4 Oct
Rawlings, D. G.	4 Oct
Coldwell, R. A.	11 Oct
Lewis, C. A.	11 Oct
Quarman, B.	8 Nov
Thomson, D.	20 Nov
Edwards, G.	27 Nov
Vaughan, M. D.	5 Dec
Beech, R. C.	20 Dec

1975

Mustard, A.	22 Jan
Wilson, G. A.	2 Feb
Cousins, C. MA	28 Feb
Lewis, R. BSc	10 Mar
Farmer, C. J.	15 Mar
Davey, M. J. S.	27 Mar
Parker, D. E.	12 Apr
Carpenter, J. J.	6 June
Jung, M. A.	15 June
Hodges, P. BSc	1 July
Clement, J.	9 July
Sheehan, D. W. MBE	11 July
Clavell, A. R. FCA	
MIMgt	29 Aug
Irlam, J. C. BSc	1 Sept
Senft, S. W.	29 Sept
Hine, M. T. BA	9 Nov
Lobb, P. J. A. MBE	9 Nov
Barker, A. A.	12 Nov
Howarth, B.	29 Nov
Spence, J. R.	29 Nov
Rooney, W.	18 Dec
Wilson, F. K. BA	29 Dec

1976

Middleton, D. J.	30 Jan
Reed, P. H.	1 Feb
Anthony, D. R.	20 Feb
Morrell, C. J.	20 Mar
Wise, P. G. BSc	9 July
Coxon, F. R. W. MBE	10 July
Edwards, M. G.	22 July
Mockeridge, P.	
MIMgt	25 July
Smith, G. J.	25 July
Wills Pope, B. W.	1 Aug
Sandford, G. S.	5 Aug

Carter, E. J. BSc	20 Sept
Briant, D. R. H.	25 Sept
Biggs, C. J.	9 Oct
Wilkie, R. M.	10 Oct
Lines, B.	16 Oct
Ball, B. J. W. GTCL	29 Oct
McCleave, M. J. MBE	4 Nov
Nicholson, J. ACA	17 Nov
Abbott, J.	20 Nov
Wright, A. G.	27 Nov
Smith, A. A.	5 Dec
Stockill, S.	16 Dec

1977

Thomas, A.	22 Jan
Green, T. B.	23 Jan
Oram, B. K.	5 Feb
Ing, P. W.	7 Feb
Owen, G. C.	19 Feb
Cook, A. BSc	20 Feb
Coomber, T. W.	24 Feb
Mans, K. D. R.	5 Apr
Drury, G. T.	21 Apr
Albone, M. S. C.	29 Apr
Osborne, A. J.	5 May
Hollands, B. F.	15 May
Chesworth, F. V.	19 May
Morris, S.	9 July
Woods, B. J.	24 Sept
Liquorish, N. J.	1 Oct
Smith, G. S.	1 Oct
Wilby, P. D.	8 Oct
Gallagher, K.	29 Oct
Walton, A. T.	3 Nov
Lark, A. J. MBE	14 Nov
Wilson, R. L.	29 Nov
Watt, K.	9 Dec
Webster, M. S.	11 Dec

1978

Russell, D.	26 Jan
Harvey, D. M.	28 Jan
Craig, G. MBE	29 Jan
Miller, C. A.	29 Jan
Lowe, B. C.	8 Feb
Mosses, J. P.	16 Feb
Place, J. K.	23 Feb
Windo, A. R.	26 Feb
North, M. J.	26 Mar
Woolliscroft, R. E.	5 Apr
Edwards, G.	10 Apr
Horsley, T. J.	1 May
Johnstone, D. A.	1 May
Richards, F. R.	3 May
Lutton, P. F. BA	4 May
Hope, D. E. BSc	3 June

Flying Officers

1978—contd

Watson, C. L.	7 June
Martin, D.	23 June
Cope, C. S.	4 July
Nowak, L. C.	7 July
Kirkland, F. B.	20 July
Fairington, R. W.	21 July
Butler, R. L. S.	26 July
Morvan, G.	28 July
McCrae, D. C.	9 Aug
Cummings, N. MBE	26 Aug
Davies, K.	26 Aug
Jones, R. P.	28 Sept
Beecroft, A. J.	11 Oct
Wells, D. J.	11 Oct
Begent, T. A.	15 Nov
Richardson, J. W. BA BEd MIMgt	20 Nov
Piper, G. R. BSc	5 Dec
Dimond, J.	6 Dec
Pardoe, D. J. D.	6 Dec
Guilbert, G. BSc	17 Dec

1979

Seymour, J. N. J.	5 Jan
Oatey, W. R.	12 Jan
Blaikie, A. R.	7 Feb
Peasgood, D. J.	7 Feb
Lyttle, T.	9 Feb
Hammond, I.	23 Feb
Burnett, W. H.	2 Mar
Moss, R.	2 Mar
Molnar, B. R.	7 Mar
Neil, J. W. G.	15 Mar
Warrender, B. R. MA	15 Mar
Tancell, P.	31 Mar
Tipper, M. S.	4 Apr
Parry, J. K. BSc	11 Apr
Kirby, R. J.	19 Apr
Miskell, T. M.	14 June
Mills, S. M.	15 June
Nichols, J. P.	22 June
Wall, J. P.	29 July
Platts, P. B.	5 Aug
Bower, P. E. L.	14 Sept
Southee, P. E. C.	21 Sept
Lawrence, T. MA	23 Sept
Richards, P. J.	4 Oct
Anderson, A.	11 Oct
Sheehan, A. V.	11 Oct
Wright, J. A.	9 Nov
Barber, D. I.	23 Nov
Coombs, P.	23 Nov
Edwards, B. R.	23 Nov

Weldon, C. A.	23 Nov
Hucker, S. J.	30 Nov
Hackett, R. PhD	1 Dec
Peace, J.	20 Dec
Bussetil, S. G.	22 Dec
Green, N. J.	22 Dec

1980

Griffin, J. W.	11 Jan
Greenhalgh, J. K.	31 Jan
Kinnon, D. McF.	7 Feb
Paterson, R. A.	7 Feb
Hepburn, R. O.	29 Feb
Catterall, R.	6 Mar
Shilladay, S. BA	6 Mar
Speakman, P. C.	6 Mar
Goldsworthy, R.	7 Mar
Cartwright, B.	8 Mar
Upham, P.	21 Mar
Clark, D. A.	22 Mar
Harris, A. R.	6 Apr
Flower, H.	25 Apr
Massey, P.	25 Apr
Molloy, S.	25 Apr
Thrussell, P. C. S.	25 Apr
Bosworth, R. J.	26 Apr
Davison, I. F.	27 Apr
Walker, J. A. BSc	19 June
Chalmers, I. MacD.	26 June
Apiafi, H.	27 June
O'Brien, D. A.	28 June
Ledamun, R.	29 June
Fradley, D.	23 July
Hadlow, R. K. J.	23 July
Geddes, R.	2 Aug
Keel, J. S.	4 Aug
Garrett, M.	12 Aug
Hills, E. R.	25 Aug
Mansfield, J.	5 Sept
Cutting, D. J. BA	12 Sept
Wilkinson, T. S.	14 Sept
Gould, C. J.	20 Sept
Symons, M. T.	20 Sept
Docking, P. W.	4 Oct
Osborne, R.	16 Oct
Austin, A. L. BA	18 Oct
Reynolds, D. A.	30 Oct
Colvin, D. P.	7 Nov
Raynor, G.	8 Nov
Whitters, P. D.	15 Nov

1981

Percival, D.	29 Jan
MacKay, D. J.	19 Feb
Swan, B.	19 Feb
Price, D.	28 Feb

Clemerson, G. C. BSc	4 Mar
Chart, D. I. J.	7 Mar
Vinnicombe, W. J.	8 Mar
Reid, M. B. BSc	9 Mar
Byng, E. F.	14 Mar
Gardner, W. J.	20 Mar
Kern, S. J. MA	29 Mar
Mackintosh, N. J.	8 May
Toon, T. H.	17 May
Challoner, E. IEng MIEIE	4 June
Jackson, B. K.	5 June
McClenagham, P. S. BEd	5 June
Jackson, T. A.	20 June
Doughty, A.	26 June
Hatch, P. F. BSc	9 July
Priest, P. T.	11 July
Seazell, P. G.	19 July
Matthews, G. R.	22 July
Gunter, N. J.	26 July
Turnbull, W. E.	26 July
Kelly, I.	30 July
Smith, R.	1 Aug
Wallace, I.	8 Aug
Walker, R. L. H. BSc	12 Aug
Christmas, K.	13 Aug
Richards, S. J.	13 Aug
Nicholls, P. T.	22 Aug
Clark, D. E.	23 Aug
Wake, G. R.	24 Aug
Duff, G. R.	3 Sept
Millar, J. B.	13 Sept
Harrison, S. D.	1 Oct
Elliott, A. G.	3 Oct
McCammont, T. T. McM	3 Oct
Murray, I. B.	3 Oct
Wood, S. MCIT	17 Oct
Acland, C. A.	23 Oct
Beardwood, P. N.	29 Oct
Ince, J. B. MCIPS	30 Oct
Miller, R. R. BTech MBCS	31 Oct
McCall, J. M.	12 Nov
Brennan, P. M. BSc	14 Nov
Aldred, J. BSc	26 Nov
Woolcock, D. H.	30 Nov
Mayes, G. J.	12 Dec
Ralph, P. S.	17 Dec
Woods, S. J. BSc	17 Dec
Walker, P.	21 Dec

1982

Thomas, G. C. J.	8 Jan
Broomfield, I. K.	14 Jan
Ellis, B. I.	14 Jan
Bowers, J. W.	30 Jan

Flying Officers

1982—contd

Doubell, P. T.	30 Jan
Hugo, R. L.	30 Jan
Yeoell, A.	30 Jan
Thirkell, C.	31 Jan
Adamson, C. J.	8 Feb
Curtis, A. J.	27 Feb
Southern, G. BDS	27 Feb
Poloczek, J. A.	7 Mar
Barton-Greenwood, G. C.	10 Mar
Thompson, A. G. F.	10 Mar
Metcalfe, J. W.	20 Mar
McArthur, A. BSc	26 Mar
Bowles, G. J.	1 Apr
Fisher, C. J.	10 Apr
Buehner-Coldrey, M. J. M.	30 Apr
White, M. E. BSc MInstP	1 May
Atherton, H. S. J.	2 May
Watts, P. A.	2 May
Wyse, A. R.	2 May
Greenslade, A. L. J.	8 May
Pitts, G. K.	9 May
Faulkner, C. R. BSc	20 May
Warren, J. S. BSc	22 May
Lever, A. J. BSc ARCS	26 May
Davis, D. J.	16 June
Dunn, D. J.	16 June
Lyons, P. C.	16 June
Taylor, W. L.	16 June
Armstrong, A. P.	17 June
Milne, T. A.	17 June
Marshall, A. E.	27 June
Woodward, I. D.	27 June
Mohammed, I. N.	30 June
Smith, A. E. BSc	9 July
Charnock, G.	11 July
Melmore, A. C.	11 July
Orr, H.	4 Aug
Kaye, M. P. BA	9 Aug
Brickley, C. J. A.	22 Aug
Slack, J. D. BSc	22 Aug
Denton, W. B.	26 Aug
Nicholls, S.	26 Aug
Chapman, G. W. MIMgt	29 Aug
Ranger, M. StJ.	29 Aug
Simpson, A. J. BSc	29 Aug
Burns, J. G.	11 Sept
Guy, S. D.	12 Sept
Semple, N. DipEE	20 Sept
Thompson, A. P. BSc	24 Sept
Biddles, D.	26 Sept
Bennett, G. E. D. BA	7 Oct
Little, G. I. BSc	7 Oct

Bailey-Woods, G. MRAeS	9 Oct
Bennett, A. R. T.	9 Oct
Dicks, C. P.	9 Oct
Lewis, M. A.	9 Oct
McKeown, B. J.	11 Oct
Cook, J. A. BA	13 Oct
Coffer, P.	28 Oct
Gibson, T. H. G.	28 Oct
Mehmet, K.	28 Oct
Swierczek, A. F. I. AIB	29 Oct
Evans, M. R. BSc	3 Nov
Chapman, J. W.	13 Nov
Walter, T. D. BA	14 Nov
Burton, P. J.	17 Nov
Melican, J. J. BA	21 Nov
Abbey, S. M. BA	26 Nov
Baker, M.	28 Nov
Jelfs, R. G. BEd	28 Nov
Measures, P. J.	8 Dec
Passfield, A.	8 Dec
Miller, B.	11 Dec
Moore, J. T.	17 Dec
Page, J. R.	17 Dec
Willman, W. T. BA MIMgt	19 Dec

1983

Harris, D. L.	6 Jan
Wilson, R. J.	6 Jan
Hill, T. J. BSc	14 Jan
Hawkes, T. I. C. BSc	19 Jan
Cox, D. C.	26 Jan
Morten, P. R.	26 Jan
Day, C. M.	27 Jan
Druce, A. G.	27 Jan
Cook, F. J.	30 Jan
Goodier, R. L.	2 Feb
Wishart, J. M.	2 Feb
Barbour, E. C.	24 Feb
Mitchell, J. A.	24 Feb
Mekins, R.	3 Mar
Borwick, J. P.	11 Mar
Hunter-Brown, D.	11 Mar
Shelbourn, P. J.	27 Mar
Freehold, D. R.	31 Mar
Quayle, S. A.	31 Mar
Sweetman, R. C.	31 Mar
Purllant, N.	16 Apr
Bond, G. F.	28 Apr
Tuff, G.	28 Apr
Clark, M.	8 May
MacDonald, J. A.	11 May
Archibald, D.	13 May
Finch, D. J.	13 May
Wood, D.	13 May
Bethell, A. H.	20 May
Gorman, F.	4 June

Jones, D. R. BA	16 June
Pettitt, B. W.	9 July
Routledge, P. W.	9 July
Stroud, J.	9 July
Forrester, A. BTech	10 July
Scott, P. R. BPharm MPS	10 July
Behenna, R. N.	17 July
Bishop, R. N. McC.	17 July
Lee, R. E.	17 July
Sherry, S. T.	17 July
James, B. R.	24 July
Crowther, A. J.	28 July
Brackston, A. M.	4 Aug
Miller, D. C. BSc	4 Aug
Rushton, F. A. StJ.	4 Aug
Coats, B.	12 Aug
Stanley, J. C.	13 Aug
Banks, H. R.	18 Aug
Cox, M.	29 Aug
Easson, S. RGN RMN DN	1 Sept
Spinks, R. D.	3 Sept
Miller, D. K.	15 Sept
Timothy, R. C.	17 Sept
Chapman, A. W.	22 Sept
Steele, R. M. G. BSc	25 Sept
English, S. A.	30 Sept
Taylor, A. T. H. BSc MIMgt	5 Oct
Brown, D.	14 Oct
Munro, B.	19 Oct
Arnold, D. H.	23 Oct
Howard-Dobson, S. P.	29 Oct
Robinson, C.	29 Oct
Southwell, G. W. PhD MSc BSc	29 Oct
Smith, G. J.	30 Oct
Birkett, B.	12 Nov
Lewis, M. A.	12 Nov
Reywer, G.	12 Nov
Bohanna, P. J.	27 Nov
Twemlow, W. J. BA	27 Nov
Thynne, D.	15 Dec

1984

Harrison, M. D.	6 Jan
Mathews, M. G. BA	6 Jan
Seaton, I. G.	6 Jan
Carter, M. A.	4 Feb
Sergeant, P. S. BEd	4 Feb
Slaney, P. J.	4 Feb
Kalamatianos, C. M. BA	12 Feb
Ensor, S. J.	19 Feb
Eaton, M. A.	2 Mar
Robins, P. R.	2 Mar
Williams, S. MBE	2 Mar
Baker, N. W.	11 Mar

Flying Officers

1984—contd

Horn, J. A.	11 Mar
Ulrich, M. P. ACA	11 Mar
Hartley, J. R. L. BSc	26 Mar
Smith, P. J.	26 Mar
Staniszewski, C. S.	26 Mar
Marshall, I. P.	30 Mar
Huntley, A. D.	1 Apr
McNamara, H. M.	10 Apr
Crook, D. J. BSc	16 Apr
Ferguson, C. G.	16 Apr
Wood, A. J.	16 Apr
Colbourne, D. J.	12 May
Davies, K.	12 May
Perriam, D. A.	12 May
Thompson, M. L.	12 May
Blundell-Pound, G. BSc MCIT	20 May
Gill, G. BA	20 May
Westgate, P. R.	20 May
Wood, P. A. W.	20 May
Barber, D. C.	2 June
Hailstone, A.	2 June
Collins, P. W.	11 June
Edwards, T. G. JP	29 June
Ely, D. E. MIMgt	29 June
Parker, G. G.	29 June
Parker, K. B. M.	29 June
Sloan, R. V.	21 July
Hoy, P. J. MIMgt	6 Aug
Hughes, D. M.	6 Aug
Swales, A. W.	6 Aug
Wilson, W. L. BSc	6 Aug
Mistry, K. K. G.	8 Aug
L'astrange, J. P.	25 Aug
Dent, M. A.	1 Sept
Gordon, J.	1 Sept
Neilson-Hansen, S. A.	7 Sept
Trueman, R.	13 Sept
Lane, P. S. BSc	14 Sept
Redmore, R. J.	17 Sept
Powell, P. J.	22 Sept
Greenow, J. W.	30 Sept
Brady, G.	4 Oct
Harper, M. E.	4 Oct
Lee, R. E. BA	4 Oct
Bennet, M. G. DFC	16 Oct
Bonfield, P. R.	3 Nov
Churnside, T. W.	3 Nov
Wilson, M. J.	3 Nov
Flynn, C. P.	11 Nov
Moffat, J. C.	11 Nov
Ritchie, W.	11 Nov
Linehan, M.	22 Nov
Callow, B.	6 Dec
Clark, A. E. C.	6 Dec

Jenkins, G. A.	8 Dec
Suddards, D. G.	8 Dec
Quarterman, R. J.	20 Dec
Willacy, B. F.	21 Dec
Fry, J. M. BSc	22 Dec

1985

Day, I. E.	3 Jan
Parsons, J.	3 Jan
Whitfield, M. A.	3 Jan
McLauchlan, W. W.	27 Jan
Nicholls, D. T.	27 Jan
Breward, R. W. MSc	1 Feb
Meath, P.	1 Feb
Silver, S. E.	7 Feb
Sucksmith, P. S.	15 Feb
Race, B. T.	16 Feb
Williams, G. N.	3 Mar
Sutton, A. J.	14 Mar
Broadbridge, I. J. D.	21 Mar
Jones, P. M.	21 Mar
Haswell, M. R. BSc MIEE	25 Mar
Streule, C. R. BSc	25 Mar
Courtney, R. B. MSc BTech	29 Mar
Heath, J. G. RMN	29 Mar
Alford, R. E. PhD BSc CChem MRSC	31 Mar
Bark, B. P.	31 Mar
Girdler, E. E. G.	3 Apr
Jones, G. D. R. PhD BSc	14 Apr
Penn, A. D.	22 Apr
Muskett, N. P.	28 Apr
Smith, D. BSc MB ChB	30 Apr
Fitzpatrick, B. J.	5 May
Gould, R. G.	11 May
Holloway, G.	11 May
Hullott, S.	11 May
Smith, P. M. BSc	18 May
Cook, W. J.	22 May
Padgham, A. J.	22 May
Gurd, T. W.	23 May
Cooper, N. C.	24 May
Oliver, A. D.	24 May
Anderson, P. B.	30 June
Bate, K. M.	30 June
Houston, T. W.	30 June
McNeill, C. T.	30 June
Milford, C.	30 June
Moore, K. S.	30 June
Parker, E. R.	28 July
Smith, J. I.	28 July
MacKay, D. J.	12 Aug
Ryder, H. C.	1 Sept
Taylor, R. S.	6 Sept
Beard, G.	19 Sept
Beardsley, C. L.	19 Sept

Sosnowski, S.	19 Sept
Steggles, T. P.	19 Sept
Foster, H.	21 Sept
Smith, M. R.	21 Sept
Williams, A. D.	21 Sept
Graham, G.	23 Sept
Allison, K. D. BA	5 Oct
Stansfield, J. D.	7 Oct
Cheeseman, G. C.	19 Oct
Standish, J. L. IPFA	20 Oct
Bratt, L. BSc	26 Oct
Whittington, J. W. BA MIL	26 Oct
Ving, I. C.	2 Nov
Dudek, M.	9 Nov
Fitch, G. R.	9 Nov
Glyde, A. K.	9 Nov
Barnes, C. R.	24 Nov
Strunwick, A.	24 Nov
Coleman, P. A. BSc	25 Nov
Igglesden, D. J.	25 Nov
Dooley, S. F.	29 Nov
Hawke, T. R.	29 Nov
Johnson, M. S.	6 Dec
Taylor, W. A.	6 Dec
Rickwood, T. R. BA	15 Dec
Naeem, S. M.	16 Dec
Price, S. M.	16 Dec
Rogers, J. C. R.	16 Dec
Tuff, V. G.	16 Dec

1986

Bean, D.	3 Jan
Cartwright, A. C.	3 Jan
Dimond, W. B.	3 Jan
Grix, A. D. H.	3 Jan
Lloyd, S.	3 Jan
Moore, P. A.	3 Jan
Warner, P. S.	3 Jan
Sheppee, P. W. V.	5 Jan
Gillespie, D.	9 Jan
Hodges, C. J. M. BA	17 Jan
Bishop, I. L. BSc	23 Jan
Ancell, T.	27 Jan
Bristow, J. C.	27 Jan
Barber, S.	1 Feb
Davey, P. R.	1 Feb
Duffin, J. E.	1 Feb
Kirczey, A. M.	1 Feb
Down, J. PhD BSc CEng MIERE	9 Feb
Ward, R. J.	16 Feb
Dignan, J. C. MIMgt	19 Feb
Newman, T. P.	3 Mar
Wiper, K. J.	7 Mar
Wright, G.	7 Mar
Longstaffe, A. J.	10 Mar
Barnett, D. A. R.	12 Mar

Flying Officers

1986—contd

Plant, J.	13 Mar
Morris, R. A. F.	19 Mar
Holt, A. BA JP	22 Mar
Loveday, P. B.	22 Mar
Nicholson, S. B.	28 Mar
Boyd, A.D. BEd	2 Apr
Mitchell, R. T. MBE	10 Apr
Levick, P.	16 Apr
Rundle, C. B.	16 Apr
Truberg, P. A.	16 Apr
Johnson, S. R. BSc	28 Apr
Cowley, W.	4 May
Hawkes, G. R.	11 May
Kelsey, G.	15 May
Mullins, C. R. J.	15 May
Bovingdon, A. D.	21 May
Scott, P. J.	21 May
Dailly, N. J. S. Dip El Eng	1 June
Sterland, R. J. MBE	11 June
Smith, R. C.	23 June
Eames, M. E.	26 June
Hick, J. K.	26 June
Lampard, J. S.	26 June
Rowland, D.	26 June
Goodier, R. E.	5 July
Higgins, D. T.	5 July
Saunders, M. J.	5 July
Matthews, S. R.	10 July
Watkins, D. V.	10 July
Gardner, T. P.	25 July
Stanley, D. S.	5 Aug
Gillott, C.	13 Aug
Gregory, T. W.	13 Aug
Foster, R. W.	28 Aug
Lipinska, A. A. E.	6 Sept
Cox, B. R.	14 Sept
Latimer, J. S.	16 Sept
Bush, R. G.	17 Sept
Hicks, R. G.	17 Sept
Chandler, K. R.	28 Sept
Crockard, R. J. M.	30 Sept
Armitage, J. P. BSc	1 Oct
Thomas, B. C.	1 Oct
McCune, A. G.	8 Oct
Hipperson, A. J.	11 Oct
Bosworth, D. PhD BSc	24 Oct
Clarke, J. BSc	24 Oct
Goodger, C. R.	24 Oct
Lark, M. A.	24 Oct
Anderson, D. J.	9 Nov
Baldock, B. F.	12 Nov
Dickinson, N. C.	15 Nov
Eccles, R. S. FCMA	15 Nov
McKinney, A.	15 Nov

Skinner, D. S.	15 Nov
Vance, W. G.	15 Nov
Carter, D. E.	17 Nov
Iliffe-Rolfe, G. D.	18 Nov
Flower, P. C.	3 Dec
Mullan, I. J.	3 Dec
Singer, J. C.	3 Dec
Roberts, T. G. BA	10 Dec
Fletcher, N. J.	14 Dec
Morgan, D. J.	14 Dec
Yates, G. J.	14 Dec
Penwarden, R. J.	16 Dec
Wood, M. R. O.	20 Dec

1987

Barrett, M. E.	9 Jan
Downhan, B. A.	9 Jan
Gibson, G. V. BSc	17 Jan
Gilleran, K. E. FCA AIPM	21 Jan
Kemp, R. A.	21 Jan
Prior, M. E.	21 Jan
French, B. S.	24 Jan
Shingler, F. J. MA	31 Jan
Anderton, K. R.	11 Feb
Bastow, J. N. MBCS	11 Feb
Byrne, M. P.	22 Feb
Cubitt, P. A.	22 Feb
Green, J. B. BSc	22 Feb
Griffiths, D.	22 Feb
Griffiths, L. M.	22 Feb
Yeomans, M. J. M.	22 Feb
Davies, A. J. BA	3 Mar
Da Silva, L. J.	8 Mar
Martin, C.	8 Mar
Nash, M. A.	8 Mar
Wilson, J.	8 Mar
Goodayle, R. C.	25 Mar
Suchorzewski, D. G.	25 Mar
Wellings, H. J.	25 Mar
Blance, L. H. BEd	28 Mar
Loynton, J. C. MA BEd	28 Mar
Kirby, W. J. MBE	8 Apr
Rogers, M. T.	9 Apr
Cairns, I. H.	24 Apr
Thomas, J. E.	28 Apr
Cooper, B. W.	30 Apr
Jones, B. R.	1 May
Ridge, J. P. MA	1 May
Bond, P. J.	2 May
Ledster, C.	2 May
Manfield, R. F. W.	8 May
Boyce, D. R.	13 May
Gould, B. J.	20 May
Pritchard, K.	20 May
Tapply, S. A. MEd BA	31 May
Riley, M. W.	3 June
Wickwar, P. J.	3 June

Shepherdson, K. A.	9 June
Cook, M. I. BSc	11 June
Davis, R. J.	11 June
Reyes, J. A. BA	28 June
Dart, N.	1 July
Davies, H. B.	1 July
Harris, R. W. BSc	1 July
Hollington, R. V.	1 July
Hoyle, R. F.	1 July
Jukes, R. W.	1 July
Parsons, P.	1 July
Sutton, B. J. N.	1 July
Aves, J. M. BSc	8 July
Bell, L. A.	8 July
Armson, T. J.	30 July
Evans, D. E.	30 July
Gregor, G. R.	30 July
Hornsey, L. BSc	30 July
Keane, L.	30 July
Kendall, D. J. BA	30 July
Smale, J. A. BEd	30 July
Souter, T. W.	30 July
Hambly, C. J.	6 Aug
Hudson, I. M.	14 Aug
Mihailovic, D.	14 Aug
Davies, M. S.	22 Aug
Brown, H. D.	29 Aug
Burchall, R. F.	3 Sept
Davies, A. J.	5 Sept
Hedley, R. L. BSc CEng MIMechE	5 Sept
Moran, J. P. BA	13 Sept
New, S. P.	19 Sept
Stacey, C.	23 Sept
Pomeroy, C. A.	28 Sept
Castleton, L. M.	30 Sept
Williamson, J. W.	30 Sept
Ross, H. S.	20 Oct
Blakey, M. P.	21 Oct
Lee, F.	21 Oct
Tunnah, J. E.	3 Nov
Goggin, J. F.	5 Nov
Gurney, R. F.	5 Nov
McLennan, J. D.	5 Nov
Bradfield, M. A. H. BA	7 Nov
Eaton, J. G.	18 Nov
Tranter, G.	26 Nov
Hincks, P. S.	2 Dec
Evans, J.	6 Dec
Rogers, A. D.	13 Dec
Swallow, R. J.	13 Dec
Howard, D.	17 Dec
Penn, B. W. BSc	18 Dec

1988

Johnson, C. D.	7 Jan
Roberts, R.	7 Jan
Lockwood, J. L.	18 Jan

Flying Officers

1988—contd

Elphick, R. W.	23 Jan
Penn, C. M.	23 Jan
Sewell, R. G.	23 Jan
Merriman, D. A. P. MA BA	2 Feb
Barton, N.	4 Feb
Kelly, L. D. BSc	14 Feb
Koscikiewicz, M. J.	14 Feb
Morse, J. E.	14 Feb
Ronaldson, D. D.	14 Feb
Walkley, J. R.	14 Feb
Yee, R.	18 Feb
MacLean, R. F.	20 Feb
Weir, D. C. J.	20 Feb
Winton, N. O.	21 Feb
Adams, P.	10 Mar
Heath, J. H.	20 Mar
Horsley, D. C.	20 Mar
Kerr, R. J. BSc CEng MIEE	20 Mar
Flynn, A. J.	11 Apr
Soughton, K. J.	11 Apr
Crew, D. R.	16 Apr
Davies, A. MBE	16 Apr
Peterkin, I. C. BA	16 Apr
Gault, R. W.	24 Apr
Murray, R. J.	24 Apr
Mulvee, B.	30 Apr
Woods, S. A. BSc	30 Apr
Ford, P.	1 May
Goodwin, D.	19 May
Totten, P. A.	19 May
Barnes, P. D.	6 June
Hector, H. M.	6 June
Huntley, J.	6 June
Pearson, D.	6 June
Stock, M. B.	23 June
Yates, P. W.	23 June
McDonald, R. L. C.	30 June
Davies, G. M.	7 July
Sumbler, B. A. BSc	7 July
Richardson, E. M.	9 July
Kidney, R. AFC	17 July
Arrowsmith, D. R.	30 July
Hepple, K. J.	30 July
Smith, S. P.	30 July
Timmins, D. AIB	30 July
Turner, D.	30 July
Vincent, J. N.	30 July
Watts, A. J.	30 July
Richardson, P. J. BSc	14 Aug
Page, A. M. BA	15 Aug
Hutton, C. R. BSc CEng MIEE JP	18 Aug
Unthank, R.	2 Sept

Beech, J. A.	8 Sept
Parker, M. C.	8 Sept
Wood, P. J.	15 Sept
Hamilton, A.	17 Sept
Leinster-Evans, S. BSc	17 Sept
Mackay, M.	17 Sept
Ward, I. M.	17 Sept
Gant, D. McK. MA	23 Sept
Shaddick, D. W. C.	23 Sept
Tippell, R. J. BA MIMgt	27 Sept
Bennett, J. E.	30 Sept
Rowan, P. R. BSc	30 Sept
Smith, R. L.	30 Sept
Lovett, M. S.	1 Oct
Warner, D. L. BSc	2 Oct
McNaught, R.	6 Oct
Mennell, B. R.	6 Oct
Paish, C. M. BA	11 Oct
Clearie, J. H. MA MSc MIL	22 Oct
Fox, A. BSc	22 Oct
Thubron, B. F.	27 Oct
Edgeworth, K. D.	28 Oct
Boden, C. G. BSc	30 Oct
Butler, A. G.	6 Nov
MacCarron, J. P. BA	6 Nov
Steed, B. P. A.	18 Nov
Green, M. H. MEd MRAeS	25 Nov
Sinclair, S. B. M.	25 Nov
Cullum, S. W. BA	4 Dec
Taylor, N. J.	4 Dec
Webb, A. W.	4 Dec
Wratten, A. J. BTech	4 Dec
Purllant, J.	10 Dec
Joynson, D. BEd	11 Dec
Godden, J. R.	15 Dec
Wort, G. L. P.	15 Dec
Beaney, V. R.	18 Dec
Hayden, A. M.	18 Dec

1989

Carr, S. J.	2 Jan
Duffin, K. E.	6 Jan
Smith, A. L.	6 Jan
Westacott, E. BA	6 Jan
Williams, R. S.	12 Jan
Dewhurst, H. J.	20 Jan
Stapleton, R.	26 Jan
Wright, M. G. BEd	26 Jan
Cooper, C. J.	27 Jan
Littleton, J. A.	27 Jan
Breedon, R. LLB	2 Feb
Brooks, B. C.	2 Feb
Jones, P. E. C.	6 Feb
Horton, J. W. C.	9 Feb
Reid, N. J. W.	9 Feb
Keen, G.	19 Feb

Beer, N. J. M.	20 Feb
Withers, N. R.	20 Feb
Cochran, A. N. MSc BSc CEng MIEE	28 Feb
Waller, A. J.	2 Mar
Thomson, B. I.	10 Mar
Butterley, J. D.	22 Mar
Britton, K. M. MSc BA	31 Mar
Browne, R. A.	31 Mar
Gale, C. A. F.	31 Mar
Guy, R. M.	31 Mar
Brown, J. A.	27 Apr
Dunnett, S. K.	27 Apr
Smith, W. H.	5 May
Cotton, E. M.	7 May
Lawrence, P. J. LLB	21 May
Spottiswood, J. D. CB CVO AFC MA	28 May
Baker, S. J.	29 May
Bickerdike, H. J.	29 May
Farndon, E. E.	29 May
Jones, J. E. M. BA	29 May
Whittenbury, W. P.	29 May
Finlay, G. F.	11 June
Jordan, A. P.	11 June
Pas, L. E. L.	15 June
Stroh, J.	18 June
Button, D. MIMgt	25 June
Humphries, J. A.	25 June
Winks, C. W. BSc	25 June
Mackay, I. F.	28 June
Budd, W. J.	2 July
Flood, E. A.	2 July
Pitt, M. R.	2 July
Broughton, B. W.	10 July
Dodd, M. S.	10 July
Hein, P. K.	10 July
Howard, B. M. RGN	10 July
Mitchell, P. V.	10 July
Cyster, C. D.	11 July
Davidson, R. H. C. MA	12 July
Evans, A. M.	13 July
Adams, D. C.	28 July
Coats, S. R.	28 July
Haygarth, P. W. J.	28 July
Hollyer, P. A.	28 July
Jefferies, N.	28 July
Wiggins, P. E.	28 July
Grover, J. D.	11 Aug
Lawrence, J. M.	13 Aug
Burford, D. P.	19 Aug
East, N. R. H.	3 Sept
Hope, M. E. MA BA	5 Sept
Down, F. C. BSc	18 Sept
Maggs, C. K.	18 Sept
Owen, J. E.	18 Sept
Snarey, C. A.	18 Sept
Bass, M.	28 Sept
Ellison, C. R.	28 Sept
Gabriel, W. A.	28 Sept

Flying Officers

1989—contd

Stephenson, B.	28 Sept
Evans, D. K.	19 Oct
Delaney, G. T.	20 Oct
Parfitt, A. P.	20 Oct
Revell, I. L.	20 Oct
Talbot, A. J.	20 Oct
Weston, P. T.	20 Oct
Winder, D.	22 Oct
Bambury, W. J.	28 Oct
Evans, J. H.	28 Oct
Laycock, J. BA	2 Nov
Palmer, J. M. BA	3 Nov
Kay, E.	9 Nov
Smith, A. C.	9 Nov
Stanton, T. M.	9 Nov
Watson, N. A.	9 Nov
Emmins, D. J.	12 Nov
White, R.	12 Nov
Wiles, H. B.	12 Nov
Crawley, E. J.	13 Nov
Hildersley, C.	13 Nov
Langfield, P. A.	13 Nov
McGrattan, C.	13 Nov
Holden, R. E.	16 Nov
Ephgrave, P. J.	18 Nov
Knight, Sir Michael KCB AFC BA DLitt FRAeS	19 Nov
Longmuir, R. W. BA	26 Nov
McMordie, A. E.	26 Nov
Simpson, A. C.	26 Nov
Morris, R. H. BEd FRGS	1 Dec
Spokes, A. J.	1 Dec
Davies, K.	10 Dec
McLachlan, R. A. P.	10 Dec
Seymour, V. R.	15 Dec
Evans, S. E. BA	18 Dec
Hodges, T. A. ACII	20 Dec
Gregory, R. J. MB BS MRCP LRCP DRCOG	21 Dec

1990

Battershall, A. E.	12 Jan
Blanche, J. D. BSc	12 Jan
Cave, A. G.	12 Jan
Franklin, S. J. W.	12 Jan
Guy, B. J.	12 Jan
Leaworthy, Y. C.	12 Jan
Smith, G. J.	18 Jan
Surtees, G. G. E.	20 Jan
Huitson, A. S.	21 Jan
Lundy, R. P.	21 Jan
Tisley, B. P. F.	24 Jan

Bage, K. M. BSc	26 Jan
Bates, J. D.	28 Jan
Tebbs, J. E.	28 Jan
Tebbs, R. C.	28 Jan
Robetts, W. C. R. MEd BA	2 Feb
Davis, H. N.	4 Feb
Lane, R. C.	4 Feb
Single, G. J.	4 Feb
Griffith, E. D.	5 Feb
Ward, D. MA MIMgt	6 Feb
Cooke, I.	19 Feb
Davies, L. S.	19 Feb
Dixon, P.	19 Feb
Edwards, D. G.	19 Feb
Hardwick, S. J.	19 Feb
Peers, J. K.	19 Feb
Young, B.	19 Feb
Grapes, N. P. P.	26 Feb
Bowyer, R. E.	1 Mar
Hair, J. L.	3 Mar
McAtamney, E. J.	3 Mar
Victory, C.	3 Mar
Walker, D. J.	3 Mar
Adgar, B.	8 Mar
Brock, J. E. BA PGCE	9 Mar
Hollands, P. A.	14 Mar
Page, B. J.	17 Mar
Dean, J. D. E. BSc	20 Mar
Lockwood, N. C.	8 Apr
Ridgway, E.	8 Apr
Sewell, M. A.	8 Apr
Trickey, A.	8 Apr
Tunstall, R.	18 Apr
Love, M. A.	28 Apr
Shimmons, R. W.	9 May
Baldwin, T. M. A. BSc MIBiol PGCE	11 May
Cohen, G.	11 May
Kerr, R. W.	11 May
Naismith, I. E.	11 May
Waller, S. E.	11 May
Hopkins, R. A.	17 May
Mayes, D. C.	24 May
Shakespeare, M. N.	24 May
Brookbank, C. K.	26 May
Wright, A. S.	26 May
McAulay, D. J.	27 May
Roy, T. D.	27 May
Day, P. J. J.	9 June
Bell, S. G.	27 June
Gillespie, A. J.	27 June
Lawrance, A. D.	30 June
Pollard, J. E.	30 June
Welborne, R. G. BA	30 June
Boggis, M. F.	2 July
Mann, M. C.	2 July
Reynolds, G. W.	4 July
Bulley, B. BSc	13 July
Rutledge, G. A. BA	14 July

Forster, J. B.	26 July
Gallagher, M.	31 July
Anderson, J. M.	2 Aug
Bracey, K. W.	2 Aug
Hansen, D.	2 Aug
Hynes, A. C. LLB	2 Aug
Morrell, S.E.	2 Aug
Parker, N. E.	2 Aug
Patterson, G. D.	2 Aug
Poulton, M. J.	2 Aug
Scott, J. G.	2 Aug
Webb, D. J.	2 Aug
Westwood, E. A. W. MIMechE	2 Aug
Wright, M. R. BSc	2 Aug
Burchell, B. L. AdDipEd CertEd	23 Aug
Kerr, A. T.	2 Sept
Shepherd, S. V.	2 Sept
Stevens, E.	2 Sept
Brittain, A. J.	4 Sept
Edmonds, R. S. P.	4 Sept
Naz, P. G.	5 Sept
Robinson, A. H.	5 Sept
Gould, H.	9 Sept
Hackshall, S. E.	9 Sept
Stancombe, K. M. BSc PGCE	12 Sept
Waters, L.	12 Sept
Baker, A. J.	14 Sept
Griffin, A. C.	14 Sept
Pavitt, R. G.	14 Sept
Kent, B. L. CertEd	16 Sept
Tebbs, R. C.	20 Sept
Bailey, M. J.	27 Sept
Carr, J. M.	27 Sept
Farrow, R. H.	27 Sept
Heathcote, S. J.	27 Sept
Ireland, D. E.	27 Sept
Midgley, R. I.	27 Sept
Roe, C. P.	27 Sept
White, M.	27 Sept
Blacklock, C. N. BA CertEd	30 Sept
Boland, W.	30 Sept
Hoskins, M. J.	4 Oct
Mead, S. M.	4 Oct
Swatridge, J. C.	6 Oct
Eckersley, E. J.	10 Oct
Graham, M. J.	10 Oct
Bartlett, A. J.	13 Oct
Palmer, P. J.	13 Oct
Bell, C. G.	24 Oct
Brown, A. J.	28 Oct
Wilkin, D.	28 Oct
Oswell, Q. M. B.	30 Oct
Sweeney, M.	31 Oct
Brad, W. G. M.	1 Nov
Martin, I. J.	2 Nov
Bloor, P. J.	4 Nov

Flying Officers

1990—contd

Anderson, I. F.	15 Nov
Hougham, S.	15 Nov
Meredith, C.	15 Nov
Newton, F. G. J.	21 Nov
Pinching, S. J.	21 Nov
Barwick, R. L.	27 Nov
Lamb, A. R. MIBiol	5 Dec
Rogers, F. C.	5 Dec
Wood, C. P.	5 Dec
Wood, J. A.	5 Dec
Aylett, G. L.	9 Dec
Pratt, B. R. D.	9 Dec
Ogden, P. J.	14 Dec
Blake, N.	22 Dec
East, C. A.	22 Dec
Hitchen, J. B.	22 Dec
Sullivan, R. J.	22 Dec

1991

Ogden, G. Y.	5 Jan
Whitehouse, J. P. BEd	5 Jan
Cook, B. J.	17 Jan
Matthews, R. S.	17 Jan
Adams, C. R.	18 Jan
Pole, H. W. M.	31 Jan
Bruguier, G. P.	6 Feb
Leduc, F. P.	6 Feb
Shipley, M. I.	8 Feb
Loxton, J. V.	9 Feb
Keable, J.	10 Feb
Bass, S.	28 Feb
Gracey, M. H. BA	28 Feb
Jenkins, D. P. BA PGCE	28 Feb
Roberts, M. A. BA	28 Feb
Stubbs, M. K.	28 Feb
Walker, S. F. BEd	28 Feb
Webster, E. D. BSc CEng MICE	28 Feb
Wardill D. H. CEng MIEE MIMechE	4 Mar
Cliffe, A. J.	14 Mar
Scanlon, N. F. J.	14 Mar
Thomas, B. A.	14 Mar
Bryan, A. S.	22 Mar
Davies, J.	25 Mar
Bruce, C. W. OBE	3 Apr
Edwards, G. G.	4 Apr
Kocbusz, G.	7 Apr
Anderson, S. D.	11 Apr
Gilvary, R. B.	12 Apr
Anderson, J. S.	15 Apr
Cowley, D. A. AFC BA	16 Apr
Howlett, M. A.	19 Apr

Johnson, K. R.	19 Apr
Stonestreet, C. J.	19 Apr
Tolley, P. J.	19 Apr
Rees, G. F. MBCS	26 Apr
Sutherland, D. F.	28 Apr
Delafield, J.	13 May
Kelly, A. J.	17 May
Kidby, M. J.	17 May
Parmenter, P. E. CertEd	17 May
Truman, W. E.	17 May
Preston, C. J.	19 May
Smith, A. M. BSc	19 May
Warrender, N. R. BSc	19 May
White, D. A. C. BSc	19 May
Deighton, D.	20 May
King, A.	25 May
Moss, D. W.	25 May
Welbourne, R. J.	25 May
Smithson, P. J.	26 May
Alexander, B. A.	13 June
Myhill, P. A.	13 June
Smitheman, G. E.	13 June
Thorrington, B. W. G.	13 June
Goodier, M. A.	14 June
Simpson, C.	14 June
Ashton, P.	21 June
Livingston, R. C.	21 June
Buckland, S.	22 June
Carter, P. A.	22 June
Moore, M. S.	22 June
Redding, S. M. BA	22 June
Flitcroft, S. E.	28 June
Murray, S. W.	29 June
Adams, J. E.	2 July
Brown, A. K. BSc	2 July
Atkinson, S. P.	4 July
King, T. R.	4 July
MacDonald, A. S.	4 July
Rattle, R.	4 July
Wood, R. P.	4 July
Boustead, S.	20 July
Lowe, J. L.	20 July
Stockill, B. M.	20 July
Walshaw, R. N. BA PGCE ARCO	20 July
Wilcock, N. BTech	20 July
Lees, A.	26 July
Taylor, J. G. MSc	26 July
Blunt, G. J.	28 July
Morton, W. J.	30 July
Carvosso, K. G.	1 Aug
Clift, A. D.	2 Aug
Reis, F.	2 Aug
Elms, D. J.	11 Aug
Slater, P. C.	11 Aug
Combe, A. G.	14 Aug
Miller, A. A. BA	14 Aug
Haller, D.	19 Aug
Davies, P. J.	21 Aug
Hall, D.	25 Aug

Hill, D. A.	25 Aug
Hooton, G. A.	25 Aug
Widdicombe, P.	25 Aug
Hill, R.	29 Aug
Cartwright, P.	4 Sept
James, D. L.	4 Sept
Lucas, J. P. MA	4 Sept
Neate, M. W. J.	4 Sept
Endean, J. P.	5 Sept
Hatch, M. L.	11 Sept
Eke, M. J.	14 Sept
Henson, D. R.	14 Sept
Williams, T. J. W.	14 Sept
Turner, Y. A.	18 Sept
Edwards, A. M.	19 Sept
Filler, I. A. BTech	19 Sept
Williams, P. M. RGN	19 Sept
Davis, A.	29 Sept
Taylor, R. D. DPhysEd	29 Sept
Henderson, D. J. PhD BSc PGCE	2 Oct
Paton, D. McL. MIMgt	2 Oct
King, G.	9 Oct
Hutchinson, S. A.	11 Oct
Mayoh, S. A.	11 Oct
Goddard, C. M.	16 Oct
Esson, D. J. M.	23 Oct
Howes, R. W.	23 Oct
Pidgeon, P. R.	23 Oct
White, A. J.	23 Oct
Biddles, D.	26 Oct
Goring, P. D.	26 Oct
Jeremiah, L.	26 Oct
Palmer, D. J.	26 Oct
Tucker, K. D.	3 Nov
Wilson, K. R.	13 Nov
Armstrong, R. T.	16 Nov
Cambra, J. M.	16 Nov
Jones, D. A.	16 Nov
Chapman, P.	25 Nov
Hallam, J. W. R.	30 Nov
Hunt, J. L.	30 Nov
Kearns, G.	30 Nov
Robinson, D. A.	30 Nov
Rogers, G. L.	30 Nov
Swinge, P. D.	30 Nov
Dasilva, M. E.	1 Dec
Ward, I. J.	7 Dec
Downs, T.	11 Dec
Rajan, G.	11 Dec
Vernon, M. BSc PGCE	12 Dec
Atkins, A. M.	20 Dec
Goodger, G.	20 Dec

1992

Burrows, G. W.	8 Jan
Davison, E. D.	8 Jan
Hamilton, M. R.	8 Jan

271

Flying Officers

1992—contd

Monro, I. W.	8 Jan
Potter, S.	8 Jan
Smith, J. H.	8 Jan
Thompson, P.	8 Jan
Brett, M. I.	13 Jan
Mitchell, A.	22 Jan
Johnson, S.	23 Jan
Mead, A. B.	24 Jan
Medhurst, P. W.	30 Jan
Brittain, V.	5 Feb
Halliday, J. W.	5 Feb
Anderson, D. N.	
CertEd	7 Feb
Hobbs, D. G.	7 Feb
Gidney, A. J.	10 Feb
Arnold, W. J. W. BA	
PGCE	15 Feb
Haggo, S. J.	15 Feb
Lee, J. F.	15 Feb
Teague, W. W. L.	15 Feb
Middleton, K. J.	
BEng	20 Feb
Miskimmin, M. D.	26 Feb
Chivers, G. C. R.	27 Feb
Jones, J.	27 Feb
Roberts, P. G.	2 Mar
Retallick, R. N.	12 Mar
Woolven, A. J.	12 Mar
Hill, C. A.	14 Mar
Hale, D. I.	20 Mar
Whitehead P. F.	23 Mar
McNeill, S. D.	28 Mar
Porter, E. A.	28 Mar
Emmins, A. M.	2 Apr
French, D.	2 Apr
Spring, D. R.	2 Apr
Cleeter, A. G.	4 Apr
Mathie, A. R. C.	4 Apr
Nutland, C. F.	4 Apr
Ford, C. A.	10 Apr
Evans, A. L. BSc	22 Apr
Bourne, P. D.	1 May
Newton, C. J.	1 May
Copsey, C.	14 May
Ditchburn, S.	14 May
Robertson, A. BSc	14 May
Deegan, P. R.	15 May
Leather, I. J.	17 May
Teggin, C. M. BA	17 May
de Labat, A. C. P.	18 May
Clarke, G. A. BA	19 May
Creveul, I. C. BA	21 May
Adam, S. D.	30 May
Jackson, A. P. BSc	
PGCE	30 May

Alburey, D.	4 June
Donnelly, D. P.	4 June
Swann, G. B. G.	4 June
Costin, G. A.	11 June
Gardner, J.	20 June
Turner, J. A.	20 June
Bragg, R. T.	4 July
Crandon, D.	4 July
Hill, K. M.	4 July
Matthewson, C. K.	4 July
Pescod, V.	4 July
Walton, E.	4 July
Filler, N. D.	16 July
Starling, P. G.	16 July
Taylor, G.	16 July
Wiggins, D. A.	16 July
Wiggins, S. J.	16 July
Worsnop, A. M.	16 July
Hawksfield, B. BA	18 July
Irving, D. J.	23 July
Smith, S. I.	23 July
Whitehead, V. G.	
MIMgt	23 July
Pyett, G. W.	24 July
Smith, N. G.	24 July
McKay, A. FIMgt	3 Aug
Morgan, A.	6 Aug
Alexander, D. A.	
BMus	9 Aug
Fox, B. J.	9 Aug
Walker, C. BA	17 Aug
Brooks, A. R.	20 Aug
Hortop, D. BA	20 Aug
Carnegie, D. N.	24 Aug
Lee, G.	24 Aug
Burke, J. R. BSc	31 Aug
Davies, S. P.	6 Sept
Godfrey, P. A.	6 Sept
Drury, C.	10 Sept
Gerrard, J. A. BEd	
FRGS	10 Sept
Jones, D. A. G.	10 Sept
Leeson, S. A.	10 Sept
O'Leary, J. A.	10 Sept
Wells, P. A.	10 Sept
Shield, M. W.	11 Sept
Westlake, R. G.	11 Sept
Kensett, C. J.	12 Sept
Perris, A. J. B.	16 Sept
Bagshaw, M. J.	19 Sept
Brunt, G. H.	19 Sept
Willis, B. A.	19 Sept
Winrow, N.	19 Sept
Rathbone, S.	21 Sept
Chandler, H. T.	22 Sept
Crawford, M. I.	25 Sept
Duff, M.	25 Sept
Reditt, J. L.	25 Sept
Gilbert, B. R.	4 Oct
Grant, D. I.	4 Oct

Brierley, J. A.	8 Oct
Harding, C. D.	8 Oct
Spencer, C. J.	8 Oct
Toth, V. M.	8 Oct
Huyton, D. G.	11 Oct
Smith, A. L. BEd	
FSERT	11 Oct
Robson, J. D.	16 Oct
Church, K. C. BSc	17 Oct
Hacksall, D.	17 Oct
Humphreys, N. A.	17 Oct
Law, D. W.	17 Oct
Caffyn, B.	25 Oct
Warwick, N. P.	25 Oct
Morrison, S. W.	30 Oct
Crawford, W. I.	1 Nov
Southwell, R.	1 Nov
Cretney, P. A.	5 Nov
Stone, J. B.	5 Nov
Stone, P.	5 Nov
Turner, S. J.	5 Nov
Walton, C. E.	5 Nov
Cambra, A.	12 Nov
Kilminster, W. B.	12 Nov
Hughes, G. W. A.	22 Nov
Pepper, I. K.	22 Nov
Podger, S.	22 Nov
Sharpe, A. J.	26 Nov
Mason, J. B.	27 Nov
Jones, N. R.	30 Nov
Metherell, M. J. BA	1 Dec
Grant, M. J. MA	
PGCE	5 Dec
Gill, J. L.	10 Dec
Smith, M. J.	10 Dec
Douglass, I. J. BSc	
PGCE	13 Dec
Tanner, H. S. T.	14 Dec
Cunningham, A. M.	17 Dec
Danson, C. A.	17 Dec
Johnson, R. G.	17 Dec
Southwell, D. L.	28 Dec

1993

Feltham, C.	7 Jan
Willey, R. E.	7 Jan
Anderson, A.	14 Jan
Hetterley, E. C.	22 Jan
Wyer, E. J.	27 Jan
Clarke, H. PhD BSc	28 Jan
Clapp, G. D.	29 Jan
Forward, A. J.	29 Jan
Foulkes, J. MSc BSc	1 Feb
Birch, F. J.	8 Feb
Rees, D. W. BSc	8 Feb
Tomlinson, J.	11 Feb
Clark, J.	15 Feb
Houghman, D. M.	18 Feb

Flying Officers

1993—contd

Artt, M. H. BA PGCE	19 Feb
Owen, D.	28 Feb
Child, R. PhD BSc PGCE	7 Mar
Weatherston, S. A.	8 Mar
Blackford, P. K.	11 Mar
Browell, A.	11 Mar
Entwistle, G. S.	11 Mar
Gilbey, S. L.	11 Mar
Hayes, G. P.	11 Mar
Pacello, L. J. BPharm BA	11 Mar
Longdon, M. E. B.	13 Mar
Stokes, R.	13 Mar
Bennett, P. J.	15 Mar
Wilson, R. C.	28 Mar
Robinson, C. I.	1 Apr
Hayr, Sir Patrick KCB KBE AFC	6 Apr
Willison, D. J. BSc	7 Apr
Marr, J. D.	8 Apr
Lawrance, M. J. B. MBE	12 Apr
Betson, C.	14 Apr
Brabner, J. R.	14 Apr
Davis, A. R.	17 Apr
Norton, W. H. W. MBE	18 Apr
Boulet, O. A. M.	19 Apr
Hatton, C. I.	19 Apr
Bolt, C.	23 Apr
Porter, A. J.	23 Apr
Bartlett, J. M.	25 Apr
Card, M. G.	25 Apr
Graddon, L. B. BA CertEd	25 Apr
Parkin, M. J. CertEd	25 Apr
Toon, S. M.	25 Apr
Gatland, G. D. LLB	26 Apr
Field, R. M. BA PGCE	29 Apr
Griffiths, R.	29 Apr
Pallister, D. H.	29 Apr
Slater, A. J.	29 Apr
Jago, T. M.	7 May
Wilson-Benn, A.	7 May
Adams, G. E.	30 May
Castle, M. E.	30 May
North, G. W.	30 May
Thomas, E. A.	30 May
Hewitt, R. S.	3 June
Atkins, P. M.	12 June
Hunter, M. J.	12 June
Kamper, R.	12 June
Machin, A. J.	25 June

Moyes, T. E.	25 June
Sansom, T. D. BEng	25 June
Shepherd, J. M.	25 June
Parkes, G. F. H. BSc PGCE	26 June
Conway, G. E.	2 July
Smith, P. R.	2 July
Barnes, M. J.	5 July
Hawthorn, M. R. CertEd	5 July
Reyes, E. J. BTh	5 July
Taylor, W. T.	5 July
Burnett, W. M.	9 July
Chapman, P. J.	9 July
Robins, M. BSc	9 July
Sutcliffe, K.	9 July
Gregory, R. J. BSc	16 July
Whitelaw, D. J. BA	18 July
Holman, B. C. L.	19 July
Parsons, J. D. F.	22 July
Cameron, W.	23 July
Craghill, W. M.	30 July
Watt, N. R.	30 July
Robson, A. A.	5 Aug
Atkins, J. S.	7 Aug
Dale, J. N.	7 Aug
Rose, J. S.	7 Aug
Watkinson, C.	7 Aug
Smart, R. W.	9 Aug
Martin, J. F. S.	11 Aug
Smith, T. J.	11 Aug
Fisher, B. A.	13 Aug
Gale, P. S.	13 Aug
Lemmon, L. J.	13 Aug
Fincher, D.	16 Aug
Nevison, C. C.	18 Aug
Musgrove, D. J.	19 Aug
Henley, P. S.	26 Aug
Marley, G.	29 Aug
McGregor, D. F.	29 Aug
Michie, J. M.	29 Aug
Cunningham, A.	2 Sept
Gillett, R. A.	2 Sept
Lindsay-Anderson, D.	3 Sept
Thomas, F. E.	4 Sept
Darnell, M. C.	9 Sept
Frowe, N. J. BA	9 Sept
Anderson, P.	11 Sept
Czarnecki, P. E.	11 Sept
Lovett, A. W.	11 Sept
Berry, D. J.	12 Sept
Budd, R. L. H.	12 Sept
Byatt, M. J. BEd	12 Sept
Robertson, A. R. BSc	12 Sept
Stump, D. R.	12 Sept
Cheek, I.	16 Sept
Quick, S. G.	16 Sept
Chaplin, R. E.	17 Sept
Fallon, J. F.	17 Sept

Leigh, J. M. BEd	17 Sept
Lloyd, J. R. BA	17 Sept
Bell, J. P.	20 Sept
McCutcheon, M.	23 Sept
Rymer, G.	23 Sept
Edmunds, A. C.	24 Sept
Easson, I. M. RGN RMN	4 Oct
Short, G.	4 Oct
Yorston, I. S.	5 Oct
Bernays, J. S.	9 Oct
Charlton, J. J. BSc PGCE	15 Oct
Taylor, I. A.	15 Oct
Cooper, J. M.	22 Oct
Doughty, P. D.	22 Oct
Gore, S. A.	22 Oct
Horncastle, S.	30 Oct
Newman, T. C. M. MA	31 Oct
Barlow, S. R. R.	4 Nov
Hutchinson, L. D.	6 Nov
McNaught, J. A. B. MA	6 Nov
Wheeler, D. J. BSc	6 Nov
Mussett, P. G.	7 Nov
Simms, V. A. M.	7 Nov
Bolton, G. A.	8 Nov
Barkey, D. C.	11 Nov
Burke, M.	11 Nov
Gridley, S. A.	11 Nov
Alexander, J. A. BA	14 Nov
Meehan, L. B.	14 Nov
Palmer, P. M.	14 Nov
Davis, P. J.	19 Nov
Mc Grath, D.	19 Nov
Morgan, L. I.	19 Nov
Davies, R. M.	21 Nov
Sumbler, K. S. BA	21 Nov
Nisbett, B.	12 Dec

1994

Bibby, A. J.	6 Jan
Bullock, S.	6 Jan
Gilbert, P.	6 Jan
Mair, D. T.	6 Jan
Mochar, A. M.	6 Jan
Pumphrey, R. J.	6 Jan
Melville, F. S.	10 Jan
Pocha, C.	12 Jan
Liddell, D.	13 Jan
Stanley, C. D. W.	13 Jan
Sked, R. F.	16 Jan
Tinson, P. J.	17 Jan
Godden, M. J.	21 Jan
Lundy, A.	21 Jan
Maclean, A. G.	23 Jan

Flying Officers

1994—contd

Grantham-Hill, M. R. BSc	24 Jan
Williams Slaven, N.	24 Jan
Hancock, D.	28 Jan
Jefferies, D. R.	28 Jan
Oram, M. C. BEng	28 Jan
Latton, K. B.	1 Feb
Andrews, W. M.	5 Feb
Bartlett, M. L.	5 Feb
Croft, P. M.	5 Feb
Freeman, D. J.	5 Feb
Grout, N. M.	5 Feb
Husbands, D. J. T.	5 Feb
Jones, G. F. MA	5 Feb
Lowe, G.	5 Feb
Martinez, R. L. M.	5 Feb
McGowan, A. P. BSc PGCE	5 Feb
Parker-Moore, D. J.	5 Feb
Picton, R.	5 Feb
Tooke, M. B.	5 Feb
Collins, I. H.	7 Feb
Hill, R. R. J.	7 Feb
McClune, J. M. BA	11 Feb
Irvine, M.	14 Feb
Lyle, R.	14 Feb
Lambert, C. R. BSc	17 Feb
Rolfe, D. G.	20 Feb
Stannard, A. P.	20 Feb
Saunders, W. L.	27 Feb
Butt, V. R.	3 Mar
Caisley, P. J.	3 Mar
Dalby, W. J.	3 Mar
Ellis, C. S.	3 Mar
Haughton-Turner, J.	3 Mar
Morgan, R. BEng	3 Mar
Parker, R. C.	3 Mar
Riley, P.	3 Mar
Robinson, I.	3 Mar
Robinson, S. A.	3 Mar
Smith, S. J.	3 Mar
Williams, M.	3 Mar
Baker, M. J. BA	4 Mar
Nolan, K. J.	9 Mar
Cremen, M. F.	10 Mar
Crichton, A. T.	10 Mar
Litting, A. D.	10 Mar
Simpson, C. R. MA BA	10 Mar
Lawrence, R. F.	11 Mar
Matheson, N. G.	11 Mar
Bidgood, S. J. BSc	20 Mar
Fox, K. A.	20 Mar
Gray, R. W.	20 Mar
Mayhew, G. A.	20 Mar

McFarlane, W. L.	20 Mar
Rennison, J. P.	20 Mar
Bone, S.	23 Mar
Upton, N. J.	23 Mar
Walker, E. M. BA	23 Mar
Beaumont, S. C. BSc	24 Mar
Lightowler, N. J,	24 Mar
Pryke, D. P.	24 Mar
Thomas, G. R. S.	24 Mar
Harris, D. G.	31 Mar
Rushen, P. C.	31 Mar
Wilson, N. J.	31 Mar
Woodman, G. PhD MSc BSc	31 Mar
Gamlin, D.G. CertEd	6 Apr
Mellish, P. W. BA	7 Apr
Mollard, D. R. G.	7 Apr
Young, A. I.	7 Apr
Gillard, J. A.	11 Apr
Bailey, G. T.	22 Apr
Cozens, D. J.	22 Apr
Diskett, D. J.	22 Apr
Dolan, K. P.	22 Apr
Fordham, A. G.	22 Apr
Kidd, J. G.	22 Apr
Weiss, R. M. J.	26 Apr
Whalvin, H. J. J. N.	27 Apr
Robins, S. E.	28 Apr
Heslin, M.	5 May
Naylor, P.	5 May
Ritson, M.	5 May
Staincliffe, A. W.	5 May
Steel, J. M.	5 May
Griffiths, D. L.	7 May
Ingham, M. J.	11 May
Brown, R. N. E.	13 May
Buckley, J. C.	13 May
Hazell, A. J. E.	13 May
Lines, M. J.	13 May
Long, D. J.	13 May
McColgan, P. E. BA	13 May
McCormick, R.	13 May
Rogers, G. R. D.	13 May
Anwar, N.	14 May
Bound, R. T.	18 May
Cairns, R. J. BA	18 May
Irvine, A. R.	19 May
Testro, B. J.	19 May
Williamson, M. A.	26 May
Woods, R. M. BSc	26 May
Winter, J. L. BSc	28 May
Horborn, M. P. BSc	30 May
Sutherland, D.	1 June
Robinson, D. K. BSc	4 June
Taylor, I.	4 June
Tipping, P. W.	4 June
Audus, A. M.	5 June
Blair, G. A.	7 June
Hutchings, C. D.	9 June
Allam, C. M.	15 June

Grinstead, M. G. P. R.	18 June
Roebuck, S. C. BSc	18 June
Roth, B. N. BSc	18 June
Sheehan, T. D.	18 June
Bennett, M. S.	29 June
Collins, D. P.	29 June
Crewe, I. L.	29 June
Bateman, A. J. BSc	30 June
Brain, T.	30 June
Human, A. R. D.	30 June
Mayes, C. R.	30 June
Stuart, B. G.	30 June
Walters, S. A.	30 June
Griffiths, M. E.	1 July
Eccles, P. J.	3 July
Davies, H. M.	6 July
Fish, L. A.	6 July
Hickie, K. M.	6 July
Gilbert, J. M.	13 July
McCracken, J.	13 July
Sneider, A. J. BA	13 July
Longhurst, S. E.	17 July
Montgomery, N.	17 July
Temple, D. R.	17 July
Miller, R.	20 July
Hamlen, W. W.	28 July
Parfrey, C. J.	28 July
Taylor, T. H.	1 Aug
Lee, C. P.	13 Aug
Rodford, R. P.	13 Aug
Knight, O. J. A.	17 Aug
Roberts, A. P.	18 Aug
Lovering, M. L. BA	23 Aug
Pallett, B. J.	28 Aug
Downham, D. A.	3 Sept
Price, M. J.	3 Sept
Long, D. BSc	6 Sept
Thum, M. J.	9 Sept
Jardine, A.	10 Sept
McCammont, L. E. W.	10 Sept
Wadsworth, M. E.	20 Sept
Hake, A. A. S.	21 Sept
Fenner, J. M. BSc PGCE	23 Sept
Rood, P.	23 Sept
Counsell, R.	25 Sept
Eckersley, M. A.	25 Sept
Fitzpatrick, I. A.	25 Sept
Goacher, M.	25 Sept
Plessis, J. K. BSc PGCE	25 Sept
Adair, C. R.	27 Sept
Baron, A. R.	28 Sept
Collins, A. S.	28 Sept
Lee, B.	28 Sept
Stanley, T. J.	28 Sept
Stobbie, J. A.	28 Sept
Wellings, D. J.	28 Sept
Whittaker, S. M.	28 Sept

Flying Officers

1994—contd

Campbell, H. N. MSc BA	29 Sept
Burns, J. C. S. BA PGCE	30 Sept
Reid-Johnson, M. J.	30 Sept
Sims, P. G. D. BSc CEng	3 Oct
Hammersley, C. D.	5 Oct
Cheveron, C. E. BSc PGCE	6 Oct
Anderson, S. J.	8 Oct
McFadden, H. K. BSc	8 Oct
Westley, P. J.	8 Oct
Bayliss, J. R. N.	20 Oct
Thomson-Clark, C. L.	20 Oct
Tziros, N. A. L. B.	21 Oct
Butterworth, R. BSc	22 Oct
Terrett, A. L.	25 Oct
Turner, P. D. C.	25 Oct
Burchett, K. J.	28 Oct
Loft, N. L.	28 Oct
Basnett, L.	2 Nov
Oldham, W. P.	2 Nov
Jackson, C. A.	4 Nov
Oakley, N. W.	4 Nov
Coleman, M. R.	6 Nov
Bees, R. G.	7 Nov
Gamble, J. R.	9 Nov
Williams, D. R.	9 Nov
Baxter, D. S.	12 Nov
Lansley, A. P. BEd	12 Nov
MacLeod, J. A.	12 Nov
Stubbs, P. N. MA	12 Nov
Waugh, M. K.	12 Nov
Bradley, L. Y.	19 Nov
Davies, G.	19 Nov
Davies, J. P. MA PGCE	19 Nov
Dixon, S. A. E. MA BD	19 Nov
Elliott, S. D.	19 Nov
Parks, T.	19 Nov
Peck, M.	19 Nov
Fagg, A. D.	23 Nov
Foskett, R. K.	23 Nov
Parsons, A. G.	23 Nov
Thompson, E. J.	23 Nov
Dowley, T. J.	24 Nov
Green, R. E.	30 Nov
Higgins, G. A.	30 Nov
Trevena, M. J.	1 Dec
Woods, I. R.	1 Dec
Collins, P. W.	7 Dec
Brock, M. J. B. BA	15 Dec
Caulfield, G. A. BA	15 Dec
Jennings, A. E. BA	15 Dec
Maycock, S.	15 Dec
McAdam, N. W. E. MA	15 Dec
Turley, R. C.	15 Dec
Wells, A. J.	16 Dec

1995

Harvey, S. J.	5 Jan
Tegg, B. A.	9 Jan
Blakenborough, S. F.	11 Jan
Davies, R. RGN	11 Jan
Dods, R. M.	11 Jan
Green, I. M. BEd	11 Jan
Lewry, G. J.	11 Jan
Macleod, S. L.	11 Jan
Smith, M. J.	11 Jan
Tickell, R.	11 Jan
Wheatley, R. P.	11 Jan
Woods, T. E.	11 Jan
Dacre, J. P.	13 Jan
Harris, S. J.	14 Jan
Boothroyd, J. M.	25 Jan
Dingwall, J. A.	25 Jan
Humphreys, M.	25 Jan
Iles, S. D.	25 Jan
Ruskin, D. J. BA PGCE	28 Jan
Hynett, M. T.	29 Jan
Hullis, S. BA	4 Feb
Thorpe, J. E. BA PGCE	10 Feb
Warman, J. L.	15 Feb
Clark, N. S.	18 Feb
Flower, A.	18 Feb
Jones, N. A.	18 Feb
Norton, P. D.	18 Feb
O'Connell, B. C.	18 Feb
Ransome, P.	18 Feb
Raper, T. D.	18 Feb
Westwood, E. A.	18 Feb
Wohlgemuth, J. F.	18 Feb
Haley, J. G.	22 Feb
Smyth, F. D. MA	22 Feb
Serle, J. C.	24 Feb
Turner, S. J.	24 Feb
White, J. E.	24 Feb
Perry, P. J.	27 Feb
Quinn, J. J.	27 Feb
Meadows, P. BEng	2 Mar
Usher, G. R. MA LTCL	3 Mar
Hakes, M. D. BEd CertEd	4 Mar
Bennett, J. K.	8 Mar
Brown, K. A.	8 Mar
Hibberd, J. P.	8 Mar
Tanner, R. J.	8 Mar
Thompson, S. T.	8 Mar
Grant, S. J.	15 Mar

Cobbold, D. J.	17 Mar
O'Neill, G. L. BA PGCE	17 Mar
Sime, V. J. MA PGCE	17 Mar
Wilkinson, M.	17 Mar
Wood, S. W.	17 Mar
Flower, L. E.	18 Mar
Tapsell, A.	20 Mar
Nickson, A. J.	24 Mar
Vasey, D. C.	24 Mar
Maddox, J. P. MA	29 Mar
Metcalfe, R.	1 Apr
Hiley, P.	2 Apr
Lawn, D. K.	2 Apr
McGhie, S.	2 Apr
Parkinson, A. G.	2 Apr
Strand, A. M.	2 Apr
Joslin, I. E. BSc	7 Apr
Bremner, G. A.	10 Apr
Flitcroft, S. K.	11 Apr
Carter, R. I.	14 Apr
Libby, K. A.	14 Apr
Nugent, J. M. B. P.	14 Apr
Dickson, J. J.	21 Apr
Ferguson, B. A.	26 Apr
Hoe, W. J. BSc	26 Apr
Ward, M. C. J. BSc	26 Apr
Brant, T. D.	29 Apr
Buscombe, C. B.	29 Apr
Woodbury, M. J.	29 Apr
Rowles, S.	2 May
Coleman, D. P.	6 May
Connolly, M. T.	6 May
Hinchliffe, D. A. R.	6 May
Maggs, S. K.	6 May
Pike, G. J. S.	6 May
Price, R. A.	6 May
Bellamy, M. G. FCA	14 May
Cottrell, S. E. BEd	14 May
Daniel, B. L.	14 May
Davies, E. M. G.	14 May
Henderson, G. P.	14 May
Smith, I. P.	14 May
Stanley, M. T.	14 May
Harvey, R. E.	18 May
Hellings, T. C. L. BA	19 May
O'Shaughnessy, S. E.	19 May
Chart, P. L.	27 May
Greenow, K. F.	27 May
Hall, A. J.	27 May
Simmons, D. C.	27 May
Todd, D.	27 May
Keech, R. A.	7 June
Kidley, M. F.	7 June
Levett, M. J.	7 June
Botten, L. D.	10 June
Dewhurst, R. M.	10 June
Pilbeam, L. M.	10 June
Fusedale, J. S.	16 June
Bland, T. J.	22 June

Flying Officers

1995—contd

Coxon, P. R.	22 June
Mathieson, P.	22 June
Ryan, J. L.	22 June
Vincent, R. A.	22 June
White, C. M.	22 June
Dunkley, D. I.	25 June
Willis, T. C.	25 June
Ash, T. A. BA PGCE	5 July
Billingham, N. J.	5 July
Charlton, D. A.	5 July
Green, I. M.	5 July
Maitland, P.	5 July
McCarthy, M.	5 July
Scruton, S. D.	5 July
Jones, L. S.	7 July
Logan, A.	7 July
Marks, F. M.	7 July
Coe, D. F.	17 July
Hibbert, C. J. MSc BA	18 July
Clift, S. A.	19 July
Gilham, J. K.	19 July
Lawton, S. M.	19 July
Parsons, J. J.	19 July
Pearce S. J.	19 July
Saunders, D.	19 July
Smith, A. P.	21 July
Fox, A. C.	23 July
Evans, S. E.	5 Aug
Mahoney, M. F.	13 Aug
Farrell, L. N. RGN	15 Aug
Hunt, W. G.	15 Aug
Noble, J. P. BSc	15 Aug
Ashpole, C. E.	16 Aug
Ballard, G. G.	16 Aug
Christmas, K. H.	16 Aug
Delves, D. J.	16 Aug
Dempsey, P. D.	16 Aug
Donaldson, L. S.	16 Aug
Tindall, N. M.	16 Aug
Woodcock, P.	16 Aug
Stevens, K. R.	26 Aug
Ward, V. E.	26 Aug
Wootton, S.	26 Aug
Mellors, W. C.	24 Aug
Taylor, G. E.	24 Aug
Downie, J. C. P.	27 Aug
Duncan, P. A. BSc	27 Aug
Fishley, J. F. MA	1 Sept
Canning, T.	6 Sept
Cooper, T.	6 Sept
Scott, J. BSc	6 Sept
Tarttelin, R. B.	6 Sept
Walkling, N J.	6 Sept
Donovan, K. B.	9 Sept
Hudson, C. D.	9 Sept

Kenny, S.	9 Sept
Russell, M. J.	9 Sept
Hawkins, P. W. BSc	12 Sept
Taylor, T. R. D.	13 Sept
Bex, P. R.	14 Sept
Coalfield, I. P.	14 Sept
Meacock, A. P.	14 Sept
Taylor, S. V.	14 Sept
Bullock, S. L.	19 Sept
Barnfather, C. R.	23 Sept
Steele, J. R.	23 Sept
Rankin, L.	24 Sept
Battram, J. M.	30 Sept
Skillman, J. J.	30 Sept
Tandy, G. F.	30 Sept
Allanson, D. BSc	4 Oct
McMillan, A. B.	4 Oct
Abington, M. B.	5 Oct
Hollings, J. I.	6 Oct
Pounder, M. L.	6 Oct
Elliott, G. L. BSc	13 Oct
Mumford, C. M.	13 Oct
Oram, R. M. D. BA ARCM DipTh	13 Oct
Yates, C. E. BSc	14 Oct
Pirie, A. L.	21 Oct
Chalmers, M. BSc	27 Oct
Donald, G. D.	27 Oct
Downie, L.	27 Oct
MacPherson, I. G. BEM	27 Oct
Showell, A. C. SRN	31 Oct
Benham, D. A.	2 Nov
Bennett, K. D. BA	2 Nov
Capon, G. J. C.	2 Nov
Jenkins, P. C.	2 Nov
Milner, M. J.	2 Nov
Norton, S. D.	2 Nov
Carlton, N.	9 Nov
Brown, J. E.	10 Nov
Graham, D. H.	11 Nov
Austing, D. R.	15 Nov
Cameron, A.	15 Nov
Hassanali, A.	15 Nov
Jackson, K. L.	15 Nov
Patel, R. K.	15 Nov
Rogers, D. J. P.	18 Nov
Grogan, R.	20 Nov
Mottram, J. M.	23 Nov
Dethierry, A. M. A. BA PGCE	25 Nov
O'Connor, F. P.	25 Nov
Payne, D. J.	25 Nov
Shelley, D. I.	25 Nov
Cairns, S.	6 Dec
Coutts, S. BSc	6 Dec
Murray, A.	6 Dec
Catcheside, S. J.	10 Dec
Dodman, L. M.	10 Dec

Growcott, J. A. BSc PGCE	10 Dec
McKee, J. V.	10 Dec
Sacre, J. F.	10 Dec
Smith, A. J. BSc	10 Dec
Smith, V. J.	10 Dec
Elvins, L. J.	20 Dec
Gardner, J. A.	20 Dec
Southern, L. W.	20 Dec
Thorn, T. G. AFC FRAeS	29 Dec

1996

Loftus, P. BEng	4 Jan
Brennan, G. J. P.	6 Jan
Atherton, V. A.	10 Jan
Healing, C. A.	10 Jan
Smith, C. F. BSc	10 Jan
Wilson, B. B.	10 Jan
Braddon, R.	12 Jan
Searl, P. D.	12 Jan
Watson, D. A.	12 Jan
McMullan, T. A. BSc PGCE	13 Jan
Vincent, P. J.	16 Jan
Bell, J.	18 Jan
Fairhurst, D. T.	18 Jan
Warner, A. J.	18 Jan
Barnes, S. BSc	21 Jan
Everett, A. M.	21 Jan
McFall, A. BSc PGCE	21 Jan
Walker, M. J. BSc PGCE	21 Jan
Sawyer, M. G. BSc MIBiol	25 Jan
Davies, D. L.	27 Jan
Pearson, T. A.	27 Jan
Prigmore, G. T.	27 Jan
Duke, C. M.	31 Jan
Felton, P. H.	2 Feb
Haywood, C. C.	2 Feb
Henry, M. W.	2 Feb
Hickin, J. V.	2 Feb
Hutchings, A. W.	2 Feb
Lee, P. A.	2 Feb
Lewis, R. J.	2 Feb
Phillips, B. E.	2 Feb
Prele, P.	2 Feb
Reed, E. C.	2 Feb
Smith, A. M.	2 Feb
Willows, S. L.	2 Feb
Downes, K. F. BSc	5 Feb
Blain, R. T.	10 Feb
Rolfe, M. J.	10 Feb
Feehan, P. J. D.	15 Feb
Grimshire, L. K. BEd	15 Feb
Harrison, I.	15 Feb
Hillier, M. A. T.	15 Feb

Flying Officers

1996—contd

Venn, J. C.	15 Feb
Wingrove, D. J.	15 Feb
Kelso, C. W.	16 Feb
Noyce, R. A.	16 Feb
Patterson, R.	16 Feb
Perera, T. E.	16 Feb
Farnworth, A.	19 Feb
Camwell, A.	22 Feb
Rillie, G.	22 Feb
Knowles, D.	25 Feb
Schofield, N. C.	25 Feb
Vickers, D. J.	27 Feb
Pearson, I. D. BA	1 Mar
Watt, L. J. MSc	4 Mar
Bartley, D.	9 Mar
Cruse, A. M.	9 Mar
D'Anna, G. W. S. MSc BSc	9 Mar
Walker, R. C. S.	9 Mar
Collins, L.	11 Mar
Loftus, K. B.	11 Mar
Steed, A.	11 Mar
Still, B. J.	11 Mar
Tait, I. A.	11 Mar
Lowery, M. D.	15 Mar
Achilles, L. E. A.	21 Mar
Mellor, A. D.	21 Mar
Monksfield, M. E.	21 Mar
Newton, M. E.	21 Mar
Nicholson, J. D. PhD BSc	21 Mar
Brearey, M. N. BSc	24 Mar
Butcher, A. J.	24 Mar
Gough, C. F.	24 Mar
Murphy, S. D.	24 Mar
Rose, I. K.	24 Mar
Jenkins, D. J.	29 Mar
Rayson, J. A.	29 Mar
Webb, J. F.	29 Mar
Walker, I. A.	1 Apr
Williams, R. T.	1 Apr
Stean, P. M.	2 Apr
Neil, R. A.	10 Apr
Achilles, B. K.	11 Apr
Butler, C.	11 Apr
Plane, R. P.	11 Apr
Harvey, J. D.	19 Apr
Greenall, B. W.	20 Apr
Malling, S. H. BEd	23 Apr
Clark, P. W.	26 Apr
Reed, G. M.	26 Apr
Tilson, N.	26 Apr
Bellis, J. P. BA	30 Apr
Callister, J. W. BA	30 Apr
Bett, S. G. BSc	3 May

Baldwin, J.	9 May
Bateman, L. A. BA	9 May
Clark, P.	9 May
Montgomery, D. W. MA	9 May
Reid, C. B.	9 May
Dickie, A. D. BSc	11 May
McQuillan, B.	11 May
Plews, A. H.	11 May
Hogben, R. J. J.	25 May
Powell, V. E.	25 May
Williamson, J. M. C.	25 May
Browne, W. F.	31 May
Byrne, J. T.	31 May
Stretton, A. I.	31 May
Tilton, D. R. BSc	31 May
Bevan, C. J.	2 June
Cross, R.	2 June
Dennis, K. M.	2 June
Freeman, P. R.	2 June
Lunt, C. J.	2 June
MacDonald, J. P. BSc	2 June
Drew, R. W. F.	7 June
Ferriman, N. T.	7 June
Harris, P. R.	7 June
Mackenzie, P. J.	7 June
Moule, J. S. BA	7 June
Rickerby, C. D.	7 June
Rodger, G. N.	7 June
Webb, R. G.	7 June
Spain, A. R.	10 June
Higgins, K. M.	13 June
Kaye, M. L. BEng PGCE	13 June
Head, L.	14 June
Marsh, C. J.	14 June
Abubakar, A. B. PhD MSc BSc	16 June
Clarke, A. G.	20 June
Brittain, M.	22 June
Greenman, D.	22 June
Allen, A. J. BSc	27 June
Elliott, J. L.	27 June
Steadman, J. A. PhD BA PGCE	27 June
Agate, J. J.	30 June
Evans, R. M.	30 June
Squires, V. J.	30 June
Sully, A. J. BSc	1 July
Hawkins, D. J.	2 July
Morton, E. M.	6 July
Peach, D. G.	6 July
Steven, R.	6 July
Duffey, M. G.	10 July
Jones, A. N. B.	11 July
Robinson, C. E.	11 July
Leggott, S. P. BSc	15 July
Mott, J. F.	15 July
Bevan, K. J.	20 July
Dodd, P. J. BEng	20 July

Millar, J. D.	20 July
Stones, M. D. BEng	20 July
Cleeter, N. Y.	25 July
Jordan, M. J.	25 July
Shakespeare, I. J.	25 July
Roberts, D. MBCS MIPD	26 July
Balshaw, H. S. BA	31 July
Bonneywell, J. E. BSc PGCE	3 Aug
Stanbury, P. W. BWng PGCE	3 Aug
Edwards, I.	5 Aug
Todd, A. D. BA MPhil	8 Aug
Kennedy, I. D. BSc	6 Aug
Barker, N. G.	9 Aug
Green, K. J.	9 Aug
Kirby, O. J. A.	9 Aug
Richards, K. F.	9 Aug
Daly, J. M.	12 Aug
Stewart, M. J.	12 Aug
Pope, J. R. BSc	14 Aug
Jones, J. W.	16 Aug
Moss, R. M.	21 Aug
Borthwick, J. H.	23 Aug
Edney, M. R.	23 Aug
Pemberton, A. L. BSc	23 Aug
Thomson, G.	23 Aug
Wall, D.	23 Aug
Wiltshire, M. J.	23 Aug
Durling, A. M. BA	25 Aug
Barnes, J. A.	1 Sept
Graham, A.	1 Sept
Hannent, P. A.	1 Sept
Mottershead, J. C.	1 Sept
Archibald, S. J.	7 Sept
Cawood, E. A.	7 Sept
Clarke, A. C.	7 Sept
Connery, P. J. MA	7 Sept
Griffiths, J. A.	7 Sept
Harrison, S. J.	7 Sept
Martin. K. H. D. BA	7 Sept
Williamson, M. A.	7 Sept
Fielder, C. BSc	13 Sept
Forrester, J. PhD BSc	13 Sept
Gill, S.	13 Sept
Hickie, L. RGN RMN	13 Sept
Hirst, S. A. J. MA BSc	13 Sept
Jones, M. A.	13 Sept
Bates, D. L.	20 Sept
Baynes, T. M. J.	20 Sept
Bissell, K. D.	20 Sept
Walters, K.	20 Sept
Evans, W. A.	27 Sept
King, N. J. BSc PGCE	27 Sept
Lee, D. P.	27 Sept
Martin, H. S.	27 Sept
Dixon, G. BSc PGCE	28 Sept
Humphrey, R.	1 Oct
Woodland, R. K. BSc	1 Oct

277

Flying Officers

1996—contd

Timms, S. J.	2 Oct
Davies, P. J.	3 Oct
Dow, S. M. MA PhD	3 Oct
Harris, C. V.	3 Oct
Thomas, D.	3 Oct
Haskell, G. BSc	5 Oct
Cooper, S. R.	6 Oct
Harpur, K. M. T.	6 Oct
Phillips, R. M.	6 Oct
Slack, R. A.	6 Oct
King, B. W.	7 Oct
Warren, L. C.	7 Oct
Egerton, C. J.	11 Oct
Stear, Sir Micheal KCB CBE MA	11 Oct
Armit, A.	14 Oct
Allen, N. J.	21 Oct
Munro, I. R.	21 Oct
Rennison, S. RGN RMN	22 Oct
Hendry, R. S.	25 Oct
Brown, J. A.	31 Oct
Green, M.	31 Oct
Smith, D. P.	31 Oct
Cox, J. M.	4 Nov
Le Worthy, D. A.	5 Nov
Madge, A. BA	7 Nov
Rishman, G. BSc	14 Nov
Glover, A. M.	16 Nov
Davies, C. G.	22 Nov
Hanks, W. G.	22 Nov
Murray, H. D.	22 Nov
Wainwright, G. J.	22 Nov
Clayson, T. P. S.	24 Nov
Foster, M. J.	24 Nov
Jones, G. C.	24 Nov
Jones, G. D.	24 Nov
Judge, C. P. B.	24 Nov
Kett, J. T. LLB	24 Nov
Lane, D.	24 Nov
Whitehead, M. S.	24 Nov
Smith, A. L.	25 Nov
Booth, S. J.	30 Nov
Harper, S.	30 Nov
Davies, A. R.	3 Dec
Doling, G. J.	3 Dec
Hicks, S. D. BA	3 Dec
Abbott, M. I.	5 Dec
Jordan, J.	5 Dec
Pal, R. R.	5 Dec
Angell, M. J. BEng	13 Dec
Brackett, L. A.	13 Dec
Foster, J.	13 Dec
Greenman, H. E.	13 Dec
Hutchison, L. B.	13 Dec

Laidler, P.	13 Dec
McElroy, G. F.	13 Dec
Renshaw, I.	13 Dec
Stephenson, T.	13 Dec
Sullivan, D. B. BA	13 Dec
Corteen, J. B.	20 Dec
Fairhurst, A. G.	20 Dec
Hallowes, R. A. D.	20 Dec
Thornby, T. J.	20 Dec
Bostock, S. N. MSc FIMgt	24 Dec
Hurt, T. S. BEng	25 Dec

1997

Adcock, C. B. BA	1 Jan
Burdess, S. BEng CEng FRAeS	2 Jan
Aitken, T. A. BSc	7 Jan
Cox, R. I.	9 Jan
Addison, G. BSc PGCE	11 Jan
Faulkner, M. A.	11 Jan
Bodger, M. A. BEng	17 Jan
Breward, C. J. W. BA	17 Jan
Ellen, G. P.	17 Jan
Parker, N. BSc	17 Jan
Ward, P. D.	17 Jan
Brooke, A. J. BA PGCE	19 Jan
Cousins, P.T. BSc	21 Jan
Balson, J. D.	25 Jan
Gay, A. J.	1 Feb
Barry, J. D.	3 Feb
Beasant, N. C. A. BSc	5 Feb
Abbott, P. J. MSc BTech CertEd	6 Feb
Butchers, M. J.	6 Feb
Horsley, N. J. BA	6 Feb
Pettengell, N. C.	6 Feb
Stannard, I. N. BA	6 Feb
Donne, R. H. S. MA PGCE	10 Feb
Chandler, N. J.	15 Feb
Mamoany, T. J.	15 Feb
Sawyer, M. A. G.	15 Feb
Turley, K. E.	15 Feb
Gough, B.	18 Feb
Legatt, C. P.	26 Feb
Astin, D. A.	27 Feb
Bain, C. A. BEng	27 Feb
Hill, D. L. BSc	27 Feb
Jones, K. W.	28 Feb
Jones, M. A.	28 Feb
Mawson, S. J. BTech	3 Mar
Singer, M. J.	3 Mar
Fletcher, G. C. A.	4 Mar
Avery, G. J.	5 Mar
Hawkins, T. R. A.	5 Mar

Coombs, T. E.	7 Mar
Hale, D. H.	7 Mar
Hicks, C. J.	7 Mar
Watson, M.	7 Mar
Withams, S. J. A. BSc	11 Mar
Pursehouse, A. J.	13 Mar
Rogers, R. M.	13 Mar
Bulgin, J. P.	14 Mar
Gilchrist, K.G.	14 Mar
Hurrell, A. J. BA	14 Mar
Patel, H. S.	14 Mar
Davidson, M. D. MA	18 Mar
King, A. K. BEng	18 Mar
Wetherall, M.	23 Mar
Cooper, A. C. BA PGCE	24 Mar
Colman, D. J.	28 Mar
Hutchins, D. J.	28 Mar
Kerr, E. R.	28 Mar
Laird, S. P.	28 Mar
Mustafa. S.	28 Mar
Southern, L. A.	28 Mar
Whyte, P. G. BA	28 Mar
Baxby, D. R.	30 Mar
King, H. R.	30 Mar
Williams, C. G.	30 Mar
Adams, G. BA	12 Apr
Best, J. T.	12 Apr
Boulton, P.	12 Apr
Dunlop, C. A.	12 Apr
Harding, A. J.	12 Apr
Marriott, G. A. BTech	12 Apr
McGarva, A. R.	12 Apr
Morris, J. N.	12 Apr
Niven, S. O.	12 Apr
Park, D. MSc	12 Apr
Shepherd, C. E.	12 Apr
Surry, D. D. BSc	12 Apr
Tatar, P. N.	12 Apr
Tidman, J. E.	12 Apr
Tenison-Collins, J. A. BSc	22 Apr
Collins, M. S.	24 Apr
Curtis, T.	24 Apr
Harrison, S. D.	24 Apr
Duran, P. M. S. BA PGCE	25 Apr
Valentine, P. A. BSc	25 Apr
Lavender, B. W. OBE AFC	26 Apr
Riach, C. J.	30 Apr
Arthur, L. O.	2 May
Bell, J. M.	2 May
Cairns, R. S. PhD MSc BSc	2 May
Dale, N. T.	2 May
Michel, R. G. BA	2 May
O'Connor, M. J. OBE	2 May
Parry, C.	2 May
Simmons, C. J.	2 May

Flying Officers

1997—contd

Stamp, G. D.	2 May	Gough, C. G.	17 July
Thompson, W. C.	2 May	Jarvis, I.	17 July
Warman, A. D.	2 May	Kendall, T. N. BSc	17 July
Spinks, J. C.	3 May	Morgan, A. D.	17 July
Fay, J. C. BA	7 May	Payne, A. G.	17 July
Wright, S. L.	10 May	Sheehan, P. J. BEng	17 July
Saunderson, K.	15 May	Sinfield, A. J.	17 July
Severs, A. D.	15 May	Smith, M. G. BSc	17 July
Stapleton, K. R.	15 May	Stilgoe, G. P. BSc	17 July
Stanford, R. K. BEd	16 May	Swatridge, E. L.	17 July
Stokoe, A. M.	17 May	Torrell, C. A.	17 July
Walker, A. P. BA PGCE	17 May	Webb, J. F.	17 July
Austin, Sir Roger KCB AFC FRAeS	22 May	Westgate, A. J. BEd	17 July
Flitton, D. C.	24 May	Lambert, S.	21 July
Goodacre, R. G.	24 May	Morten, J. A.	21 July
Hannaford, P. F.	24 May	Williams, J. T. BA	21 July
Hooper, C. P.	24 May	Fletcher, R. M. BSc	26 July
Reeves, M. C.	24 May	Gerrish, D. J.	27 July
Banks, T. J.	25 May	Alford, A. M.	28 July
Beswick, G. T. W.	25 May	Bishop, G. P.	28 July
McChristie, R. S.	25 May	Exton, D. V.	28 July
Whitcombe, P. J. BSc PGCE	25 May	Jackson, N.	28 July
Bracci, M. S.	1 June	Lovell, P. M.	28 July
Cletheroe, B. G. BSc	1 June	May, S. J.	28 July
Greene, C. D.	1 June	Muggridge, S. J.	28 July
King, A. C.	1 June	Barker, D. BSc	30 July
Pattenden, C. E.	1 June	Joyce, T. J.	6 Aug
Perring, I. D.	1 June	Byng, E. F.	12 Aug
Sherlock, L. M. BA	1 June	Armstrong, I. G.	14 Aug
Miller, H. A. BSc	4 June	Cantwell, P. J. BSc	14 Aug
Young, A. J.	4 June	Ackerley, D. J.	15 Aug
Hourican, D. M.	8 June	Betts, J. D. BEng	15 Aug
Screen, D. A.	8 June	Cotton, D. A.	15 Aug
Smith, R. G.	9 June	Dudgeon, P.	15 Aug
Hunt, H.	10 June	Jackson, N.	15 Aug
Colbron, S. L.	15 June	Lewis, N. M.	15 Aug
Hughes, G. P.	15 June	Stamp, M. R.	15 Aug
Waters. R. D.	23 June	Walker, P. J.	15 Aug
Jancis, A. BSc PGCE	24 June	Hawthorne, M. E. BSc	24 Aug
Warburton, R. G.	24 June	Priestly, R. M. BSc	24 Aug
Brady, J. P. BA	3 July	Henderson, J.	25 Aug
Cockrill, M. J. MBE	9 July	Kay, R.	25 Aug
Falle, P. R.	9 July	Pender, W. D.	1 Sept
Williams, R. J. BSc	9 July	Seabrook, R. J.	5 Sept
Barlow, P.	17 July	Boulton, R. P.	6 Sept
Bissell, E. I.	17 July	Cork, S. J.	6 Sept
Blackwell, T. W.	17 July	Davies, A. M.	6 Sept
Brown, D. W.	17 July	Ford, M. P.	6 Sept
Butler, S. P.	17 July	Ridge, J. G.	6 Sept
Carlisle, A.	17 July	Thompson Ambrose, W. I.	6 Sept
Dunn, R. A.	17 July	Alcock, R. J. F. BEng	12 Sept
Dunn, S. S.	17 July	Bewley, J. W.	12 Sept
		Golding, S. T.	12 Sept
		Martin, J. W.	12 Sept
		Perkins, A. D.	17 Sept
		Hunt, G. J. JP PhD MBA BA MInstAM MIMgt	18 Sept

Gardiner, C. D.	19 Sept
McQueen, S. E.	19 Sept
Molloy, M. P.	19 Sept
Sherwood, R. J.	19 Sept
Eyers, I. A.	20 Sept
Jones, J. T. D.	20 Sept
Napier, M. J. W. BSc	21 Sept
Dabell, S. W. BSc	26 Sept
Melrose, W.	26 Sept
Axon, P. J. W.	29 Sept
Burns, I. A.	29 Sept
Grant, P. E.	29 Sept
Jago, M.	29 Sept
Pudney, K. W.	29 Sept
Ratinon, J. G. A.	29 Sept
Tyler, F. M.	29 Sept
Joy, C. A. BEd	3 Oct
Beesley, M. J.	6 Oct
Fraser, I. E.	6 Oct
Haworth, D. BSc	6 Oct
Hinchliffe, S. K.	6 Oct
Ireland, D. P. BEng PGCE	6 Oct
Jones, A. D.	6 Oct
Lennie, A. W.	6 Oct
Nolan, A. D. BSc	6 Oct
Slater, A. D.	6 Oct
Smith, F. M. BSc	6 Oct
Thompson, C. W.	6 Oct
Freeney, D.	10 Oct
Hall, M. I.	10 Oct
Sparry, P. M.	10 Oct
Hodge, R. J. W. BSc	13 Oct
Coombes, G. R.	17 Oct
Evans, J. R.	17 Oct
Gregory, K.	17 Oct
Kilby, D. J.	17 Oct
Roberts, P. M.	17 Oct
Baker, R.	23 Oct
Mitchell, C. BA	23 Oct
Sibley, J. BEd	23 Oct
Echevarria, J. MA BA PGCE	24 Oct
Lakeland, A. J.	24 Oct
Millar, M. W. MSc PGCE	24 Oct
Walker, D. K. BTech	24 Oct
Edwards, P. J.	29 Oct
Balsillie, I.	31 Oct
Dean, R. J.	31 Oct
Keenan, A.	31 Oct
Rankin, D. M.	31 Oct
Whiteman, R. C.	31 Oct
Joynson, J. BA	14 Nov
Aala, R. MA ACA	20 Nov
Banks, N. K. M.	20 Nov
Brown, D. BA	20 Nov
Ireland, C. BA PGCE	20 Nov
Rogers, N. S.	20 Nov
Turner, R. R.	20 Nov

Flying Officers

1997—contd

Plane, K. L.	21 Nov
Barnett, I. C. BEng	25 Nov
Cooper, A. H. C. BSc	27 Nov
Laycock, P. M. BSc	2 Dec
Hawkins, D. G. PhD BSc	3 Dec
Bagnall, R. D. A.	4 Dec
Denton, D. J.	4 Dec
Taylor, C. L. BA	7 Dec
Cowell, A. C.	7 Dec
Davison, M. G.	7 Dec
King, A. P.	7 Dec
Milligan, D. R.	7 Dec
Partridge, J. M. BSc	7 Dec
Thomas, J. N.	7 Dec
Young, J. S.	7 Dec
Coram-Wright, N. H. MA	8 Dec
Feakes, C. J. MSc BSc	8 Dec
Grace, M. J. BSc PGCE	8 Dec
Penny, S. D. BA BSc MBCS MIEE MRAeS	8 Dec
Bone, K. L.	19 Dec
Pym, J. D.	19 Dec
Abdy, M. J.	20 Dec
Jensen, F. LLB ACIS	20 Dec
Kocbusz, M. D.	20 Dec

1998

Manktelow, J. A.	4 Jan
Strand, S.	7 Jan
Boughton, R. P.	10 Jan
Johnson, A. G.	10 Jan
Martin, P. M.	10 Jan
Gant, I. S.	12 Jan
Wilson, E. R. BSc	14 Jan
Bayles, J. M.	16 Jan
Allard, C. E.	17 Jan
Bell, M. F.	17 Jan
Crane, N. M.	17 Jan
Bailey, A. J.	25 Jan
Galley, P. T. PhD BSc	25 Jan
George, S. J.	25 Jan
Kuschirow, D. K.	25 Jan
Banks, S.	26 Jan
Braithwaite, S. M.	26 Jan
Braybrook, D. R. MA DPhil	26 Jan
Curry, P. D. BA	26 Jan
Kay, M.	26 Jan

Masters, D. A.	26 Jan
Mogford, A. S.	26 Jan
Schenk, K. S. R.	28 Jan
Fry, R.	31 Jan
Geary-Andrews, C.	31 Jan
Rees, D. E.	31 Jan
Kirsopp, G. N. J.	2 Feb
Smith, I.	2 Feb
Hindley, K. L. BA	9 Feb
Jones, E. G. BSc MB ChB	10 Feb
Bennett, M. J.	12 Feb
MacDonald, B.	12 Feb
Alderton, R. C.	16 Feb
Lamb, S. G. MA PGCE	16 Feb
Gee, M. J.	19 Feb
Hall, M. J.	19 Feb
Higginson, S. J.	19 Feb
Salt, G. T. BEng	19 Feb
Davies, D. I.	21 Feb
McLachlan, S. C. J.	21 Feb
Moore, M. J.	21 Feb
McCotter, B. W.	27 Feb
Green, P. D.	2 Mar
Crighton, D. S. BSc	7 Mar
Mulroy, M. C.	11 Mar
Collick, A. J.	12 Mar
Fox, C. J.	12 Mar
Hogg, A. R. BA	13 Mar
Lardner, N. J. BA PGCE	13 Mar
Lynch, K.	13 Mar
Makepeace, C. J.	13 Mar
Quinn, M. S.	13 Mar
Thompson, G. BEd	13 Mar
Thurtle, G. R.	13 Mar
Treutlein, J.	13 Mar
Xavier, F. Y.	13 Mar
Hudson, J.	20 Mar
O'Brien, P. S.	20 Mar
Platt, M. A.	20 Mar
Shepherd, D. J. BSc	20 Mar
Gunstone, J. P.	25 Mar
Impey, M. J.	25 Mar
Pace, S.	25 Mar
Routledge, S.	27 Mar
Lawton, S. R.	29 Mar
Organ, A.	29 Mar
Gadd, S. I.	7 Apr
Riley, S. C.	8 Apr
Smith, T. R.	8 Apr
Armstrong, P. W.	9 Apr
Glover, R. G.	9 Apr
Belshaw, A. M. T.	15 Apr
Madge, A. D.	15 Apr
Carter, R. S. BEd	17 Apr
Siddall, P. J. BSc	17 Apr
Forward, W. J.	19 Apr
Perkins, C.	19 Apr

Wingfield-Griffin, J. A.	19 Apr
Sherring, I. D.	22 Apr
Whiten, P. R.	22 Apr
Cowan, J. A. BA	23 Apr
Angelosanto, A. BSc PGCE	30 Apr
Jarvis, K. W.	5 May
Parsons, M. G.	5 May

Pilot Officers

1990

Hunter, L. M.	27 Feb
Rotherham, D. J. BEd	20 Mar

1991

McLintock, C. M. BSc	25 June
Cameron, J.	2 July
Cooper, P. R. BEng	2 July
Sawyer, J. N. CBE	17 Sept
Alexander, A. J.	9 Dec
Bailey, G. M. B.	9 Dec
Cheetham, M. K.	9 Dec
Green, H. J.	9 Dec
Coates, N. D.	10 Dec
Davies, M. R.	10 Dec
Dix, R.	10 Dec
Bird, I. N.	12 Dec
Blood, C. ARCM	18 Dec

1992

Marshall, G. P. B.	9 June
Cherry, R. F. N.	4 Aug
Brennan, M. I.	18 Aug
Child, J. J.	18 Aug
Davies, P. A.	18 Aug
Hart, D. L.	28 Aug
Elliot, S. D.	19 Nov

1993

Garwood, R. MIMgt	5 July
Langdon, N. G.	19 July
Wilkes, C. A. BA PGCE	6 Oct
Redican, S. N.	4 Dec
Rhodes, K. P.	9 Dec
Leech, E. J.	10 Dec
Moy, A. J.	10 Dec

Pilot Officers

1993—contd

Van Rhyn, S. J.	10 Dec
Bentley, K. LTCL	12 Dec
Seward, C. M.	12 Dec
Paul, C.	16 Dec
Nash, D. J.	18 Dec

1994

Vickers, D. J.	27 Feb
Spinks, J. C.	3 May
Whalley, A. L. BSc PGCE	7 Sept
Symonds, D. C. BA	19 Oct

1995

Moore, E.	24 Mar
Peat, C. I. BSc	25 Apr
Banks, D. S.	10 May
Reeves, M. C.	24 May
Webb, C. J.	15 Aug
Dolby, R. A.	6 Oct
Hayward, P. J.	6 Oct
Davidson, G.	20 Dec
Dengate, K. MEd	20 Dec

1996

Jenkins, L. C.	16 Jan
Chipman, P. D. PhD BSc PGCE	5 Feb
Burton, G. C.	7 Feb
James, P.	19 Feb
Cheesman, D. A. J. BSc	13 Mar
Grafham, D.	13 Mar
Higson, A. L. BSc	13 Mar
Morris, M. R.	13 Mar
Parfitt, M. A.	13 Mar
Elliott, M. A.	20 Mar
Norman, P. E.	25 Mar
France, J. C.	15 Apr
Train, N. M.	15 Apr
Head, D. P.	9 May
Knowles, C. A. BEng	9 May
McGuire, J. A.	9 May
Purkiss, A.	9 May
Staincliffe, R. E. BA	9 May
Terry, S. J. BA	9 May
Allanson, W. J.	13 May
Fortune, A. R. BA	13 May

Robinson, S. M. BEng	14 May
Lewis, C. R. BA	20 May
Adkins, M. J.	31 May
Alexander, S. C.	31 May
Baker, E. A. BA	31 May
Davies, J. R.	31 May
Dixon, S. E.	31 May
Flint, R. S. B.	31 May
Howard, D. F.	31 May
Hudson, A. C.	31 May
Laird, J. E.	31 May
Marshall, S. W.	31 May
Milne, A. C.	31 May
Mollan, M. S. J. BSc	31 May
Parkes, S. M.	31 May
Pollock, J. M.	31 May
Ross, A. I.	31 May
Rylatt, A. J. BEng	31 May
Sie, E. R. H. B. PhD BSc	31 May
Smith, P. J.	31 May
Voce, H. B.	31 May
Brown, R. C.	5 June
Jones, M. G.	5 June
Shepherd, D. M.	5 June
Bonner, B. A.	7 June
Rennie, A. E. W. BSc	7 June
Smith, D. E.	7 June
Anderson, D. I.	10 June
Johnson, H. M.	10 June
Robb, I. R.	10 June
Rule, N. W.	13 June
Bain, J. B.	18 June
Crumpton, D. L.	18 June
Fisher, T.	18 June
Lobban, A.	18 June
McTeir, J.	18 June
Thom, A. G.	18 June
Bull, M. M.	4 July
Edwards, R. T. MInstAM	4 July
Herniman, M. C. J.	4 July
Marriott, G. E.	4 July
Saunders, P.	4 July
Weston, N. S.	4 July
Allan, J.	8 July
Duplock, S. J.	8 July
Turner, K. P.	8 July
Walters, A. M.	8 July
Balmford, S. J.	9 July
Bass, C. R. BA	9 July
Taylor, M. A.	9 July
Morris, K. R. BSc PGCE	12 July
Kinnear, N. R. MA	16 July
Connolly, G. M.	19 July
Holmes, I. G.	19 July
Jones, T. M.	19 July
Piccavey, S. K. E.	19 July

Williamson, D. BA	19 July
Holmes, A. T.	22 July
Stead, J. L.	23 July
Hall, J. E. BA	6 Aug
Heckel, P. A.	6 Aug
Morton, D. R.	6 Aug
Walker, M. A.	6 Aug
Cassidy, S. BSc	8 Aug
Creswell, P. N. BSc	9 Aug
Fairley, G. J.	9 Aug
Taylor, S. R.	9 Aug
Stone, C. A.	21 Aug
Stubbs, C. M.	21 Aug
Burrett, T. J.	28 Aug
Maguire, B. J.	28 Aug
Porter, S. A.	28 Aug
Fitton, N. J.	I Sept
Milne, D. D.	1 Sept
Philpott, A.	1 Sept
Riding, P. M.	1 Sept
Fitton, R. J. BSc	11 Sept
Arrowsmith, C. E.	13 Sept
Bragg, D.	13 Sept
Fowler, L. D.	13 Sept
Poole, C. J.	13 Sept
Pratt, E. V.	13 Sept
Blythe, R. T. C.	19 Sept
Coppack, D. M.	19 Sept
Bailey, S. M.	24 Sept
Burnham, K. A. BSc	24 Sept
Chesher, K. W.	24 Sept
MacMillan, L. D. BSc	24 Sept
Ryder, D. J.	25 Sept
Amey, R. J.	7 Oct
Crust, A. C BSc	7 Oct
Evans, T. W.	7 Oct
Eyre, P. S.	7 Oct
Farrell, D. P.	7 Oct
Fox, P. E.	7 Oct
Nowlan, K. A.	7 Oct
Palmer, R. F.	7 Oct
Smith, M.	7 Oct
Titley, S. K. BSc	7 Oct
Watson, M. S. J. BA PGCE	7 Oct
Arnold, R. J.	11 Oct
Capron-Tee, J. A.	11 Oct
Deadman, I. A. BA	11 Oct
McFall, A. J. BA	11 Oct
Watson, L. B.	11 Oct
Hardy, L. R.	14 Oct
Little, S. P.	14 Oct
Rowbotham, P.	14 Oct
Bacon, R. R.	15 Oct
Barre, G. R.	15 Oct
Brayford, S.	15 Oct
Flux, M. J.	15 Oct
Foster, C. T.	15 Oct
Laurence, P. E.	15 Oct
Manning, D. A.	15 Oct

Pilot Officers

1996—contd

Shearer, L. E.	15 Oct
Walvin, J. C.	15 Oct
Allen, H. F. BMus	
PGCE	23 Oct
Abbott, S. J.	6 Nov
Finck, P. H.	6 Nov
Pickup, G. R.	6 Nov
Taylor, S. R.	6 Nov
Walters, R. J.	6 Nov
Colverson, A.	11 Nov
English, H.	11 Nov
Woods, A. J.	11 Nov
Bird, J. BSc	25 Nov
Frazer, A. T. W. BA	25 Nov
Henderson, N. T.	25 Nov
Ashby, A. P.	27 Nov
Bell, M. J.	27 Nov
Castleton, J. R.	27 Nov
Cottier, K. J. BSc	27 Nov
Dawson, A.	27 Nov
Holmes, A. N. BA	27 Nov
Howlett, S. A.	27 Nov
MacDonald, J. A.	27 Nov
Reed, S. J.	27 Nov
Shaw, T. L. BA	27 Nov
Squance, K. L.	27 Nov
Hayward, J. L.	3 Dec
McCormack, W. J.	
BSc	3 Dec
Muller, J. V.	3 Dec
Shorthouse, L. J.	
MSc	3 Dec
White, A. J. BSc	
PGCE	3 Dec
Hemsil, K. I.	5 Dec
Ross, I. S. PhD BSc	5 Dec
Ruscoe, R. M.	5 Dec
Smith, A. N. W.	5 Dec
Chandler, N. A.	9 Dec
Dyos, M. B.	9 Dec
Lillywhite, G. J.	9 Dec
Burton, S. B.	12 Dec
Derrick, L. M. H.	12 Dec
Gay, S. J. BSc	12 Dec
Johnson, N. I.	12 Dec
Pass, A. C.	12 Dec
Powell, K. D. BSc	
PGCE	12 Dec
Smith, R.	12 Dec
Baron, J. St. J. BSc	
PGCE	13 Dec
Childs, M. E. BA	
PGCE	13 Dec
Baines. N.	17 Dec
Clifton, W. A. H.	17 Dec

Cooper, S. L.	17 Dec
McDonnell, S. M.	17 Dec
Stockill, J. L.	17 Dec
Fray, H. A.	19 Dec
Howarth, S.	19 Dec
Lloyd, J.	19 Dec
Thomas, J. S.	19 Dec
Tyson, N. K.	19 Dec

1997

Bailey, J.	6 Jan
Bailey, S. E.	6 Jan
Blatchford, A. M.	
TEng	6 Jan
Blease, M.	6 Jan
Furley, S. J.	6 Jan
Gilson, D. R. BPhil	6 Jan
Bishop, M. S.	9 Jan
Brewer, E.	9 Jan
O'Shaughnessy, K. E.	
	9 Jan
Anderson, S. J.	10 Jan
Campbell, R. I.	10 Jan
Coyle, J. M.	10 Jan
Adamson, M. BSc	
PGCE	15 Jan
Davies, C. V. BSc	15 Jan
MacMillan, D. J.	15 Jan
Giess, N. P.	21 Jan
Leese, J. BA	21 Jan
Shoebridge, T. C.	21 Jan
Ali, M.	24 Jan
Bridges, S.	24 Jan
Haynes, C.	24 Jan
Deere, G. W.	27 Jan
Kenchington, N.	27 Jan
Pendlebury, S. R.	27 Jan
Williams, R. M.	27 Jan
White, H. J. PhD BSc	
PGCE	28 Jan
Bennett, N. A. D.	3 Feb
Courtnadge, S. E.	3 Feb
Coyne, C. P.	3 Feb
King, K. A.	3 Feb
Williams, J. D. BSc	
PGCE	3 Feb
Hammond, G. G.	6 Feb
Knight, T. F. BSc	
PGCE	6 Feb
Bullock, R. E.	18 Feb
Conley, C. R.	18 Feb
Faulkner, S. C.	18 Feb
Greenland, L. S.	18 Feb
Hoddinott, V. K. BA	
PGCE	18 Feb
Miller, P. D. BA PGCE	
MIMgt	18 Feb
Hayton, P.	19 Feb

Taylor, A. B. BSc	19 Feb
Bennett, D. J.	26 Feb
Hughes, K. E. BA	
PGCE	26 Feb
Bartlett, J. D.	4 Mar
Frizzle, R. W.	4 Mar
Gildea, A. C.	4 Mar
Greaves, D. W.	4 Mar
Moore, H.	4 Mar
Pocock, M. D.	4 Mar
Walker, S.	4 Mar
Cullen, R. J. BEd	5 Mar
Bullingham, M. C.	7 Mar
Carroll, I. H.	7 Mar
Hyde, M. A.	7 Mar
Brocklebank, J. M.	13 Mar
Curran, I. J.	13 Mar
Hopkins, M. J.	13 Mar
Le Worthy, S. L.	13 Mar
Lynch, C. BA	13 Mar
Todd, D.	13 Mar
Willies, A. M.	13 Mar
Yaku, L.	13 Mar
Day, J. P. DPhil BSc	
PGCE	24 Mar
Houlihan, M. S. BSc	24 Mar
Knell, R. E. BA PGCE	27 Mar
Appleby, R. C.	2 Apr
Smith, B. A.	2 Apr
Streeton, R. W.	2 Apr
Armstrong, C. J.	14 Apr
Ball, H. G.	14 Apr
Bellamy, C. H.	14 Apr
Cobb, J.	14 Apr
Gallop, M. P.	14 Apr
Taylor, P. J.	14 Apr
White, B. J.	14 Apr
Hart, D. J. BD	16 Apr
Close-Ash, W. P.	28 Apr
MacIntosh, F. I.	28 Apr
Smith, B. D.	28 Apr
Lawson, J. R.	2 May
Shere-Massey, M.	2 May
Wright, D. M.	2 May
Balchin, A. W.	7 May
Bell, G. M.	7 May
Jenkins, K. F.	7 May
Moore, D. A. S.	7 May
Silver, B. R.	7 May
Colley, P.	12 May
Williamson, M. A.	12 May
Farr, J. E.	20 May
Hughes, P. M.	20 May
Lawson, P. S.	20 May
Revill, G. D.	20 May
Mewes, C. A.	21 May
Eade, F. R. PhD	22 May
Pressley, J. W. BA	
PGCE	22 May
Duncan, J. A.	23 May

Pilot Officers

1997—contd

Parry, D. H.	23 May
Warrender, M.	23 May
Burgess, L. A.	29 May
Smith, P. J.	29 May
Turner. P. L.	29 May
Whitehead, S. J.	29 May
Allen, L. I.	4 June
Anthony, G.	4 June
Brannan, R. J.	4 June
Bromley, G. L.	4 June
Brooksbank, R. E.	4 June
Hill, Z. M.	4 June
Lemmon, D. S.	4 June
Rafferty, D. M.	4 June
Smith, M. J. MEng MICE	4 June
Adams, S. L. BSc	6 June
Fry, A. W. BEM	6 June
Morris, A.	6 June
Scott, W. G. BA	6 June
Newell, D. R.	9 June
Wilson, N.	9 June
Wilson, P.	9 June
Driscoll, K. J. S.	11 June
Mayfield, P. S. BA PGCE	11 June
Wood, R.	11 June
Ayre, A. M.	16 June
Hatton, T. J.	16 June
Mason, A. C.	16 June
Rigby, S. I.	16 June
Scudder, D. R. M.	16 June
Clark, J. E.	20 June
Moore, R. A.	30 June
Pinckston, P. K.	30 June
Searle, G. R.	30 June
Withersby, E. D.	30 June
Booth, T. N. BSc	3 July
Kendall, A. R.	4 July
Gilhooly, D. BA DipEd	9 July
Cepelak, A.	10 July
Edwards, A. J.	10 July
Mortimer, D. F.	10 July
Pearce, G. M.	10 July
Durkin, C. B. J. BSc	14 July
Sharrard-Williams, E. L. BEd	14 July
Wheatley, J. L.	14 July
Hick, S.	17 July
Reece, D. J.	17 July
Williams, J. D. BSc	17 July
Fulbrook, I. S.	21 July
Partington, J. E.	21 July
Prentice, K. J. BA BSc	21 July
Pursehouse, M. C.	21 July
Gillespie, J. W. C.	29 July
Booth, L. A.	31 July
Butterfield, J. BSc	31 July
Fitzgerald, A. C. BSc	31 July
Berry, I. C.	4 Aug
Divver, J. A.	4 Aug
Hunt, R. A. J.	4 Aug
Thomas, L. C.	4 Aug
Macher, D.	5 Aug
Pick, J. A.	5 Aug
Swierczek, J.	5 Aug
Bartlett, J. F.	12 Aug
Davenport, L. F.	12 Aug
Davies, M. J.	12 Aug
Thijs, N.	12 Aug
MacMillan, D. F.	28 Aug
Oldham, C. M.	18 Aug
Carrington, J. F.	2 Sept
Collins, M. J.	2 Sept
Carr, M.	5 Sept
Darwin, K. A.	5 Sept
French, M. J.	5 Sept
Head, G. M. M. BA IEng MIEIE	5 Sept
Byford, J. E. BSc PGCE	10 Sept
Caseman, P. M.	10 Sept
Sutherland, S.	10 Sept
Cooper, N. L.	18 Sept
Dalrymple, I. V. J.	18 Sept
Daly, N. T.	18 Sept
Davies, A. S.	18 Sept
Davies, J. T.	18 Sept
Elliott, K. F. BA	18 Sept
Forster, D. MA	18 Sept
Gough, S. J.	18 Sept
Izzard, V. E. L.	18 Sept
Malik, S. BEng	18 Sept
Roberts, P. F.	18 Sept
Smith, D. P.	18 Sept
Lambert, B. J. BSc CertEd	19 Sept
Quarmby, C. A. MA PGCE	19 Sept
Ravenhall, S. R. MPhil BA	19 Sept
Ripley, J. K. PhD BSc	19 Sept
Adam, K. J. BA PGCE	26 Sept
Draper, C. BSc PGCE	26 Sept
Elder, L. N.	26 Sept
Kuperus, S.	26 Sept
Vardon, A. J. BEd FRSA	26 Sept
McGovern, R.	3 Oct
Smith, J. A. BA	3 Oct
Tucker, K. A. E.	10 Oct
Bone, P. J.	13 Oct
Britton, P. J.	13 Oct
Crane, M. A. J.	13 Oct
Edwards, J. O. LTCL	13 Oct
Head, K. L.	13 Oct
Hockin, M. J. BEng	13 Oct
Smart, M. Z. BEd	13 Oct
Allen, G. D.	15 Oct
Gibson, D. J.	15 Oct
Jones, W. H.	15 Oct
Nadin, R. T. BEng	15 Oct
Cameron, W. H. M. LLB BD	23 Oct
Evans, B. J. BSc(Eng)	23 Oct
Roderick, J. G. MA BSc	23 Oct
Smith, T. D. BA PGCE	23 Oct
Dunn, R. J.	6 Nov
Inglis, J. H.	6 Nov
Symmons, G. J. JP	6 Nov
Cole, P. A.	11 Nov
Gordon, J. A. BSc	11 Nov
Gunner, P. A.	11 Nov
Knell, G. C.	11 Nov
Millyard, P. A.	11 Nov
Tucker, J. M. BSc	11 Nov
Brown, E. L. BA	14 Nov
Furze, J. A. BA	14 Nov
Simms, N. J. BSc	14 Nov
Aldis Neil, J. E. MSc BSc	18 Nov
Jenkins, S. R.	18 Nov
Mimpress, P. J.	18 Nov
Moreton, D. K.	18 Nov
Fotheringham, J. T.	19 Nov
Norris, S. T.	19 Nov
Berry-Robinson, J. A. S.	24 Nov
McNicholas, J. A.	24 Nov
Rosewarn, P. J.	24 Nov
Stedman, L. S.	24 Nov
Brewster, R. A. BSc	25 Nov
Holdsworth, B. J. BA	25 Nov
Brayford, M. A.	27 Nov
Andrews, R. P.	1 Dec
Briggs, A. D. PhD BSc	1 Dec
Yates, F. L.	1 Dec
Costain, J. P. BA	2 Dec
Power, C. P.	5 Dec
Pugsley, G. D.	5 Dec
Cornell, G. W.	11 Dec
Donoghue, I. D.	11 Dec
Jennings, R. D.	15 Dec
Clark, G. J.	16 Dec

1998

Colling, T.	5 Jan
Doveton, L. J.	5 Jan
Fisher, H. J.	5 Jan
Howell, R.	5 Jan
Lee, A. G. C. Y.	5 Jan

Pilot Officers

1998—contd

Lester, M. S.	5 Jan
Machin, J. G.	5 Jan
Melia, C. P.	5 Jan
Richards, S. A.	5 Jan
Smith, A. M. R.	5 Jan
Twist, S. L. BA	5 Jan
Walker, R. A.	5 Jan
Burt, D. J.	12 Jan
Cornish, P. M.	12 Jan
Merchant, G. H. L.	12 Jan
Armitstead, A. R.	16 Jan
Collier, D.	16 Jan
MacQuarrie, J. B.	16 Jan
McDonnell, G. T. MSc	16 Jan
Ramage, C. A.	16 Jan
Branson, F. S. BA PGCE	26 Jan
Cave, S.	26 Jan
Longmuir, M. C. BA PGCE	26 Jan
Mann, J. CertEd	26 Jan
O'Connor, P.	26 Jan
Randle, M. J.	26 Jan
Rogers, G. T.	26 Jan
Cook, S. M.	27 Jan
Crebbin, C. B. BEng	27 Jan
Davidson, A.	27 Jan
Hardy, D.	27 Jan
Hawksfield, D.	27 Jan
John, J. K.	27 Jan
Miller, J. D. BEng	27 Jan
Morrissey, S. M.	27 Jan
Sumner, A. J.	27 Jan
Woodburn, B. W.	27 Jan
Brooks-Johnson, A. J.	28 Jan
Penberthy, M. P.	28 Jan
Young, S-D.	28 Jan
Hogan, J. F.	3 Feb
Ward, G.	3 Feb
Williams, E. C. BA PGCE	3 Feb
Brekke, J. K.	6 Feb
Carter, M.	6 Feb
Evans, A.	6 Feb
Cope, J.	9 Feb
Gibson, S. M. BA PGCE	9 Feb
Last, G. A. BA PGCE	9 Feb
James, M. D.	16 Feb
Pears, J. S. BA MIIM	16 Feb
Sault, D. A.	16 Feb
Tazzyman, J. C. BA PGCE	16 Feb
Edwards, N. McM.	25 Feb
Gilmour, K.	25 Feb

Leith, D. McK.	25 Feb
Shields, H.	25 Feb
Walmsley, D. MIFireE	25 Feb
Bradshaw, R.	26 Feb
Davis, M. L. BSc	26 Feb
Hadley, L. J. BA	26 Feb
Izzard, T. C. BSc	26 Feb
Lane, D. M.	26 Feb
Wilson, C. S.	26 Feb
Dyer, J. J.	27 Feb
Baron, N.	12 Mar
Bassett, J. B.	12 Mar
Beal, S.	12 Mar
Burr, L.	12 Mar
Caffrey, C. M.	12 Mar
Erasmuson, H. J.	12 Mar
Fleming, M. E.	12 Mar
Gillies, S.	12 Mar
Horton, J. M. BSc	12 Mar
Hutchinson, C. A.	12 Mar
Middlemiss, J. J.	12 Mar
Payne, C. J.	12 Mar
Pickering, C. M. BSc	12 Mar
Tucker, J. H.	12 Mar
Jones, R. Y.	18 Mar
Morris, D. W.	18 Mar
Parkinson, S. L.	18 Mar
Baradoe, S. J.	19 Mar
Corfield, A. G.	19 Mar
Marshallsay, P. J. BEd	19 Mar
Rigsby, A. E.	19 Mar
Rowlands, J. A. J.	19 Mar
Taylor, A. G. BSc PGCE	27 Mar
Robertson, L.	31 Mar
Vernon, P. I.	31 Mar
Webb, S. L.	31 Mar
Foy, N.	1 Apr
Bryce, M. BSc PGCE	6 Apr
Basnett, D.	8 Apr
Jones, A. G.	8 Apr
Bryans, E. P. BEd	20 Apr
Ellis, W.	20 Apr
Glennon, A. M.	20 Apr
Pimm, J. A.	20 Apr
Sadler, D. A.	20 Apr
Herd, G. D.	21 Apr
Openshaw, R. A.	21 Apr
Prestage, S. D.	21 Apr
Austin, K. L. BA PGCE	22 Apr
Clark, A. R. D.	22 Apr
Mixture, D. BEng	22 Apr
Skinner, A. J.	22 Apr
Wellsteed, M. A.	22 Apr
Ayre, J.	23 Apr
Di Domenico, A. J. MSc BEng	23 Apr
Richards, M.	23 Apr
Sewart, P. R. BSc	23 Apr
Freeman, S. R.	29 Apr

Kidd, N. S.	29 Apr
Long, D. P.	29 Apr
Marmion, M. S. BEd	29 Apr
Milton, P. BEd	29 Apr
Milner, E.	5 May
Patel, Y. BSc PGCE	5 May
Shaw, D. A. T. BSc	5 May
Wood, C. S. MSc BSc PGCE	5 May
Thompson, D. MSc BSc PGCE	7 May
Lentell, S. D.	14 May
Dicks, M. A. BA	18 May
Roper, B. F.	18 May
Thornell, P. J.	18 May

BATTLE HONOURS—RAF SQUADRONS

(**BOLD** PRINT INDICATES HONOURS ACTUALLY EMBLAZONED ON THE EXISTING STANDARD)

1 SQUADRON RAF

1st STANDARD PRESENTED 24 APRIL 1953 BY AVM SIR CHARLES LONGCROFT.
2nd STANDARD PRESENTED 27 JUNE 1983 BY MRAF SIR DERMOT BOYLE.

HONOURS WITH THE RIGHT TO EMBLAZONMENT

WESTERN FRONT, 1915–1918 YPRES, 1915 NEUVE CHAPPELLE LOOS **SOMME, 1916** ARRAS YPRES, 1917 LYS AMIENS SOMME, 1918 HINDENBERG LINE **INDEPENDENT FORCE & GERMANY, 1918 FRANCE & LOW COUNTRIES, 1939–1940 BATTLE OF BRITAIN, 1940** CHANNEL & NORTH SEA, 1941–1945 HOME DEFENCE, 1940–1945 **FORTRESS EUROPE, 1941–44** ARNHEM NORMANDY, 1944 **FRANCE & GERMANY, 1944–1945** BISCAY, 1944–1945 RHINE **SOUTH ATLANTIC, 1982**

HONOURS WITHOUT THE RIGHT TO EMBLAZONMENT

KURDISTAN, 1922–1925   IRAQ, 1923–1925

2 SQUADRON RAF

1st STANDARD PRESENTED 31 OCTOBER 1953 BY ACM SIR ROBERT M FOSTER.
2nd STANDARD PRESENTED 30 MAY 1984 BY ACM SIR ALASDAIR STEEDMAN.

HONOURS WITH THE RIGHT TO EMBLAZONMENT

WESTERN FRONT, 1914–1918 MONS **NEUVE CHAPPELLE YPRES, 1915** LOOS **SOMME, 1916** ARRAS SOMME, 1918 LYS **FRANCE & LOW COUNTRIES, 1939–1940 DUNKIRK** FORTRESS EUROPE, 1942–1944 FRANCE & GERMANY, 1944–1945 **NORMANDY, 1944 ARNHEM** WALCHEREN RHINE **GULF, 1991**

3 SQUADRON RAF

1st STANDARD PRESENTED 11 DECEMBER 1953 BY ACM SIR PHILIP JOUBERT de la FERTE.
2nd STANDARD PRESENTED 3 JUNE 1983 BY AM SIR PATRICK B HINE.

HONOURS WITH THE RIGHT TO EMBLAZONMENT

WESTERN FRONT, 1914–1918 MONS NEUVE CHAPELLE LOOS SOMME, 1916 CAMBRAI, 1917 **SOMME, 1918** HINDENBERG LINE **FRANCE & LOW COUNTRIES, 1940 BATTLE OF BRITAIN, 1940** HOME DEFENCE, 1940–1945 FORTRESS EUROPE, 1942–1944 CHANNEL AND NORTH SEA, 1943–1945 **NORMANDY, 1944 ARNHEM** RHINE **FRANCE & GERMANY, 1944–1945**

4 SQUADRON RAF

1st STANDARD PRESENTED 20 NOVEMBER 1953 BY MRAF SIR JOHN SLESSOR.
2nd STANDARD PRESENTED 6 JULY 1984 BY AM SIR PATRICK B HINE.

HONOURS WITH THE RIGHT TO EMBLAZONMENT

WESTERN FRONT, 1914–1918 MONS NEUVE CHAPPELLE SOMME, 1916 **YPRES, 1917** LYS **SOMME, 1918**
FRANCE & LOW COUNTRIES, 1939–1940 FORTRESS EUROPE, 1942–1944 **FRANCE & GERMANY, 1944–1945**
NORMANDY, 1944 ARNHEM RHINE

5 SQUADRON RAF

1st STANDARD PRESENTED 24 APRIL 1954 BY ACM SIR LESLIE N HOLLINGHURST.
2nd STANDARD PRESENTED 11 AUGUST 1983 BY AVM G A WHITE.

HONOURS WITH THE RIGHT TO EMBLAZONMENT

WESTERN FRONT, 1914–1918 **MONS** NEUVE CHAPPELLE **YPRES, 1915 LOOS ARRAS** SOMME, 1918 **AMIENS**
HINDENBERG LINE **ARAKAN, 1942–1944** MANIPUR, 1944 **BURMA, 1944–1945**

HONOURS WITHOUT THE RIGHT TO EMBLAZONMENT

WAZIRISTAN, 1920–1925 MOHMAND, 1927 NORTH WEST FRONTIER, 1930–1931 NORTH WEST FRONTIER, 1935–1939

6 SQUADRON RAF

1st STANDARD PRESENTED 31 JANUARY 1954 BY AM SIR CLAUDE B R PELLY.
2nd STANDARD PRESENTED 31 OCTOBER 1980 BY ACM SIR KEITH WILLIAMSON.

HONOURS WITH THE RIGHT TO EMBLAZONMENT

WESTERN FRONT, 1914–1918 NEUVE CHAPPELLE YPRES, 1915 LOOS **SOMME, 1916** YPRES, 1917 AMIENS
HINDENBURG LINE **EGYPT & LIBYA, 1940–1943 EL ALAMEIN** EL HAMMA **ITALY, 1944–1945**
SOUTH EAST EUROPE, 1944–1945 GULF, 1991

HONOURS WITHOUT THE RIGHT TO EMBLAZONMENT

IRAQ, 1919–1920 KURDISTAN, 1922–1924 PALESTINE, 1936–1939

7 SQUADRON RAF

1st STANDARD PRESENTED 9 OCTOBER 1953 BY MRAF SIR JOHN SALMOND.
2nd STANDARD PRESENTED 8 JUNE 1978 BY HRH PRINCESS ALICE DUCHESS OF GLOUCESTER.

HONOURS WITH THE RIGHT TO EMBLAZONMENT

WESTERN FRONT, 1915–1918 YPRES, 1915 LOOS **SOMME, 1916** YPRES, 1917 **FORTRESS EUROPE, 1941–1944**
BISCAY PORTS, 1941–1944 RUHR, 1942–1945 GERMAN PORTS, 1942–1945 **BERLIN, 1943–1945**
FRANCE & GERMANY, 1944-1945 NORMANDY, 1944 RHINE GULF, 1991

8 SQUADRON RAF

1st STANDARD PRESENTED 9 APRIL 1954 BY SIR TOM HICKINBOTHAM.
2nd STANDARD PRESENTED 25 FEBRUARY 1967 BY HIS EXCELLENCY SIR RICHARD TURNBALL.
3rd STANDARD PRESENTED 28 MAY 1992 BY HRH THE DUKE OF GLOUCESTER.

HONOURS WITH THE RIGHT TO EMBLAZONMENT

WESTERN FRONT, 1915–1918   **LOOS**   **SOMME, 1916**   **ARRAS**   **CAMBRAI, 1917**   SOMME, 1918   AMIENS
HINDENBURG LINE   **EAST AFRICA, 1940–1941**   **EASTERN WATERS, 1942–1945**   **BURMA, 1945**

HONOURS WITHOUT THE RIGHT TO EMBLAZONMENT

KURDISTAN, 1922–1924   ADEN, 1928   ADEN, 1929   ADEN, 1934

9 SQUADRON RAF

1st STANDARD PRESENTED 9 OCTOBER 1956 BY ACM SIR HUGH LLOYD.
2nd STANDARD PRESENTED 23 MAY 1984 BY ACM SIR DAVID CRAIG.

HONOURS WITH THE RIGHT TO EMBLAZONMENT

WESTERN   FRONT, 1915–1918   **SOMME, 1916**   **YPRES, 1917**   AMIENS   HINDENBURG LINE
CHANNEL & NORTH SEA, 1939–1945   BALTIC, 1939–1945   FRANCE & LOW COUNTRIES, 1940   NORWAY, 1940
GERMAN PORTS, 1940–1945   **FORTRESS EUROPE, 1940–1944**   **BERLIN, 1941–1945**   BISCAY PORTS, 1940–1945
RUHR, 1941–1945   FRANCE & GERMANY, 1944–1945   **TIRPITZ**   **THE DAMS**   RHINE   **GULF, 1991**

10 SQUADRON RAF

1st STANDARD PRESENTED 21 OCTOBER 1958 BY HRH THE PRINCESS MARGARET.
2nd STANDARD PRESENTED 30 SEPTEMBER 1988 BY RT HON MARGARET THATCHER.

HONOURS WITH THE RIGHT TO EMBLAZONMENT

WESTERN   FRONT, 1915–1918   LOOS   SOMME, 1916   **ARRAS**   **SOMME 1918**   **INVASION PORTS, 1940**
CHANNEL & NORTH SEA, 1940–1945   NORWAY, 1940   **FORTRESS EUROPE, 1940–1944**   BISCAY PORTS, 1940–1945
RUHR, 1940–1945   GERMAN PORTS, 1940-1945   **NORMANDY, 1944**   **BERLIN, 1940–1945**
FRANCE & GERMANY, 1944-1945   RHINE

HONOURS WITHOUT THE RIGHT TO EMBLAZONMENT

GULF, 1991

11 SQUADRON RAF

1st STANARD PRESENTED 28 AUGUST 1954 BY AM SIR OWEN JONES.
2nd STANDARD PRESENTED 17 AUGUST 1984 BY AVM P S COLLINS.

HONOURS WITH THE RIGHT TO EMBLAZONMENT

WESTERN FRONT, 1915–1918   **LOOS**   SOMME, 1916   ARRAS   **CAMBRAI, 1917**   **SOMME, 1918**   AMIENS
HINDENBURG LINE   EAST AFRICA, 1940   **EGYPT & LIBYA, 1940–1942**   GREECE, 1941   SYRIA, 1941
CEYLON, APRIL 1942   **ARAKAN, 1943–1944**   **NORTH BURMA, 1943–1944**   MANIPUR, 1944   **BURMA, 1944–1945**

HONOURS WITHOUT THE RIGHT TO EMBLAZONMENT

NORTH WEST FRONTIER, 1930–1931   NORTH WEST FRONTIER, 1935–1939

12 SQUADRON RAF

1st STANDARD PRESENTED 23 JUNE 1954 BY MRAF THE LORD NEWALL.
2nd STANDARD PRESENTED 21 FEBRUARY 1975 BY AM SIR NIGEL MAYNARD.

HONOURS WITH THE RIGHT TO EMBLAZONMENT

WESTERN FRONT, 1915–1918 **LOOS** SOMME, 1916 ARRAS **CAMBRAI, 1917 SOMME, 1918** HINDENBURG LINE **FRANCE & LOW COUNTRIES, 1939–40** **MEUSE BRIDGES** FORTRESS EUROPE, 1940–1944 GERMAN PORTS, 1941–1945 BISCAY PORTS, 1940–1945 **BERLIN, 1941–1945** **RUHR, 1941–1945** FRANCE & GERMANY, 1944–1945 **RHINE GULF 1991;**

13 SQUADRON RAF

1st STANDARD PRESENTED 3 MAY 1957 BY FM SIR JOHN HARDING.
2nd STANDARD PRESENTED 12 FEBRUARY 1993 BY HRH DUKE OF KENT.

HONOURS WITH THE RIGHT TO EMBLAZONMENT

WESTERN FRONT, 1915–1918 SOMME, 1916 **ARRAS CAMBRAI, 1917 SOMME, 1918** HINDENBURG LINE **FRANCE & LOW COUNTRIES, 1939–1940 DIEPPE NORTH AFRICA, 1942–1943** MEDITERRANEAN, 1943 **ITALY, 1944–1945** GUSTAV LINE GOTHIC LINE **GULF, 1991**

14 SQUADRON RAF

1st STANDARD PRESENTED 21 AUGUST 1954 BY AVM T C TRAILL.
2nd STANDARD PRESENTED 26 NOVEMBER 1982 BY ACM SIR KEITH WILLIAMSON.

HONOURS WITH THE RIGHT TO EMBLAZONMENT

EGYPT, 1915–1917 ARABIA, 1916–1917 PALESTINE, 1917–1918 GAZA MEGIDDO **EAST AFRICA, 1940–1941 EGYPT & LIBYA, 1941–1942 MEDITERRANEAN, 1941–1943 SICILY, 1943 ATLANTIC, 1945** GULF, 1991

HONOURS WITHOUT THE RIGHT TO EMBLAZONMENT

TRANSJORDAN, 1924 PALESTINE,1936–1939

17 SQUADRON RAF

1st STANDARD PRESENTED 12 JULY 1960 BY MRAF SIR DERMOT BOYLE.
2nd STANDARD PRESENTED 8 FEBURARY 1985 BY AM SIR PATRICK HINE.

HONOURS WITH THE RIGHT TO EMBLAZOMENT

EGYPT, 1915–1916 PALESTINE, 1916 MACEDONIA, 1916–1918 FRANCE & LOW COUNTRIES, 1940 DUNKIRK HOME DEFENCE, 1940 **BATTLE OF BRITAIN, 1940 BURMA, 1942** ARAKAN, 1943 **BURMA, 1944–1945** GULF, 1991

18 SQUADRON RAF

1st STANDARD PRESENTED 14 JUNE 1962 BY HRH THE PRINCESS MARGARET.
2nd STANDARD PRESENTED 3 FEBRUARY 1989 BY ACM SIR PETER HARDING.

HONOURS WITH THE RIGHT TO EMBLAZONMENT

WESTERN FRONT, 1915–1918 SOMME, 1916 **SOMME, 1918** LYS **HINDENBURG LINE** FRANCE & LOW COUNTRIES, 1940 **INVASION PORTS, 1940** FORTRESS EUROPE, 1940–1942 **CHANNEL & NORTH SEA, 1940–1941** GERMAN PORTS, 1940–1941 **MALTA, 1941–1942** EGYPT & LIBYA, 1942 **NORTH AFRICA, 1942–1943** MEDITERRANEAN, 1943 SICILY, 1943 SALERNO SOUTH EAST EUROPE, 1943–1944 **ITALY, 1943–1945** GOTHIC LINE **SOUTH ATLANTIC, 1982 GULF, 1991**

22 SQUADRON RAF

1st STANDARD PRESENTED 20 OCTOBER 1960 BY AM SIR RALPH SORLEY.
2nd STANDARD PRESENTED 15 MARCH 1978 BY ACM SIR DAVID EVANS.

HONOURS WITH THE RIGHT TO EMBLAZONMENT

WESTERN FRONT, 1916–1918 SOMME, 1916 YPRES, 1917 CAMBRAI, 1917 SOMME, 1918 LYS AMIENS **HINDENBURG LINE CHANNEL & NORTH SEA, 1939–1941** FRANCE & LOW COUNTRIES, 1940 INVASION PORTS, 1940 BISCAY PORTS, 1940–1941 **MEDITERRANEAN 1942 EASTERN WATERS, 1942–1944 BURMA, 1944–1945**

23 SQUADRON RAF

1st STANDARD PRESENTED 28 JUNE 1957 BY MRAF SIR JOHN SLESSOR.
2nd STANDARD PRESENTED 2 FEBRUARY 1987 BY AM SIR ANTHONY SKINGSLEY

HONOURS WITH THE RIGHT TO EMBLAZONMENT

HOME DEFENCE, 1916 WESTERN FRONT, 1916–1918 SOMME, 1916 ARRAS **YPRES, 1917 SOMME, 1918 CHANNEL & NORTH SEA, 1939–1940** FORTRESS EUROPE, 1940–1944 **NORTH AFRICA, 1943** SICILY, 1943 **ITALY, 1943–1944 ANZIO & NETTUNO FRANCE & GERMANY 1944–1945** RUHR 1944–1945

24 SQUADRON RAF

1st STANDARD PRESENTED 4 MARCH 1954 BY AM SIR CHARLES E N GUEST.
2nd STANDARD PRESENTED 15 SEPTEMBER 1981 BY HRH THE PRINCESS ANNE.

HONOURS WITH THE RIGHT TO EMBLAZONMENT

WESTERN FRONT, 1916–1918 SOMME, 1916 SOMME 1918 **AMIENS HINDENBURG LINE** FRANCE & LOW COUNTRIES, 1939–1940 **MALTA, 1942 NORTH AFRICA, 1942–1943** ITALY, 1943–1944 **BURMA, 1944–1945**

HONOURS WITHOUT THE RIGHT TO EMBLAZONMENT

GULF, 1991

25 SQUADRON RAF

1st STANDARD PRESENTED 21 JUNE 1954 BY AM SIR DERMOT BOYLE.
2nd STANDARD PRESENTED 15 MAY 1984 BY ACM SIR THOMAS KENNEDY.

HONOURS WITH THE RIGHT TO EMBLAZONMENT

HOME DEFENCE, 1916 **WESTERN FRONT, 1916–1918** SOMME 1916 ARRAS **YPRES, 1917 CAMBRAI, 1917 SOMME, 1918** LYS HINDENBURG LINE CHANNEL & NORTH SEA, 1939–1941 **BATTLE OF BRITAIN, 1940 FORTRESS EUROPE, 1943–1944 HOME DEFENCE, 1940–1945 FRANCE & GERMANY, 1944–1945**

27 SQUADRON RAF

1st STANDARD PRESENTED 7 JANUARY 1955 BY AVM A E BORTON.
2nd STANDARD PRESENTED 22 JUNE 1979 BY ACM SIR DAVID EVANS.

HONOURS WITH THE RIGHT TO EMBLAZONMENT

WESTERN FRONT, 1916–1918 SOMME 1916 ARRAS **YPRES, 1917 CAMBRAI, 1917** SOMME, 1918 LYS AMIENS HINDENBURG LINE **MALAYA, 1941–1942 ARAKAN, 1942–1944 NORTH BURMA, 1944 BURMA, 1944–1945 GULF, 1991**

HONOURS WITHOUT THE RIGHT TO EMBLAZONMENT

MAHSUD, 1920 WAZIRISTAN, 1920–1925 MOHMAND, 1927
NORTH WEST FRONTIER, 1930–1931 MOHMAND, 1933
NORTH WEST FRONTIER, 1935–1939

28 SQUADRON RAF

1st STANDARD PRESENTED 16 MARCH 1955 BY AM F J FRESSANGES.
2nd STANDARD PRESENTED 29 JUNE 1977 BY HE SIR MURRAY MACLEHOSE.

HONOURS WITH THE RIGHT TO EMBLAZONMENT

ITALIAN FRONT & ADRIATIC, 1917–1918 PIAVE VITTORIO VENETO BURMA, 1942 ARAKAN, 1943–1944 MANIPUR, 1944 BURMA, 1944–1945

HONOURS WITHOUT THE RIGHT TO EMBLAZONMENT

WAZIRISTAN, 1921–1925 NORTH WEST FRONTIER, 1939

29 SQUADRON RAF

1st STANDARD PRESENTED 18 JULY 1956 BY ACM SIR DERMOT BOYLE.
2nd STANDARD PRESENTED 30 JUNE 1987 BY HRH THE PRINCESS MARGARET.

HONOURS WITH THE RIGHT TO EMBLAZONMENT

WESTERN FRONT, 1916–1918 SOMME, 1916 ARRAS **YPRES, 1917 SOMME, 1918** LYS **CHANNEL & NORTH SEA, 1939–1940 BATTLE OF BRITAIN, 1940 HOME DEFENCE, 1940–1945** FORTRESS EUROPE, 1943–1944 NORMANDY, 1944 **FRANCE & GERMANY 1944–1945** ARNHEM

HONOURS WITHOUT THE RIGHT TO EMBLAZONMENT

GULF, 1991

30 SQUADRON RAF

1st STANDARD PRESENTED 1 JULY 1954 BY ACM SIR JAMES M ROBB.
2nd STANDARD PRESENTED 18 MAY 1978 BY HRH THE PRINCESS ANNE.

HONOURS WITH THE RIGHT TO EMBLAZONMENT

EGYPT, 1915   **MESOPOTAMIA, 1915–1918**   **EGYPT & LIBYA, 1940–1942**   **GREECE, 1940–1941**
MEDITERRANEAN, 1940–1941   **CEYLON APRIL, 1942**   **ARAKAN, 1944**   **BURMA, 1944–1945**

HONOURS WITHOUT THE RIGHT TO EMBLAZONMENT

IRAQ, 1919-1920   NORTH WEST PERSIA, 1920   KURDISTAN, 1922–1924   IRAQ, 1923–1925   IRAQ, 1928–1929
KURDISTAN, 1930–1931   NORTHERN KURDISTAN, 1932   GULF, 1991

31 SQUADRON RAF

1st STANDARD PRESENTED 13 SEPTEMBER 1956 BY ACM SIR ALEC CORYTON.
2nd STANDARD PRESENTED 14 NOVEMBER 1986 BY AM SIR LESLIE MAVOR.

HONOURS WITH THE RIGHT TO EMBLAZONMENT

NORTH WEST FRONTIER, 1916–1918   **IRAQ, 1941**   SYRIA, 1941   **EGYPT & LIBYA, 1941–1942**   **BURMA, 1941–1942**
NORTH BURMA, 1943–1944   **ARAKAN, 1943–1944**   **MANIPUR, 1944**   **BURMA, 1944–1945**   GULF,1991

HONOURS WITHOUT THE RIGHT TO EMBLAZONMENT

AFGHANISTAN 1919,   MAHSUD, 1919–1920,   WAZIRISTAN,1919–1925   NORTH WEST FRONTIER, 1939

32 (THE ROYAL) SQUADRON RAF

1st STANDARD PRESENTED 6 JUNE 1957 BY ACM SIR JAMES M ROBB.
2nd STANDARD PRESENTED 6 JUNE 1987 BY ACM SIR MICHAEL KNIGHT.

HONOURS WITH THE RIGHT TO EMBLAZONMENT

WESTERN FRONT, 1916–1918   **SOMME, 1916–1918**   ARRAS   **YPRES, 1917**   **AMIENS**   **FRANCE & LOW COUNTRIES, 1939–1940**   **BATTLE OF BRITAIN, 1940**   HOME DEFENCE, 1940–1942   **DIEPPE**   **NORTH AFRICA, 1942–1943** ITALY, 1943   **SOUTH EAST EUROPE, 1944–1945**

HONOURS WITHOUT THE RIGHT TO EMBLAZONMENT

GULF, 1991

33 SQUADRON RAF

1st STANDARD PRESENTED 24 APRIL 1958 BY ACM SIR PHILIP JOUBERT de la FERTE.
2nd STANDARD PRESENTED 19 MAY 1988 BY ACM SIR DENIS SMALLWOOD.

HONOURS WITH THE RIGHT TO EMBLAZONMENT

HOME DEFENCE, 1916–1918   **EGYPT & LIBYA, 1940–1943**   **GREECE, 1941**   **EL ALAMEIN**
FRANCE & GERMANY, 1944–1945 NORMANDY, 1944 WALCHEREN RHINE GULF, 1991

HONOURS WITHOUT THE RIGHT TO EMBLAZONMENT

PALESTINE, 1936–1939

39(1 PRU) SQUADRON RAF

1st STANDARD PRESENTED 26 JUNE 1954 BY AM SIR CLAUDE B R PELLY.
2nd STANDARD PRESENTED 25 SEPTEMBER 1981 BY ACM SIR KEITH WILLIAMSON.

HONOURS WITH THE RIGHT TO EMBLAZONMENT

HOME DEFENCE, 1916–1918 EAST AFRICA, 1940   **EGYPT & LIBYA, 1940–1943**   **GREECE, 1941**
MEDITERRANEAN, 1941–1943   MALTA, 1942 NORTH AFRICA, 1942–1943   SOUTH EAST EUROPE, 1944–45

HONOURS WITHOUT THE RIGHT TO EMBLAZONMENT

NORTH WEST FRONTIER, 1930–1931   MOHMAND, 1933   NORTH WEST FRONTIER, 1935–1939

41 SQUADRON RAF

1st STANDARD PRESENTED 14 JULY 1957 BY AM SIR THEODORE MCEVOY.
2nd STANDARD PRESENTED 5 DECEMBER 1985 BY ACM SIR PETER HARDING.

HONOURS WITH THE RIGHT OF EMBLAZONMENT

WESTERN FRONT, 1916–1918 SOMME, 1916 ARRAS **CAMBRAI, 1917** SOMME, 1918 LYS **AMIENS**
BATTLE OF BRITAIN, 1940 HOME DEFENCE, 1940–1944 **FORTRESS EUROPE, 1940–1944** **DIEPPE**
FRANCE & GERMANY, 1944–1945 ARNHEM WALCHEREN GULF, 1991

43 SQUADRON RAF

1st STANDARD PRESENTED 4 JUNE 1957 BY HM QUEEN ELIZABETH II.
2nd STANDARD PRESENTED 26 MAY 1988 BY HM QUEEN ELIZABETH II.

HONOURS WITH THE RIGHT TO EMBLAZONMENT

WESTERN FRONT, 1917–1918 ARRAS **YPRES, 1917** CAMBRAI, 1917 **SOMME, 1918** LYS AMIENS **DUNKIRK**
BATTLE OF BRITAIN, 1940 HOME DEFENCE, 1940–1942 FORTRESS EUROPE, 1942 DIEPPE
NORTH AFRICA, 1942–1943 SICILY, 1943 SALERNO ITALY, 1943–1945 **ANZIO AND NETTUNO** GUSTAV LINE
FRANCE & GERMANY, 1944

HONOURS WITHOUT THE RIGHT TO EMBLAZONMENT

GULF,1991

47 SQUADRON RAF

1st STANDARD PRESENTED 25 MARCH 1955 BY MRAF SIR JOHN SLESSOR.
2nd STANDARD PRESENTED 3 MAY 1984 BY HRH THE PRINCESS ANNE.

HONOURS WITH THE RIGHT TO ENBLAZONMENT

**MACEDONIA, 1916–1918   EAST AFRICA, 1940–1941   EGYPT & LIBYA, 1942   MEDITERRANEAN, 1942–1943
BURMA, 1945**

HONOURS WITHOUT THE RIGHT TO EMBLAZONMENT

SOUTH ATLANTIC, 1982   GULF, 1991

51 SQUADRON RAF

STANDARD PRESENTED 9 JULY 1968 BY ACM SIR WALLACE KYLE.

HONOURS WITH THE RIGHT TO EMBLAZONMENT

HOME DEFENCE, 1916–1918   CHANNEL & NORTH SEA, 1940–1943   **NORWAY, 1940   FRANCE & LOW
COUNTRIES, 1940   RUHR, 1940–1945   FORTRESS EUROPE, 1940–1944**   GERMAN PORTS, 1940–1945   INVASION
PORTS, 1940   BISCAY PORTS, 1940–1944   BERLIN, 1940–1944   **BALTIC, 1940–1944**   BISCAY, 1942   **ITALY, 1943
FRANCE & GERMANY, 1944–1945**   NORMANDY, 1944   WALCHEREN   RHINE

HONOURS WITHOUT THE RIGHT TO EMBLAZONMENT

SOUTH ATLANTIC, 1982   GULF, 1991

54 SQUADRON RAF

1st STANDARD PRESENTED 24 MAY 1963 BY MAJOR K K HORN RFC.
2nd STANDARD PRESENTED 21 JANUARY 1988 BY ACM SIR PETER HARDING.

HONOURS WITH THE RIGHT TO EMBLAZONMENT

WESTERN FRONT, 1916–1918   **ARRAS   YPRES, 1917   CAMBRAI, 1917   AMIENS**   HOME DEFENCE, 1940–1945
FRANCE & LOW COUNTRIES, 1940   **DUNKIRK   BATTLE OF BRITAIN, 1940   FORTRESS EUROPE, 1941   EASTERN
WATERS, 1943–1945**   GULF, 1991

70 SQUADRON RAF

1st STANDARD PRESENTED 16 JULY 1955 BY AVM SIR HAZELTON NICHOLL.
2nd STANDARD PRESENTED 3 MAY 1984 BY HRH THE PRINCESS ANNE.

HONOURS WITH THE RIGHT TO EMBLAZONMENT

WESTERN FRONT, 1916–1918   SOMME, 1916   ARRAS   **YPRES, 1917**   SOMME, 1918   MEDITERRANEAN, 1940–1943
EGYPT & LIBYA, 1940–1943   GREECE, 1940–1941   SYRIA, 1941   **IRAQ, 1941**   EL ALAMEIN   **NORTH
AFRICA, 1942–1943**   EL HAMMA   SICILY, 1943   **ITALY, 1943–1945**   SALERNO   ANZIO & NETTUNO   GUSTAV LINE
GOTHIC LINE   **SOUTH EAST EUROPE, 1944–1945**

HONOURS WITHOUT THE RIGHT TO EMBLAZONMENT

KURDISTAN, 1922–1924   IRAQ, 1928–1929   KURDISTAN, 1930–1931   NORTHERN KURDISTAN, 1932
NORTH WEST FRONTIER, 1937   SOUTH ATLANTIC, 1982   GULF, 1991

72 SQUADRON RAF

STANDARD PRESENTED 30 JUNE 1966 BY AM SIR RONALD LEES.

HONOURS WITH THE RIGHT OF EMBLAZONMENT

MESOPOTAMIA, 1918   CHANNEL & NORTH SEA, 1939–1942   **DUNKIRK   BATTLE OF BRITAIN, 1940**
FORTRESS EUROPE, 1941–1942   NORTH AFRICA, 1942–1943   MEDITERRANEAN, 1942–1943   **SICILY, 1943**
ITALY, 1943–1945 **SALERNO   ANZIO & NETTUNO**

78 SQUADRON RAF

STANDARD PRESENTED 11 FEBRUARY 1965 BY Lt Gen SIR CHARLES HARINGTON

HONOURS WITH THE RIGHT TO EMBLAZONMENT

HOME DEFENCE, 1916–1918   FORTRESS EUROPE, 1940–1944   RUHR, 1940–1945   INVASION PORTS, 1940
BISCAY PORTS, 1940–1943   **BERLIN, 1940–1944   CHANNEL & NORTH SEA, 1942–1945   NORMANDY, 1944**
WALCHEREN   **FRANCE & GERMANY, 1944–1945   RHINE**

84 SQUADRON RAF

1st STANDARD PRESENTED 5 JANUARY 1956 BY ACM SIR FRANCIS FOGARTY.
2nd STANDARD PRESENTED 23 OCTOBER 1980 BY AM SIR KEITH WILLIAMSON.

HONOURS WITH THE RIGHT TO EMBLAZONMENT

WESTERN FRONT, 1917–1918   CAMBRAI, 1917   **SOMME, 1918**   AMIENS   **HINDENBURG LINE   EGYPT &
LIBYA, 1940–1942   GREECE, 1940–1941   IRAQ, 1941**   HABBANIYA   SYRIA, 1941   **MALAYA, 1942
NORTH BURMA, 1944**   MANIPUR, 1944

HONOURS WITHOUT THE RIGHT TO EMBLAZONMENT

IRAQ, 1920   IRAQ, 1923–1925   IRAQ, 1928–1929

100 SQUADRON RAF

1st STANDARD PRESENTED 21 OCTOBER 1955 BY AM SIR GEORGE MILLS.
2nd STANDARD PRESENTED 14 DECEMBER 1984 BY MRAF SIR MICHAEL BEETHAM.

HONOURS WITH THE RIGHT TO EMBLAZONMENT

**WESTERN FRONT, 1917–1918   YPRES, 1917   SOMME, 1918   INDEPENDENT FORCE & GERMANY, 1918
MALAYA, 1941–1942   FORTRESS EUROPE, 1943–1944**   BISCAY PORTS, 1943–1945   **RUHR, 1943–1945
BERLIN, 1943–1945**   GERMAN PORTS, 1943–1945   BALTIC, 1943–1945   FRANCE & GERMANY, 1944–1945
NORMANDY, 1944   WALCHEREN

101 SQUADRON RAF

1st STANDARD PRESENTED 14 JUNE 1962 BY HRH THE PRINCESS MARGARET.
2nd STANDARD PRESENTED 24 JUNE 1988 BY ACM SIR PETER HARDING.

HONOURS WITH THE RIGHT TO EMBLAZONMENT

WESTERN FRONT, 1917–1918   **YPRES, 1917**   **SOMME, 1918**   LYS   HINDENBURG LINE
FORTRESS EUROPE, 1940–1944   **INVASION PORTS, 1940**   **RUHR, 1940–1945**   **BERLIN, 1941**   CHANNEL & NORTH
SEA, 1941–1944   BISCAY PORTS, 1941–1944   GERMAN PORTS, 1941–1944   BALTIC, 1942–1945   BERLIN, 1943–1944
FRANCE & GERMANY 1944–1945   **NORMANDY, 1944**   WALCHEREN

HONOURS WITHOUT THE RIGHT TO EMBLAZONMENT

SOUTH ATLANTIC, 1982   GULF, 1991

111 SQUADRON RAF

1st STANDARD PRESENTED 30 APRIL 1957 BY ACM SIR HARRY BROADHURST.
2nd STANDARD PRESENTED 2 AUGUST 1987 BY ACM SIR PATRICK HINE.

HONOURS WITH THE RIGHT TO EMBLAZONMENT

PALESTINE, 1917–1918   MEGIDDO   **HOME DEFENCE, 1940–1942**   FRANCE & LOW COUNTRIES, 1940   **DUNKIRK**
BATTLE OF BRITAIN, 1940   **FORTRESS EUROPE, 1941–1942**   DIEPPE   **NORTH AFRICA, 1942–1943**   SICILY, 1943
ITALY, 1943–1945   SALERNO   ANZIO & NETTUNO   GUSTAV LINE   **FRANCE & GERMANY, 1944**

120 SQUADRON RAF

1st STANDARD PRESENTED 14 AUGUST 1961 BY HM THE QUEEN.
2nd STANDARD PRESENTED 26 MAY 1988 BY HRH THE DUKE OF EDINBURGH,

HONOURS WITH THE RIGHT TO ENBLAZONMENT

ATLANTIC, 1941–1945   BISCAY, 1941–1944   ARCTIC, 1942–1944   CHANNEL & NORTH ATLANTIC, 1941–1944

HONOURS WITHOUT THE RIGHT TO EMBLAZONMENT

SOUTH ATLANTIC, 1982   GULF, 1991

201 SQUADRON RAF

1st STANDARD PRESENTED 16 DECEMBER 1955 BY AVM G W TUTTLE.
2nd STANDARD PRESENTED 9 NOVEMBER 1984 BY HRH THE DUKE OF EDINBURGH.

HONOURS WITH THE RIGHT TO EMBLAZONMENT

WESTERN FRONT, 1915–1918   ARRAS   YPRES, 1917   SOMME, 1918   AMIENS   HINDENBURG LINE   CHANNEL &
NORTH SEA, 1939–1945   **NORWAY, 1940   ATLANTIC, 1941–1945   BISMARCK**   BISCAY, 1941–1945   **NORMANDY, 1944**

HONOURS WITHOUT THE RIGHT TO EMBLAZONMENT

SOUTH ATLANTIC, 1982   GULF, 1991

202 SQUADRON RAF

1st STANDARD PRESENTED 6 SEPTEMBER 1957 BY ACM SIR DOUGLAS EVILL.
2nd STANDARD PRESENTED 16 JUNE 1987 BY ACM SIR PETER TERRY.

HONOURS WITH THE RIGHT TO EMBLAZONMENT

WESTERN FRONT, 1916–1918 ATLANTIC, 1939–1945 **MEDITERRANEAN, 1940–1943** **NORTH AFRICA, 1942–1943**
BISCAY, 1942–1943

206 SQUADRON RAF

1st STANDARD PRESENTED ON 28 JULY 1966 BY HRH THE PRINCESS MARGARET.
2nd STANDARD PRESENTED 21 MAY 1992 BY HRH THE DUKE OF EDINBURGH.

HONOURS WITH THE RIGHT TO EMBLAZONMENT

WESTERN FRONT, 1916–1918 ARRAS, 1917 LYS **CHANNEL & NORTH SEA, 1939–1945 ATLANTIC 1939, 1941–1945**
DUNKIRK INVASION PORTS, 1940 **FORTRESS EUROPE 1940, 1942** GERMAN PORTS 1940, 1942
BISCAY 1941, 1943–1944 BISMARCK BALTIC, 1945

HONOURS WITHOUT THE RIGHT TO EMBLAZONMENT

SOUTH ATLANTIC, 1982 GULF, 1991

216 SQUADRON RAF

1st STANDARD PRESENTED ON 24 MAY 1957 BY ACM SIR DONALD HARDMAN.
2nd STANDARD PRESENTED ON 24 JUNE 1988 BY ACM SIR PETER HARDING.

HONOURS WITH THE RIGHT TO EMBLAZONMENT

INDEPENDENT FORCE AND GERMANY, 1917–1918 GREECE, 1940–1941 **EGYPT & LIBYA 1940–1942** SYRIA, 1941
EL ALAMEIN EL HAMMA **NORTH AFRICA, 1943** MEDITERRANEAN, 1943 MANIPUR, 1944 **NORTH BURMA, 1944**
SOUTH EAST EUROPE, 1944–1945

HONOURS WITHOUT THE RIGHT TO EMBLAZONMENT

GULF, 1991

230 SQUADRON RAF

1st STANDARD PRESENTED ON 26 OCTOBER 1962 BY HRH THE DUKE OF GLOUCESTER.
2nd STANDARD PRESENTED ON 27 OCTOBER 1992 BY HRH THE DUKE OF GLOUCESTER.

HONOURS WITH THE RIGHT TO EMBLAZONMENT

HOME WATERS, 1918 MEDITERRANEAN, 1940–1943 **EGYPT & LIBYA, 1940–1943** GREECE, 1940–1941
MALTA, 1940–1942 EASTERN WATERS, 1943–1945 **NORTH BURMA, 1944** BURMA, 1945 **GULF, 1991**

617 SQUADRON RAF

1st STANDARD PRESENTED ON 14 MAY 1959 BY HM QUEEN ELIZABETH.
2nd STANDARD PRESENTED ON 13 JANUARY 1988 BY THE QUEEN MOTHER.

HONOURS WITH THE RIGHT TO EMBLAZONMENT

**FORTRESS EUROPE, 1943–1944   THE DAMS   BISCAY PORTS, 1944   FRANCE & GERMANY, 1944–1945
NORMANDY, 1944   TIRPITZ   CHANNEL & NORTH SEA, 1944–1945   GERMAN PORTS, 1945**   GULF, 1991

RAF RESERVE SQUADRONS

15 (RESERVE) SQUADRON RAF

1st STANDARD PRESENTED ON 3 MAY 1961 BY HRH THE DUCHESS OF KENT.
2nd STANDARD PRESENTED ON 8 MAY 1981 BY SQN LDR P J S BOGGIS.

HONOURS WITH THE RIGHT TO EMBLAZONMENT

WESTERN FRONT, 1915–1918   SOMME, 1916   ARRAS   **CAMBRAI, 1917**   SOMME, 1918   **HINDENBURG LINE**
FRANCE & LOW COUNTRIES, 1939–1940   **MEUSE BRIDGES**   DUNKIRK   INVASION PORTS, 1940
FORTRESS EUROPE, 1941–1944   **RUHR, 1941–1945   BERLIN, 1941–1945**   BISCAY PORTS, 1941–1945   FRANCE &
GERMANY, 1944–1945   **NORMANDY, 1944   GULF, 1991**

16 (RESERVE) SQUADRON RAF

1st STANDARD PRESENTED ON 6 APRIL 1956 BY HRH PRINCESS MARINA.
2nd STANDARD PRESENTED ON 12 JULY 1985 BY AVM D PARRY-EVANS

HONOURS WITH THE RIGHT TO EMBLAZONMENT

WESTERN FRONT, 1915–1918   NEUVE CHAPPELLE   LOOS   **SOMME, 1916   ARRAS   YPRES, 1917**   FRANCE & LOW
COUNTRIES, 1940   **DUNKIRK   FORTRESS EUROPE, 1943–1944**   FRANCE & GERMANY, 1944   **NORMANDY, 1944
ARNHEM**   RUHR, 1944–1945   GULF, 1991

19 (RESERVE) SQUADRON RAF

1st STANDARD PRESENTED 11 JULY 1956 BY ACM SIR DONALD HARDMAN
2nd STANDARD PRESENTED 19 JANUARY 1988 BY AM SIR ANTHONY SKINGSLEY

HONOURS WITH THE RIGHT TO EMBLAZONMENT

WESTERN FRONT, 1916–1918   SOMME, 1916   ARRAS   **YPRES, 1917**   SOMME, 1918   LYS   AMIENS
HINDENBURG LINE   **DUNKIRK**   HOME DEFENCE, 1940–1942   **BATTLE OF BRITAIN, 1940**   CHANNEL &
NORTH SEA, 1941–1942   **FORTRESS EUROPE, 1942–1944**   DIEPPE   **NORMANDY, 1944   ARNHEM**
FRANCE & GERMANY, 1944–1945

20 (RESERVE) SQUADRON RAF

1st STANDARD PRESENTED 13 JULY 1954 BY HRH THE PRINCESS MARGARET
2nd STANDARD PRESENTED 26 NOVEMBER 1982 BY ACM SIR KEITH WILLIAMSON.

HONOURS WITH THE RIGHT TO EMBLAZONMENT

WESTERN FRONT, 1916–1918 **SOMME, 1916 ARRAS YPRES, 1917 SOMME, 1918** LYS HINDENBURG LINE **NORTH BURMA, 1943–1944 ARAKAN, 1943–1944 MANIPUR, 1944 BURMA, 1944–1945** GULF, 1991

HONOURS WITHOUT THE RIGHT TO EMBLAZONMENT

MAHSUD, 1919–1920 WAZIRISTAN, 1919–1925 MOHMAND, 1927 NORTH WEST FRONTIER, 1930–1931 MOHMAND, 1933 NORTH WEST FRONTIER, 1935–1939

42 (RESERVE) SQUADRON RAF

STANDARD PRESENTED 14 JULY 1966 BY HM THE QUEEN.

HONOURS WITH THE RIGHT TO EMBLAZONMENT

WESTERN FRONT, 1916–1918 ITALIAN FRONT & ADRIATIC, 1917–1918 SOMME, 1916 ARRAS, 1917 YPRES, 1917 LYS **CHANNEL & NORTH SEA, 1939–1942 BISCAY, 1940 BALTIC, 1941** FORTRESS EUROPE, 1941 PACIFIC, 1943–1945 **EASTERN WATERS, 1943 ARAKAN, 1943–1944 MANIPUR, 1944** BURMA, 1944–1945

HONOURS WITHOUT THE RIGHT TO EMBLAZONMENT

SOUTH ATLANTIC, 1982 GULF, 1991

45 (RESERVE) SQUADRON RAF

1st STANDARD PRESENTED 9 FEBRUARY 1955 BY AM F J FRESSANGES.
2nd STANDARD PRESENTED 4 OCTOBER 1994 BY ACM SIR ANDREW WILSON.

HONOURS WITH THE RIGHT TO EMBLAZONMENT

WESTERN FRONT, 1916–1917 SOMME, 1916 YPRES, 1917 **ITALIAN FRONT & ADRIATIC, 1917–1918** PIAVE **INDEPENDENT FORCE & GERMANY, 1918 EGYPT & LIBYA, 1940–1942 EAST AFRICA, 1940** SYRIA,1941 **BURMA, 1942 ARAKAN, 1943–1944 BURMA, 1944–1945**

HONOURS WITHOUT THE RIGHT TO EMBLAZONMENT

KURDISTAN, 1922–1924 IRAQ, 1923–1925

55 (RESERVE) SQUADRON RAF

1st STANDARD PRESENTED 20 JULY 1962 BY PRINCESS MARINA, DUCHESS OF KENT.

HONOURS WITH THE RIGHT TO EMBLAZONMENT

WESTERN FRONT, 1917–1918 ARRAS **YPRES, 1917 INDEPENDENT FORCE & GERMANY, 1918 EGYPT & LIBYA, 1940–1943 EL ALAMEIN EL HAMMA** NORTH AFRICA, 1943 SICILY, 1943 SALERNO ITALY, 1943–1945 GUSTAV LINE **GOTHIC LINE** SOUTH ATLANTIC, 1982 GULF, 1991

HONOURS WITHOUT THE RIGHT TO EMBLAZONMENT

IRAQ, 1920 KURDISTAN, 1922–1924 IRAQ, 1928–1929 KURDISTAN, 1930–1931 NORTHERN KURDISTAN, 1932

56 (RESERVE) SQUADRON RAF

1st STANDARD PRESENTED 27 APRIL 1956 BY HRH PRINCESS MARINA.
2nd STANDARD PRESENTED 23 OCTOBER 1986 BY ACM SIR JOHN ROGERS.

HONOURS WITH THE RIGHT TO EMBLAZONMENT

WESTERN FRONT, 1917–1918 ARRAS **YPRES, 1917** CAMBRAI, 1917 **SOMME, 1918** AMIENS HINDENBURG LINE FRANCE & LOW COUNTRIES, 1940 **DUNKIRK BATTLE OF BRITAIN, 1940** FORTRESS EUROPE, 1942–1944 DIEPPE **FRANCE & GERMANY, 1944–1945 NORMANDY, 1944** HOME DEFENCE, 1942–1945 **ARNHEM**

57 (RESERVE) SQUADRON RAF

STANDARD PRESENTED 20 JULY 1962 BY HRH PRINCESS MARINA.

HONOURS WITH THE RIGHT TO EMBLAZONMENT

WESTERN FRONT, 1916-1918 AMIENS FRANCE & LOW COUNTRIES, 1939–1940 NORWAY, 1940 CHANNEL & NORTH SEA, 1940 RUHR, 1941–1943 FORTRESS EUROPE, 1941–1944 **BERLIN, 1941–1943** WALCHEREN **FRANCE & GERMANY, 1944–1945**

HONOURS WITHOUT THE RIGHT TO EMBLAZONMENT

SOUTH ATLANTIC, 1982

60 (RESERVE) SQUADRON RAF

1st STANDARD PRESENTED 6 MAY 1955 BY ACM SIR JOHN BAKER.
2nd STANDARD PRESENTED 18 MAY 1984 BY ACM SIR DAVID LEE.

HONOURS WITH THE RIGHT TO EMBLAZONMENT

WESTERN FRONT, 1916-1918 SOMME, 1916 ARRAS SOMME, 1918 **HINDENBURG LINE BURMA, 1941–1942 MALAYA, 1941–1942 ARAKAN, 1942–1944** NORTH BURMA, 1944 **MANIPUR, 1944 BURMA, 1944–1945**

HONOURS WITHOUT THE RIGHT TO EMBLAZONMENT

WAZIRISTAN, 1920–1925 MOHMAND, 1927 NORTH WEST FRONTIER 1930–1931 MOHMAND, 1933 NORTH WEST FRONTIER, 1935–1939

74 (RESERVE) SQUADRON RAF

1st STANDARD PRESENTED 3 JUNE 1965 BY HRH THE PRINCESS MARGARET.
2nd STANDARD PRESENTED 11 MAY 1990 BY AVM B L ROBINSON WHO DEPUTISED FOR ACM SIR FREDERICK ROSIER.

HONOURS WITH THE RIGHT TO EMBLAZONMENT

WESTERN FRONT, 1918   FRANCE & LOW COUNTRIES, 1940   DUNKIRK   BATTLE OF BRITAIN, 1940   FORTRESS EUROPE, 1940–1941 & 1944   HOME DEFENCE, 1940–1941   **MEDITERRANEAN 1943**   WALCHEREN   **NORMANDY, 1944 FRANCE & GERMANY, 1944–1945**   RHINE

203 (RESERVE) SQUADRON RAF

STANDARD PRESENTED 6 JUNE 1963 BY HRH PRINCESS MARGARET.

HONOURS WITH THE RIGHT TO EMBLAZONMENT

WESTERN FRONT, 1914–1918   INDEPENDENT FORCE & GERMANY 1914–1918   AEGEAN, 1915   HELLES   **ANZAC** SUVLA   **ARRAS**   LYS   **SOMME, 1918**   HINDENBURG LINE   EAST AFRICA, 1940–1941   **MEDITERRANEAN, 1941–1943 IRAQ, 1941**   HABBANIYA   SYRIA, 1941   EGYPT & LIBYA 1941, 1942   NORTH AFRICA, 1943   SICILY, 1943 EASTERN WATERS, 1944–1945   **BURMA, 1945**

208 (RESERVE) SQUADRON RAF

1st STANDARD PRESENTED 15 NOVEMBER 1955 BY AVM SIR GEOFFREY BROMET
2nd STANDARD PRESENTED 1 JUNE 1984 BY SIR HUMPHREY EDWARDES-JONES.

HONOURS WITH THE RIGHT TO EMBLAZONMENT

WESTERN FRONT, 1916–1918   ARRAS   YPRES, 1917   LYS   **SOMME, 1918   EGYPT & LIBYA, 1940–1942   GREECE, 1941** IRAQ, 1941   SYRIA, 1941   **EL ALAMEIN   ITALY, 1944–1945**   GUSTAV LINE   GOTHIC LINE   **GULF, 1991**

ROYAL AIR FORCE REGIMENT SQUADRONS

1 SQUADRON RAF REGIMENT

1st STANDARD PRESENTED 8 APRIL 1959 BY AM SIR HUGH CONSTANTINE.
2nd STANDARD PRESENTED 3 NOVEMBER 1988 BY AM SIR HUGH SKINGSLEY.

HONOURS WITH THE RIGHT TO EMBLAZONMENT

IRAQ, 1941   EGYPT & LIBYA, 1941–1943   GULF, 1991   HABBANIYA

HONOURS WITHOUT THE RIGHT TO EMBLAZONMENT

KURDISTAN, 1922–1923   KURDISTAN, 1930–1931   PALESTINE, 1936

2 SQUADRON RAF REGIMENT

1st STANDARD PRESENTED 25 NOVEMBER 1959 BY ACM SIR HUBERT PATCH.
2nd STANDARD PRESENTED 5 JUNE 1989 BY ACM SIR PATRICK HINE.

HONOURS WITH THE RIGHT TO EMBLAZONMENT

EGYPT & LIBYA, 1940–1943   IRAQ, 1941   SYRIA, 1941   EL ALAMEIN   NORTH AFRICA, 1943

HONOURS WITHOUT THE RIGHT TO EMBLAZONMENT

TRANSJORDAN, 1924   PALESTINE, 1936–1939

3 (FIELD) SQUADRON RAF REGIMENT

STANDARD PRESENTED 15 JUNE 1996 BY HRH DUKE OF YORK

HONOURS WITH THE RIGHT TO EMBLAZONMENT

FRANCE & GERMANY, 1944–45

HONOURS WITHOUT THE RIGHT OF EMBLAZONMENT

IRAQ, 1923–1925

15 SQUADRON RAF REGIMENT

STANDARD PRESENTED 10 OCTOBER 1975 BY ACM SIR ANDREW HUMPHREY.

16 SQUADRON RAF REGIMENT

STANDARD PRESENTED 26 MAY 1977 BY AM SIR MICHAEL BEETHAM.

26 SQUADRON RAF REGIMENT

STANDARD PRESENTED 28 NOVEMBER 1979 BY AM SIR PETER TERRY.

HONOURS WITHOUT THE RIGHT TO EMBLAZONMENT

GULF, 1991

27 SQUADRON RAF REGIMENT

STANDARD PRESENTED 4 JUNE 1980 BY ACM SIR DAVID EVANS.

34 SQUADRON RAF REGIMENT

STANDARD PRESENTED 4 OCTOBER 1979 BY ACM SIR DAVID EVANS.

HONOURS WITHOUT THE RIGHT TO EMBLAZONMENT

GULF, 1991

37 SQUADRON RAF REGIMENT

STANDARD PRESENTED 26 NOVEMBER 1980 BY AM SIR PETER TERRY.

48 SQUADRON RAF REGIMENT

STANDARD PRESENTED 22 MAY 1980 BY ACM SIR DAVID EVANS.

THE QUEEN'S COLOUR SQUADRON OF THE RAF - 63 SQUADRON RAF REGIMENT

STANDARD PRESENTED 27 MAY 1976 BY HRH THE PRINCESS ANNE.

HONOURS WITH THE RIGHT OF EMBLAZONMENT

ITALY, 1943–1944   FRANCE & GERMANY, 1945   SOUTH ATLANTIC, 1982

QUEEN'S COLOURS TO THE ROYAL AIR FORCE

RAF COLLEGE CRANWELL

1st COLOUR PRESENTED 6 JULY 1948 BY HM KING GEORGE VI.
2nd COLOUR PRESENTED 25 JULY 1960 BY HM THE QUEEN.
3rd COLOUR PRESENTED 30 MAY 1975 BY HM THE QUEEN.
4th COLOUR PRESENTED 27 JULY 1989 BY HM THE QUEEN.

RAF IN THE UNITED KINGDOM

1st COLOUR PRESENTED 26 MAY 1951 BY HRH THE PRINCESS ELIZABETH.
2nd COLOUR PRESENTED 3 JULY 1964 BY HM THE QUEEN.
3rd COLOUR PRESENTED 29 JULY 1977 BY HM THE QUEEN.
4th COLOUR PRESENTED 1 APRIL 1993 BY HM THE QUEEN.

No 1 SCHOOL OF TECHNICAL TRAINING

1st COLOUR PRESENTED 25 JULY 1952 BY HM THE QUEEN.
2nd COLOUR PRESENTED 6 APRIL 1968 BY HRH THE PRINCESS MARGARET.
3rd COLOUR PRESENTED 25 SEPTEMBER 1990 BY HRH THE DUKE OF KENT.

ROYAL AIR FORCE REGIMENT

1st COLOUR PRESENTED 17 MARCH 1953 BY HM THE QUEEN.
2nd COLOUR PRESENTED 16 JUNE 1967 BY HM THE QUEEN.
3rd COLOUR PRESENTED 30 OCTOBER 1992 BY HM THE QUEEN.

NEAR EAST AIR FORCE
(TITLE CHANGED FROM MIDDLE EAST AIR FORCE ON 11 APRIL 1961)

COLOUR PRESENTED 14 OCTOBER 1960 BY HRH THE DUKE OF GLOUCESTER.

FAR EAST AIR FORCE

COLOUR PRESENTED 13 JANUARY 1961 BY THE EARL OF SELKIRK.

CENTRAL FLYING SCHOOL

1st COLOUR PRESENTED 26 JUNE 1969 BY HM THE QUEEN.
2nd COLOUR PRESENTED 4 JUNE 1992 BY HM THE QUEEN MOTHER.

ROYAL AIR FORCE GERMANY

COLOUR PRESENTED 16 SEPTEMBER 1970 BY HRH THE PRINCESS ANNE.

ROYAL AUXILIARY AIR FORCE
(Known as Sovereign's Colour)

COLOUR PRESENTED 12 JUNE 1989 BY HM THE QUEEN.

IMPORTANT NOTES CONCERNING RAF BATTLE HONOURS

The Battle Honours to which Royal Air Force Squadrons are entitled, and the conditions under which they are awarded are set out in AP 3327, originally published in 1957.

The Battle Honours Committee was first convened in 1947 to consider Honours for World War 1, World War 2 and the Inter War Years, however since the Army did not then award honours for battles between the wars the RAF fell in step and considered just World War 1 and World War 2. These recommendations were approved by the Air Council in AC 58 (47) of Nov 47.

The Standard will be awarded by order of the Monarch in every case, to Operational Squadrons qualifying in one of the following two respects:

1. By completion of 25 years of existence in the RAF, the Royal Flying Corps or the Royal Naval Air Service. This includes Squadrons with continuous or non-continuous service.

2. By having earned the Monarch's appreciation of specially outstanding operations.

Battle Honours awarded for operations during the First and Second World Wars, up to maximum of 8 in number, may be displayed on Squadron Standards. If a Squadron has been awarded more than 8, the Squadron Commander is to select those which are to be displayed. Battle Honours for operations during the period between the two wars were awarded to Squadrons but may not be emblazoned on Standards. Battle Honours awarded for operations occurring after the Second World War have been awarded both with and without the right to emblazonment. Only those Battle Honours with the Sovereign's permission to emblazon may be displayed but subject to a maximum of 15.

It was also agreed that only flying squadrons were entitled to receive a Squadron Standard, however in January 1952 Standards were to be awarded to RAF Regiment and Royal Auxiliary Air Force Squadrons.

The first Squadron to receive its Standard was No 1 Squadron and the first Regiment squadron to receive its Standard was No 2 Armoured Car Company RAF Regiment.

Since 1945, 3 Battle Honours have been granted namely, "Korea 1950–1953", "South Atlantic 1982" and "Gulf 1991". However, no right to emblazonment was granted in the case of "Korea 1950–53", and the three Squadrons awarded their Battle Honours in 1987 have been disbanded in the intervening years. In the case of "South Atlantic 1982" 3 precidents were created;

a. For the first time, authority was given to emblazon an honour awarded outside the time frame of the 2 World Wars.

b. The right to emblazon was accorded to 3 Squadrons only (Numbers 1 and 18 Squadrons and Number 63 Squadron RAF Regiment) rather than being extended to all the Squadrons which were granted the battle honour, thus creating a two-tier battle-honours system. The review of post-war operations conducted in 1987 considered that a distinction should be drawn between the award of the battle honours and the right of emblazonment. It was decided that the latter should be the ultimate accolade and be reserved to those Squadrons which were in direct confrontation with the enemy and had demonstrated gallantry and spirit under fire.

For seniority purposes an RAF Regiment Squadron is entitled to claim its service as a armoured car squadron.

WILKINSON SWORD OF PEACE

1995—RAF Laarbruch
1996—RAF Stornoway

WILKINSON BATTLE OF BRITAIN SWORD

1992/94—No IX Squadron
1994/96—No 399 Signals Unit

THE ROYAL AIR FORCES ESCAPING SOCIETY TROPHY

1996—No Award
1997—No Award

QUEEN'S MEDAL FOR CHAMPION SHOTS OF THE AIR FORCE

1997—Sergeant J. T. Prictor
1998—Flight Lieutenant L. F. Smith, BEng

JOLLIFFE TROPHY

1996—Competition Suspended for 1 year
1997—RAF Woodvale

THE ARTHUR BARRATT MEMORIAL PRIZE

1995—Mr. T. Thompson
1996—Hercules Wing Rodeo 96 Team

THE "L. G. GROVES" MEMORIAL PRIZES & AWARDS

Air Safety Prize

1995—Mr. D. G. Murray
      Mr. G. Stephens
      Mr. R. Hansford
1996—Wing Commander J. Cugley, OBE MB BS

Meteorology

1995—Dr. M. S. J. Harrison
1996—Dr D. Pick
      Mr B. Greener

Meteorological Observation Award

1995—Dr. A. Lapworth
1996—Mr N. Price

Ground Safety Award

1995—No Award
1996—No Award

ADRIAN RAY MEMORIAL AWARD FOR RAF ENGINEERING

1996—No Award
1997—Squadron Leader R. D. A. Tulloch, MBE BSc

"HYDE-THOMSON" MEMORIAL PRIZE

General Duties Officer Award

1995—No Award
1996—Flying Officer I. D. Bland

Engineering Officer Award

1995—Flight Lieutenant K. Rosbotham
1996—Flight Lieutenant A. K. Stanley, BEng

"GORDON SHEPHARD" MEMORIAL PRIZE ESSAY

1996—Squadron Leader W H. Milroy, MA BTh MIPD
1997—No Award

ROYAL AIR FORCE COMMAND TROPHIES

(listed in Command order of precedence)

HEADQUARTERS STRIKE COMMAND

GEORGE STAINFORTH TROPHY

1996—RAF Brize Norton
1997—RAF Coltishall

SMALLWOOD ELECTRONIC WARFARE TROPHY

1996—No Award
1997—Flight Sergeant R. C. Boatman

YELLOWGATE TROPHY

1996—Sergeant P. Hooper
1998—Not yet awarded

HQ No 11/18 Group

ABERPORTH TROPHY

1996—Not Awarded
1997—No 43 Squadron

DACRE TROPHY

1995/96—No 25 Squadron
1996/97—No 25 Squadron

INGPEN TROPHY

1994/95—No Award
1995/96—Not yet Awarded

SEED TROPHY

1995/96—No 29 Squadron
1996/97—No 5 Squadron

SMALL STATIONS TROPHY

1995—RAF Saxa Vord
1996—Not yet Awarded

AIRD WHYTE TROPHY

1996—No 120 Squadron
1997—No 206 Squadron

FINCASTLE TROPHY

1996—Royal Canadian Air Force
1997—Royal New Zealand Air Force

INTER SQUADRON PHOTOGRAPHIC TROPHY

1996—No 42(R) Squadron
1997—No 42(R) Squadron

HARRIS TROPHY

1996—Flight Lieutenant C. S. H. Watson
1997—Flight Lieutenant A. K. Stratton

NAIRN TROPHY

1996—NLS (North) RAF Kinloss
1997—NLS RAF Kinloss

SKYFAME TROPHY

1995/96—No 202 Squadron

HQ MATO

COSSOR TROPHY

1996—Cottesmore
1997—Not yet awarded

SHORTS TROPHY

1996—Flying Officer C. J. Edie

THE BOMBARDIER SUPPORT SERVICES ATC TROPHY

1997—Sergeant J. W. Wylie

HEADQUARTERS ROYAL AIR FORCE PERSONNEL & TRAINING COMMAND

DISTINGUISHED PASSES IN FLYING TRAINING

1996—No Award
1997—No Award

HEADQUARTERS ELEMENTARY FLYING TRAINING

HACK TROPHY

1997—Aberdeen, Dundee & St Andrews UAS
1998—To be Notified

THE COOPER TROPHY

1997—No Competition
1998—To be Notified

DE HAVILLAND TROPHY

1997—Cambridge UAS
1998—To be Notified

REID TROPHY

1997—Liverpool UAS
1998—To be Notified

SCONE TROPHY

1997—Aberdeen, Dundee, St Andrews UAS
1998—To be Notified

ROYAL AIR FORCE REGIMENT

LLOYDS CUP (ROYAL AIR FORCE REGIMENT SKILL AT ARMS)

1996—Not Awarded
1997—Armament Defence Squadron (RAF Honington) RAF Regiment

HIGGINSON TROPHY (EXCEPTIONAL PROFESSIONAL ACHIEVEMENT)

1996—3 Squadron RAF Regiment
1997—1 Squadron RAF Regiment

ARTHUR BARNARD TROPHY

1996—Not Awarded
1997—Not Awarded

ROBERTS LEADERSHIP TROPHY FOR THE RAF REGIMENT

1996—Flight Lieutenant N. J. Trown
1997—Flight Lieutenant P. T. W. Holland

RAF REGIMENT ESSAY COMPETITION

1996—Flight Lieutenant T. E. Uren, BSc
1997—Flight Lieutenant G. J. Powell

THE RAF REGIMENT OFFICERS DINNER CLUB PRIZE AND KAPUSCINSKI SWORD

(Top Student on the Junior Regiment Officer's Course)

1996—Course 1—Flying Officer R. L. Morgan, BSc
1997—Course 1—Flying Officer M. Bottrill
 Course 2—Pilot Officer G. M. Wood

THE VAUX TROPHY

(Student on the Junior Regiment Officer's Course displaying the greatest development of leadership qualities)

1996—Course 1—Flying Officer S. Magee, BSc
1997—Course 1—Flying Officer S. Booth
 Course 2—Flying Officer J. H. Liston, BSc

ROYAL AIR FORCE MEDICAL SERVICES

"RICHARD FOX LINTON" MEMORIAL PRIZE

1996—Wing Commander D. P. Gradwell, PhD BSc MB ChB DAvMed MRAeS
1997—Wing Commander R. J. M. Broadbridge, MB BS MRCGP DRCOG DAvMed

THE LADY CADE MEDAL

1995—Group Captain W. J. Coker, OBE MB ChB BA BSc FRCP
1996—Wing Commander M. J. Spittal, MB ChB

THE SIR ANDREW HUMPHREY MEMORIAL MEDAL

1997—Wing Commander A. Wingham, MB BS DRCOG
1998—Squadron Leader B. Wroe, CertEd

LEAN MEMORIAL AWARD

1997—Squadron Leader G. N. Wilson, BDS
1998—Group Captain J. Reid, BDS MGDSRCPS(Glas)

STEWART MEMORIAL PRIZE

1997—Squadron Leader D Newman, RAAF
1998—Major A. Manton RAMC

THE SIR HAROLD WHITTINGHAM MEMORIAL PRIZE

1997—Dr A. J. F. Macmillan BSc MB ChB MFOM
1998—Air Commodore S. A. Cullen, QHS MB ChB FRCPath FRAeS DCP

ROYAL AIR FORCE MUSIC SERVICES—Competition Winners

SIR FELIX CASSEL CHALLENGE CUP

1997—The Band of the Royal Air Force Regiment
 Director of Music—Flight Lieutenant
 D. W. Compton, ARCM
1998—The Band of the Royal Air Force Regiment
 Director of Music—Flight Lieutenant
 D. W. Compton, ARCM

SIMS CEREMONIAL CUP

1997—The Band of the Royal Air Force College
Director of Music—Flight Lieutenant D. J. G. Stubbs,
BA PGCE ARCM LGSM
1998—Squadron Leader S. L. Stirling, MA BMus FTCL
LRAM ARCM

BOOSEY AND HAWKES TROPHY

1997—The Band of the Royal Air Force College
Director of Music—Flight Lieutenant D. J. G. Stubbs,
BA PGCE ARCM LGSM
1998—Flight Lieutenant G. J. Bain, BA MIL LRAM ARCM

WORSHIPFUL COMPANY OF MUSICIANS' SILVER MEDAL

1997—Headquarters Music Services
Flight Sergeant C. Weldon
1998—Not yet awarded

THE SIR FELIX CASSEL SILVER MEDAL

1997—The Band of the Royal Air Force College
Junior Technician R. Taylor
1998—Not yet awarded

THE SIR FELIX CASSEL BRONZE MEDAL

1997—Headquarters Music Services
Junior Technician J. M. Ness
1998—Not yet awarded

SUPPLY BRANCH

THE GILL SWORD AWARD

1997—Flight Lieutenant K. S. Muskett, BSc
1998—Flight Lieutenant P. J. Warwick

ADMINISTRATIVE (SECRETARIAL BRANCH)

ROYAL AIR FORCE HALTON

Secretarial Cup Winners

1997—Flying Officer J. M. Moore
Flying Officer A. D. Aston
Flight Lieutenant J. L. Hamilton-Wilkes, BSc
1998—Flying Officer L. M. Bolton, LLB
Flight Lieutenant N. P. Sloan

THE WORSHIPFUL COMPANY OF CHARTERED SECRETARIES AND ADMINISTRATORS' PRIZES

1997—Flying Officer S. L. Scott, BA
Senior Aircraftwoman L. M. Reid
1998—Flying Officer S. Rowlands LLB
Senior Aircraftwoman L. M. Coffill

ADMINISTRATIVE (CATERING BRANCH)

THE HEREFORD TROPHY

1996—Flying Officer J. Barnett
1997—Flying Officer C. Gunn-Wilson, BA

R AUX AF TROPHIES & AWARDS

ROBINS TROPHY

1995/96—No 2 (City of Edinburgh) Maritime Headquarters
Unit RAuxAF
1996/97—No 2622 (Highland) Squadron RAuxAF Regiment
RAF Lossiemouth

STRICKLAND TROPHY

1997—No 2622 (Highland) Squadron RAuxAF Regiment
1998—No 2503 (County of Lincoln) Squadron RAuxAF
Regiment

ROYAL MILITARY COLLEGE OF SCIENCE

COMMANDANTS PRIZE

1996—Acting Pilot Officer H. B. Davies, BEng
Lieutenant S. B. George, RE
1997—Acting Pilot Officer J. H. R. Franklin, BEng

ROYAL AIR FORCE HISTORICAL SOCIETY

"THE TWO AIR FORCES" AWARD

1996—Squadron Leader P. C. Emmett, PhD BSc CEng MIEE
1997—Wing Commander M. P. Brzezicki, MPhil MIL

The Awards Shown on this page are made at the Royal Air Force College, Cranwell

DEPARTMENT OF INITIAL OFFICER TRAINING

QUEEN'S MEDAL AND R. S. MAY MEMORIAL PRIZE

1995—Flight Lieutenant J. F. Elliot, MB ChB
1996—Flying Officer J. M. Murnane, BA

WILKINSON SWORD OF HONOUR AND R. S. MAY MEMORIAL PRIZE

1995—Flying Officer S. Lindsell, BSc
1996—Flying Officer S. J. Brett, BEng

PRINCE BANDAR TROPHY AND PRIZE

1995—Flight Lieutenant J. E. Savage, BSc
1996—Flying Officer C. J. Layden, BA

SWORD OF MERIT

1996—Flying Officer I. A. Davies, BSc
Pilot Officer J. M. Murnane, BA
Pilot Officer S. J. Brett, BEng
Pilot Officer J. D. Scourfield, BSc
1997—Flying Officer W. G. Smith, BEng
Flying Officer C. R. Lynham, BA
Flying Officer J. A. Watson
Pilot Officer J. W. Ixer, BA
Flying Officer S. A. Bateman
Flying Officer M. L. Parker, MA

HENNESSY TROPHY AND PHILIP SASSOON MEMORIAL PRIZE

1996—Flying Officer R. G. P. Shand, BA
Pilot Officer A. D. C. Floyd, BEd
Pilot Officer C. E. White, BSc
Pilot Officer M. S. A. Potter, BSc
1997—Flight Lieutenant J. I. M. Tomlinson, BEng
Pilot Officer R. T. D. Hollin, MA BSc
Flying Officer J. E. Atack
Flying Officer I. Wright
Pilot Officer G. M. Wood
Flying Officer S. M. Trollone

BRITISH AIRCRAFT CORPORATION TROPHY

1996—Flight Lieutenant J. B. Osborne, BEng
Pilot Officer J. M. Greenhowe, BSc
Flying Officer N. R. Hawthorn
Pilot Officer S. A. B. Mattocks, MA
1997—Flying Officer C. J. McKee, BSc
Flying Officer R. K. J. McPhee, BEng
Pilot Officer J. A. A. Schofield, BSc
Flying Officer A. G. Corner
Flying Officer P. J. Duffield
Pilot Officer B. Hall

OVERSEAS STUDENT'S PRIZE

1996—Officer Cadet H. J. Hishamuddin Abidin, RBAF
Captain E. F. Dixon, BSc JDF
Pilot Officer S. S. S. Al-Munaijri, RAFO
2nd Lieutenant M. E. Junaidi, RBAF
1997—Second Lieutenant K. O. K. Al-Khayareen QEAF
Flying Officer F. Odoi-Wellington, BA GAF
Officer Cadet C. Kis, HAF
Second Lieutenant H. M. A. S. Noeh, RBAF
Second Lieutenant J. J. M. E. Vital, SPDF

DEPARTMENT OF ELEMENTARY FLYING TRAINING

KINKEAD TROPHY

1995—Not Awarded
1996—Flying Officer R. G. P. Shand, BA

MICHAEL HILL MEMORIAL PRIZE

1995—Not Awarded
1996—Flying Officer R. G. P. Shand, BA

R. M. GROVES MEMORIAL PRIZE

1996—Flying Officer R. A. Caine
Flight Lieutenant N. C. B. Morton, BEng
Flying Officer H. R. Bond, MSc BSc
Flying Officer A. E. Wells, BSc
Flying Officer P. S. Francis, BSc
Flying Officer R. G. P. Shand, BA
Pilot Officer A. P. D. Fowle
1997—Flying Officer A. Mickellides, BEng
Flying Officer J. A. Waterson, BA
Flying Officer S. V. Bowell, BEng
Acting Pilot Officer P. A. Boyce
Flying Officer S. J. Kovach, BA
Acting Pilot Officer W. D. R. Saunders
Flight Lieutenant D. S. Jamieson
Flying Officer R. K. McPhee, BEng
Acting Pilot Officer D. A. Robinson

DICKSON TROPHY

1996—Sub Lieutenant D. Denham
Lieutenant J. T. Mazdon
Flying Officer M. C. Lindley, BCom
Flying Officer A. E. Wells, BSc
Flying Officer P. S. Francis, BSc
Flying Officer R. G. P. Shand, BA
Pilot Officer A. P. D. Fowle
1997—Sub Lieutenant S. Alsop
Flying Officer J. A. Waterson, BA
Flying Officer S. V. Bowell, BEng
Acting Officer P. A. Boyce
Lieutenant P. M. Kelly
Sub Lieutenant S. B. Gamble
Flight Lieutenant D. S. Jamieson
Sub Lieutenant K. M. Thomson
Acting Pilot Officer D. A. Robinson

BATTLE OF BRITAIN TROPHY

1996—Flying Officer K. B. Dyer, BA
Flying Officer A. P. Millikin, BSocSc
1997—Flying Officer J. B. Sheldon, BSc
Flying Officer A. L. Adams, LLB
Lieutenant P. M. Kelly

HICKS MEMORIAL TROPHY

1996—Not Awarded
1997—Not Awarded

DEPARTMENT OF SPECIALIST GROUND TRAINING

WHITTLE PRIZE

1996—Squadron Leader P. Martin, BSc
1997—Flight Lieutenant A. G. Jacopino, BEng RAAF

SHIRLEY MEMORIAL CUP AND MINERVA SOCIETY PRIZE

1995—Flight Lieutenant J. Rolf, BA
1996—Flight Lieutenant A. C. McLeod, BEng

HALAHAN PRIZE

1995—Flight Lieutenant P. R. Blevins
1996—Flight Lieutenant A. C. McLeod, BEng

HERBERT SMITH MEMORIAL TROPHY

1996—Flight Lieutenant G. Stewart, BEng RAAF
1997—Squadron Leader A. M. Sansom, BEng CEng MRAeS

SUPPLY PRIZE

1995—Flying Officer J. C. Louca, LLB
1996—Flight Lieutenant I. S. Stoneley, BA

WORSHIPFUL COMPANY OF ENGINEERS' PRIZE

1995—Flight Lieutenant R. J. Knighton, MA CEng MIMechE
1996—Flight Lieutenant S. Harris, BEng

STUART BOULTON MEMORIAL PRIZE

1995—Flight Lieutenant P. R. Blevins
1996—Flight Lieutenant R. D. Longden, BEng

BECKWITH TROPHY AND PRIZE

1996—Acting Pilot Officer S. J. Dyke
1997—Acting Pilot Officer J. E. Dodwell

ROYAL NEW ZEALAND AIR FORCE PRIZES

1996—Acting Pilot Officer R. P. Barr, BEng
Flying Officer S. J. Austin
1997—Acting Pilot Officer D. M. Lawson, BEng
Acting Pilot Officer B. D. Morris, BEng

COLLEGE AWARDS
LOWE-HOLMES TROPHY

1996—Sergeant R. Payne
1997—Officer Cadet S. M. Lansdell

OPERATIONAL DOCTRINE AND TRAINING
(AIR WARFARE CENTRE)

ANDREW HUMPHREY MEMORIAL GOLD MEDAL

1996—Major A. W. Geisse, GAF
1997—Major A. G. Glodowski, MSc BSc USAF

ARIES TROPHY

1996—Flight Lieutenant R. A. McCormick, BSc
1997—Flight Lieutenant M. J. Gunn, BSc

SIR ROBERT BROOKE-POPHAM TROPHY

(Awarded to the member of the Advanced Staff Course at
the RAF Staff College, Bracknell who submits the best
Service paper)

1996—Squadron Leader A. D. Gunby
1997—Not Awarded

BRABYN TROPHY

(Awarded annually to the winner of the individual
aerobatics competition for Hawk instructors from Royal
Air Force Personnel and Training Command)

1997—Not Awarded
1998—Not Awarded

WRIGHT JUBILEE TROPHY

(Awarded annually to the overall winner of the aerobatics
competition for instructors from Royal Air Force
Personnel and Training Command)

1997—Flight Lieutenant K. A. Lewis, BEng
1998—Flight Lieutenant R. A. Harrison, BSc

BRITISH AEROSPACE BULLDOG TROPHY

(Awarded annually to the winner of the Aerobatics
Competition for Bulldog instructors from Royal Air Force
Personnel and Training Command)

1997—Not Awarded
1998—Flight Lieutenant P. R. Margetts, BSc

SPITFIRE TROPHY FOR JET PROVOST AND TUCANO

(Awarded annually to the winner of the individual
Aerobatics Comptition for instructors from Royal Air Force
Personnel and Training Command) Tucano

1997—Not Awarded
1998—Not Awarded

OBITUARY

ACTIVE LIST

Officers and Warrant Officers
whose deaths have been reported since September 1997

Rank and Name	Date of Death	Rank and Name	Date of Death
Group Captain		RAFR	
A. J. Parsons, OBE BSc (Eng) CEng FRAeS ACGI...	8.1.98	*Wing Commander* J. D. Douglas-Boyd, MBE BA MIMgt...	3.5.98
Wing Commander D. N. H. Stone, MB ChB DRCOG DAvMed	7.7.98	*Flight Lieutenant* N. G. Preston	24.8.98
Squadron Leaders		RAFVR(T)	
P. L. Marsland	20.2.98	*Flying Officers*	
P. C. Pullen	14.7.98	J. C. Lodge, BA	25.12.97
A. Storey, BSc	21.2.98	J. C. Nute	12.2.98
A. J. Streeter	26.4.98	J. H. Snowden, MEd	12.2.98
W. M. Vivian	15.6.98		
Flight Lieutenants		*Pilot Officer* C. R. Morris, BA PGCE ...	13.2.98
R. A. Barker, BA	28.8.98		
G. N. Dunlop, BSc	4.6.98		
D. S. Lacey, BSc	15.6.98		
I. A. Leddra	26.8.98		
D. N. Mills...	16.11.97		
Flying Officer J. M. Collier	6.2.98		
Warrant Officer D. J. Ruddock	29.9.98		

LIST OF RETIRED OFFICERS OF THE ROYAL AIR FORCE

Officers who have retired since July 1997

ACKROYD D. F. W. MMedSci MB BS MRCGP MFOM DRCOG DAvMed. Born 4/1/54. Commd 17/2/80. Wg Cdr 18/8/91. Retd MED 4/12/97.
ADAMS C. J. Born 30/5/39. Commd 1/8/61. Sqn Ldr 1/1/74. Retd GD 1/1/98.
ALLAWAY W. J. Born 12/1/45. Commd 30/4/81. Sqn Ldr 1/1/89. Retd GD 7/10/97.
ALLEN C. R. Born 15/6/47. Commd 8/9/77. Sqn Ldr 1/1/85. Retd ENG 16/6/97.
AMROLIWALLA F. K. BSc MB BS FRCP DPH DIH DAvMed. Born 21/2/33. Commd 2/5/66. A Cdre 19/11/91. Retd MED 21/2/98.
ANDERSON J. D. MBE. Born 18/3/57. Commd 20/5/82. Sqn Ldr 1/1/91. Retd ADMIN 18/3/98.
ANDREWS G. N. Born 14/1/43. Commd 10/11/80. Sqn Ldr 1/7/91. Retd ADMIN 14/1/98.
ANDREWS M. L. Born 19/5/60. Commd 11/1/79. Flt Lt 11/7/84. Retd GD 19/5/98.
ARMSTRONG J. M. Born 29/5/60. Commd 28/6/79. Flt Lt 28/12/84. Retd GD 31/7/98.
ATKINSON P. R. Born 31/7/59. Commd 25/9/80. Flt Lt 25/3/86. Retd GD 31/7/97.
ATKINSON R. C. AFC. Born 4/12/41. Commd 9/10/64. Sqn Ldr 1/1/82. Retd GD 11/10/97.
AUBREY-REES I. G. BA. Born 16/1/44. Commd 17/12/65. Sqn Ldr 1/1/82. Retd GD 1/8/97.

BAGGLEY K. J. Born 31/1/60. Commd 11/1/79. Sqn Ldr 1/7/90. Retd GD 31/1/98.
BAKER B. A. F. Born 13/4/47. Commd 26/8/66. Flt Lt 17/12/72. Retd OPS SPT 7/4/98.
BANNISTER R. A. Born 19/1/54. Commd 1/7/76. Sqn Ldr 1/7/90. Retd GD 1/2/98.
BARBER R. Born 23/9/95. Commd 5/4/79. Sqn Ldr 1/1/91. Retd GD 23/9/97.
BARLOW D. E. Born 23/7/59. Commd 15/8/85. Flt Lt 5/9/88. Retd OPS SPT 23/7/97.
BARNARD J. B. Born 3/5/44. Commd 6/7/62. Sqn Ldr 1/7/88. Retd GD 1/6/98.
BARNES D. J. Born 6/8/44. Commd 29/7/83. Sqn Ldr 1/7/92. Retd ADMIN 2/12/97.
BARNETT J. C. Born 12/4/38. Commd 22/5/64. Flt Lt 22/5/68. Retd GD 3/2/80.
BARRASS K. Born 10/7/58. Commd 15/2/90. Flt Lt 15/2/92. Retd ENG 15/2/98.
BARRATT The Rev P. Born 25/3/56. Commd 5/4/79. Flt Lt 20/9/82. Retd GD 2/9/87. Re-entered 2/7/90. Retd 31/12/97. Sqn Ldr
BARTER J. F. Born 21/4/61. Commd 5/2/81. Sqn Ldr 1/1/94. Retd OPS SPT.
BECKETT J. R. MCIPS. Born 18/9/42. Commd 23/9/66. Sqn Ldr 1/7/74. Retd SUP 18/9/97.
BENNISON S. W. BSc CEng MIEE. Born 10/11/59. Commd 6/9/81. Sqn Ldr 1/1/91. Retd ENG 10/11/97.
BENOIST J. D. Born 2/10/46. Commd 27/2/75. Sqn Ldr 1/1/88. Retd OPS SPT 2/4/98.
BERESFORD S. E. Born 24/2/53. Commd 12/3/87. Flt Lt 12/3/89. Retd ENG 31/10/97.
BILLINGS E. H. Born 14/1/43. Commd 22/1/80. Flt Lt 22/5/83. Retd GD 14/1/98.
BILLINGS S. J. BSc DipEd. Born 26/9/54. Commd 6/9/81. Flt Lt 6/3/84. Retd ENG 6/9/97.
BISHOP A. M. Born 14/7/47. Commd 23/10/86. Flt Lt 23/10/88. Retd GD 15/7/97.
BOGG R. Born 14/6/42. Commd 11/5/62. A Cdre 11/5/62. Retd GD 14/6/97.
BOORMAN P. S. Born 19/7/49. Commd 6/11/80. Sqn Ldr 1/1/91. Retd OPS SPT 1/10/97.
BOOTHBY P. E. Born 16/10/56. Commd 20/9/79. Flt Lt 20/3/85. Retd GD 2/3/98.
BOURNE L. Born 16/10/54. Commd 31/1/80. Sqn Ldr 1/1/94. Retd OPS SPT 31/10/97.
BOWSHER D. S. Born 24/7/59. Commd 17/5/79. Flt Lt 17/11/84. Retd GD 24/7/97.
BRACKPOOL M. J. BA. Born 31/7/46. Commd 15/10/81. Sqn Ldr 1/1/91. Retd ENG 26/5/98.
BRADSHAW K. M. J. BEng. Born 26/11/57. Commd 6/7/80. Sqn Ldr 1/7/89. Retd ENG 9/6/97.
BRAITHWAITE S. M. Born 13/10/63. Commd 24/3/83. Flt Lt 24/9/88. Retd GD 1/10/97.
BRAY D. B. Born 27/12/44. Commd 22/5/64. Sqn Ldr 1/1/81. Retd GD 2/12/97.
BRENNAN C. Born 6/3/57. Commd 16/6/88. Flt Lt 21/4/94. Retd MED(T) 15/8/97.
BRIDGE B. J. Born 25/9/47. Commd 8/12/83. Sqn Ldr 1/7/93. Retd ENG 2/4/98.
BRIGGS J. F. BSc. Born 23/10/48. Commd 8/9/74. Sqn Ldr 1/1/91. Retd GD 2/9/97.

BROWN C. N. A. BSc CEng MIMechE. Born 27/8/52. Commd 22/6/75. Sqn Ldr 1/1/84. Retd ENG 2/6/97.
BROWN J. R. Born 12/1/45. Commd 25/3/64. Wg Cdr 1/1/88. Retd GD 8/12/97.
BROWN K. M. A. Born 1/5/46. Commd 9/3/72. Sqn Ldr 1/7/90. Retd ADMIN 1/1/98.
BROWN M. R. MIIM MIMgt. Born 2/6/43. Commd 4/11/82. Sqn Ldr 1/1/91. Retd ENG 2/6/98.
BRUCE D. V. Born 25/8/58. Commd 22/6/89. Flt Lt 22/6/91. Retd ENG 22/6/97.
BRUNING M. P. W. C. E. W. M. Born 1/11/42. Commd 6/11/67. Sqn Ldr 1/7/85. Retd OPS SPT 1/11/97.
BRUNSDEN J. P. Born 14/3/43. Commd 28/4/65. Sqn Ldr 1/7/79. Retd GD 14/3/98.
BUCHAN D. J. Born 20/9/42. Commd 3/8/62. Sqn Ldr 1/7/80. Retd OPS SPT 20/9/97.
BUCKBY D. M. Born 7/3/58. Commd 18/10/81. Flt Lt 18/10/85. Retd ADMIN 18/10/97.
BUCKLEY T. P. MIMgt. Born 18/5/43. Commd 3/1/64. Wg Cdr 1/7/92. Retd ADMIN 18/5/98.
BURKE K. S. MSc BSc. Born 28/11/58. Commd 17/1/82. Sqn Ldr 1/1/91. Retd ENG 17/1/98.
BURKE R. H. Born 28/6/39. Commd 21/7/61. Sqn Ldr 1/1/74. Retd GD 28/6/97.
BURNETT D. J. Born 3/4/45. Commd 17/12/65. Flt Lt 1/7/68. Retd GD 17/9/97.
BUSH G. R. Born 21/10/48. Commd 17/3/67. Gp Capt 1/7/94. Retd OPS SPT 7/4/98.
BUSSEREAU V. R. D. Born 7/7/42. Commd 21/4/65. Wg Cdr 1/7/94. Retd GD 7/7/97.
BUSUTTIL W. MB ChB. Born 5/11/59. Commd 9/7/81. Wg Cdr 1/8/97. Retd MED 5/11/97.
BYWATER R. D. Born 20/3/64. Commd 30/8/84. Flt Lt 20/2/90. Retd GD 30/3/98.

CADWALLADER D. G. Born 2/12/44. Commd 3/3/67. Sqn Ldr 1/1/79. Retd GD 19/10/97.
CALVERT D. T. Born 4/1/44. Commd 15/9/67. Wg Cdr 1/1/87. Retd GD 11/10/97.
CAMPBELL D. A. Born 23/11/58. Commd 2/3/78. Sqn Ldr 1/1/94. Retd GD 1/9/97.
CAMPBELL R. D. Born 25/4/60. Commd 3/7/80. Flt Lt 3/1/87. Retd OPS SPT 25/4/98.
CAMPBELL R. S. Born 7/6/45. Commd 3/7/80. Sqn Ldr 1/7/91. Retd ENG 6/2/98.
CARLETON G. W. CB. Born 22/9/35. Commd 18/6/59. Plt Offr 24/12/59. Retd LGL 12/7/61. Re-entered 31/5/65. AVM 1/1/93. Retd LGL 22/9/97.
CARR P. H. Born 7/11/59. Commd 11/6/81. Sqn Ldr 1/7/91. Retd GD 4/1/98.
CARROLL P. Born 9/7/59. Commd 7/8/87. Flt Lt 15/7/91. Retd ENG 9/7/97.
CATTLE A. P. Born 26/9/37. Commd 9/2/62. Sqn Ldr 1/7/89. Retd GD 26/9/97.
CHAMBERS B. R. G. BSc CEng MIMechE MRAeS. Born 23/1/43. Commd 25/11/68. Wg Cdr 1/1/88. Retd ENG 23/1/98.
CHARLTON D. Born 8/5/49. Commd 8/5/86. Wg Cdr 1/7/96. Retd ADMIN 1/7/97.
CHARLTON G. K. BSc. Born 24/3/47. Commd 1/9/70. Sqn Ldr 1/7/86. Retd GD 25/9/97.
CHASE S. W. BA FIPD FBIFM FIMgt MInstAM. Born 22/5/55. Commd 16/9/73. Gp Capt 1/1/95. Retd ADMIN 10/7/97.
CHEAL T. Born 31/7/59. Commd 20/7/78. Sqn Ldr 1/1/91. Retd GD 31/7/97.
CHEW C. P. BA BArch. Born 19/8/56. Commd 6/9/81. Flt Lt 6/12/82. Retd GD 6/9/97.
CHICK S. D. BSc. Born 11/3/64. Commd 17/11/83. Flt Lt 15/1/88. Retd GD 15/7/97.
CHICKEN S. H. BSc. Born 17/8/60. Commd 4/8/78. Sqn Ldr 1/7/94. Retd ENG 23/1/98.
CHILDS I. J. Born 24/6/42. Commd 17/12/64. Wg Cdr 1/7/89. Retd GD 24/6/97.
CHOTHIA G. M. Born 31/1/67. Commd 28/7/67. Wg Cdr 1/7/96. Retd OPS SPT 10/4/98.
CHRISTY M. P. BSc. Born 2/5/60. Commd 28/1/82. Sqn Ldr 1/1/95. Retd GD 2/5/98.
CLARK D. MSc BA. Born 13/12/43. Commd 12/8/79. Sqn Ldr 1/1/88. Retd ADMIN 1/11/97.
CLARKE M. C. A. Born 12/12/42. Commd 6/7/62. Sqn Ldr 1/1/85. Retd OPS SPT 12/12/97.
CLEGG M. A. Born 10/8/42. Commd 17/12/64. Gp Capt 1/1/91. Retd GD 2/4/98.
CLEMENTS R. E. Born 18/6/43. Commd 3/5/68. Sqn Ldr 1/7/79. Retd GD 21/9/97.
CLIFFORD R. I. MIMgt. Born 25/4/44. Commd 25/6/65. Flt Lt 25/12/70. Retd GD 26/1/73. Re-entered 6/6/74. Sqn Ldr 1/7/87. Retd ADMIN 5/1/98.
CLOUGH D. B. Born 19/8/47. Commd 14/7/66. Flt Lt 4/5/72. Retd GD 28/2/78. Re-entered 30/8/85. Flt Lt 2/11/79. Retd OPS SPT 18/11/97.
COE M. J. Born 18/10/42. Commd 11/5/78. Sqn Ldr 1/1/92. Retd ENG 18/10/97.
COLE D. J. R. BA DPhysEd. Born 21/12/44. Commd 7/8/67. Wg Cdr 1/7/89. Retd ADMIN 21/6/97.

COLE G. E. Born 5/12/59. Commd 27/3/80. Flt Lt 27/9/86. Retd OPS SPT 5/12/97.
COLE P. L. Born 12/5/46. Commd 26/4/84. Sqn Ldr 1/7/92. Retd ENG 12/5/98.
COLEMAN P. T. Born 14/6/42. Commd 29/6/72. Wg Cdr 1/1/96. Retd ENG 14/6/97.
COLES R. E. BSc. Born 20/10/57. Commd 19/9/76. Sqn Ldr 1/1/91. Retd ENG 1/10/97.
COLES R. G. Born 30/11/41. Commd 22/2/63. Flt Lt 12/11/69. Retd GD(G) 1/10/75. Re-entered 8/7/81. Sqn Ldr 1/7/87. Retd OPS SPT 8/7/97.
COLLIER-BAKER A. D. Born 6/2/57. Commd 15/2/90. Flt Lt 15/2/92. Retd ENG 15/2/98.
COLLINS A. F. MLitt BA. Born 19/9/45. Commd 20/8/67. Sqn Ldr 1/1/92. Retd GD 16/3/98.
COOK D. E. MMedSci MB ChB DIH DAvMed AFOM MRAeS. Born 31/5/56. Commd 18/1/77. Wg Cdr 1/8/93. Retd MED 18/6/97.
COSGROVE J. A. OBE. Born 13/10/43. Commd 21/7/65. Gp Capt 1/1/92. Retd GD 22/5/98.
COURTENAY R. T. MB BS DAvMed. Born 29/9/59. Commd 18/6/81. Wg Cdr 1/8/97. Retd MED 29/9/97.
COVENEY A. J. Born 21/2/43. Commd 6/11/67. Sqn Ldr 1/1/78. Retd SUP 5/12/97.
COWAN J. A. BA. Born 8/10/45. Commd 27/2/70. Sqn Ldr 1/1/86. Retd GD 23/4/98.
COWNIE A. G. H. BSc. Born 20/10/56. Commd 1/2/79. Sqn Ldr 1/7/91. Retd GD 4/4/98.
COX S. B. BSc. Born 25/11/42. Commd 24/1/66. Sqn Ldr 1/1/88. Retd GD 25/11/97.
COYLE P. J. Born 15/3/57. Commd 22/3/81. Sqn Ldr. Retd ENG 22/9/97.
CRESSWELL R. F. BA MCIPS MILog MIMgt. Born 23/4/44. Commd 15/7/66. Sqn Ldr 1/7/77. Retd SUP 27/10/97.
CROMBIE K. S. Born 16/8/53. Commd 25/4/82. Sqn Ldr 1/1/94. Retd GD 25/4/98.
CROSBY M. A. Born 20/12/63. Commd 24/3/83. Sqn Ldr 1/7/94. Retd GD 31/12/97.
CROSS M. J. BA. Born 7/1/59. Commd 11/4/82. Sqn Ldr 1/1/92. Retd ADMIN 11/4/98.
CROWE P. A. BSc(Eng) MMS MIMgt. Born 3/1/42. Commd 30/9/62. Sqn Ldr 1/1/78. Retd GD 3/11/97.
CULMER B. E. Born 4/11/43. Commd 22/5/75. Flt Lt 22/5/77. Retd OPS SPT 3/4/98.
CURRY P. M. Born 22/6/47. Commd 19/8/66. Sqn Ldr 1/1/91. Retd GD 10/2/98.
CUTHILL R. T. Born 19/1/46. Commd 1/3/68. Wg Cdr 1/7/86. Retd GD 15/6/97.

DAVENPORT-GOOD A. M. Born 2/12/61. Commd 11/6/81. Sqn Ldr 1/7/93. Retd OPS SPT 1/8/97.
DAVIDGE E. H. MIPD. Born 12/3/50. Commd 14/1/88. Flt Lt 14/1/92. Retd ADMIN 13/11/97.
DAVIES T. C. BSc CEng FIEE FRAeS MInstP. Born 21/10/42. Commd 13/4/64. A Cdre 1/1/91. Retd ENG 21/10/97.
DAWSON W. E. BEng. Born 13/2/57. Commd 20/11/78. Flt Lt 20/8/80. Retd GD 1/12/97.
DHESE I. R. Born 17/4/43. Commd 24/7/81. Sqn Ldr 1/1/89. Retd ADMIN 17/4/98.
DIBB P. G. R. Born 9/7/60. Commd 12/9/86. Sqn Ldr 1/1/94. Retd GD 2/12/97.
DICK I. C. H. MBE AFC. Born 23/7/42. Commd 18/12/62. Gp Capt 1/7/86. Retd GD 23/11/97.
DICKINSON D. P. Born 15/9/42. Commd 24/3/83. Flt Lt 24/3/87. Retd ENG 18/9/97.
DOBBY V. Born 20/3/43. Commd 11/6/81. Flt Lt 11/6/84. Retd GD 12/10/97.
DOLAN D. M. Born 6/12/50. Commd 14/8/70. Flt Lt 14/2/76. Retd GD 31/1/98.
DOVE B. AFC. Born 25/11/43. Commd 8/12/61. Wg Cdr 1/7/81. Retd GD 18/10/97.
DOYE C. C. Born 2/2/45. Commd 8/4/82. Wg Cdr 1/7/95. Retd ENG 10/4/98.
DRUREY S. J. Born 25/12/58. Commd 28/6/79. Sqn Ldr 1/1/95. Retd GD 1/1/98.
DUGGAN T. E. Born 1/5/47. Commd 28/2/69. Sqn Ldr 1/7/81. Retd GD 1/6/98.
DUMMER P. J. BA. Born 30/10/38. Commd 28/9/60. Sqn Ldr 1/7/73. Retd GD 10/10/97.
DYDE S. A. J. Born 19/2/60. Commd 28/2/80. Sqn Ldr 1/1/91. Retd GD 30/6/97.

EASTON S. J. BSc. Born 14/7/64. Commd 29/9/83. Flt Lt 15/1/88. Retd GD 15/7/97.
EDKINS A. C. Born 31/12/46. Commd 21/3/74. Flt Lt 29/6/80. Retd OPS SPT 6/7/97.
EDWARDS I. P. BSc. Born 4/6/64. Commd 18/8/85. Flt Lt 18/2/88. Retd GD 28/8/97.
EDWARDS T. A. BSc. Born 23/6/63. Commd 10/11/85. Flt Lt 10/5/88. Retd GD 28/11/97.
EELES T. BA. Born 14/9/42. Commd 30/7/63. Gp Capt 1/7/90. Retd GD 14/9/97.

ELIOT R. C. Born 7/5/60. Commd 13/12/79. Flt Lt 13/6/85. Retd GD 7/5/98.
EMERSON J. E. Born 24/9/43. Commd 8/6/84. Sqn Ldr 1/7/93. Retd ENG 12/10/97.
EMMERSON J. G. Born 21/5/43. Commd 6/9/65. Flt Lt 6/9/69. Retd GD 6/9/81. Re-entered
   3/11/86. Sqn Ldr 1/7/94. Retd GD 21/5/98.
ERSKINE CRUM W. S. OBE. Born 26/3/42. Commd 30/7/63. Wg Cdr 1/1/86. Retd GD 26/6/97.
EUSTACE P. H. Born 5/8/42. Commd 12/1/62. A Cdre 1/1/91. Retd GD 3/4/98.
EVANS G. H. BSc. Born 25/11/59. Commd 6/9/81. Flt Lt 6/12/82. Retd GD 25/11/97.
EVANS M. J. Born 22/8/42. Commd 25/1/63. Wg Cdr 1/7/85. Retd GD 22/8/97.
EVANS P. I. MSc MBA BSc. Born 15/2/60. Commd 23/11/80. Sqn Ldr 1/1/92. Retd ENG 15/2/98.

FAIERS J. H. Born 19/4/43. Commd 14/8/80. Sqn Ldr 1/1/90. Retd ENG 19/4/98.
FAIRBAIRN J. M. Born 7/1/59. Commd 25/9/80. Sqn Ldr 1/1/95. Retd GD 6/10/97.
FEATHERSTONE J. C. Born 15/4/43. Commd 17/12/64. Gp Capt 1/7/91. Retd ADMIN 15/4/98.
FELLOWS T. A. Born 3/1/57. Commd 13/12/79. Sqn Ldr 1/7/94. Retd SUP 13/7/97.
FENLON-SMITH P. A. Born 4/5/60. Commd 12/7/79. Sqn Ldr 1/1/93. Retd GD 4/5/98.
FENN A. K. BDS. Born 20/3/58. Commd 1/9/86. Sqn Ldr 28/6/93. Retd DEL 20/3/98.
FENNELL J. R. Born 9/6/42. Commd 31/8/62. Sqn Ldr 1/7/94. Retd GD 9/6/97.
FISHER C. J. Born 5/3/43. Commd 24/11/67. Sqn Ldr 1/7/81. Retd SUP 1/7/84. Re-entered
   17/2/89. Sqn Ldr 17/2/86. Retd SUP 5/3/98.
FISHER R. I. Born 9/5/43. Commd 28/4/67. Wg Cdr 1/1/94. Retd GD 9/5/98.
FLAVELL D. M. Born 21/4/43. Commd 11/4/85. Sqn Ldr 1/7/95. Retd ENG 24/4/98.
FLETCHER R. M. BSc. Born 29/11/57. Commd 26/7/81. Flt Lt 26/10/81. Retd GD 26/7/97.
FLETCHER W. D. M. CEng MRAeS. Born 12/7/42. Commd 7/12/65. Wg Cdr 1/7/82. Retd ENG
   12/7/97.
FLINT C. J. MILog MIMgt. Born 22/2/43. Commd 26/5/67. Wg Cdr 1/7/84. Retd SUP 22/2/98.
FORD J. A. F. FIMgt. Born 19/6/44. Commd 24/6/65. A Cdre 1/7/94. Retd GD 24/5/98.
FOREMAN M. C. Born 3/8/59. Commd 29/8/77. Sqn Ldr 1/7/97. Retd GD 3/8/97.
FOWLE A. P. D. Born 10/4/76. Commd 5/10/95. Plt Offr 5/10/96. Retd GD 16/2/98.
FRAZER K. D. Born 18/7/42. Commd 16/9/71. Sqn Ldr 1/7/79. Retd ENG 18/7/98.
FREEMAN B. G. OBE. Born 20/3/45. Commd 27/5/71. Gp Capt 1/1/94. Retd GD 1/1/98.
FULLER A. B. Born 18/2/46. Commd 5/3/65. Sqn Ldr 1/1/77. Retd GD 27/4/98.
FULTON T. J. N. BSc. Born 10/2/42. Commd 30/8/66. Wg Cdr 1/1/89. Retd GD 10/2/98.

GALE I. T. Born 4/2/60. Commd 12/7/79. Sqn Ldr 1/7/91. Retd GD 4/2/98.
GALLAGHER R. Born 11/1/43. Commd 6/9/63. Sqn Ldr 1/7/84. Retd GD 11/1/98.
GARGETT J. P. Born 31/5/44. Commd 26/11/81. Sqn Ldr 1/7/90. Retd ENG 3/12/97.
GARTON A. C. Born 8/9/45. Commd 10/6/66. Sqn Ldr 1/1/78. Retd GD 28/10/97.
GASSON D. R. MBE. Born 21/11/44. Commd 31/3/68. Sqn Ldr 1/1/81. Retd GD 31/3/84. Re-
   entered 2/6/86. Wg Cdr 1/7/90. Retd GD 15/8/97.
GEDGE P. W. Born 19/12/42. Commd 28/4/67. Sqn Ldr 1/7/90. Retd SUP 19/12/97.
GEORGE G. H. E. Born 9/7/46. Commd 22/7/71. Flt Lt 11/12/77. Retd OPS SPT 7/4/98.
GIBBON R. M. Born 3/6/43. Commd 17/7/75. Wg Cdr 1/1/91. Retd ENG 3/6/98.
GIBSON T. J. MBA BSc. Born 17/2/50. Commd 11/8/74. Sqn Ldr 1/1/88. Retd ENG 1/12/97.
GILBERT P. N. Born 4/3/59. Commd 28/2/85. Flt Lt 2/11/87. Retd OPS SPT 4/8/97.
GILL P. H. R. MSc MFOM MRCS LRCP DAvMed. Born 30/1/42. Commd 11/1/65. Gp Capt 5/9/92.
   Retd MED 14/1/98.
GLENTON J. A. Born 25/1/43. Commd 28/9/62. Flt Lt 1/7/68. Retd GD 25/1/98.
GODDARD P. J. AFC. Born 17/10/43. Commd 22/3/63. AVM 1/1/94. Retd GD 17/4/98.
GODDEN D. R. P. BDS MB ChB FDSRCS(Eng) FRCS(Eng). Born 28/12/58. Commd 13/1/80.
   Plt Offr 13/1/80. Retd DEL 8/12/86. Re-entered 28/8/88. Sqn Ldr 1/8/92. Retd DEL 28/9/97.
GOODE The Rev A. T. R. MA Born 10/12/42. Commd 18/7/71. Retd 10/12/97. Wg Cdr
GOODMAN A. M. Born 14/4/37. Commd 16/12/58. Sqn Ldr 1/1/71. Retd GD 14/10/97.
GOODWIN C. W. D. Born 3/8/57. Commd 29/7/76. Sqn Ldr 1/1/91. Retd GD 1/6/98.

GORMAN A. BSc. Born 23/10/56. Commd 17/1/82. Flt Lt 17/4/85. Retd OPS SPT 17/1/98.
GOULDING B. S. Born 16/2/57. Commd 26/9/90. Flt Lt 13/5/95. Retd MED(T) 12/10/97.
GRAEME-COOK B. G. Born 1/3/60. Commd 4/9/81. Sqn Ldr 1/1/95. Retd GD 1/5/98.
GRAHAM K. P. BSc. Born 3/11/59. Commd 20/3/79. Flt Lt 15/10/82. Retd GD 3/11/97.
GRAHAM R. Born 28/4/47. Commd 21/1/66. Sqn Ldr 1/1/81. Retd GD 4/9/97.
GRIFFIN C. A. BEng. Born 15/4/59. Commd 29/11/81. Flt Lt 29/2/84. Retd ENG 29/11/97.
GROOMBRIDGE R. C. Born 17/11/39. Commd 6/10/60. Sqn Ldr 1/7/74. Retd GD 17/11/77.

HAIGH C. F. MBE. Born 7/2/43. Commd 2/9/63. Sqn Ldr 1/7/85. Retd GD 7/2/98.
HAKIN L. OBE psc(m) cfs. Born 9/7/42. Commd 6/9/63. Gp Capt 1/7/90. Retd GD 9/7/97.
HALL A. T. Born 3/10/50. Commd 5/4/91. Sqn Ldr 5/4/89. Retd ENG 14/7/97.
HALL M. R. BA. Born 6/1/43. Commd 13/4/66. Wg Cdr 1/1/86. Retd GD 17/10/97.
HAMILTON D. R. Born 24/7/48. Commd 28/4/67. Gp Capt 1/1/95. Retd GD 12/9/97.
HAMILTON N. I. Born 13/8/43. Commd 10/5/64. A Cdre 1/1/96. Retd GD 1/2/98.
HAMMANS M. P. Born 3/8/59. Commd 20/1/81. Sqn Ldr 1/1/95. Retd GD 1/1/98.
HAMMOND L. C. Born 16/6/42. Commd 9/11/70. Sqn Ldr 1/1/80. Retd SUP 16/6/97.
HAND V. M. RRC. Born 2/4/44. Commd 2/10/67. Flt Lt 2/10/69. Retd 2/10/71.
HANSON P. C. Born 26/1/54. Commd 11/2/93. Flt Lt 11/2/97. Retd ADMIN 15/9/97.
HARDING P. J. CB CBE AFC. Born 1/6/40. Commd 12/3/60. AVM 1/1/89. Retd GD 1/6/98.
HARLOW E. J. A. Born 10/3/43. Commd 17/7/64. Flt Lt 17/1/70. Retd GD 10/3/98.
HARPER B. L. S. Born 9/3/43. Commd 10/11/61. Sqn Ldr 1/7/81. Retd GD 9/3/98.
HARRISON A. J. CB CBE. Born 9/11/43. Commd 22/2/63. AVM 1/1/95. Retd GD 4/5/98.
HARRISON J. D. BA. Born 22/1/53. Commd 6/3/77. Flt Lt 6/12/78. Retd GD 1/10/97.
HAWKINS D. G. PhD BSc. Born 1/6/41. Commd 21/1/68. Gp Capt 1/1/87. Retd GD 3/12/97.
HEARD A. W. Born 7/1/59. Commd 25/2/62. Flt Lt 25/8/87. Retd GD 19/10/97.
HEARD N. J. BSc. Born 21/12/59. Commd 4/9/78. Sqn Ldr 1/7/93. Retd GD 21/12/97.
HEARN P. J. MBE MIMgt. Born 22/8/42. Commd 2/4/65. Sqn Ldr 1/1/82. Retd GD 31/12/97.
HENDERSON J. S. Born 18/9/42. Commd 1/11/63. Flt Lt 4/5/72. Retd OPS SPT 18/9/97.
HENRY P. G. BEng. Born 15/11/59. Commd 2/9/84. Flt Lt 23/6/87. Retd ENG 13/11/97.
HERON S. W. Born 5/1/60. Commd 1/7/82. Sqn Ldr 1/7/91. Retd ENG 5/1/98.
HILDAGE A. R. MIMgt. Born 31/12/52. Commd 8/9/83. Wg Cdr 1/7/96. Retd ADMIN 1/5/98.
HILL B. H. Born 30/6/42. Commd 12/4/73. Wg Cdr 1/1/92. Retd GD 30/6/97.
HILL D. Born 15/7/45. Commd 2/6/67. Sqn Ldr 1/1/80. Retd GD 1/6/98.
HIRST C. W. Born 24/6/52. Commd 27/1/77. Flt Lt 7/12/80. Retd OPS SPT 1/10/97.
HOAR R. J. Born 2/7/42. Commd 2/6/67. Sqn Ldr 1/1/88. Retd GD 2/7/97.
HOLLETT R. A. F. Born 31/12/42. Commd 4/11/82. Sqn Ldr 1/1/92. Retd ENG 31/12/97.
HORLOCK R. E. BA. Born 24/10/57. Commd 18/10/81. Sqn Ldr 1/1/90. Retd ENG 18/10/97.
HORSHAM-BATLEY D. J. W. BTech. Born 18/5/58. Commd 29/3/90. Flt Lt 29/3/92. Retd
    MED(SEC) 29/3/98.
HORSTED K. T. Born 26/5/59. Commd 22/6/89. Flt Lt 22/6/91. Retd ENG 22/6/97.
HOSKINS P. J. BA MIL. Born 6/2/48. Commd 28/2/69. Gp Capt 1/7/91. Retd GD 1/5/98.
HOULBROOK L. Born 3/3/60. Commd 19/11/87. Flt Lt 19/11/89. Retd OPS SPT 3/3/98.
HOURSTON D. I. Born 14/12/59. Commd 5/4/79. Sqn Ldr 1/1/92. Retd SUP 14/12/97.
HOWE I. MCG. G. Born 11/5/57. Commd 5/8/76. Wg Cdr 1/7/94. Retd GD 1/12/97.
HUGHES B. M. Born 7/3/64. Commd 18/11/90. Flt Lt 25/1/93. Retd GD 21/4/98.
HUGHES D. N. Born 4/8/59. Commd 11/6/81. Flt Lt 11/12/87. Retd OPS SPT 4/8/97.
HUGHES S. D. Born 4/10/59. Commd 15/10/81. Sqn Ldr 1/7/93. Retd GD 4/10/97.
HUMPHREYS G. A. BSc. Born 17/7/58. Commd 11/9/77. Sqn Ldr 1/7/89. Retd GD 1/12/97.
HUNT N. B. BSc. Born 1/8/59. Commd 11/9/77. Sqn Ldr 1/1/95. Retd GD 1/1/98.
HURRELL D. A. CB AFC. Born 29/04/43. Commd 2/12/63. AVM 1/7/95. Retd GD 29/4/98.
HUTCHINS P. F. W. CEng MIEE. Born 14/6/42. Commd 15/6/65. Wg Cdr 1/7/88. Retd ENG
    14/6/97.
HUTCHINS T. J. BA. Born 14/12/53. Commd 24/7/81. Sqn Ldr 1/7/90. Retd OPS SPT 14/12/97.

HUTCHINSON J. C. Born 24/12/58. Commd 11/4/82. Flt Lt 11/4/87. Retd ENG 11/4/98.
HUTCHISON P. D. J. BSc. Born 8/3/63. Commd 13/9/81. Flt Lt 15/10/85. Retd GD 15/7/97.
HYGATE J. P. Born 3/1/43. Commd 3/11/77. Flt Lt 3/11/79. Retd ENG 3/1/98.

IZZARD P. W. MBE. Born 10/11/42. Commd 4/10/63. Wg Cdr 1/1/94. Retd GD 10/11/97.

JACKSON D. H. BSc. Born 3/11/42. Commd 6/8/63. Wg Cdr 1/1/94. Retd GD 3/11/97.
JAMES M. F. C. MBE MSc BSc CEng MRAeS. Born 20/4/46. Commd 7/1/71. Wg Cdr 1/7/89. Retd ENG 25/8/97.
JARDINE J. A. BA. Born 20/9/44. Commd 27/2/75. Flt Lt 27/2/77. Retd GD(G) 27/2/83. Re-entered 30/4/90. Flt Lt 30/4/86. Retd OPS SPT 22/5/98.
JENSEN F. D. MSc BSc CEng MIEE. Born 21/10/49. Commd 24/9/72. Wg Cdr 1/7/91. Retd ENG 1/10/97.
JOCELYN M. A. BSc. Born 12/9/53. Commd 3/9/72. Wg Cdr 1/7/91. Retd GD 12/9/97.
JONES D. C. Born 28/5/60. Commd 24/7/81. Sqn Ldr 1/1/94. Retd GD 28/5/98.
JONES E. G. BSc MB ChB. Born 2/2/53. Commd 30/8/78. Wg Cdr 1/7/93. Retd GD 30/8/97.
JONES P. F. P. BSc. Born 17/3/48. Commd 11/8/74. Sqn Ldr 1/7/86. Retd GD 13/4/98.
JONES P. K. BEng. Born 9/10/61. Commd 20/1/85. Flt Lt 20/7/87. Retd GD 30/9/97.
JONES T. R. Born 16/5/39. Commd 20/1/69. Gp Capt 1/1/87. Retd LGL 3/11/97.
JONES W. C. MBE. Born 3/7/48. Commd 16/6/92. Flt Lt 16/6/94. Retd ADMIN 1/9/97.
JOOSSE C. A. Born 2/1/44. Commd 11/1/79. Sqn Ldr 1/7/89. Retd ENG 2/12/97.

KEELING T. W. Born 16/1/45. Commd 13/9/70. Sqn Ldr 1/7/84. Retd ENG 9/6/97.
KENDRICK K. R. IEng. Born 4/12/42. Commd 9/2/66. Sqn Ldr 1/7/79. Retd ENG 4/7/97.
KENNEDY C. G. MSc MB BS MRCGP DRCOG DAvMed. Born 8/6/54. Commd 20/8/78. Wg Cdr 20/8/91. Retd MED 31/7/97.
KENNELL J. M. MSc. Born 11/11/42. Commd 26/11/60. Gp Capt 1/7/93. Retd GD 11/5/98.
KENT K. J. Born 26/9/42. Commd 31/7/86. Flt Lt 31/7/90. Retd OPS SPT 26/9/97.
KILLINGRAY A. J. Born 24/5/44. Commd 3/7/80. Sqn Ldr 1/1/90. Retd ENG 19/11/97.
KING J. G. Born 30/8/42. Commd 22/7/71. Sqn Ldr 1/7/80. Retd ENG 7/6/97.
KING W. F. Born 18/1/43. Commd 21/2/74. Sqn Ldr 1/1/87. Retd ADMIN 18/1/98.
KINGS A. F. BSc. Born 2/7/59. Commd 3/9/79. Sqn Ldr 1/1/91. Retd ENG 2/7/97.
KIRKPATRICK W. J. BA. Born 10/8/53. Commd 19/10/75. Wg Cdr 1/7/91. Retd GD 1/2/98.
KNILL T. S. MSc BSc(Eng). Born 30/1/60. Commd 4/9/78. Sqn Ldr 1/7/91. Retd ENG 30/1/98.
KYLE R. H. CB MBE BSc(Eng) CEng FRAeS. Born 4/1/43. Commd 30/9/61. AVM 1/1/92. Retd ENG 8/9/97.

LAITE B. C. Born 8/6/44. Commd 19/4/63. Air Cdre 1/1/94. Retd GD 4/6/98.
LAKER J. G. S. MIMgt. Born 25/5/48. Commd 8/11/68. Sqn Ldr 1/1/87. Retd OPS SPT 25/5/98.
LAMBERT The Rev I. A. MTh BA. Born 9/12/43. Commd 5/11/75. Retd 10/2/98. Retd WG CDR.
LANE R. W. Born 28/1/44. Commd 11/8/77. Sqn Ldr 1/1/85. Retd ENG 15/8/97.
LANGLEY M. J. Born 15/2/44. Commd 9/3/62. Wg Cdr 1/1/85. Retd GD 2/3/98.
LARBEY J. P. S. Born 10/10/42. Commd 7/5/64. Flt Lt 4/11/70. Retd OPS SPT 10/10/97.
LAW S. A. T. BA MB ChB MRCGP DA DAvMed. Born 21/12/53. Commd 14/8/83. Wg Cdr 14/8/92. Retd MED 15/12/97.
LEE G. A. CEng MIEE MRAeS MIMgt. Born 20/9/43. Commd 15/7/64. Sqn Ldr 1/7/77. Retd ENG 2/12/97.
LEE R. K. CEng MIMechE. Born 25/10/45. Commd 7/3/71. Flt Lt 7/8/74. Retd ENG 29/5/98.
LEONARD A. OBE BEM. Born 15/3/42. Commd 14/8/80. Wg Cdr 1/7/93. Retd ENG 3/1/98.
LEWINS D. M. Born 10/8/59. Commd 12/7/79. Sqn Ldr 1/7/91. Retd GD 10/8/97.
LEWIS D. H. Born 6/5/51. Commd 24/1/74. Sqn Ldr 1/1/89. Retd GD 1/10/97.
LILLEY E. C. J. MHCIMA. Born 19/1/55. Commd 8/4/82. Sqn Ldr 1/7/93. Retd ADMIN 1/6/98.
LIVERMORE N. K. BA. Born 7/1/57. Commd 20/3/80. Flt Lt 2/6/81. Retd GD 1/10/97.

LIVESEY N. J. BSc. Born 2/12/58. Commd 18/10/81. Flt Lt 18/7/82. Retd GD 18/10/97.
LOGAN S. T. BSc. Born 17/3/44. Commd 30/8/66. Flt Lt 30/5/68. Retd GD 2/12/97.
LOOSELEY K. D. Born 18/12/46. Commd 14/7/66. Flt Lt 8/3/72. Retd GD 10/1/98.
LUCKHURST T. E. MBE. Born 17/7/42. Commd 3/11/77. Sqn Ldr 1/1/85. Retd ENG 16/7/97.
LUXTON J. D. BEM. Born 14/9/43. Commd 8/9/77. Sqn Ldr 1/1/86. Retd ENG 14/9/97.
LYNN-MACRAE A. H. Born 27/1/43. Commd 30/8/62. Sqn Ldr 1/1/79. Retd OPS SPT 27/1/98.

MACDONALD I. A. Born 25/3/60. Commd 11/1/79. Sqn Ldr 1/7/91. Retd GD 25/3/98.
MACEVOY R. I. Born 17/11/43. Commd 2/8/68. Wg Cdr 1/7/94. Retd OPS SPT 1/1/98.
MACKINLAY G. CEng MIEE. Born 10/12/42. Commd 15/7/65. Wg Cdr 1/7/80. Retd ENG
    10/12/97.
MACKINNON N. J. Born 10/2/43. Commd 26/11/81. Flt Lt 26/11/85. Retd OPS SPT 10/2/98.
MACRAE A. Born 9/5/60. Commd 17/7/87. Flt Lt 21/11/89. Retd ENG 9/5/98.
MACRAE J. R. A. BSc. Born 7/7/57. Commd 12/8/79. Sqn Ldr 1/1/91. Retd GD 7/4/98.
MANDER R. M. J. Born 15/11/46. Commd 1/11/79. Flt Lt 21/12/81. Retd ENG 16/6/97.
MARKEY P. D. OBE MSc BA FCIPS FILog FIMgt. Born 28/3/43. Commd 17/12/64. AVM 1/7/95.
    Retd SUP 28/8/97.
MARSH N. Born 18/7/47. Commd 28/4/67. Sqn Ldr 1/7/83. Retd ENG 18/7/97.
MARSHALL J. C. W. Born 20/8/42. Commd 29/11/63. Wg Cdr 1/1/97. Retd GD 20/8/97.
MARSHALL R. A. Born 23/6/43. Commd 3/10/69. Sqn Ldr 1/1/93. Retd GD 22/10/97.
MASSEY R. G. MIMgt. Born 10/12/42. Commd 22/7/71. Sqn Ldr 1/7/80. Retd ADMIN 10/12/97.
MATHIESON D. Born 12/12/59. Commd 14/8/80. Flt Lt 14/2/86. Retd GD 12/12/97.
MATTHEWS S. I. Born 3/8/46. Commd 29/11/68. Sqn Ldr 1/1/95. Retd GD 31/5/98.
MAYNARD G. J. D. CBE. Born 30/6/42. Commd 17/12/63. A Cdre 1/7/90. Retd SUP 30/6/97.
MCBRIEN T. Born 27/4/53. Commd 8/12/83. Flt Lt 8/12/85. Retd ENG 8/12/97.
MCCLYMONT D. BSc. Born 5/7/59. Commd 26/7/81. Sqn Ldr 1/1/92. Retd GD 26/7/97.
MCCORD A. W. IEng. Born 18/7/39. Commd 3/11/77. Sqn Ldr 1/7/87. Retd ENG 18/7/97.
MCDONALD-GIBSON J. H. Born 25/5/49. Commd 20/5/82. Flt Lt 20/11/88. Retd OPS SPT
    18/1/98.
MCGETTIGAN F. H. P. Born 23/8/42. Commd 19/7/84. Sqn Ldr 1/1/92. Retd SUP 23/8/97.
MCKEOWN J. D. P. Born 22/9/51. Commd 4/5/72. Flt Lt 12/4/77. Retd OPS SPT 1/1/98.
MCKINLAY K. P. MB BS MRCP MRCS LRCP. Born 17/6/57. Commd 28/5/86. Wg Cdr 4/8/94.
    Retd MED 15/10/97.
MCLAUGHLIN S. AFC BSc. Born 1/12/59. Commd 9/11/78. Flt Lt 15/4/81. Retd GD 1/12/97.
MCNEE I. R. MBE. Born 25/6/42. Commd 9/12/76. Sqn Ldr 1/1/85. Retd ENG 25/6/97.
MEDCALF D. Born 30/5/58. Commd 10/5/90. Flt Lt 10/5/92. Retd ADMIN 10/5/98.
MERRILL M. Born 6/8/59. Commd 22/2/79. Flt Lt 22/8/84. Retd GD 6/8/97.
MILLAR P. CB FRAeS MInstD. Born 20/06/42. Commd 30/7/63. AVM 1/1/95. Retd GD 31/5/98.
MILLER R. Born 23/3/42. Commd 15/3/84. Sqn Ldr 1/7/94. Retd ADMIN 1/7/97.
MILLINGTON N. D. MCs BChD BDS MGDSRCS(Eng). Born 22/6/58. Commd 1/2/81. Flt Lt
    10/12/81. Retd DEL 10/12/86. Re-entered 11/12/87. Wg Cdr 17/12/94. Retd DEL 10/2/98.
MINSHULL J. S. Born 24/12/54. Commd 26/9/91. Flt Lt 26/9/95. Retd ENG 20/4/98.
MITCHELL P. MBE. Born 8/9/42. Commd 4/7/69. Wg Cdr 1/7/92. Retd ENG 8/7/97.
MONCASTER C. J. BSc. Born 8/4/54. Commd 17/9/72. Wg Cdr 1/1/94. Retd GD 8/4/98.
MOORE R. C. Born 13/12/42. Commd 30/7/63. Wg Cdr 1/1/87. Retd GD 13/12/97.
MORGAN G. I. BSc CEng MIProdE. Born 26/11/54. Commd 17/1/82. Sqn Ldr 1/1/91. Retd
    ENG 17/1/98.
MORRIS A. G. BSc CEng MIEE. Born 7/4/55. Commd 16/9/73. Sqn Ldr 1/1/91. Retd ENG
    17/5/98.
MORRIS S. J. BA. Born 10/12/51. Commd 25/9/71. Gp Capt 1/7/95. Retd ADMIN
    3/12/97.
MOULE D. E. DFC. Born 28/12/56. Commd 6/11/80. Sqn Ldr 1/7/89. Retd GD 7/7/97.
MOULTON J. E. Born 22/3/43. Commd 14/6/63. Wg Cdr 1/1/85. Retd SUP 22/3/98.

MULDOWNEY A. J. Born 8/2/60. Commd 23/4/87. Flt Lt 23/4/89. Retd ENG 8/2/98.
MULHALL T. A. Born 29/9/51. Commd 15/8/85. Sqn Ldr 1/7/95. Retd ENG 22/1/98.
MURTAGH M. L. BA. Born 12/2/53. Commd 18/10/81. Flt Lt 18/1/85. Retd ADMIN 18/10/97.

NAPIER M. J. W. BSc(Eng). Born 20/9/59. Commd 4/9/78. Sqn Ldr 1/1/92. Retd GD 20/9/97.
NEWMAN R. A. Born 20/10/42. Commd 21/7/65. Sqn Ldr 1/7/90. Retd GD 20/10/97.
NEWTON R. J. BSc(Eng). Born 24/7/45. Commd 26/9/66. Flt Lt 24/1/68. Retd GD 25/10/97.
NICHOL C. R. Born 13/5/60. Commd 11/1/79. Flt Lt 11/7/84. Retd GD 13/5/98.
NOBLE K. G. BSc. Born 15/6/59. Commd 17/8/80. Sqn Ldr 1/7/92. Retd GD 15/6/97.
NORGAN K. A. BSc. Born 25/11/42. Commd 12/1/62. Flt Lt 12/7/67. Retd GD 6/5/72. Re-entered 6/9/76. Sqn Ldr 1/7/87. Retd ENG 25/11/97.
NORTH D. E. Born 2/12/44. Commd 15/7/66. Gp Capt 1/1/91. Retd GD 1/9/97.
NORTHEY H. MVO. Born 27/11/46. Commd 2/8/68. Wg Cdr 1/1/92. Retd GD 2/5/98.
NUTTALL J. A. Born 10/9/54. Commd 20/9/79. Sqn Ldr 1/1/92. Retd GD 1/10/97.

OLIVER M. S. MSc BSc. Born 4/8/47. Commd 18/9/66. Gp Capt 1/1/91. Retd SUP 7/10/97.
ONLEY M. J BSc. Born 12/5/59. Commd 17/1/82. Sqn Ldr 1/1/92. Retd GD 17/1/98.
ORR J. S. Born 1/1/43. Commd 1/4/76. Sqn Ldr 1/1/92. Retd GD 1/2/98.
OSWALD T. J. Born 11/2/43. Commd 20/8/65. Sqn Ldr 1/7/88. Retd GD 11/2/98.
OSZCZYK M. S. BSc CertEd. Born 8/4/55. Commd 6/9/81. Flt Lt 6/9/82. Retd ADMIN 6/9/97.
OTRIDGE D. Born 5/4/43. Commd 10/6/66. Flt Lt. Retd GD 5/4/98.
OVENDEN D. A. RVM IEng FIEIE MIMgt. Born 7/9/43. Commd 14/8/80. Sqn Ldr 1/7/89. Retd ENG 25/10/97.
OWEN P. C. Born 9/11/57. Commd 8/12/83. Sqn Ldr 1/1/93. Retd ADMIN 2/12/97.
OXBORROW M. D. Born 30/5/52. Commd 11/1/79. Flt Lt 21/2/83. Retd GD 20/12/97.

PAISEY M. A. C. BA. Born 6/8/64. Commd 5/9/82. Flt Lt 15/10/86. Retd GD 15/7/97.
PARKER R. Born 26/1/43. Commd 24/3/61. Wg Cdr 1/7/87. Retd GD 26/1/98.
PARSLEY R. R. C. OBE. Born 22/3/43. Commd 17/12/65. Wg Cdr 1/7/84. Retd GD 22/3/98.
PARSONS C. J. MIMgt. Born 6/2/45. Commd 6/5/65. Wg Cdr 1/1/88. Retd ADMIN 24/1/98.
PARSONS G. C. MSc BSc ARCS. Born 20/8/42. Commd 28/9/80. Sqn Ldr 1/1/88. Retd ADMIN 20/8/97.
PATTERSON J. R. CEng MIEE. Born 30/6/43. Commd 18/7/63. Wg Cdr 1/1/88. Retd ENG 18/7/97.
PEARCE R. S. Born 1/6/60. Commd 4/9/81. Sqn Ldr 1/7/93. Retd GD 1/6/98.
PEARSON M. L. MEng. Born 18/12/70. Commd 14/12/89. Fg Offr 15/1/92. Retd ENG 5/8/97.
PENNY S. D. BA BSc CEng MBCS MIEE MRAeS. Born 3/1/58. Commd 19/9/76. Wg Cdr 1/7/94. Retd ENG 1/7/97.
PENTON-VOAK M. J. Born 15/1/43. Commd 8/6/62. Wg Cdr 1/1/91. Retd GD 15/1/98.
PERKINS N. J. Born 18/1/60. Commd 22/2/79. Flt Lt 22/8/85. Retd GD(G) 22/8/87. Re-entered 19/4/91. Flt Lt 17/10/86. Retd OPS SPT 1/10/97.
PETRE B. Born 26/10/46. Commd 4/7/85. Flt Lt 4/7/89. Retd ENG 6/12/97.
PHILIP R. J. Born 21/9/42. Commd 28/2/85. Sqn Ldr 1/7/93. Retd ADMIN 21/9/97.
PHILLIPS G. T. BSc. Born 9/10/45. Commd 25/7/71. Sqn Ldr 1/7/84. Retd ADMIN 1/2/98.
PHILLIPS G. W. BSc. Born 1/2/52. Commd 2/9/84. Sqn Ldr 1/1/93. Retd GD 1/10/97.
PHILLIPS J. J. Born 1/5/43. Commd 15/10/81. Flt Lt 15/10/86. Retd ENG 1/2/98.
PHILLIPS S. A. Born 12/3/60. Commd 11/1/79. Sqn Ldr 1/1/91. Retd GD 12/3/98.
PLANT M. E. Born 20/6/42. Commd 14/8/70. Flt Lt 14/8/72. Retd GD 20/6/97.
PLUMMER R. A. MCIPS. Born 9/7/42. Commd 29/3/68. Gp Capt 1/7/90. Retd SUP 9/7/97.
POOK J. J. MBE DFC. Born 20/4/45. Commd 15/7/66. Sqn Ldr 1/1/79. Retd GD 15/6/97.
POOLE D. R. BSc. Born 17/5/60. Commd 6/9/81. Sqn Ldr 1/7/91. Retd GD 17/5/98.
POPPLE J. R. Born 23/11/56. Commd 25/11/82. Sqn Ldr 1/7/92. Retd SUP 19/12/97.
POWELL L. G. Born 2/5/54. Commd 17/9/72. Sqn Ldr 1/7/91. Retd ENG 2/5/98.

PRIDDLE A. L. BSc. Born 29/12/58. Commd 6/9/81. Flt Lt 6/12/81. Retd GD 6/9/97.
PRINCE M. J. Born 11/5/60. Commd 15/12/88. Flt Lt 15/12/90. Retd ENG 11/5/98.
PRIOR A. R. J. MBE BSc MB BS. Born 3/11/52. Commd 19/11/74. Wg Cdr 1/8/92. Retd MED 2/4/98.
PRITCHARD M. MIMgt. Born 25/4/44. Commd 31/10/63. Sqn Ldr 1/7/74. Retd ADMIN 3/10/97.

RAGG W. L. Born 2/5/42. Commd 15/3/79. Sqn Ldr 1/1/89. Retd GD 2/11/97.
RALPH A. BSc. Born 21/5/59. Commd 29/11/81. Flt Lt 28/2/83. Retd GD 29/11/97.
RAMSEY S. Born 27/9/59. Commd 15/6/83. Sqn Ldr 1/1/92. Retd ENG 8/2/98.
RANCE F. S. Born 2/6/43. Commd 6/4/62. Gp Capt 1/7/90. Retd GD 2/6/98.
RANDS J. E. OBE. Born 23/11/59. Commd 5/4/79. Sqn Ldr 1/1/91. Retd GD 23/11/97.
RAYFIELD G. BA CIMS FMS FInstAM MIMgt. Born 25/3/43. Commd 24/6/65. Wg Cdr 1/1/93. Retd GD 20/12/97.
REDMORE M. A. Born 22/6/42. Commd 11/5/62. Sqn Ldr 1/7/74. Retd GD 22/6/97.
REEVE R. J. Born 18/12/47. Commd 1/3/68. Sqn Ldr 1/7/80. Retd GD 26/5/98.
REID D. C. MRAeS. Born 20/4/43. Commd 22/2/63. Wg Cdr 1/1/90. Retd GD 20/4/98.
REID D. E. MACD. BSc. Born 8/2/59. Commd 9/11/80. Sqn Ldr 1/7/92. Retd GD 29/7/97.
RELF B. R. F. DipEurHum AIPM. Born 23/12/42. Commd 18/8/61. Sqn Ldr 1/1/81. Retd OPS SPT 23/12/97.
RENSHAW S. J. Born 22/4/51. Commd 26/11/81. Flt Lt 26/5/88. Retd OPS SPT 27/7/97.
RICE V. J. BA IEng. Born 7/6/42. Commd 3/7/80. Sqn Ldr 1/7/88. Retd ENG 7/6/97.
RICHARDSON B. T. MBE. Born 24/2/51. Commd 23/4/87. Sqn Ldr 1/1/97. Retd ADMIN 21/4/98.
ROBB B. S. Born 11/12/56. Commd 2/2/84. Flt Lt 14/3/86. Retd GD 1/6/98.
ROBERTS D. BEng. Born 1/3/58. Commd 18/11/79. Flt Lt 18/2/81. Retd GD 1/10/97.
ROBERTSON G. Born 23/7/43. Commd 28/2/85. Sqn Ldr 1/7/94. Retd ENG 24/10/97.
ROBINSON M. L. R. MA. Born 27/6/59. Commd 4/9/78. Flt Lt 15/10/82. Retd GD 27/6/97.
ROBINSON P. N. Born 15/4/45. Commd 11/11/65. Wg Cdr 1/7/88. Retd ENG 14/4/98.
ROCHE T. J. BA. Born 30/3/60. Commd 4/8/78. Sqn Ldr 1/7/91. Retd GD 30/3/98.
ROGERS N. C. Born 14/11/58. Commd 18/10/81. Sqn Ldr 1/1/94. Retd GD 18/10/97.
ROOUM J. E. CBE AFC. Born 14/10/42. Commd 23/12/60. A Cdr 1/7/91. Retd GD 11/11/97.
ROSCOE C. W. Born 21/5/51. Commd 22/6/89. Flt Lt 22/6/91. Retd ADMIN 22/6/97.
ROSE J. OBE MIISec. Born 15/9/45. Commd 21/10/66. Gp Capt 1/7/91. Retd ADMIN 20/7/97.
ROSS D. FInstAM MIPD. Born 30/9/42. Commd 5/1/78. Sqn Ldr 1/7/89. Retd ADMIN 12/7/97.
RUDD M. C. AFC. Born 12/5/49. Commd 1/4/69. A Cdre 1/7/95. Retd GD 3/12/97.
RYCROFT D. H. CEng MIEE. Born 11/12/42. Commd 6/1/69. Flt Lt 4/5/72. Retd ENG 11/12/97.

SALTER R. M. Born 19/12/45. Commd 30/4/81. Flt Lt 30/4/85. Retd ENG 22/9/97.
SAUNDERS D. J. CBE MSc BSc CEng FIMechE FRAeS. Born 12/6/43. Commd 15/7/64. AVM 1/7/91. Retd ENG 1/9/97.
SCHOLEFIELD J. N. MIMgt. Born 28/12/47. Commd 16/9/76. Wg Cdr 1/7/91. Retd ADMIN 1/5/98.
SEARLE P. E. Born 6/4/43. Commd 4/3/71. Sqn Ldr 1/7/79. Retd SUP 6/4/98.
SEATON D. J. MBE. Born 8/8/45. Commd 7/6/68. Sqn Ldr 1/7/81. Retd ENG 8/6/97.
SELBY-DAVIES R. BA. Born 9/9/42. Commd 13/6/71. Flt Lt 13/3/75. Retd OPS SPT 9/9/97.
SENIOR S. E. MBE. Born 18/4/60. Commd 13/8/82. Sqn Ldr 1/7/93. Retd ADMIN 12/4/98.
SHACKLEY G. J. MSc BSc CEng MIEE. Born 9/4/45. Commd 6/9/81. Sqn Ldr 1/1/90. Retd ENG 6/9/97.
SHARP J. A. H. Born 25/8/52. Commd 19/3/78. Wg Cdr 1/1/96. Retd ENG 1/5/98.
SHARPE D. I. Born 20/4/58. Commd 29/11/81. Sqn Ldr 1/1/90. Retd ENG 29/11/97.
SHERRINGTON T. B. CB OBE FIMgt MHCIMA. Born 30/9/42. Commd 12/9/63. AVM 1/1/92. Retd ADMIN 30/9/97.
SHUSTER R. C. AFC. Born 2/9/44. Commd 15/7/66. Flt Lt 15/1/69. Retd GD 26/9/97.
SILLS C. J. Born 18/5/38. Commd 5/2/57. Sqn Ldr 1/1/80. Retd GD 18/5/98.

SIMPSON A. Born 28/4/46. Commd 4/1/68. Flt Lt 1/12/75. Retd OPS SPT 1/6/98.
SINCLAIR R. E. Born 8/12/45. Commd 2/4/65. Sqn Ldr 1/1/89. Retd GD 1/6/98.
SKILLICORN B. W. AFC. Born 16/2/43. Commd 7/12/64. Flt Lt 12/11/69. Retd GD 15/2/98.
SLATER T. G. Born 13/10/59. Commd 21/12/89. Flt Lt 21/12/91. Retd OPS SPT 21/12/97.
SMART M. D. BA FIPD. Born 18/3/42. Commd 15/12/60. AVM 1/9/96. Retd ADMIN 25/4/98.
SMITH B. I. Born 17/8/59. Commd 5/1/78. Sqn Ldr 1/7/90. Retd GD 17/8/97.
SMITH G. D. Born 31/7/41. Commd 8/12/83. Sqn Ldr 1/7/94. Retd ENG 1/7/97.
SMITH G. M. Born 14/5/46. Commd 25/2/82. Sqn Ldr 1/7/91. Retd SUP 6/4/98.
SMITH J. Born 24/9/41. Commd 11/8/67. Sqn Ldr 1/7/76. Retd ADMIN 3/4/82. Re-entered
    5/11/90. Sqn Ldr 2/2/85. Retd ADMIN 5/6/98.
SMITH J. A. Born 9/12/42. Commd 27/10/67. Sqn Ldr 1/1/85. Retd OPS SPT 12/6/97.
SMITH J. M. Born 6/11/71. Commd 5/10/95. Plt Offr 5/10/96. Retd GD 26/7/97.
SMITH R. H. FIMgt psc. Born 11/7/42. Commd 26/5/61. Gp Capt 1/1/88. Retd ADMIN 11/7/97.
SMITH S. C. Born 7/9/52. Commd 30/8/73. Sqn Ldr 1/1/88. Retd GD 1/10/97.
SMULOVIC P. S. V. BSc. Born 22/11/46. Commd 15/6/83. Sqn Ldr 1/7/95. Retd ENG 24/1/98.
SPEAR C. W. P. Born 27/4/43. Commd 15/7/64. Wg Cdr 1/7/89. Retd ENG 27/4/98.
SQUIRES S. B. Born 27/5/59. Commd 28/7/88. Flt Lt 28/7/90. Retd ADMIN 27/5/98.
STAFFERTON P. MIPD AIIP. Born 2/12/42. Commd 24/6/67. Sqn Ldr 1/7/82. Retd ENG 2/12/97.
STEELE J. Born 22/10/42. Commd 11/4/85. Flt Lt 11/4/89. Retd ENG 22/10/97.
STEER M. J. FIPD FIMgt. Born 21/5/47. Commd 10/7/90. Gp Capt 1/1/90. Retd ADMIN 2/12/97.
STENSON R. BA. Born 20/1/46. Commd 20/8/65. Flt Lt 20/2/71. Retd OPS SPT 18/5/98.
STEPHENS M. J. Born 6/10/59. Commd 24/3/83. Flt Lt 19/1/89. Retd OPS SPT 18/5/98.
STEWART A. W. J. Born 19/5/51. Commd 25/2/72. Wg Cdr 1/1/93. Retd GD 6/4/98.
STEWART I. G. Born 1/3/47. Commd 4/11/82. Sqn Ldr 1/7/94. Retd ENG 13/7/97.
STRAW D. P. E. Born 6/9/42. Commd 11/5/62. Wg Cdr 1/7/88. Retd GD 6/9/97.
STRETEN M. W. BSc. Born 12/2/43. Commd 22/9/63. Wg Cdr 1/1/82. Retd GD 12/2/98.
STRICKLAND D. Born 21/5/51. Commd 25/8/71. Wg Cdr 1/7/91. Retd ADMIN 31/5/98.
SUMNER A. W. Born 7/12/47. Commd 17/2/67. Wg Cdr 1/7/91. Retd GD 1/7/97.
SUMNER D. G. Born 22/2/54. Commd 15/10/81. Flt Lt 15/10/83. Retd OPS SPT 22/2/98.
SWETMAN K. M. TD. Born 9/5/44. Commd 13/4/86. Flt Lt 13/12/87. Retd ADMIN 13/4/98.
SYMES D. B. Born 2/12/45. Commd 28/4/67. Gp Capt 1/7/91. Retd GD 2/4/98.
SYMMANS T. Born 29/4/48. Commd 25/4/69. Plt Offr 29/4/69. Retd GD 19/8/70. Re-entered
    1/11/81. Flt Lt 1/11/87. Retd OPS SPT 1/11/97.
SYMONDS J. B. MIPD. Born 18/6/42. Commd 21/10/65. A Cdre 1/1/94. Retd ADMIN 18/6/97.

TAME P. H. Born 10/1/43. Commd 22/2/63. Sqn Ldr 1/1/77. Retd GD 8/6/97.
TAYLOR G. T. Born 6/3/43. Commd 15/7/66. Sqn Ldr 1/1/97. Retd GD 30/10/97.
TAYLOR M. J. BSc. Born 9/4/54. Commd 3/9/72. Sqn Ldr 1/1/91. Retd GD 9/4/98.
TEAGER J. F. N. Born 21/3/58. Commd 21/4/77. Wg Cdr 1/7/94. Retd GD 1/1/98.
THOMAS A. Born 9/3/44. Commd 25/9/80. Sqn Ldr 1/7/94. Retd SUP 7/1/98.
THOMAS M. R. MB BS FRCS(Edin). Born 24/11/55. Commd 22/2/81. Wg Cdr 8/8/93. Retd
    MED 21/7/97.
THOMAS R. J. M. Born 27/5/47. Commd 21/1/66. Sqn Ldr 1/7/93. Retd GD 27/5/98.
THORNHAM A. B. Born 9/7/59. Commd 18/12/80. Sqn Ldr 1/1/94. Retd ADMIN 9/7/97.
THROWER B. S. Born 2/6/46. Commd 28/8/75. Wg Cdr 1/7/91. Retd ENG 1/11/97.
TISBURY J. A. MBE MIMgt. Born 7/1/45. Commd 27/1/77. Sqn Ldr 1/7/85. Retd ADMIN 6/4/98.
TIWARI I. B. MB BS FRCS(Ed). Born 13/11/35. Commd 24/3/69. Gp Capt
    4/4/85. Retd MED 2/12/97.
TOMALIN A. M. Born 2/5/43. Commd 17/12/65. Sqn Ldr 1/1/79. Retd GD 2/5/98.
TOOGOOD W. R. Born 5/3/48. Commd 16/12/66. Sqn Ldr 1/1/91. Retd OPS SPT 1/5/98.
TOOTS R. I. Born 15/2/56. Commd 7/11/85. Flt Lt 7/5/92. Retd ADMIN 8/7/97.
TRUEMAN D. A. Born 7/9/42. Commd 20/11/75. Sqn Ldr 1/1/84. Retd GD 7/9/97.
TURNER S. BSc. Born 15/8/59. Commd 29/8/77. Sqn Ldr 1/7/93. Retd ENG 15/8/97.

TYACK G. E. MTech BSc CEng MIEE MBCS MIMgt. Born 23/12/40. Commd 10/9/63. Wg Cdr 1/7/79. Retd ENG 29/9/97.

VAN DER VEEN M. MA CEng FIEE. Born 22/1/46. Commd 28/9/64. AVM 1/1/96. Retd ENG 3/1/98.
VAUGHAN S. A. Born 12/10/56. Commd 22/11/84. Sqn Ldr 1/7/94. Retd ENG 1/7/97.
VEARNCOMBE M. G. Born 8/8/55. Commd 22/2/79. Wg Cdr 1/1/97. Retd ADMIN 1/2/98.
VENUS L. C. Born 22/7/58. Commd 19/10/81. Sqn Ldr 1/1/94. Retd ADMIN 19/10/97.

WAITE B. Born 22/10/47. Commd 9/2/81. Sqn Ldr 1/7/94. Retd ADMIN 1/7/97.
WALKER A. R. BSc. Born 10/11/59. Commd 5/1/86. Flt Lt 15/3/90. Retd ENG 10/11/97.
WALKER S. G. Born 11/7/58. Commd 13/8/82. Flt Lt 13/2/89. Retd OPS SPT 12/4/98.
WALL A. J. CEng MRAeS. Born 7/4/58. Commd 20/5/82. Sqn Ldr 1/1/91. Retd ENG 7/12/97.
WALSH P. Born 11/11/42. Commd 12/4/73. Flt Lt 12/4/75. Retd GD 10/11/97.
WARD J. C. W. BMet. Born 16/6/59. Commd 2/5/80. Flt Lt 15/4/83. Retd GD 16/6/97.
WATKIN G. Born 17/4/49. Commd 2/2/70. Wg Cdr 1/7/94. Retd OPS SPT 31/1/98.
WATSON P. R. Born 14/2/41. Commd 22/5/75. Wg Cdr 1/7/90. Retd ADMIN 14/2/98.
WATSON S. W. IEng MIEIE. Born 19/11/46. Commd 15/3/84. Sqn Ldr 1/7/97. Retd ENG 31/1/98.
WEAVER I. W. Born 31/1/60. Commd 6/6/89. Flt Lt 31/1/85. Retd GD 4/12/97.
WEBB E. A. H. FISM MInstAM MIMgt MIPD. Born 18/4/43. Commd 23/7/80. Sqn Ldr 1/7/88. Retd ADMIN 18/4/98.
WELLS J. MCIPS. Born 26/4/42. Commd 2/1/70. Wg Cdr 1/7/87. Retd SUP 1/9/97.
WENSLEY G. Born 2/8/42. Commd 4/10/63. Wg Cdr 1/1/84. Retd GD 2/8/97.
WESTON G. A. C. Born 10/10/55. Commd 27/3/80. Flt Lt 5/6/82. Retd GD 3/12/97.
WESTON J. R. BSc. Born 18/2/58. Commd 18/10/81. Flt Lt 18/7/82. Retd GD 18/10/97.
WHITE D. A. MB ChB FRCS FFARCS DRCOG. Born 7/12/48. Commd 14/3/82. Wg Cdr 14/3/88. Retd MED 14/3/98.
WHITE D. A. C. Born 28/8/42. Commd 31/10/69. Flt Lt 4/5/72. Retd OPS SPT 28/2/98.
WHITE R. J. BSc CEng MRAeS. Born 4/9/42. Commd 15/7/64. Sqn Ldr 1/7/76. Retd ENG 31/5/98.
WHITTINGHAM I. C. Born 26/10/58. Commd 2/2/84. Sqn Ldr 1/7/92. Retd ADMIN 1/7/97.
WHYTE W. L. Born 19/1/46. Commd 2/12/66. Wg Cdr 1/1/86. Retd GD 26/11/97.
WILKINSON A. T. B. MBE BA MIMIS MCIPS MRAeS. Born 19/4/43. Commd 30/1/70. Wg Cdr 1/1/96. Retd SUP 19/4/98.
WILKINSON R. E. LRAM ARCM. Born 28/1/42. Commd 9/12/76. Wg Cdr 1/7/95. Retd DM 1/6/98.
WILKS B. P. BEM MLitt. Born 21/12/42. Commd 20/5/82. Fl Lt 20/5/86. Retd ADMIN 21/12/97.
WILLIAMS B. Born 27/1/45. Commd 14/1/88. Flt Lt 14/1/92. Retd ADMIN 30/4/98.
WILLIAMS J. Born 6/12/46. Commd 1/11/81. Flt Lt 1/11/86. Retd ENG 1/11/97.
WILLIAMS K. L. D. Born 5/5/43. Commd 23/11/78. Sqn Ldr 1/7/89. Retd ADMIN 5/5/98.
WILLIAMS M. A. Born 16/12/59. Commd 22/2/79. Flt Lt 22/8/84. Retd GD 16/12/97.
WILLIAMS T. G. BSc. Born 4/6/60. Commd 4/9/78. Flt Lt 15/4/84. Retd GD 4/6/98.
WILLIAMSON C. R. Born 2/4/46. Commd 20/8/65. Wg Cdr 1/1/90. Retd GD 9/8/97.
WILLIAMSON-NOBLE S. M. D. MA MS CEng FRAeS. Born 18/5/43. Commd 30/9/62. A Cdre 1/1/93. Retd ENG 1/8/97.
WILLIS. GBE KCB. Born 27/10/37. Commd 29/7/58. ACM 4/4/95. Retd GD 10/1/98.
WILLMOTT R. A. Born 26/6/44. Commd 2/2/84. Flt Lt 2/2/88. Retd ADMIN 2/12/97.
WILSON B. G. R. Born 31/12/59. Commd 1/11/79. Flt Lt 1/5/85. Retd GD 31/12/97.
WILSON J. S. Born 21/6/47. Commd 2/8/68. Wg Cdr 1/7/90. Retd GD 20/5/98.
WINNING R. M. J. Born 14/3/43. Commd 17/3/67. Wg Cdr 1/7/87. Retd OPS SPT 14/3/98.
WINTERBOURNE S. J. Born 12/12/57. Commd 3/11/77. Sqn Ldr 1/7/90. Retd ADMIN 12/6/97.
WOLSEY A. K. Born 18/7/49. Commd 27/5/71. Sqn Ldr 1/7/85. Retd ADMIN 30/9/97.
WOOD M. H. MBE. Born 11/9/44. Commd 10/12/65. Wg Cdr 1/1/94. Retd GD 10/10/97.
WOOLLEY R. Born 26/5/56. Commd 7/11/91. Flt Lt 7/11/95. Retd MED(SEC). 15/10/97.

WRATTEN. KBE CB AFC CIMgt FRAeS. Born 15/8/39. Commd 13/12/60. ACM 1/9/94. Retd GD 5/11/97.
WREN R. J. Born 6/7/59. Commd 11/8/77. Sqn Ldr 1/7/93. Retd GD 8/5/98.
WRIGHT R. M. Born 14/7/39. Commd 11/5/62. Flt Lt 11/11/67. Retd GD 14/7/97.
WRIGHT T. B. BA. Born 10/2/43. Commd 22/7/71. Wg Cdr 1/1/86. Retd ENG 10/2/98.
WYATT A. V. Born 15/2/43. Commd 21/1/66. Sqn Ldr 1/1/92. Retd GD 15/2/98.
WYATT D. A. Born 3/2/61. Commd 31/1/80. Sqn Ldr 1/1/92. Retd GD 4/2/98.

YATES J. S. BA. Born 20/6/59. Commd 28/12/80. Flt Lt 28/6/84. Retd OPS SPT 20/6/97.
YOUNG A. M. BA. Born 22/5/59. Commd 4/9/78. Flt Lt 14/10/82. Retd GD 21/8/97.
YOUNG M. J. R. MA BA CertEd MIPD. Born 28/1/47. Commd 24/1/74. Flt Lt 8/6/80. Retd GD(G) 1/10/89. Re-entered 13/3/91. Flt Lt 18/11/81. Retd OPS SPT 1/6/98.
YOUNG T. B. BSc CEng MIEE. Born 20/10/59. Commd 6/9/81. Sqn Ldr 1/7/90. Retd ENG 20/10/97.

LIST OF RETIRED OFFICERS OF
THE PRINCESS MARY'S ROYAL AIR FORCE
NURSING SERVICE

HAND V. M. RRC Born 2/4/44. Commd 2/10/67. Flt Lt 2/10/69. Retd 2/10/71. Re-entered 10/7/72. A Cdr 1/7/95. Retd 1/7/97.

OBITUARY

RETIRED LIST

Retired Officers whose deaths have been reported since July 97

Rank and Name	Date of Death	Rank and Name	Date of Death
ABBOTT S. A. G. Flt Lt ...	11.4.98	BEDFORD T. J. Sqn Ldr... ...	12.7.97
ABELL J. B. Flt Lt	7.1.98	BELL H. O. Sqn Ldr	17.8.97
ADAMS J. Flt Lt	6.7.98	BENNETT A. O. W. Flt Lt ...	17.1.98
ADAMS N. FCA Gp Capt	20.5.98	BENNETT H. A. CEng MIMechE	
AINGER J. C. L. Sqn Ldr	12.3.98	Sqn Ldr	16.10.97
ALLAN J. Sqn Ldr	21.5.98	BENTLEY R. R. Flt Lt	26.10.97
ALLEN R. H. Flt Lt	25.2.98	BERNSTEIN T. Flt Lt	19.1.98
ALLEN R. H. Sqn Ldr	17.2.98	BERRYMAN J. D. Sqn Ldr ...	29.3.98
ALLEN-JONES M. A. Sqn Offr ...	24.2.98	BINDLOSS K. W. C. OBE Wg Cdr	26.3.98
ALLSOPP A. E. Sqn Ldr	27.11.97	BIRCHALL L. W. Sqn Ldr ...	2.6.98
ALLSWORTH M. W. Flt Lt	13.4.98	BIRD D. Le R. CEng MRAeS	
ANGUS C. F. Flt Lt	30.5.98	Wg Cdr	8.6.98
ANSTESS J. MSc CEng MRAeS		BIRD E. W. Flt Lt	21.1.98
MIMgt Wg Cdr	4.4.98	BIRD G. D. Flt Lt	8.5.98
APPLETON E. P. CBE Gp Capt ...	9.2.98	BISHOP H. F. Flt Lt	5.9.97
ARDEN B. DFC Wg Cdr	12.2.98	BLACKBURN J. G. Flt Lt ...	22.1.98
ARTHUR J. Fg Offr	10.2.98	BLACKMORE D. McK. DFC Sqn Ldr	9.1.98
ASHBY S. L. Flt Lt	4.1.98	BLANKS T. V. G. Flt Lt	31.3.98
ATKINSON G. B. MBE DFC Wg Cdr	16.9.97	BOARDMAN J. B. J. Gp Capt	19.1.98
ATKINSON P. D'A. Flt Lt	11.8.97	BOND G. R. W. Sqn Ldr ...	27.3.98
AVERY F. W. Wg Cdr	16.1.98	BONSER S. H. CB MBE BSc CEng	
AZZARO V. E. MBE DFC* Flt Lt	26.7.97	FRAeS AVM	12.11.97
BAILEY C. G. AFC Flt Lt	6.1.98	BORMAN V. R. D. Sqn Ldr ...	25.9.97
BAILEY H. C. Wg Cdr	13.6.98	BOULT N. De W. DFC AFC Cp Capt	5.2.98
BAILEY R. K. Sqn Ldr...	31.12.97	BOWDEN E. G. MBE Flt Lt ...	19.1.98
BAINES E. L. Sqn Ldr...	2.3.98	BOXALL F. G. Fg Offr	9.12.97
BAKER-CARR Sir John KBE CB		BOXER Sir Alan KCVO CB DSO	
AFC AM	9.7.98	DFC AVM	26.4.98
BALLARD D. A. W. Flt Lt	25.9.97	BRADBURY K. G. MBE BA MIMgt	
BARKER F. W. DFC Sqn Ldr ...	8.11.97	Sqn Ldr	9.5.98
BARRETT F. Sqn Ldr	3.2.98	BRADLEY L. J. Flt Lt	3.11.97
BARTLEY W. E. L. Flt Lt	7.3.98	BRADLEY O. P. Flt Lt	25.6.98
BATCHELOR H. M. Flt Lt	18.1.98	BRAIN F. T. OBE Wg Cdr ...	31.8.97
BATES E. K. G. Flt Lt	3.2.98	BRIDGER A. R. S. MIEE Sqn Ldr	2.1.98
BAX N. B. W. Sqn Ldr	28.12.97	BRIDLE P. J. Flt Lt	3.2.98
BAYLEY J. W. MBE CEng MRAeS		BROOKE L. Flt Lt	2.10.97
A Cdre	23.10.97	BROUGHTON Sir Charles KBE CB	
BAYLEY N. O. S. DFC Wg Cdr ...	20.6.98	AM	17.5.98
BAYLISS G. A. Sqn Ldr	26.10.97	BROWN G. A. DFC Gp Capt ...	20.2.98
BEACH G. A. Sqn Ldr...	20.11.97	BROWN G. C. Flt Lt	6.6.98
BECKETT S. L. Flt Lt	4.5.98	BROWN J. D. Flt Lt	8.1.98

Rank and Name	Date of Death	Rank and Name	Date of Death
BROWN W. A. Flt Lt	23.10.97	CROWDY R. L. Flt Lt	2.2.98
BRUCE C. M. Sqn Ldr	15.8.97	CROWE A. H. DFC* AFC Sqn Ldr	16.10.97
BURBERRY U. L. OBE Gp Capt...	25.12.97	CULLEN F. A. Flt Lt...	24.12.97
BURGESS T. E. Gp Capt	5.2.98	de BRETT R. J. H. Gp Capt ...	15.9.97
BURROUGH R. J. DFC Wg Cdr...	2.1.98	DAGGER A. CEng MIEE MIMgt	
BURWELL R. H. C. CBE DFC		Sqn Ldr	14.6.98
A Cdre	22.4.98	DALE G. DFC MIMgt Wg Cdr	29.7.98
BUTLER-DAVIS W. St.G. Flt Lt ...	6.11.97	DALEY J. W. A. Sqn Ldr ...	31.10.97
CADWALLADER H. G. CB FIMgt		DALLAS W. M. Sqn Ldr... ...	21.1.98
AVM...	13.6.98	DANIEL H. B. R. Flt Lt	25.12.97
CAHILL M. J. Flt Lt	13.9.97	DANIELS A. G. Flt Lt	8.1.98
CALLOW H. W. LDS Wg Cdr ...	19.7.98	DARBY P. W. J. Flt Lt	1.11.97
CALLOW R. C. BEM Flt Lt	9.12.97	DARK K. F. Sqn Ldr	6.6.98
CAMERON F. H. O. M. Sqn Ldr	30.1.98	DASTGIR G. CEng MIMechE Flt Lt	21.4.98
CAMPBELL E. D. MBE Sqn Ldr...	8.12.97	DAVIES J. C. Flt Lt	31.10.97
CANNIFORD W. H. CBE Gp Capt	15.1.98	DAVIES Sir Alan. KCB CBE AM	27.1.98
CARDWELL I. AFC Sqn Ldr ...	15.5.98	DAVIS G. D. Flt Lt	15.2.98
CARMICHAEL L. D. Flt Lt	9.2.98	DAWES D. C. MB ChB DavMed	
CASSELS R. K. CBE DFC AFC		LLB MIMgt Wg Cdr	9.11.97
Gp Capt	22.11.97	DAWSON V. A. Sqn Ldr ...	17.7.98
CASTELL M. F. MIMgt Flt Lt ...	29.3.98	DAY N. Flt Lt	20.4.98
CHALLIS C. R. A. DFC* Flt Lt ...	24.9.97	DEAKIN T. A. Flt Lt	3.6.98
CHAMBERLAIN A. P. BSc DIC		DELANEY C. G. J. Sqn Ldr ...	27.7.98
Gp Capt	27.6.98	DEVLIN B. E. Sqn Ldr	17.1.98
CHARLWOOD K. Sqn Ldr	14.7.98	DIMBERLINE R. CEng MIMEchE	
CHRISTIE F. J. Flt Lt	1.10.97	Sqn Ldr	24.2.98
CHRISTOPHER P. F. MBE DFC		DONOGHUE M. J. FLt Lt ...	11.6.98
Sqn Ldr	25.8.97	DORMER D. E. CEng FIEE MRAeS	
CLARKE G. D. C. Flt Lt	27.10.97	FIMgt Wg Cdr	1.12.97
COLDBECK H. G. DFC Sqn Ldr...	31.5.98	DOSSETT W. S. DFM Flt Lt ...	23.8.97
COLE R. J. AFC Sqn Ldr	18.8.97	DOUGLAS-BOYD J. D. MBE BA	
COLES M. A. BEM Flt Lt	20.6.98	MIMgt Wg Cdr	3.5.98
COLLIER S. C. W. MBE Sqn Ldr	17.6.98	DYSON C. H. MBE DFC* Wg Cdr	12.8.97
COLLINS R. G. AFC Sqn Ldr ...	23.12.97	EASTWOOD F. Flt Lt	22.6.98
CONAN-DOYLE Dame Jean. DBE		EATON G. R. H. Flt Lt	8.5.98
AE A Cdre	18.11.97	EDGE V. J. Sqn Ldr	31.8.97
CONNOLLY B. C. Sqn Ldr	30.9.97	EDRUPT B. C. R. Sqn Ldr ...	29.8.97
COONEY J. A. MB ChB Wg Cdr	30.8.97	EDWARDS J. D. BA Sqn Ldr	10.12.97
COOPER A. S. DFM Sqn Ldr ...	21.9.97	EDWARDS R. BSc Gp Capt ...	11.6.98
COOPER B. G. FIMgt Gp Capt ...	11.6.98	EDWARDS R. DSO Sqn Ldr ...	27.1.98
COOPER M. G. OBE Wg Cdr ...	18.6.98	EDWARDS W. S. Plt Offr ...	13.3.98
COOPER R. K. D. MBE Flt Lt ...	26.6.98	ELWORTHY R. E. Sqn Ldr ...	27.9.97
COOTE B. P. MC MIMgt Wg Cdr	5.11.97	EYNON W. H. Sqn Ldr	5.9.97
COOTE L. G. Flt Lt	1.12.97	FAIRHURST J. Flt Lt	29.4.98
COX F. R. DFC DFM Wg Cdr ...	22.4.98	FANTHORPE K. MBE Sqn Ldr	8.1.98
CRAWFORD W. BA Flt Lt	20.3.98	FARREN R. B. DFC Sqn Ldr ...	29.9.97
CRICHTON D. MBE MB ChB DPH		FEARN P. G. MVO Sqn Ldr ...	22.2.98
DIH A Cdre	24.1.98	FELDON F. K. Flt Lt...	4.11.97
CRISP H. I. B. Flt Lt	11.8.97	FENTON I. G. O. DFC Sqn Ldr	6.8.97
CROSSLEY P. DFC Wg Cdr ...	27.12.97	FERGUSON J. Flt Lt	18.10.97

Rank and Name	Date of Death
FERNAND A. H. DFC* Sqn Ldr ...	1.8.98
FERRE H. A. G. DFM Flt Lt... ...	14.7.98
FIELD K. C. B. MIMgt Sqn Ldr ...	9.5.98
FISHER V. L. Sqn Ldr	17.4.98
FLETCHER A. C. Flt Lt	19.7.98
FLETCHER D. C. Sqn Ldr	23.1.98
FOLLAND E. P. MBE BSc Wg Cdr	6.7.98
FORD A. Sqn Ldr...	21.5.98
FORSTER K. A. Flt Lt	20.9.97
FORWARD J. M. P. Flt Lt	22.8.97
FOSTER K. S. Sqn Ldr	8.2.98
FOX J. J. Sqn Ldr	31.1.98
FRAME T. J. Flt Lt	5.11.97
FRANSMAN E. V. MRAeS Flt Lt	27.7.98
FREEMAN K. H. W. Sqn Ldr ...	3.3.98
FRY W. J. DFC Flt Lt	25.4.98
GARDINER F. H. BEM Sqn Ldr ...	22.12.97
GARLICK R. K. MBE Sqn Ldr ...	24.1.98
GASKELL R. S. Flt Lt	20.9.97
GEGG D. G. Sqn Ldr	2.9.97
GILKS R. E. Sqn Ldr	7.2.98
GILL E. G. Flt Lt	1.7.98
GILPIN R. C. Flt Lt	12.4.98
GLEAVE G. CEng MIEE MIMgt Wg Cdr	30.11.97
GODMON T. W. R. MBE MIMgt Sqn Ldr	9.1.98
GOLIGHTLY R. H. OBE DFC AFC Wg Cdr	6.2.98
GOMM R. F. Flt Lt	17.8.97
GOODWIN F. Flt Lt	1.12.97
GOSS The Rev T. A. MA Wg Cdr	10.12.97
GOTHAM V. L. Sqn Ldr	28.12.97
GREEN A. A. DFC Sqn Ldr ...	6.8.97
GREENBROOK P. Flt Lt	1.7.98
GREENFIELD G. Wg Cdr	21.9.97
GRIFFIN C. E. Flt Lt	10.4.98
GRIFFITHS D. R. DFC Gp Capt ...	3.7.98
GRIFFITHS W. A. CBE DFC FIMgt Gp Capt	18.1.98
GROOMS J. W. Flt Lt	24.1.98
HALLETT H. S. Sqn Ldr	16.3.98
HARDING H. G. Sqn Ldr	23.1.98
HARPER The Rev D. M. MA Wg Cdr	23.3.98
HARRIS A. G. Wg Cdr	5.10.97
HARVEY N. O. Sqn Ldr	14.8.97
HARVEY N. T. MIPD Gp Capt ...	16.12.97
HARVEY R. A. AFC Sqn Ldr ...	2.3.98
HAWKINS R. H. Sqn Ldr	19.3.98

Rank and Name	Date of Death
HAYES A. G. OBE Wg Cdr ...	11.9.97
HEAL P. W. D. AFC Gp Capt ...	31.12.97
HEAL W. F. S. Flt Lt	19.2.98
HEALY F. H. Sqn Ldr	10.5.98
HENDERSON R. J. Flt Lt ...	21.6.98
HENRY J. J. MB BCh BAO DPH Gp Capt	17.12.97
HENSON L. DFC* Flt Lt... ...	29.5.98
HESELTINE F. BA MIPD MMS MIWM MIMgt Sqn Ldr ...	30.8.97
HESTER W. G. Sqn Ldr	18.11.97
HEWITT A. H. OBE Gp Capt ...	8.6.98
HICK R. H. N. DFC Flt Lt ...	26.11.97
HICKOX A. MIMgt Wg Cdr ...	3.1.98
HIDER S. A. DFC Flt Lt	6.11.97
HIGGINBOTTOM J. Flt Lt ...	31.10.97
HILL I E. Wg Cdr	2.12.97
HILL J. A. MB BS FRCP DCH Gp Capt	25.7.97
HILL W. J. BEM Sqn Ldr ...	9.5.98
HILL-TURNER P. G. Wg Cdr ...	22.10.97
HINDLE F. K. DFC Wg Cdr ...	30.8.97
HISLOP C. B. CEng MRAeS MIMgt Sqn Ldr	21.12.97
HODGES E. A. Sqn Ldr	8.3.98
HOGG H. B. Sqn Ldr	27.7.97
HOLDEN N. FIMLS Sqn Ldr ...	9.11.97
HOOPER W. D. OBE AFC MA Wg Cdr	28.5.98
HORNER J. G. Sqn Ldr	20.11.97
HORTON J. E. OBE Wg Cdr ...	10.3.98
HOWE W. F. Wg Cdr	28.10.97
HOWLETT C. R. C. A Cdre ...	25.11.97
HUDSON W. J. J. Flt Lt... ...	18.10.97
HUNTER J. A. Wg Cdr	5.6.98
HUXHAM G. H. Gp Capt ...	20.1.98
INGHAM T. W. Flt Lt	19.12.97
IRELAND-BLACKBURNE R. G. R. Sqn Ldr	27.12.97
JACKSON D. R. Sqn Ldr ...	12.1.98
JACKSON E. M. Sqn Ldr ...	1.6.98
JARRETT G. H. MBE Sqn Ldr	20.6.98
JEFFERY D. I. Sqn Ldr	10.2.98
JOEL L. J. DFC* Gp Capt ...	28.4.98
JOHN T. Sqn Ldr	21.3.98
JONES B. A. Sqn Ldr	27.3.98
JONES F. V. Flt Lt	11.10.97
JONES K. DFC Sqn Ldr... ...	27.6.98
JORDAN T. W. Flt Lt	30.3.98

Rank and Name	Date of Death	Rank and Name	Date of Death
JUKES I. J. N. MIPD MIMgt Flt Lt...	10.11.97	MARTIN W. CEng MRAeS MIMgt Wg Cdr	15.5.98
KELLEHER P. Fg Offr	3.7.97	MASON G. D. Flt Lt	16.1.98
KELLY W. M. Sqn Ldr...	22.4.98	MASTERS D. Sqn Ldr	11.5.98
KEMISH W. L. Flt Lt	2.8.97	MATTHEWS L. R. Sqn Ldr ...	4.2.98
KEMP C. W. OBE Wg Cdr	22.7.97	MATTHEWS S. C. Sqn Ldr ...	3.2.98
KEMP P. A. Flt Lt	28.10.97	MAURICE A. D. Sqn Offr ...	11.3.98
KENNEDY F. F. LDSRCS Gp Capt	21.5.98	MAYDEW G. F. Flt Lt	6.6.98
KENNEDY N. Flt Lt	28.1.98	MAYNARD Sir Nigel. KCB CBE	
KENNEDY T. S. OBE Gp Capt ...	24.11.97	DFC AFC ACM	19.6.98
KENYON E. Sqn Ldr	15.3.98	MEAD D. J. Flt Lt	7.9.97
KERSE A. S. Sqn Ldr	27.7.97	MERMAGEN H. W. CB CBE AFC	
KING D. MBE MIMgt Gp Capt ...	29.4.98	A Cdre...	10.1.98
KINGSBURY J. H. AFC Flt Lt ...	9.1.98	MILLER J. D. CBE A Cdre ...	18.4.98
KNIGHT H. A. S. Flt Lt	6.11.97	MILLER J. Sqn Ldr...	2.4.98
KNIGHT R. H. Sqn Ldr	31.3.98	MILLER W. E. DFC Sqn Ldr ...	24.8.97
KNOWLES E. C. H. DFM Flt Lt ...	15.10.97	MILLS R. AFM Flt Lt	3.7.97
KNOWLES E. DFM Flt Lt	14.8.97	MOLLOY T. L. Sqn Ldr	4.11.97
LAING R. T. W. FIMgt Gp Capt ...	2.10.97	MORGAN D. K. Wg Cdr ...	6.8.97
LAMBERT W. R. Flt Lt	17.5.98	MORRIS G. T. Flt Lt	5.5.98
LANDREY F. AFC AFM Wg Cdr...	5.6.98	MOSS A. F. Sqn Ldr	19.12.97
LANGTON L. N. Sqn Ldr	20.11.97	MOSS E. Flt Lt	13.4.98
LASBREY F. J. O. Wg Cdr	2.9.97	MOTHERSDALE G. H. Flt Lt ...	22.9.97
LAUNDON V. G. Flt Lt	29.4.98	MUTH B. MBE DFC Flt Lt ...	17.6.98
LAW W. A. Flt Lt	3.1.98	McADAM A. Sqn Ldr	4.10.97
LAWSON I. D. N. CB CBE DFC* AVM...	22.1.98	McARTHUR S. BEM Flt Lt ...	6.8.97
LEE N. R. C. Flt Lt	8.6.98	McBREARTY The Rev J. Gp Capt	21.2.98
LEWER F. H. P. OBE CEng FIIP MRAeS FIMgt Gp Capt... ...	17.9.97	McINTYRE F. G. Sqn Ldr ...	16.5.98
LEWIS E. N. AFC AFM Sqn Ldr	21.11.97	McKAY J. J. DSO DFC Gp Capt	25.2.98
LEWIS G. D. Flt Lt	21.3.98	McLAVERTY M. T. Flt Lt ...	30.6.97
LEWIS H. H. B. MRAeS Wg Cdr	25.10.97	NELSON M. Wg Cdr	17.11.97
LISTER G. L. Wg Cdr	26.3.98	NEVILLE C. R. G. CBE MA A Cdre	9.6.98
LISTER R. C. F. DFC Gp Capt ...	7.3.98	NEWMAN C. P. N. OBE DFC* DL Gp Capt	14.1.98
LOCKHART R. DFM AFM Sqn Ldr	11.3.98	NORBURY G. McN. DFC Flt Lt	2.11.97
LONGHURST M. J. Flt Lt	13.4.98	NORMAN R. C. Flt Lt	7.2.97
LOWE F. Sqn Ldr...	9.1.98	NORRIS H. N. Flt Lt	17.12.97
LUCAS B. AFC Wg Cdr	2.5.98	OAKES G. B. AFM Flt Lt ...	31.3.98
LUCY R. F. BEM Wg Cdr	26.10.97	ORR S. N. Flt Lt	6.4.98
LUTON K. J. Sqn Ldr	9.3.98	OULTON W. E. CB CBE DSO DFC AVM	31.10.97
MACKENZIE K. F. Wg Cdr	17.10.97	OWEN C. D. DFC Sqn Ldr ...	25.3.98
MACKENZIE S. E. CBE Gp Capt	13.9.97	PAGE G. A. Sqn Ldr	16.7.98
MACLAINE F. V. MB BCh BAO DPH A Cdre	31.1.98	PARKER H. M. G. MRAeS Gp Capt	5.4.98
MAGINESS L. Flt Lt	1.1.98	PATTISON H. G. DFC Sqn Ldr	20.2.98
MANGAN W. Flt Lt	28.3.98	PAYNTER N. S. CB A Cdre ...	16.3.98
MANLY T. F. DFM Flt Lt	7.1.98	PEARCE D. MBE Wg Cdr ...	11.8.97
MARTIN G. Flt Lt...	15.10.97	PEARCE W. R. Fg Offr	1.12.97
		PEARSON A. R. Flt Lt	22.3.98
		PEDDER A. A. Wg Cdr	23.4.98

Rank and Name	Date of Death	Rank and Name	Date of Death
PENDER W. Sqn Ldr	11.1.98	ROBINSON W. H. MBE DFC DFM	
PENFOLD H. K. Sqn Ldr	20.6.98	Sqn Ldr	26.4.98
PERRY A. J. Flt Lt	30.1.98	ROE P. W. BA Sqn Ldr	12.6.98
PERRY R. L. MIMgt Sqn Ldr ...	15.10.97	ROGERS R. G. Flt Lt	14.8.97
PETERS B. J. Flt Offr	10.7.98	ROLL J. W. AFC Sqn Ldr ...	2.9.97
PHILLIPS D. MBE DFC Wg Cdr ...	5.10.97	ROSE C. B. Flt Lt	23.3.98
PHILLIPS R. H. Sqn Ldr	27.1.98	ROSS J. Wg Cdr	30.5.98
PHILLIPS S. H. Sqn Ldr	5.3.98	ROTHERAM J. K. CB CBE BA DIC	
PHILLIPS V. G. J. DFC Flt Lt	27.12.97	CEng FRAeS AVM	14.5.98
PLANT A. F. H. Sqn Ldr	25.3.98	ROWBOTHAM P. V. Sqn Ldr...	14.8.97
PLUCKNETT R. F. MRAeS Sqn Ldr	7.2.98	ROWE J. M. DFC Wg Cdr ...	9.9.97
POLLING R. E. Flt Lt	27.9.97	ROWLANDS R. F. Sqn Ldr ...	13.9.97
POOLE C. A. Flt Lt	26.10.97	RUSSELL W. A. MBE BSc MIEE	
POPHAM L. A. OBE Gp Capt ...	27.2.98	Wg Cdr	23.2.98
PORTLOCK J. G. MBE Wg Cdr ...	2.4.98	RUTHERFORD-JONES A. D.	
POULTON H. R. G. DFC Flt Lt ...	21.5.98	Wg Cdr	21.6.98
POWELL E. E. Flt Lt	14.4.98	SANDS P. P. W. MBE DFC Gp Capt	8.1.98
PRATT R. H. MB BCh DPH DIH		SAUNDERS R. J. Fg Offr ...	25.2.98
A Cdre	4.8.97	SAUNDERS T. O. OBE Sqn Ldr	31.3.98
PRICE S. A. Wg Cdr	23.8.97	SAVAGE T. B. Sqn Ldr	2.11.97
PRIDE R. E. FRSA MSCD MIMgt		SCANLON C. J. Flt Lt	17.2.98
Flt Lt...	22.3.98	SCARBOROUGH J. Flt Lt ...	13.7.98
PRUDENCE L. J. O. Sqn Ldr ...	18.7.98	SCARTH R. Sqn Ldr	26.7.98
PRYER E. C. Flt Lt	10.2.98	SCHOFIELD C. J. D. BEM MRAeS	
QUIN The Rev T.R. MA Gp Capt	6.2.98	MIMgt Sqn Ldr	13.9.97
QUINN J. Fg Offr	10.11.97	SCOTT D. J. DSO OBE DFC	
RAMPLING B. M. L. Sqn Ldr ...	27.1.98	Sqn Ldr	8.10.97
RAMSCAR L. MHCIMA Flt Lt ...	31.5.98	SEELEY E. C. MBE Wg Cdr ...	14.7.98
RAMSDEN J. H. OBE CEng MRAeS		SENIOR G. K. DFC Flt Lt ...	7.9.97
MIMgt Gp Capt	8.6.98	SHARLAND P. H. Sqn Ldr ...	15.6.98
RANDLE K. S. DFM Flt Lt	24.8.97	SHARP W. W. Sqn Ldr	16.11.97
READ R. W. Sqn Ldr	5.11.97	SHARPE R. C. Sqn Ldr	27.10.97
REBBECK D. J. N. MBE Sqn Ldr	24.4.98	SHAW R. Flt Lt	14.8.98
REECE A. DSO OBE DFC AFC		SHIELD L. G. Sqn Ldr	6.4.98
FIMgt Gp Capt	18.5.98	SHORE D. R. DFC AFC Gp Capt	18.9.97
REED C. F. Sqn Ldr	27.11.97	SINCLAIR J. Flt Lt	10.2.98
REES D. A. J. Flt Lt	18.9.97	SKIDMORE D. Flt Lt	27.8.97
REX J. MRAeS DCAe Sqn Ldr ...	28.10.97	SKINNER A. W. Sqn Ldr ...	21.1.98
RICHARDS R. D. Flt Lt	25.10.97	SKINNER S. E. Sqn Ldr... ...	24.7.98
RICHARDSON J. D. Wg Cdr ...	19.3.98	SLATER G. D. Flt Lt	21.8.97
RICHARDSON J. H. Flt Lt	20.6.98	SMALLWOOD W. F. Flt Lt ...	6.9.97
RIDGE S. G. MBE Sqn Ldr... ...	15.3.98	SMITH B. V. Sqn Ldr	17.8.97
ROBERTS C. L. C. Wg Cdr... ...	10.1.98	SMITH E. B. St. E. Flt Lt ...	6.6.98
ROBERTS C. S. Sqn Ldr	9.1.98	SMITH N. F. Flt Lt	15.7.97
ROBERTS R. A. Flt Lt	20.7.97	SMITH P. R. MIMgt Sqn Ldr ...	14.9.97
ROBERTSON J. G. MB BS LMSSA		SORENSEN M. I. Flt Lt	2.12.97
Wg Cdr	15.6.98	SPALDING V. G. Sqn Ldr ...	27.1.98
ROBINSON B. CB CBE AVM ...	20.5.98	SPICER W. J. Flt Lt...	16.9.97
ROBINSON F. A. DFC Sqn Ldr ...	19.3.98	SPURGEON C. E. Sqn Ldr ...	22.11.97
ROBINSON H. E. Sqn Ldr	18.2.98	STAFFORD C. J. Flt Lt	30.9.97

Rank and Name	Date of Death	Rank and Name	Date of Death
STAFFORD T. OBE FIMgt Gp Capt	3.9.97	WALL A. OBE Gp Capt	3.7.98
STATE H. E. Flt Lt	6.4.98	WAND S. P. MBE Flt Lt	27.11.97
STATHAM G. N. Flt Lt	2.4.98	WARCUP P. E. CBE A Cdr ...	5.6.98
STEER W. H. BEM Sqn Ldr ...	12.10.97	WATLING J. B. B. MBE Sqn Ldr	20.1.98
STEVENS G. T. Flt Lt	17.8.98	WATSON B. J. MIMgt Sqn Ldr	15.8.97
STEWART E. MacR. Flt Lt	11.2.98	WATSON K. MBE Sqn Ldr ...	18.4.98
STONHAM P. D. MBE Sqn Ldr ...	14.1.98	WATTS G. E. AFM MIMgt Sqn Ldr	3.4.98
STOVIN T. H. L. Flt Lt	18.1.98	WEBBER T. M. BA Sqn Ldr ...	13.4.98
SUMMERS J. T. MA Sqn Ldr ...	10.12.97	WEBSTER D. V. Sqn Ldr ...	3.7.98
SWEET A. H. P. MIMgt Sqn Ldr	24.12.97	WELLS E. W. L. Flt Lt	23.5.98
SWIFT W. J. CVO FIMgt Gp Capt	4.7.98	WELSH G. P. Sqn Ldr	9.3.98
TAIT N. A. OBE MRAeS A Cdre	21.1.98	WESTWOOD J. A. G. Flt Lt ...	9.2.98
TATEM K. A. G. Flt Lt	4.12.97	WHEELER F. J. DFC AFC Sqn Ldr	16.8.97
TAYLOR B. M. Flt Lt	2.5.98	WHITE J. A. MIMgt Sqn Ldr...	21.5.98
TAYLOR C. AFC* Sqn Ldr	19.3.98	WHITE K. J. Sqn Ldr	8.2.98
TAYLOR G. S. Wg Cdr ...	15.3.98	WHITLEY Sir John. KBE CB DSO	
TAYLOR P. B. BSc Sqn Ldr ...	4.1.98	AFC* AM	26.12.97
TEBBOTH G. H. OBE Gp Capt ...	10.11.97	WHYBROW J. H. H. Flt Lt ...	25.11.97
THACKERAY J. R. A. MITD MIPD		WIGLEY P. DFC Sqn Ldr ...	12.7.98
Sqn Ldr	30.7.97	WILKINSON G. Flt Lt	26.4.98
THOMAS A. J. Sqn Ldr	3.5.98	WILKINSON J. P. T. Flt Lt ...	22.10.97
THOMAS G. J. CEng MIEE MRAeS		WILKINSON W. MIMgt Flt Lt	29.6.97
Wg Cdr	15.6.98	WILLIAMS D. E. MBE Sqn Ldr	12.6.98
THOMAS M. R. MB BS FRCS(Edin)		WILLSON B. J. Sqn Ldr... ...	14.2.98
Wg Cdr	10.10.97	WILSON F. H. Flt Offr	6.5.98
THOMPSON D. MCIPS Sqn Ldr	9.12.97	WILSON J. A. OBE MA Wg Cdr	29.1.98
THOMPSON J. BEM Flt Lt... ...	18.1.98	WINN A. L. Flt Lt	17.6.98
THOMPSON R. G. OBE Gp Capt	14.5.98	WOOD B. A. C. DFC Gp Capt	16.4.98
THORNTON-PETT G. P. BA Flt Lt	3.8.97	WOOD L. A. Flt Lt	6.11.97
THORP R. W. BSc Flt Lt	26.2.98	WOOD-GLOVER H. H. MBE	
THOUARD F. G. Sqn Ldr	10.11.97	Gp Capt	9.1.98
THROWER W. J. Fg Offr	20.5.98	WOODALL J. C. G. BSc Flt Lt	17.1.98
TINSLEY J. DFM Sqn Ldr	3.11.97	WOODS W. G. Flt Lt	11.7.98
TITMUSS H. MRAeS Flt Lt ...	22.5.98	WOODWARD R. W. Sqn Ldr...	20.6.98
TODD A. G. DFC Wg Cdr	9.6.98	WOOLLEY F. Flt Lt	12.6.98
TODD E. J. Flt Lt	6.10.97	WOOLLEY J. P. M. Wg Cdr ...	17.9.97
TOMPKINS B. Sqn Ldr	5.5.98	WRAY J. B. DFC Gp Capt ...	31.1.97
TOYNBEE-HOLMES A. Flt Lt ...	28.7.98	WRIGHT G. E. Flt Lt	19.1.98
TRAIN F. A. DFC Flt Lt	4.8.97	WRIGHT G. Sqn Ldr	27.1.98
TROTTER S. H. DFC Sqn Ldr ...	14.3.98	WYNZAR R. BA Flt Lt	3.8.97
TROTTER T. A. Gp Capt	12.3.98	YOUNG W. R. Flt Lt	31.8.97
TURNBULL R. A. Sqn Ldr	26.6.98		
TURNER L. Sqn Ldr	16.6.98		
UBEE S. R. CB AFC AVM	7.7.98	**Princess Mary's Royal Air Force**	
VALENTINE A. F. C. Flt Lt	5.1.98	**Nursing Service**	
VISAN G. D. Sqn Ldr	12.6.98		
VISAN S. Wg Offr	11.6.98	BEAUVOISIN T. J. M. SRN	
WALKER N. C. Gp Capt	1.12.97	Sqn Offr	14.8.98
WALKER R. B. Sqn Ldr	21.9.97	BOUNDEN P. E. SRN Flt Offr	9.6.98
WALKER T. D. MBE Wg Cdr ...	13.8.97		

Rank and Name	Date of Death
WALKER G. E. K. ARRC SRN	
Sqn Offr	1.8.98
WALLER W. M. ARRC SRN	
Sqn Offr	28.9.97
WOODS S. E. ARRC SRN	
Sqr Offr	18.9.97

INDEX

Personal No	Page No	Personal No	Page No	Personal No	Page No
A		8106241 Acland, C. A.	265	8186915 Adey, D. D.	202
		4335541 Acons, E. G. N. . .	9, 142	5204657 Adey, E. J.	144
2615302 Aspinall, R. M.	64	5208164 Acres, S. P.	220	8304283 Adey, S. K.	133
214157 Aala, R.	279	4272153 Acton, A.	233	209957 Adgar, B.	270
210482 Abbey, S. M.	266	2625748 Adair, C. R.	274	300887 Adkin, M. E.	243
8025993 Abbot, A. C.	118	2627644 Adair, P. G.	241	214271 Adkins, M. J.	281
8023070 Abbott, C. J.	144	609378 Adam, I. W.	162	8138361 Adkinson, S.	125
Abbott, C. J. A.	207	2628435 Adam, J.	121	8028476 Adlam, R. H.	114
209364 Abbott, J.	264	214619 Adam, K. J.	283	5208366 Adrain, J. M.	155
5202893 Abbott, J. D. F.	161	212669 Adam, S. D.	272	213784 Agate, J. J.	277
4278642 Abbott, J. E.	237	8174955 Adams, A. D.	173	8028806 Ager, J. N.	114
213883 Abbott, M. I.	278	2639274 Adams, A. L. . . 137, 310		8234393 Ager, L. J.	243
Abbott, N. J. S.	26	8025070 Adams, C. K. . . . 52, 102		2625171 Ahearn, A. S.	257
213925 Abbott, P. J.	278	3517109 Adams, C. R.	271	5208575 Ahmad, O.	156
8238442 Abbott, P. K.	186	211954 Adams, D. C.	269	210250 Ailes, M. K. G.	255
206975 Abbott, P. L.	264	Adams, D. N. . . 30, 96		Ainge, D. R.	157
1961438 Abbott, P. L.	237	213980 Adams, G.	278	4335470 Ainslie, I. McP. . . 69, 143	
3528097 Abbott, R. J.	251	212873 Adams, G. E.	273	8032454 Ainsworth, A. M. . . .	183
5202781 Abbott, S. 15, 142		8019445 Adams, I. M.	184	2628484 Ainsworth, D. P.	125
214390 Abbott, S. J.	282	416895 Adams, J. E.	271	8250071 Ainsworth, M. S. A. . .	197
Abbott, Sir Peter. . .	5, 7	5207944 Adams, M. P.	199	5203703 Ainsworth, S. J.	182
8152394 Abbs, M. R.	173	8027388 Adams, N. M.	113	8191718 Aird, B. G.	216
306273 Abdy, D. L.	204	8023231 Adams, P.	269	5208339 Airey, A. M. R.	137
214181 Abdy, M. J.	280	Adams, P. D.	14	8027193 Airey, N. D.	113
5202999 Abell, Rev P. J.	224	5204609 Adams, R. C.	164	2628413 Airey, S. M.	241
4231716 Aber, C. P. 37, 102		2622400 Adams, R. M.	163	8138143 Aitchison, D. F.	171
213545 Abington, M. B. . . .	276	8028724 Adams, R. M.	115	8026563 Aitken, A. P-D.	110
688933 Abra, J. E.	162	214545 Adams, S. L.	283	8026563 Aitken, A. P. D.	66
5207374 Abra, S. M.	132	5207992 Adamson, A. P. W. .	151	8127576 Aitken, D. S.	239
2627894 Abraham, D. L.	127	1945434 Adamson, C. J.	266	5207037 Aitken, J..	208
2637544 Abrahams, M. D. . . .	136	91426 Adamson, G. D. W.	144	1937895 Aitken, J. O.	231
306032 Abram, E. A.	256	5208066 Adamson, J. P. M. .	132	0687868 Aitken, R. C.	231
213772 Abubakar, A. B.	277	9798 Adamson, M.	282	8026098 Aitken, R. T.	108
8067852 Achilles, B. K.	277	608182 Adcock, C. B.	278	2630940 Aitken, T. A.	278
8043185 Achilles, L. E. A. . . .	277	8029342 Adcock, M. R.	128	5203024 Akehurst, P. B.	159
214087 Ackerley, D. J.	279	686516 Adcock, T. R.	107	8032302 Akehurst, P. L.	148
213892 Ackland, E. C.	154	8235107 Addison, E.	152	8027764 Akehurst, R.	114
2636128 Ackland, P. M.	131	213911 Addison, G.	278	8209943 Akerman, C.	171
8032634 Ackroyd, C. A.	200	8212303 Addison, J. M.	125	8100663 Akers, P. A.	232
5208386 Ackroyd, R. D.	154	5206076 Aderyn, A. A.	196	91491 Akhatar, S.	260
Acland, B. J.	84	Ades, A. V.	100	Akhurst, G. R.	64

INDEX

INDEX

INDEX

INDEX

Personal No		Page No	Personal No		Page No	Personal No		Page No

D

8302702	D Albertanson, K. . .	153
8300440	D'Albertanson, S. R.	244
213678	D'Anna, G. W. S. . .	277
8028466	D'Arcy, Q. N. P. . . .	113
8119396	D'Ardenne, P. J. . . .	195
2616454	D'Aubyn, J. A.	117
2626546	D'Lima, D. J.	122
2636096	D'Lima, L. J. V.	151
4230194	Da Costa, F. A.	108
211409	Da Silva, L. J.	268
8028703	Da'Silva, C. D.	115
5205875	Dabell, S. W.	279
8023849	Dabin, N. R. S.	182
5208140	Daborn, D. K. R. . . .	210
5205100	Dabrowski, M. R. . .	169
8141667	Dack, G. T.	128
8024069	Dack, J. R.	183
	Dacre, J. P.	88
4231721	Dacre, J. P.	275
4277291	Dadds, J.	234
8020882	Daffarn, G. C. . . 37,	103
8024333	Daft, R. E.	125
8304793	Dahroug, M.	138
211249	Dailly, N. J. S.	268
8024426	Dainton, S. D.	183
2630987	Dairon, L. J. T.	122
306111	Daisley, L. S.	152
5205606	Daisley, R. M.	146
	Dakin, Dr S. D.	19
2621405	Dakin, A. G.	110
2647784	Dalboozi, F.	259
5204902	Dalby, A. P.	220
2642566	Dalby, N. L.	136
5207676	Dalby, R. P.	199
213091	Dalby, W. J.	274
212627	Dale, A. L.	128
2634286	Dale, B. E.	130
8001834	Dale, D. C.	184
5203224	Dale, I. P.	165
8023427	Dale, J.	194
8302542	Dale, J.	244
212911	Dale, J. N.	273
214004	Dale, N. T.	278
2642461	Dales, N. M. C.	135
8024272	Dallas, A. W.	149
2630609	Dalley, G. P.	115
4335080	Dalley, K. P.	143
	Dalley, R. J.	85
5206624	Dalley, S. L.	166
300902	Dalling, R.	252
594103	Dally, M. J.	238

4292104	Dalrymple, I. V. J. . .	283
5208183	Dalrymple, P. M. . . .	211
8028557	Dalton, A. G.	124
	Dalton, A. M.	43
5206292	Dalton, G.	173
8102198	Dalton, G. S.	173
8300388	Dalton, M. J.	152
5204255	Dalton, R. A.	116
	Dalton, S. G. G.	99
8027227	Dalton, S. M.	198
213895	Daly, B. J.	204
8029684	Daly, C. A.	130
5205755	Daly, Rev J. A.	224
213811	Daly, J. M.	277
214603	Daly, N. T.	283
4335165	Danby, C. I.	242
5202397	Dancey, A. N.	110
	Dandy, D. J.	221
3515713	Dane, M. B.	244
5204187	Dangerfield, M. J. . .	167
213437	Daniel, B. L.	275
	Daniel, D.	18
4253246	Daniel, N. S.	255
5208576	Daniel, R. C.	156
8025492	Daniels, G. A.	107
306009	Daniels, J. C.	196
	Daniels, R. A.	43
0687877	Daniels, R. A.	232
2638530	Daniels, S. M.	133
8021279	Daniels, S. R.	163
5202699	Danks, P. I.	161
8304329	Dann, G. J.	133
	Dannatt, S. R.	15
8300825	Danso, K. G.	156
212796	Danson, C. A.	272
8289165	Dant, A. C.	185
5206310	Danton, S. J.	173
9763	Darby, S. J.	258
8300715	Dargan, R. J.	154
213718	Dargan, S.	259
2640345	Dark, E. A.	135
1949750	Dark, W. J.	232
8402430	Darling, S. J.	152
1930449	Darling, T.	245
212934	Darnell, M. C.	273
8304114	Darnley, P. R.	132
208202	Darrant, J. G.	263
	Dart, G. C.	93
8026350	Dart, J. N.	109
211469	Dart, N.	268
5206300	Dart, P. G.	174
214595	Darwin, K. A.	283
8015412	Dasilva, M. E.	271
	Datchler, C.	43
5205948	Dathan, C. H.	184

2640855	Datson, R. I.	132
8076341	Daughney, R.	109
5203981	Daughtrey, P. S.	193
2628438	Daulby, K. J.	122
8152948	Daulby, P. R.	173
5202593	Davenall, D. S.	67
5202593	Davenall, D. S.	105
2640971	Davenhill, J. C. M. . .	132
8023276	Davenport, A. J. R. . .	180
	Davenport, C.	9
5208376	Davenport, D. A. . . .	155
409507	Davenport, J.	216
214588	Davenport, L. F.	283
5203129	Davey, G. J.	111
8140923	Davey, G. R.	111
8260506	Davey, M. F.	135
209083	Davey, M. J. S.	264
8028866	Davey, P. M.	125
211162	Davey, P. R.	267
214698	Davidson, A.	284
	Davidson, A. F.	30
8028471	Davidson, A. G. G. . .	124
5202276	Davidson, C. S. . . 47,	190
214182	Davidson, G.	281
8029291	Davidson, G. S.	128
306088	Davidson, H. R.	247
8026807	Davidson, I.	119
4232447	Davidson, I. F. . . . 37,	104
4285799	Davidson, J. H.	233
0595559	Davidson, M. A.	232
5203183	Davidson, M. C. F. . .	165
262728	Davidson, M. D.	278
2627287	Davidson, M. F.	241
8300407	Davidson, N.	185
8031743	Davidson, P. M.	182
8013847	Davidson, R.	239
8024604	Davidson, R. B.	184
2619835	Davidson, R. H. C. . .	269
688663	Davidson, W. A.	163
609483	Davie, A. 67,	142
211647	Davies, A.	269
8007638	Davies, A. E.	237
210705	Davies, Rev A. J. . . .	225
211522	Davies, A. J.	268
2620494	Davies, A. J.	268
8024016	Davies, A. J.	148
8300688	Davies, A. J.	204
214104	Davies, A. M.	279
5207602	Davies, A. R.	245
8094933	Davies, A. R.	278
214604	Davies, A. S.	283
8008628	Davies, A. T.	174
8095945	Davies, B.	235
8406130	Davies, B.	154
8025276	Davies, C. D.	109

H

INDEX

INDEX

INDEX

INDEX

INDEX

INDEX

INDEX

INDEX

INDEX

INDEX

INDEX

INDEX

INDEX

INDEX

INDEX

INDEX

INDEX

INDEX

INDEX

INDEX

INDEX

INDEX

INDEX

442

INDEX

Honorary Agents to the Royal Air Force

The Agent's role is to provide a service of personal financial advice to all members of the Royal Air Force no matter whether they bank with the Agent Banks or elsewhere. The advice is unbiased and free of charge and may range from the simplicity of opening an account to constructive advice on commutation and investment at the time of resettlement. The Agents also specialise in dealing with technical financial matters relating to Units and formations.

The Royal Air Force Agents are:

Cox's & King's
PO Box 1190
7 Pall Mall
London SW1Y 5NA
Freephone: 0800 317053

Cox's & King's is a branch of Lloyds Bank Plc which specialises in military business. Advice given is impartial and tailored to each individual. The branch has access to a very broad range of specialists within Lloyds Bank Group.

Holt's Branch, The Royal Bank of Scotland plc
Lawrie House
Victoria Road
Farnborough
Hampshire
GU14 7NR

Telephone: 0345 465871
Facsimile: 01252 370 291

(Holt's Services Agency Limited is attached to Holt's Farnborough Branch of The Royal Bank of Scotland plc and can call upon a wide range of financial "expertise" in providing individual independent adivce to service personnel of all ranks.)

LADY GROVER'S HOSPITAL FUND
FOR OFFICERS' FAMILIES

Registered under the Friendly Societies Acts 1896 to 1974

Registered No. 474F

The OBJECT of the Fund is to help Officers to defray expenses incurred by the illness of their dependants, as shown below.

MEMBERSHIP is open to serving and retired male and female Officers of the three Services, for the benefit of their dependants; and to widows/widowers, daughters/sons, divorced wives/husbands of Officers, for their own benefit (UNDER CERTAIN CONDITIONS).

RATES OF BENEFITS

GRANTS. The amount of each grant is assessed on the basis of the actual expenses incurred, with maximum rates as follows: –

		Scale 'Y'
(a)	For the expenses of temporary residence in a hospital or nursing home	£1050 weekly
(b)	For the expenses of a temporary privately employed nurse	£280 weekly
(c)	For convalescence away from home	£280 weekly
(d)	For the expenses of a temporary Home Help	£140 weekly
(e)	In special cases, at the Committee's discretion, ex-Gratia payments	

The maximum period for which benefit is payable is payable in any period of twelve months is EIGHT weeks
TWELVE weeks for Home Help ONLY

ANNUAL SUBSCRIPTION RATE:- SCALE 'Y'—£30

For particulars apply to: –

The Secretary, Lady Grover's Hospital Fund for Officers' Families
48 Pall Mall, London SW1Y 5JY

(enclose 30p to include postage, for Book of Rules)

RFEA LIMITED
FINDING JOBS FOR EX FORCES PERSONNEL
49 PALL MALL,
LONDON, SW1Y 5JG

Telephone: 0171-321 2011
Fax: 0171-839 0970

Patrons

H.M. THE QUEEN

H.M. QUEEN ELIZABETH, THE QUEEN MOTHER

Chairman: Vice Admiral Sir GEOFFREY DALTON, KCB

Vice-Chairman: Major General B T PENNICOTT, CVO

Chief Executive: Major General M F L SHELLARD, CBE

"The Association operates a network of 39 Branches throughout the UK and exists for the express purpose of assisting men and women to find employment and return to civilian life when they leave the regular Forces. They may register, as often as they wish, up to the national retirement age, provided they served in the ranks for a minimum of three years (or less if medically discharged) and left with a "Good" or above character assessment. In 1997/98 the Association registered 9,754 ex-servicemen and women and placed 3,782 and of those 1,195 were from the RAF."

NATIONAL BRANCH NETWORK

ABERDEEN	LINCOLN
BEDFORD	LONDON
BELFAST	MANCHESTER
BIRMINGHAM	MIDDLESBROUGH
BRISTOL	NEWCASTLE-UPON-TYNE
BURY ST EDMUNDS	NORTHAMPTON
CARDIFF	NORWICH
CARLISLE	NOTTINGHAM
CHATHAM	PLYMOUTH
CHELMSFORD	PORTSMOUTH
CHELTENHAM	PRESTON
CHESTER	READING
DERBY	SALISBURY
DUNDEE	SHEFFIELD
EDINBURGH	SHROPSHIRE
EXETER	STOKE-ON-TRENT
GLASGOW	SURREY/SUSSEX
HULL	SWANSEA
LEEDS	

"For contact details see Yellow Pages and local directories or contact head office"

Established 1885.   Registered under the Charities Act 1960:   Registered No: 1061212

Company Registration No: 3270369

THE
ROYAL PATRIOTIC FUND CORPORATION

FOUNDED 1854

REORGANISED UNDER THE PATRIOTIC FUND REORGANISATION ACT 1903,

AND THE ROYAL PATRIOTIC FUND CORPORATION ACT, 1950

President: H.R.H. Prince MICHAEL of KENT, KCVO

Vice-President: General Sir ROBERT PASCOE, KCB MBE

Secretary: Brigadier T. G. Williams, CBE

The Corporation administers a number of Funds for the benefit of widows, children and dependants of deceased officers and other ranks of the Naval, Military and Air Forces of the Crown.

Over £300,000 is distributed annually in allowances and grants.

Regular allowances are paid to widows of officers and other ranks with at least 5 year's regular service with the Colours where need exists.

Television sets and/or licences may be provided for widows of former members of the Armed Services.

Grants are made from time to time to meet particular requirements.

In addition bursaries and educational grants are available to children of deceased servicemen to assist with school fees.

Applications for assistance should be made through local branches of S.S.A.F.A. or the War Pensions Agency.

Further information may be obtained from the Secretary, Royal Patriotic Fund Corporation, 40 Queen Anne's Gate, London, SW1H 9AP. Telephone 0171-233 1894. Fax 0171-233 1799.

THE ROYAL AIR FORCES ASSOCIATION

(Incorporated by Royal Charter)

MOVING WITH THE TIMES

RAFA, the Royal Air Forces Association, is a unique membership organisation with over 100,000 'RAF family' members worldwide. As a charity we provide support to all serving and retired RAF personnel and their dependants through our worldwide network of Branches. We help over 50,000 individuals each year and provide a range of services – from resettlement and war pensions advice to a family recuperation unit; our aim is to respond quickly and positively to all requests for help.

- We provide support and resettlement advice for RAF leavers to help ease the transition into civilian life.

- We have a family recuperation unit at Rothbury, near Newcastle upon Tyne.

- We have three convalescent and respite care homes – at Lytham St Annes, at Rothbury near Newcastle upon Tyne and at Weston super Mare.

- We run sheltered and supportive housing schemes.

- We provide 24 hour nursing care at Sussexdown, our nursing home near Storrington in West Sussex.

- We run a scheme enabling those in need of residential care to be treated close to their own home.

- Trained volunteer Welfare Officers offer free advice and assistance to those in need.

- RAFA Liaison Officers (RAFALOs) on stations act as a link between the Association and serving RAF personnel.

If you would like information about membership please contact your RAFALO on station or

The Membership Director
The Royal Air Forces Association
Portland Road
Malvern
Worcs WR14 2TA
Tel 01684 891020

Membership is only £8.00 per year (£9.50 in the first year)

Registration No 226686

King Edward VII's
HOSPITAL FOR OFFICERS

Where amidst the bustle of central London will you find an independent hospital which...

- welcomes serving and retired officers, their families and those holding territorial or reserve commissions
- offers day case and complex surgery
- has state of the art diagnostic facilities
- offers unparalleled nursing care
- has a superb physiotherapy department with hydrotherapy facilities
- serves fine food and wines
- offers subsidised nursing accommodation for uninsured officers

...this is King Edward VII's Hospital for Officers, where technology works with tradition.

✂--*Registered Charity Number 208944*--

For further information, please telephone 0171 486 4411
or post to: King Edward VII's Hospital for Officers,
1 Bentinck Street, London. W1M 5RN

Name:_____Address:_____

_____Postcode:_____AFL

QUEEN VICTORIA SCHOOL

DUNBLANE, PERTHSHIRE, FK15 0JY

Patron: HRH THE DUKE OF EDINBURGH, KG, KT, OM, GBE

The School provides boarding school education for the children of Scottish servicemen and women and those who have served in Scotland.   Quality education, including school clothing is provided at a low cost of £165 per term.   Set in 45 acres of beautiful Perthshire countryside, QVS is easily accessible by road, rail or air.

Pupils may be registered for entry from the age of 7 but the main entry is at Primary 7 (i.e. age 10.5/11 years).   Applications must reach the School by 31 December so that they may be considered for the Admissions Board which convenes in February. However, consideration will also be given, in particular circumstances, to applications made after these dates.

The School offers a wide curriculum following the Scottish educational system and includes courses at Standard and Higher Grade as well as Certificate of Sixth Year Studies and SCOTVEC modules.   Career links with the services remain strong, but increasingly pupils move on to Higher and Further Education.   Pastoral care is afforded a very high priority along with Careers Guidance and Personal and Social Education.

Queen Victoria School is a unique boarding school and, as such, looks to achieve the best that is possible academically for all its pupils.   The School prides itself also on developing the pupil in the widest possible sense and, as well as academically, aims to achieve success in activities such as sport, music, drama and many other extra-curricular areas.   The traditional ceremonial side adds a very special and unique dimension.

For further information, write to
The Headmaster
Queen Victoria School
Dunblane
Perthshire FK15 0JY

Telephone: 01786 822288 (Exchange)
0131 3102901 (Direct Line to HM's Secretary)
Fax No: 0131 310 2926

THE OFFICERS' ASSOCIATION

The Officers' Association provides services which are available to ex-officers of the Royal Navy (including Royal Marines), the Army and the Royal Air Force, and their widows and dependants, including those who held Commissions in the Womens' Services.

Services include:

- **EMPLOYMENT** – an efficient Employment Department to assist ex-officers of all ages and ranks to find suitable employment, both those just leaving the Services and those who are changing their civilian jobs. Many hundreds of ex-officers are found jobs every year over a wide salary range.

- **BENEVOLENCE** – financial assistance is given in a number of ways such as cash grants and allowances to those in their own homes in financial distress, and for the elderly in Residential or Nursing Home Care and towards shortfalls in Home fees.

- **HOMES ADVICE** – advice and information on independent sector Homes and Homes run by service charities and other voluntary organisations; sheltered accommodation for the elderly; convalescence homes; advice on financial assistance towards Homes fees.

- **A COUNTRY HOME** – running "Huntly" a delightful country home at Bishopsteignton, South Devon, which affords comfort and security for lonely ex-officers at or over the age of 65, both male and female, who do not need special nursing care. Selection is made with due regard to need.

- **BUNGALOWS** – running a 12 bungalow estate at Leavesden, Herts, for disabled ex-officers and their families.

The Association has offices in London and Dublin. The Officers' Association (Scotland) has offices in Glasgow and Edinburgh.

All enquiries should be made to the General Secretary, The Officers' Association, 48 Pall Mall, London SW1Y 5JY. (Tel: 0171 930 0125).

THE ROYAL AIR FORCE BENEVOLENT FUND

Head Office: 67, PORTLAND PLACE, LONDON W1N 4AR

Telephone: 0171-580 8343

Fax: 0171-636 7005

www.raf-benfund.org.uk

(Registered under the Charities Act, 1960)

Patron: HER MAJESTY THE QUEEN

President: H.R.H. THE DUKE OF KENT, KG GCMG GCVO ADC

Chairman of Council: SIR ADRIAN SWIRE

Controller: AIR CHIEF MARSHAL SIR DAVID COUSINS, KCB AFC BA

★   ★   ★

Purpose of the Fund. The Benevolent Fund exists to provide assistance to those of the extended Royal Air Force family who need support as a consequence of sickness, disability, accident, infirmity, poverty or other adversity. This extended family embraces all ranks, male and female, who are serving, or who have served, in the Royal Air Force or its associated Air Forces, their spouses, and their other dependants.

Welfare. The Fund's Welfare work can be divided into 4 areas:

Housing – where death or severe disablement has occurred in service the Fund may assist with the provision of housing. Help may take the form of a secured loan to provide the balance needed for house purchase, or possibly the use of a Fund-owned property.

Education – where a parent's death or severe disablement has occurred whilst serving, the Fund may assist with the costs of education until the completion of 'A' levels and exceptionally, to first degree level. Such children, known as Foundationers, may attend a boarding school of choice at both the preparatory and secondary stages of education; Fund help is based on need and limited to a maximum of the fees at appropriate benchmark schools.

Homes – the Fund has two Homes of its own, Alastrean House in Tarland, Scotland, providing residential and nursing accommodation and Princess Marina House on the Sussex coast, providing residential and respite care. The Fund also shares two other homes, Rothbury House in Northumberland and Flowerdown House at Weston-Super-Mare with the Royal Air Forces Association. Where nursing home care, or an alternative form of residential care is needed, the Fund may be able to assist in cases where the statutory provision is inadequate.

General Needs – this category forms the bulk of the Fund's welfare work and embraces circumstances which falls within the Fund's scope but not covered above. One-off help is normally by grant, except where the help is property-related, when a loan is considered more appropriate. Loans attract interest at the Fund's current rate, but repayment may be deferred. Help might be the provision of wheelchairs or specialist furniture. For pensioners in need, a small regular addition to income may be provided.

Measure of the Assistance. Expenditure on all forms of relief continues to rise, year on year, and is currently over £14 million per annum.

How to Help. The Chairman and Council hope that the Service and general public will continue to respond generously and so enable the Fund to meet all its commitments. Donations, preferably under deed of covenant, attending events, purchasing merchandise from the Fund's mail order catalogues or leaving something in a Will are all valued ways of helping the Fund. Requests for further information on Wills and donations should be addressed to Director Appeals.

Those who may be in need of assistance. Should you, as a member of the RAF family, be in need of our help, please contact us. Equally, if you know someone else who is, please encourage them to get in touch, at the address above.

The Royal Air Force Benevolent Fund
Helping Colleagues who need a brighter future

COMBAT *STRESS*

WITH
EX-SERVICES MENTAL WELFARE SOCIETY
Broadway House, The Broadway, Wimbledon, London SW19 1RL
Telephone: 0181-543 6333.   Fax: 0181-542 7082

The Ex-Services Mental Welfare Society was founded in 1919 and is the only organisation specialising in helping men and women, of all ranks, who have served in the Armed Forces or the Merchant Navy and who are suffering from psychiatric disability.

The Society has a national network of twelve welfare officers and its activities, which cover the UK and Eire, include assistance with claims and appeals for War Disablement Pensions; domiciliary and psychiatric hospital visits; assessment and treatment in one of the short stay homes; provision of long term residential accommodation and limited financial help.

A veterans' home offers long stay residential accommodation for those service-men who are unable to manage for themselves in the community, and three other centres are available for short stay assessment, treatment and respite care.

The work of the Society requires about £4.0 million annually to help those who suffer from psychiatric disability. Currently, the Society is providing help for over 4,200 veterans, men and women, of the Second World War and other conflicts including Palestine, Korea, Malaya, Kenya, Cyprus, Suez, the Arabian Peninsula, Northern Ireland, the Falklands, the Gulf and Bosnia.

For further information contact:
The Director
Combat Stress
Broadway House
The Broadway
London SW19 1RL
Telephone: 0181 543 6333
Facsimile: 0181 542 7082

BLESMA

BRITISH LIMBLESS EX-SERVICE MEN'S ASSOCIATION

ARE YOU ELIGIBLE FOR HELP?

BLESMA is a National Charity specifically for limbless Ex-Service men and women. The Association also accepts responsibility for the dependants of its members and, in particular, their widows.

BLESMA wants to help 5,000 more eligible men and women. The Association promotes the welfare of men or women who have lost a limb or limbs or one or both eyes as a result of service in any branch of Her Majesty's Forces or Auxiliary Forces and to assist needy dependants of such Service limbless.

BLESMA CAN HELP:

Provide permanent residential and convalescent holiday accommodation through its two nursing and residential Homes at Blackpool and Crieff in Perthshire.

Provide financial assistance to Members and Widows in the form of Grants.

Assist in finding suitable employment for Amputees.

Furnish advice on Pensions, Allowances, makes representation to Government Departments on individual entitlements and, where necessary, represent Members and their dependants at Pensions Appeal Tribunals.

A LEGACY MEANS A LOT TO THE LIMBLESS

Help the disabled by helping BLESMA with a donation now and a legacy in the future. We promise you that not one penny will be wasted.

For further information contact:
HQ BLESMA,
Frankland Moore House,
185-187 High Road,
Chadwell Heath, Romford,
Essex RM6 6NA

Telephone: 0181 590 1124 Fax: 0181 599 2932
Registered as a Charity under the Charities Act, 1960. No. 207621

455

THE ROYAL AIR FORCE MUSEUM

The Royal Air Force Museum was established in 1964 to collect, preserve and exhibit articles and records relating to the history and tradition of the Royal Air Force, and of aviation in general. The collections include aircraft, uniforms and flying clothing, personal relics, equipment and trophies, as well as important private papers of RAF personnel and others. The Museum complex includes art galleries, library and archive, and a cinema/lecture theatre.

The Aircraft Hall has a world-class collection of aircraft, ranging from the days of Louis Bleriot to the Tornado GRI and a new exhibition, "Higher, Further, Faster" which tells the story of aviation developments between the wars. The neighbouring galleries tell the story of aviation, from the legend of Icarus to "the RAF 2000" gallery, where a multi-screen video presentation, models and graphics illustrate life, in the air and on the ground, in the RAF today, and looking towards the next millenium, with a dramatic simulation of a mission in Eurofighter 2000.

THE BATTLE OF BRITAIN EXPERIENCE

The Battle of Britain Experience, housed in a separate purpose-built hall, concentrates on the epic struggle of 1940. This exhibition includes a unique collection of the British, German and Italian aircraft which were engaged in the Battle. Among the British aircraft are the immortal Hurricane and Spitfire, and the sole surviving example of the Defiant. Messerschmitt Bf 109, Junkers 87 "Stuka" dive-bomber, and Heinkel He 111 are included in the German line-up, and Italy is represented by the Fiat CR 42. Later German onslaughts on the British Isles are highlighted by a V.1 flying bomb and a V.2 rocket. Since 1995 visitors to the Battle of Britain Exhibition Hall have been able to round off their visit by "walking through" the Museum's Sunderland Flying Boat.

BOMBER COMMAND HALL

The Bomber Command Hall, the latest addition to the Museum complex, displays a collection of aircraft which have taken part in bombing operations throughout the years, together with some of the aircraft which have opposed or co-operated with them. They range from the BE2b of the First World War to the towering delta-winged Vulcan, in service into the 1980's.

The RAF Museum is open from 10.00 am to 6.00 pm, seven days a week, except 1 January and 24, 25 and 26 December.

The admission charge covers admission to the whole complex, including film shows and the art galleries, and includes a FREE RETURN VISIT within 6 months. Additional discounts are allowed for families, and parties of ten or more. Serving RAF personnel and their immediate families are admitted free, on production of RAF Form 1250 at the Museum entry point.

The new interactive *fun 'n' flight* gallery opened in April allowing visitors to learn more about the theory of flight and related scientific principles in an entertaining and informative way. There will be a wide range of hands on experiments to try and experience.

"Wings", the Museum's restaurant, offers snacks, lunches and a licensed bar. A souvenir shop has an extensive range of gifts, clothing, books, models and videos, and a full mail order service.

The Museum's flight simulator offers the visitor the next best thing to actually flying in an aircraft with a choice of exciting programmes, including a ride in a Tornado with 617 "Dambusters" Squadron. With the support of The Friends of the Museum, visitors can now benefit from free "Plane and Simple" demonstrations on the principles of flight and guided tours of the exhibitions on most open days.

Visitors can operate the controls of a Jet Provost T3 Trainer to gain an understanding of how the aircraft flies or walk through a Sunderland flying boat.

Access is well signposted from the M1, A1, A5, A41, M25 and North Circular, and there is a large free car park. The nearest Underground is Colindale on the Northern Line, and the nearest British Rail station is Mill Hill, Broadway, on Thames Link. Bus route 303 connects the stations with the Museum.

The Royal Air Force Museum, Grahame Park Way, Hendon, London, NW9 5LL. Telephone 0181-205 2266 (GPTN 95271 7210). Fax: 0181-205 8044.

SSAFA Forces Help is the national caseworking charity helping serving and ex-Service men and women and their families, in need. It is the only charity which provides such a breadth of support to the serving and ex-Service communities both in the UK and around the world.

- **In the serving community overseas** we offer: a professional, comprehensive, confidential and cost-effective range of welfare and social work services, including marital counselling, to Armed Forces personnel and their families. This is available in Western Europe, Brunei, Gibraltar and Cyprus

  - We employ midwives, health visitors, community psychiatric nurses, practice nurses, practice managers and pharmacists within the Health Alliance in Germany

- **In the serving community in the UK,** SSAFA Forces Help Social workers advise and assist with welfare support within RAF Command. Our Community Volunteers, who are selected and trained Service personnel and family members, offer friendship and support

- **In the ex-Service community,** we offer: practical and personal welfare support; financial advice and support; training; residential care; short-stay accommodation and a Housing Advisory Service

- We have over 7,000 trained volunteers in the UK at over 100 branches helping more than 85,000 people annually

- More than 14 million people are estimated to be eligible for our help and this need is expected to grow into the next century

For more information please contact:

THE SOLDIERS, SAILORS, AIRMEN AND FAMILIES ASSOCIATION – FORCES HELP
19 Queen Elizabeth Street London SE1 2LP Telephone: 0171 403 8783 Facsimile: 0171 403 8815
Registered Charity Number 210760.   Est 1885

461

THE ROYAL HOMES FOR OFFICERS' WIDOWS AND DAUGHTERS

Queen Alexandra's Court, Wimbledon
(A Branch of SSAFA – Forces Help)
Chairman: Brigadier R. W. M. Lister

The accommodation comprises unfurnished self-contained flats for Widows and Daughters of deceased Officers of all three Services.

For full particulars application should be made in writing to:

The Manager, Queen Alexandra's Court, St. Mary's Road, Wimbledon SW19 7DE. Tel: 0181-946 5182.

ROYAL UNITED SERVICES INSTITUTE
FOR DEFENCE STUDIES

Many members of the RUSI, men and women, are drawn from the ranks of the Royal Air Force.

We believe that the armed services will always need, and have always needed, a platform on which to debate issues of the moment and to be able to voice their concerns. The RUSI, as the professional association of the armed services, fulfils these roles – and more.

Since our foundation in 1831 RUSI has responded to its Royal Charter which urges "the promotion and advancement of military sciences" by focussing upon the practical application of military power and associated political, economic and technological affairs – with a strong operational flavour designed to appeal to all service (or ex-service) personnel. Members can attend lectures, seminars and conferences at our premises in Whitehall, as well as using our library and reading room, all of which were refurbished during 1995 to improve the facilities available for members and Institute activities. Those serving too far from London to attend such events can still benefit from our range of excellent publications – the RUSI *Journal, Newsbrief, Whitehall Papers* and annual International Security Review – which not only cover strictly military issues but also give something of the wider context of international affairs within which the RAF operates.

Further details of membership may be obtained from the Membership Secretary, RUSI, Whitehall, London SW1A 2ET, telephone 0171-930 5854.

Director: Rear Admiral Richard Cobbold CB FRAeS

Director of Studies: Dr Jonathan Eyal

Telephone: 0171-930-5854. / Fax: 0171-321-0943
Web Site: http://www.rusi.org